CHORLEY AND SMART
LEADING CASES
IN THE
LAW OF BANKING

Sixth Edition

by

P. E. SMART, LL.B., Hon. F.I.B.

LONDON
SWEET & MAXWELL
1990

First Edition 1953
Second Edition 1966
Third Edition 1973
Fourth Edition 1977
Second Impression 1979
Fifth Edition 1983
Sixth Edition 1990

Published by
Sweet & Maxwell Limited of
South Quay Plaza, 183 Marsh Wall, London, E14 9FT
in association with
The Chartered Institute of Bankers.

Laserset by P.B. Computer Typesetting, Pickering, N. Yorks.
Printed in Great Britain by
Richard Clay (The Chaucer Press) Ltd., Bungay, Suffolk

A CIP catalogue record
for this book is available
from the British Library

£16 95

LEADING CASES
IN THE

LAW OF BANKING

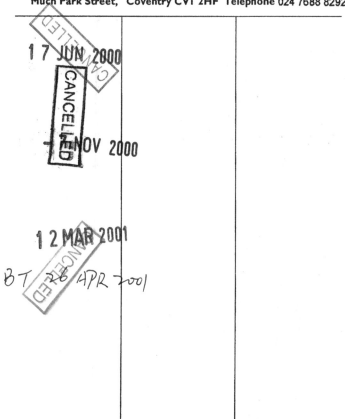

AUSTRALIA
The Law Book Company Ltd.
Sydney : Melbourne : Brisbane : Perth

CANADA
The Carswell Company Ltd.
Toronto : Calgary : Vancouver : Ottawa

INDIA
N. M. Tripathi Private Ltd.
Bombay
and
Eastern Law House Private Ltd.
Calcutta

M.P.P. House
Bangalore

ISRAEL
Steimatzky's Agency Ltd.
Jerusalem : Tel Aviv : Haifa

PAKISTAN
Pakistan Law House
Karachi

PREFACE TO SIXTH EDITION

Since the previous edition of this book the Chartered Institute of Bankers has welcomed the republication by Professional Books, now a division of Butterworths, of the eight original volumes of *Legal Decisions affecting Bankers*, which carried the series to 1966, supplemented by two new volumes to bring the coverage to 1986. The appropriate new L.D.B. references are included in this volume.

New cases calling for inclusion have not been as numerous as they were in the previous edition. Bankers must regret that in the *Tai Hing Cotton Mill* case the Privy Council refused to extend the customer's responsibilities to include the checking of their bank statements; but against that disappointment they may set relief that in the *Morgan* decision the House of Lords defined more strictly the principles of liability in the undue influence cases. There has been some development of the *Mareva* restrictions in the granting of orders freezing accounts suspected of holding the proceeds of crime, and on occasion restraining defendants from leaving the country; while in the area of confidentiality the Police and Criminal Evidence Act 1984, has opened a new avenue of access to information about the customer's account, and the Drug Trafficking Offences Act 1986 and the Prevention of Terrorism (Temporary Provisions) Act 1989 have imposed heavy responsibilities on the banks which have yet to appear in the law reports.

There has been other legislation with relevance to banking. The Banking Act 1987 has had marginal effect on the banker's traditional business, and the Financial Services Act 1986 may be said to affect bankers principally as they have expanded their activities into less traditional areas. But the insolvency legislation, with its radical reorganisation of the whole area of bankruptcy and winding up procedures, has made a substantial impact on the banker's daily work, and its first effects are reflected in this edition. Not so, unfortunately, with the further changes, including the virtual abolition of the *ultra vires* rule, in the Companies Act, 1989, which reached the statute book after the text of this edition was in print.

For the future, we have advance notice of many possibilities for more changes in the extensive recommendations of Professor R. B. Jack's Committee in their Report on *Banking Services: Law and Practice*. A few of these recommendations are noted in the pages that follow.

As with all previous editions of the book, the law section of the Library of the Chartered Institute and the willing cooperation of its staff have been of great help to me. And I am particularly grateful to Mr Geoffrey Reeday, who has read the text and, in saving me from errors of omission and commission, has contributed much to the work.

December 1989   P. E. Smart

PREFACE TO FIRST EDITION

THE absence of an elementary case book on the Law of Banking
is a serious impediment to the successful study of the subject,
especially where library facilities are not available, and this
book is an attempt to fill the gap. Even professional law
students working under expert supervision often encounter
difficulties in the use of the different sets of law reports, and
find it helpful to have recourse to the various volumes of leading
cases which have appeared over the last thirty years or so. We
think that this type of book is even more necessary for the
young bank officer, struggling to understand a difficult branch of
the law in which the decisions of the Courts are all-important,
and working sometimes with little or no tutorial assistance.

The Institute of Bankers has, of course, long made available
its own volumes of *Legal Decisions affecting Bankers*, admirable
compilations produced under the most distinguished editorship,
but more detailed and elaborate than is needed by any but the
most gifted and industrious students, while their chronological
arrangement does not lend itself to the study of any particular
aspect of the subject.

We have had in mind in compiling this volume the needs of
the ordinary candidate for the Diploma Examination of the
Institute of Bankers. The method employed is that which has
become usual in this type of book: a sufficient summary of the
facts of a case to enable the student to grasp what it is about;
the decision; and, where appropriate, an apposite quotation
from one or more of the judgments of the Court. To this, the
leading case, is appended a Note in which attention is drawn to
other cases relevant to the decision, to passages in textbooks or
articles which we think may help the student, and to any other
material which appears likely to be useful. The general plan of
the subject-matter follows the first author's *Law of Banking*,
which embodies the results of a number of years of teaching in
this subject.

We are most grateful to Mr. John Tonkyn, an Assistant
General Manager of Barclays Bank Limited, who read the
manuscript and made a large number of valuable suggestions.

We are also grateful to the Incorporated Council of Law Reporting for England and Wales for permission to make use of their various series of law reports, to the proprietors of the All England Law Reports and *The Times* Law Reports for their like permission, to the Council of the Institute of Bankers for allowing quotation from their *Legal Decisions affecting Bankers*, and from the *Journal* of the Institute, and to Messrs. Benn Bros. for permission to quote from *The Miller*.

The first author, while accepting full responsibility for the contents of this book, would like to make it clear that the main burden and heat of the day in connection with its preparation have fallen upon the second one, who shouldered the onerous task not only of digesting the leading cases, but of preparing the materials for the Notes.

The second author, in his turn, wishes to record his grateful appreciation of the encouragement given to him by the Trustees of the Houblon-Norman Fund in their award of a grant to further the studies of which this book is in part the product; and to express his thanks for the unfailing co-operation he has found at the Library of the Institute of Bankers. Without this co-operation his share of the work would have been impossible.

LONDON   CHORLEY
August, 1952   P. E. SMART

In addition to those acknowledged in the Preface to the First Edition the following are acknowledged:

Extracts from various HMSO Publications are reproduced by kind permission of Her Majesty's Stationery Officer.

The extract from Publication No. 400 copyright c. 1983 (Uniform Customs and Practice for Documentary Credits, Art. 8 1974 Revision), published by The International Chamber of Commerce, Paris. Available from: ICC United Kingdom, Centre Point, 103 New Oxford Street, London WC1A 1QB; or from: ICC Publishing S.A. 38 Cours Albert, 1ER 75008 Paris.

The extract from The Law Society's Gazette by kind permission of the same.

Extracts from Lloyd's Law Reports by kind permission of Lloyd's of London Press.

CONTENTS

Preface to Sixth Edition   v

Preface to First Edition   vii

Table of Cases   xi

Table of Statutes   xliii

Table of Abbreviations   xlix

Introduction   liii

1.   RELATIONSHIP OF BANKER AND CUSTOMER   1

2.   NEGOTIABLE INSTRUMENTS   37
     The Bills of Exchange Act 1882   40

3.   THE PAYING BANKER   78

4.   THE COLLECTING BANKER   156
     Negligence under section 4 of the Cheques Act   162

5.   SPECIAL ACCOUNTS   194
     Joint Accounts   194
     Partners   201
     Executors   205
     Unincorporated Associations   209
     Limited Companies   212

6.   FINANCING BY BANKERS   223
     Combination of Accounts   233
     Discounts of Bills   238
     Exchange Rates   241
     Banker's Commercial Credits   244

7. SECURITIES FOR ADVANCES 276
    Bankers' Lien 276
    Pledge 280
    Guarantees 291
    Mortgages 319

8. TERMINATION OF RELATIONSHIP BETWEEN
    BANKER AND CUSTOMER 362
    Notice 362
    Mental Disorder 364
    Insolvency 366
    Preferences 371
    Administration Orders 377
    Receivers 379
    Winding Up 383

9. BANKING ADMINISTRATION 400

Index 409

TABLE OF CASES

*[References in **bold** type indicate where the facts of a case are set out in detail.]*

A/S AWILCO OF OSLO v. Fulvia S.p.A. di Navigazione of Cagliari; Chikuma, The [1981] 1 W.L.R. 314; (1981) 125 S.J. 184; [1981] 1 All E.R. 652; [1981] 1 Lloyd's Rep. 371; [1981] Com.L.R. 64 75

A/S Tankexpress v. Compagnie Financière Belge de Pétroles S.A. [1949] .A.C. 76; [1949] L.J.R. 170; 93 S.J. 26; [1948] 2 All E.R. 939; 82 Ll.L.Rep. 43 72

AGIP (Africa) v. Jackson *The Times*, June 5, 1989 85

Addis v. Gramophone Co. Ltd. [1909] A.C. 488; 78 L.J.K.B. 1122; 101 L.T. 466 130

Admiralty Commissioners v. National Provincial and Union Bank of England Ltd. (1922) 127 L.T. 452; 38 T.L.R. 492; 66 Sol.Jo. 422 141

Afovos Shipping Co. S.A. v. Pagnan (R.) and Lli (F.); Afovos, The [1983] 1 W.L.R. 195; (1983) 127 S.J. 98; [1983] 1 All E.R. 449; [1983] Com.L.R. 83; [1983] 1 Lloyd's Rep. 335; [1984] 2 L.M.C.L.Q. 189; 10 L.D.B. 386 .... 75, 149

Akbar Khan v. Attar Singh [1936] 2 All E.R. 545; 80 Sol.Jo. 718, P.C. 39

Akrokerri (Atlantic) Mines v. Economic Bank [1904] 2 K.B. 465; 73 L.J.K.B. 742; 91 L.T. 175; 52 W.R. 670; 20 T.L.R. 564; 48 S.J. 454; 9 Com.Cas. 281; 2 L.D.B. 63 186

Alan (W.J.) & Co. Ltd. v. El Nasr Export & Import Co. [1972] 2 Q.B. 189; [1972] 2 W.L.R. 800; 116 S.J. 139; [1972] 2 All E.R. 127; [1972] 1 Lloyd's Rep. 313 256

Alcom v. Republic of Colombia, First National Bank of Boston [1984] A.C. 580; [1984] 2 W.L.R. 750; [1984] 2 All E.R. 6; [1984] 2 Lloyd's Rep. 24; (1984) 81 L.S.Gaz. 1837 270

Alicia Hosiery Ltd. v. Brown Shipley & Co. Ltd. [1970] 1 Q.B. 195; [1969] 2 W.L.R. 1268; 113 S.J. 466; [1969] 2 All E.R. 504; *sub nom.* Alicia Hosiery v. Brown, Shipley & Co., and Allied Shippers [1969] 2 Lloyd's Rep. 179 290

Allcard v. Skinner (1887) 36 Ch.D. 145; 56 L.J.Ch. 1052; 57 L.T. 61; 36 W.R. 251; 3 T.L.R. 751 302

Allester (David) Ltd., *Re* [1922] 2 Ch. 211; 91 L.J.Ch. 797; 127 L.T. 434; 38 T.L.R. 611; 66 S.J. 486; [1922] B. & C.R. 190; 3 L.D.B. 264 .... **285**, 288, 346

Alliance Bank v. Kearsley (1871) L.R. 6 C.P. 433; 40 L.J.C.P. 249; 24 L.T. 552; 19 W.R. 822 .... **201**, 202

Al Nahkel for Contracting and Trading Ltd. v. Lowe [1986] Q.B. 235; [1986] 2 W.L.R. 317; (1986) 130 S.J. 130; [1986] 1 All E.R. 729; (1986) L.S.Gaz. 525; (1985) 126 New L.J. 164 123

Al Saudi Banque v. Clarke Pixley [1989] 3 All E.R. 361; (1989) 5 BCC 822; (1989) N.L.J. 1341 24

Alton Corporation, *Re* [1985] 27 BCLC 27 341

Aluminium Industrie Vaasen BV v. Romalpa Aluminium Ltd. [1976] 1 W.L.R. 676; 120 S.J. 95; [1976] 2 All E.R. 552; [1976] 1 Lloyd's Rep. 443, C.A.; 9 L.D.B. 426 .... 110, **358**, 359, 360

xi

Amalgamated Investment & Property Co. (in liquidation) v. Texas Commerce International Bank [1982] Q.B. 84; [1981] 3 W.L.R. 565; (1981)
125 S.J. 623; [1981] 3 All E.R. 577; [1981] Com.L.R. 236 .... 312, 403
Amirteymour (decd.), Re [1979] 1 W.L.R. 63; [1978] 3 All E.R. 637; sub
nom. Bank Melli Iran v. Personal Representatives of Amirteymour
(decd.) (1978) 122 S.J. 525 208
Anns v. Merton London Borough Council [1978] A.C. 728; [1977] 2 W.L.R.
1024; (1977) 121 S.J. 377; (1977) 75 L.G.R. 555; [1977] J.P.L. 514;
(1977) 243 E.G. 523, 591; sub nom. Anns v. London Borough of
Merton [1977] 2 All E.R. 492, H.L.; affirming sub nom. Anns v.
Walcroft Property Co. (1976) 241 E.G. 311 23
Arab Bank v. Ross [1952] 2 Q.B. 216; [1952] 1 T.L.R. 811; 96 S.J. 229; [1952]
1 All E.R. 709 .... **56**, 58
Arden v. Bank of New South Wales (1956) 7 L.D.B. 85 200
Arnold (R.M.) & Co., Re (1984) 128 S.J. 659; [1984] C.I.L.L. 119; (1984) 81
L.S.Gaz. 2140 346
Arora v. Barclays Bank Ltd. (unreported) [1979] C.L.Y. 20; C.L.B.
16 .... 232, 233
Ashbury Carriage & Iron Co. v. Riche (1875) L.R. 7 H.L. 653; 44 L.J.Ex.
185; 33 L.T. 450; 24 W.R. 794, H.L.; varying S.C. sub nom. Riche v.
Ashbury Railway Carriage Co. (1874) L.R. 9 Exch. 224, Ex.Ch. 213
Att.-Gen. v. National Provincial Bank Ltd. (1928) 44 T.L.R. 701; 14 T.C.
111 14
Attwood v. Griffin (1826) 2 C. & P. 368; sub nom. Attwood v. Griffin Ry. &
M. 425, N.P. 65
―― v. Munnings (1827) 7 B. & C. 278; 1 Man. & Ry.K.B. 66; 108 E.R. 727;
sub nom. Atwood v. Munnings 6 L.J.O.S. K.B. 9 176
Auchteroni & Co. v. Midland Bank Ltd. [1928] 2 K.B. 294; 97 L.J.K.B. 625;
139 L.T. 344; 44 T.L.R. 441; 72 S.J. 337; 33 Com.Cas. 345; 4 L.D.B.
164 .... 145, 147
Augustus Barnett & Sons, Re [1986] PCC 167; The Times, December 7,
1985 398
Austin-Fell v. Austin-Fell [1989] Fam.Law 437; (1989) 139 New L.J. 1113 337
Australia and New Zealand Bank Ltd. v. Ateliers de Construction Electri-
que de Charleroi [1967] 1 A.C. 86; [1966] 2 W.L.R. 1216; 110 S.J. 467;
[1966] 2 Lloyd's Rep. 463; 9 L.D.B. 2 175
Awilco A/S v. Fulvia S.p.A. di Navigazione. See A/S Awilco v. Fulvia S.p.A.
di Navigazione.
Aziz v. Knightsbridge Gaming and Catering Services and Supplies (1982) 79
L.S.Gaz. 1412 54

BACHE & CO. (LONDON) LTD. v. Banque Vernes et Commerciale de Paris
(1973) 117 S.J. 483; [1973] 2 Lloyd's Rep. 437 299
Backhouse v. Backhouse [1978] 1 W.L.R. 243; [1978] 1 All E.R. 1158; [1977]
Fam.Law 212; sub nom. B. v. B. (1977) 121 S.J. 710 .... 208, 333
Baden Delvaux and Lecuit v. Société Générale pour Favoriser le Développe-
ment du Commerce et de l'Industrie en France S.A. [1983] Com.L.R.
88; [1983] B.C.L.C. 325 84
Bailey (T.D.) Son & Co. v. Ross T. Smyth & Co. Ltd. (1940) 67 W.R. 147 245
Baines v. National Provincial Bank Ltd. (1927) 96 L.J.K.B. 801; 137 L.T.
631; 4 L.D.B. 87; 32 Com.Cas. 216 .... **146**
Baker v. Australia and New Zealand Bank Ltd. [1958] N.Z.L.R. 907; 7
L.D.B. 186 .... 131, **133**, 134

Baker v. Barclays Bank Ltd. [1955] 1 W.L.R. 822; 99 S.J. 491; [1955] 2 All
E.R. 571; 7 L.D.B. 26 .... 180, 199
Banbury v. Bank of Montreal [1918] A.C. 626; 87 L.J.K.B. 1158; 119 L.T.
446; 34 T.L.R. 518; 62 S.J. 665, H.L.; 3 L.D.B. 189 .... 22, 25
Bank Melli Iran v. Barclays Bank (D.C. & O.) [1951] 2 T.L.R. 1057; [1951] 2
Lloyd's Rep. 367; 6 L.D.B. 215 .... 259, 263, 265
Bank Negara Indonesia 1946 v. Lariza (Singapore) Pte. [1988] A.C. 583;
[1988] 2 W.L.R. 374; (1988) 132 S.J. 125; [1988] F.L.R. 197; [1988] 1
Lloyd's Rep. 407 250
Bank of Baroda v. Shah [1988] 3 All E.R. 24; (1988) 138 New L.J. 98 303
Bank of Credit and Commerce v. Bawany (unreported) (1981) C.L.Y. 405 226
Bank of Credit and Commerce International S.A. v. Aboody [1989] 2 W.L.R.
759; [1989] Fam.Law 435 304
—— v. Dawson and Wright [1987] F.L.R. 342 146
Bank of Cyprus (London) Ltd. v. Gill [1980] 2 Lloyd's Rep. 51 326
Bank of England v. Vagliano Bros. [1891] A.C. 107; 60 L.J.Q.B. 145; 64 L.T.
353; 39 W.R. 657; 7 T.L.R. 333; 1 L.D.B. 130 ...... 45, 48, 49, 54, 125, 126
Bank of India v. Trans Continental Commodity Merchants [1983] 2 Lloyd's
Rep. 298 308
Bank of Ireland v. Trustees of Evans' Charities in Ireland (1855) 5 H.L.Cas.
389 172
Bank of Montreal v. Dominion Gresham Guarantee and Casualty Company
Ltd. [1930] A.C. 659; 99 L.J.P.C. 202; 144 L.T. 6; 46 T.L.R. 575; 36
Com.Cas. 28; 4 L.D.B. 248 174
—— v. Stuart and Another [1911] A.C. 120; 80 L.J.P.C. 75; 103 L.T. 641; 27
T.L.R. 117; 3 L.D.B. 1 .... 302, 328
Bank of New South Wales v. Goulburn [1902] A.C. 543; 71 L.J.P.C. 112; 87
L.T. 88; 51 W.R. 367; 18 T.L.R. 735 104
—— v. Milvain (1884) 1 V.L.R. 3 130
—— v. Owston (1879) 4 App.Cas. 270; 48 L.J.P.C. 25; 40 L.T. 500; 43 J.P.
476; 14 Cox, C.C. 267 407
Bank of Scotland v. Grimes [1985] Q.B. 1179; [1985] 3 W.L.R. 294; (1985)
129 S.J. 331; [1985] 2 All E.R. 254; 1985 F.L.R. 322; (1985) 15
Fam.Law 314; (1985) 82 L.S.Gaz. 1857; (1985) 135 New L.J. 411 327
Bank of Tokyo Ltd. v. Magid Karoon [1986] 3 W.L.R. 414 402
Bankers Trust Co. v. Shapira and Others [1980] 1 W.L.R. 1274; (1980) 124
S.J. 480; [1980] 3 All E.R. 353 .... 17, 110
Banque Belge pour l'Etranger v. Hambrouck and Others [1921] 1 K.B. 321;
90 L.J.K.B. 322; 37 T.L.R. 76; 65 Sol.Jo. 74; 26 Com.Cas. 72 ... 106, **107**,
108, 109
Banque de l'Indochine et de Suez v. Euroseas Group Finance Co. Ltd. [1981]
3 All E.R. 198; [1981] Com.L.R. 77 .... 53, 263
Barber & Nicholls v. R. & G. Associates Ltd. (1985) C.L.Y. 129; C.A.T.
81/455 53
Barclay-Johnson v. Yuill [1980] 1 W.L.R. 1259; (1980) 124 S.J. 594; [1980] 3
All E.R. 190 118
Barclays Bank Ltd. v. Aschaffenberger Zellstoffwerke AG [1967] 1 Lloyd's
Rep. 387; 111 S.J. 350; 117 New L.J. 268 .... 71, **238**, 240, 241
—— v. Astley Industrial Trust Ltd. [1970] 2 Q.B. 527; [1970] 2 W.L.R. 876;
[1970] 1 All E.R. 719; 9 L.D.B. 135 .... 159, 278
—— v. Bank of England [1985] 1 All E.R. 385; [1985] F.L.R. 209; (1985) 135
New L.J. 104; 10 L.D.B. 482 148
—— v. Beck [1952] 2 Q.B. 47; [1952] 1 T.L.R. 595; 96 S.J. 194; [1952] 1 All
E.R. 549; 6 L.D.B. 258 .... **319**, 320

Barclays Bank Ltd. *v.* Commissioners of Customs and Excise [1963] 1 Lloyd's
Rep. 81; 8 L.D.B. 138 285
—— *v.* Fisher (unreported) 226
—— *v.* Harding (April 1962) 83 J.I.B. 109; *The Guardian*, January 27,
1962 158
—— *v.* Kiley [1961] 1 W.L.R. 1050; 105 S.J. 569; [1961] 2 All E.R. 849; 8
L.D.B. 27 323
—— *v.* Okenarhe [1966] 2 Lloyd's Rep. 87; 8 L.D.B. 525 .... 33, **233**
—— *v.* Parry (1979) C.A.T. 277 327
—— *v.* Quistclose Investments [1970] A.C. 567; [1968] 3 W.L.R. 1097; 112
S.J. 903; [1968] 3 All E.R. 651; 9 L.D.B. 105; affirming *sub nom.*
Quistclose Investments *v.* Rolls Razor (in liquidation) [1968] Ch. 540;
[1968] 2 W.L.R. 478; *sub nom.* Quistclose Investments *v.* Rolls
Razor (in voluntary liquidation) [1968] 1 All E.R. 613; [1967] C.L.Y.
514 .... 103, 237
—— *v.* Simms (W.J.) Son and Cooke (Southern) Ltd. and Another [1980]
Q.B. 677; [1980] 2 W.I.R. 218; (1979) 123 S.J. 785; [1979] 3 All E.R.
522; [1980] 1 Lloyd's Rep. 225; 10 L.D.B. 127 .... 135, **136**, 140
—— *v.* Taylor [1974] Ch. 137; [1973] 2 W.L.R. 293; 117 S.J. 109; [1973] 1 All
E.R. 752; 25 P. & C.R. 172; 9 L.D.B. 322 .... 340, 341
—— *v.* Taylor; Trustee Savings Bank of Wales and Border Countries *v.*
Taylor [1989] 1 W.L.R. 1066; (1989) 133 S.J. 1372; [1989] 3 All E.R.
563 16
—— *v.* Tennet (unreported) [1985] C.A.T. 84/242 325
—— *v.* Thienel (1978) 122 S.J. 472; 247 E.G. 385; C.L.B. 38 305
—— *v.* Trevanion [1933] *The Banker* 98 .... 306, 312
Barclays Bank International Ltd. *v.* Levin Brothers (Bradford) Ltd. [1976] 3
W.L.R. 852 243
Barclays Bank of Swaziland *v.* Hahn [1989] 1 W.L.R. 506; [1989] 2 All E.R.
398 72
Barker *v.* Wilson [1980] 1 W.L.R. 884; (1980) 124 S.J. 326; [1980] 2 All E.R.
81; (1980) 70 Cr.App.R. 283; [1980] Crim.L.R. 373 13
Barnes *v.* Addy (1874) L.R. 9 Ch.App. 244; 43 L.J.Ch. 513; 30 L.T. 4; 22
W.R. 505 83
Barnett (Augustus) & Son, *Re. See* Augustus Barnett & Son, *Re.*
Barrows and Others *v.* Chief Land Registrar, *The Times*, October 20, 1977;
C.L.B. 51 382
Barwick *v.* English Joint Stock Bank (1867) L.R. 2 Ex. 259; 36 L.J.Ex. 147; 16
L.T. 461; 15 W.R. 877 .... 25, **406**
Bavins Junr. & Sims *v.* London and South Western Bank [1900] 1 Q.B. 270;
69 L.J.Q.B. 164; 81 L.T. 655; 48 W.R. 210; 16 T.L.R. 61; 5 Com.Cas.
1; 1 L.D.B. 293 44
Bayer AG *v.* Winter [1986] 1 W.L.R. 497; (1985) 130 S.J. 246; [1986] 1 All
E.R. 733; [1986] F.S.R. 323; (1985) 83 L.S.Gaz. 974; (1985) 136 New
L.J. 187; 10 L.D.B. 578 123
—— *v.* —— (No. 2) [1986] 1 W.L.R. 540; (1985) 130 S.J. 373; [1986] 2 All
E.R. 43 123
Baylis *v.* Bishop of London [1913] 1 Ch. 127 139
Beale *v.* Caddick (1857) 2 H. & N. 326; 26 L.J.Ex. 356; 29 L.T.(o.s.) 355; 157
E.R. 135 202
Beavan, *Re*, Davies, Banks & Co. *v.* Bevan [1913] 2 Ch. 595; 83 L.J.Ch. 109;
109 L.T. 538; 58 S.J. 31 .... **364**, 365

Bechuanaland Exploration Co. *v.* London Trading Bank Ltd. [1898] 2 Q.B.
658; 67 L.J.Q.B. 986; 79 L.T. 270; 14 T.L.R. 587; 3 Com.Cas. 285; 1
L.D.B. 279 38
Beckett *v.* Addyman (1882) 9 Q.B.D. 783; 51 L.J.Q.B. 597 318
Beevers and Another *v.* Mason (1978) 37 P. & C.R. 452; (1978) 122 S.J. 610;
(1978) 248 E.G. 781; 10 L.D.B. 119 .... **71**, 72
Bell *v.* London North-Western Railway Co. (1852) 15 Beav. 548; 19
L.T.(o.s.) 292; 51 E.R. 651 345
Bellamy *v.* Marjoribanks (1852) 7 Ex. 389; 21 L.J.Ex. 70; 18 L.T.(o.s.) 277;
16 Jur. 106; 155 E.R. 999 186
Belmont Finance Corporation *v.* Williams Furniture [1979] Ch. 250; [1978] 3
W.L.R. 712; (1977) 122 S.J. 743; [1979] 1 All E.R. 118, C.A. 84
——— *v.* ——— (No. 2) [1980] 1 All E.R. 393 84
Beresford *v.* Royal Insurance Co. Ltd. [1938] 2 All E.R. 602; [1938] A.C. 586;
107 L.J.K.B. 464; 158 L.T. 459; 54 T.L.R. 789; 82 S.J. 431; 5 L.D.B.
145 .... **354**, 355, 356
Berry *v.* Gibbons (1873) 8 Ch.App. 747; 29 L.T. 88; 38 J.P. 4; 21 W.R. 754 207
Bevan *v.* National Bank Ltd.; Bevan *v.* Capital & Counties Bank Ltd. (1906)
23 T.L.R. 65; 2 L.D.B. 135 186
Beverley Acceptances Ltd. *v.* Oakley [1982] R.T.R. 417 289
Bhogal *v.* Punjab National Bank; Basna *v.* Same [1988] 2 All E.R. 296; [1988]
1 F.T.L.R. 161; [1988] F.L.R. 97 237
Biddell Bros. *v.* E. Clemens Horst Co. [1911] 1 K.B. 934; 80 L.J.K.B. 584;
104 L.T. 577; 27 T.L.R. 331; 55 Sol.Jo. 383; 12 Asp.M.L.C.I., C.A.;
reversed on other grounds, *sub nom.* E. Clemens Horst Co. *v.* Biddell
Brothers [1912] A.C. 18 244
Bishop (decd.), *Re*, National Provincial Bank *v.* Bishop [1965] Ch. 450;
[1965] 2 W.L.R. 188; 109 S.J. 107; [1965] 1 All E.R. 249 197
Bodenham *v.* Hoskins (1852) 21 L.J.Ch. 864; 19 L.T.(o.s.) 294; 16 Jur.
721 .... 80, 105
Bolivinter Oil S.A. *v.* Chase Manhattan Bank [1984] 1 W.L.R. 392; (1984)
128 S.J. 153; [1984] 1 Lloyd's Rep. 251 273
Bonalumi *v.* Secretary of State for the Home Department [1985] Q.B. 675;
[1985] 2 W.L.R. 722; (1985) 129 S.J. 223; [1985] 1 All E.R. 797; (1985)
82 L.S.Gaz. 1336 401
Bondina Ltd. *v.* Rollaway Shower Blinds [1986] 1 W.L.R. 517; (1985) 130 S.J.
264; [1986] 1 All E.R. 564; [1986] F.L.R. 266; [1986] E.C.C. 260; 1986
PCC 325; (1986) 136 New L.J. 116; (1986) 83 L.S.Gaz. 36 51
Bond Worth, *Re* [1980] Ch. 228; [1979] 3 W.L.R. 629; (1979) 123 S.J. 216;
[1979] 3 All E.R. 919; C.L.B. 54 360
Borden (U.K.) Ltd. *v.* Scottish Timber Products Ltd. and McNicol Brownlie
[1981] Ch. 25; [1979] 3 W.L.R. 672; (1979) 123 S.J. 688; [1979] 3 All
E.R. 961; [1980] 1 Lloyd's Rep. 160; C.L.B. 53 360
Boundy *v.* Bhagwanami (1979) C.A.T. 834 68
Bourne, *Re*, Bourne *v.* Bourne [1906] 2 Ch. 427; 75 L.J.Ch. 779; 95 L.T. 131;
54 W.R. 559; 50 S.J. 575; 2 L.D.B. 107 .... **203**, 205
Bower *v.* Foreign and Colonial Gas Co. Ltd., Metropolitan Bank, Garnishees
(1874) 22 W.R. 740 115
Box *v.* Midland Bank Ltd. [1981] 1 Lloyd's Rep. 434; 10 L.D.B. 127 .... 18, **20**,
21, 22, 24
Bradford Banking Co. Ltd. *v.* Briggs Son & Co. Ltd. (1886) 12 App.Cas. 29;
56 L.J.Ch. 364; 56 L.T. 62; 35 W.R. 521; 3 T.L.R. 170 340

Bradford Old Bank v. Sutcliffe [1918] 2 K.B. 833; 34 T.L.R. 619; 62 S.J. 753; 24 Com.Cas. 27, C.A.; 88 L.J.K.B. 85; 119 L.T. 727 .... 236, 313, **314**, 318, 322

Bradley Egg Farm Ltd. v. Clifford and Others [1943] 2 All E.R. 378 .... **209**

Brandao v. Barnett (1846) 12 Cl. & Fin. 787; 3 C.B. 519; 8 E.R. 1622, H.L.; reversing S.C. sub nom. Barnett v. Brandao (1843) 6 Man. & G. 630, Ex.Ch.; restoring S.C. sub nom. Brandao v. Barnett (1840) 1 Man. & G. 908 276

Brandt v. Liverpool Brazil and River Plate Steam Navigation Co. Ltd. [1924] 1 K.B. 575; [1923] All E.R.Rep. 656; 93 L.J.K.B. 646; 130 L.T. 392; 16 Asp.M.L.C. 262; 29 Com.Cas. 57 .... 282, **283**

Brandt's (William) Sons & Co. v. Dunlop Rubber Co. Ltd. [1905] A.C. 454; [1904–7] 74 L.J.K.B. 898; 93 L.T. 495; 21 T.L.R. 710; 11 Com.Cas. 1 .... **348**, 351

Brettel v. Williams (1849) 4 Ex. 623; 19 L.J.Ex. 121; 14 L.T.(o.s.) 255; 154 E.R. 1363 202

Brewer v. Westminster Bank Ltd. [1952] 2 T.L.R. 568; [1952] 2 All E.R. 650; 6 L.D.B. 344 .... 93, 199, 200

Brightlife, Re [1987] Ch. 200; [1987] 2 W.L.R. 197; (1987) 131 S.J. 132; [1986] 3 All E.R. 673; 1986 PCC 435; (1987) 84 L.S.Gaz. 653 389

Brimnes, The; Tenax Steamship Co. Ltd. v. The Brimnes (Owners) [1975] Q.B. 929; [1974] 3 W.L.R. 613; 118 S.J. 808; sub nom. Brimnes, The; Tenax Steamship Co. v. Owners of the Motor Vessel Brimnes [1974] 3 All E.R. 88; sub nom. Tenax Steamship Co. v. Brimnes, The (Owners); Brimnes, The [1974] 2 Lloyd's Rep. 241, C.A.; affirming sub nom. Tenax Steamship Co. v. Reinante Transoceanica Navegacion S.A.; Brimnes, The [1973] 1 W.L.R. 386; 117 S.J. 244; sub nom. Tenax Steamship Co. v. Brimnes, The (Owners) [1972] 2 Lloyd's Rep. 465; [1973] 1 All E.R. 769 .... 74, 77, 149

Bristol & West Building Society v. Henning [1985] 1 W.L.R. 778; (1985) 129 S.J. 363; [1985] 2 All E.R. 606; (1985) 50 P. & C.R. 237; (1985) 17 H.L.R. 432; (1985) 135 New L.J. 508; (1985) 82 L.S.Gaz. 1788 332

British Airways Board v. Parish (1979) 123 S.J. 319; [1979] 2 Lloyd's Rep. 361; C.L.B. 7 53

British Bank of the Middle East v. Sun Life Assurance Co. of Canada (U.K.) [1983] 2 Lloyd's Rep. 9; [1983] Com.L.R. 187; (1983) 133 New L.J. 575 221

British and North European Bank Ltd. v. Zalzstein [1927] 2 K.B. 92; 96 L.J.K.B. 539; 137 L.T. 127; 43 T.L.R. 299; 4 L.D.B. 76 100

British Imex Industries Ltd. v. Midland Bank Ltd. [1958] 1 Q.B. 542; [1958] 2 W.L.R. 103; 102 S.J. 69; [1958] 1 All E.R. 264; [1957] 2 Lloyd's Rep. 591; 7 L.D.B. 171 .... 260, 261

Brown v. Cork [1986] PCC 78; [1986] F.L.R. 118 310

—— v. Westminster Bank Ltd. [1964] 2 Lloyd's Rep. 187; 8 L.D.B. 286 .... 92, 93

Buck v. Robson (1878) 3 Q.B.D. 686; 48 L.J.Q.B. 250; 39 L.T. 325; 26 W.R. 804 351

Buckingham v. London & Midland Bank Ltd. (1895) 12 T.L.R. 70; 1 L.D.B. 219 236

Bunge Corp. v. Vegetable Vitamin Foods (Pte) [1985] 1 Lloyd's Rep. 613; (1984) 134 New L.J. 125 267

Burnes v. Trade Credits Ltd. [1981] 1 W.L.R. 805; (1981) 125 S.J. 198; [1981] 2 All E.R. 122; 10 L.D.B. 276 307

Burnett v. Westminster Bank Ltd. [1966] 1 Q.B. 742; [1965] 3 W.L.R. 863;
  109 S.J. 533; [1965] 3 All E.R. 81; [1965] 2 Lloyd's Rep. 218; 8 L.D.B.
  424 .... 35, 129
Burton v. Gray (1873) 8 Ch.App. 932; 43 L.J.Ch. 229 299
Bute (Marquess of) v. Barclays Bank Ltd. [1955] 1 Q.B. 202; [1954] 3 W.L.R.
  741; 98 S.J. 805; [1954] 3 All E.R. 365 .... 65, 165, **181**, 183
Byfield (a bankrupt), Re, ex p. Hill (Samuel) & Co. v. The Trustee of the
  Bankrupt [1982] Ch. 267; [1982] 2 W.L.R. 613; [1982] 1 All E.R. 249;
  10 L.D.B. 301 368

CBS v. Robinson (1988) C.L.Y. 503 123
C.B.S. United Kingdom v. Lambert [1983] Ch. 37; [1982] 3 W.L.R. 746;
  (1982) 126 S.J. 691; [1982] 3 All E.R. 237; (1983) 80 L.S.Gaz. 36;
  [1983] F.L.R. 127, C.A. 120
C.T.I. International Inc. v. Oceanus Mutual Underwriting Association
  (Bermuda). See Container Transport International Inc. v. Oceanus
  Mutual Underwriting Association.
C.W. and A.L. Huges Ltd., Re [1966] 2 All E.R. 702 397
Calico Printers' Association v. Barclays Bank Ltd. & Anglo-Palestine Co.
  Ltd. (1931) 1 All E.R. Rep. 350; 145 L.T. 51; 36 Com.Cas. 197 405
Calzaturificio Fiorella S.p.A. v. Walton and Another (unreported) (1979)
  C.L.Y. 23; C.L.B. 8 .... 53, 68
Caparo Industries plc v. Dickman (1988) 138 New L.J. 289, C.A. 24
Cape Asbestos Co. Ltd. v. Lloyds Bank Ltd. [1921] W.N. 274; 3 L.D.B.
  314 .... **246**, 248
Capital and Counties Bank Ltd. v. Gordon, London, City & Midland Bank
  v. Gordon [1903] A.C. 240; 72 L.J.K.B. 451; 88 L.T. 574; 51 W.R.
  671; 19 T.L.R. 402; sub nom. London, City & Midland Bank v.
  Gordon, Capital & Counties Bank v. Gordon 8 Com.Cas. 221 158
Carl Zeiss Stiftung v. Herbert Smith & Co. and Another [1969] 2 All E.R.
  367 .... 83, 84
Carlisle and Cumberland Banking Co. v. Bragg [1911] 1 K.B. 489; 80
  L.J.K.B. 472; 104 L.T. 121 .... 297, 298
Carpenters' Company v. British Mutual Banking Co. Ltd. [1937] 3 All E.R.
  811; [1938] 1 K.B. 511; 107 L.J.K.B. 11; 157 L.T. 329; 53 T.L.R. 1040;
  81 Sol.Jo. 701; 43 Com.Cas. 38 .... **141**, 173
Carreras Rothmans v. Freemans Mathews Treasure [1985] Ch. 207; [1984] 3
  W.L.R. 1016; (1984) 128 S.J. 614; [1985] 1 All E.R. 155; (1984) 81
  L.S.Gaz. 2375; 1985 PCC 222 103
Catlin v. Cyprus Corporation (London) Ltd. [1983] Q.B. 759; [1983] 2
  W.L.R. 566; (1982) 126 S.J. 744; [1983] 1 All E.R. 809; (1983) 80
  L.S.Gaz. 153 199
Cebora S.N.C. v. S.I.P. (Industrial Products) Ltd. [1976] 1 Lloyd's Rep. 271;
  9 L.D.B. 381 .... 62, **66**, 69
Cedar Holdings Ltd. v. Green [1981] Ch. 129; [1979] 3 W.L.R. 31; (1979) 123
  S.J. 302; [1979] 3 All E.R. 117; (1979) 38 P. & C.R. 673; C.L.B. 39 337
Central Motors (Birmingham) Ltd. v. P.A. and S.N. Wadsworth [1983]
  C.A.T. 82/231 .... 52, 203
Centrax Trustees Ltd. v. Ross [1979] 2 All E.R. 952 327
Chambers v. Miller (1862) 13 C.B.(N.S.) 125; 1 New Rep. 95; 32 L.J.C.P. 30;
  7 L.T. 856; 9 Jur.(N.S.) 626; 11 W.R. 236; 143 E.R. 50 138
Chan Man-Sin v. Att.-Gen. of Hong Kong [1988] 1 W.L.R. 196; (1988) 132
  S.J. 126; [1988] 1 All E.R. 1; (1988) 86 Cr.App.R. 303; [1988]
  Crim.L.R. 319; (1988) 85 L.S.Gaz. 36 229

Chan Man-Sin v. The Queen. See Chan Man-Sin v. Att.-Gen. of Hong Kong.
Chapman v. Smethurst [1909] 1 K.B. 927; 78 L.J.K.B. 654; 100 L.T. 465; 25
    T.L.R. 383; 53 S.J. 340; 14 Com.Cas. 94; 16 Mans. 171   51
—— v. Walton (1834) 10 Bing. 57; 3 Moo. & S. 389; [1824–34] All E.R.Rep.
    384; 2 L.J.C.P. 910; 131 E.R. 826   163
Charge Card Services, Re [1988] 3 W.L.R. 764; (1988) 132 S.J. 1458; (1988) 4
    BCC 524; 1988 PCC 390; [1988] 3 All E.R. 702; (1988) 138 New L.J.
    201; [1988] BCLC 711; [1988] L.S.Gaz. November 16, 46, C.A.;
    affirming [1987] Ch. 150; [1986] 3 W.L.R. 697; [1987] B.C.L.C. 17;
    1978 PCC 36; [1987] F.L.R. 1; (1986) 130 S.J. 801; [1986] 3 All E.R.
    289; (1986) 83 L.S.Gaz. 3424   229
Charterbridge Corporation Ltd. v. Lloyd's Bank Ltd. [1970] Ch. 62; [1969] 3
    W.L.R. 122; (1968) 113 S.J. 465; [1969] 2 All E.R. 1185; 9 L.D.B. 111;
    sub nom. Charterbridge Corporation v. Lloyd's Bank and Pomeroy
    Developments (Castleford) [1969] 2 Lloyd's Rep. 24   215
Chase Manhattan Bank Ltd. N.A. v. Israel-British Bank (London) Ltd.
    [1981] Ch. 105; [1980] 2 W.L.R. 202; (1979) 124 S.J. 99; [1979] 3 All
    E.R. 1025 .... 109, 138, 141
Chatterton v. London & County Banking Co. Ltd. The Miller, February 2,
    1891, The Times, January 21, 1891   95
Chetwynd-Talbot v. Midland Bank Ltd. (1982) 102 J.I.B. 214 .... 303, 328, 333
Chic Fashions (West Wales) v. Jones [1968] 2 Q.B. 299; [1968] 2 W.L.R. 201;
    132 J.P. 175; 112 S.J. 16; [1968] 1 All E.R. 229; reversing sub nom.
    Chic Fashions v. Chief Constable of Carmarthenshire and Cardigan-
    shire [1967] Crim.L.R. 484, Cty.Ct. Petition for leave to appeal to the
    House of Lords granted [1968] 1 W.L.R. 463   122
Chief Constable of Kent v. V. and Another [1983] Q.B. 34; [1982] 3 W.L.R.
    462; (1982) 126 S.J. 536; [1982] 3 All E.R. 36; 10 L.D.B. 337   122
Chief Constable of Leicestershire v. M. [1989] 1 W.L.R. 20; (1989) 133 S.J.
    47; [1988] 3 All E.R. 1015   122
Chief Constable of Surrey v. A. and Another The Times, October 27, 1988   123
Chikuma, The. See A/S Awilco v. Fulvia S.p.A. de Navigazione; Chikuma,
    The.
Choice Investments Ltd. v. Jeromnimon; Midland Bank (Garnishee) [1981]
    Q.B. 149; [1980] 2 W.L.R. 80; (1980)) 124 S.J. 883; [1981] 1 All E.R.
    225   116
City of London Building Society v. Hegg [1988] A.C. 54; [1987] 2 W.L.R.
    1266; (1987) 131 S.J. 806; [1987] 3 All E.R. 435; (1987) 19 H.L.R. 484;
    (1987) 54 P. & C.R. 337; (1988) 18 Fam.Law 17; [1988] 1 F.L.R. 98;
    (1987) 137 New L.J. 475; (1987) 84 L.S.Gaz. 1966; reversing [1986]
    Ch. 605; [1986] 2 W.L.R. 616; (1985) 130 S.J. 300; [1986] 1 All E.R.
    989; (1986) 52 P. & C.R. 193; (1986) 136 New L.J. 311; (1986) 83
    L.S.Gaz. 1394   332
Clare & Co. v. Dresdner Bank [1915] 2 K.B. 576; 84 L.J.K.B. 1443; 133 L.T.
    93; 31 T.L.R. 278; 21 Com.Cas. 62   401
Claydon v. Bradley [1987] 1 W.L.R. 521; (1987) 131 S.J. 593; [1987] 1 All
    E.R. 522; [1987] F.L.R. 111; (1987) 84 L.S.Gaz. 1571; (1987) 137 New
    L.J. 57 .... 40, 109, 151, 152, 153
Clayton's Case. v. Devaynes v. Noble.
Clemens Horst (E.) Co. v. Biddell Bros. [1912] A.C. 18; 81 L.J.K.B. 42; 105
    L.T. 563; 28 T.L.R. 42; 56 S.J. 50; 12 Asp.M.L.C. 80; 17 Com.Cas. 55;
    [1911–13] All E.R.Rep. 10 ....   **244**
Cleveland Manufacturing Co. Ltd. v. Muslim Commercial Bank Ltd. [1981]
    Com.L.R. 247; [1981] 2 Lloyd's Rep. 646; 10 L.D.B. 292 .... 60, 220

Clifford Maersk, The [1982] 1 W.L.R. 1292; (1982) 126 S.J. 446; [1982] 3 All
 E.R. 905; [1982] 2 Lloyd's Rep. 251; (1982) 79 L.S.Gaz. 988 75
Clifton Place Garage Ltd., Re [1970] Ch. 477; [1970] 2 W.L.R. 243; (1969) 113
 S.J. 895; [1970] 1 All E.R. 353 393
Clinch v. I.R.C. [1974] Q.B. 76; [1973] 2 W.L.R. 862; 117 S.J. 342; [1973] 1
 All E.R. 977; [1973] S.T.C. 155; [1973] T.R. 157; 49 T.C. 52 14
Clough Mill v. Martin [1985] 1 W.L.R. 111; (1984) 128 S.J. 850; [1984] 3 All
 E.R. 982; (1985) 82 L.S.Gaz. 116; [1985] L.M.C.L.Q. 15; reversing
 [1984] 1 W.L.R. 1067; (1984) 128 S.J. 564; [1984] 1 All E.R. 721;
 (1984) L.S.Gaz. 2375 361
Clovertogs Ltd. v. Jean Scenes Ltd. [1982] Com.L.R. 88 68
Clutton v. Attenborough [1897] A.C. 90; 66 L.J.Q.B. 221; 75 L.T. 556; 45
 W.R. 276; 13 T.L.R. 114; 1 L.D.B. 247 48
Cocks v. Masterman (1829) 9 B. & C. 902; Dan. & Ll. 329; 4 Man. & Ry.K.B.
 676; 8 L.J.(os.) K.B. 77; 109 E.R. 335 140
Coldunell v. Gallon [1986] Q.B. 1184; [1986] 2 W.L.R. 466; (1986) 130 S.J.
 88; [1986] 1 All E.R. 429; [1986] F.L.R. 183; (1986) 82 L.S.Gaz. 520 ... 303
Cole v. Milsome [1951] W.N. 49; [1951] 1 All E.R. 311; 6 L.D.B. 171 43
Coleman v. Bucks and Oxon Union Bank [1897] 2 Ch. 243; 66 L.J.Ch. 564; 76
 L.T. 684; 45 W.R. 616; 41 S.J. 491 .... 81, 103, 104
—— v. London County and Westminster Bank Ltd. [1916] 2 Ch. 353; 85
 L.J.Ch. 652; 115 L.T. 152 339
Commercial Bank of Scotland v. Rhind (1860) 3 Macq. 643 98
Commercial Banking Company of Sydney Ltd. v. Brown (R.H.) & Co. [1972]
 2 Lloyd's Rep. 360 26
—— v. Jalsard Pty. [1973] A.C. 279; [1972] 3 W.L.R. 566; 116 S.J. 695;
 [1972] 2 Lloyd's Rep. 529 .... 260, 265
Commissioners of Taxation v. English Scottish and Australian Bank. See
 Taxation, Commissioners of v. English, Scottish and Australian Bank.
Company, A, Re (No. 005009 of 1987) (1988) 4 BCC 424 399
Conley (Trading as Caplan & Conley), ex p., The Trustee v. Barclays Bank
 Ltd.; Same v. Lloyd's Bank Ltd. 2 All E.R. 127; 107 L.J.Ch. 257; 158
 L.T. 323; 54 T.L.R. 641; 82 S.J. 292; 5 L.D.B. 121 373
Consumer and Industrial Press, Re [1988] BCLC 177 377
Container Transport International Inc. v. Oceanus Mutual Underwriting
 Association (Bermuda) [1984] 1 Lloyd's Rep. 476 358
Cooper v. National Provincial Bank Ltd. [1945] 2 All E.R. 641; [1946] K.B. 1;
 115 L.J.K.B. 84; 173 L.T. 368; 62 T.L.R. 36; 89 S.J. 477; 5 L.D.B.
 426 293
Cooper (Gerald) Chemicals, Re [1978] Ch. 262; [1978] 2 W.L.R. 866; (1977)
 121 S.J. 848; [1978] 2 All E.R. 49 399
Cordoba Shipping Co. Ltd. v. National State Bank, Elizabeth, New Jersey;
 Albaform, The [1984] 2 Lloyd's Rep. 91; (1984) 81 L.S.Gaz. 1360;
 [1985] L.M.C.L.Q. 6 26
Coutts & Co. v. Browne-Lecky and Others [1947] K.B. 104; 115 L.J.K.B.
 508; 62 T.L.R. 421; 90 S.J. 489; [1946] 2 All E.R. 207; 5 L.D.B. 443 312
—— v. Irish Exhibition in London, The (1891) 7 T.L.R. 313; 1 L.D.B. 127 ... 210
Crédit Lyonnais v. Barnard (P.T.) & Associates [1976] 1 Lloyd's Rep. 557 298
Cresswell v. Potter [1978] 1 W.L.R. 255n 208, 333
Cripps (R.A.) & Son v. Wickenden; Cripps (Pharmaceuticals) v. Wickenden
 [1973] 1 W.L.R. 944; (1972) 117 S.J. 446; [1973] 2 All E.R. 606; 9
 L.D.B. 306 381
Crouch v. Credit Foncier of England (1873) L.R. 8 Q.B. 374; 42 L.J.Q.B.
 183; 29 L.T. 259; 21 W.R. 946 38

Crumplin v. London Joint Stock Bank Ltd. (1913) 109 L.T. 856; 30 T.L.R. 99;
    19 Com.Cas. 69; 3 L.D.B. 69 .... 177, **187**, 189, 190
Cuckmere Brick Co. Ltd. v. Mutual Finance Ltd. [1971] Ch. 949; [1971] 2
    W.L.R. 1207; 115 S.J. 288; 22 P. & C.R. 624; 9 L.D.B. 212; *sub nom.*
    Cuckmere Brick Co. v. Mutual Finance; Mutual Finance v. Cuckmere
    Brick Co. [1971] 2 All E.R. 633 .... 305, **324**, 326
Curtice v. London City & Midland Bank Ltd. [1908] 1 K.B. 293; 77 L.J.K.B.
    341; 98 L.T. 190; 24 T.L.R. 176; 52 S.J. 130; 2 L.D.B. 156 .... **126**, 129
Czarnikow (C.) Ltd. v. Centrala Handlu Zagranicznego Rolinipex [1979]
    A.C. 351; [1978] 3 W.L.R. 274; (1978) 122 S.J. 506; [1978] 2 All E.R.
    1043; [1978] 2 Lloyd's Rep. 305 270

DALTON, Re (A bankrupt), ex p. Herrington and Carmichael (A Firm) v. The
    Trustee [1963] Ch. 336; [1962] 3 W.L.R. 140; 106 S.J. 510; [1962] 2 All
    E.R. 499; 8 L.D.B. 70 393
Davidson v. Barclays Bank [1940] 1 All E.R. 316; 164 L.T. 25; 56 T.L.R. 343;
    84 S.J. 117; 5 L.D.B. 232 .... **132**, 133, 134, 135
Dearle v. Hall; Loveridge v. Cooper (1828), [1824–34] All E.R.Rep. 28; 3
    Russ. 1; 38 E.R. 475 351
Debtor (No. 5 of 1967), Re A, ex p. National Westminster Bank v. Official
    Receiver [1972] 1 Ch. 197; [1971] 2 W.L.R. 1477; 22 P. & C.R. 688;
    sub nom. Debtor (No. 5 of 1967), Re A, ex p. National Provincial Bank
    v. Official Receiver, 115 S.J. 325; *sub nom.* Rushton (A bankrupt),
    Re, ex p. National Westminster Bank v. Official Receiver (Trustee of
    the Property of the Bankrupt) [1971] 2 All E.R. 937; 9 L.D.B. 202 370
Deeley v. Lloyds Bank Ltd. [1912] A.C. 756; 81 L.J.Ch. 697; 107 L.T. 465; 29
    T.L.R. 1; 56 S.J. 734; 2 L.D.B. 230 .... 151, 152, 343
Despina, R., The. See Services Europe Atlantique Sud (SEAS) v. Stock-
    holms Rederiaktiebolag Svea of Stockholm; Despina R., The; Folias,
    The.
Devaynes v. Noble, Clayton's Case (1816) 1 Mer. 529, 572; 35 E.R. 767,
    781 .... **150**, 151, 279, 316, 317, 343, 384, 388, 395, 396
Diamond v. Bank of London and Montreal Ltd. [1979] Q.B. 333; [1979] 2
    W.L.R. 228; (1978) 122 S.J. 814; [1979] 1 All E.R. 561; [1979] 1
    Lloyd's Rep. 335; C.L.B. 24 26
——— v. Graham [1968] 1 W.L.R. 1061; 112 S.J. 396; [1968] 2 All E.R. 909; 9
    L.D.B. 45 56
D.P.P. v. Turner [1974] A.C. 357; [1973] 3 W.L.R. 352; 117 S.J. 664; [1973] 3
    All E.R. 124; 57 Cr.App.R. 932; [1974] Crim.L.R. 186, H.L.;
    reversing *sub nom.* R. v. Turner [1973] 1 W.L.R. 653; 117 S.J. 303;
    [1973] 2 All E.R. 828; [1973] Crim.L.R. 370; *sub nom.* R. v. Turner
    (John Eric), 57 Cr.App.R. 650 231
——— v. Withers [1975] A.C. 842; [1974] 3 W.L.R. 751; 118 S.J. 862; [1974] 3
    All E.R. 984; 60 Cr.App.R. 85; [1975] Crim.L.R. 95, H.L.; reversing
    sub nom. R. v. Withers [1974] Q.B. 414; [1974] 2 W.L.R. 26; *sub nom.*
    R. v. Withers (Ian Douglas); R. v. Withers (Stuart Robert); R. v.
    Gearing (Helen); R. v. Withers (Phyllis) (1973) 58 Cr.App.R. 187 8
Discount Records Ltd. v. Barclays Bank Ltd. and Another [1975] 1 W.L.R.
    315; (1974) 119 S.J. 133; [1975] 1 All E.R. 1071; [1975] 1 Lloyd's Rep.
    444 249
Domenico v. Shimco (U.K.). See Montecchi v. Shimco (U.K.); Domenica v.
    Shimco.

Donoghue (or McAlister) v. Stephenson [1932] A.C. 562; 101 L.J.P.C. 119;
    48 T.L.R. 494; 37 Com.Cas. 850; 1932 S.C. (H.L.) 31; sub nom.
    McAlister (or Donoghue) v. Stevenson 147 L.T. 281; 76 Sol.Jo. 396;
    sub nom. Donoghue (or McAllister) v. Stevenson [1932] All E.R.
    Rep. 1; 1932 S.L.T. 317 .... 21, 23
Douglass v. Lloyds Bank Ltd. (1929) 34 Com.Cas. 263; 4 L.D.B. 220 .... **153**
Dow Banking Corporation v. Bank Mellatt, The Financial Times, January
    12, 1983 318
Drouby v. Wassif and Others (unreported) (1978) C.L.Y. 17   69
Durham Fancy Goods Ltd. v. Jackson (Michael) (Fancy Goods) [1968] 2
    Q.B. 839; [1968] 3 W.L.R. 225; 112 ??? 582; [1968] 2 All E.R. 987; 9
    L.D.B. 61; sub nom. Durham Fancy Goods v. Jackson (Michael)
    (Fancy Goods) and Jackson [1968] 2 Lloyd's Rep. 98 .... 52, 53
Durrant v. Ecclesiastical Commissioners (1880) 6 Q.B.D. 234; 50 L.J.Q.B.
    30; 44 L.T. 348; 45 J.P. 270; 29 W.R. 443 139
Dutton, Massey & Co., ex p. Manchester and Liverpool District Banking Co.
    Ltd. Re [1924] 2 Ch. 199; 93 L.J.Ch. 547; 131 L.T. 622; 68 S.J. 536; 3
    L.D.B. 319 .... **369**, 370

EAGLEHILL LTD. v. Needham Builders Ltd. [1973] A.C. 992; [1972] 3 W.L.R.
    789; 116 S.J. 861; [1972] 3 All E.R. 895; [1973] 1 Lloyd's Rep. 143; 9
    L.D.B. 296 .... **61**, 62
Earl of Sheffield v. London Joint Stock Bank. See Sheffield (Earl) v. London
    Joint Stock Bank.
Eckman v. Midland Bank Ltd. [1973] 1 Q.B. 519; [1973] I.C.R. 71; [1973] 3
    W.L.R. 284; (1972) 117 S.J. 87; [1973] 1 All E.R. 609; sub nom. Goad,
    Re v. Amalgamated Union of Engineering Workers (Engineering
    Section); Eckman v. Midland Bank and Hill Samuel & Co. [1973] 1
    Lloyd's Rep. 162   17
Edward Owen Engineering Ltd. v. Barclays Bank International Ltd. See
    Owen (Edward) Engineering Ltd. v. Barclays Bank International Ltd.
Egbert v. National Crown Bank [1918] A.C. 903; 87 L.J.P.C. 186; 119 L.T.
    659; 35 T.L.R. 1; 3 L.D.B. 200 318
Elian & Rabbath (Trading as Elian & Rabbath) v. Matsas and Matsas;
    McLaren (J.D.) & Co. and Midland Bank [1966] 2 Lloyd's Rep. 495 274
Elliott v. Bax-Ironside [1925] 2 K.B. 301; 94 L.J.K.B. 807; 133 L.T. 624; 41
    T.L.R. 631   52
Emmardart Ltd., Re [1979] Ch. 540; [1979] 2 W.L.R. 868; (1978) 123 S.J. 15;
    [1979] 1 All E.R. 599; C.L.B. 52 382
Equitable Trust Company of New York v. Dawson Partners Ltd. (1927) 27
    Ll.L.Rep. 49 259
Esal (Commodities) and Relton v. Oriental Credit and Wells Fargo Bank
    N.A.; Banque du Caire S.A.E. v. Wells Fargo Bank N.A. [1985] 2
    Lloyd's Rep. 546; [1986] F.L.R. 70 275
Esso Petroleum Co. Ltd. v. Mardon [1976] Q.B. 801; [1976] 2 W.L.R. 583;
    (1976) 120 S.J. 131; [1976] 2 All E.R. 5; [1976] 2 Lloyd's Rep. 305   23
Etablissement Esefka International Anstalt v. Central Bank of Nigeria [1979]
    1 Lloyd's Rep. 445; C.L.B. 33 254
European Asian Bank AG v. Punjab Sind Bank (No. 2) [1983] 1 W.L.R. 642;
    (1983) 127 S.J. 379; [1983] 2 All E.R. 508; [1983] 1 Lloyd's Rep. 611;
    [1983] Com.L.R. 128; 10 L.D.B. 411 258
Evans v. London and Provincial Bank Ltd. (1917) 3 L.D.B. 152 131

F.L.E. Holdings Ltd., *Re* [1967] 1 W.L.R. 1409; 111 S.J. 600; [1967] 3 All
E.R. 553; 9 L.D.B. 34 375
Farhall *v.* Farhall, *ex p.* London & County Banking Co. (1871) 7 Ch.App.
123; 41 L.J.Ch. 146; 25 L.T. 685; 20 W.R. 157 .... **205**
Federal Commerce and Navigation Co. *v.* Tradax Export S.A.; Maratha
Envoy, The [1978] A.C. 1; [1977] 3 W.L.R. 126; (1977) 121 S.J. 459;
[1977] 2 All E.R. 849; [1977] 2 Lloyd's Rep. 301 242
Fern *v.* Bishop Burns & Co. Ltd. and Lloyds Bank Ltd. [1980] New L.J., July
10; C.L.B. 13 115
Ferson Contractors Ltd. *v.* Ferris (unreported) [1982] C.L.Y. 14 68
First National Finance Corporation *v.* Goodman [1983] Com.L.R. 184;
Financial Times, May 19, 1982 313
First National Securities Ltd. *v.* Hegerty (1985) 126 S.J. 836; *The Times*,
November 2, 1982 .... **333**
Flach *v.* London and South Western Bank Ltd. (1915) 31 T.L.R. 334; 3
L.D.B. 123 .... 133, 134
Foley *v.* Hill (1848) 2 H.L.Cas. 28; 9 E.R. 1002 .... **1**, 3, 4, 5
Ford & Carter Ltd. *v.* Midland Bank Ltd. (1979) 129 New L.J. 543; 10 L.D.B.
182 .... **308**, 310, 314, 383
Forestal Mimosa Ltd. *v.* Oriental Credit Ltd. [1986] 1 W.L.R. 631; (1986) 130
S.J. 202; [1986] 2 All E.R. 400; [1986] 1 Lloyd's Rep. 329; [1986]
F.L.R. 171; (1986) 83 L.S.Gaz. 779 254
Foxton *v.* Manchester and Liverpool District Banking Co. (1881) 44 L.T.
406 .... 81, 82
Freeman & Lockyer (A Firm) *v.* Buckhurst Park Properties (Mangal) Ltd.
[1964] 2 Q.B. 480; [1964] 2 W.L.R. 618; 108 S.J. 96; [1964] 1 All E.R.
630; 8 L.D.B. 228 .... 216, **217**, 219, 220
Frost *v.* London Joint Stock Bank Ltd. (1906) 22 T.L.R. 760; 2 L.D.B. 116 134

Gader *v.* Flower (1979) 129 New L.J. 1266 .... 43, 53
Galaxia Maritima S.A. *v.* Mineral Importexport; Eleftherios, The [1982] 1
W.L.R. 539; (1982) 126 S.J. 115; [1982] 1 All E.R. 796; [1982] 1
Lloyd's Rep. 351; [1982] Com.L.R. 38 120
Galbraith *v.* Grimshaw and Baxter [1910] A.C. 508; [1908–10] All E.R.Rep.
561; 79 L.J.K.B. 1011; 103 L.T. 294; 54 S.J. 634; 17 Mans. 183 112
Gallie *v.* Lee. *See* Saunders (formerly Gallie) *v.* Anglia Building Society.
Garnett *v.* McKewan (1872) L.R. 8 Ex. 10; 42 L.J.Ex. 1; 27 L.T. 560; 21 W.R.
57 .... 234, 235, 237, 363, 402
Garrard *v.* James [1925] 1 Ch. 616; 94 L.J.Ch. 234; 133 L.T. 261; 69 S.J. 622 ... 311
Gaunt *v.* Taylor (1834) 3 My. & K. 302; 3 L.J.Ch. 135; 40 E.R. 115 207
Gibbons *v.* Westminster Bank Ltd. [1939] 3 All E.R. 577; [1939] 2 K.B. 882;
108 L.J.K.B. 841; 161 L.T. 61; 55 T.L.R. 888; 83 Sol.Jo. 674 .... **129**
Gill *v.* Cubitt (1824) 3 B. & C. 466; 5 Dow. & Ry.K.B. 324; 3 L.J.(o.s.)K.B.
48; 107 E.R. 806 144
Glyn Mills Currie & Co. *v.* East and West India Dock Co. (1882) 7 App.Cas.
591; [1881–5] All E.R.Rep. 674; 52 L.J.Q.B. 146; 47 L.T. 809; 31
W.R. 201; 4 Asp.M.L.C. 580 284
Goldsworthy *v.* Brickell [1987] Ch. 378; [1987] 2 W.L.R. 133; (1987) 131 S.J.
102; [1987] 1 All E.R. 853; (1987) 84 L.S.Gaz. 654 303
Golodetz (M.) & Co. Inc. *v.* Czarnikow-Rionda Co. Inc.; Galatia, The [1980]
1 W.L.R. 495; (1979) 124 S.J. 201; [1980] 1 All E.R. 501; [1980] 1
Lloyd's Rep. 453 262

Gomba Holdings U.K. v. Homan; Same v. Johnson Matthey Bankers [1986]
  1 W.L.R. 1301; [1986] 130 S.J. 821; [1986] 3 All E.R. 94; 1986 PCC
  449; (1987) 84 L.S.Gaz. 36 .... **379**
Goodwin v. Robarts (1876) 1 App.Cas. 476; [1874–80] All E.R.Rep. 628; 45
  L.J.Q.B. 748; 35 L.T. 179; 24 W.R. 987 .... **37, 38**
Gorman (Siebe) & Co. v. Barclays Bank; Same v. McDonald (R.H.) and
  Baclays Bank [1979] 2 Lloyd's Rep. 142; 9 L.D.B. 94 .... 279, 347
Gowers v. Lloyds and National Provincial Foreign Bank Ltd. [1938] 1 All
  E.R. 766; 158 L.T. 467; 54 L.T.R. 550; 82 S.J. 232; 5 L.D.B.
  86 .... **191**, 193
Graham (James) & Co. (Timber) v. Southgate-Sands [1986] Q.B. 80; [1985] 2
  W.L.R. 1044; (1985) 129 S.J. 331; [1985] 2 All E.R. 344; 1985 F.L.R.
  194; (1985) 35 New L.J. 290; (1985) 82 L.S.Gaz. 1408 307
Grant v. Edwards [1986] Ch. 638; [1986] 3 W.L.R. 114; (1986) 130 S.J. 408;
  [1986] 2 All E.R. 426; [1987] 1 F.L.R. 87; (1986) 16 Fam.Law 300;
  (1986) 136 New L.J. 439; (1986) 83 L.S.Gaz. 1996 332
Gray v. Johnston (1868) L.R. 3 H.L. 1; 16 W.R. 842 .... 101, **102**, 103, 104, 112
Grays Inn Construction Co. Ltd., Re [1980] 1 W.L.R. 711; (1979) 124 S.J.
  463; [1980] 1 All E.R. 814; 10 L.D.B. 189 .... 367, **390**
Great Western Railway Co. v. London and County Banking Co. Ltd. [1901]
  A.C. 414; 70 L.J.K.B. 915; 85 L.T. 152; 50 W.R. 50; 17 T.L.R. 700; 45
  S.J. 690; 6 Com.Cas. 275; 2 L.D.B. 10 .... **30**, 189
Green v. Green (Barclays Bank Ltd. Third Party) [1981] 1 W.L.R. 391; [1981]
  1 All E.R. 97 333
Greenhalgh (W.P.) & Sons v. Union Bank of Manchester Ltd. [1924] 2 K.B.
  153; 93 L.J.K.B. 844; 131 L.T. 637; 3 L.D.B. 341 235
Greenwood v. Martins Bank Ltd. [1933] A.C. 51; 101 L.J.K.B. 623; 147 L.T.
  441; 48 T.L.R. 601; 76 S.J. 544; 38 Com.Cas. 54; 4 L.D.B. 337; ... 86, 87,
                                                      88, **90**, 91, 92, 93, 94, 230
Griffiths v. Dalton [1940] 2 K.B. 264; 109 L.J.K.B. 656; 163 L.T. 359; 56
  T.L.R. 784; 84 S.J. 467; 5 L.D.B. 247 66
Gross, Re, ex p. Kingston (1871) 6 Ch.App. 632; 40 L.J.Bcy. 91; 25 L.T. 250;
  19 W.R. 910; affirming S.C. sub nom., Re Gross, ex p. Adair (1871) 24
  L.T. 198 .... **78**, 80, 237
Gur Corp. v. Trust Bank of Africa [1987] Q.B. 599; [1986] 3 W.L.R. 583 271

Habib v. Ladup (1981) C.A.T. 82/316 68
Habib Bank Ltd. v. Tailor [1982] 1 W.L.R. 1218; (1982) 126 S.J. 448; [1982] 3
  All E.R. 561 327
Haigh, ex p. (1805) 11 Ves. 403; 32 E.R. 1143 338
Halesowen Presswork and Assemblies Ltd. v. Westminster Bank Ltd. See
  National Westminster Bank Ltd. v. Halesowen Presswork and
  Assemblies Ltd.
Halifax Building Society v. Clark and Another [1973] Ch. 307; [1973] 2
  W.L.R. 1; 116 S.J. 883; [1973] 2 All E.R. 33; 24 P. & C.R. 339 333
Hall (William) (Contractors) (In Liquidation) [1967] 1 W.L.R. 948; 111 S.J.
  472; sub nom. Hall (William) (Contractors), Re [1967] 2 All E.R.
  1150 .... 375, 397
Hallett's Estate, Re, Knatchbull v. Hallett (1880) 13 Ch.D. 696; [1874–80] All
  E.R.Rep. 793; sub nom. Hallett's Estate, Re, Knatchbull v. Hallett,
  Cotterell v. Hallett 49 L.J.Ch. 415; 42 L.T. 421; 28 W.R. 732 ... **106**, 108,
                                                      109, 110, 153, 359, 360
Halstead v. Patel [1972] 1 W.L.R. 661; 116 S.J. 218; [1972] 2 All E.R. 147; 56
  Cr.App.R. 334; [1972] Crim.L.R. 235 232

Hamilton v. Watson (1845) 12 Cl. & Fin. 109; 8 E.R. 1339 .... **291**, 295

Hamilton, Young & Co., Re, ex p. Carter [1905] 2 K.B. 772; 74 L.J.K.B. 905;
93 L.T. 591; 54 W.R. 260; 21 T.L.R. 757; 12 Mans. 365; 2 L.D.B.
98 .... 285, **287**, 289

Hampstead Guardians v. Barclays Bank Ltd. (1923) 39 T.L.R. 229; 67 S.J.
440; 3 L.D.B. 282 169

Hamzeh Malas v. British Imex Industries. See Malas (Hamzeh) v. British
Imex Industries.

Hancock v. Smith (1889) 41 Ch.D. 456; 58 L.J.Ch. 725; 61 L.T. 341; 5 T.L.R.
459 113

Hansson v. Hamel & Horley Ltd. [1922] 2 A.C. 36; [1922] All E.R.Rep. 237;
91 L.J.K.B. 433; 127 L.T. 74; 38 T.L.R. 466; 66 Sol.Jo. 421; 15
Asp.M.L.C. 546; 27 Com.Cas. 321; 10 Ll.LR. 199, 507 .... 262, 265

Harbottle (R.D.) (Mercantile) Ltd. v. National Westminster Bank Ltd.
[1978] Q.B. 146; [1977] 3 W.L.R. 752; (1977) 121 S.J. 745; [1977] 2 All
E.R. 862 272

Harman v. Glencross [1987] Fam. 81; [1986] 2 W.L.R. 637; (1986) 130 S.J.
224; [1986] 1 All E.R. 545; [1986] 2 F.L.R. 241; (1986) 16 Fam.Law
215; (1986) 136 New L.J. 69; (1985) 83 L.S.Gaz. 870, C.A.; [1984]
Fam. 49; [1984] 3 W.L.R. 759; (1984) 128 S.J. 662; [1984] 2 All E.R.
577; (1984) 14 Fam.Law 182; (1984) 81 L.S.Gaz. 1763 337

Harris Simons Construction Ltd., Re [1989] 1 W.L.R. 368; 1989 PCC 229;
(1989) 133 S.J. 122; [1989] BCLC 202; (1989) 5 BCC 11; [1989]
L.S.Gaz. February 22, 43 378

Harrods Ltd. v. Tester [1937] 2 All E.R. 236; 157 L.T. 7; 81 S.J. 376; 5 L.D.B.
31 113

Harrold v. Plenty [1901] 2 Ch. 314; 70 L.J.Ch. 562; 85 L.T. 45; 49 W.R. 646;
17 T.L.R. 545; 8 Mans. 304 .... **337**, 338

Harse v. Pearl Life Assurance Co. [1904] 1 K.B. 558; 73 L.J.K.B. 373; 90 L.T.
245; 52 W.R. 457; 20 T.L.R. 264; 48 Sol.Jo. 275 356

Hasan v. Willson [1977] 1 Lloyd's Rep. 431 .... 55, 56

Haynes v. Forshaw (1853) 11 Hare 93; 1 Eq.Rep. 527; 22 L.J.Ch. 1060; 22
L.T.(o.s.) 62; 17 Jur. 930; 1 W.R. 346; 68 E.R. 1201 206

Hedley Byrne & Co. Ltd. v. Heller & Partners [1964] A.C. 465; [1963] 3
W.L.R. 101; 107 S.J. 454; [1963] 2 All E.R. 575; [1963] 1 Lloyd's Rep.
485; 8 L.D.B. 155 .... **18**, 20, 21, 22, 23, 24, 25, 269

Heppenstall v. Jackson, Barclays Bank Ltd., Garnishees [1939] 2 All E.R. 10;
[1939] 1 K.B. 585; 108 L.J.K.B. 266; 160 L.T. 261; 55 T.L.R. 489; 83
S.J. 276; 5 L.D.B. 197 114

Hirschorn v. Evans [1938] 3 All E.R. 491; [1938] 2 K.B. 801; 107 L.J.K.B.
756; 159 L.T. 405; 54 T.L.R. 1069; 82 S.J. 664; 5 L.D.B. 155 ..... 115, 196

Hispano Americano Mercantil S.A. v. Central Bank of Nigeria (1979) 123
S.J. 336; [1979] 2 Lloyd's Rep. 277; C.L.B. 36 .... 269, 270

Holland v. Manchester and Liverpool District Banking Co. (1909) 25 T.L.R.
386; 14 Com.Cas. 241; 2 L.D.B. 221 .... **97**, 98

Holt v. Markham [1923] 1 K.B. 504; [1922] All E.R.Rep. 134; 92 L.J.K.B.
406; 128 L.T. 719; 67 S.J. 314; 3 L.D.B. 293 .... 98, 100, 139, 141

Hone (a bankrupt), Re ex p. The Trustee v. Kensington Borough Council
[1951] Ch. 85; 66 T.L.R. (Pt. 2) 350; 114 J.P. 495; [1950] 2 All E.R.
716; 6 L.D.B. 132; sub nom. Re A Bankrupt, 43 R. & I.T. 608 72

Hong Kong & Shanghai Banking Corporation v. Kloeckner & Co. A.G.
[1989] 3 All E.R. 513 .... 256, 384

Hopkinson v. Rolt (1861) 9 H.L.Cas. 514; 34 L.J.Ch. 468; 5 L.T. 90; 7
    Jur.(N.S.) 1209; 9 W.R. 900; 11 E.R. 829; affirming S.C. sub nom. Rolt
    v. Hopkinson (1858) 3 De G. & J. 177 .... **342**, 343
Houghland v. Low (R.R.) (Luxury Coaches) Ltd. [1962] 1 Q.B. 694; [1962] 2
    W.L.R. 1015; 106 S.J. 243; [1962] 2 All E.R. 159; 8 L.D.B. 48 280
House Property Co. of London Ltd. and Others v. London County and
    Westminster Bank Ltd. (1915) 84 L.J.K.B. 1846; 113 L.T. 817; 31
    T.L.R. 479 .... **185**, 187
Howe Richardson Scale Co. Ltd. v. Polimpex-Cekop and Another [1978] 1
    Lloyd's Rep. 161; C.L.B. 49 274
Hubbard, Re, Re Hardwick (1886) 17 Q.B.D. 690; 55 L.J.Q.B. 490; 59 L.T.
    172n.; 35 W.R. 2; 2 T.L.R. 904; 3 Morr. 246 286
Hughes (C.W. & A.L.) Ltd., Re [1966] 1 W.L.R. 1369; (1966) 110 S.J. 404;
    [1967] 2 All E.R. 1150 297
Hunter v. Hunter and Others [1936] A.C. 222; 105 L.J.Ch. 97; 154 L.T. 513 ... 323

I CONGRESO DEL PARTIDO, THE. See Playa Larga (Cargo Owners) v. I
    Congreso del Partido (Owners); Marble Islands (Cargo Owners) v. I
    Congreso del Partido (Owners).
Ian Stach v. Baker Bosley [1958] 2 Q.B. 130; [1958] 2 W.L.R..419; 102 S.J.
    177; [1958] 1 All E.R. 542; sub nom. Ian Stach v. Baker Bosly [1958] 1
    Lloyd's Rep. 127 267
Imperial Bank of Canada v. Bank of Hamilton [1903] A.C. 49; 72 L.J.P.C. 1;
    87 L.T. 457; 51 W.R. 289; 19 T.L.R. 56; 2 L.D.B. 51 140
Importers Company Ltd. v. Westminster Bank Ltd. [1927] 2 K.B. 297; 96
    L.J.K.B. 919; 137 L.T. 693; 43 T.L.R. 639; 32 Com.Cas. 369; 4 L.D.B.
    118 .... 34, 186
International Factors Ltd. v. Rodriguez [1979] Q.B. 351; [1978] 3 W.L.R.
    877; (1978) 122 S.J. 680; [1979] 1 All E.R. 17; C.L.B. 17 183
International Sales and Agencies Ltd. v. Marcus [1982] 3 All E.R. 551; [1982]
    2 C.M.L.R. 46 214
Interpool Ltd. v. Galani [1988] Q.B. 738; [1987] 3 W.L.R. 1042; (1987) 131
    S.J. 1392; [1987] 2 All E.R. 981; [1987] 2 F.T.L.R. 315; (1987) 137
    New L.J. 613 116
Intraco Ltd. v. Notis Shipping Co. of Liberia Bhoja Trader, The [1981]
    Com.L.R. 184; [1981] 2 Lloyd's Rep. 256 275
Introductions Ltd. v. National Provincial Bank Ltd. [1970] Ch. 199; [1969] 2
    W.L.R. 791; 113 S.J. 122; [1969] 1 Lloyd's Rep. 229; 9 L.D.B. 124; sub
    nom. Introductions, Re Introductions v. National Provincial Bank
    [1969] 1 All E.R. 887; affirming [1968] 2 All E.R. 1221 .... **212**
Irani Finance v. Singh [1971] Ch. 59; [1970] 3 W.L.R. 330; (1970) 114 S.J. 636;
    [1970] 3 All E.R. 199; (1970) 21 P. & C.R. 843 336
Isaacs v. Barclays Bank Ltd. and Barclays Bank (France) Ltd. [1943] 2 All
    E.R. 682; 169 L.T. 370; 88 S.J. 36; 5 L.D.B. 350 6
Islington Metal and Plating Works, Re [1984] 1 W.L.R. 14; (1984) 128 S.J. 31;
    [1983] 3 All E.R. 218; (1984) 81 L.S.Gaz. 354; [1983] Com.L.R. 176;
    (1983) 133 New L.J. 847 386

J.E.B. FASTENERS v. Marks, Bloom & Co. [1983] 1 All E.R. 583 23
Jackson v. White and Midland Bank Ltd. [1967] 2 Lloyd's Rep. 68; 9 L.D.B.
    13 .... **198**, 199
Jade International Steel Stahl and Eisen GmbH & Co. K.G. v. Nicholas
    (Robert) (Steels) Ltd. [1978] Q.B. 917; [1978] 3 W.L.R. 39; (1978) 122
    S.J. 294; [1978] 3 All E.R. 104; [1978] 2 Lloyd's Rep. 13; C.L.B. 20 69

Jayson v. Midland Bank Ltd. [1968] 1 Lloyd's Rep. 409; 9 L.D.B. 41   134

Joachimson v. Swiss Bank Corporation [1921] 3 K.B. 110; 90 L.J.K.B. 973;
      125 L.T. 338; 37 T.L.R. 534; 65 S.J. 434; 26 Com.Cas. 196; 3 L.D.B.
      233 .... 1, **2**, 4, 5, 8, 147, 155, 322, 323, 363

John v. Dodwell & Co. [1918] A.C. 563; 87 L.J.P.C. 92; 118 L.T. 661; 34
      T.L.R. 261   82

Jones v. Gordon (1877) 2 App.Cas. 616; 47 L.J.Bcy. 1; 37 L.T. 477; 26 W.R.
      172; affirming S.C. sub nom. Gomersall, Re (1875) 1 Ch.D. 137   145

——— v. Maynard [1951] Ch. 572; [1951] 1 T.L.R. 700; [1951] 1 All E.R. 802 ...   197

K., Re, The Independent, July 4, 1989   235

Kahler v. Midland Bank Ltd. [1950] A.C. 24; [1949] L.J.R. 1687; 65 T.L.R.
      663; [1949] 2 All E.R. 621; 6 L.D.B. 70   406

Kalish v. Manufacturers Trust Co. 191 N.Y.S. (2d) 61 (1959); 7 L.D.B. 238 ...   129

Karak Rubber Co. Ltd. v. Burden (No. 2) [1972] 1 W.L.R. 602; (1971) 115
      S.J. 888; [1972] 1 All E.R. 1210; [1972] 1 Lloyd's Rep. 73 .... 83, 85

Kayford Ltd. (in Liquidation), Re [1975] 1 W.L.R. 279; (1974) 118 S.J. 752;
      [1975] 1 All E.R. 604   237

Keever, Re, ex p. Cork v. Midland Bank. See Keever, Re, A Bankrupt ex p.
      Trustee of the Property of the Bankrupt v. Midland Bank.

———, Re, A Bankrupt, ex p. Trustee of the Property of the Bankrupt v.
      Midland Bank [1967] Ch. 182; [1966] 3 W.L.R. 779; 110 S.J. 847;
      [1966] 3 All E.R. 631; sub nom. Keever, Re, ex p. Cork v. Midland
      Bank [1966] 2 Lloyd's Rep. 475 .... 160, 278

Keller (Samuel) (Holdings) v. Martins Bank, Lawton (Henry W.) [1971] 1
      W.L.R. 43; sub nom. Keller (Samuel) (Holdings) v. Martins Bank
      (1970) 114 S.J. 951; [1970] 3 All E.R. 950; 22 P. & C.R. 68   325

Kendall v. Hamilton (1879) 4 App.Cas. 504; [1874–80] All E.R.Rep. 932; 48
      L.J.Q.B. 705; 41 L.T. 418; 28 W.R. 97, H.L.   202

Kent & Sussex Sawmills Ltd., Re [1947] Ch. 177; [1947] L.J.R. 534; 176 L.T.
      167; 62 T.L.R. 747; 91 S.J. 12; [1946] 2 All E.R. 638; 5 L.D.B.
      450 .... **345**, 346

Kenton v. Barclays Bank Ltd., The Banker, March 1977, p. 18 .... 186, 187

Kepitigalla Rubber Estates Ltd. v. National Bank of India Ltd. [1909] 2 K.B.
      1010; 78 L.J.K.B. 964; 100 L.T. 516; 100 L.T. 516; 25 T.L.R. 402; 53
      S.J. 377; 14 Com.Cas. 116; 16 Mans. 234 .... 92, 93, 95

Kings North Trust Ltd. v. Bell [1986] 1 W.L.R. 119   303

Kingsnorth Finance Co. v. Tizard [1986] 1 W.L.R. 783; (1985) 130 S.J. 244;
      [1986] 2 All E.R. 54; (1985) 51 P. & C.R. 296; (1985) 83 L.S.Gaz.
      1231   332

Kleinwort Benson v. Malaysia Mining Corp. Berhad [1989] 1 W.L.R. 379;
      [1989] 1 All E.R. 785; [1989] 1 Lloyd's Rep. 556; (1989) 133 S.J. 262;
      (1989) 139 New L.J. 221; [1989] L.S.Gaz. April 26, 35   399

Kinlan v. Ulster Bank Ltd. [1928] I.R. 171   130

Koch v. Dicks [1933] 1 K.B. 307; 102 L.J.K.B. 97; 148 L.T. 208; 49 T.L.R. 24;
      38 Com.Cas. 66; 4 L.D.B. 354   65

——— v. Mineral Ore Syndicate (London & South Western Bank Ltd.,
      Garnishees) (1910) 54 S.J. 600; 2 L.D.B. 264   114

Korea Exchange Bank Ltd. v. Debenhams (Central Buying) Ltd. (1979) 123
      S.J. 163; [1979] 1 Lloyd's Rep. 548; 10 L.D.B. 144   45

Kraut (Jean) A.G. v. Albany Fabrics [1977] Q.B. 182; [1976] 3 W.L.R. 872;
      [1977] 1 All E.R. 116; [1976] 2 Lloyd's Rep. 350   243

Kum and Another v. Wah Tat Bank Ltd. [1971] 1 Lloyd's Rep. 439   39

Kushler (M.) Ltd., *Re* [1943] 2 All E.R. 22; [1943] Ch. 248; 112 L.J.Ch. 194;
   169 L.T. 17; 59 T.L.R. 328; 87 S.J. 265; 5 L.D.B. 345 373
Kydon Compania Naviera S.A. *v.* National Westminster Bank Ltd.; Lena,
   The [1981] 1 Lloyd's Rep. 68; [1980] Com.L.R. 12 .... 260, 261

LADBROKE *v.* Todd (1914) 111 L.T. 43; 30 T.L.R. 433; 19 Com.Cas. 256; 3
   L.D.B. 89 .... 32, 169
Lamont (James) & Co. Ltd. *v.* Hyland Ltd. (No. 2) [1950] W.N. 205; 66
   T.L.R. (Pt. 1) 940; 94 S.J. 336; [1950] 1 All E.R. 929 69
Lancaster Motor Co. (London) Ltd. *v.* Bremith Ltd. [1941] 2 All E.R. 11;
   [1941] 1 K.B. 675; 110 L.J.K.B. 398; 165 L.T. 134; 57 T.L.R. 418;
   [1940–41] B. & C.R. 24; 5 L.D.B. 310 113
Landes *v.* Marcus and Davids (1909) 25 T.L.R. 478; 2 L.D.B. 203 51
Larner *v.* London County Council [1949] 2 K.B. 683; [1949] L.J.R. 1363; 65
   T.L.R. 316; 113 J.P. 300; 93 S.J. 371; [1949] 1 All E.R. 964 .... 99, 139
Latchford *v.* Beirne [1981] 3 All E.R. 705 .... 305, 306
Leeman *v.* Leeman (unreported) (1979) C.L.Y. 124; C.L.B. 40 334
Lewes Sanitary Steam Laundry Co. Ltd. *v.* Barclay & Co. Ltd. (1906) 95 L.T.
   444; 22 T.L.R. 737; 11 Com.Cas. 255 92
Lex Services plc. *v.* Johns, *The Times*, September 29, 1989 72
Libyan Arab Foreign Bank *v.* Bankers Trust Company [1987] 2 F.T.L.R. 509;
   [1988] 1 Lloyd's Rep. 259 6
Liggett (B.) (Liverpool) Ltd. *v.* Barclays Bank Ltd. [1928] 1 K.B. 48; 97
   L.J.K.B. 1; 137 L.T. 443; 43 T.L.R. 449; 4 L.D.B. 99 .... 221, 366
Lines Bros. Ltd. (In Liquidation), *Re* [1982] 2 W.L.R. 1010; (1982) 126 S.J.
   197; [1982] 2 All E.R. 183; [1982] Com.L.R. 81 .... 243, 386
Lipkin Gorman (a firm) *v.* Cass, *The Times*, May 29, 1985 123
—— *v.* Karpnale, [1989] F.L.R. 137 .... **78**, **79**, 83
Lloyds and Scottish Trust Ltd. *v.* Britten and Another (1982) 44 P. & C.R.
   249; (1982) 79 L.S.Gaz. 1291 312
Lloyds Bank Ltd. *v.* Bank of America National Trust and Savings Association
   [1938] 2 All E.R. 63; [1938] 2 K.B. 147; 107 L.J.K.B. 538; 158 L.T.
   301; 54 T.L.R. 599; 82 S.J. 312; 43 Com.Cas. 209; 5 L.D.B. 109 290
—— *v.* Brooks (1950) 72 J.I.B. 114; 6 L.D.B. 161 99
—— *v.* Bundy [1975] Q.B. 326; [1974] 3 W.L.R. 501; 118 S.J. 714; [1974] 3
   All E.R. 757; [1974] 2 Lloyd's Rep. 366 .... 22, 302, 303
—— *v.* Chartered Bank of India, Australia and China [1929] 1 K.B. 40; 97
   L.J.K.B. 609; 139 L.T. 126; 44 T.L.R. 534; 4 L.D.B. 171 .... **171**, 184,
   220
—— *v.* Harrison (1925) 4 L.D.B. 12 294
—— *v.* Hornby (1933) 54 J.I.B. 372 58
—— *v.* Margolis and Others [1954] 1 W.L.R. 644; 98 S.J. 250; [1954] 1 All
   E.R. 734; 6 L.D.B. 416 .... 315, 320, **321**
—— *v.* Savory (E.B.) & Co. [1933] A.C. 201; 102 L.J.K.B. 224; 49 T.L.R.
   116; 38 Com.Cas. 115; *sub nom.* Savory & Co. *v.* Lloyds Bank 148
   L.T. 291; 6 L.D.B. 416 .... **162**, 165, 166, 167, 170, 174
—— *v.* Suvale Properties Ltd. (unreported) (1981) C.L.Y. 271; C.L.B.
   16 .... 232, 233, 328
Lock International *v.* Beswick [1989] 1 W.L.R. 1268; [1989] 3 All E.R. 373;
   (1989) 139 New L.J. 644; (1989) 133 S.J. 1297 123
Lockwood *v.* Wood (1844) 6 Q.B. 50; 13 L.J.Q.B. 365; 3 L.T.(o.s) 139; 5 Jur.
   543; 115 E.R. 19 39
London and River Plate Bank *v.* Bank of Liverpool [1896] 1 Q.B. 7; 65
   L.J.Q.B. 80; 73 L.T. 473; 1 Com.Cas. 170; 1 L.D.B. 209 140

London City and Midland Bank Ltd. *v.* Gordon [1903] A.C. 240; 72 L.J.K.B. 451; 88 L.T. 574; 51 W.R. 671; 19 T.L.R. 402; *sub nom.* London, City & Midland Bank *v.* Gordon, Capital & Counties Bank *v.* Gordon 8 Com.Cas. 221; 2 L.D.B. 35 45

London Intercontinental Trust Ltd. *v.* Barclays Bank Ltd. [1980] 1 Lloyd's Rep. 241; C.L.B. 11 .... 93, 96

London Joint Stock Bank Ltd. *v.* Macmillan & Arthur [1918] A.C. 777; 119 L.T. 387; 34 T.L.R. 509; 62 S.J. 650; 3 L.D.B. 165 .... 66, **85**, 87, 88, 89, 92, 93, 94

—— *v.* Simmons [1892] A.C. 201; 61 L.J.Ch. 723; 66 L.T. 625; 56 J.P. 644; 41 W.R. 108; 8 T.L.R. 478; 36 S.J. 394; reversing S.C. *sub nom.* Simmons *v.* London Joint Stock Bank; Little *v.* London Joint Stock Bank [1891] 1 Ch. 270; 1 L.D.B. 169 .... 105, 145, **280**, 281, 282

London Provincial & South Western Bank Ltd. *v.* Buszard (1918) 35 T.L.R. 142; 63 S.J. 246; 3 L.D.B. 204 .... 129, 402

Lucas *v.* Dorrien (1817) 1 Moore C.P. 29; 7 Taunt. 278; 129 E.R. 112 279

Lumsden & Co. *v.* London Trustee Savings Bank [1971] 1 Lloyd's Rep. 114; 9 L.D.B. 198 .... 88, 174

Lyons (J.S.), *ex p.* Barclays Bank Ltd. *v.* The Trustee (1934) 51 T.L.R. 24; 4 L.D.B. 460 .... **371**, 373

McEvoy *v.* Belfast Banking Co. Ltd. [1935] A.C. 24; [1934] All E.R. Rep. 800; 103 L.J.P.C. 137; 151 L.T. 501; 40 Com.Cas. 1; 4 L.D.B. 447 .... **194**, 196

McInerny *v.* Lloyds Bank Ltd. [1974] 1 Lloyd's Rep. 246 23

McKinnon *v.* Donaldson, Lufkin and Jenrette Securities [1986] Ch. 482; [1986] 2 W.L.R. 453; (1985) 130 S.J. 224; [1986] 1 All E.R. 653; [1987] E.C.C. 139; [1986] F.L.R. 225; (1986) 83 L.S.Gaz. 1226 401

Mackenzie *v.* Royal Bank of Canada [1934] A.C. 468; 103 L.J.P.C. 81; 151 L.T. 486; 78 S.J. 471; 4 L.D.B. 439 .... **295**

Mackersy *v.* Ramsays Bonar & Co. (1843) 9 Cl. & Fin. 818; 8 E.R. 628 404

Madras, Official Assignee *v.* Mercantile Bank of India [1934] All E.R.Rep. 237; [1935] A.C. 53; 104 L.J.P.C. 1; 152 L.T. 170; 40 Com.Cas. 143 288

Malas (Hamzeh) & Sons *v.* British Imex Industries [1958] 2 Q.B. 127; [1958] 2 W.L.R. 100; 102 S.J. 68; [1958] 1 All E.R. 262; [1957] 2 Lloyd's Rep. 549 248

Mal Bowers Macquaries Electrical Centre Pty. Ltd. [1974] 1 N.S.W.L.R. 254 392

Manhattan Bank N.A. *v.* Israel-British Bank (London) Ltd. [1979] 3 All E.R. 1025 109

Mansouri *v.* Singh [1986] 1 W.L.R. 1393; [1986] 2 All E.R. 619; (1986) 130 S.J. 801; [1986] F.L.R. 143; (1986) 136 New L.J. 260; (1986) 83 L.S.Gaz. 3508, C.A.; affirming in part (1984) 134 New L.J. 991 ... 68, 254

Maratha Envoy, The. *See* Federal Commerce and Navigation Co. *v.* Tradax Export S.A.; Maratha Envoy, The.

Mardorf Peach & Co. *v.* Attica Sea Carriers Corp. of Liberia [1977] A.C. 850; [1977] 2 W.L.R. 286; (1977) 121 S.J. 134; [1977] 1 All E.R. 545; [1977] 1 Lloyd's Rep. 315 75

Mareva Compagnia Naviera S.A. of Panama *v.* International Bulk Carriers S.A. (1975) 119 S.J. 660; [1975] 2 Lloyd's Rep. 509; 9 L.D.B. 393 .... 117, 242

Marfani & Co. Ltd. *v.* Midland Bank Ltd. [1968] 1 W.L.R. 956; 112 S.J. 396; [1968] 2 All E.R. 573; [1968] 1 Lloyd's Rep. 411; 9 L.D.B. 49 ... 162, **164**, 167

Marreco v. Richardson [1908] 2 K.B. 584; [1908–10] All E.R.Rep. 655; 77
    L.J.K.B. 859; 99 L.T. 486; 24 T.L.R. 624; 52 S.J. 516 72
Marshal v. Crutwell (1875) L.R. 20 Eq. 328; 44 L.J.Ch. 504; 39 J.P. 775 196
Marten v. Rocke, Eyton & Co. (1885) 53 L.T. 946; 34 W.R. 253; 2 T.L.R.
    140 105
Marzetti v. Williams (1830) 1 B. & Ad. 415; 1 Tyr. 77n.; 9 L.J.O.S.K.B. 42;
    109 E.R. 842 130
Matthews v. Brown & Co. (1894) 63 L.J.Q.B. 494; sub nom. Matthews v.
    Brown & Co. 10 T.L.R. 386; sub nom. Matthews v. Williams Brown &
    Co. 10 R. 210; 1 L.D.B. 200 34
Matthews (F.P. & C.H.) Ltd., Re [1982] Ch. 257; [1982] 2 W.L.R. 495;
    [1982] 1 All E.R. 338 376
Maxform S.p.A. v. Mariani & Goodville Ltd. [1981] 2 Lloyd's Rep. 54 52
May v. Chapman (1847) 16 M. & W. 355; 8 L.T.O.S. 369; 153 E.R. 1225 144
Mecca, The [1897] A.C. 286; 66 L.J.P. 86; 76 L.T. 597; 45 W.R. 667; 13
    T.L.R. 339; 8 Asp.M.L.C. 266 153
Metropolitan Police Commissioner v. Charles [1976] 3 W.L.R. 431; 120 S.J.
    588; [1976] 3 All E.R. 112; (1976) 63 Cr.App.R. 252, H.L.; affirming
    sub nom. R. v. Charles [1976] 1 W.L.R. 248; (1975) 120 S.J. 147;
    [1976] 1 All E.R. 659; (1976) 63 Cr.App.R. 252; [1976] Crim.L.R.
    196 .... 226, 228
Midland Bank Ltd. v. Conway Corporation [1965] 1 W.L.R. 1165; 129 J.P.
    466; 109 S.J. 494; [1965] 2 All E.R. 972; 8 L.D.B. 416 4
Midland Bank v. Dobson and Dobson [1986] 1 FLR 171; (1985) F.L.R. 314;
    (1985) 16 Fam.Law 55; (1985) 135 New L.J. 751 332
—— v. Harris (R.V.) Ltd. [1963] 1 W.L.R. 1021; [1963] 2 All E.R. 685; 8
    L.D.B. 150 .... 60, 160, 161
—— v. Reckitt [1933] A.C. 1; 102 L.J.K.B. 297; 148 L.T. 374; 48 T.L.R. 271;
    76 S.J. 165; 37 Com.Cas. 202; 4 L.D.B. 298 .... 82, 176, 184, 235
—— v. Seymour [1955] 2 Lloyd's Rep. 147; 7 L.D.B. 42 .... **256**, 258
—— v. Shephard [1988] 3 All E.R. 17 303
Miliangos v. Frank (George) (Textiles) Ltd. [1976] A.C. 443; [1975] 3
    W.L.R. 758; 119 S.J. 774; [1975] 3 All E.R. 801; [1975] 2 C.M.L.R.
    585; [1976] 1 Lloyd's Rep. 201; 9 L.D.B. 408 .... 116, **241**, 243
Misa v. Currie (1876) 1 App.Cas. 554; 45 L.J.Q.B. 852; 35 L.T. 414; 24 W.R.
    1049 278
Moledina v. Gandesha [1980] New L.J., January 31 68
Momm v. Barclays Bank International Ltd. [1977] Q.B. 790; [1977] 2 W.L.R.
    407; sub nom. Delbrueck & Co. v. Barclays Bank International (1976)
    120 S.J. 486; [1976] 2 Lloyd's Rep. 341 .... 35, 114, 148, 149, 346
Montague's Settlement, Re (1985) 84 L.S.Gaz. 1057 84
Montebianceo Industrie Tessili S.p.A. v. Carlyle Mills (London) Ltd. [1981]
    1 Lloyd's Rep. 509 68
Montecchi v. Shimco (U.K.); Navone v. Same [1979] 1 W.L.R. 1180; (1978)
    123 S.J. 551; sub nom. Montecchi v. Shimco (U.K.); Domenica v.
    Same [1980] 1 Lloyd's Rep. 50; C.L.B. 19 .... 70, 255
Moore v. Woolsey (1854) 4 E. & B. 243; 3 C.L.R. 207; 24 L.J.Q.B. 40; 24
    L.T.O.S. 155; 1 Jur.N.S. 468; 3 W.R. 66; 19 E.R. 93 .... 355, 356
Morel (E.J.) (1934) Ltd., Re [1961] 1 All E.R. 796; [1962] Ch. 21; [1961] 3
    W.L.R. 57; 105 S.J. 156; 7 L.D.B. 272 236
Morison v. London County and Westminster Bank Ltd. [1914] 3 K.B. 356;
    [1914–15] All E.R.Rep. 853; 83 L.J.K.B. 1202; 111 L.T. 114; 30
    T.L.R. 481; 58 S.J. 453; 19 Com.Cas. 273; 3 L.D.B. 91 .... 95, 172, 173,
    177, 184, 189

Mortimer (Thomas) Ltd., *Re* (1938) 4 L.D.B. 3; 46 J.I.B. 259; 4 L.D.B. 3   388
Motor Traders Guarantee Corporation Ltd. *v.* Midland Bank Ltd. [1937] 4
    All E.R. 90; 157 L.T. 498; 54 T.L.R. 10; 81 S.J. 865; 5 L.D.B.
    68 ....   170, **177**, 179
Murphy (Elijah) (decd.), *Re*, Merton *v.* Marchanton (1930) 74 Sol.Jo. 321; 4
    L.D.B. 328   207
Mutual Life and Citizens Assurance *v.* Evatt (Clive Raleigh) [1971] A.C. 793;
    [1971] 2 W.L.R. 23; *sub nom.* Mutual Life and Citizens' Assurance
    Co. *v.* Evatt, 114 S.J. 932; [1971] 1 All E.R. 150; [1970] 2 Lloyd's Rep.
    441   23

NATHAN *v.* Ogdens Ltd. (1906) 95 L.T. 458   45
National Bank *v.* Silke [1891] 1 Q.B. 435; 60 L.J.Q.B. 199; 63 L.T. 787; 39
    W.R. 361; 7 T.L.R. 156; 1 L.D.B. 118   186
National Bank of Egypt *v.* Hannevig's Bank (1919) 3 L.D.B. 213   261
National Bank of Greece S.A. *v.* Pinios Shipping Co., No. 1; Maira, The (No.
    3) [1988] 2 F.T.L.R. 9; [1988] F.L.R. 249, C.A.   225
National Provincial Bank Ltd. *v.* Ainsworth [1965] A.C. 1175; [1965] 3
    W.L.R. 1; 109 S.J. 415; [1965] 2 All E.R. 472; reversing *sub nom.*
    National Provincial Bank *v.* Hastings Car Mart [1964] Ch. 665; [1964] 2
    W.L.R. 751; 108 S.J. 115; [1964] 1 All E.R. 688; [1964] C.L.Y. 1742;
    [1963] C.L.Y. 1689   331
—— *v.* Freedman and Rubens (1934) 4 L.D.B. 444 ....   **394**
—— *v.* Glanusk [1913] 3 K.B. 335; 3 L.D.B. 63   293
National Provincial Bank of England *v.* Brackenbury (1906) 22 T.L.R.
    797   310
—— *v.* Jackson (1886) 33 Ch.D. 1; 55 L.T. 458; 34 W.R. 597   353
National Westminster Bank Ltd. *v.* Barclays Bank International Ltd. and
    Another [1975] Q.B. 654; [1975] 2 W.L.R. 12; 118 S.J. 627; [1974] 3
    All E.R. 834; [1974] 2 Lloyd's Rep. 506; 9 L.D.B. 349 .... 91, 100, **136**,
                                                                                        141, 230
—— *v.* Halesowen Presswork & Assemblies Ltd. [1972] A.C. 785; [1972] 2
    W.L.R. 455; 116 S.J. 138; [1972] 1 All E.R. 641; [1972] 1 Lloyd's Rep.
    101, H.L.; 9 L.D.B. 253; reversing *sub nom.* Halesowen Presswork &
    Assemblies *v.* Westminster Bank [1971] 1 Q.B. 1; [1970] 3 W.L.R.
    625; [1970] 3 All E.R. 473, C.A. 235, 236, 278, 279, **383**, 385
—— *v.* Morgan [1985] A.C. 686; [1985] 2 W.L.R. 588; (1985) 129 S.J. 205;
    [1985] 1 All E.R. 821; (1985) 17 H.L.R. 360; 1985 F.L.R. 266; (1985)
    135 New L.J. 254; (1985) 82 L.S.Gaz. 1485, H.L.; 10 L.D.B. 510;
    reversing [1983] 3 All E.R. 85; (1983) 133 New L.J. 378 .... 22, **301**,
                                                                                        302, 303
—— *v.* Stockman [1981] 1 W.L.R. 67; (1980) 124 S.J. 810; [1981] 1 All E.R.
    800; *sub nom.* National Westminster Bank *v.* Stockton, *The Times*,
    August 19, 1980   336
Neste Oy. *v.* Lloyds Bank plc [1983] 2 Lloyd's Rep. 658; [1982] Com.L.R.
    145; (1983) 133 New L.J. 597 ....   103, 238
Newport County Association Football Club, *Re* [1987] BCLC 582; (1987) 3
    BCC 635   378
Nippon Yusen Kaisha *v.* Karageorgis [1975] 1 W.L.R. 1093; (1975) 119 S.J.
    441; [1975] 3 All E.R. 282; [1975] 2 Lloyd's Rep. 137   117
Nocton *v.* Ashburton (Lord) [1914] A.C. 932   19
Norman *v.* Ricketts (1886) 3 T.L.R. 182   72

North and South Insurance Corp. Ltd. *v.* National Provincial Bank Ltd. [1935] All E.R.Rep. 640; [1936] 1 K.B. 328; 105 L.J.K.B. 163; 154 L.T. 255; 52 T.L.R. 71; 80 S.J. 111; 41 Com.Cas. 80; 4 L.D.B. 489 ...... 42, 43
North & South Wales Bank Ltd. *v.* Macbeth, North & South Wales Bank Ltd. *v.* Irvine [1908] A.C. 137; 77 L.J.K.B. 464; 98 L.T. 470; 24 T.L.R. 397; 52 S.J. 353, 354; 13 Com.Cas. 219; affirming *sub nom.* Macbeth *v.* North & South Wales Bank [1908] 1 K.B. 13 .... 45, **47**, 48
North Western Bank *v.* Poynter, Son & Macdonalds [1895] A.C. 56; 64 L.J.P.C. 27; 72 L.T. 93; 11 R. 125 287
Northern Counties of England Fire Insurance Co. *v.* Whipp (1884) 26 Ch.D. 482; 53 L.J.Ch. 629; 51 L.T. 806; 32 W.R. 626 339
Nova (Jersey) Knit Ltd. *v.* Kammgarn Spinnerei GmbH, 120 S.J. 351; [1976] 2 Lloyd's Rep. 155 .... 70, 241
Nu-Stilo Footwear Ltd. *v.* Lloyds Bank Ltd. (1956) 7 L.D.B. 121 169
Nye (C.L.), *Re* [1971] Ch. 442; [1970] 3 W.L.R. 158; 114 S.J. 413; [1970] 3 All E.R. 1061; 9 L.D.B. 144 346

OCEANICA CASTELANA ARMADORA S.A. *v.* Mineral Importexport Seawind; Maritime Inc. *v.* Romanian Bank for Foreign Trade, *The Times,* February 5, 1983 120
Official Assignee of Madras *v.* Mercantile Bank of India [1935] A.C. 53 288
Official Solicitor to the Supreme Court *v.* Thomas [1986] 2 E.G.L.R. 1; (1986) 279 E.G. 407 72
Offord *v.* Davies and Another (1862) 12 C.B.(N.S.) 748; 31 L.J.C.P. 319; 6 L.T. 579; 9 Jur.N.S. 22; 10 W.R. 758; 142 E.R. 1336 311
Offshore International S.A. *v.* Banco Central S.A. [1977] 1 W.L.R. 399; (1977) 121 S.J. 252; [1976] 3 All E.R. 749; *sub nom.* Offshore International S.A. *v.* Banco Central S.A. and Hijos de J. Barreras S.A.; [1976] 2 Lloyd's Rep. 402; C.L.B. 31 262
O'Hara *v.* Allied Irish Bank [1985] BCLC 52; *The Times,* February 7, 1984 300
Oliver *v.* Davis [1949] 2 K.B. 727; [1949] L.J.R. 1661; (1949) 93 S.J. 562; [1949] 2 All E.R. 353 .... **54**, 55, 56
Orbit Mining & Trading Co. Ltd. *v.* Westminster Bank Ltd. [1963] 1 Q.B. 794; [1962] 3 W.L.R. 1256; 106 S.J. 937; [1962] 3 All E.R. 565; 8 L.D.B. 97 .... **41**, 43, 44, 88, 167, 174, 184
Oriel (in liquidation), *Re* [1986] 1 W.L.R. 180; (1985) 129 S.J. 669; [1985] 3 All E.R. 216; 1986 PCC 11; (1985) 82 L.S.Gaz. 3446; 10 L.D.B. 528 347
Orwell Steel (Erection and Fabrication) *v.* Asphalt and Tarmac (U.K.) [1984] 1 W.L.R. 1097; (1984) 128 S.J. 597; [1985] 3 All E.R. 747; (1984) 81 L.S.Gaz. 2935 118
Osterreichische Länderbank *v.* S'Elite Ltd. [1981] Q.B. 565; [1980] 3 W.L.R. 356; (1980) 124 S.J. 326; [1980] 2 All E.R. 651; [1980] 2 Lloyd's Rep. 139 376
Owen Decd., *Re,* Owen *v.* I.R.C. [1949] W.N. 201; [1949] L.J.R. 1128; 93 S.J. 287; 1 All E.R. 901; [1949] T.R. 189 73
Owen (Edward) Engineering Ltd. *v.* Barclays Bank International Ltd. [1977] 3 W.L.R. 764; (1977) 121 S.J. 617; [1978] 1 All E.R. 976; [1978] 1 Lloyd's Rep. 166; (1977) 6 Build.L.R. 1; 10 L.D.B. 50 .... **271**, 273, 325

PACLANTIC FINANCING CO. INC. *v.* Moscow Narodny Bank Ltd., *The Times,* May 5, 1982 226
Paddington Building Society *v.* Mendelsohn (1985) 50 P. & C.R. 244; (1987) 17 Fam.Law 121 332

Parkside Leasing Ltd. *v.* Smith (Inspector of Taxes) [1985] 1 W.L.R. 310; (1984) 128 S.J. 855; (1984) 58 T.C. 282; [1985] S.T.C. 63; (1985) 82 L.S.Gaz. 125 73

Parr's Banking Corporation Ltd. *v.* Yates [1898] 2 Q.B. 460; 67 L.J.Q.B. 851; 79 L.T. 321; 47 W.R. 42; 1 L.D.B. 276 315

Parsons *v.* Barclay & Co. Ltd. & Goddard (1910) 103 L.T. 196; 26 T.L.R. 628; 2 L.D.B. 248 .... 10, 25

Paul *v.* Constance [1977] 1 W.L.R. 527; [1977] 1 All E.R. 195; (1977) 121 S.J. 320; (1976) 7 Fam.Law 18 208

Pavia & Co. SpA *v.* Thurmann-Nielsen [1952] 2 Q.B. 84; [1952] 1 T.L.R. 586; 96 S.J. 193; [1952] 1 All E.R. 492; [1952] 1 Lloyd's Rep. 153 ...... **265**, 267

Peat *v.* Clayton [1906] 1 Ch. 659; 75 L.J.Ch. 344; 94 L.T. 465; 54 W.R. 416; 22 T.L.R. 312; 50 S.J. 291; 13 Mans. 117 353

—— *v.* Gresham Trust Ltd. (1934) 50 T.L.R. 345 372

Penmount Estates Ltd. *v.* National Provincial Bank Ltd. (1945) 173 L.T. 344; 89 S.J. 566; 5 L.D.B. 418 .... 179, 190

Perry *v.* National Provincial Bank Ltd. [1910] 1 Ch. 464; 79 L.J.Ch. 509; 102 L.T. 300; 54 S.J. 233; 2 L.D.B. 223 308

Perrylease *v.* Imecar AG [1988] 1 W.L.R. 463; (1988) 132 S.J. 536; [1987] 2 All E.R. 373; (1986) 136 New L.J. 987; [1988] L.S.Gaz. May 4, 32 313

Pertamina, The. *See* Rasu Maritima S.A. *v.* Perusahaan Pertambangan Minyak Dan Gas Bumi Negara (Pertimina) and Government of Republic of Indonesia (Intervener).

Pettit *v.* Pettit [1970] A.C. 777; [1969] 2 W.L.R. 966; 113 S.J. 344; [1969] 2 All E.R. 385; 20 C. & P.R. 991 198

Philippine Admiral, The; Philippine Admiral (Owners) *v.* Wallem Shipping (Hong Kong) [1976] 2 W.L.R. 214; (1975) 119 S.J. 865; *sub nom.* Owners of the Ship Philippine Admiral *v.* Wallem Shipping (Hong Kong); [1976] 1 All E.R. 78; *sub nom.* Wallem Shipping (Hong Kong) and Telfair Shipping Corp. *v.* Owners of the Ship Philippine Admiral; Philippine Admiral, The [1976] 1 Lloyd's Rep. 234; affirming *sub nom.* Wallem Shipping (Hong Kong) and Telfair Shipping Corp. *v.* Owners of the Ship Philippine Admiralty; Philippine Admiral, The [1974] 2 Lloyd's Rep. 568 269

Piller (Anton) K.B. *v.* Manufacturing Processes [1976] Ch. 55; [1976] 2 W.L.R. 162; (1975) 120 S.J. 63; [1976] 1 All E.R. 779; [1976] F.S.R. 129; [1976] R.P.C. 719 123

Pittoriou (A Bankrupt), Re, *ex p.* Trustee of the Property of the Bankrupt [1985] 1 W.L.R. 58; (1985) 129 S.J. 42; [1985] 1 All E.R. 285; (1985) 82 L.S.Gaz. 680 334

Place & Sons Ltd. *v.* Turner, *The Times*, February 7, 1951 88

Playa Larga (Cargo Owners) *v.* I Congreso del Partido (Owners); Marble Islands (Cargo Owners) *v.* Same [1981] 3 W.L.R. 328; (1981) 125 S.J. 528; [1981] 2 All E.R. 1064; [1981] Com.L.R. 190; [1981] 2 Lloyd's Rep. 367 270

Plunkett *v.* Barclays Bank Ltd. [1936] 1 All E.R. 653; [1936] 2 K.B. 107; 105 L.J.K.B. 379; 154 L.T. 465; 52 T.L.R. 353; 80 S.J. 225; 4 L.D.B. 495 .... 110, **111**, 113, 133

Pospischal *v.* Phillips, *The Times*, January 20, 1988 120

Pott *v.* Clegg (1847) 16 M. & W. 321; 16 L.J.Ex. 210; 8 L.T.O.S. 493; 11 Jur. 289; 153 E.R. 1212 3

Potters Oils, *Re* (No. 2) [1986] 1 W.L.R. 201; (1985) 130 S.J. 166; [1986] 1 All E.R. 890; 1986 PCC 185; (1985) 83 L.S.Gaz. 869 380

Potton Homes v. Coleman Contractors (Overseas) (1984) 128 S.J. 282; (1984) 28 Build.L.R. 19; (1984) 81 L.S.Gaz. 1044 274

Power Curber International Ltd. v. National Bank of Kuwait S.A.K. [1981] 1 W.L.R. 1233; (1981) 125 S.J. 585; [1981] 3 All E.R. 607; [1981] 2 Lloyd's Rep. 394; [1981] Com.L.R. 224 .... 255, 256, 400

Prekookeanska Plovidba v. L.N.T. Lines Srl (1988) 132 S.J. 1215; [1988] 3 All E.R. 897; (1988) 138 New L.J. 196; [1988] L.S.Gaz. September 14, 42 106

President of India v. Taygetos Shipping Company S.A. [1985] 1 Lloyd's Rep. 155 244

Primrose (Builders) Ltd., Re [1950] Ch. 561; 66 T.L.R. (Pt. 2) 99; [1950] 2 All E.R. 334; 6 L.D.B. 128 395

Prosperity Ltd. v. Lloyds Bank Ltd. (1923) 39 T.L.R. 372; 3 L.D.B. 287 .... 362, 363

Provincial Bank of Ireland v. O'Donnell [1934] N.I. 33 299

Pyke v. Hibernian Bank Ltd. [1950] I.R. 195; 6 L.D.B. 33 .... 134, 135

R. v. Beck (Brian) [1985] 1 W.L.R. 22; (1985) 149 J.P. 276; (1984) 128 S.J. 871; [1985] 1 All E.R. 571; (1984) 80 Cr.App.R. 355; (1985) 82 L.S.Gaz. 762, C.A. 229

—— v. Bevan (1987) 84 Cr.App.R. 143; [1987] Crim.L.R. 129; [1987] E.C.C. 372 229

—— v. Central Criminal Court, ex p. Adegbesan [1986] 1 W.L.R. 1292; (1986) 130 S.J. 821; [1986] 3 All E.R. 113; (1987) 84 Cr.App.R. 219; [1986] Crim.L.R. 691; (1986) 136 New L.J. 704; (1986) 83 L.S.Gaz. 3672 16

—— v. Dadson (1983) 127 S.J. 306; (1983) 77 Cr.App.R. 91; [1983] Crim.L.R. 540 13

—— v. Davies [1982] 1 All E.R. 513; [1982] 74 Cr.App.R. 94; [1982] Crim.L.R. 458 60

—— v. Fazackerley [1973] 1 W.L.R. 632; 117 S.J. 303; [1973] 2 All E.R. 819; [1973] Crim.L.R. 368; sub nom. R. v. Fazackerly (Eric Baker) 57 Cr.App.R. 578 231

—— v. Fisher (1988) 4 BCC 360 233

—— v. Gilmartin [1983] Q.B. 953; [1983] 2 W.L.R. 547; [1983] 1 All E.R. 829; (1983) 76 Cr.App.R. 238; [1983] Crim.L.R. 330 231

—— v. Governor of Pentonville Prison, ex p. Osman, The Times, April 13, 1988 232

—— v. Grantham [1984] Q.B. 675; [1984] 2 W.L.R. 815; (1984) 128 S.J. 331; [1984] 3 All E.R. 166; (1984) 79 Cr.App.R. 86; [1984] Crim.L.R. 492; (1984) 81 L.S.Gaz. 1437; 10 L.D.B. 473 397

—— v. Greenstein; R. v. Green [1975] 1 W.L.R. 1353; 119 S.J. 742; [1975] 1 All E.R. 1; sub nom. R. v. Greenstein (Allan); R. v. Green (Monty) (1975) 61 Cr.App.R. 296; [1975] Crim.L.R. 714 232

—— v. Grossman (1981) 73 Cr.App.R. 302; [1981] Crim.L.R. 396; 10 L.D.B. 282 .... 13, 400, 401

—— v. Hamid Shadrok-Cigaril [1988] Crim.L.R. 465 232

—— v. Hayat (Masood) 120 S.J. 434; (1976) 63 Cr.App.R. 181; [1976] Crim.L.R. 508; C.L.B. 30 233

—— v. Hazleton (1874) L.R. 2 C.C.R. 134; 44 L.J.M.C. 11; 31 L.T. 451; 39 J.P. 37; 23 W.R. 139; 13 Cox, C.C. 1, C.C.R. 231

—— v. Kohn (1979) 69 Cr.App.R. 395; [1979] Crim.L.R. 675; C.L.B. 8 350

R. v. Kovacs [1974] 1 W.L.R. 370; (1973) 118 S.J. 116; [1974] 1 All E.R.
    1236; *sub nom.* R. v. Kovacs (Stephanie Janika) (1973) 58 Cr.App.R.
    412; [1974] Crim.L.R. 183 227
—— v. Kritz [1950] 1 K.B. 82; [1949] L.J.R. 1535; 65 T.L.R. 505; 113 J.P.
    449; 93 S.J. 648; [1949] 2 All E.R. 406; 33 Cr.App.R. 169; 48 L.G.R.
    88 232
—— v. Lambie [1982] A.C. 449; [1981] 3 W.L.R. 88; (1981) 125 S.J. 480;
    [1981] 2 All E.R. 776; [1981] Crim.L.R. 712; (1981) 73 Cr.App.R.
    294 228
—— v. Manchester Crown Court, *ex p.* Taylor [1988] 1 W.L.R. 705; (1988)
    132 S.J. 899; [1988] 2 All E.R. 769; [1988] Crim.L.R. 386 16
—— v. Marlborough Street Stipendiary Magistrate, *ex p.* Simpson (1980) 70
    Cr.App.R. 291; [1980] Crim.L.R. 305 13
—— v. Navvabi [1986] 1 W.L.R. 1311; (1986) 150 J.P. 474; [1986] 3 All E.R.
    102; (1986) 83 Cr.App.R. 271; [1987] E.C.C. 366; [1987] Crim.L.R.
    57; (1986) 150 J.P.N. 558; (1986) 136 New L.J. 893; (1986) 83 L.S.Gaz.
    1919 229
—— v. Nottingham City Justices, *ex p.* Lynn (1984) 79 Cr.App.R. 238;
    [1984] Crim.L.R. 554 13
—— v. Registrar of Companies, *ex p.* Central Bank of India [1986] Q.B.
    1114; [1986] 2 W.L.R. 177; (1985) 129 S.J. 755; [1986] 1 All E.R. 105;
    1986 PCC 235 346
—— v. Shadrock-Cigaril (Hamid) [1988] Crim.L.R. 465 232
—— v. Southwark Crown Court, *ex p.* Customs and Excise; R. v. Same *ex p.*
    Bank of Credit and Commerce International S.A. [1989] 3 W.L.R.
    1054; [1989] 3 All E.R. 673 15
—— v. Townshend (1884) 15 Cox C.C. 466 289
—— v. Turner [1973] 1 W.L.R. 653; 117 S.J. 303; [1973] 2 All E.R. 828
    (C.A.); reversed [1974] A.C. 357 (H.L.) 231
—— v. Watkins [1976] 1 All E.R. 578; C.L.B. 30 231
—— v. Withers [1974] Q.B. 414; [1974] 2 W.L.R. 26; (1973) 58 Cr.App.R.
    187, C.A.; reversed [1975] A.C. 842, H.L. 8
Rae v. Yorkshire Bank [1988] F.L.R. 1; *The Times*, October 12, 1987 131
Rampgill Mill Ltd., *Re* [1967] Ch. 1138; [1967] 2 W.L.R. 394; 111 S.J. 130;
    [1967] 1 All E.R. 56; [1966] 2 Lloyd's Rep. 527 396
Raphael v. Bank of England (1855) 17 C.B. 161; 25 L.J.C.P. 33; 26 L.T.O.S.
    60; 4 W.R. 10; 139 E.R. 1030 .... **143**
Rasu Maritima S.A. v. Perusahaan Pertambangan Minyak Dan Gas Bumi
    Negara (Pertamina) and Government of Republic of Indonesia
    (Intervener) [1978] Q.B. 644; [1977] 3 W.L.R. 518; (1977) 121 S.J.
    706; [1977] 3 All E.R. 324; [1977] 2 C.M.L.R. 470; [1977] 2 Lloyd's
    Rep. 397 118
Rayner (J.H.) & Co. Ltd. v. Hambro's Bank Ltd. [1942] 2 All E.R. 649;
    [1943] 1 K.B. 37; 112 L.J.K.B. 27; 167 L.T. 380; 59 T.L.R. 21; 5
    L.D.B. 334 .... 259, 261, 275
Reckitt v. Barnett, Pembroke and Slater Ltd. [1929] A.C. 176; [1928] All
    E.R.Rep. 1; 98 L.J.K.B. 136; 140 L.T. 208; 45 T.L.R. 36; 34
    Com.Cas. 126, H.L.; 4 L.D.B. 205 176
Reigate v. Union Manufacturing Co. (Ramsbottom) [1918] 1 K.B. 592;
    [1918–19] All E.R.Rep. 143; 87 L.J.K.B. 724; 118 L.T. 479 200
Rekstin v. Severo Sibirsko Gosudarstvernnoe Akcionernoe Obschestvo
    Komseverputj & Bank for Russian Trade [1933] 1 K.B. 47; 102
    L.J.K.B. 16; 147 L.T. 231; 48 T.L.R. 578; 76 S.J. 494; 4 L.D.B.
    328 .... 114, 346, 404

Resinoid and Mica Products, Re [1983] Ch. 132; [1982] 3 W.L.R. 979; [1982] 3
    All E.R. 67 346
Rimmer v. Rimmer [1953] 1 Q.B. 63; [1952] 2 T.L.R. 767; 96 S.J. 801; [1952]
    2 All E.R. 863 197
Ringham v. Hackett and Another (1980) 124 S.J. 201; The Times, February 9,
    1980; 10 L.D.B. 206 .... 52, 63, 203
Robarts v. Tucker (1851) 16 Q.B.D. 560; 20 L.J.Q.B. 270; 15 Jur. 987; 117
    E.R. 994 .... 49, **124**, 125
Roberts Petroleum v. Kenney (Bernard) [1983] A.C. 192; [1983] 2 W.L.R.
    305; (1983) 127 S.J. 138; [1983] 1 All E.R. 564; [1983] Com.L.R. 564;
    [1982] 1 W.L.R. 301; [1982] 1 All E.R. 685; 10 L.D.B. 393 .... **335**, 336,
                                                                                                            337
Robinson v. Midland Bank Ltd. (1925) 41 T.L.R. 402; 69 S.J. 428, 792; 4
    L.D.B. 19 49
Rogers v. Whiteley [1892] A.C. 118; 61 L.J.Q.B. 512; 66 L.T. 303;
    S.T.T.L.R. 418; 1 L.D.B. 181 .... **110**, 113
Rolfe, Lubell & Co. v. Keith and Another (1978) 123 S.J. 32; [1979] 1 All
    E.R. 860; [1979] 2 Lloyd's Rep. 75 .... **50**
Rolin v. Steward (1854) 14 C.B. 595; 23 L.J.C.P. 148; 18 Jur. 536; 2 C.L.R.
    959; 139 E.R. 245; sub nom. Rollin v. Steward 23 L.T.O.S. 114; 2
    W.R. 467 .... 130, 131
Rolled Steel Products (Holdings) v. British Steel Corporation [1986] Ch. 246;
    [1985] 2 W.L.R. 908; (1984) 128 S.J. 629; [1985] 3 All E.R. 1; (1984) 81
    L.S.Gaz. 2357 215
Ross v. London County Westminster and Parr's Bank Ltd. [1919] 1 K.B. 678;
    88 L.J.K.B. 927; 120 L.T. 636; 35 T.L.R. 315; 63 S.J. 411; 3 L.D.B.
    205 .... 179, 265
Rowlandson v. National Westminster Bank Ltd. [1978] 1 W.L.R. 798; (1977)
    122 S.J. 347; [1978] 3 All E.R. 370; [1978] 1 Lloyd's Rep. 523; C.L.B.
    25 82
Royal Bank of Canada v. I.R.C. [1972] 665; [1972] 2 W.L.R. 106; 115 S.J.
    968; [1972] 1 All E.R. 225; (1971) 47 T.C. 565 147
Royal Bank of Scotland v. Christie (1841) 8 Cl. & Fin. 214; 8 E.R. 84; 2 Robin
    App. 118 .... 153, 205
—— v. Greenshields [1914] S.C. 259; 51 Sc.L.R. 260; 3 L.D.B. 80 294
Royal British Bank, The v. Turquand (1856) 6 E. & B. 327; 25 L.J.Q.B. 317; 2
    Jur.N.S. 663; 119 E.R. 886 .... **216**
Royal Products Ltd. v. Midland Bank [1981] Com.L.R. 93; [1981] 2 Lloyd's
    Rep. 194; 10 L.D.B. 393 .... 114, 149, 346, **403**
Royal Trust Company of Canada v. Markham [1975] 1 W.L.R. 1416; 119 S.J.
    643; [1975] 3 All E.R. 433; 30 P. & C.R. 317; 9 L.D.B. 399 327
Rudd & Son, Re; Fosters & Rudd, Re The Times, January 22, 1986 321
Rumball v. Metropolitan Bank (1877) 2 Q.B.D. 194; 46 J.Q.B. 346; 36 L.T.
    240; 25 W.R. 366 38
Rushton (A Bankrupt), Re; ex p. National Westminster Bank v. Official
    Receiver (Trustee of the Property of the Bankrupt). See Debtor (No. 5
    of 1967) A, Re; ex p. National Westminster Bank v. Official Receiver.
Russel v. Russel (1873) 1 Bro.C.C. 269 338
Russell v. Bank America National Trust and Savings Association (1978)
    (unreported) 135, 364
Rutherford (James R.) & Sons, Re Lloyd's Bank v. Winter [1964] 1 W.L.R.
    1211; 108 S.J. 563; [1964] 3 All E.R. 137; 8 L.D.B. 311 396

SCF Finance Co. *v.* Masri (No. 3) (Masri, garnishee) [1987] Q.B. 1028;
   [1987] 2 W.L.R. 81; (1987) 131 S.J. 22; [1987] 1 All E.R. 194; (1987) 84
   L.S.Gaz. 37 .... 116, 118
St. Ives Windings, *Re* (1987) 3 BCC 634 378
Sarflax, *Re* [1979] Ch. 592; [1979] 2 W.L.R. 202; (1978) 123 S.J. 97; [1979] 1
   All E.R. 529 399
Sass, *Re*, *ex p.* National Provincial Bank of England [1896] 2 Q.B. 12; 65
   L.J.Q.B. 481; 74 L.T. 383; 44 W.R. 588; 12 T.L.R. 333; 40 Sol.Jo. 686;
   3 Mans. 125 370
Satis House, Datchett, Bucks., *Re*; Sowman *v.* Samuel (David) Trust Ltd.
   (1977) (unreported) 382
Saunders *v.* Anglia Building Society. *See* Saunders (Executrix of the Estate of
   Rose Maud Gallie) *v.* Anglia Building Society.
Saunders (Executrix of the Estate of Rose Maud Gallie) *v.* Anglia Building
   Society [1971] A.C. 1004; [1970] 3 W.L.R. 1078; *sub nom.* Saunders *v.*
   Anglia Building Society, 114 S.J. 885; 9 L.D.B. 180; *sub nom.*
   Saunders (Executrix of the Estate of Rose Maud Gallie) *v.* Anglia
   Building (formerly Northampton Town and County Building Society)
   [1970] 3 All E.R. 961 298
Savory (E.B.) & Co. *v.* Lloyds Bank [1932] 2 K.B. 122 163
Scarth *v.* National Provincial Bank Ltd. (1930) 4 L.D.B. 241 365
Scholefield *v.* Earl of Londesborough [1896] A.C. 514; 1 L.D.B. 215 .... 87, 89
Scholefield Goodman & Sons *v.* Zyngier [1986] A.C. 562; [1985] 3 W.L.R.
   953; (1985) 129 S.J. 811; [1985] 3 All E.R. 105; [1986] F.L.R. 1; (1985)
   135 New L.J. 985; (1985) 82 L.S.Gaz. 3529, P.C. 240
Schorsch Meier GmbH *v.* Hennin [1975] Q.B. 416; [1974] 3 W.L.R. 823; 118
   S.J. 881; [1975] 1 All E.R. 152; [1975] 1 C.M.L.R. 20; [1975] 1 Lloyd's
   Rep. 1 242
Schroeder *v.* Central Bank (1876) 34 L.T. 735; 24 W.R. 710; 2 Char. Pr. Cas.
   77 350
Scott *v.* Barclays Bank Ltd. [1923] 2 K.B. 1; 3 L.D.B. 278 259
Securities and Investment Board *v.* Pantell S.A. [1989] 3 W.L.R. 698; [1989] 2
   All E.R. 673; [1989] BCLC 590; (1989) 139 New L.J. 754 121
Selangor United Rubber Estates Ltd. *v.* Cradock (a bankrupt) (No. 3) [1968]
   1 W.L.R. 1555; 112 S.J. 744; [1968] 2 All E.R. 1073; [1968] 2 Lloyd's
   Rep. 289; 9 L.D.B. 66 .... 82, 83, 84, 85, 149, 168, 181, 408
Services Europe Atlantique Sud (SEAS) *v.* Stockholms Rederiaktiebolag
   Svea of Stockholm; Despina R., The; Folias, The [1979] A.C. 685;
   [1978] 3 W.L.R. 804; (1978) 122 S.J. 758; [1979] 1 All E.R. 421; [1979]
   1 Lloyd's Rep. 1; affirming [1978] 2 W.L.R. 887; [1977] 3 W.L.R. 597;
   (1978) 122 S.J. 366; (1977) 121 S.J. 574; [1978] 2 All E.R. 764; *sub*
   nom. Owners of the M.V. Eleftherotria *v.* Owners of the M.V.
   Despina R. [1979] Q.B. 491; [1977] 3 All E.R. 874; [1978] 1 Lloyd's
   Rep. 535; [1977] 2 Lloyd's Rep. 319 243
Settebello *v.* Banco Totta and Acores [1985] 1 W.L.R. 1050; (1985) 129 S.J.
   683; [1985] 2 All E.R. 1025; [1985] 2 Lloyd's Rep. 448; [1986] E.C.C.
   11; (1985) 135 New L.J. 658; (1985) 82 L.S.Gaz. 2658, C.A. 275
Sewell *v.* Burdick (1884) 10 App.Cas. 74 .... **282**, 284
Seymour, *Re*, *ex p.* Trustee [1937] 1 Ch. 668; *sub nom.* Seymour, *Re*, Trustee
   v. Barclays Bank [1937] 3 All E.R. 499; 157 L.T. 472; 53 T.L.R. 940;
   81 Sol.Jo. 629; [1936–7] B. & C.R. 178 .... 261, 367
Shamji *v.* Johnson Matthey Bankers [1986] BCLC 278; *Financial Times*,
   January 17, 1986, C.A. 380
Shaw (John) (Rayners Lane) Ltd. *v.* Lloyds Bank Ltd. (1944) 66 J.I.B. 105 104

Sheffield Corpn. v. Barclay [1905] A.C. 392; 74 L.J.K.B. 747; 93 L.T. 83; 69
  J.P. 385; 54 W.R. 49; 21 T.L.R. 642; 49 S.J. 617; 3 L.G.R. 992; 10
  Com.Cas. 287; 12 Mans. 248 .... 137, 282, **351**, 353
Sheffield (Earl) v. London Joint Stock Bank (1888) 13 App.Cas. 333; 57
  L.J.Ch. 986; 58 L.T. 735; 37 W.R. 33; 4 T.L.R. 389, H.L.; reversing
  S.C. sub nom. Easton v. London Joint Stock Bank (1886) 34 Ch.D.
  95 281
Sherry, Re, London & County Banking Company v. Terry (1884) 25 Ch. 692;
  53 L.J.Ch. 404; 50 L.T. 227; 32 W.R. 394 .... **316**, 317
Siebe Gorman & Co. v. Barclays Bank. See Gorman (Siebe) & Co. v.
  Barclays Bank.
Simm v. Anglo-American Telegraph Co., Anglo-American Telegraph Co. v.
  Spurling (1879) 5 Q.B.D. 188 137
Simms, Re [1930] 2 Ch. 22; 99 L.J.Ch. 235; 46 T.L.R. 258; [1929] B. & C.R.
  129; sub nom. Simms, Re, ex p. Trustee 143 L.T. 326 367
Sinason-Teicher Inter-American Grain Corporation v. Oilcakes and Oilseeds
  Trading Co. Ltd. [1954] 1 W.L.R. 1394; 98 S.J. 864; [1954] 3 All E.R.
  468; [1954] 2 Lloyd's Rep. 327; 6 L.D.B. 460 .... 266, 267
Singer (A.) & Co. (Hat Manufacturers) Ltd., Re [1943] 1 Ch. 121; [1943] 1 All
  E.R. 225; 112 L.J.Ch. 113; 168 L.T. 132; 59 T.L.R. 176; 87 S.J. 102,
  C.A.; 5 L.D.B. 339 .... 373, 374
Singh (Gian) & Co. v. Banque de l'Indochine [1974] 1 W.L.R. 1234; 118 S.J.
  644; [1974] 2 All E.R. 754; [1974] 2 Lloyd's Rep. 1 253
Siskina, The [1979] A.C. 210; [1977] 3 W.L.R. 818; 121 S.J. 744; [1977] 3 All
  E.R. 803; [1978] 1 C.M.L.R. 190; sub nom. Siskina (Owners of Cargo
  Lately on Board) v. Distos Compania Naviera (1977) 121 S.J. 744;
  [1977] 3 All E.R. 803; [1978] 1 Lloyd's Rep. 1, H.L.; reversing (1977)
  121 S.J. 461; [1977] 2 Lloyd's Rep. 230; sub nom. Siskina v. Distos
  Compania Naviera S.A. sub nom. Ibrahim Shanker v. Distos Compania Naviera S.A., The Times, June 2, 1977 121
Skyring v. Greenwood (1825) 4 B. & C. 281; 6 Dow. & Ry.K.B. 401;
  [1924–34] All E.R.Rep. 104; 107 E.R. 1064 97
Slingsby v. District Bank [1932] 1 K.B. 544; 101 L.J.K.B. 281; 146 L.T. 377;
  48 T.L.R. 114; 37 Com.Cas. 39; 4 L.D.B. 275 .... 59, **63**, 65, 88, 89,
                                                                      175, 183, 184
——— v. Westminster Bank Ltd. (No. 2) [1931] 2 K.B. 583; 101 L.J.K.B.
  291n.; 146 L.T. 89; 47 T.L.R. 1; 36 Com.Cas. 61; 4 L.D.B. 258 64
Smith v. Eric S. Bush; Harris v. Wyre Forest District Council [1989] 2 W.L.R.
  790; (1989) 133 S.J. 597; (1989) 21 H.L.R. 424; [1989] 2 All E.R. 514;
  (1989) 139 New L.J. 576; [1989] 17 E.G. 68; 18 E.G. 99 24
Smith and Baldwin v. Barclays Bank Ltd. (1944) 5 L.D.B. 370 179
Société Générale de Paris v. Walker (1885) 11 App.Cas. 20; 55 L.J.Q.B. 169;
  54 L.T. 389; 34 W.R. 662; 2 T.L.R. 200 340
Souhrada v. Bank of New South Wales [1976] 2 Lloyd's Rep. 444 175
Space Investments Ltd. v. Canadian Imperial Bank of Commerce Trust Co.
  (Bahamas) [1986] 1 W.L.R. 1072; [1986] 3 All E.R. 75; (1986) 130 S.J.
  612; (1986) 83 L.S.Gaz. 2567, P.C. 5
Spencer v. Clarke (1878) 9 Ch.D. 137; 47 L.J.Ch. 692; 27 W.R. 133 ..... 338, 340
Stach (Ian) Ltd. v. Baker Bosley. See Ian Stach v. Baker Bosley.
Standard Chartered Bank v. Walker [1982] 1 W.L.R. 1410; (1982) 126 S.J.
  479; [1982] 3 All E.R. 938; (1982) 264 E.G. 345; [1982] Com.L.R. 233;
  (1982) 79 L.S.Gaz. 1137; 10 L.D.B. 365 .... 304, 306, 326
Standish v. Ross (1849) 3 Ex. 527; 19 L.J.Ex. 185; 12 L.T.(o.s.) 495; 13 J.P.
  269; 154 E.R. 954 139

Stanley (G.) & Co. Ltd., *Re* [1925] 1 Ch. 148; 94 L.J.Ch. 187; 133 L.T. 37; 69
    S.J. 36; [1925] B. & C.R. 1 373
State of Norway's Application (Nos. 1 & 2), *Re* [1989] 2 W.L.R. 458; (1989)
    133 S.J. 290; [1989] 1 All E.R. 745 15
State Trading Corporation of India, The *v*. Man (E.D. & F.) (Sugar) [1981]
    Com.L.R. 235 274
Stenning, *Re*, Wood *v*. Stenning [1895] 2 Ch. 433; 73 L.T. 207; 13 R. 807 153
Stewart (Alexander) & Son of Dundee Ltd. *v*. Westminster Bank Ltd. [1926]
    W.N. 271; (1926) 4 L.D.B. 40 219
Stewart Chartering *v*. C. & O. Management S.A.; Venus Destiny, The 1
    W.L.R. 460; (1979) 124 S.J. 205; [1980] 1 All E.R. 718; [1980] 2
    Lloyd's Rep. 116 118
Stone *v*. Compton (1838) 5 Bing.N.C. 142; 1 An. 436; 6 Scott 846; 2 Jur. 1042;
    132 E.R. 1059 297
Stony Stanton Supplies (Coventry) *v*. Midland Bank (1965) 109 S.J. 255; *sub*
    nom. Stoney Stanton Supplies (Coventry) *v*. Midland Bank [1966] 2
    Lloyd's Rep. 373; 8 L.D.B. 342 .... 34, 49
Suffell *v*. Bank of England (1882) 9 Q.B.D. 555; 51 L.J.Q.B. 401; 47 L.T.
    146; 46 J.P. 500; 30 W.R. 932; 1 L.D.B. 41 65
Sunderland *v*. Barclays Bank Ltd., *The Times*, November 25, 1938; 5 L.D.B.
    163 9
Swan *v*. Bank of Scotland (1836) 10 Bli.(N.S.) 627; 1 Deac. 746; 2 Mart. & A.
    656; 6 E.R. 231, H.L. 312
—— *v*. North British Australasian Company (1862) 7 H. & N. 603; (1863) 2
    H. & C. 175 172
Swift *v*. Jewsbury (1874) L.R. 9 Q.B. 301; 43 L.J.Q.B. 56; 30 L.T. 31; 22
    W.R. 319; varying S.C. *sub nom.* Swift *v*. Winterbotham (1873) L.R. 8
    Q.B. 244 .... 25, 27
Sztejn *v*. Schroder (J. Henry) Banking Corp. 31 N.V.S. 2d 631 (1941) .. 249, 273

T.C.B. *v*. Gray [1987] Ch. 458; [1987] 3 W.L.R. 1144; [1988] 1 All E.R. 108;
    [1988] BCLC 281; [1988] F.L.R. 116; (1987) 3 BCC 503, C.A. 215
T.W. Construction Ltd.., *Re* [1954] 1 W.L.R. 540; (1954) 98 S.J. 216; [1954] 1
    All E.R. 744 393
Tai Hing Cotton Mill Ltd. *v*. Lin Chong Hing Bank [1986] A.C. 80; [1985] 3
    W.L.R. 317; (1985) 129 S.J. 503; [1985] 2 All E.R. 947; [1986] FLR 14;
    [1985] 2 Lloyd's Rep. 313; (1985) 135 New L.J. 680; (1985) 82
    L.S.Gaz. 2995; 10 L.D.B. 541 .... 87, 91, **93**, 96
Tankexpress A/S *v*. Compagnie Financière Belge des Pétroles S.A. *See* A/S
    Tankexpress *v*. Compagnie Financière Belge des Pétroles S.A.
Tapp *v*. Jones (1875) L.R. 10 Q.B. 591; 44 L.J.Q.B. 127; 33 L.T. 201; 23
    W.R. 694 114
Tassell *v*. Cooper (1850) 9 C.B. 509; 14 L.T.(o.s.) 466; 137 E.R. 990 ... **101**, 103
Tatung (U.K.) *v*. Galex Telesure Ltd. [1989] 5 B.C.C. 25 361
Taxation, Commissioners of *v*. English, Scottish & Australian Bank [1920]
    A.C. 683; 89 L.J.P.C. 181; 123 L.T. 34; 36 T.L.R. 305 .... 30, **31**, 34,
                                                          163, 169
Teale *v*. William Williams Brown & Co. (1894) 11 T.L.R. 56 105
Thackwell *v*. Barclays Bank [1986] 1 All E.R. 676 181
Thai-Europe Tapioca Service *v*. Government of Pakistan, Ministry of Food
    and Agriculture, Directorate of Agricultural Supplies (Import and
    Shipping Wing); Harmattan, The [1975] 1 W.L.R. 1485; 119 S.J. 745;
    [1975] 3 All E.R. 961; [1976] 1 Lloyd's Rep. 1 269

Thairlwall v. Great Northern Railway Co. [1910] 2 K.B. 509; 79 L.J.K.B. 924;
103 L.T. 186; 26 T.L.R. 555; 54 S.J. 652; 17 Mans. 247; 2 L.D.B.
259 45
Thames Guaranty v. Campbell [1985] Q.B. 210; [1984] 3 W.L.R. 109; (1984)
128 S.J. 301; [1984] 2 All E.R. 585; (1984) 47 P. & C.R. 575; (1984) 81
L.S.Gaz. 2294, C.A. 337, 342
Third Chandris Shipping Corporation v. Unimarine S.A.; Aggelikai Ptera
Compania Maritima S.A. v. Same; Western Sealanes Corporation v.
Same; Genie, The; Pythia, The; Angelic Wings, The [1979] Q.B. 645;
[1979] 3 W.L.R. 122; (1979) 123 S.J. 389; [1979] 2 All E.R. 972; [1979]
2 Lloyd's Rep. 184 118
Thomas v. Nottingham Incorportated Football Club [1972] Ch. 596; [1972] 2
W.L.R. 1025; (1971) 116 S.J. 96; [1972] 1 All E.R. 1176; 9 L.D.B.
245 316
Thompson v. Barke (J.) & Co. (Caterers) Ltd. 1975 S.L.T. 67 212
Thomson v. Clydesdale Bank Ltd. [1893] A.C. 282; 62 L.J.P.C. 91; 69 L.T.
156; I.R. 255 105
Thoni GmbH & Co., K.G. v. R.T.P. Equipment Ltd. [1979] 2 Lloyd's Rep.
282; C.L.B. 20 69
Thornton v. Maynard (1875) L.R. 10 C.P. 695; 44 L.J.C.P. 382; 33 L.T. 433 .. 239
Tournier v. National Provincial and Union Bank of England [1924] 1 K.B.
461; 93 L.J.K.B. 449; 130 L.T. 682; 40 T.L.R. 214; 68 S.J. 441; 29
Com.Cas. 129; 3 L.D.B. 305 .... 6, 8, 9, 10, 11, 14
Transvaal and Delagoa Bay Investment Co. v. Atkinson [1944] 1 All E.R.
579; 5 L.D.B. 358 108
Trendtex Trading Corporation v. Central Bank of Nigeria [1977] Q.B. 529;
[1977] 2 W.L.R. 356; 121 S.J. 85; [1977] 1 All E.R. 881; [1977] 2
C.M.L.R. 465; [1977] 1 Lloyd's Rep. 581; 10 L.D.B. 8 .... 268, 269, 270
Tse Kwong Lam v. Wong Chif Sen [1983] 1 W.L.R. 1394; (1983) 127 S.J. 632;
[1983] 3 All E.R. 54; (1983) New L.J. 829; (1983) 80 L.S.Gaz. 2368,
P.C. 326
Turner v. London and Provincial Bank Ltd. (1903) 2 L.D.B. 33; Journal of
Institue of Bankers Vol. xxiv, p. 220 .... 169, 170
Turquand v. Marshall (1869) 4 Ch.App. 376; 38 L.J.Ch. 639; 20 L.T. 766; 33
J.P. 708; 17 W.R. 935, L.C. 219, 221
Tyler, Re ex p. Official Receiver [1907] 1 K.B. 865; 76 L.J.K.B. 541; 97 L.T.
30; 23 T.L.R. 328; 51 S.J. 291; 14 Mans. 73 368

UBAF v. European American Banking Corp.; Pacific Colocotronis, The
[1984] Q.B. 713; [1984] 2 W.L.R. 508; (1984) 128 S.J. 243; [1984] 2 All
E.R. 226; [1984] 1 Lloyd's Rep. 258; (1984) 81 L.S.Gaz. 429, C.A.; 10
L.D.B. 456 .... 26, 408
Underwood (A.L.) Ltd. v. Bank of Liverpool and Martins; Same v. Barclays
Bank Ltd. [1924] 1 K.B. 775; 93 L.J.K.B. 690; 131 L.T. 271; 40 T.L.R.
302; 68 S.J. 716; 29 Com.Cas. 182; 3 L.D.B. 323 .... 115, 158, 173, 179,
184, 219
United Bank of Kuwait v. Hammond [1988] 1 W.L.R. 1051; (1988) 132 S.J.
1388; [1988] 3 All E.R. 418; (1988) 138 New L.J. 281, C.A.; reversing
(1987) 137 New L.J. 921 203
United City Merchants (Investments) and Glass Fibres and Equipments v.
Royal Bank of Canada, Vitrofuertos S.A. and Banco Continental
S.A.; American Accord, The [1983] A.C. 168; [1982] 2 W.L.R. 1039;
[1982] 2 All E.R. 720; [1982] Lloyd's Rep. 1; [1982] Com.L.R. 142; 10
L.D.B. 350 .... 250, 254, 259, 260, 267

United Dominions Trust v. Kirkwood [1966] 2 Q.B. 431; [1966] 2 W.L.R. 1083; 110 S.J. 169; [1966] 1 All E.R. 968; [1966] 1 Lloyd's Rep. 418; 8 L.D.B. 490 .... **27**, 30, 216

—— v. Western; B.S. Romanay (Trading as Romanay Car Sales) Third Party [1976] Q.B. 513; [1976] 2 W.L.R. 64; 119 S.J. 792; [1975] 3 All E.R. 1017 298

United Overseas Bank v. Jiwani [1976] 1 W.L.R. 964; 120 S.J. 329; 10 L.D.B. 1 99

United Railways of the Havana and Regla Warehouses, Re [1961] A.C. 1007; [1960] 2 W.L.R. 969; 104 S.J. 466; [1960] 2 All E.R. 332 241

United Service Co., Re, Johnston's Claim (1870) 6 Ch.App. 212; 40 L.J.Ch. 286; 24 L.T. 115; 19 W.R. 457 277

United Trading Corp. S.A. v. Allied Arab Bank; Murray Clayton v. Rafidair Bank [1985] 2 Lloyd's Rep. 554, C.A. 273, 275

Universal Guarantee Pty. v. National Bank of Australasia [1965] 1 W.L.R. 691; 109 S.J. 331; [1965] 2 All E.R. 98; [1965] 1 Lloyd's Rep. 525; 65 S.R.(N.S.W.) 102 186

Urquhart Lindsay & Co. v. Eastern Bank Ltd. [1922] 1 K.B. 318; 91 L.J.K.B. 274; 126 L.T. 534; 27 Com.Cas. 124; 3 L.D.B. 250 .... 246, **247**

Uttamchandani v. Central Bank of India (1989) 133 S.J. 262; (1989) 139 New L.J. 222; [1989] L.S.Gaz. March 8, 41 237

VICTORS LTD. v. Lingard [1927] 1 Ch.D. 323; 96 L.J.Ch. 132; 136 L.T. 476; 70 S.J. 1197; 4 L.D.B. 43 221

Vinden v. Hughes [1905] 1 K.B. 795; 74 L.J.K.B. 410; 53 W.R. 429; 21 T.L.R. 324; 49 S.J. 351; 2 L.D.B. 81 48

WALKER v. Manchester and Liverpool District Banking Co. Ltd. (1913) 108 L.T. 728; 29 T.L.R. 492; 57 Sol.Jo. 478 95

—— v. —— [1952] 2 All E.R. 650 95

Wallis, Re [1902] 1 K.B. 719; 71 L.J.K.B. 465; 18 T.L.R. 414; 9 Mans. 136 340

Wealden Woodlands (Kent) Ltd. v. National Westminster Bank Ltd. (1983) 133 New L.J. 719 96

Welch v. Bank of England [1955] Ch., 508; [1955] 2 W.L.R. 757; 99 S.J. 236; [1955] 1 All E.R. 811 199

Weld-Blundell v. Synott [1940] 2 All E.R. 580; [1940] 2 K.B. 107; 109 L.J.K.B. 684; 163 L.T. 39; 56 T.L.R. 677; 84 S.J. 502; 45 Com.Cas. 218 139

West v. Williams [1899] 1 Ch. 132; 68 L.J.Ch. 127; 79 L.T. 575; 47 W.R. 308 .... 343, 344

West Mercia Constabulary v. Wagener [1982] 1 W.L.R. 127; (1981) 125 S.J. 860; [1981] 3 All E.R. 378 122

Western Bank Ltd. v. Schindler [1976] 3 W.L.R. 341; 120 S.J. 301; [1976] 2 All E.R. 393 .... 324, **325**, 327

Westminster Bank Ltd. v. Cond (1940) 46 Com.Cas. 60; 5 L.D.B. 263 .... 152, 293, 315

—— v. Hilton (1926) 136 L.T. 315; 43 T.L.R. 124; 70 S.J. 1196; sub nom. Hilton v. Westminster Bank Ltd. 162 L.T.Jo. 450 .... 88, 126, **128**, 129

—— v. Sassoon (1927) 48 J.I.B. 4; 5 L.D.B. 19 314

—— v. Zang [1966] A.C. 182; [1966] 2 W.L.R. 110; 109 S.J. 1009; [1966] 1 All E.R. 114; [1966] 1 Lloyd's Rep. 49; [1965] C.L.Y. 210; 8 L.D.B. 448 .... 58, 60, 62, 115, **156**, 157, 158, 159, 160, 161, 232

Whitbread Flowers v. Thurston (unreported) (1979) C.L.Y. 22; C.A.T. 483 .. 116

Whittingham v. Whittingham [1979] Fam. 19; [1978] 2 W.L.R. 936; (1978)
    122 S.J. 247; [1978] 3 All E.R. 805; (1978) 36 P. & C.R. 164; (1978) 8
    Fam.Law 171; (1978) 36 P. & C.R. 164; 104 L.D.B. 87 333
Whyte (G.T.) & Co. Ltd., Re, Financial Times, December 14, 1982 ...... 389, 403
Wickens, ex p. [1898] 1 Q.B. 543; 67 L.J.Q.B. 397; 46 W.R. 385; 5 Mans.; sub
    nom. Wickens v. Shuckburgh, 78 L.T. 213 325
Wigzell, Re, ex p. Hart [1921] 2 K.B. 835; 3 L.D.B. 240; sub nom. Wigzell,
    Re, ex p. Trustee 90 L.J.K.B. 897; [1921] B. & C.R. 42; sub nom.
    Wigzell, Re, ex p. Trustee v. Barclays Bank Ltd. 125 L.T. 361; sub
    nom. Wigzell, Re, Hart v. Barclays Bank 37 T.L.R. 526; 65 Sol.Jo.
    493 .... 366, 367, 368
Williams v. Barclays Bank [1988] Q.B. 161; [1987] 3 W.L.R. 790; (1987) 131
    S.J. 1214; [1987] 3 All E.R. 257; [1988] 1 F.L.R. 455; (1988) 18
    Fam.Law 204; [1987] 2 F.T.L.R. 393; (1987) F.L.R. 361; (1987) 84
    L.S.Gaz. 2455, C.A. 13
—— v. Summerfield [1972] 2 Q.B. 513; [1972] 3 W.L.R. 131; 116 S.J. 413;
    [1972] 2 All E.R. 1334; 56 Cr.App.R. 597; [1972] Crim.L.R. 424; 9
    L.D.B. 289 11
—— v. Williams; Tucker v. Williams. See Williams v. Barclays Bank.
Williams & Glyn's Bank Ltd. v. Barnes [1981] Com.L.R. 205; 10 L.D.B.
    220 .... 223, 224, 225, 353
—— v. Boland; Same v. Brown [1981] A.C. 487; [1980] 3 W.L.R. 138; (1980)
    124 S.J. 443; [1980] 2 All E.R. 408; (1980) 40 P. & C.R. 451; 10 L.D.B.
    243 .... 328, 331, 332, 333, 337, 357
Williams & Humbert v. W & H Trade Marks (Jersey); Rumasa S.A. v.
    Multinvest (UK) [1986] A.C. 368; [1986] 2 W.L.R. 24; [1986] 1 All
    E.R. 129; (1986) 83 L.S.Gaz. 362; (1986) 83 L.S.Gaz. 37; (1986) 136
    New L.J. 15, H.L. 275
Wilson & Meeson v. Pickering [1946] 1 All E.R. 394; [1946] K.B. 422; [1947]
    L.J.R. 18; 175 L.T. 65; 62 T.L.R. 223; 5 L.D.B. 435 190
Wiltshire Iron Co., Re, ex p. Pearson (1868) 3 Ch.App. 443; 37 L.J.Ch. 554;
    18 L.T. 423; 16 W.R. 682 392
Windsor Refrigerator Co. Ltd. v. Branch Nominees Ltd. [1961] Ch. 375;
    [1961] 2 W.L.R. 196; 105 S.J. 205; [1961] 1 All E.R. 277 381
Winkworth v. Baron (Edward) Development Co. [1986] 1 W.L.R. 1512;
    [1987] 1 All E.R. 114; [1987] BCLC 193; [1987] 1 F.T.L.R. 176; (1987)
    53 P. & C.R. 378; [1987] 1 F.L.R. 525; (1987) 17 Fam.Law 166; (1986)
    130 S.J. 954; (1987) 84 I.S.Gaz. 340, H.L. 332
Wise v. Perpetual Trustee Co. [1903] A.C. 139; 72 L.J.P.C. 31; 87 L.T. 569;
    51 W.R. 241; 19 T.L.R. 125 211
Woodland v. Fear (1857) 7 E. & B. 519; 26 L.J.Q.B. 202; 29 L.T.(o.s.) 106; 3
    Jur.(N.S.) 587; 5 W.R. 624; 119 E.R. 1339 401
Woodroffes (Musical Instruments), Re [1986] Ch. 366; [1985] 3 W.L.R. 543;
    (1985) 129 S.J. 589; [1985] 2 All E.R. 908; 1985 PCC 318; (1985) 82
    L.S.Gaz. 3170; 10 L.D.B. 497 389
Woods v. Martins Bank [1959] 1 Q.B. 55; [1958] 1 W.L.R. 1018; 102 S.J. 655;
    [1958] 3 All E.R. 166; 7 L.D.B. 192 .... 22, 33, 408
Woodstead Finance v. Petrou (1985) 136 New L.J. 188 303
Woolcott v. Excess Insurance Co. and Miles, Smith Anderson and Game
    (No. 2) [1979] 2 Lloyd's Rep. 210 357
—— v. Sun Alliance & London Insurance [1978] 1 W.L.R. 493; (1977) 121
    S.J. 744; [1978] 1 All E.R. 1253; [1978] 1 Lloyd's Rep. 129; C.L.B.
    45 357

X v. Y and Y Establishment [1989] 3 W.L.R. 910; [1989] 3 All E.R. 689;
(1989) 133 S.J. 945 121
XAG v. A Bank, [1983] 2 All E.R. 464; [1983] 2 Lloyd's Rep. 535; [1983]
Com.L.R. 134; (1983) New L.J. 400 15

YEOVIL GLOVE CO. LTD., Re [1965] Ch. 148; [1964] 3 W.L.R. 406; 108 S.J.
499; [1964] 2 All E.R. 849; 8 L.D.B. 267 .... **387**, 388
Yeung Kai Yung v. Hong Kong and Shanghai Banking Corporation [1981]
A.C. 787; [1980] 3 W.L.R. 950; (1980) 124 S.J. 591; [1980] 2 All E.R.
599; 10 L.D.B. 208 353
Young, Re, Trye v. Sullivan (1885) 28 Ch.D. 705 198
―― v. Grote (1827) 4 Bing. 253; 12 Moore C.P. 484; 5 L.J.(o.s.)C.P. 165;
130 E.R. 764 .... 87, 88, 92
―― v. Sealey [1949] Ch. 278; [1949] L.J.R. 529; 93 S.J. 58; [1949] 1 All E.R.
92; 6 L.D.B. 8 198
Yourell v. Hibernian Bank Ltd. [1918] A.C. 372; 87 L.J.P.C. 1; 117 L.T.
729 225

Z. v. A-Z and AA-LL [1982] Q.B. 558; [1982] 2 W.L.R. 288; (1982) 126 S.J.
100; [1982] 1 All E.R. 556; [1982] 1 Lloyd's Rep. 240; 10 L.D.B. 309 .... **117**
Zivnostenska Banka National Corporation v. Frankman [1950] A.C. 57;
[1949] 2 All E.R. 671; reversing sub nom. Frankman v. Prague Credit
Bank [1949] 1 K.B. 199; 92 S.J. 705; [1948] 2 All E.R. 1025; reversing
[1948] 1 K.B. 730; restoring [1948] 1 K.B. 730 .... 401, 402, 406

TABLE OF STATUTES

Administration of Justice Act 1956 (4 & 5 Eliz. 2, c. 46)—
s. 35 336
Administration of Justice Act 1970 (c. 31)—
s. 36 327
Administration of Justice Act 1973 (c. 15)—
s. 8 327
Administration of Justice Act 1977 (c. 38) 243
s. 26 341
Agricultural Credits Act 1928 (18 & 19 Geo. 5, c. 43) 319
Bank Charter Act 1844 (7 & 8 Vict. c. 32)—
s. 11 40
Bankers' Books Evidence Act 1879 (42 & 43 Vict. c. 11)—
s. 7 .... 16, 30
Banking Act 1979 (c. 37) 29
s. 47 175
Sched. 6, para. 1 13
Banking Act 1987 (c. 22) 29
Banking and Financial Dealings Act 1971 (c. 80) 75
Bankruptcy Act 1914 (4 & 5 Geo. 6, c. 59) 370, 383
s. 31 .... 384, 385
s. 44 .... 373, 376
s. 45 368
s. 46 368
s. 155 (a) 233
s. 167 370
Bankruptcy (Amendment) Act 1926 (16 & 17 Geo. 5, c. 7)—
s. 4 .... 368, 374
Bills of Exchange Act 1882 (45 & 46 Vict. c. 61) 38, **40**, 45, 53, 59, 289
s. 2 .... 28, 60
s. 3 (1) 40, 42, 44
(2) 42
(4) (a) 66
s. 5 (2) 40, 53, 54
s. 7 (3) 45, 46, 125
s. 11 45
s. 13 (2) 129
(6) 271
s. 20 66
(2) 66
s. 21 (2) (b) 69
s. 23 .... 52, 203
(2) 203
s. 24 220
s. 25 51
s. 26 50
(1) 50, 51
(2) 51, 53
s. 27 (1) 54

Bills of Exchange Act 1882—*cont.*
  s. 27 (1)—*cont.*
       (*a*) 54, 55
       (*b*) 54, 55, 56
    (2) 56
    (3) 159
  s. 29 .... 56, 57, 146, 376
    (1) 57, 159
       (*a*) 58
       (*b*) 58
    (2) 376
  s. 30 (2) 57, 68
  s. 32 56
  s. 34 59
    (1) 60
  s. 38 (2) 57
  s. 45 63
  s. 49 .... 61, 62
  s. 50 (2) (*c*) 140
  s. 53 350
  s. 57 (2) 243
  s. 60 .... 40, 49, 64, 125, 126, 141, 142, 143
  s. 64 .... 63, 64
    (1) 64
    (2) 65
  s. 72 (4) 243
  s. 73 .... 40, 41, 42
  s. 75 127
  s. 79 186
  s. 80 64
  s. 81 190
  s. 82 .... 30, 32, 40, 41, 44, 47, 50, 142, 162, 163, 165, 170, 171, 176, 178,
                                180, 182, 183, 189, 190
  s. 90 145
  s. 91 (1) 203
  s. 108 .... 52, 53
Bills of Exchange (Crossed Cheques) Act 1906 (6 Edw. 7, c. 17) 158
Bills of Lading Act 1855 (18 & 19 Vict. c. 111)—
  s. 1 284
Bills of Sale Act 1878 (41 & 42 Vict. c. 31) 287, 288, 289
  s. 4 .... 286, 287, 288
Building Societies Act 1986 (c. 37)—
  Sched. 41 (1) 324
Charging Orders Act 1979 (c. 53) 336
Cheques Act 1957 (5 & 6 Eliz. 2, c. 36) 44, 45, 59, 73, 145, 187, 189
  s. 1 144
  s. 2 .... 156, 157, 159, 160
  s. 3 .... 74, 144, 160
  s. 4 .... 30, 40, 44, 47, 50, 141, 142, 162, 165, 175, 183, 186
    (1) 41
    (2) (*b*) 41, 42
  s. 5 44
Civil Jurisdiction and Judgements Act 1982 (c. 27)—
  s. 25 121

Civil Liability (Contribution) Act 1978 (c. 47) 115, 202, 354
Companies Act 1862 (25 & 26 Vict. c. 89)—
  s. 30 340
Companies Act 1929 (19 & 20 Geo. 5, c. 23)—
  s. 79 345
  s. 264 395
    (3) 394
Companies Act 1947 (10 & 11 Geo. 6, c. 47)—
  s. 115 375
Companies Act 1948 (11 & 12 Geo. 6, c. 38) 213, 375, 383
  s. 95 .... 346, 348, 360, 361, 375
  s. 98 (2) 346
  s. 106 347
  s. 108 (4) 52
  s. 227 .... 390, 391, 392
  s. 316 386
  s. 317 .... 384, 385, 386
  s. 319 395
    (4) 394
  s. 321 375
    (1) 374
    (3) 374, 375
  s. 322 .... 387, 388, 389, 398, 399
  s. 325 336
Companies Act 1967 (c. 81) 29, 213
Companies Act 1981 (c. 62)—
  s. 20 180
  s. 30 180
  s. 119 180
Companies Act 1985 (c. 6)—
  s. 35 214
  s. 349 (4) 52
  s. 360 340
  s. 395 .... 286, 345
  s. 396 286
    (1) 345
  s. 401 346
  s. 404 346
  s. 409 347
  s. 458 398
Companies (Consolidation) Act 1908 (8 Edw. 7, c. 69)—
  s. 93 (1) (c), (e) 286
Company Securities (Insider Dealing) Act 1985 (c. 8) 233
Consumer Credit Act 1974 (c. 39) 27
Drug Trafficking Offences Act 1986 (c.32) 14, 235
Employment Agencies Act 1973 (c. 35) 106
Estate Agents Act 1979 (c. 38) 106
European Communities Act 1972 (c. 68) 218
  s. 9 (1) 214, 215
Evidence (Proceedings in Other Jurisdictions) 1975 (c. 34) 16
Factors Act 1889 (52 & 53 Vict. c. 45)—
  s. 2 (1) 290
  s. 3 289
Finance Act 1950 (c. 15) 351

Financial Services Act 1986 (c. 60) 14, 121
Gaming Act 1845 (8 & 9 Vict. c. 109) 79
Income Tax Act 1918 (8 & 9 Geo. 5, c. 40)—
    s. 103 14
Insolvency Act 1976 (c. 60) 395
Insolvency Act 1986 (c. 45) 366, 370, 383
    ss. 8–27 378
    s. 8 (1) 377
       (3) 377
    s. 45 367
    s. 127 390
    s. 183 336
    s. 213 398
    s. 214 399
    s. 215 398
    s. 239 373
    s. 241 (1) (e) 375
    s. 245 .... 388, 389
    s. 278 367
    s. 284 (5) 368
    s. 323 385
    s. 330 395
    s. 340 373
    s. 342 (1) (e) 375
    s. 386 394
    Sched. 6 394
    Sched. 8 385
Insurance Brokers (Registration) Act 1977 (c. 46) 106
Land Registration Act 1925 (15 & 16 Geo. 5, c. 21) 330
    s. 3 329
          (xv) 329
          (xvi) 329
    s. 70 329
       (1) (g) 329
    s. 106 341
       (2) 341
Law of Property Act 1925 (15 & 16 Geo. 5, c. 20)—
    s. 34 336
    s. 36 336
    s. 70 333
    s. 94 344
    s. 136 350
Law Reform (Contributory Negligence) Act 1945 (8 & 9 Geo. 6, c. 28) 174
Law Reform (Married Women and Tortfeasors) Act 1935 (25 & 26 Geo. 5,
    c. 30) 91
Limitation Act 1939 (2 & 3 Geo. 6, c. 21) 322
Limitation Act 1980 (c. 58) 322
Marine Insurance Act 1906 (6 Edw. 7, c. 41)—
    s. 18 357
Matrimonial Causes Act 1973 (c. 18) 303
    s. 24 333
    s. 37 .... 333, 334
Matrimonial Homes Act 1967 (c. 75) 331
Mental Health Act 1959 (7 & 8 Eliz. 2, c. 72) 365

Mercantile Law Amendment Act 1856 (19 & 20 Vict. c. 60)—
s. 5 311
Minors' Contracts Act 1987 (c. 13) 312
Moneylenders Act 1900 (63 & 64 Vict. c. 51) 27, 29, 216
s. 6 28
Partnership Act 1890 (53 & 54 Vict. c. 39)—
s. 5 203
s. 38 204
Police and Criminal Evidence Act 1984 (c. 60)—
s. 9 (1) 16
s. 9 16
Powers of Attorney Act 1971 (c. 27)—
s. 10 176
Registration of Business Names Act 1916 (6 & 7 Geo. 5, c. 58) 180
Revenue Act 1883 (46 & 47 Vict. c. 55)—
s. 17 .... 41, 44
Sale of Goods Act 1893 (56 & 57 Vict. c. 71) 359
Solicitors Act 1933 (23 & 24 Geo. 5, c. 24) 111
Solicitors Act 1974 (c. 47) 111
s. 85 105
Stamp Act 1853 (16 & 17 Vict. c. 59)—
s. 19 .... 125, 143
State Immunity Act 1978 (c. 33) 269
Statute of Frauds Amendment Act 1828 (9 Geo. 4, c. 14)—
s. 6 .... 25, 27
Suicide Act 1961 (9 & 10 Eliz. 2, c. 60) 355
Supreme Court Act 1981 (c. 54) 401
s. 27 (3) 118
s. 37 (1) 122, 123
Supreme Court of Judicature Act 1873 (36 & 37 Vict. c. 66) 386
Theft Act 1968 (c. 60) 230, 232
s. 3 (1) 229
s. 15 230
s. 16 .... 229, 230
(1) 227, 228
s. 20 (2) 229
Torts (Interference with Goods) Act 1977 (c. 32)—
s. 11 (1) 175
Unfair Contract Terms Act 1977 (c. 50) 24, 300, 306

AUSTRALIA
Bills of Exchange Act 1909—
s. 88 31

INDIA
Contract Act 1872 289
Negotiable Instruments Act 1881 171

ISLE OF MAN
Bankers' Books Evidence Act 1935 400

TABLE OF ABBREVIATIONS

[Square brackets around the date in a citation indicate that the date is an essential part of the reference. Round brackets are used where the report is in a numbered series, the date being added for information only.]

The Incorporated Society of Law Reporting have since 1865 published various series of reports of which the following are referred to in this book—

L.R.C.P.	Common Pleas		
L.R.Ch.	Chancery		
L.R.Eq.	Exchequer		
L.R.H.L.	English and Irish Appeal Cases	....	1865–75
L.R.P.C.	Privy Council Appeal Cases		
L.R.Q.B.	Queen's Bench		
Ch.App.	Chancery Appeals		

App.Cas.	Appeal Cases (House of Lords)		
Q.B.D.	Queen's Bench Division	....	1876–90
Ch.D.	Chancery Division		

A.C.	Appeal Cases (House of Lords)		
Ch.	Chancery Division	....	1891—current
Q.B. or K.B.	Queen's or King's Bench Division		

W.N.	Weekly Notes	1866–1952
W.L.R.	Weekly Law Reports	1953—current

Other series of reports cited in this book, and the years covered by them, are—

A. & E.	Adolphus and Ellis	Q.B. 1834–42
All E.R.	All England Reports	1936—current
B. & A.	Barnewall and Alderson	K.B. 1817–22
B. & Ad.	Barnewall and Adolphus	K.B. 1830–34
B. & C.	Barnewall and Creswell	K.B. 1822–30
B. & C.R.	Bankruptcy and Companies (Winding-up) Cases ...	1918–1941
B. & S.	Best and Smith	Q.B. 1861–70
Bing.	Bingham	C.P. 1822–34
Bing.N.C.	Bingham's New Cases	C.P. 1834–40
Bli. (N.S.)	Bligh, New Series	H.L. 1827–37
Bro.C.C.	Brown's Chancery Reports	1778–94
Burr.	Burrow	K.B. 1757–71
C.B.	Common Bench Reports	1845–56
C.B., N.S.	Common Bench Reports New Series	1856–65

C. & P.	Carrington and Payne	N.P. 1823–41
Cl. & Fin.	Clark and Finelly	H.L. 1831–46
Com.Cas.	Commercial Cases	1895–1941
Cox C.C.	Cox's Criminal Cases	1843–1940
Cr. & M.	Crompton and Meeson	Exch. 1832–34
De G.M. & G.	De Gex, Macnaghten and Gordon	Ch. 1851–57
E. & B.	Ellis and Blackburn	Q.B. 1852–58
Esp.	Espinasse	N.P. 1793–1807
Ex.	Exchequer Reports (Welsby, Hurlstone and Gordon)	1847–56
H. & N.	Hurlstone and Norman	Exch. 1856–62
H.L.Cas.	House of Lords Cases (Clark)	1847–66
Hare	Hare's Vice Chancellor's Reports	1841–53
I.R.	Irish Law Reports	1894—current
Jur (N.S.)	The Jurist, New Series	1855–66
L.J.Ch.	Law Journal, Chancery Reports	1831–1949
L.J.C.P.	Law Journal, Common Pleas	1831–1949
L.J.P.C.	Law Journal, Privy Council	1831–1949
L.J.Q.B.	Law Journal, Queen's Bench	1831–1949
Ll.L.R.	Lloyd's List Law Reports	1919–50
Lloyd's Rep.	Lloyd's List Law Reports	1951—current
L.T.	Law Times Reports	1859–1947
Macq.	Macqueen	1851–65
M. & G.	Manning and Grainger	C.P. 1840–45
M. & R.	Moody and Robinson	N.P. 1830–44
M. & W.	Meeson and Welsby	Exch. 1836–47
Mer.	Merivale	Ch. 1815–17
Moo.J.B.	J.B. Moore's Common Pleas Reports	1817–27
N.I.	Northern Ireland Reports	1925—current
N.Z.L.R.	New Zealand Law Reports	1883—current
P. & C.R.	Planning & Compensation Reports	1949—current
Q.B.	Queen's Bench Reports (Adolphus and Ellis, New Series)	1841–52
R.T.R.	Road Traffic Reports	1970—current
Russ.	Russell	Ch. 1823–29
S.C.	Court of Sessions Cases, Scotland	1906—current
Sid.	Siderfin	K.B. 1657–70
S.J.	Solicitors' Journal	1856—current
T.L.R.	Times Law Reports	1885–1952
T.R.	Term Reports (Durnford and East)	1785–1800
Taun.	Taunton	C.P. 1808–19
V.L.R.	Victoria (Australia) Law Reports	1874—current
Ves.Jr.	Vesey Junior	Ch. 1789–1816
W.R.	Weekly Reporter	1853–1906

Other abbreviations used are—

C.L.Y.	*Current Law Yearbook*
J.B.L.	*Journal of Business Law*
J.I.B.	*Journal of the Institute of Bankers*
L.D.B.	*Legal Decisions affecting Bankers*

Textbooks mainly cited are—

Ellinger, *Modern Banking Law.*
Holden, *Law and Practice of Banking* (4th ed.) (Vol. 1 *Banker and Customer*).
(7th ed.) (Vol. 2 *Securities for Bankers' Advances*).
Paget, *Law of Banking* (9th ed.).
Penn, Shea & Arora, *Banking Law* (Vol. 1 *The Law Relating to Domestic Banking*). (Vol. 2 *The Law and Practice of International Banking*).
Reeday, *The Law Relating to Banking* (5th ed.).

INTRODUCTION

As far as possible legal technicalities have been avoided in this book, but the reader with little previous knowledge of the English legal system may find the following notes useful. The dangers of attempting to deal with so wide a subject in so short a space are obvious, as is the desirability of further reading for anyone who wishes to obtain a clearer picture of the law.[1]

The present structure of the courts was established by the Administration of Justice Act 1970, and the Courts Act 1971. It comprises (1) the magistrates' courts; (2) the county courts; (3) the Crown Court, a superior court of record, which can sit anywhere in England and Wales; (4) the High Court, organised in three divisions — Queen's Bench, Chancery and Family — which can also sit anywhere in England and Wales, thus replacing the earlier assize courts; (5) the Court of Appeal; and (6) the House of Lords. Broadly speaking appeal lies from the magistrates' courts first to the High Court and thence to the Court of Appeal (or in certain special circumstances direct to the House of Lords). From the county courts appeal is to the Civil Division of the Court of Appeal, and the Criminal Division of the Court of Appeal hears appeals from the Crown Courts. Appeal thence lies to the Court of Appeal. The House of Lords takes appeals from the Court of Appeal.

In this book we are principally concerned with the High Court, the Court of Appeal and the House of Lords, which need further elaboration.

The House of Lords has for centuries been the highest court in the realm. Only a small number of legally qualified peers take part in the judicial work of the House of Lords. They are mostly life peers, and are known as Lords of Appeal in Ordinary. The Lords of Appeal serve also as members of the Judicial Committee of the Privy Council, which hears, *inter alia*, appeals from such parts of the Commonwealth as have not

---

[1] *Learning the Law*, by E. Glanville Williams, gives an admirable outline of the whole subject, and a useful description of the legal system in a banking context is to be found in *Banking: the Legal Environment*, by David Palfreman.

removed themselves from its jurisdiction. Its opinions are given great weight by English and Scottish courts, but are not formally binding on them, in contrast to decisions of the House of Lords, which are binding upon all courts, and normally upon itself, although the House is now prepared exceptionally to overrule an earlier decision.

In the absence of any precedent in the English cases the courts will consider precedents from other jurisdictions, especially Scotland, Ireland, the Dominions and the United States, but of course none of these is in any way binding: they are in greater or less degree persuasive merely.

A High Court judge is "Mr. Justice Smith," and this is written "Smith J." The regular members of the Court of Appeal have the title of Lord Justice: Smith J., becomes Smith L.J. The Chairman of the Court of Appeal is the Master of the Roles— M.R. Upon elevation to the House of Lords as a Lord of Appeal in Ordinary, Smith L.J. becomes Lord Smith (or whatever other title he chooses). There are a number of examples in the pages that follow of individual judges referred to variously as J., L.J., or Lord, as they have moved from High Court to Court of Appeal, or from Court of Appeal to House of Lords.

The head of the Queen's Bench Division is the Lord Chief Justice, who normally sits in this court, although he is entitled to, and sometimes does, sit in the House of Lords, or even in the Court of Appeal. The Lord Chancellor is the head of the whole judicial system.

The only change in this part of the legal system effected by the 1970 Act was in the organisation of the divisions of the High Court, one of which had previously been Probate, Divorce and Admiralty. This is now replaced by the Family Division, Admiralty jurisdiction being transferred to the Queen's Bench, which also includes the Commercial Court.[2]

Queen's Bench,[3] Chancery and Probate, Divorce and Admiralty dated from 1875, when the Judicature Act of 1873 radically reformed the whole legal system. There were initially five divisions of the High Court, but Exchequer and Common Pleas were merged with Queen's Bench in 1880.

Before 1875 the whole legal system was much more

---

[2] The so-called Commercial Court is merely one of the courts of the Queen's Bench Division to which a judge specially conversant with commercial law has been assigned for duty. Naturally many cases involving points of banking law are dealt with in this court.

[3] King's Bench from 1901 to 1952.

complicated than it is now, and it is not possible to summarise it adequately in the space of this note. There were then a larger number of uncoordinated courts; the banking student is concerned mainly with the decisions of Queen's Bench, Common Pleas, and Exchequer (the Common Law Courts), Exchequer Chamber (a court of appeal for certain common law cases) and the Courts of Chancery, which administered the separate body of law known as Equity. Trusts and mortgages were within the equitable jurisdiction, and are still the concern of the Chancery Division; contract (including the relationship of banker and customer) was a common law matter, and is still dealt with mainly in the Queen's Bench Division.[4] But since 1875 there is no conflict between the two jurisdictions, judges in either being competent to deal with matters touching upon the other, and precedence being given to equitable rules where there would otherwise be conflict between equitable and common law rules.

The simplification of the legal system brought about by the Judicature Act was preceded by a formalisation of what had been previously a highly individual system of reporting the law. The Table of Abbreviations includes such of the earlier reports as are cited in this book, and it will be seen that they are nearly all named after the reporters themselves. In 1865 the Incorporated Council of Law Reporting started the Law Reports, and the "private" reporters began to be superseded. Certain series belonging to firms of publishers, e.g. the Law Journal reports, have continued to the present day, and others have been started since.

Thus The Times Law Reports (not to be confused with the law reports that appear in The Times newspaper) were published from 1885 until 1952, the All England Reports have been published since 1936, and the Lloyd's List Reports since 1919.

There can be discrepancies between different reports of the same case (although these are minimal in the major series), and it is sometimes desirable to examine two or more reports of the same case in order to discover its true effect. As this book is chiefly designed for students it has not been considered necessary to give a multiplicity of citiations in the text. The Table of Cases includes, however, all the major references as

---

[4] But since company law and some important aspects of security work, such as mortgage and charges, are normall dealt with in the Chancery Division, the banking student is often concerned with that Division also.

well as the appropriate citation for cases which are to be found in *Legal Decisions affecting Bankers.*

The reporting of any case depends upon its importance as extending or explaining the law, and many cases which do neither are not reported in any of the series. Sometimes a case of real importance is omitted, and although this happens less often today than ever before, it will be seen that some cases in this book have as their only citation the *Journal of the Institute of Bankers*, or *Legal Decisions affecting Bankers.* These are cases which are not reported, or are not reported in any detail, elsewhere. One case, *Chatterton* v. *London & County Banking Co. Ltd.*,[5] is of particular interest: the trade paper, *The Miller*, contained the only full report of it.

In a few cases in this book[6] the plaintiff or the defendant is described as the "public officer" of a bank partnership. Until 1826 an action by or against a banking partnership involved the recital of all the partners' names, and this, as the joint stock principle slowly developed, became a troublesome matter. The Bank Act of 1826 made provision for such banking partnership (which had to be within 65 miles of London) to sue or be sued through a duly appointed and registered officer, the "public officer." In 1858 banks of limited liability were first permitted but the public officers continued to act for those registered under the 1826 Act (or the 1833 Act, which made similar provision) that did not avail themselves of the new privilege.

It may be added finally that while in a High Court action the role of plaintiff and defendant is clear enough, care is sometimes needed to distinguish, in appeal reports, between the appellant, who is bringing the appeal against the decision of the lower court, and the respondent. The appellant of course may have been the plaintiff or the defendant in the court below: thus in the *Savory* case the bank were defendants in the High Court, and appellants in the Court of Appeal and the House of Lords. And the *Savory* case is an example also of the way in which the name of a case may change: on appeal to the Court of Appeal the name is unchanged, even when the defendant is appellant, but in the House of Lords the appellant is named first. So it was *E. B. Savory and Co.* v. *Lloyds Bank Ltd.* in the High Court and the Court of Appeal, but *Lloyds Bank Ltd.* v. *E. B. Savory & Co.* in the House of Lords.

An unusual change took place when *Gallie* v. *Lee* reached the

---

[5] *Post*, p. 152.
[6] *cf. post*, pp. 174, 265 and 310.

House of Lords, for there the original plaintiff had died and the second defendant did not appeal, so the case reached the Lords as *Saunders* v. *Anglia Building Society*[7]: *i.e.* the executrix of the original plaintiff and the building society which had been the second defendant.

Chapter 1

RELATIONSHIP OF BANKER AND CUSTOMER

Foley v. Hill

(1848) 9 E.R. 1002

Joachimson v. Swiss Bank Corporation

[1921] 3 K.B. 110

The relationship between banker and customer is that of debtor and creditor; but one of the terms of the implied contract is that money lent to the banker is not payable except on demand

Facts of Foley v. Hill

In 1829, an account in the name of the plaintiff was opened with the defendant banker, the initial credit being for £6,117 10s. It was agreed that 3 per cent. per annum interest should be allowed. There were later two debits on the account, for £1,700 and £2,000. Interest entries were shown in a separate column, and interest was not credited to the main account.

In 1838, the plaintiff sought to recover the money outstanding by an action in Chancery for an account. The account, being so simple, was held not to be a matter for a Court of Equity, and the plaintiff thereupon claimed that the relationship of a banker with his customer was analogous to that of an agent and his principal, and that he was entitled to an account on this basis; and that therefore, the relationship being of a fiduciary nature, the Statute of Limitations did not apply.

Decision

The House of Lords held that the relationship was that of debtor and creditor, and that therefore the matter was not a suitable one for an account in Equity.

In the course of his judgment, Lord Cottenham L.C. said:

Money, when paid into a bank, ceases altogether to be the money of the principal; it is then the money of the banker, who is bound to

1

return an equivalent by paying a similar sum to that deposited with him when he is asked for it. The money paid into the banker's is money known by the principal to be placed there for the purpose of being under the control of the banker; it is then the banker's money; he is known to deal with it as his own; he makes what profit of it he can, which profit he retains to himself, paying back only the principal, according to the custom of bankers in some places, or the principal and a small rate of interest, according to the custom of bankers in other places. The money placed in the custody of a banker is, to all intents and purposes, the money of the banker, to do with it as he pleases; he is guilty of no breach of trust in employing it; he is not answerable to the principal if he puts it into jeopardy, if he engages in a hazardous speculation; he is not bound to keep it, or deal with it, as the property of his principal, but he is of course answerable for the amount, because he has contracted, having received that money, to repay to the principal, when demanded, a sum equivalent to that paid into his hands.

That has been the subject of discussion in various cases.... That being established to be the relative situations of banker and customer, the banker is not an agent, or factor, but he is a debtor.[1]

And Lord Brougham said:

This trade of a banker is to receive money, and use it as if it were his own, he becoming debtor to the person who has lent or deposited with him the money to use as his own.[2]

Facts of Joachimson v. Swiss Bank Corporation

The plaintiff firm was a partnership between two Germans and a naturalised Englishman, carrying on business in Manchester. On August 1, 1914, one of the Germans died and the partnership was thus dissolved. On the outbreak of war three days later the other German became an enemy alien. On August 1, the firm's account with the defendant bank was £2,321 in credit.

On June 5, 1919, the naturalised partner commenced an action in the name of the firm to recover this sum, the cause of action being alleged to have arisen on or before August 1, 1914. The firm had not made any demand on or before that date for payment of the sum in question and the bank (which had counter-claimed for a larger sum than the balance of the account) pleaded on the point here at issue (*inter alia*) that there had thus accrued no cause of action to the firm on August 1, 1914, and that therefore the action was not maintainable.

---

[1] At pp. 1005–1006.
[2] At p. 1008.

Decision

On appeal, the Court of Appeal held that where money was standing to the credit of a customer on current account at a bank, a previous demand was necessary before an action could be maintained against the bank for the money, and the Court therefore entered judgment for the defendant bank. In his judgment, Atkin L.J. said:

I think that there is only one contract made between the bank and its customer. The terms of that contract involve obligations on both sides, and require careful statement. They appear upon consideration to include the following provisions. The bank undertakes to receive money and to collect bills for its customer's account. The proceeds so received are not to be held in trust for the customer, but the bank borrows the proceeds and undertakes to repay them. The promise to repay is to repay at the branch of the bank where the account is kept, and during banking hours. It includes a promise to repay any part of the amount due against the written order of the customer, addressed to the bank at the branch, and as such written orders may be outstanding in the ordinary course of business for two or three days, it is a term of the contract that the bank will not cease to do business with the customer except upon reasonable notice. The customer on his part undertakes to exercise reasonable care in executing his written orders so as not to mislead the bank or to facilitate forgery. I think it is necessarily a term of such contract that the bank is not liable to pay the customer the full amount of his balance until he demands payment from the bank at the branch at which the current account is kept. Whether he must demand it in writing it is not necessary now to determine.[3]

And Bankes L.J. said:

Having regard to the peculiarity of that relation there must be, I consider, quite a number of implied superadded obligations beyond the one specifically mentioned in *Foley* v. *Hill*[4] and *Pott* v. *Clegg*.[5] Unless this were so, the banker, like any ordinary debtor, must seek out his creditor and repay him his loan immediately it becomes due—that is to say, directly after the customer has paid the money into his account— and the customer, like any ordinary creditor, can demand repayment of the loan by his debtor at any time and place.... It seems to me impossible to imagine the relation between banker and customer as it exists today, without the stipulation that, if the customer seeks to withdraw his loan, he must make application to the banker for it.[6]

[3] At p. 127.
[4] *Supra*.
[5] (1847) 16 M. & W. 321.
[6] At pp. 119–121.

Notes[7]

The importance of *Foley* v. *Hill* was that it authoritatively established the legal basis of the relationship of banker and customer as that of debtor and creditor, a position which on the earlier cases was by no means clear. Originally the goldsmith-banker had accepted gold and valuables for safe custody, and his position had been that of a bailee. As the relationship began to assume its modern form, a fundamental aspect of which is that the customer draws bills of exchange (now usually in the form of cheques) upon the banker, the bailment basis became quite inadequate for the solution of the legal problems arising, and an attempt was made to equate the position with that of agent and principal. An agent holding the moneys of his principal is under very strict obligations, and in particular must meticulously account for its use within the terms of his authority. If bankers had so to account the practice of banking as we know it today would be hardly possible. Bankers in fact often act as agents for their customers; for example, the banker is his customer's agent when on the presentation of the customer's cheque he pays out to a third party money from the customer's account, and in doing so he must act in accordance with the customer's mandate. But the decision in *Foley* v. *Hill* definitely rejected the suggestion that the banker/customer relationship was itself one of agency, and established instead a basis for the relationship which left the banker quite free in his use of moneys received from his customers. It is accordingly a case of the first importance.[8]

The simple debtor-creditor relationship was accepted as fundamental, but it is not altogether satisfactory without refinements on the ordinary rules of debtor and creditor. For example, the enforcement of the rule that the debtor must seek out his creditor would give rise to obvious difficulty. The second case, *Joachimson* v. *Swiss Bank Corporation*, initiated the development of these refinements and carried the implications of *Foley* v. *Hill* a stage further, in deciding not only that the

[7] The nature of the contract between banker and customer is discussed at length in Chorley, *Law of Contract in Relation to the Law of Banking* (Gilbart Lectures, 1964). *cf.* Holden, *Banker and Customer* (3rd ed.) pp. 1–111, and Reeday, *The Law relating to Banking* (5th ed.) pp. 1–55.

[8] *cf. Midland Bank Ltd.* v. *Conway Corporation* [1965] 1 W.L.R. 1165 for a surprising attempt to extend the relationship to one of general agency. It was held that the fact that the bank had paid rates and received rent for a customer who lived overseas did not make it an agent for the management of the property concerned.

money is lent to the banker, who is thus able to do what he likes with it, but also that it is not repayable until demand is made. If the rule as to the debtor seeking out his creditor were applied to the banker, not only would his customer be entitled at any time to issue a writ against him for the balance of his account (as happened in effect in the *Joachimson* case) but on his side the banker could close the account without notice by repaying that balance. Either proposition would clearly not be in accord with the recognised function of the banker, and the (theoretical) dislocation of business which would have resulted from any other ruling was a reason which weighed with the Court in reaching the decision they did.

An interesting application of the principle of *Foley* v. *Hill* by the Privy Council was seen in *Space Investments Ltd.* v. *Canadian Imperial Bank of Commerce Trust Co. (Bahamas) Ltd.*[9] where Mercantile Bank and Trust Co. Ltd. was appointed trustee of certain settlements which empowered it, *inter alia*, to open bank accounts and to deposit in them any part of the trust funds. Such funds were deposited by M.B.T. as trustees with M.B.T. as bankers, and upon M.B.T. becoming insolvent the Supreme Court and the Court of Appeal in the Bahamas ruled that money so deposited was subject to a trust, and that the trust beneficiaries were entitled to payment in priority to other customers and other unsecured creditors. But the appeal of the other unsecured creditors to the Privy Council succeeded: M.B.T. as trustees had been expressly authorised to make the deposits and no breach of trust was involved. The money deposited "became the property of M.B.T. in law and in equity and M.B.T. was entitled to use that money for the purposes of M.B.T. in any manner that M.B.T. pleased."

The *Joachimson* decision was concerned with current accounts; in the case of deposit accounts there are usually other considerations precedent to the right to withdraw—a fixed period of notice (seldom enforced, an appropriate deduction of interest taking its place) and the production of deposit receipt or deposit book where either has been issued. In such cases the balance is clearly not payable until the conditions have been fulfilled, but the rule in the *Joachimson* case would presumably apply in the case of a demand deposit if the book was (as quite often happens) left in the hands of the bank.

The demand must be at the branch at which the account is kept—*cf.* in addition to the statement of Atkin L.J. itself, *Isaacs*

[9] [1986] 3 All E.R. 75.

v. *Barclays Bank Ltd. and Barclays Bank (France) Ltd.*,[10] where
the position was discussed but not decided.

There was a recent example of the customer's right to
demand his money in cash in the unusual circumstances of
Libyan Arab Foreign Bank v. *Bankers Trust Company*.[11] The
bank claimed $131m, the balance of its account with Bankers
Trust in London on January 8, 1986, plus $161m held in the
New York branch of Bankers Trust which it was claimed ought
to have been transferred to London before the executive order
freezing Libyan funds came into effect in the afternoon of
January 8.

Staughton J. said that the contract between banker and
customer was governed by the law of the place where the
account was kept, and there were no grounds here for holding
that this general law did not apply; the London account was
under English law, and could operate unless an infringement of
United States law on United States territory was involved.
There were various payment methods which would have
infringed United States law, but cash in United States dollars
had been demanded, and "although it would be a formidable
operation to transport $131m in cash from New York," no
breach of New York law would be involved. And the claim for
$161m arising from Bankers Trust's breach of contract was to be
added to the first claim.

Tournier v. National Provincial and Union Bank of England

[1924] 1 K.B. 461

*It is a further term of the implied contract that the bank enters into a
qualified obligation not to disclose information concerning the customer's
affairs without his consent*

Facts

The plaintiff was a customer of the defendant bank. In April
1922, his account being £9 8s. 6d. overdrawn, he signed a
document agreeing to pay this amount off by weekly instalments
of £1. On the document the plaintiff wrote the name and
address of a firm, Kenyon & Co., whose employ he was about
to enter as a traveller, on a three months' contract.

When the agreement to repay was not observed the manager
of the branch telephoned Kenyon & Co. to ascertain the

---

[10] [1943] 2 All E.R. 682.
[11] [1987] 2 F.T.L.R. 509.

plaintiff's private address, and there followed conversation between him and two of the company's directors. The plaintiff said that in this conversation the manager had disclosed the facts of the overdraft and that promises for repayment were not being carried out, and had expressed the opinion that the plaintiff was betting heavily, the bank having traced a payment or payments passing from the plaintiff to a bookmaker. The plaintiff said that as a matter of fact the payment to the bookmaker was in respect of goods bought, and not of betting. The branch manager's version of the telephone conversation differed from that of the plaintiff in accent rather than in fact.

As a result of the conversation, Kenyon & Co. refused to renew the plaintiff's employment when the three months had expired. The plaintiff sued the defendant bank ior slander, and also for breach of an implied contract that they would not disclose to third persons the state of the account or any transactions relating to it. Judgment was entered for the bank, and the plaintiff now appealed.

Decision

The Court of Appeal allowed the appeal and ordered a new trial. In the course of his judgment, Bankes L.J. said:

> At the present day I think it may be asserted with confidence that the duty [of non-disclosure] is a legal one arising out of contract, and that the duty is not absolute, but qualified. It is not possible to frame any exhaustive definition of the duty.... On principle, I think that the qualifications can be classified under four heads: (*a*) where disclosure is under compulsion by law; (*b*) where there is a duty to the public to disclose; (*c*) where the interests of the bank require disclosure; (*d*) where the disclosure is made by the express or implied consent of the customer.[12]

And Atkin L.J. said:

> The first question is: To what information does the obligation of secrecy extend? It clearly goes beyond the state of the account, that is, whether there is a debit or a credit balance, and the amount of the balance. It must extend at least to all the transactions that go through the account, and to the securities, if any, given in respect of the account; and in respect of such matters it must, I think, extend beyond the period when the account is closed, or ceases to be an active account.... I further think that the obligation extends to information obtained from other sources than the customer's actual account, if the

[12] At pp. 471–473.

occasion upon which the information was obtained arose out of the banking relations of the bank and its customers—for example, with a view to assisting the bank in conducting the customer's business, or in coming to decisions as to its treatment of its customers...In this case, however, I should not extend the obligation to information as to the customer obtained after he had ceased to be a customer.... I do not desire to express any final opinion on the practice of bankers to give one another information as to the affairs of their respective customers, except to say it appears to me that if it is justified it must be upon the basis of an implied consent of the customer.[13]

Notes

As we have seen, the scope of the implied contract between banker and customer is a wide one, and the term recognised in the *Tournier* decision as a part of it is in addition to those outlined by Atkin L.J. in the *Joachimson* case. It is of course obvious that no such obligation of secrecy attached to the normal relationship of debtor to his creditor, so that this additional qualification is of substantial importance.

The general secrecy covering the customer's account, which of course continues after the account is closed, has long been recognised in practice as fundamental.[14]

The Younger Committee[15] heard evidence from *The Guardian* of a breach of confidentiality involving two banks which were alleged to have given details of an account over the telephone. The Committee of London Clearing Bankers found it hard to believe that any bank employee would give such details in answer to a telephone inquiry, but the Committee were satisfied that "information was obtained, possibly by deception," and urged the banks "to look to the arrangements they have for protecting the details of their clients' accounts." It is to be noted that the Committee appears to have heard of only the one example of fault, and the testimony of the clearing banks which the Report quotes makes it clear that they already took the matter very seriously, as of course they always have done.

A most important part of the *Tournier* decision is the scope of the qualifications on the duty, and all four classes of qualification outlined by Bankes L.J. need the careful consideration of bankers. The first, compulsion by law, is considered in the next section.[16] The second qualification, where there is a

---

[13] At pp. 485–486.
[14] *cf.*, *e.g. Tassell* v. *Cooper post*, p. 101.
[15] See The Report of the Committee on Privacy, 1972, Cmnd. 5012.
[16] *Post*, p. 11.

duty to the public to disclose, is much less frequently seen in practice. The banker who knew that an account on his books was that of a revolutionary body, for example, or that it was being used in time of war in connection with trade with the enemy, would owe a duty to the public to report the facts to the proper authorities; but he would clearly need to be extremely circumspect in his actions. There are many examples of the third qualification—where the interests of the bank require disclosure—one of which is when, upon suing a guarantor, the state of the account guaranteed must be shown—as it must, also, when the bank sues the customer on his overdraft.

Another such example is seen in *Sunderland* v. *Barclays Bank Ltd.*[17] There the customer, a woman, issued a cheque to her dressmaker. The bank dishonoured it, as there were insufficient funds on the account; as they knew of the customer's bookmaking transactions they did not wish to allow any overdraft on the account. The customer protested about the dishonour to her husband, a doctor, and he told her to take the matter up with the bank. She did so, by telephone, and after a while the husband interrupted the conversation to add his own protest. The bank then disclosed to him that cheques had previously been drawn payable to bookmakers. Upon the wife's bringing an action against the bank for breach of duty in making this disclosure, the bank contended that the conversation with the husband was a continuation of that with the wife, and that they had her implied consent to the disclosure. This the wife denied; but it was held by du Parcq L.J. sitting as an additional King's Bench judge, that on the facts the bank must succeed, the disclosure being in their interests, within the third of the qualifications on the duty of secrecy in the *Tournier* case.[18]

The last type of permissible disclosure, with the customer's consent, is of course the one most often seen in practice. The customer may instruct his banker to give some or all of the particulars of his account to, say, his accountant; and in such a case there is no difficulty. It is sometimes less easy to deal with the questions asked by a proposing guarantor about the account he is to guarantee: has the customer in such a case given his implied consent to disclosure (where his express consent is lacking) by seeking to obtain the guarantee or should this

---

[17] *The Times*, November 25, 1938; 5 L.D.B. 163.
[18] However it has been questioned whether the disclosure of the gambling activities was justified. The dishonour was justified by the insufficiency of funds, *cf.* Ellinger, *Modern Banking Law*, p. 104.

properly be regarded as another example of the third group? This is a matter in which the reasonableness or otherwise of the questions must be the chief criterion, for while the guarantee may be avoided by misrepresentation there must clearly be no unnecessary disclosure.[19]

The greatest difficulty, however, and that most often discussed, has been caused by the answering of credit inquiries. Bankers' references are a useful part of the machinery of commerce, and the practice of using them has more than once received judicial approval, perhaps most notably in *Parsons* v. *Barclay & Co. Ltd.*,[20] where Cozens-Hardy M.R. spoke (at p. 252) of:

> ... that very wholesome and useful habit by which one banker answers in confidence, and answers honestly, to another banker, the answer being given at the request and with the knowledge of the first banker's customer.... [21]

There are however obvious dangers for the banker answering the inquiry. In the passage just quoted the customer's request and knowledge are seen (in 1910) as essential parts of the "wholesome habit." Atkin L.J. in the passage quoted from his judgment in the *Tournier* case, 14 years later, saw the practice as justified only with the implied consent of the customer. His consent is plainly enough implied when he himself gives his banker as a referee; but the practice has grown up of answering all inquiries, provided that they come from other banks, with no knowledge whether the customer has himself given the bank as referee, or indeed whether he would or would not wish the inquiry to be answered. The banks could easily enough, if challenged, prove the existence of this usage, but it might not be possible to prove that it is understood and accepted by the general public.[22]

The clearing banks told the Younger Committee[23] that to notify a customer when an inquiry is made about his financial

---

[19] *cf. post*, pp. 291 *et seq.*
[20] (1910) 2 L.D.B. 248. *cf. post*, p. 25.
[21] *cf. post*, p. 132, for the comments of Hilbery J., on the qualified privilege that arises in these circumstances.
[22] The Jack Report, which attaches considerable importance to the principle of confidentiality, and argues against any unnecessary limitation of it, recommends, *inter alia*, that the fourth *Tournier* exception should be amended to "where the disclosure is made by the express consent of the customer."
[23] *Supra.*

standing might damage the relationship between the customer and the enquirer. But the Committee thought otherwise.

We doubt whether there is any serious or widespread abuse of the bank reference system, but we do not believe that the practice is as well-known and accepted among customers, particularly individuals, as the banks assert. Nor are we convinced that it would be undesirable for a customer to know what inquiries had been made about him and what replies had been given. On the contrary, we think the present system is undesirable. We recommend that the banks should make clear to all customers, existing or prospective, the existence and manner of operation of their reference system, and give them the opportunity either to grant a standing authority for the provision of references or to require the bank to seek their consent on every occasion.

The banks, agreeing that there is no "serious or widespread abuse" of the system, or indeed any public dissatisfaction with it, have not taken any of the kind of action recommended by the committee. But there are aspects of the reference system that give some cause for concern. There is growing pressure on the banks by credit agencies to supplement their opinions on credit worthiness with more or less detailed information on their customers' accounts. Even an opinion, given direct to any enquirer other than another bank, might be challenged as being outside the scope of the "wholesome and useful" habit; its extension into a wider area of inquiry would enlarge the danger of infringing the *Tournier* principle.

It is unfortunate that a system so widely used, and useful, in commerce should present problems to the bankers operating it. They can only seek to keep within the bounds of what has become normal banking practice, and hope that it does not prove to be legally unjustified. Certainly any departure from that practice should be entertained only with a full appreciation of its possible perils.[24]

Williams and Others v. Summerfield
[1972] 2 Q.B. 513

Disclosure of information concerning the customer's affairs by compulsion of law

Facts
When the Bristol police sought to inspect the banking

---

[24] The liability of the banker to his customer discussed here is to be compared with his liability to the enquirer when answering the inquiries he receives, *post*, pp. 18–20, 24–27.

accounts of certain defendants in a criminal prosecution the magistrate made the order required under section 7 of the Bankers' Books Evidence Act 1879. The defendants appealed, arguing, *inter alia*, that the Act was intended only to provide a procedural method to allow evidence not otherwise admissible, and did not alter the fundamental proposition that a defendant in criminal proceedings should not be required to incriminate himself.

Section 7 provides:

> On the application of any party to a legal proceeding a court or judge may order that such party be at liberty to inspect and take copies of any entries in a banker's book for any of the purposes of such proceedings. . . .

Decision

The divisional court dismissed the appeal. Lord Widgery C.J. pointed out that acceptance of the appellants' argument would mean in practice that the Act does not apply to any criminal proceedings, whereas the Act is explicit that it does. But, he said:

> . . . One must I think recognise that an order under section 7 can be a very serious interference with the liberty of the subject. It can be a gross invasion of privacy; it is an order which clearly must only be made after the most careful thought and on the clearest grounds . . . I think that in criminal proceedings, justices should warn themselves of the importance of the step which they are taking in making an order under section 7; should always recognise the care with which the jurisdiction should be exercised; should take into account amongst other things whether there is other evidence in the possession of the prosecution to support the charge; or whether the application under section 7 is a fishing expedition in the hope of finding some material on which the charge can be hung.[25]

Notes

As Lord Widgery remarked, this was the first case in close on a 100 years since the Bankers' Books Evidence Act was passed in which its application to criminal proceedings had been tested. In civil cases, he said, "the courts have set their face against section 7 being used as a kind of searching inquiry or fishing expedition beyond the ordinary rules of discovery," and it may be taken that his statement regarding the care that should be

---

[25] At p. 518.

exercised in the making of a section 7 order is relevant to civil as well as to criminal cases.

The Act is probably the best known example of the first of the four qualifications to the "no disclosure" rule set out by Bankes L.J.[26] In fact the primary purpose of the Act was, in Lord Widgery's words, "to enable entries in a banker's books to be proved in legal proceedings without the disruption of the bank which would result if the original books had to be taken away and kept in court," and it is not until section 7 "that one finds any kind of provision in this Act whereby an application of a hostile character can be made." Even here there was no change in substantive law: "the ordinary rules of discovery" cannot be extended by means of the section.

Lord Widgery's cautionary words to magistrates were repeated and amplified in *R. v. Marlborough Street Stipendiary Magistrate, ex p. Simpson and Others*[27] where the divisional court quashed 26 orders obtained by the police under the 1879 Act. The orders had been obtained *ex parte*—notice had not been given to the parties affected—and the court held that although there was nothing in section 7 to prevent *ex parte* applications, there was much to be said for notice being given. They held further that orders under the Act should be limited in time, as otherwise investigations might continue indefinitely, and that orders should not extend beyond the true purpose of the relevant charges.

In *Barker v. Wilson*[28]; the divisional court held that microfilm records were within the scope of the Act, a point given statutory force by the Banking Act 1979, which provides in paragraph 1 of Schedule 6 that for the purposes of the Act bankers' books include records used in the ordinary business of the bank, whether written or "a microfilm, magnetic tape or any other form of mechanical or electronic data retrieval mechanism."[29]

In *Williams v. Williams; Tucker and Others v. Williams and Another*[30] disclosure was sought of documents, including paid cheques and paying-in slips, and an order under the Bankers' Books Evidence Act was made. But the Court of Appeal

[26] *Ante*, p. 7.
[27] (1980) 70 Cr.App.R. 291; see also *R. v. Nottingham City Justices* [1984] Crim.L.R. 554.
[28] [1980] 2 All E.R. 81.
[29] See also *R. v. Grossman, post*, p. 400, and *cf. R. v. Dadson* [1983] Crim.L.R. 540, where the Court of Appeal held that "bankers' books" did not include bank correspondence.
[30] [1987] 3 All E.R. 257.

allowed the bank's appeal: Sir John Donaldson M.R., said that he was unable to accept that an individual cheque or paying-in slip could be regarded as an "entry" in the bank's records. But he so decided with considerable regret; it should be possible to obtain such records, and "this is something which I hope can be looked at by the relevant rule committee."

However, there are other circumstances in which the banker's duty of secrecy is qualified by compulsion of law; the range of this exception to the *Tournier* principle is still increasing, and is likely to increase still further.[31]

Income tax legislation has long provided for access to bankers' books. In 1924 Sir John Paget, in the third volume of Legal Decisions affecting Bankers, commented on the Revenue's requisitions for information from bankers, and remarked "It would be interesting to know on what statutory authority such demands are based. Possibly on a very dubious interpretation of sec.103 of the Income Tax Act 1918." It was under that s.103 that in 1928, in *Att.-Gen* v. *National Provincial Bank Ltd*.[32] it was held that in certain circumstances the banks must name all persons for whom it receives interest on certain government stocks.

In *Clinch* v. *I.R.C.*[33] Ackner J. rejected the claim by the managing director of the London subsidiary of a Bermuda bank that the relevant legislation did not authorise questions to an intermediary about unidentified transactions on behalf of unidentified principals; but he did not accept the Revenue's initial contention, questioning the court's power to interfere with an act of executive authority: "One of the vital functions of the courts is to protect the individual from any abuse of power by the executive, a function which nowadays grows more and more important as governmental interference increases."

Company legislation, too, has seen expansion of powers of compelling disclosure, a recent example being the wide powers in the Financial Services Act 1986 to obtain information regarding insider trading. And the passing of the Drug Trafficking Offences Act 1986, which imposes *inter alia* a duty to report suspicions that an offence under the Act has been committed, is of particular interest in the possibility which it

---

[31] *cf.* Penn, Shea & Arora, *Banking Law I*, 4–04–18.
[32] (1928) 44 T.L.R. 701.
[33] [1974] Q.B. 76.

raises that similar draconian measures might be extended to other crimes.[33a]

There have been in recent years a number of cases in which confidentiality has been an international issue. Thus in *X A G v. A Bank*[34] a New York court had issued a *subpoena* to the London branch of an American bank to produce documents relating to the business of three companies banking there. The companies obtained interim injunctions restraining the bank from producing the documents, and on their application to continue the injunctions until trial, Leggatt J., remarking that refusal to continue the injunctions "would potentially cause very considerable harm to the companies, by suffering the bank to act for its own purposes, in breach of the duty of confidentiality," said that the court had to consider the balance of convenience between impeding the New York court in the exercise in England of powers which by English standards were excessive, and the possibility that doing so might cause very considerable commercial harm to the companies. The balance was in favour of renewing the injunctions.

The issue in *In re State of Norway's Application*[35] eventually produced a decision of wider constitutional significance than the initial confidentiality question. It concerned Norway's request by letters rogatory[36] for an oral examination as witnesses of officers of Lazard Brothers, on a disputed tax assessment in a charitable trust for which Lazards had acted as bankers. Neill J. made the order, but the Court of Appeal by a majority allowed the witnesses' appeal on the grounds that the request (a) went far beyond the elicitation of evidence: it was a fishing expedition; and (b) breached the requirement for confidentiality: the witnesses would be compelled to disclose wide-ranging banking confidences. The State of Norway appealed, with revised terms, but the witnesses raised again the argument that taxation did not fall within the "civil or commercial" categories which alone were eligible for the order sought under the Evidence (Proceedings in Other Jurisdictions)

[33a] *cf. R.* v. *Southwark Crown Court, ex parte Customs and Excise and Bank of Credit and Commerce International*, [1989] 3 W.L.R. 1054, where an officer of the bank and a customer had been indicted in the United States for drug offences, and the Divisional Court held that an order to produce documents found in the officer's office in London was not to be conditional on an undertaking that they be not disclosed to a foreign law enforcement agency.

[34] [1983] 2 All E.R. 464.

[35] [1989] 2 W.L.R. 458.

[36] See Penn, Shea & Arora, *op. cit.* I, 4, 09 for description of the process.

Act 1975, and, the Court agreeing, the appeal failed. But the House of Lords held on Norway's further appeal that "civil and commercial" in the 1975 Act was not to be equated with the French text of the Hague Convention of 1970. The phrase went back in English legislation for 70 years before the Convention. In the present context the only requirement was that the proceedings must be civil or commercial according to the laws of the two countries involved. The judge was entirely justified in finding that in Norway the proceedings would be classified as civil, and the appeal was allowed.

A new area of incursion into the banker's duty of confidentiality has been opened by the Police and Criminal Evidence Act 1984, s.9(1), which empowers a constable to obtain access to "special procedure material" for the purpose of a criminal investigation, such material being defined as including confidential material acquired in the course of any business. In *R. v. Manchester Crown Court, ex parte Taylor*[37] the police had obtained orders addressed to a number of banks under section 9 giving them access to ledger accounts, correspondence and business records relating to a person and companies suspected of conspiracy to defraud the banks involved. The orders were executed, and in the present action Kevin Taylor sought judicial review of one of the orders, and a declaration that it was invalidly made by reason of no proper notice of intention to apply for it having been given to the bank.

The Court of Appeal dismissed the application. Glidewell L.J. examined the provisions of the Act, which "were, when they came into force, new provisions in our law." The orders had been sought because, *inter alia*, the material could not be obtained under the Bankers' Books Evidence Act because no legal proceedings had been started, nor could be until the investigation was completed. The safeguards in the Act for obtaining special procedure material were for the protection of the persons against whom an order was sought, and not to protect the suspect, who was protected by the fact that the judge making the order had to be satisfied that the access conditions had been met. Here there were no grounds for granting the application.

In another case under section 9, *Barclays Bank plc* v. *Taylor*; *Trustee Savings Bank of Wales and Border Counties* v. *Taylor*,[37a]

---

[37] [1988] 1 W.L.R. 705; and *cf. R. v. Central Criminal Court, ex parte Adegbesan*, [1986] 1 W.L.R. 1292.
[37a] [1989] 3 All E.R. 563.

the defendants counterclaimed against the banks alleging breach of the duty of confidentiality in that they had not opposed court orders authorising the police to inspect their accounts, and had not told the defendants that the orders had been sought. The Court of Appeal held that there was no duty on the banks to contest disclosure by compulsion of law, and while the banks might be free to ignore the police request that the customers be not informed, there was no basis for an implied obligation to act in a way which might in some circumstances hinder police inquiries.

Bankers Trust Company v. *Shapira and Others*[38] was an unusual example of the overruling of the banker's duty of confidentiality. The plaintiff wished to trace the proceeds of two forged cheques, totalling $700,000, the product of an elaborate fraud, which were alleged to have been paid in for the credit of two personal accounts with the Discount Bank (Overseas). The account holders, the first two defendants, had not been served with the writ, one being in prison in Switzerland and the other being untraceable. The Discount Bank, the third defendant, although "very properly" remaining neutral, put forward the confidentiality argument, but the Court of Appeal made the very wide order for discovery sought: it was justified when the evidence of fraud against the customer was very strong, but the plaintiffs should give an undertaking in damages to the bank, pay all the expenses involved, and use the documents disclosed only for the purpose of tracing the funds.

It is important in the whole of this area that the banker should disclose no more than the law compels him to. An interesting example of a bank's caution in this regard is *Eckman* v. *Midland Bank Ltd.*[39] When the Amalgamated Union of Engineering Workers refused to pay the fine of £5,000 imposed by the National Industrial Relations Court, a sequestration order was made, and the Union's bankers, Midland Bank and Hill, Samuel Ltd., were required to disclose the assets held by them and to pay the fine. The banks argued that while the writ of sequestration entitled them to give the information sought, it did not oblige them to give it. The relationship between banker and customer was not one that consisted wholly of legal rights and duties, and a banker should not take any action of this kind of which his customer would disapprove unless compelled (in this case by an order of the court) to do so. Donaldson J.

---

[38] [1980] 1 W.L.R. 1245.
[39] [1973] 1 Q.B. 519.

agreed "that strict compliance with obligations which bind in honour only is one of the hallmarks of the most respected members of the banking community," but he rejected the argument in the present case; the third party in a writ of sequestration must not knowingly take any action that would obstruct the operation of the writ, and a demand by sequestrators for disclosure of property must be answered promptly, fully and accurately.

It is also to be noted that Donaldson J. discussed in some detail, albeit *obiter*, the general effect of a sequestration order in connection with a banking account. He remarked that where there has been an agreed overdraft limit which has not been fully taken up "this facility is part of the property of the contemnor which the sequestrators are entitled to have transferred to them and which they can operate by authority of the writ of sequestration." Securities lodged to secure borrowing are also subject to the sequestration order, as to any margin not required to cover the borrowing.

Hedley Byrne & Co. Ltd. v. Heller & Partners Ltd.

[1964] A.C. 465

Box v. Midland Bank Ltd.

[1979] 2 Lloyd's Rep. 391

There can be a special relationship between banker and customer, over and above that of contract

Facts of Hedley Byrne & Co. Ltd. v. Heller & Partners Ltd.

The plaintiffs, advertising agents, inquired through their bankers, the National Provincial Bank, Bishopsgate, as to the credit of their clients, Easipower Ltd., who banked with the defendant merchant bank. Satisfactory replies were given to two such inquiries, and the plaintiffs, relying on these replies, placed orders for advertising space in connection with which, on the subsequent liquidation of Easipower Ltd., they lost more than £17,000. They brought an action against the defendant bank alleging that the replies had been given negligently.

One of the inquiries was made, and replied to, in writing. The reply began with the words—

CONFIDENTIAL

For your private use and without responsibility
on the part of the bank or its officials.

The other inquiry was made by telephone, but it was agreed by the parties that a similar disclaimer of responsibility was accepted by the inquiring bank. McNair J. held that the bank had in fact been negligent,[40] but he considered that, quite apart from the effect of the disclaimer, if any, he was bound by precedent to hold that a bank was not liable for damage resulting from mere statements of this kind, however negligently made. His judgment was affirmed by the Court of Appeal.

Decision

The House of Lords, after reviewing the earlier cases, held that if a person such as a banker, upon receiving a request for information or advice in circumstances that show that his skill or judgment is being relied upon, gives that information or advice without a clear disclaimer of responsibility, he accepts a legal duty to exercise proper care in doing so even though he is not under any contractual or fiduciary obligation to the inquirer, and if hc is ncgligent an action for damages will lie.

Lord Devlin said:

I think, therefore, that there is ample authority to justify your lordships in saying now that the categories of special relationships, which may give rise to a duty to take care in word as well as in deed, are not limited to contractual relationships, but include also relationships which, in the words of Lord Shaw in *Nocton* v. *Lord Ashburton*,[41] are "equivalent to contract", that is, where there is an assumption of responsibility in circumstances in which, but for the absence of consideration, there would be a contract.[41a]

However, in the circumstances of the present case, the bank's disclaimer was held to be sufficient to free them from liability:

A man cannot be said voluntarily to be undertaking a responsibility if at the very moment when he is said to be accepting it he declares that in fact he is not.[42]

And Lord Morris said:

They stated that they only responded to the inquiry on the basis that their reply was without responsibility. If the inquirers chose to receive

---

[40] The bank strenuously denied having been negligent, but the point was not in issue in the Court of Appeal or the House of Lords, in view of the findings of law in those courts.

[41] [1914] A.C. 932.

[41a] At pp. 528–529.

[42] At p. 533.

and act upon the reply they cannot disregard the definite terms upon which it was given. They cannot accept a reply given with a stipulation and then reject the stipulation.[43]

Facts of Box v. Midland Bank Ltd.

The plaintiff was anxious to obtain the additional finance needed to enable the company he controlled to carry out a contract with a Manitoba company. The manager of the Wells branch of the bank told the plaintiff that he would like to make the advance, which would require the sanction of his regional head office, and that if an E.C.G.D. policy was obtained, sanction would be a mere formality. But he did not explain the difference between an E.C.G.D. policy, which was obtainable, and an E.C.G.D. Bankers Guarantee (Bills and Notes) policy, which was not.

The application for sanction was duly submitted, and three days later, the manager forwarded the E.C.G.D. quotation for a comprehensive policy, which he assumed to be the policy itself. Regional head office then said that there was no possibility that the advance would be granted. The plaintiff later applied, unsuccessfully, for the Bankers Guarantee policy, and his subsequent financial difficulties culminated in his bankruptcy. He then brought this action against the bank, claiming damages totalling £250,000 for negligence, in that his losses resulted from the manager's careless statements about the availability of finance, upon which he had relied in proceeding with the contract negotiations.

The bank argued (a) that the plaintiff had not come to the bank for advice, but had submitted a proposition; and (b) that a statement regarding the possibility of entering into a contract, made by a party reserving the right not to enter into the contract, could not found an action for negligence.

Decision

Lloyd J. rejected both arguments. As to the first, the *Hedley Byrne* principle is not confined to negligent advice, but to negligent statements generally. And while he saw the force of the second, he could not accept it: "the *Hedley Byrne* principle ought not to be surrounded with too many limitations and qualifications." If the manager had said that his prediction was without responsibility the bank would have escaped liability, as the defendants did in *Hedley Byrne*; but "he certainly did not

---

[43] At p. 504.

say so expressly, and I refuse to draw that inference from what he did say, namely that the ultimate decision rested with regional head office."

[The manager] was not obliged to predict the outcome of his application to regional head office... But if he did predict the outcome he was under a duty to take reasonable care, since he knew that his prediction would be relied upon. Secondly, [he] failed to exercise reasonable care—that is to say the care to be expected of an ordinary competent bank manager—in that he gave Mr Box the impression, as he intended, that the granting of a facility up to £45,000 would be a mere formality once the E.C.G.D. policy had been obtained, whereas there was never the slightest prospect of the facility being made available, as [he] ought to have known. Thirdly, Mr Box did rely on [the] negligent prediction, in continuing to draw on his account... thereby suffering damage.[43a]

However, he awarded damages of only £5,000 on the first of the eight heads of claim[44] and he allowed the bank's counter-claim for the amount of the overdraft, £40,000.

Notes

In the general law of negligence the *Hedley Byrne* decision is of major importance, establishing for the first time that there can be liability for financial loss resulting from negligent words (as contrasted with physical injury resulting from negligent actions) even when the parties have no contractual or fiduciary relationship.[45]

Earlier decisions reviewed in the judgments in *Hedley Byrne* included cases in which plaintiffs had succeeded by suing in contract and asserting that there had been some kind of consideration. The House of Lords here held that the same result "can and should be achieved by the application of the law of negligence and that it is unnecessary and undesirable to construct an artificial consideration."

Lord Devlin remarked in his judgment that while their

[43a] At p. 399.

[44] In *Box* v. *Midland Bank Ltd.* [1981] 1 Lloyd's Rep. 434, the bank successfully appealed against the judge's order against them for costs of the claim *and the counterclaim*. Lord Denning said "On [the] substantive issue the bank undoubtedly won, at least in the sum of £35,000"; the judgment should have been for the balance, with costs accordingly.

[45] In 1932, in *Donoghue* v. *Stevenson* [1932] A.C. 562, the House of Lords had held that the manufacturer of a dangerous product could be liable in damages to the ultimate purchaser who suffered injury, although he had no contractual relationship with the manufacturer.

Lordships' decision concerned relationships equivalent to contract, "cases may arise in the future in which a new and wider proposition, quite independent of contract, will be needed." Such cases would require consideration of whether there could be evolved from the general conception of proximity a specific proposition to fit the case. *Hedley Byrne* has indeed had wideranging implications which are still being explored; of later cases *Box* v. *Midland Bank Ltd.* seems to have been the first in which a bank was held liable under the principle, the plaintiff being the customer to whom the negligent statement was made, but the bank's liability being for the tort of negligence, not for breach of the contract with the customer.

The "special relationship" on which the liability apart from contract was based took a different form in *Lloyds Bank Ltd.* v. *Bundy*[46] where the Court of Appeal held that the relationship of confidence between the bank and its elderly farmer customer imposed on the bank a duty of care of which the bank was in breach. Although in *Morgan's* case[47] the House of Lords did not follow Lord Denning's reliance on inequality of bargaining power, *Morgan* did not upset the principle of the special relationship, on which the majority of the Court in *Bundy* based their finding.

An earlier decision than *Bundy* can be regarded as within the special relationship principle. *Woods* v. *Martins Bank Ltd. and Another*[48] established that advice on investments is within the scope of a bank's business and the gross negligence of the branch manager in the advice he gave to the plaintiff gave the plaintiff his case in damages against the bank and the manager. The bank had relied on *Banbury* v. *Bank of Montreal*[49] where the House of Lords by a majority had held that such advice was outside the scope of banking business, but Salmon J. said that what was true of the Bank of Montreal in 1918 was not necessarily true of Martins Bank in 1958. The banking developments of the past 40 years, which have added so considerably to the area in which the banks act as financial advisers, have given added point to his comparison.

In the *Woods* case he held that a fiduciary relationship existed between the plaintiff and the defendants, and although in *Morgan's* case Lord Scarman warned against the loose use of

---

[46] [1975] Q.B. 326 *post*, pp. 302, 303.
[47] *Post*, p. 301.
[48] [1959] 1 Q.B. 55.
[49] [1918] A.C. 626.

"fiduciary" and "confidential" it seems clear that *Woods* was a special relationship case.

In *Mutual Life and Citizens Assurance* v. *Evatt*[50] a majority of the Privy Council held that the *Hedley Byrne* principle did not extend to negligent advice given by one whose business did not include the giving of advice and who had not held himself out as an expert. As a Privy Council decision this was not binding on the English Courts. It was criticised at the time,[51] and in *Esso Petroleum Co. Ltd.* v. *Mardon*[52] the Court of Appeal upheld Lawson J. in following the Privy Council minority: *Hedley Byrne* is not to be thus restricted.

In *McInerny* v. *Lloyds Bank Ltd.*,[53] a bank manager had made certain statements in a telex message to his customer, and at the customer's request had repeated the telex to the plaintiff, with whom the customer was doing business. In the plaintiff's action, based in part on an allegation of negligence in those statements, Kerr J. expressed the view that the court should be cautious in extending the *Hedley Byrne* principle to include statements made to a particular person with his interests in mind, even if they were likely to be shown to a third party.[54]

However, in *J.E.B. Fasteners* v. *Marks, Bloom & Co.*[55] accountants were held to have been negligent within the *Hedley Byrne* principle in preparing the company accounts in a misleading manner. They knew that the accounts were likely to be shown to parties from whom the company was seeking support, although they did not know to whom the accounts would in fact be shown.[56] This brings the principle close to the physical damage cases, based on the earlier decision in *Donoghue* v. *Stevenson*[57]; and in *J.E.B. Fasteners* Woolf J. quoted Lord Salmon, in a quite different case of negligence[58]:

---

[50] [1971] A.C. 793.
[51] *cf. The Banker* (March, 1971), Vol. 121, p. 332.
[52] [1976] Q.B. 801.
[53] [1973] 2 Lloyd's Rep. 389.
[54] The bank succeeded here and in the Court of Appeal ([1974] 1 Lloyd's Rep. 246) although the judgments in the Court of Appeal did not repeat the judge's *caveat* quoted here.
[55] [1981] 3 All E.R. 289.
[56] But the judge held that the plaintiffs, who had taken over the company, would have done so even if the accounts had not been misleading; and the Court of Appeal dismissed their subsequent appeal [1982] C.M.L.R. 226.
[57] *Supra.*
[58] *Anns* v. *London Borough of Merton* [1977] 2 All E.R. 492.

There are a wide variety of instances in which a statement is negligently made by a professional man which he knows will be relied on by many people besides his clients, *e.g.* a well-known firm of accountants certifies in a prospectus the annual profits of the company issuing it and unfortunately, due to negligence on the part of the accountants, the profits are seriously overstated. Those persons who invested in the company in reliance on the accuracy of the accountants' certificate would have a claim for damages against the accountants for any money they might have lost as a result of the accountants' negligence: see the *Hedley Byrne* case.[58a]

That comment was *obiter*, but it stands as a significant pointer to the possible future development of *Hedley Byrne*.[59] The *Box* decision is a notable addition to the cases which have widened the range of dangers to which the banker is exposed.

The fact that the bank escaped liability in *Hedley Byrne* through its disclaimer of responsibility is of obvious interest to bankers, although the decision merely recognised the effectiveness of the practice that bankers had followed for many years before 1963.

Conscious however of the possibility that "without responsibility" may one day be challenged under the Unfair Contract Terms Act 1977, they must note with interest, and indeed some surprise, Lord Hodson's approval of the words of Pearson L.J. in the Court of Appeal:

Apart from authority, I am not satisfied that it would be reasonable to impose on a banker the obligation suggested, if that obligation really adds anything to the duty of giving an honest answer. It is conceded by counsel for the plaintiffs that the banker is not expected to make outside inquiries to supplement the information which he already has. Is he then expected, in business hours in the bank's time, to expend time and trouble in searching records, studying documents, weighing and comparing the favourable and unfavourable features and producing a well-balanced and well-worded report? That seems wholly unreasonable. Then, if he is not expected to do any of these things, and if he is permitted to give an impromptu answer in the words that immediately come to his mind on the basis of the facts which he happens to remember or is able to ascertain from a quick glance at the file or one

---

[58a] At p. 294.
[59] *cf.*, *e.g. Caparo Industries plc* v. *Dickman and Others, The Times,* August 5, 1988 (auditors of public companies owe duty to shareholders but not to potential investors); *Al Saudi Banque* v. *Clarke Pixley,* (1989) N.L.J. 1341 (auditors of public companies owe no duty to banks, either as actual or potential lenders); *Smith* v. *Eric S Bush* [1989] 2 All E.R. 514 (valuers of houses for mortgage purposes owe duty to purchasers, and disclaimers in the case were held unreasonable under the Unfair Contract Terms Act 1977).

of the files, the duty of care seems to add little, if anything, to the duty of honesty.[60]

Lord Hodson went on to remark that "this is to the same effect as the opinion of Cozens-Hardy M.R." in *Parsons* v. *Barclay & Co. Ltd.*[61] With respect, it seems to go further, for in that case the Master of the Rolls, having rejected the argument that before answering an inquiry the banker should make inquiries himself, still required that he answer "honestly according to his own knowledge of what he knows from the books before him, and from any other actual knowledge he has." This is rather less casual than the conduct Pearson L.J. would seem to have permitted.[62] It need hardly be said that bankers themselves, however careful they may be to disclaim responsibility, do in practice take this aspect of their business very seriously.

There does not appear to be any reported case in which the inquirer and the object of the inquiry had their accounts with the same bank. In such a case there would be a contractual relationship between the inquirer and the bank answering the inquiry; and it is to be noted that in the *Hedley Byrne* case, Lord Pearce said of the disclaimer "I do not . . . accept that, even if the parties were already in contractual or other special relationship, the words would give no immunity to a negligent answer." This view was *obiter*, but it may well be taken as indicating the courts' probable attitude were such a case to be brought.

Section 6 of the Statute of Frauds Amendment Act 1828, provides that no action can be brought against a person making a false representation regarding another person's credit unless such representation is in writing and signed.[63] In *Swift* v. *Jewsbury*,[64] where the manager was joined as defendant, he was held personally liable, but the bank escaped, both under the 1828 Act and because Coleridge C.J. considered that the inquiry was made to the manager personally.

---

[60] At pp. 512–513.
[61] *Ante*, p. 10.
[62] *cf.* L.D.B. Vol. 8, p. 212, where the learned editor, commenting on this passage, says "It is permissible to wonder if this view is not a little at variance with the facts of the situation . . . one would have thought, even if a manager relied on his memory and his files, there was a duty of care in addition to a duty to be honest."
[63] In the *Banbury* case (*supra*) the House of Lords held that the section applies only to the fraudulent representation.
[64] (1874) L.R. 9 Q.B. 301. *cf. Barwick's* case, *post*, p. 406, where the St Frauds defence was not pleaded.

More recently in *Commercial Banking Company of Sydney Ltd.* v. *R.H. Brown & Co.*[65] the Australian High Court held the bank liable for its manager's fraudulent reply to a credit inquiry, and rejected the bank's argument that, *inter alia*, the reply had been sent not to the plaintiffs but to their bankers, and had been expressed to be "confidential and for your private use." The fact that it was also "without responsibility" also failed to save the bank. But the Statute of Frauds defence was not raised, so the case, which as an Australian decision is anyhow not of binding authority in England, leaves that defence still available.

It was advanced by the bank in *Diamond* v. *Bank of London and Montreal Ltd.*[66] where the plaintiff alleged that he had suffered damage as a result of telephone and telex messages from the bank's Nassau manager, which he claimed were false, to the knowledge of the manager. On a preliminary issue the Court of Appeal held that the plaintiff's writ could be issued outside the jurisdiction: the tort of misrepresentation is committed in the place where it is received and acted upon.[67] Here the plaintiff had not shown that he had suffered the losses alleged but they considered that the 1828 Act might have protected the bank on the manager's statement as to the creditworthiness of the brokers involved. (Although they did not discuss the bank's plea that the telex message was expressed to be without responsibility, Lord Denning doubted "very much" whether they could be liable when that phrase had been used.)

The Statute of Frauds defence made a late and unexpected appearance[68] in *U.B.A.F. Ltd.* v. *European American Banking Corporation*[69] where the first issue was the defendants' claim that it freed them from liability for a representation made in a letter signed by their assistant secretary. Ackner L.J., after reviewing the authorities, found no impediment there against deciding that the signature on behalf of a company of its duly authorised agent acting within the scope of his authority is, for

---

[65] [1972] 2 Lloyd's Rep. 360.

[66] [1979] 1 All E.R. 561.

[67] *cf. Cordoba Shipping Co. Ltd.* v. *National State Bank, Elizabeth, New Jersey* [1984] 2 Lloyd's Rep. 91: "The UK was an obvious place for the owners to start proceedings especially having regard to the fact that the substance of the tort was committed in the UK in relation to a transaction negotiated in the UK through brokers carrying on business in the U.K.": *per* Robert Goff L.J.

[68] Even more unexpected (and arguably "disquieting": see A. H. Hermann, *The Financial Times*, March 9, 1989) was the Department of Trade's use of the defence in the International Tin Council litigation.

[69] [1985] 1 W.L.R. 585.

the purpose of section 6 of the 1828 Act, the signature of the company.

If "without responsibility" were ever successfully challenged, the 1828 Act, which is not open to such challenge, might be increasingly relied upon. Whether this would be desirable is perhaps questionable. It is improbable that a bank would resist liability in a case of what one might call gross fraud by one of its managers, but there are degrees of fraud: in the Australian case the manager had been concerned to nurse his customer through difficulties which he believed to be temporary, and it cannot be regarded as satisfactory that in such circumstances, which cannot be unique, his employers can escape liability merely because the reply to an inquiry is unsigned.

It is not without interest to note that immediately following the decision in *Swift* v. *Jewsbury*, an article in *The Economist* for February 7, 1874, strongly criticised the finding that the inquiry was addressed to the manager personally, and the "very technical" application of the 1828 Act; "...certainly, whatever the present law may be, few business men will question the expediency of having the law so framed that people who authorise their servants to make statements as to the credit of others in the ordinary course of their business should be held responsible for such statements."

United Dominions Trust v. Kirkwood

[1966] 2 Q.B. 431

The definition of a banker

Facts

The defendant was managing director of a company that had financed the purchase of cars in its garage business through "stocking loans" from United Dominions Trust, the company accepting bills for £5,000 drawn by UDT, and the defendant indorsing them. When the bills were not met and the company went into liquidation, UDT brought the present action against the defendant as indorser. His only defence was that as unlicensed moneylenders UDT were not entitled to recover the debt.

The Moneylenders Act 1900,[70] which required moneylenders

---

[70] Repealed by the Consumer Credit Act 1974.

to be licensed, provided in section 6 for the exemption from this requirement of, *inter alia*, persons carrying on the business of banking. The plaintiffs claimed to be within this banking exemption, producing evidence that they received money on deposit, and operated current accounts; that other bankers recognised them as bankers; and that the Inland Revenue allowed them to account for stamp duty on cheques by composition fee.

Mocatta J. finding for the plaintiffs, the defendant appealed.

Decision

The Court of Appeal upheld the finding in favour of the plaintiffs by a majority. Lord Denning M.R. said:

> There are therefore two characteristics usually found in bankers today: (i) They accept money from, and collect cheques for, their customers and place them to their credit; (ii) They honour cheques or orders drawn on them by their customers when presented for payment and debit their customers accordingly. These two characteristics carry with them also a third, namely, (iii) They keep current accounts, or something of that nature, in their books in which the credits and debits are entered. Those three characteristics are much the same as those stated in Paget's *Law of Banking* (6th ed., 1961), p. 8; "No-one and nobody, corporate or otherwise, can be a 'banker' who does not (i) take current accounts; (ii) pay cheques drawn on himself; (iii) collect cheques for his customers."[71]

Notes

It is a continuing anomaly that we lack precise definition of "bank," "banker" and "banking."[71a] Section 2 of the Bills of Exchange Act states that " 'Banker' includes a body of persons whether incorporated or not who carry on the business of banking." The purpose of that section was, not to define the business of banking, but to make it clear at a time when joint stock banks were still not as familiar as they are today that companies and firms, as well as individuals, could be bankers. But the several other statutory references did not carry definition appreciably further, and the Jenkins Committee[72] declined the invitation of the Board of Trade to provide a definition that would relieve the Board of its duty under the

---

[71] At p. 447.

[71a] *cf.* Ellinger, *Modern Banking Law*, Chap. 3, for discussion of the variety of statutory definitions of banking.

[72] *cf. post*, p. 213 and (October 1962) 83 J.I.B. 318.

Companies Act of deciding which companies do and which do not rank as banking companies.

The question had not come before the courts in recent years until in 1966 United Dominions Trust were to everyone's surprise challenged in this remarkable case—remarkable not least because the plaintiffs' success was plainly contrary to the court's view as to the proper definition of banking. All three judges found that on the guidance before them UDT fell short of the requirements that all three agreed must be satisfied to constitute a banker; but Lord Denning and, with less conviction, Diplock L.J. based their finding in favour of the plaintiffs on their *reputation* as bankers: the banking community should know a banker when they see one. Harman L.J., perhaps more consistently, could not go with his brethren here, and although he recognised the unfortunate consequences that would have followed his decision, he would have rejected the UDT case. And Lord Denning made it clear that other companies in the same situation as UDT could not rely upon a similar decision being reached again: they should seek a certificate from the Board of Trade. The Companies Act 1967 expressly provided that such a certificate should be conclusive evidence of the status of banker for the purposes of the Moneylenders Act.

But the Court of Appeal's decision in the particular case did not remove the confusion of a multiplicity of definitions for different purposes: statutes had in some instances allowed the authorities to decide on individual applications for recognition, and in others had provided that lists should be maintained of institutions to which recognition was given for the purposes of the particular Acts.

The problem of definition was eased but not entirely removed by the Banking Acts of 1979 and 1987. The purpose of both Acts was the regulation of the taking of banking deposits, which is only one of the banker's functions, but the prohibition of the use by anyone except an authorised institution of words indicating that the user "is a bank or banker or is carrying on a banking business" goes a long way to meet the danger of such words being used to mislead the public as to the standing of less reputable businesses.

It does not meet it completely. It was considered necessary to provide for some exceptions, including in particular overseas institutions, which may in certain circumstances use the names by which they are known in their own countries. And it is still possible for questions of definition to arise outside the scope of the Banking Act. But in considering any such question the courts are likely to have in mind, as well as the three characteristics of the *Kirkwood* decision, and the *Kirkwood* recognition of the possible relevance of reputation, the wider criteria of the Banking Act.

Great Western Railway Co. v. London and County Banking Co. Ltd.

[1901] A.C. 414

Commissioners of Taxation v. English, Scottish and Australian Bank

[1920] A.C. 683

A customer of a bank is one who has an account with that bank; but the relationship is not one of which duration is the essence

Facts of Great Western Railway Co. v. London and County Banking Co. Ltd.

One Huggins, over a course of years, exchanged cheques with the respondent bank, although he had no account with them. In 1898 he obtained from the appellant company, by false pretences, a cheque drawn in his favour and crossed "Not Negotiable," for £142 10s., and this too he exchanged, as to £117 10s. for cash, the balance of £25 being credited by the branch manager, at Huggins's request, to the local Council. The cheque was paid on presentation.

Upon discovery of the fraud, Huggins was convicted and action brought against the bank to recover the money, on the grounds, *inter alia*, that Huggins was not a customer of the bank within section 82 of the Bills of Exchange Act 1882.[73]

Bigham J. gave judgment for the bank, and this judgment was upheld by the Court of Appeal. The railway company now further appealed.

Decision

The House of Lords allowed the appeal, holding that Huggins was not a customer of the bank.

In the course of his judgment, Lord Lindley said:

I cannot think that Huggins was in any sense a customer of the bank; no doubt he was known at the bank as a person accustomed to come

---

[73] Now s.4 of the Cheques Act 1957.

and get cheques cashed, but he had no account of any sort with the bank. Nothing was put to his debit or credit in any book or paper kept by the bank . . . Lord Justice Romer thought he was a customer because the bank had for years collected cheques for him; but in my view the bank collected money for themselves, not for him, in this particular transaction, and the evidence only shows that previous transactions were similar to this.[74]

Facts of Commissioners of Taxation v. English, Scottish and Australian Bank

On June 6, 1917, an Australian taxpayer delivered to the offices of the Commissioner of Taxation, in Sydney, a cheque payable to bearer for £786 18s. 3d., in payment for taxes owing. The Commissioner required all payments made at his office to be in cash, and it was for this reason that the cheque was made payable to bearer. The cheque was stolen from the offices by some person unknown.

On June 7, a person calling himself Stewart Thallon opened an account with the respondent bank, with a deposit of £20 in cash, and gave as his address certain well-known residential chambers in the town. On June 8 he paid in the stolen cheque for £786 18s 3d. On June 9, 11, 12, cheques were presented for £483 16s 6d., £260 10s., and £50 12s. 6d. Thallon was not seen again; the name was unknown at the address given and was presumably fictitious.

The Commissioner of Taxation brought an action against the bank for conversion. The bank pleaded section 88 of the Bills of Exchange Act 1909 (Commonwealth of Australia) (which substantially reproduced section 82 of the Bills of Exchange Act 1882). The Commissioner contended that (*a*) the bank had been negligent and (*b*) Thallon was not a customer within the meaning of the Act. The trial judge and, on appeal, the Supreme Court for New South Wales, found for the bank. The Commissioner now further appealed.

Decision

The Judicial Committee of the Privy Council dismissed the appeal, holding that the bank had not been negligent and that Thallon was a customer within the meaning of the Act.

In delivering their judgment Lord Dunedin said:

Their Lordships are of opinion that the word "customer" signifies a relationship in which duration is not of the essence. A person whose

---

[74] At p. 425.

money has been accepted by a bank on the footing that they undertake to honour cheques up to the amount standing to his credit is, in the view of their Lordships, a customer of the bank in the sense of the statute, irrespective of whether his connection is of short or long standing. The contrast is not between an habitué and a newcomer, but between a person for whom the bank performs a casual service, such as, for instance, cashing a cheque for a person introduced by one of their customers, and a person who has an account of his own at the bank.[75]

Notes

In a line of cases, including the first case above, it had been held that an account is necessary to the relationship of banker and customer in addition to some degree of use and custom. In *Ladbroke* v. *Todd*[76] the plaintiffs were bookmakers, who posted to a client, Jobson, a cheque drawn to his order and crossed "Account Payee." The cheque was stolen and the thief, fraudulently endorsing Jobson's name upon it, took it to the defendant banker and with it opened an account in Jobson's name. At his request the cheque was specially cleared, and on the following day he drew the proceeds and disappeared. The plaintiffs issued a new cheque to Jobson and sued the bank to recover the proceeds of the first cheque as money had and received to their use, contending that the thief was not a customer of the bank within the meaning of section 82 and that the defendants were therefore not entitled to protection of the section. They argued that "a person does not become a customer of a bank until the first cheque is collected." Judgment was given for the plaintiffs, on the grounds of the banker's negligence in not taking reasonable precautions to safeguard the interests of persons who might be the true owners of the cheque; but Bailhache J. said that in his opinion, but for the negligence, the defendant would have been entitled to the protection of the section as having received payment for a customer:

It is true that it was the first transaction that had taken place between them; but I have to look at the relationship between the parties created by the receipt of the cheque. Was he a customer of the bank when he handed the cheque to the defendant? I think he was. There must be a time when he began to be a customer. In my opinion a person becomes a customer of a bank when he goes to the bank with money or a cheque and asks to have an account opened in his name,

[75] At p. 687.
[76] (1914) 19 Com.Cas. 256.

and the bank accepts the money or cheque and is prepared to open an account in the name of that person; after that he is entitled to be called a customer of the bank. I do not think it is necessary that he should have drawn any money or even that he should be in a position to draw money. I think such a person becomes a customer the moment the bank receives the money or cheque and agrees to open an account.[77]

This decision was criticised as being in conflict with previous decisions, but the Privy Council decision in the second case here dealt with goes far to confirm the view of Bailhache J. Privy Council cases are not technically binding on the other English courts, but the greatest weight short of binding precedent is attached to them, and more recently, in *Barclays Bank Ltd.* v. *Okenarhe*,[78] Mocatta J. quoted Bailhache J.'s dictum with approval.

The Bailhache view would almost certainly be followed in any fresh case on the point. Indeed, it has been argued[79] that the mere offer by the prospective customer to open an account, and its acceptance by the bank, creates as binding a contract as any other offer and acceptance.

This reasoning is in line with common banking usage. A person who has completed the bank's formalities for opening an account would be regarded as a customer even if he had not paid in at all, and a cheque book would be issued even before any credit was received, although an initial credit is the normal course of events upon the opening of an account.

In *Woods* v. *Martins Bank Ltd.*,[80] Salmon J. took the matter further, holding that when the bank, several weeks before an account was opened, accepted instructions to receive money and invest it on behalf of the plaintiff, the relationship of banker and customer was set up. Although limited to its special facts this decision must make the older view even less tenable; and although the banker would still be reluctant to regard as a customer a person for whom he merely exchanged cheques from time to time, it may be that even here a banker/customer relationship will some day be imported. It may be noted, however, as a point of academic interest, that the crediting to an account headed "Sundry Customers' Account" of cheques

---

[77] At p. 261.
[78] *Post*, p. 233.
[79] See Chorley, Gilbart Lectures, 1955, cited by Mocatta J. in *Barclays Bank Ltd.* v. *Okenarhe, supra.*
[80] *Ante*, p. 22. *cf.* Chorley, Gilbart Lectures, 1964, for further discussion of the point here referred to.

thus cashed for persons with no account does not make those persons customers.[81]

In the light of the increasing diversity of the business of the commercial banks, a question may arise in the future as to whether a person dealing with a specialist division of a bank is a customer of the bank in the full sense. The holder of a bank credit card who has no bank account would presumably not be a customer of the bank where the credit card operation is entirely separate from the bank, but, where the credit card is operated by the bank, it could clearly be argued that the card-holder is a customer of the bank, even though he has no banking account in the accepted sense.

With regard to the apparent negligence of the bank in the *Commissioners of Taxation* case, in not taking up references regarding their customer, see *ante*, p. 31.

It may be noted that a bank can itself be the customer of another bank. In *Importers Company Ltd.* v. *Westminster Bank Ltd.*,[82] Atkin L.J. said:

> The remaining point was that Heilmanns, being a bank, could not be a "customer." In my opinion, on the evidence, they were customers in every sense of the word. They had a drawing account with the respondents. But if they were in a different position, it seems to me that if a non-clearing bank regularly employs a clearing bank to clear its cheques, the non-clearing bank is the "customer" of the clearing bank.[83]

Stony Stanton Supplies (Coventry) Ltd. v. *Midland Bank Ltd.*[84] is an interesting but quite exceptional case of an account opened in the name of a company eventually proving to have founded no banker/customer relationship at all. In 1960, one Fox, an undischarged bankrupt, formed a company which later had the name Stony Stanton Supplies (Coventry) Ltd., the two directors being the proprietors of the company registration firm through which he had formed the company. Fox had entered into negotiations for the purchase of an old-established wholesale grocery business, R.H. Taylor (Coventry) Ltd. Mr. Taylor agreed to sell, and introduced Fox to the manager of his own branch of the Midland Bank. Fox in due course produced to the branch manager the forms necessary for opening an

---

[81] *Matthews* v. *Brown & Co.* (1894) 10 T.L.R. 386.
[82] [1927] 2 K.B. 297 *cf. post*, p. 186.
[83] At p. 310.
[84] [1966] 2 Lloyd's Rep. 373.

account in the name of the Stony Stanton Company, the forms purporting to be signed by the two directors as chairman and secretary. These signatures were forgeries. Money thereafter coming into the Taylor business was paid in to the new account, and drawn upon by Fox, on forged signatures, for his own purposes. When the fraud was discovered Fox received a prison sentence, and Mr. Taylor's company obtained a winding-up order against the Stony Stanton Company. The present action was for the recovery of some £9,000, the amounts drawn by Fox from the account in the company's name. The Court of Appeal, upholding the decision of McNair J. in favour of the bank, held that the company had given no authority to Fox to buy the grocery business, no contract between the company and R.H. Taylor Ltd. had been signed, the company had never had any title to the funds passing through the account (in the opening of which, in the circumstances, there had been no negligence), and there had been no banker/customer relationship between the bank and the company, to which therefore the bank owed no duty.

Reference may be made here to *Burnett* v. *Westminster Bank Ltd.*,[85] widely commented upon as the first case concerning the bank's automated book-keeping, which is of legal interest primarily in its relevance to the contract between banker and customer.

On the introduction of automated book-keeping,[86] the bank printed on the covers of cheque books a warning that the cheques (and credit slips) in the books, all of which bore magnetic ink characters, would "be applied to the account for which they have been prepared. Customers must not, therefore, permit their use on any other account." The plaintiff, who had accounts at two branches of the bank, at only one of which the book-keeping was automated, altered a cheque on this branch with the intention of drawing on his account at the other branch. He later instructed the non-automated branch to stop payment of the cheque; but the magnetic ink coding took the cheque to the automated branch, where it was paid, no one noticing the handwritten alteration. Mocatta J. held that the wording on the cover of the cheque book was not adequate

---

[85] [1966] 1 Q.B. 742.
[86] cf. *Momm* v. *Barclays Bank International, post*, p. 148.

notice to alter the pre-existing contractual relationship, unless the bank could show that the customer had read the words, or had agreed in writing to their effect. He said that he would have been prepared to accept the signature on the cheque as signifying such agreement if the warning had been printed on the cheque itself (in the way, it will be noted, that the right to refuse payment against uncleared effects is reserved on credit slips[87]); he said also that the position *might* have been different if the cheque book had been the first issued to a new customer, instead of one issued to an established customer who had previously received other cheque books that did not bear any terms of the contract.

The case raises points of interest also regarding the nature of the cheque as a mandate, and the possibility, not at issue before the Court, that a bank might be held to be negligent in not scrutinising automated cheques.[88]

[87] *cf. post*, pp. 157 *et seq.*
[88] *cf.* Chorley, Gilbart Lectures, 1966, and *The Banker* (August 1965), Vol. 55, p. 528.

Chapter 2

NEGOTIABLE INSTRUMENTS

Goodwin v. Robarts

(1876) 1 App.Cas. 476

Mercantile usage can confer negotiability

Facts

The plaintiff had bought certain Russian and Hungarian Government scrip, expressed to be exchangeable for bonds. He deposited the certificates with his broker, Clayton, who fraudulently lodged them with the defendant, his banker, as security for a loan to himself. In this action by the plaintiff to recover the scrip the defendant banker claimed that title in it had passed to him, and proved 50 years' usage by which such scrip had been treated as negotiable by delivery.

Decision

The House of Lords upheld the decision of the Court of Exchequer Chamber that such usage did in fact make the scrip negotiable legally, and that the plaintiff's case failed.

In the Court of Exchequer Chamber,[1] Lord Cockburn C.J. said:

It is true that the law merchant is sometimes spoken of as a fixed body of law, forming part of the common law, and as it were coeval with it. But as a matter of legal history, this view is altogether incorrect. The law merchant, thus spoken of with reference to bills of exchange and other negotiable securities, though forming part of the general body of the *lex mercatoria*, is of comparatively recent origin. It is neither more nor less than the usages of merchants and traders in the different departments of trade, ratified by the decisions of Courts of Law, which, upon such usages being proved before them, have adopted them as settled law with a view to the interests of trade, and public

[1] (1875) L.R. 10 Ex. 337.

37

convenience.... Why is it to be said that a new usage which has sprung up under altered circumstances, is to be less admissible than the usages of past times?...

We must by no means be understood as saying that mercantile usage, however extensive, should be allowed to prevail if contrary to positive law.... But so far from that being the case, we are, on the contrary, in our opinion, only acting on an established principle of that law in giving legal effect to a usage, now become universal, to treat this form of security... as assignable by delivery.[2]

Notes

The negotiability of cheques and bills of exchange is largely taken for granted by bankers, but they are concerned with the principle in other areas of their work, not least where other instruments may or may not have the quality of negotiability.[3]

To be negotiable an instrument must be "capable of being sued upon by the holder of it *pro tempore* in his own name; and it must be, by the custom of trade, transferable like cash by delivery (including indorsement and delivery in the case of an instrument payable to order)."[4] Mercantile custom had long recognised cheques, bills and promissory notes as negotiable when statutory recognition was accorded them in 1882 by the Bills of Exchange Act.[5] But there had been considerable doubt as to whether mercantile usage was fixed or expandable. In 1873 it had been held in a case concerning a bearer debenture[6] that the instrument could not be regarded as negotiable merely because the business community had so treated it. *Goodwin* v. *Robarts* showed that this proposition could not be maintained, and a later decision recognised as negotiable scrip certificates for shares in an English company.[7] In 1898, when the question arose again regarding bearer debentures,[8] Kennedy J. held that they were negotiable, *Goodwin* v. *Robarts* having virtually overruled the earlier decision.

---

[2] At pp. 346, 352, 357.
[3] *cf. Post*, pp. 280 *et seq.*, as to the pledge of negotiable securities. *cf.* also pp. 187 *et seq.*
[4] Halsbury's *Laws of England*, Vol. 4, Chapter 513.
[5] See Holden, *The History of Negotiable Instruments in English Law*, for the development of the principle of negotiability.
[6] *Crouch* v. *Credit Foncier of England* (1873) I.R. 8 Q.B. 374.
[7] *Rumball* v. *Metropolitan Bank* (1877) 2 Q.B.D. 194.
[8] *Bechuanaland Exploration Co.* v. *London Trading Bank Ltd.* [1898] 2 Q.B. 658.

The combined effect of these decisions is to make all such documents, whether English or foreign, negotiable,[9] provided always that they satisfy the general requirements of negotiability. But they are of wider importance in that they established, finally, that proof of mercantile usage can confer legal negotiability on instruments not previously so recognised.[10]

The Privy Council considered the effect of mercantile custom in *Kum and Another* v. *Wah Tet Bank Ltd.*[11] There it had been claimed that mate's receipts were documents of title by local custom in Sarawak and Singapore, and their Lordships said that there was no reason why local custom should not create a document of title: Lord Devlin said "it was by the custom of merchants that the bill of lading became such a document."

There must be proof in the first place that the custom is generally accepted by those who habitually do business in the trade or market concerned. Moreover, the custom must be so generally known that an outsider who makes reasonable enquiries could not fail to be made aware of it. The size of the market or the extent of the trade affected is neither here nor there. It does not matter that the custom alleged in this case applies only to part of the shipping trade within the State of Singapore, so long as the part can be ascertained with certainty, as it can here, as the carriage of goods by sea between Sarawak and Singapore. A good and established custom "... obtains the force of a law, and is, in effect, the common law within that place to which it extends" (*Lockwood* v. *Wood* (1844) 6 Q.B. 31 *per* Tindal C.J. at p. 64).[12]

However, "a negotiable bill of lading is not negotiable in the strict sense: it cannot, as can be done by negotiation of a bill of exchange, give to the transferee a better title than the transferor has got, but it can by endorsement and delivery give as good a title." And in the present case the fact that the mate's receipts bore the words "Not negotiable" was fatal to even that limited negotiability, despite the fact that the words had been ignored by everybody connected with the trade: "the rule is plain and clear that inconsistency with the document defeats the custom."

It may be noted that in *Akbar Khan* v. *Attar Singh*[13] a Privy

---

[9] See Holden, *op. cit.*, II Chap. 16, for a description of these documents, with which bankers are mainly concerned as security for loans.
[10] *cf.* Holden, *The History of Negotiable Instruments in English Law*, pp. 251 *et seq.*
[11] [1971] 1 Lloyd's Rep. 439.
[12] At p. 444.
[13] [1936] 2 All E.R. 545.

Council case concerning deposit receipts, Lord Atkin said that negotiable instruments "come into existence for the purpose only of recording an agreement to pay money and nothing more, though of course they may state the consideration."[14] The implied promise to pay, in the documents in question, was not enough to make them promissory notes. The Court of Appeal adopted the same reasoning in *Claydon* v. *Bradley*.[14a]

The negotiability of the banker's draft has never been challenged in the courts, although when it is drawn by a bank upon itself it is not a bill of exchange, which by section 3(1) of the Bills of Exchange Act 1882 is an order "addressed by one person to another."[14b] In the improbable event of such a challenge there would be no difficulty in showing it to be negotiable by mercantile custom; and in any case the court might well hold it negotiable by virtue of section 5(2), which gives the holder of such a document the option of treating it as a bill of exchange or a promissory note.

It may be noted finally that a banker's draft must always be to order: a bearer draft would be in effect a bank-note, and no bank in this country now retains the right of note issue except the Bank of England.[15]

THE BILLS OF EXCHANGE ACT 1882

The Act provides the ground rules regarding bills of exchange, promissory notes, and, of more frequent concern to practising bankers, cheques. Of most concern to bankers are sections 60 and 82, providing protection for paying and collecting bankers respectively (section 82 is replaced and extended by section 4 of the Cheques Act 1957).[16] These sections arise frequently in the chapters on the paying banker and the collecting banker, but of course the whole Act is relevant to banking. Section 73, the first of 10 sections dealing specifically with "Cheques drawn on a banker," defines a cheque as "a bill of exchange drawn on a banker payable on demand," and provides that "except as otherwise

---

[14] At p. 550.
[14a] [1987] 1 All E.R. 532.
[14b] But *cf. Slingsby* v. *Westminster Bank Ltd.* [1931] 1 K.B. 173.
[15] *cf.* Bank Charter Act 1844, s.11; Paget, *op. cit.* p. 216.
[16] As to the Bills of Exchange Act and the Cheques Act generally, see *Chalmers on Bills of Exchange Act* (13th ed.) D.A.L. Smout, and Reeday, *op. cit.*, pp. 329–452.

provided in this part, the provisions of this Act applicable to a bill of exchange payable on demand apply to a cheque."[16a]

Following are a number of cases dealing with the formalities of bills and cheques. They demonstrate the interchangeability, within this context, of the two instruments.

Orbit Mining & Trading Co. Ltd. v. Westminster Bank Ltd.

[1963] 1 Q.B. 794

The definition of a Bill of Exchange in section 3

An order to a banker in the words "pay cash or order" is not a cheque but merely a mandate

Facts

The plaintiff company had two directors, who were authorised to sign cheques jointly on the company's account. One of them, Epstein, had some years prior to his joining the plaintiff company opened an account with the defendant bank. The bank was not informed of his new employment when he joined Orbit.

Epstein's co-director, on going abroad for short visits, left crossed cheques with Epstein signed in blank, and in August, 1957, and August and October, 1958, Epstein paid in three of these cheques, completed with his own (virtually illegible) signature and made payable to "Cash or Order," for the credit of his private account. When his fraud was discovered the company brought an action against the bank for conversion of the cheques, totalling some £1,800.

MacKenna J. held that the three instruments were not cheques within section 73 of the Bills of Exchange Act, but were documents intended to enable a person to obtain payment from a banker within section 17 of the Revenue Act 1883, and section 4(2)(*b*) of the Cheques Act 1957.[17] But he held further that the bank had lost the protection of section 4(1) of the 1957 Act by their negligence.

[16a] The Jack Report recommends extensive changes in this area, to be embodied in a new Act, the Cheques and Bank Payment Orders Act, covering the law relating to cheques, and a new Negotiable Instruments Act, covering all other negotiable instruments.

[17] The subsection applies the protection of s.82 of the 1882 Act, as extended by s.4(1) of the 1957 Act to: any document issued by a customer of a banker which, though not a bill of exchange, is intended to enable a person to obtain payment from that banker of the sum mentioned in the document.

Decision

The Court of Appeal, allowing the bank's appeal on the negligence issue, upheld MacKenna J.'s finding as to the nature of the documents.[18]

Harman L.J. said:

> In order to be a cheque within section 73, the document must be a bill of exchange. This is defined by section 3(1) of the Act of 1882, under which there must be a sum payable "to the order of a specified person or to 'bearer.' " Clearly "cash" is not a specified person, and I do not think that unless made expressly in favour of the bearer it is enough to argue that "cash or order" in the end as a matter of construction means "bearer," and I agree with the judge below that the mandate to pay bearer must be expressed and not implied. As to section 4(2)(b), this is clearly a document intended to enable a person to obtain payment of the sum mentioned in the document. "Person" here means any person, and does not require a named person: therefore "cash" is good enough. The question is whether the document was "issued by a customer of a banker." In my opinion, this clearly was so issued. It was a good cheque so far as the plaintiff company was concerned. . . . A written document is intended to bring about that which its written terms indicate. It is not legitimate to inquire into the mind of the creator of the document.[19]

Notes

Section 3(1) provides

> A bill of exchange is an unconditional order in writing, addressed by one person to another, signed by the person giving it, requiring the person to whom it is addressed to pay on demand or at a fixed and determinable future time, a sum certain in money to or to the order of a specified person, or to bearer.

And section 3(2) reinforces the definition:

> An instrument which does not comply with these conditions, or which orders any act to be done in addition to the payment of money, is not a bill of exchange.

The *Orbit* decision is the most notable of the "Pay cash" cases. In *North and South Insurance Corporation Ltd.* v. *National Provincial Bank Ltd.*[20] an instrument in the form "Pay Cash or Order" was paid by the defendant bank a few days

---

[18] cf. *post*, pp. 167 and 174, for other points involved.
[19] At pp. 821–822.
[20] [1936] 1 K.B. 328.

after a winding-up petition had been presented, unknown to the bank, and the liquidator claimed that the bank had wrongly paid an order instrument without an indorsement. Branson J. held that the document was not a cheque, and that it must therefore be construed in accordance with the apparent wishes of the drawers. The words "or Order" must therefore be ignored as being inconsistent with the apparent intention, and the document was thus a valid order to the bank.

It cannot have been intended that "Cash," which is a purely impersonal collection of letters, should indorse this draft. That being so, I think the four words "Pay Cash or Order" cannot be read so as to give any sensible meaning to the whole four, and the result is that the printed words "or Order" must be disregarded, and we have a direction to pay cash—by necessary implication, to pay it to the bearer of the document. . . . "[21]

There was some discussion following the *North and South Insurance* decision as to whether instruments in the form in question (and "Pay Wages or Order" is analogous) could be treated as equivalent to "Pay Bearer" cheques. On the one hand, the rule that a bill payable to a fictitious payee is regarded as a bearer bill could be viewed as supporting the wider view, as indeed could the words of Branson J. just quoted. On the other hand it was argued that the decision should be treated with caution, and regarded as meaning no more than that if the amount of the instrument is received by the person intended to receive it the drawer cannot claim it back from the bank. This narrower view received support from the decision in *Cole* v. *Milsome*,[22] where Lloyd-Jacob J. held that the plaintiff, who had innocently received a "Pay Cash or Order" instrument from a fraudulent third party, was not entitled to recover from the defendant as drawer of the instrument; he considered that the *North and South Insurance* case "did not decide that . . . a payment [in this form] was a payment to bearer."[23]

The decision of the Court of Appeal in the *Orbit*[24] case confirms this view: instruments in this form are *not* to be regarded as payable to bearer, although for some purposes the

---

[21] At pp. 335–336.
[22] [1951] 1 All E.R. 311.
[23] *cf. Gader* v. *Flower post*, p. 53.
[24] *cf.* Megrah, Gilbart Lectures, 1962, where the case is discussed at some length.

practical effect is the same as if they were. It will be noted that the period during which the fraudulent cheques in the *Orbit* case were issued, included the passing of the Cheques Act 1957, so that the provisions of that Act fell to be applied to the later cheques; but the 1957 Act has not affected the position as regards the point here discussed, and it is still appropriate to quote the advice given on the matter in 72 J.I.B. at p. 200 (October 1951):

> The following rules may, perhaps, be taken as a guide in dealing with an instrument drawn "pay cash or order" (which is assumed to be otherwise in order)—
>
> (*a*) if uncrossed it may safely be paid over the counter only to the drawer or his known agent and whether indorsed or not (the indorsement of the drawer does not make the instrument transferable);
>
> (*b*) if crossed and bearing no sign of having been transferred, it may be paid through the clearing or over the counter to another bank without question, whether indorsed by the drawer or not;
>
> (*c*) it should not be collected, if uncrossed, except for a responsible customer, who, anyhow, should be asked to cross it.

Other decisions have turned on other aspects of section 3(1). Its relevance to the banker's draft drawn by a bank on itself has already been noted.[25] That a bill (and therefore a cheque) must be an unconditional order was applied in *Bavins Jnr. & Sims* v. *London and South Western Bank Ltd.*,[26] where an instrument in the form of a cheque but with the order followed by the words "provided the receipt form at foot hereof is duly signed...," was stolen, and later collected for a customer by the defendant bank. They claimed to be protected by section 82 of the Act (now section 4 of the Cheques Act 1957). The trial judge ruled that the instrument, being conditional, was not a cheque, so that section 82 did not cover it. The bank appealed, claiming that by section 17 of the Revenue Act, 1883 (now section 5 of the Cheques Act) the provisions of section 82 were extended to instruments other than cheques. The Court of Appeal held that the bank had in fact been negligent, and so anyhow lost the protection of section 82; but they upheld the view that the receipt requirement was a condition which made the instrument not a cheque.

[25] *Ante*, p. 40.
[26] (1899) 81 L.T. 655.

The use of receipt forms on cheques, whether combined with indorsements or in addition to them, has very substantially diminished since the passing of the Cheques Act made it generally known that the paid cheque is itself prima facie evidence of payment. Thus the earlier cases on the subject, which established that the effect of such receipts depended on the wording of the document, are now largely of academic interest.[27] In practice the banks have long required of customers using any such form of receipt an indemnity which puts them, as regards the protective sections of the Bills of Exchange Act and the Cheques Act, in the same position as if they were handling ordinary cheques. It is to be noted also that as the Cheques Act relieves the banker of the liability to examine indorsements on cheques, that small minority of cheques for which receipts/indorsements are required carry a large R on the face.

In a more recent case, *Korea Exchange Bank Ltd.* v. *Debenhams (Central Buying) Ltd.*[28] it was the "fixed and determinable future time" that was in issue. A bill had been drawn "at 90 days D/A," and it was argued that the words meant "90 days after acceptance." Megaw L.J., held that even if the words were so read they did not give a determinable future time, for that is defined by section 11 as including "a fixed period after the occurrence of a specified event which is certain to happen, though the time of happening may be uncertain." Acceptance of a bill can never be certain, and the section expressly provides that "an instrument expressed to be payable on a contingency is not a bill, and the happening of the event does not cure the defect."

Bank of England v. Vagliano Bros.

[1891] A.C. 107

North & South Wales Bank Ltd. v. Macbeth

[1908] A.C. 137

The meaning of a "fictitious or non-existing person" under section 7(3) of the Bills of Exchange Act 1882

Facts of Bank of England v. Vagliano Bros.

Vagliano carried on business in London as a merchant and

---

[27] See, *e.g. London, City and Midland Bank Ltd.* v. *Gordon* [1903] A.C. 240; *Nathan* v. *Ogdens Ltd.* (1906) 94 L.T. 126; *Thairlwall* v. *Great Northern Railway Co.* [1910] 2 K.B. 509.
[28] [1979] 1 Lloyd's Rep. 549; 10 L.D.B. 144.

foreign banker in the name of Vagliano Brothers, and banked with the Bank of England. One of his clerks, by name Glyka, with another clerk managed the foreign correspondence of the firm, and over a period forged the signature of Vucina, an Odessa correspondent of Vagliano, as drawer of a number of bills on Vagliano to a total of £71,500. All these bills were drawn in favour of a firm, Petridi & Co., in whose favour Vucina had drawn genuine bills on Vagliano. Glyka also forged letters of advice from Vucina, and the bills were duly accepted by Vagliano in the course of routine of the office, which also involved monthly advice to the Bank of England of these and other bills due to become payable during the month. Glyka obtained the forged bills again after acceptance and forged the indorsements of Petridi & Co., making the bills payable to B. Maratis or N. Maratis, non-existing persons, and obtained payment of the bills in cash at the Bank of England. He was later arrested, admitted the forgeries, and was sentenced to 10 years' penal servitude.

The bank had debited Vagliano's account with the amounts of the bills, and Vagliano now claimed that the bank must recredit him with such amounts. The bank contended, *inter alia*, that the bills were, in the circumstances, payable to fictitious or non-existing persons within the meaning of section 7(3) of the Bills of Exchange Act 1882, and were therefore payable to bearer.

That subsection provides that:

Where the payee is a fictitious or non-existing person the bill may be treated as payable to bearer.

Decision

On appeal the House of Lords held (on this point) that the payees named on the bills were fictitious or non-existing within the meaning of the subsection, that the bills were payable to bearer, and that the bank was therefore entitled to debit Vagliano with the amounts paid by them on the bills. In the course of his judgment, Lord Macnaghten said:

On behalf of Vagliano Brothers it was contended that a bill payable to a fictitious person is not payable to bearer unless the acceptor is proved to have been aware of the fiction; and further it was contended that nothing but a creature of the imagination can properly be described as a fictitious person. I do not think that either of these contentions...can be maintained.... Then it was said that the proper meaning of "fictitious" is "imaginary." I do not think so. I think the proper meaning of the word is "feigned" or "counterfeit." It seems to me that the C. Petridi & Co. named as payees on these pretended bills were, strictly speaking, fictitious persons. When the bills came before Vagliano for acceptance they were fictitious from beginning to end. The drawer was fictitious; the payee was fictitious; the person indicated as agent for presentation was fictitious. One and all they were feigned or counterfeit persons put forward as real persons, each in a several and distinct capacity; whereas, in truth, they were mere make-believes for the persons whose names appeared on the instrument. They were not, I think, the less fictitious because there were in existence real persons for whom these names were intended to pass muster.[29]

Facts of North & South Wales Bank Ltd. v. Macbeth

One White fraudulently induced Macbeth to draw a cheque for £11,250 in favour of Kerr or order. Kerr was an existing person, and Macbeth, although in fact misled by the fraud, intended him to receive the money. White, obtaining the cheque, forged Kerr's indorsement and paid the cheque into his account with the appellant bank who in due course received payment of it. On discovering the fraud, Macbeth brought action against the bank to recover the money on the basis that by collecting a cheque to which their customer had no title they were guilty of the tort of conversion. Since the cheque had not been crossed, the bank were unable to rely for protection upon section 82 of the Bills of Exchange Act 1882.[30] However, they contended, *inter alia*, that the payee was a fictitious person within the meaning of section 7(3) of the Act, and that as the cheque must therefore be regarded as payable to bearer, they could not have been guilty of conversion in collecting it.

Decision

The House of Lords held that the subsection did not apply; as the drawer of the cheque intended that the payee or his transferee should receive the money it could not be said, although this intention was induced by fraud, that the payee was fictitious.

In his judgment, Lord Loreburn L.C. said:

If the argument for the appellants were to prevail, namely, that the payee was a fictitious person because White (who was himself no party to the cheque) did not intend the payee to receive the proceeds of the cheque, most serious consequences would ensue. It would follow, as it seems to me, that every cheque to order might be treated as a cheque

---

[29] At pp. 160–161.
[30] Now s.4 of the Cheques Act 1957, which extends the protection to uncrossed cheques.

to bearer if the drawer had been deceived, no matter by whom, into drawing it. To state such a proposition is to refute it.... As to the authorities, I agree with the Court of Appeal in thinking that neither *Bank of England* v. *Vagliano*,[31] nor *Clutton* v. *Attenborough*[32] governs the present case. I will not discuss the former of those authorities beyond saying that it was not a case in which the drawer intended the payee to receive the proceeds of the bill. And in the latter authority the payee was a non-existent person whom no one either could or did mean to be the recipient of the proceeds of the cheque.[33]

Notes[34]

In *Clutton* v. *Attenborough* the appellants, a firm of land agents, were fraudulently induced by their clerk to draw cheques in favour of Brett, there being actually no such person. The clerk forged indorsements in the name of Brett, and induced a third party to cash the cheques for him; the third party, the respondents in the present case, who acted in good faith, eventually obtained payment of the cheques, and upon Cluttons' suing them for the money they had received it was held that the cheques, being payable to a person who by any showing was fictitious, could be considered as payable to bearer, and that Cluttons' could not therefore recover.

In *Vinden* v. *Hughes*[35] a cashier filled in a number of cheques with the names of customers of his employers, obtained the firm's signature, forged the indorsements and negotiated the cheques to an innocent third party, who obtained payment from the firm's bankers. When the firm sued the third party for the amounts he had received, it was held that on the facts of the case the payees could not be regarded as fictitious or non-existing.

The importance of the rule that a bill payable to a fictitious or non-existing payee may be treated as payable to bearer arises from the fact that it enables any indorsement which may be forged upon it to be disregarded. The decision in the *Macbeth* case, however, deprives it of most of its practical value, since banks are for the most part concerned with cheques, and it will rarely be the case that a person who signs a cheque as drawer will do so without some knowledge of the payee. In this connection the reports of *Clutton* v. *Attenborough* are not at all

---

[31] *Supra.*
[32] [1897] A.C. 90.
[33] At pp. 139–140.
[34] As to the effect of the *Vagliano* decision on the law regarding indorsements, see *post*, p. 125.
[35] [1905] 1 K.B. 795.

satisfactory, but the case is intelligible only on the basis that Brett did not in fact exist. Occasionally, however, the whole business may be fictitious from the opening of the account, as in *Robinson* v. *Midland Bank Ltd.*[36] In that case, the report of which is of unusual interest for reasons not here relevant,[37] there had been a blackmailing conspiracy against an Eastern potentate, called in the case Mr. A, who had been discovered in compromising circumstances with the wife of the plaintiff. The plaintiff was held not to have been a party to the conspiracy. Mr. A issued a cheque for £150,000 to prevent the plaintiff from bringing divorce proceedings, and the conspirators, without the plaintiff's knowledge, opened an account with the defendants in the name of the plaintiff. They paid into this account the cheque in question, and later drew out the proceeds. The plaintiff's action for money had and received failed because, *inter alia*, it was held that the bank was dealing wth a fictitious customer, notwithstanding the use of plaintiff's name.

In the *Vagliano* case the drawer of the bill was in fact the forger, only the acceptance being genuine. But since it is the intention of the drawer which is vital, the bill could properly be regarded as payable to a fictitious payee. This situation could not arise in the case of a cheque, because if the drawer's signature is forged it is quite immaterial that the payee is fictitious, since the paying bank must, unless there is an estoppel against the customer, be liable in any event.

It may be noted that the drawers of the cheques could not recover from their own banks because of the protection given to the paying banker by section 60; but this covers cheques only and there is no such protection either for the acceptor of a bill who pays the wrong person on a forged indorsement or for the banker who debits to his customer's account such a bill which has been accepted payable at the bank.[38] Lord Bramwell's dissenting judgment in the *Vagliano* case was based on a principle which would have left the banker unprotected even in the circumstances of that case: "...[A] banker cannot," he said, "charge his customer with the amount of a bill paid to a person who had no right of action against the customer, the acceptor." The banker may be grateful that the majority of the Court considered this an over-simplification of the law.

---

[36] (1924) 41 T.L.R. 170. *cf. Stony Stanton Supplies (Coventry) Ltd.* v. *Midland Bank Ltd.* [1966] 2 Lloyd's Rep. 373; *ante*, p. 34.

[37] See (October 1981) 102 J.I.B. 163.

[38] See *Robarts* v. *Tucker* (1851) 16 Q.B.D. 560; *post*, p. 124.

It may be noted also that had the cheques signed by Macbeth been crossed the defendant bank would in all probability have been able to plead section 82 of the Bills of Exchange Act 1882 successfully (see pp. 162 *et seq.*). The protection given by that section is extended by section 4 of the Cheques Act 1957, which replaces it, to uncrossed cheques.

Rolfe Lubell & Co. v. Keith and Another

[1979] 1 All E.R. 860

Signature in a representative capacity: section 26

Facts

The plaintiff agreed to supply goods to a company, Grafton Manquest Ltd., provided that bills of exchange in payment were personally indorsed by two officers of the company. The bills were duly accepted by the managing director and the company secretary, who also signed the backs of the bills within a rubber-stamped "For and on behalf of" the company, and the designations "Director" and "Secretary." The bills were dishonoured, and the company went into receivership. The plaintiffs then sued the two signatories, claiming that they were personally liable on the bills. The action against the secretary was not pursued, but the first defendant, the managing director, argued that by virtue of section 26(1) of the 1882 Act his personal liability was excluded. The subsection provides:

Where a person signs a bill as drawer, indorser or acceptor, and adds words to his signature, indicating that he signs for or on behalf of a principal, or in a representative character, he is not personally liable thereon; but the mere addition to his signature of words describing him as an agent or as filling a representative character, does not exclude him from personal liability.

Decision

Kilner-Brown J. found for the plaintiffs. He rejected the defendant's argument that no evidence could be admitted to give a different meaning to words which have an accepted meaning. He said:

By signing [thus] on the back of the bill they produced what counsel for the plaintiffs described as a mercantile nonsense. An indorsement on the back of a bill amounts to a warrant that the bill will be honoured and imposes in certain circumstances a transfer of liability to the indorser. No one can transfer liability from himself to himself. The only way in which validity can be given to this indorsement is by construing it to bind someone other than the acceptor. As soon therefore as it becomes obvious that the indorsement as worded is meaningless and of no value there is a patent ambiguity which allows evidence to be accepted to give effect to the intentions of the parties.

And the evidence thus admitted satisfied him that the defendant knew that he was expected to accept personal liability.

Notes

In so finding the judge in effect accepted the plaintiffs' contention that section 26(2) was relevant:

> In determining whether a signature on a bill is that of the principal or that of the agent by whose hand it is written, the construction most favourable to the validity of the instrument shall be adopted.

The circumstances of the case were unusual. In earlier cases[39] the courts have not always applied the section in the way businessmen would have expected. Thus in *Landes* v. *Marcus and Davids*[40] a cheque with the company name stamped at the top was signed by two directors with "Director" after each name. But even though the cheque had been given for goods supplied to the company, it was held that the directors were personally liable, the judge so interpreting the second clause in section 26(1). But in *Chapman* v. *Smethurst*[41] a promissory note signed by the defendant as managing director of the company named above his signature was held to be the company's note, the Court of Appeal overruling the trial judge's view that the wording of the note—"I promise to pay"—showed that the signature was a personal one.[42] And in *Bondina Ltd.* v. *Rollaway Shower Blinds Ltd.*,[43] where a director had signed a cheque without adding the capacity in which he signed, the Court of Appeal rejected the plaintiff's argument that this showed that he was personally liable. When he signed the cheque he adopted all the printing and writing on it, including

[39] As to which *cf.* Chalmers, *op. cit.* pp. 82 *et seq.*
[40] (1909) 35 T.L.R. 478; 2 L.D.B. 203.
[41] [1909] 1 K.B. 927.
[42] *cf.* the discussion in (1963) 84 J.I.B. 133 of two Canadian cases reaching opposite conclusions on similar facts; and see *post*, p. 177 as to the effect of s.25, covering procuration signatures.
[43] [1986] 1 All E.R. 564.

the company's name: "the drawer of the cheque was the company."[44]

In the case of a company it is possible on occasion to establish the personal liability of the signatory of a cheque by virtue of section 108(4) of the Companies Act 1948[45] which provides, *inter alia*, that

> . . . if an officer of a company . . . signs or authorises to be signed on behalf of the company any bill of exchange . . . cheque or order for money or goods wherein its name is not mentioned in manner aforesaid . . . he shall be liable to a fine not exceeding fifty pounds and shall be further liable to the holder of a bill of exchange [or] cheque . . . for the amount thereof unless it is duly paid by the company.[46]

In *Durham Fancy Goods Ltd.* v. *Michael Jackson (Fancy Goods) Ltd.*[47] Donaldson J. remarked that it was the first recorded case for over half a century on a provision that could be traced back to 1856. The plaintiffs had drawn a bill on the defendants, wrongly naming them as "M. Jackson (Fancy Goods) Ltd." and preparing the form of acceptance in the same way. The director and secretary of the company signed the acceptance without noticing the misdescription. The bill was dishonoured, the director having left the company, and the company having gone into liquidation. It was held that by section 108 the director was personally liable on the bill, but that the company was estopped from enforcing his liability, as they were responsible for the error, and had represented that they would treat the acceptance as regular.

Since then there have been several other cases on section 108. In *Maxform S.p.A.* v. *Mariani and Goodville Ltd.*[48] the director of Goodville Ltd., a company that traded as Italdesign, its registered business name, was held by Mocatta J. personally

---

[44] See also *Elliott* v. *Bax-Ironside* [1925] 2 K.B. 301. *cf.* cases on s.23: *Ringham* v. *Hackett* and *Central Motors (Birmingham)* v. *P.A. & S.N. Wadsworth, post*, p. 203.

[45] Now Companies Act 1985, s.349(4).

[46] See *The Company Lawyer*, (1982) Vol. 3, p. 156 for discussion of the subsection as "harsh and rigid, and not constrained by any particular bounds of fairness, common sense, or presumed legislative policy."

[47] [1968] 2 All E.R. 987; 9 L.D.B. 61.

[48] [1979] 2 Lloyd's Rep. 385.

liable on the acceptance of bills drawn on Italdesign, without mention on the bills of Goodville Ltd: "name" in section 108 could mean only the company's registered corporate name. The Court of Appeal dismissed his appeal[49]: section 26(2) of the 1882 Act was intended to ensure that a bill is looked at as a whole, and hence it was clear that the defendant purported to sign on behalf of the drawers.

In *British Airways Board* v. *Parish*[50] and in *Calzaturificio Fiorella S.p.A.* v. *Walton and Another*[51] the directors of limited companies were held personally liable on cheques on which "Ltd." was omitted from the company names. But in *Banque de l'Indochine et de Suez* v. *Euroseas Group Finance Co. Ltd.*,[52] a challenge under section 108 on the grounds that the abbreviation "Co." for "Company" was ambiguous, was successfully resisted: "Ltd." had long been established as an acceptable abbreviation, and as there was no practical possibility of confusion when "Co." was used, that too was permissible.

In *Gader* v. *Flower*,[53] where the defendant's signature to a cheque payable to "Cash or order" was irregular under section 108, the Court of Appeal allowed him unconditional leave to appeal on the grounds that this was not a cheque under the Bills of Exchange Act, and it was not clear beyond argument that "cheque" in section 108 had a different meaning.

In *Barber & Nicholls* v. *R. & G. Associates (London) Ltd.*[54] the plaintiffs obtained judgment on seven dishonoured cheques, and the second defendant appealed against the finding that he was personally liable on them. The cheques had been printed with the company's name, but omitting, as a result of the bank's mistake, "(London)," and he claimed that the defendants were estopped from relying on section 108, as they had received the cheques without question. But his appeal was dismissed, Stephenson L.J. distinguishing the *Durham Fancy Goods* case. There the plaintiff had been responsible for the wrong description; here the fault was that of the defendants' bank.

Section 5(2) of the Act provides that where the drawee of a

[49] [1981] 2 Lloyd's Rep. 54.
[50] [1979] 2 Lloyd's Rep. 361.
[51] (Unreported) (1979) C.L.Y. 23.
[52] [1981] 3 All E.R. 198.
[53] (1979) 129 New L.J. 1266.
[54] (1985) C.L.Y. 129; C.A.T. 81/455.

bill is a fictitious person the holder may treat the instrument at his option as a bill of exchange or a promissory note. In *Aziz* v. *Knightsbridge Gaming Services*[55] Hobhouse J, holding that an instrument drawn on a non-existent bank was still a cheque, said that section 5(2) clearly indicated that a document might satisfy the definition on its face even though later investigation showed that it did not literally comply with the definition. And he added that the *Vagliano* decision supported the proposition that bills of exchange "have to be judged on their appearance, and be capable of passing from one hand to another without investigation of the facts lying behind their issue."

Oliver v. Davis and Woodcock

[1949] 2 K.B. 727

Consideration: section 27(1)

Facts

The plaintiff lent £350 to Davis, who gave him a post-dated cheque for £400. Davis could not have met the cheque, and he persuaded Miss Woodcock to send the plaintiff her cheque for £400. Before it was presented she learned more of the facts of the case, and stopped her cheque; and in the plaintiff's action against her she contended that there had been no consideration for the cheque. The plaintiff succeeded in the High Court, and Miss Woodcock appealed.

Section 27(1) provides

Valuable consideration for a bill may be constituted by
(*a*) Any consideration sufficient to support a simple contract;
(*b*) An antecedent debt or liability. Such a debt or liability is deemed valuable consideration whether the bill is payable on demand or at a future time.

Decision

The Court of Appeal allowed the appeal, holding that
(i) "antecedent debt" within the meaning of the subsection, did not include the debt of a third party, but must be that of the maker or negotiator of the instrument, so that the plaintiff could not rely on subsection (*b*);
(ii) the plaintiff had given no promise, express or implied, to abstain from any action he might have against Davis, nor, as a

---

[55] (1982) 79 L.S.Gaz. 1412.

result of the cheque, had he changed his position as regards Davis's cheque, and so there was no consideration under subsection (a).
Sir Raymond Evershed M.R. said[56]:

> I think, for myself, that the proper construction of the words in para (b), "an antecedent debt or liability," is that they refer to an antecedent debt or liability of the promisor or drawer of the bill and are intended to get over what would otherwise have been prima facie the result at common law by which the giving of a cheque for an amount for which the drawer was already indebted imported no consideration since the obligation was past.... It is, at any rate, plain that, if the antecedent debt or liability of a third party is to be relied on as supplying "valuable consideration for a bill," there must at least be some relationship between the receipt of the bill and the antecedent debt or liability. For practical purposes it is difficult to see how there can be any distinction between a case in which there is a sufficient relationship for this purpose... and a case in which, as a result of that relationship, there is in the ordinary sense a consideration passing from the payee to the drawer of the bill. Otherwise the creditor might recover both on the debt from the third party and on the cheque from the drawer.

Notes

In *Hasan* v. *Willson*[57] the plaintiff sued the defendant on a dishonoured cheque for £50,000. The cheque, payable to the plaintiff, had been obtained by fraud by one Smith, who owed the plaintiff this sum. Smith gave the defendant, by way of consideration, a cheque drawn on a company with which he said he was associated. That cheque was dishonoured when the defendant presented it, and the defendant thereupon stopped payment of the cheque payable to the plaintiff which he had handed to Smith. When the present action was brought he pleaded (1) that the consideration for his cheque had wholly failed, and (2) that his signature to the cheque had been obtained by fraud.

As to the second argument, Robert Goff J. held that it could succeed only if the defendant could prove that the plaintiff knew of the fraud, and this he had not done. But the plaintiff had argued that Smith's debt to him was consideration for the defendant's cheque, and his Lordship, applying the rule in *Oliver* v. *Davis*, held that as the antecedent debt of a third party

---

[56] At p. 735.
[57] [1977] 1 Lloyd's Rep. 431.

the debt was not good consideration, and the defendant had been entitled to stop payment of his cheque.

Some doubt had been expressed as to the third party rule following the decision of the Court of Appeal in *Diamond* v. *Graham*.[58] There the plaintiff gave a cheque for £1,650 to a third party on the condition that he arranged for the defendant to give the plaintiff a cheque for £1,665. Both cheques were dishonoured, and in this action on the cheque for £1,665 the defendant argued that no consideration had passed from the plaintiff to him. But all three members of the Court of Appeal held that the plaintiff's cheque to the third party was sufficient consideration.

However, Danckwerts L.J. went further, holding that consideration was also provided by the third party's cheque to the defendant. He based this finding on the provision of section 27(2) of the 1882 Act that where value has at any time been given for a bill, the holder is deemed a holder for value; the subsection does not require that value has been given by the holder. This last finding was advanced by the plaintiff in *Hasan* v. *Willson*, but Robert Goff J. pointed out that it was the view of only one of the three Lords Justices in a case in which neither section 27(1)(*b*) nor the decision in *Oliver* v. *Davis* was considered.

It is a fundamental principle of the law of contract that consideration must move from the promisee...If Lord Justice Danckwerts is to be understood as having stated that, as between immediate parties to a bill, valid consideration may move otherwise than from the promisee, I have to say, with the greatest respect, that I find it impossible to reconcile this statement with the analysis of the law by the Court of Appeal in *Oliver* v. *Davis*.[58a]

Arab Bank Ltd. v. Ross

[1952] 2 Q.B. 216

The holder in due course: section 29

Requirements of a regular indorsement: section 32

Facts

In part payment for certain shares the defendant gave two promissory notes for £10,000 each, made payable to Fathi and

[58] [1968] 1 W.L.R. 1061.
[58a] *Hasan* v. *Wilson* [1977] 1 Lloyd's Rep. 431 at p. 442.

Fathi Nabulsy Company. The notes were indorsed to the plaintiff bank, who claimed that they had given value for them and were holders in due course. At first instance, McNair J. rejected the defendant's allegation in the pleadings of lack of good faith and held that the bills had been discounted for value and that the bank were holders in due course.

The defendants then raised a further point that had not been pleaded: that the indorsements, omitting the word "Company," were irregular. The judge did not agree: the indorsements would leave nobody in any doubt that the payee intended to pass property in the notes to the bank. The defendant appealed.

Decision

The Court of Appeal upheld the judge's findings on the points pleaded. On the indorsement point they did not agree with him: the indorsements were irregular, and so the notes were not "complete and regular" so as to make the bank holders in due course within section 29 of the Bills of Exchange Act. But as the point had not been included in the pleadings the defendants were not entitled to rely on it, and the appeal was dismissed: the bank was entitled to succeed as holders for value.

Notes

The distinction between holder in due course and holder for value can be, as it was here, of considerable importance to bankers, for only the holder in due course holds the bill (in the words of section 38(2) of the 1882 Act) "free from any defect of title of prior parties . . . and may enforce payment against all parties liable on the bill."[59] Section 30(2) provides:

> Every holder of a bill is prima facie deemed to be a holder in due course; but if in an action on a bill it is admitted or proved that the acceptance, issue, or subsequent negotiation of the bill is affected with fraud, duress, or force and fear, or illegality, the burden of proof is shifted, unless and until the holder proves that subsequent to the alleged fraud or illegality, value has in good faith been given for the bill.

The conditions to be met to establish title as holder in due course are set out in section 29(1) of the Act:

> A holder in due course is a holder who has taken the bill, complete and regular on the face of it, under the following conditions: namely

---

[59] *cf.* Reeday, *op. cit.* pp. 355 *et seq.*

(a) That he became the holder of it before it was overdue, and without knowledge that it had previously been dishonoured, if such was the fact;

(b) That he took the bill in good faith and for value, and that at the time the bill was negotiated to him he had no notice of any defect in the title of the person who negotiated it.

Section 29(3) provides that a holder deriving his title in good faith through a holder in due course has himself the rights of a holder in due course.

The holder cannot be a holder in due course if he fails to satisfy any one of the conditions: the notes in the *Arab Bank* case were not "complete and regular" on their face because the court held that the indorsements were irregular. But "without negligence" is not one of the conditions, and in *Lloyds Bank Ltd.* v. *Hornby*,[59a] where the defendant claimed that the bank had been negligent in opening an account without a proper introduction, Branson J. held that this was not relevant in the bank's action on the defendant's cheque, against which they had paid on a newly opened account; they were suing as holders in due course.

There are numerous examples in the cases of the importance of holder in due course status to bankers[60]; the *Arab Bank* case provides also an unusual examination by the court of indorsement law, for although the rules regarding indorsements are extensive, they have produced little litigation.

In his judgment Denning L.J. after remarking that "strangely enough no one doubts that the 'face' of a bill includes the back of it," went on to distinguish between regularity on the one hand and validity and liability on the other: an indorsement can be valid although irregular; equally, the maker of an irregular indorsement can still be liable on it.

He considered that an indorsement is irregular when it gives rise to doubt whether it is the indorsement of the payee.

But if it is asked: When does an indorsement give rise to doubt? I would say that that is a practical question which is, as a rule, better answered by a banker than a lawyer. Bankers have to consider the regularity of indorsements every week and every day of every week,

---

[59a] (1933) 54 J.I.B. 372.
[60] *cf., e.g. Westminster Bank Ltd.* v. *Zang, post,* p. 156.

and every hour of every day, whereas the judges sitting in this court have not had to consider it for these last 20 years.

He pointed out that bankers had insisted on strict conformity between the indorsement and the name of the payee for long before the passing of the Bills of Exchange Act.

The truth is, I think, that the bankers adopted this strict attitude both in their own interests and also in the interests of their customers. It would be quite impossible for them to make inquiries to see that all the indorsements on a bill are, in fact, genuine; but they can at least see that they are regular on the face of them . . . That is some safeguard against dishonesty. It is a safeguard which the bankers have taken for the past 120 years at least, and I do not think we should throw any doubt today on the correctness of their practice.

Section 34 of the Act provides rules for the validity of indorsements, but the Act does not cover their regularity. However, doubtless for the reason suggested by Denning L.J., bankers through the years developed elaborate guide lines as to conformity, which used to occupy many pages of banking textbooks.[61] Some of the more subtle rules have an appearance of artificiality, and there is something less than complete unanimity amongst bankers on some of the practice involved,[62] but the general principle underlying them is clear enough: that the indorsement should prima facie show that the payee and no other made it.[63]

The importance of indorsements to the banker has been very greatly reduced, although not entirely removed, by the Cheques Act 1957.[64] But although the banker is perhaps no longer concerned with indorsements "every hour of every day," indorsements are still scrutinised by the paying banker when cheques are paid over the counter,[65] and by the collecting banker when cheques are paid in for the credit of persons other

---

[61] Questions 486–546 in *Questions on Banking Practice* (11th ed.) are concerned with indorsements.

[62] There is perhaps discernible a tendency to move from the extreme strictness of earlier years.

[63] *cf. Slingsby and Others* v. *District Bank, post*, p. 63, for an example of a particular indorsement requirement.

[64] See *Jones and Holden's Studies in Practical Banking* (6th ed.), pp. 296 *et seq*; and *Chalmers on Bills of Exchange* (13th ed.), pp. 300 *et seq.* for events leading to the passing of the Act, and discussion of its provisions.

[65] *cf. Paget, op. cit.*, p. 190 as to whether such "indorsements" are strictly necessary.

than the payees,[66] while on certain instruments other than cheques indorsements are still generally required. In these circumstances, in which the overwhelming majority of instruments handled by the banks do not require indorsement, it is perhaps even more necessary than it was before for the banker to keep in mind the requirements for the indorsements that remain necessary.

By section 34(1) of the Act, "an indorsement in blank specifies no indorsee, and a bill so indorsed becomes payable to bearer." The subsection is relevant for the banker in, for example, the discussion as to the position when he pays a cheque to the payee, who has indorsed it: he is then paying the bearer, not the payee as such, and is not affected by the fact that the "delivery," which section 2 requires to complete the effect of indorsement, is lacking.[67]

But the provision does not always give the protection to the bearer that he may claim. In *Cleveland Manufacturing Co. Ltd.* v. *Muslim Commercial Bank Ltd.*[68] the bank argued, *inter alia*, that the draft they had paid was indorsed in blank, and so was payable to bearer. But Robert Goff J. rejected the defence: the person indorsing had no authority to make the indorsements, and there was no evidence that the bank had relied on the indorsement in paying against the cheque.

And in *R.* v. *Davies*,[69] where the manager of an old people's home obtained indorsed cheques from two old ladies and misappropriated the proceeds, the Court of Appeal rejected his argument that as cheques payable to bearer the documents were the property of anyone holding them. Eveleigh L.J. said:

Counsel's submission to this court, with respect to him, is based on the error of examining the nature of the article which constituted the gift, rather than on the very act of giving. It follows, as night follows day, that if [the ladies] did not know that they were signing the cheques, but gave the accused the pieces of paper, they were clearly

---

[66] cf. *Westminster Bank Ltd.* v. *Zang, post,* p. 156. In *Midland Bank Ltd.* v. *R.V. Harris Ltd. post,* p. 160 the bank was unsuccessfully challenged on the absence of indorsement on a cheque paid in for the credit of the payee's account.

[67] cf. Paget, *op. cit.* pp. 189 *et seq.*

[68] [1981] Com L.R. 247; see also *post,* p. 220.

[69] [1982] 1 All E.R. 513.

not intending to give a cheque ... Consequently the property, in other words those cheques, never passed to the accused at any time.

Eaglehill Ltd. v. Needham Builders Ltd.

[1973] A.C. 992

Notice of dishonour of a bill of exchange: section 49

Facts

The defendants were drawers of a bill of exchange for £7,660 on a furniture company, payable on December 31, 1970, and accepted payable at Lloyds Bank, High Wycombe. It was dicounted by the plaintiff company. By December 28, the furniture company was in liquidation, and both plaintiffs and defendants knew this, and that the bill could not be paid. But notice of dishonour is necessary regardless of the knowledge of the parties, and Eaglehill prepared a notice, dating it January 1, the day after the bill was to be presented. A secretary at the company mistakenly posted it on December 30, and it reached the defendants by the first post on December 31. On the same day the bill was delivered to the bank by the first post.

The defendants argued that notice is ineffective if it is given before the dishonour takes place. Here it could not be proved that this had not happened, and therefore they could not be liable on the bill. A majority of the Court of Appeal reluctantly accepted this argument, Lord Denning dissenting.

Decision

The House of Lords unanimously allowed the appeal, holding that (1) a notice of dishonour is not vitiated by the mere fact that it was posted before the due date for payment of the bill; it constitutes a good notice unless it is received before the bill itself is dishonoured; and (2) a notice of dishonour is given at the time when the drawers receive it, and is (*per* Lord Cross) "when it is opened in the ordinary course of business, or would be so opened if the ordinary course of business was followed."[70] And in the absence of evidence as to the precise times at which notice and bill were received, Lord Cross said:

> If two acts have been done, one of which ought to have been done after the other if it was to be valid and the evidence which could

[70] At p. 1001.

reasonably be expected to be available does not show which was done first they will be presumed to have been done in the proper order.[71]

Notes

The bill of exchange is now much less frequently seen in domestic banking than it once was, but its continuing use in international commerce[72] makes it important for bankers still to be familiar with the formalities of its handling, so long as the laws of England apply, while it has always to be remembered that the cheque is itself a bill of exchange, and where, for example, the bank, having given value for a cheque or having a lien on it, intends to sue on it, the cheque must be retained and notice of dishonour, normally given by the return of the cheque to the customer, must be given separately.[73]

The *Eaglehill* case, although no bank was directly involved, is a good example of one of the formalities of dishonour, the rules as to which are set out at considerable length in section 49 of the 1882 Act. In the event, the House of Lords, on the special and unusual facts of the case, unanimously upheld Lord Denning's powerful dissenting judgment in the Court of Appeal. But the judgments in the latter, of Sachs and Stamp L.JJ., should not be forgotten. Sachs L.J. said:

It is now a very long time since Lord Mansfield stressed the importance of certainty in the law merchant. For well over a century there has been certainty that to establish due notice of dishonour it must be shown that it was notice after presentment and dishonour. In this technical sphere of the law merchant it would be no good service to introduce complexity and uncertainty by grafting artificial exceptions on to a well-known rule—exceptions moreover which run contrary to the plain meaning of the words of the 1882 Act and which would make an inroad on its provisions.[74]

It is to be noted that he made the same point in a different context in the *Cebora* case.[75] The two different approaches to the facts of the present case may be regarded as reflecting the recurring difference between what may be termed the strict and the liberalising schools of thought in the law. In practice the prudent course is to seek to satisfy the former.

---

[71] At p. 1011.
[72] *cf. post*, pp. 238 *et seq.*
[73] *cf. Westminster Bank Ltd.* v. *Zang, post*, p. 156.
[74] [1972] 2 A.C. 8 at p. 24; 9 L.D.B. 296.
[75] *Post*, p. 66.

Section 45 of the 1882 Act provides

Subject to the provisions of this Act a bill must be duly presented for payment. If it be not so presented the drawer and indorsers shall be discharged.

In *Ringham* v. *Hackett and Another*[76] the plaintiff had presented the cheque at the branch at which it was drawn, and was told that he should pay it in at his own bank, but as he was also told that in fact it had been stopped, he did not pay it in. The defendant argued, *inter alia*, that a crossed cheque can be presented within section 45 only through a banking account, so that the cheque had never been presented. But the Court of Appeal rejected the argument. It was a misconception that presentation must be through a bank: the crossed cheque provisions of the Act were intended to protect the bank and its customer, and had no effect on the payee. The fact that those provisions might prevent the payee from getting the money when he presented the cheque in person did not make it any less due presentation.

Slingsby and Others v. District Bank Ltd.

[1932] 1 K.B. 544

Material alteration of a bill of exchange: section 64

Facts

The plaintiffs, who were executors of an estate, had as solicitors a firm, Cumberbirch and Potts, who assisted them in work connected with the estate, the partner Cumberbirch being the acting partner. The plaintiffs had an account with the defendant bank. Cumberbirch, who regularly drew cheques for the plaintiffs' signatures, drew one such for £5,000 representing an investment of trust funds, in the form "Pay John Prust & Co. . . . or order," with a space between the word "Co." and the word "or." The executors signed the cheque, and Cumberbirch then added in the blank space the words "per Cumberbirch and Potts." The whole of the cheque with the exception of the signatures being in Cumberbirch's writing, there was no apparent alteration or addition. He then indorsed the cheque "Cumberbirch and Potts" and paid it to the credit of an account with the Westminster Bank in the name of the Palatine

[76] (1980) 124 S.J. 201; *post*, p. 203.

Industrial Finance Co. Ltd., in which he was interested. The cheque was duly collected and paid.

When the fraud was discovered the plaintiffs brought an action against the collecting bank, the Westminster Bank, which they lost.[77] For technical reasons they did not appeal but brought the present action against the District Bank, and Wright J. finding for them, the bank appealed.

Decision

The Court of Appeal upheld Wright J.'s decision, holding, *inter alia*, that:

(i) The cheque having been materially altered within section 64 of the Bills of Exchange Act it was avoided as between the plaintiffs and the defendants, and the latter therefore lost the protection both of sections 60 and 80.

(ii) If the description of the payee as altered was a permissible one, the indorsement without mention of John Prust & Co. was invalid, and the defendants were negligent in honouring the cheque.

In the course of his judgment, Scrutton L.J. said:

> The cheque, having been signed by the executors in a form which gave Cumberbirch no rights, was fraudulently altered by Cumberbirch before it was issued and, it was not disputed, altered in a material particular ...The cheque was thereby avoided under section 64 of the Bills of Exchange Act. A holder in due course might not be affected by an alteration not apparent, such as this alteration. But [the Westminster Bank were not holders in due course and] could not therefore justifiably claim on the District Bank, and the cheque when presented to the District Bank was invalid, avoided, a worthless piece of paper, which the District Bank was under no duty to pay. This invalidity comes before any question of indorsement. Secondly I am of opinion, as already stated, that if valid the cheque was not properly indorsed. The indorsement should have been "John Prust & Co., *per pro* Cumberbirch and Potts." Any attempt to prove a custom failed.[78-79]

Notes

The Bills of Exchange Act 1882, s.64(1), provides that a bill (or of course a cheque) materially altered without the assent of all parties liable upon it is avoided except against a party who has made or assented in the alteration, and subsequent indorsers. If the banker pays a void instrument he cannot debit his customer with the amount of it.

---

[77] *Slingsby* v. *Westminster Bank Ltd. (No. 2)* [1931] 2 K.B. 583.
[78-79] At p. 559. See also *post*, p. 88.

Section 64(2) of the Act provides:

In particular the following alterations are material, namely any alteration of the date, the sum payable, the time of payment, the place of payment, and, where a bill has been accepted generally, the addition of a place of payment without the acceptor's assent.

This leaves a number of points that may or may not be material including for example the alteration of "bearer" to "order" in *Attwood* v. *Griffin*[80] (where the alteration was held in the circumstances to be not material), and an alteration of the place of drawing, as in *Koch* v. *Dicks*[81] (where the alteration from London to a German town was held to be material, Greer L.J. pointing out that an alteration from London to Southampton would not be material as it would not affect rights in the bill). The test of what is material is clear enough: in *Suffell* v. *Bank of England*,[82] Brett L.J. said: "Any alteration of any instrument seems to be material which would alter the business effect of the instrument...."[83] But it is plainly undesirable that bills and cheques should be altered at all, and in *Koch* v. *Dicks*, Scrutton L.J. in placing upon the person setting up the altered instrument the onus of proving the non-materiality of the alteration, provided a salutary check upon any tendency to regard any such alterations as immaterial.

The significance of this one of the three *Slingsby* decisions[84] lies in its emphasis that a cheque materially altered, as the cheque of £5,000 was altered, becomes a nullity upon which the paying banker cannot properly pay, even though the position of a holder in due course *vis-à-vis* the drawer might not be affected by a non-apparent alteration; and in the fact that it lays down the correct form of indorsement for a cheque made out in the unusual, but by no means unknown, form of the £5,000 cheque.[85] The placing by Scrutton L.J. of the principal's name before "*per pro,*" although etymologically accurate, is not in accordance with common usage; "*per pro* Prust & Co., Cumberbirch and Potts" is the normal form. In any case, the important point is that the fact that it is an agent's signature must be apparent in the indorsement itself.

[80] (1826) 2 C. & P. 368.
[81] (1932) 49 T.L.R. 24.
[82] (1882) 9 Q.B.D. 555.
[83] At p. 568.
[84] cf. *ante*, p. 50 and n. 77 *supra*.
[85] cf. *Marquess of Bute* v. *Barclays Bank Ltd.*, *post*, p. 181.

Reference should be made to p. 88 regarding the refusal of the Court here to apply the principle of the *Macmillan* case to facts only slightly different from those in that case.

The "opening" of a crossed cheque is the alteration most commonly seen in practice. Its dangers led to the resolution of the Committee of London Clearing Bankers in 1912 under which no such cheque was to be cashed without the full signature of the drawer to the alteration, and even so only for the drawer personally or his known agent.

It is to be noted that the completion of an incomplete bill is expressly authorised by section 20 of the Act: "... when a bill is wanting in any material particular the person in possession of it has a prima facie authority to fill up the omission in any way he thinks fit." But this must be done "within a reasonable time, and strictly in accordance with the authority given." In *Griffiths* v. *Dalton*[86] an undated cheque was issued in August 1931, the plaintiff eventually completing it with a date in February 1933. The cheque was dishonoured, but the plaintiff's action on it failed, the court holding that an unreasonable time had elapsed.

The practice of bankers in refusing payment of undated cheques has been questioned, but although a cheque is not invalid merely because it is undated,[87] section 20(2) provides that the filling up of any omission must be "strictly in accordance with the authority given," and "it is difficult to see what authority the customer can be supposed to have given to the banker in the circumstances."[88]

In *Griffiths* v. *Dalton*, 18 months was held to be unreasonable delay in completing the cheque. The position would have been different had the cheque been negotiated to a third party, who took it in good faith and for value, for section 20(2) provides further that "if any such instrument after completion is negotiated to a holder in due course it shall be valid and effectual for all purposes in his hands, and he may enforce it as if it had been filled up within a reasonable time. . . ."

Cebora S.N.C. v. S.I.P. (Industrial Products) Ltd.

[1976] 1 Lloyd's Rep. 271

The cash equivalence of the bill of exchange

Facts

The plaintiffs, an Italian manufacturing company, entered into

---

[86] [1940] 2 K.B. 264.
[87] Bills of Exchange Act, s.3(4)(*a*).
[88] *Questions on Banking Practice* (11th ed.), Question 405.

an agreement with the defendants, an English company, granting them exclusive rights to sell the plaintiffs' products in the United Kingdom. Following disputes between the parties the plaintiffs terminated the agreement and set up their own distributing company in England. The defendants gave instructions that five outstanding bills of exchange, for a total of £56,000, should be dishonoured. Upon the plaintiffs claiming summary judgment on the bills, the defendants counterclaimed for delivery of defective goods and loss of profit. The District Registrar entered judgment for the plaintiffs on the bills, and the defendants appealed, applying for a stay pending trial of the counterclaim, and alleging that in all the circumstances, including the fact that the plaintiffs were outside the jurisdiction, there was considerable doubt whether any judgment that might be obtained on the counterclaim would be enforceable. But May J. refused the stay, and the defendants appealed.

Decision

The Court of Appeal dismissed the appeal. Sir Eric Sachs said:

Any erosion of the certainties of the application by our Courts of the law merchant relating to bills of exchange is likely to work to the detriment of this country, which depends on international trade to a degree that needs no emphasis. For some generations one of those certainties has been that the bona fide holder for value of a bill of exchange is entitled, save in truly exceptional circumstances, on its maturity to have it treated as cash, so that in an action upon it the Court will refuse to regard either as a defence or as grounds for a stay of execution any set off, legal or equitable, or any counterclaim, whether arising on the particular transaction upon which the bill of exchange came into existence, or, a fortiori, arising in any other way. This rule of practice is thus, in effect, pay up on the bill of exchange first and pursue claims later. . . .

In my judgment, the Courts should be really careful not to whittle away the rule of practice by introducing unnecessary exceptions to it under the influence of sympathy-evoking stories, and should have due regard to the maxim that hard cases make bad law. Indeed, in these days of international interdependence and increasing need to foster liquidity of resources, the rule may be said to be of special import to the business community. Pleas to leave in Court large sums to deteriorate in value while official referee proceedings are fought out may well to that community seem rather divorced from business realities, and should perhaps be examined with considerable caution.[89]

[89] At pp. 278–279.

Notes

Sir Eric Sachs emphasised the importance of the bill's cash equivalence in international trade, and most of the cases establishing the principle are concerned with that trade. But of course the principle applies equally to domestic transactions; and while the cases are for the most part on bills of exchange, the principle applies equally to cheques and to promissory notes.

The rule was applied to the cheques in issue in the *Calzaturificio Fiorella* case[90]; and in a promissory note case, *Ferson Contractors Ltd.* v. *Ferris*[91] the Court of Appeal unanimously rejected the argument of the defence that as the cases were mainly on bills of exchange and their importance in international commerce, it was open to the courts in cases on promissory notes to depart from the rule more frequently and more generously.[92]

The principle is restricted to the refusal to the defendant of the right to delay payment on account of any kind of counterclaim: the bill (or cheque or promissory note) is a contract in itself, apart from whatever contract underlies it. This does not mean that there is no defence to an action on a bill of exchange: the bill can be challenged on its own defects— including the "fraud, duress, or force and fear, or illegality" which by section 30(2) of the 1882 Act can deny the holder the rights of a holder in due course.[93] And in *Clovertogs Ltd.* v. *Jean Scenes Ltd.*[94] the Court of Appeal held that alleged misrepresentation, although not fraudulent, can amount to an arguable defence, Eveleigh L.J. remarking that "the effect of misrepresentation upon a bill of exchange is a matter on which it is not easy to discover the law."

One of such defences is failure of consideration. Partial failure of consideration can be a defence *pro tanto*, as between immediate parties, and when the failure is an ascertained and liquidated amount, Stephenson L.J., distinguished between total and partial failure in *Montebianceo Industrie Tessili S.p.A.* v.

---

[90] *Ante*, p. 53; *cf. Habib* v. *Ladup* (1981) C.A.T. 82/316; *Mansouri* v. *Singh* [1986] 2 All E.R. 619.
[91] (Unreported) (1982) C.L.Y. 14.
[92] *cf. Boundy* v. *Bhagwanami* (Unreported) (1981) C.L.Y. 400.
[93] *cf.* Chalmers, *op. cit.*, pp. 99 *et seq.* for discussion of these defences and *cf. Moledina* v. *Gandesha*, New L.J. January 31, 1980, where the defendant had refused payment of a promissory note, and in the Court of Appeal was given unconditional leave to defend on his allegation of fraud.
[94] [1982] Com.L.R. 88.

Carlyle Mills (London) Ltd.[95] where the defendants appealed against summary judgment on dishonoured bills: "we cannot consider this case as a case of total failure of consideration, when, of course, it would be beyond argument that the defendants should have leave to defend, so we are in the position of partial failure of consideration, where we have a discretion." In the circumstances of that case the Court applied the cash equivalence rule (which his Lordship had referred to as "a rule of practice almost amounting to a rule of law"), and rejected the appeal.

But in *Thoni GmbH & Co., K.G.* v. *R.T.P. Equipment Ltd.*[96] where the defendants were appealing against summary judgment on a bill for one million Austrian Schillings, alleging that they owed only half of that amount, the Court of Appeal refused a stay of execution but on the information before them, "clouded and confused though it is in some respects," held that there seemed to be an arguable case for the disputed amount and gave the defendants leave to defend in respect of that balance, provided that they brought into court its sterling equivalent.[97]

There can be other direct defences in actions on bills. In *Drouby* v. *Wassif and Others*[98] for example, a cheque was held to have been issued on a condition that had not been fulfilled, and by virtue of section 21(2)(*b*) of the 1882 Act the issue was "not for the purpose of transferring property in the bill."

Even apart from such defences, it is clear that the courts have a discretion to order a stay of execution in an action on bills of exchange. But the *Cebora* decision underlines the fact that this discretion will be exercised only in "truly exceptional circumstances." It will not be exercised when the counter-claim is for unliquidated damages[99] or otherwise than between immediate parties to the bill. Thus in *Jade International Steel Stahl and Eisen GmbH* v. *Robert Nicholas (Steels) Ltd.*[1] the defendants had dishonoured a bill drawn by the plaintiffs, alleging delivery of faulty goods. Donaldson J, giving the plaintiffs immediate

---

[95] [1981] 1 Lloyd's Rep. 509.
[96] [1979] 2 Lloyd's Rep. 282.
[97] The defendants in arguing for a stay drew an analogy with the *Mareva* injunction (see p. 117 *post*) on the grounds that the plaintiffs were a company outside the jurisdiction and without assets in the jurisdiction apart from the fruits of the present action. Presumably the Court's requirement to bring the money in issue into court was based on the same reasoning.
[98] (Unreported) (1978) C.L.Y. 17.
[99] See *James Lamont & Co. Ltd.* v. *Hyland (No. 2)* [1950] 1 All E.R. 929.
[1] [1978] 3 W.L.R. 39.

judgment on the bill, refused the defendant's application for leave to defend. They argued that he had discretion to vary the rule where the dispute was between immediate parties to the bill, but he held that the plaintiffs were no longer immediate parties: they had lost the capacity of drawers when they discounted the bill, and were now holders in due course, having received it back from the bankers, who had been holders in due course. The Court of Appeal upheld his decision, Geoffrey Lane L.J. expressing surprise that in close on 100 years since the passing of the Bills of Exchange Act the point seemed not to have arisen before.

In *Nova (Jersey) Knit Ltd.* v. *Karngarn Spinnerei GmbH*[2] there was a dispute between the English plaintiffs and the German defendants, and the defendants resisted immediate payment of dishonoured bills of exchange on the grounds that German arbitration was pending on the whole issue in dispute. The Court of Appeal granted the stay, but on appeal the House of Lords reversed their decision by a majority,[3] Lord Wilberforce saying:

> I fear that the Court of Appeal's decision, if it had been allowed to stand, would have made a very substantial inroad upon the commercial principle on which the bills of exchange have always rested.[4]

That principle he had described thus:

> ...I must emphasise, since it seems to be suggested that all the merits require the whole dispute to go to arbitration in Germany, that it is not mere technicality that supports the appellants' claim. When one person buys goods from another it is often, one would think generally, important for the seller to be sure of his price: he may (as indeed have the appellants here) have bought the goods from someone else whom he has to pay. He may demand payment in cash; but if the buyer cannot provide this at once, he may agree to take bills of exchange payable at future dates... Unless they are to be treated as unconditionally payable instruments... which the seller can negotiate for cash, the seller might just as well give credit. And it is for this reason that English law (and German law appears to be no different) does not allow cross-claims, or defences, except such limited defences as those based on fraud, invalidity, or failure of consideration, to be made.[5]

---

[2] [1976] 2 Lloyd's Rep. 155.
[3] [1977] 2 All E.R. 463.
[4] At p. 470.
[5] At p. 470; and *cf. Domenica* v. *Shimco, post*, p. 255.

But the decision in this case does not mean that the cash equivalence rule can never be affected by pending arbitration proceedings.[6] The argument in the House of Lords turned largely on whether the arbitration agreement, which was governed by German law, and on which there was conflicting expert evidence, could be held to cover the bills of exchange. Lord Wilberforce considered that it could not, and his brethren agreed, with the exception of Lord Salmon, who delivered a dissenting judgment and would have dismissed the appeal. He too recognised the basic rule (and made a particular point on it: "certainly there could be no question of a stay if the bills had been discounted and the holders in due course were the plaintiffs in the action".)[7] But he held that the agreement covered the bills, and he seemed to accept the defendants' argument "that if the circumstances of this case were not exceptional, it is difficult to imagine any that could be." It seems clear that if the majority had agreed with him on both points the stay would have been granted.

Beevers and Another v. Mason

(1978) 37 P. & C.R. 452

Payment of a debt by cheque: when effected

Facts

The defendant was a farm tenant long accustomed to pay rent by post to the landlord. He was told to make future payments to the farmer's agent. He had frequently been in arrear in payment; and in a letter dated October 21, 1975, he was given two months in which to pay rent already due. He sent a cheque to the landlord, postmarked December 22, the landlord receiving it on December 24. He was given notice to quit, and when in the county court it was held that he had failed to pay the rent in time, he appealed.

Decision

The Court of Appeal allowed the appeal: the cheque posted within the two months of the notice was, subject only to its being honoured, payment within the period. And the fact that the new instruction for payment was ignored was not relevant:

---

[6] *cf. Barclays Bank Ltd.* v. *Aschaffenberger Zellstoffwerke AG, post*, p. 238.
[7] At p. 475.

"a payment direct to a creditor, other things being equal, can hardly be less effective in law than a payment... to the agent. It might be otherwise if, for example, the creditor is out of England, or his whereabouts are uncertain." Shaw L.J., delivering the judgment of the Court, cited Lord Esher M.R. in *Norman* v. *Ricketts*[8]: "If asked to pay through the post the putting the letter in the post with the money is sufficient," and Lord du Parcq in *Tankexpress A/S* v. *Compagnie Financière Belge des Pétroles SA*.[9]

It seems to me to be hopeless to contend that the owner's acceptance of the method of payment was subject to a condition, unexpressed but implied, that if the cheque did not arrive in London on [the due date] the charterers, though they were not to blame for the delay, should be treated as having made default.

Notes

The general rule as to the time at which payment by cheque is effected was stated in *Marreco* v. *Richardson*[10] by Farwell, L.J.: "... the giving of a cheque for a debt is conditional on the cheque being met, that is, subject to a condition subsequent, and if the cheque is met it is an actual payment *ab initio* and not a conditional one." The rule was recognised in the *Beevers* decision in the proviso "subject only to its being honoured"; and it was underlined in *Official Solicitor to the Supreme Court* v. *Thomas*[11] where the Court of Appeal rejected the argument that *Beevers* covered a case where the cheque was delivered but never cashed by the payee.[11a]

The eventual payment of the cheque does not operate to make the initial payment absolute for all purposes. Between the receipt of the cheque and its payment by the drawee bank, payment may be regarded as still conditional as regards an external event occurring during the period. Thus in *Re Hone ex*

---

[8] (1886) 3 T.L.R. 182.
[9] [1948] 2 All E.R. 939.
[10] [1908] 2 K.B. 584.
[11] [1986] 2 E.G.L.R. 1.
[11a] As to questions regarding postal delivery, *cf. Barclays Bank of Swaziland* v. *Hahn, The Times*, May 19, 1989 (service of a writ through the defendant's letter box when he is out of the jurisdiction is effective if it is shown that within seven days it has been seen by the defendant within the jurisdiction); and *Lex Service plc* v. *Johns, The Times*, September 19, 1989 (when a landlord's notice sent by recorded delivery is recorded as having been received at the address, the tenant's denial that he has received it does not have the effect of proving that the notice has not been served).

parte the Trustee v. *Kensington Borough Council*[12] Harman
J., referring to Farwell L.J.'s dictum, said "I cannot take
that view as between the trustee in bankruptcy and the
bankrupt." In that case the council received a cheque in
payment of rates on November 3, and paid it into their
account on November 4. On that day, after the cheque was
paid in, the debtor filed her petition in bankruptcy, was
made bankrupt at once and adjudicated on the same day.
The council submitted payment had been made within the
meaning of the section on November 3. But it was held that
payment had not been made until the cheque had been
collected: "...the council...got their money when they
were richer by £55."

That was a case in bankruptcy, in which, it is to be
noted, the bank could not have succeeded if the action had
been brought against them. An earlier decision to the same
effect without that complication, by Romer J., was that in
Re Owen deceased, Owen v. *Inland Revenue
Commissioners*,[13] where the deceased had intended some
years before his death to make certain gifts, and accordingly
cheques were issued on May 21, 1941, to the three donees.
The first cheque was presented for payment on June 4, the
second on June 5, and the third on July 2. The donor died
on June 1, 1944, and the question arose as to whether the
gifts were subject to estate duty, or whether they had been
made more than three years before the death. It was held
that they were so subject, as the gifts were not complete
until the cheques had been paid by the drawee bank.

Scott J.'s decision in *Parkside Leasing Ltd.* v. *Smith
(Inspector of Taxes)*[14] was to the same effect: a cheque
received on April 9, and paid into the bank on April 11,
was taxable in the period beginning on April 10, not, as the
Revenue contended, in the period ending on April 9.
"...mere receipt of the cheque did not place the proceeds
at the taxpayer's disposal: the cheque might not have been
honoured."

It is of course only in exceptional circumstances that there
is any difficulty in the matter. Since the passing of the
Cheques Act 1957, receipts are not issued so regularly for

[12] [1951] Ch. 85.
[13] [1949] 1 All E.R. 901.
[14] [1985] 1 W.L.R. 310.

payments made by cheque as they were previously[15]; but it is normal business practice for such receipts as are issued to be sent on the generally understood condition that if the cheque is dishonoured the receipt is ineffective; and the increasing tendency to issue such receipts without qualification is possibly a recognition of the fact that in any event the payee has an action against the drawer on the dishonoured cheque itself, irrespective of the original debt.[16]

Payment by other forms of money transfer: when effected

The time at which payment is effected can be questioned in regard to other forms of money transfer in the banking system. Thus in *The Brimnes: Tenax Steamship Co. Ltd.* v. *The Brimnes (Owners)*[16a] the payment in dispute was a transfer from one account to another in the books of Morgan Guaranty Trust in New York, the transfer being initiated by a telex message from Hambros in London. The Court of Appeal held that payment was effected, not when the telex was received, but some two hours later, after the message had been "processed" and the decision to effect the transfer made.

At the trial Brandon J. had said that the words "payment in cash" in the charterparty

cannot mean only payment in dollar bills or other legal tender of the United States. They must...have a wider meaning, comprehending any commercially recognised method of transferring funds the result of which is to give the transferee the unconditional right to the immediate use of the funds transferred.[16b]

That ruling was adopted by the Court of Appeal and has

---

[15] It was a curious side effect of the Cheques Act that s.3, intended merely to preserve for the unindorsed paid cheque the value as evidence of receipt that had always attached to the indorsed paid cheque, drew the attention of the business community for the first time to this aspect of the cheque. It was an unjustifiable *non sequitur* that led further to the omission of stamps from many acknowledgements of payment.

[16] *cf.* the cases discussed at pp. 66 *et seq.* in which the principle is established that only in exceptional circumstances will the courts consider any kind of counter-claim as entitling the acceptor to postpone payment on a bill of exchange: the bill is a contract separate from the underlying transaction.

[16a] [1974] 3 All E.R. 88.

[16b] [1973] 1 All E.R. 769 at p. 782.

been specifically approved in later cases.[17] But its precise meaning is still not clear. In *Mardorf Peach & Co. v. Attica Sea Carriers Corp. of Liberia*[18] the instrument involved was a payment order issued under the London Currency Settlement Scheme. Such payment orders are regarded as equivalent to cash by the banks operating the scheme, even though beneficiaries cannot draw against them until they are "processed." The Court of Appeal held by a majority that payment was effected when the payment order was received by the beneficiary's bankers, any paper work thereafter being irrelevant. The House of Lords reversed their decision in favour of the plaintiffs,[19] but this was on other grounds, while dicta of Lord Russell and Lord Salmon seem to support the majority view of the Court of Appeal on the point here discussed, Lord Salmon remarking that "no doubt a certain amount of processing or paper work has to be done even in relation to a cash payment before it finds its way as a credit into the haven of the customer's account."[20]

In *Afovos Shipping Co. S.A. v. Pagnan*, another charterparty case where payment by telex of a semi-monthly instalment of hire was delayed as a result of an error in a telex directory, the question was whether the owners were justified in giving notice

---

[17] In *The Chikuma* [1981] 1 All E.R. 652 Brandon J.'s ruling was accepted in the Court of Appeal and the House of Lords, but the case did not turn on the point here discussed. The question there was whether a payment authorised on January 22, by one Italian bank by teleprinter to another and expressed to be "value 26" was effective payment of the charter hire due on January 22. The Court of Appeal held that it was; the owners were entitled to immediate use of the money on the due date, "value 26," a local banking usage and almost certainly unfamiliar to the Scandinavian hirers and their bankers, meaning merely that interest would not begin to run until January 26. But the House of Lords applied "unconditional" strictly: the payment was not unconditional as "it could only be drawn subject to a (probable) liability to pay interest."

[18] [1976] Q.B. 835.

[19] [1977] 2 W.L.R. 286.

[20] See "Two Questions of Time" (April 1977) *The Banker*, Vol. 127, p. 141, where also is discussed the question whether a payment due on a Sunday, when the banks are closed, must be made on the Friday. This was accepted without argument in the *Mardorf Peach* case, only Lord Denning, in the Court of Appeal, suggesting that the assumption was wrong. It may be thought that his view finds support in the provision of the Banking and Financial Dealings Act 1971, which makes bills of exchange due on any non-business day payable on the succeeding business day. *cf. The Clifford Maersk* [1982] 1 W.L.R. 1292, where Sheen J. held that where a contractual time set for the beginning of proceedings expires on a Sunday, the writ may be issued on the next day on which the court office is open.

of withdrawal of the vessel at 4.40 p.m. on the date payment was due. Lloyd J, at first instance[21] considered Brandon J.'s ruling and said:

> If by "immediate use of the funds" he meant that payment was not complete until all the paperwork within the bank had been done, there is support for that view in the speech of Lord Fraser [in the *Mardorf Peach* case]...; but I would prefer the views expressed, albeit tentatively, by Lord Salmon... and Lord Russell...

And he pointed out that a transferee can have the immediate right to the funds before the paperwork is complete; in practice, no bank would refuse the use of funds because a credit known to be in their hands had not been processed.

But he held that the owners were entitled to give notice when they did, it being by then impossible for payment to be received in the bank's books on the due date. He was overruled in the Court of Appeal, and their decision was upheld in the House of Lords[22] Lord Hailsham saying:

> I take it to be a general principle of law not requiring authority that where a person under an obligation to do a particular act has to do it on or before a particular date he has the whole of that day to perform his duty.... The question is not when the charterer would cease to be likely to pay in time, but when... "punctual payment" would have failed. In my opinion this moment must relate to a particular hour, and is not dependent on the modalities of the recipient bank. It is the hour of midnight to which the general rule applies.[23]

The owners' argument based on the doctrine of anticipatory breach was rejected: failure to pay one instalment was not a fundamental breach of the contract that would support the argument—it did not, in Lord Diplock's words, "have the effect of depriving the owners of substantially the whole benefit" of the rest of the contract.

For their application of the "general principle of law" it was not necessary for their Lordships to decide whether the processing of a telex (or other banking transfer system) is relevant to the time at which payment is effected, and Lord Hailsham reserved judgment on the point. However, Lord Roskill, referring to Lloyd J's comments, and his view that

---

[21] [1980] 2 Lloyd's Rep. 469.
[22] [1983] 1 W.L.R. 195.
[23] At p. 201. But *cf.* the dictum of Kerr J, quoted *post*, p. 149.

payment is complete "when the telex is received and tested by the receiving bank" and agreeing that the point was not for present decision, went on:

> But as at present advised I think that the correct answer, whatever it may be, is likely to depend, at least in most cases, upon proof of the practice of bankers current when the question arises, rather than upon any determination of it as a matter of law.[24]

So the question is still open; but the reaffirmation of the principle that a debtor has, in the absence of stipulation to the contrary, until midnight of the due date to pay his debt will remove at least some disputes from the element of doubt in the area.

———

If the question were the bank's liability for a refusal resulting from the inevitable delay in the actual crediting, the *Brimnes* ruling could found a defence. It is interesting to note that *Questions on Banking Practice*[25] in successive editions, has taken a strong line on the point: to a question whether a bank would be liable for dishonouring a specially presented cheque after the customer had paid in at a sub-branch but before the sub-branch clerk had returned to the parent branch, the answer is given: "No. Money is not available immediately it is paid in. Even in the case of notes and coin, a sufficient period must be allowed to elapse before drawing against it to enable the bank to carry out the necessary bookkeeping operations."

[24] At p. 204.
[25] 11th ed., 360.

Chapter 3

THE PAYING BANKER

Re Gross, Ex parte Kingston
(1871) 6 Ch.App. 632

Lipkin Gorman v. Karpnale and Another Ltd.
[1989] F.L.R. 137

When the banker knows that an account is composed of trust money, he must not deal with it in a manner which he knows is inconsistent with the trust

Facts of Re Gross, Ex p. Kingston

Gross was treasurer of the county rates for the eastern division of Suffolk. He kept private accounts with National Provincial Bank of England in Ipswich, and, although the other county funds were kept with Bacon's Bank, Gross kept the police rates mixed with his own principal account, and made drawings on this account for police-rate payments. Later, however, he opened two further accounts, called "Police Account" and "Superannuation Account," and transferred to them the moneys in question, thereafter keeping his private money entirely distinct from the public funds which he was handling, save that, interest being allowed on all the accounts, it was carried to his main private account.

Some time later Gross became insolvent, and disappeared. It was then found that the two police accounts were in credit to a total of £2,972 10s. 6d., but that the two other accounts in Gross's name were overdrawn to a total which left less than £300 net credit, if the four balances were amalgamated. The County Court judge at Ipswich made an order that the bank were entitled to a lien on the credit balances to satisfy the net indebtedness, and the magistrates, representing the County, appealed. The Chief Judge in Bankruptcy found against the bank, and the present case was a further appeal.

78

Decision

The appeal was dismissed, and it was held that in the circumstances the bank had no right of set-off.

In the course of his judgment, Sir W. M. James L.J. said:

> The bankers opened the account, and dealt with the account, knowing that it was a county account. The fact that, when his private account was overdrawn, he drew from it sums made up of pounds, shillings, and pence, for the purpose of paying them into the police account, conclusively shows that he paid, out of moneys which his bankers were willing to lend him, the moneys which he knew to be due from him to the county. ... In my mind this case is infinitely stronger than those referred to during the argument, in which a similar claim on the part of bankers was disallowed, for in those cases the banker relied on cheques drawn by the customers; and if a banker receives from a customer holding a trust account a cheque drawn on that account, he is not in general bound to inquire whether the cheque was properly drawn. Here the customer has drawn no cheque, and the bankers are seeking to set off the balance on his private account against the balance in his favour on what they knew to be a trust account.[1]

Facts of Lipkin Gorman v. Karpnale

The plaintiffs were a firm of solicitors. From 1978 to 1980 a partner in the firm, Norman Barry Cass, who was a compulsive gambler, used his right to sign cheques on the firm's client account with Lloyds Bank to steal for his gambling purposes more than £200,000. He was convicted of theft and sentenced to three years' imprisonment, and the firm claimed to recover their loss from the bank and from the Playboy Club, where most of the money was lost. The claim against the Club was for negligence and for money had and received; against the bank it was as constructive trustees and for breach of contract. At first instance before Alliott J. the principal claim against the Club failed, but the bank was held liable as constructive trustee for losses until the date when the firm discovered Cass's dishonesty. There were appeals and cross-appeals against these findings.

Decision

By a majority the Court of Appeal dismissed the firm's appeal against the Playboy finding: Cass's contract with the Club was not avoided under the Gaming Act 1845, and the money had been received by the Club bona fide and for value without notice of Cass's defective title to it. But the bank's appeal was

---

[1] At p. 639.

allowed. As to the finding of liability as constructive trustees it was argued, as it had been at the trial, that the pleadings in the case had only at one point alleged that the manager knew of the fraud, the allegation more generally being that he "knew or ought to have known" of it; and it was therefore not open to the judge to find that he had been aware of the fraud. The Court accepted the argument; May L.J., said that there was strong persuasive authority for the view that nothing less than knowledge of an underlying dishonest design is sufficient to found liability as a constructive trustee, and on the single relevant point in the pleadings the supporting allegations were "wholly inadequate" to found an inference of dishonesty on the part of the manager.

As to the claim in contract, a bank's basic obligation on a current account in credit is to pay the customer's cheque in accordance with the mandate, and only exceptional circumstances—in which, Parker L.J. suggested, a reasonable banker would see "a serious or real possibility" that his customer was being defrauded—would the banker be justified in questioning payment. Here the manager's knowledge of Cass's gambling, derived from the conduct of the personal account, had no obvious relevance to the cheques fraudulently drawn on the clients account, which numbered only one-seventh of the cheques properly drawn by the partnership; and the disclosure of such knowledge to the firm would have been a breach of the bank's duty of confidentiality to Cass. The bank's appeal was allowed.

Notes

The banker's knowledge of the existence of the trust may be inferred from the facts of the case. In *Re Gross* the facts were clear, and the decision in *Bodenham* v. *Hoskins*[1a] was also that the facts should have made it obvious that a trust was involved.

The plaintiff was the owner of the Rotherwas estate, and Parkes, his receiver. Parkes had a private account with the defendant banker, and on being appointed Bodenham's receiver, opened another account called "the Rotherwas account." Evidence was given that Parkes had promised to bring this account to the bankers, in consideration of their allowing him an overdraft on his private account; and that they were told that the account would be for the receipt of the rents of the estate. Later a cheque for £829 11s. 9d., drawn on the

[1a] (1852) 2 De G.M. & G. 903.

Rotherwas account, was paid to the credit of Parkes's private account, which was overdrawn, and on this being discovered, the plaintiff sought refund of the money, alleging that the bankers had knowledge not only of the fact that the money was trust money, but also that Parkes was, or was in danger of becoming, insolvent. The defendants in their defence denied all knowledge of the trust relationship. But Sir Richard Kindersley V.-C. found for the plaintiff, and on appeal his judgment was upheld.

> The bankers did not seem to feel or be aware that they had no right, and that Parkes had no right, to enter into any arrangement, the effect of which was to make the money... liable to any defalcation, any deficiency that might exist upon the private account of Mr. Parkes with the bankers.

In *Foxton* v. *Manchester and Liverpool District Banking Co.*[2] an executorship account had been opened in the joint names of Edmund and Henry Hardman, both of whom had private accounts also with the defendant bank. Both private accounts were overdrawn, and substantial sums were transferred from the executors' account to the private accounts. After the deaths of the two executors, certain beneficiaries under the will sought to recover from the bank the sums which had been so transferred, and in giving his decision against the bank, Fry J. said:

> It appears to be plain that the bank could not derive the benefit which they did from that payment, knowing it to be drawn from a trust fund, unless they were prepared to show that the payment was a legitimate and proper one, having reference to the terms of the trust. It is said that they did not know what the trust was at that time. That appears to me, I confess, to be immaterial, because those who know that a fund is a trust fund cannot take possession of that fund for their own private benefit, except at the risk of being liable to refund it in the event of the trust being broken by the payment of the money.[3]

This judgment has been approved in later cases, but whether the "benefit" to the banker must be benefit deliberately sought (as in the pressure exercised on the executors in *Foxton's* case) or may be merely incidental benefit, is not entirely clear. In *Coleman* v. *Bucks and Oxon Union Bank*[4] it was contended

---

[2] (1881) 44 L.T. 406.
[3] At p. 608.
[4] [1897] 2 Ch. 243; *post*, p. 103.

against the bank that even incidental benefit must fix them with notice of the breach of trust, but Byrne J. considered that the *Foxton* decision could not be pushed so far, and must mean rather that bankers were liable who "are going to derive a benefit from the transfer and intend and design that they should derive a benefit from it."

It is natural, in any event, that benefit gained by the person dealing with the trust funds must be a material factor in assessing his culpability. On this point reference may be made to *Midland Bank Ltd.* v. *Reckitt and Others*[5]; the fact that the bank had pressed strongly for repayment of the overdraft was held to be a fact materially against them. But benefit gained is still only one factor in the case of recovery of trust moneys. In the *Selangor* case[6] there was clearly no benefit to the bank; and in *John* v. *Dodwell & Co.*,[7] when Dodwell's manager had bought shares for himself with cheques on Dodwell's account, the firm was held to be entitled to recover the money from the brokers as being held in trust for them, on the grounds that the manner in which the cheques were drawn showed that the manager was using the firm's money for his own purposes, which left the brokers without any right to hold that money as against the firm; while further, the brokers were in the position of receiving property from someone they knew to be in a fiduciary position, knowing that he was in breach of his trust, and so were themselves under a fiduciary obligation to the agent's principal.

In *Rowlandson and Others* v. *National Westminster Bank Ltd.*[8] the bank was fixed with liability for the misappropriation of funds by their own designation of the relevant account as "Trust Account." No receipt or account card was written when the bank received money said to be for the benefit of the donor's grandchildren, but later an account card was made out on the model of an earlier account at the branch, in the names of two of the children's uncles, and marked "Trust Account," and one of the uncles having thereafter used the money for his own purposes it was held that although no express trust was created when the money was handed to the bank, the bank's fiduciary duty arose when the account was opened with its specific description.

---

[5] [1933] A.C. 1; *post*, pp. 176 and 235.
[6] *Infra.*
[7] [1918] A.C. 563.
[8] [1978] 1 W.L.R. 798.

The *Lipkin Gorman* decision is the latest in a series of cases in which very detailed consideration has been given to the question what degree of knowledge of wrong-doing is necessary to found liability in a third party where trust funds have been misappropriated.[9]

In his classic formulation of the law on the question in *Barnes* v. *Addy*[10] Lord Selborne distinguished two categories of constructive trusteeship. In the first, where a person receives trust property and deals with it in a manner inconsistent with the trust, he may be liable even though he acted innocently, if he had notice of the trust. In the second a person who, while not himself receiving the trust property, assists the trustees in a dishonest design will not be liable as a constructive trustee unless he assists with knowledge of the improper design.

The decision of Ungoed-Thomas J. in *Selangor United Rubber Estates Ltd.* v. *Cradock (a Bankrupt) and Others No. 3*[11] caused some alarm in the banks, for in a case where the "wrong-doing" was a complicated manoeuvre in which company funds were used to buy the company shares the District Bank were held liable as constructive trustees and in contract. Actual knowledge by the bank officials that the transaction was illegal was not alleged, but it was held that the circumstances should have made the position clear to them; and the judge said if a bank allows officials completely inexperienced in such transactions to conduct such business it is asking for the kind of trouble it had got in that case.[12]

This was to include in Lord Selborne's second type of constructive trustee a person with constructive knowledge of the improper design. But in *Carl Zeiss Stiftung* v. *Herbert Smith & Co. and Another*[13] in the Court of Appeal, Sachs L.J. was "inclined to the view" that there needed to be proved "both actual knowledge of the trust's existence and actual knowledge that what is being done is improperly in breach of the trust." And some years later, in the two *Belmont Finance*

---

[9] *cf.* Penn, Shea & Arora, *op. cit.* I, 10, especially at 10.08 *et seq.* "Leading and Misleading Cases."

[10] (1874) 9 Ch.App. 244.

[11] [1968] 2 All E.R. 1073.

[12] Paget's comment on *Selangor* was that the decision "places an impossibly high burden on a bank not to be negligent, in requiring its officers to be expert in finance as well as in banking": *op. cit.* 225. The decision was followed by Brightman J. in *Karak Rubber Co. Ltd.* v. *Burden (No. 2)* [1972] 1 W.L.R. 602, a case on very similar facts.

[13] [1969] 2 All E.R. 367.

cases,[14] the Court of Appeal rejected the *Selangor* view, in the first case unanimously disagreeing with it, and in the second accepting in all the judgments that actual knowledge is needed to establish constructive trusteeship in Lord Selborne's second category.

In *Baden, Delvaux and Lecuit* v. *Société Générale*[15] Peter Gibson J. suggested five categories of knowledge to be considered in such cases: (i) actual knowledge; (ii) a wilful shutting of one's eyes to the obvious; (iii) a wilful and reckless failure to make enquiries that an honest and reasonable man would have made; (iv) knowledge of facts which would have indicated the facts to an honest and reasonable man; and (v) knowledge of circumstances which would have put an honest and reasonable man on enquiry. In that case *Selangor* was not challenged, and the judge appeared to accept it, but in the event he held that Société Générale had neither actual nor constructive knowledge of the fraud, and the Court of Appeal upheld his decision without discussing constructive trusteeship.

It will be noticed that *Selangor* involved categories (iv) and (v) of what have become known as the Baden types of knowledge. In *Re Montague's Settlement*[16] Sir Robert Megarry V.-C. questioned their relevance:

> ...knowledge is not confined to actual knowledge but includes at least types (ii) and (iii) of the *Baden* knowledge...for in such cases there is a want of probity which justifies imposing a constructive trust. Whether knowledge of Baden types (iv) and (v) suffices for this purpose is doubtful; in my view it does not, for I cannot see that the carelessness involved will normally amount to a want of probity.

This dictum echoed that of Edmund Davies L.J. in *Carl Zeiss Stiftung*[17]:

> The concept of "want of probity" appears to provide a useful touchstone...it is true that not every situation where probity is lacking gives rise to a constructive trust. Nevertheless, the authorities appear to show that nothing short of it will do. Not even gross negligence will suffice.

In the *Lipkin Gorman* case at first instance Alliott J. adopted the Megarry reasoning, citing the passage quoted above, and

---

[14] *Belmont Finance Corpn.* v. *Williams Furniture* [1979] Ch. 250; *Belmont Finance Corpn.* v. *Williams Furniture (No. 2)* [1980] 1 All E.R. 393.
[15] [1983] B.C.L.C. 325.
[16] (1985) 84 L.S.Gaz. 1057.
[17] *Supra.*

finding that there had been a want of probity in the manager's conduct. In the Court of Appeal, in view of the Court's acceptance of the submission that there was no case to answer on the allegation that the manager knew of Cass's fraudulent intent, the hearing turned mainly on breach of contract. But May L.J. in a short summary of the relevant cases, on contractual liability, referred to *Selangor* and *Karak* as stating the common law duty of care of the paying banker too highly, their principal error being in his opinion equating the duty to enquire where there has been fraud and the bank is proved to have known of it, and where all that is being alleged is that the bank has been negligent.

It seems unlikely that the full rigour of *Selangor* will be repeated in future decisions; it is perhaps odd that its shadow has hung over the area for so long in view of the repeated refusal of the Court of Appeal to follow it. If "want of probity" becomes recognised as the significant test, the discussion in these notes will be largely of historic interest.

But constructive trusteeship has problems still for bankers and others involved in dealing with other people's money.[17a] In *AGIP (Africa) Ltd.* v. *Jackson and Others*[17b] the defendants, a firm of accountants in the Isle of Man, were participants in an elaborate money-laundering operation and were held liable as constructive trustees who had given knowing assistance to the fraud. Want of probity was a key factor in Millett J.'s, judgment: they made no inquiries because they thought it was none of their business, which was not "honest behaviour." And he added that "those who provide the services of nominee companies for the purpose of enabling their clients to keep their activities secret" should realise that this could make them liable as constructive trustees.

London Joint Stock Bank Ltd. v. Macmillan & Arthur

[1918] A.C. 777

 In drawing a cheque, the customer owes a duty to the bank to take reasonable precautions against possible alteration of the cheque

Facts

The respondents, customers of the London Joint Stock Bank,

[17a] The Jack Report has recommended that the Law Commission should examine the subject.
[17b] *The Times*, June 5, 1989.

entrusted to their confidential clerk the duty of filling in cheques for signature. The clerk presented a cheque to one of the partners for his signature, drawn in favour of the firm or bearer; there was no sum written in words, and in the space for the figures were the figures "2.0.0." The partner signed the cheque, and the clerk thereafter inserted the figures "1" and "0" respectively before and after the figure "2," and added the words "one hundred and twenty pounds." He presented the cheque at the bank and received £120 in cash, the bank debiting the plaintiffs' account with that sum.

The firm contended that the bank could debit their account with £2 only, and brought this action for a declaration to that effect. The bank alleged that the firm had been negligent in drawing and signing the cheque.

Decision

The House of Lords held that the relationship of banker and customer imposed a special duty on the customer, in drawing a cheque, to take reasonable and ordinary precautions against forgery, and that the alteration in this case was the direct result of a breach of that duty by the firm, whose account the bank was therefore entitled to debit with the full amount of £120 paid by them on the cheque.

In his judgment, Lord Finlay L.C. said:

A cheque drawn by a customer is in point of law a mandate to the banker to pay the amount according to the tenor of the cheque. It is beyond dispute that the customer is bound to exercise reasonable care in drawing the cheque to prevent the banker being misled. If he draws the cheque in a manner which facilitates fraud, he is guilty of a breach of duty as between himself and the banker, and he will be responsible to the banker for any loss sustained by the banker as a natural and direct consequence of this breach of duty.... As the customer and the banker are under a contractual relation in this matter, it appears obvious that in drawing a cheque the customer is bound to take usual and reasonable precautions to prevent forgery.... If the cheque is drawn in such a way as to facilitate or almost to invite an increase in the amount of forgery if the cheque should get into the hands of a dishonest person, forgery is not a remote but a very natural consequence of negligence of this description.[18]

Notes

This decision and that in *Greenwood* v. *Martins Bank Ltd.*[19]

[18] At pp. 789–790.
[19] *Post*, p. 90.

were cited in the *Tai Hing Cotton Mill* case[20] as establishing the limits of the customer's duty in the operation of a current account, Lord Scarman stating that "no duty wider than that recognised in *Macmillan* and *Greenwood* can be implied into the banking contract in the absence of express terms to that effect."

The case itself is one of the most important ever decided upon the law relating to cheques, because it makes clear for the first time the dual function of the cheque. The cheque is primarily an instrument of authority or a mandate from customer to banker used for the purpose of obtaining repayment of the customer's moneys held by the banker. Since it was at a very early stage convenient for the customer not only to be able to obtain the money, or part of it, himself, but also to have it, or part of it, paid to some third party or third party's order, it became customary to draw the mandate in the form of a bill of exchange, or, as this particular form of bill came to be called, a cheque.

The function of the cheque as a mandate was recognised as early as 1827 in *Young* v. *Grote*,[21] where the plaintiff, on going away on business, left with his wife for the purpose of his business five blank cheques signed by himself. The wife required £50 2s. 3d. to pay wages, and got one of the clerks to fill in one of the cheques for that amount. He did so, but in such a way as to allow him to make subsequent additions, and after showing it to the wife, who told him to cash it, he increased the amount to £350 2s. 3d. The defendant banker cashed the cheque, and it was held that the loss must fall on the plaintiff.

In spite of the fact that *Young* v. *Grote* was plainly founded on the mandate principle,[22] the cheque's form as a bill of exchange tended for long to obscure its mandate aspect, which becomes of such great importance when any question arises, as it did in the *Macmillan* case, as to the customer's obligation to take care of his banker's interests when making out the mandate.

---

[20] *Post*, p. 93.

[21] (1827) 4 Bing. 253. *cf. post*, p. 92.

[22] The decision in *Young* v. *Grote* was based on principles earlier enunciated by Pothier. In *Scholefield* v. *Earl of Londesborough, infra*, Watson L.J. cited Pothier as discussing "the nature of the contract which is constituted between the drawer and the acceptor of a bill, which he asserts to be *un vrai contrat de mandat, mandatum solvendae pecuniae.*" In the *Macmillan* case itself Lord Finlay said: "Pothier treats the question [of the right of the drawee to be recouped by the drawer when by reason of a fraudulent alteration in the draft he has been led to pay more than the sum really drawn for] as one of the law of mandate."

It must be here remarked that there is some difference as to the effect of the *Macmillan* decision. It clearly established (as indeed *Young* v. *Grote* had established earlier) that a customer drawing an incomplete cheque and leaving the completion of it to his agent cannot object to his banker's debiting him with the fraudulently raised amount of it. It is generally considered, however, that the decision went further than this, and set up a wider duty of care in the drawer, so that even when he completes the cheque he must not leave spaces facilitating fraudulent raising.[23] Indeed, Lord Shaw in his judgment went still further, and suggested that the customer is liable for the condition of the cheque until it is presented, and might therefore even be responsible for an erasure and substitution: in the words of the headnote to the case, "in the case of a customer's cheque, admittedly genuine, no responsibility rests upon the banker for what has happened to the cheque before its presentation to the bank, but the responsibility for what has happened to it between the dates of signature and presentation rests upon the customer."

However, in *Slingsby* v. *District Bank Ltd.*,[24] the banker was denied any such complete immunity as was contemplated in Lord Shaw's opinion and in the headnote just quoted. In this case the cheque was payable to John Prust & Co., with a blank between those words and "or order," the fraudulent solicitor adding the words "per Cumberbirch and Potts" in the blank so left. It was held that such an alteration was a form of fraud that could not reasonably be anticipated by the customer, and that therefore the customer could not be held to have been negligent in leaving the blank space in the cheque. This decision has been criticised, but it is to be noted that some banks, at least, give printed warnings in their cheque books of the danger of gaps in the words and figures of the amount, but say nothing of the danger of blanks in the designation of the payee.

It may be said that there is apparent, since the establishment of the customer's duty to take care in drawing the cheque, a tendency to establish duties of a general character in relation to the handling of the account; see, for example, the *Greenwood* case,[25] *Westminster Bank Ltd.* v. *Hilton*[26] and the *Orbit* case.[27] It is possible that

---

[23] cf. *Lumsden & Co.* v. *London Trustee Savings Bank, post,* p. 174.
[24] [1932] 1 K.B. 544; *ante,* p. 63, for facts and decisions on other points involved.
[25] *Post,* p. 90.
[26] *Post,* p. 128. But in *Place & Sons Ltd.* v. *Turner, The Times,* February 7, 1951, it was held *inter alia* by Devlin J. that the drawer of a cheque owes no duty to the drawee or to the general public to avoid such carelessness in his business (including the drawing of cheques) as may injure another financially.
[27] *Ante,* p. 41.

another case on the lines of *Slingsby* v. *District Bank* would now be decided differently.[28]

The distinction between the liability of the drawer of a cheque and that of the acceptor of a bill of exchange is seen in comparing the *Macmillan* decision with that in *Scholefield* v. *Earl of Londesborough*.[29] In this last case, the defendant accepted a bill drawn upon him for £500, but which was stamped £2—sufficient to cover a bill for £4,000. After acceptance the drawer fraudulently increased the amount of the bill to £3,500, inserting the figure "3" and the words "three thousand" in appropriate spaces which he had left in the bill when he drew it. He then indorsed the bill to a third party, who negotiated it to the plaintiff, who took it in good faith and for value. The plaintiff sued the defendant for the amount of the bill as altered. The defendant paid £500 into Court, the amount of the bill as accepted by him, and denied any further liability. The plaintiff contended (*inter alia*) that the defendant was negligent in accepting the bill in that form, and with a £2 stamp upon it.

On appeal the House of Lords decided that the acceptor of a bill of exchange was not under any duty to take precautions against a subsequent alteration of the bill, and that the defendant had not been negligent, Lord Watson saying:

> The duty which the appellant's argument assigns to an acceptor is towards the public, or what is much the same thing towards those members of the public who may happen to acquire right to the bill, after it has been criminally tampered with. Apart from authority, I do not think the imposition of such a duty can be justified on any sound legal principle. In many if not most cases which occur in the course of business, the bill is written out by the drawer, and sent by him to the acceptor, who is under an obligation to sign it. Assuming the appellant's argument to be well founded, it would be within the right of the acceptor to return the bill unsigned, if it were not drawn so as to exclude all reasonable possibilities of fraud or forgery. The exercise of that right might lead to very serious complications in commercial transactions.... I am therefore unwilling in the case of an acceptor to affirm the doctrine, upon which the appellant relies, unless it can be shown to be established by authority as part of the English law merchant.... The result of the English authorities is, in my opinion, decidedly adverse to the appellant.[30]

---

[28] *cf.* Penn, Shea & Arora, *op. cit.* I 7.18, where it is submitted that a customer "is not in breach of his duty if he gives a cheque so drawn to an apparently worthy and trustworthy solicitor."

[29] [1896] A.C. 514.

[30] At pp. 537–542.

The contrast between cheque and bill in this connection may be otherwise expressed: between a banker and his customer there is a contractual relationship under which the discharge of the banker's primary obligation is effected by means of the mandate, in the drawing up of which the customer can reasonably be expected to take care. But between the acceptor of a bill and the payee or holder of the instrument there is no such relationship, under which it would be proper to hold the acceptor responsible for the drawing of the instrument.

Greenwood v. Martins Bank Ltd.

[1933] A.C. 51

The customer also has a duty to inform the bank if he knows that a cheque on his account has been forged

Facts

The plaintiff had an account with the defendant bank. His wife kept the pass book and cheque book, and gave him cheques as he required them. In October, 1929, he asked her for a cheque, saying that he wished to draw £20. She thereupon told him that there was no money in the bank, as she had drawn it all out to help her sister in legal proceedings in which she was involved. The wife had in fact forged her husband's name on cheques over a period. Upon the urgent request of the wife, the husband refrained from notifying the bank of the frauds.

Eight months later he discovered that the explanation his wife had given him, regarding her sister's legal proceedings, was false, and he then told her that he would notify the bank, whereupon she committed suicide. The plaintiff afterwards brought an action against the defendants for the amount paid by them on the forged signatures.

Decision

The House of Lords held that the plaintiff owed a duty of disclosure to the bank on his first discovery of the fraud, and that as his conduct had, in the event, deprived them of their right of action against the forger he was estopped from asserting the forgery.

In his judgment Lord Tomlin, after summarising the essentials of estoppel—a representation, an act or omission resulting from that representation by the person to whom it was made, and detriment suffered by him as a result—went on to say:

The deliberate abstention from speaking in those circumstances seems to me to amount to a representation to the respondents that the forged cheques were in fact in order, and assuming that detriment to the respondents followed there were, it seems to me, present all elements essential to estoppel.[31]

In the Court of Appeal,[32] Scrutton L.J. had said:

[There is] a continuing duty on either side to act with reasonable care to ensure the proper working of the account. It seems to me that the banker, if a cheque were presented to him which he rejected as forged, would be under a duty to report this to the customer to enable him to inquire into and protect himself against the circumstances of the forgery. This, I think would involve a corresponding duty on the customer, if he became aware that forged cheques were being presented to his banker, to inform his banker in order that the banker might avoid loss in the future. If this is correct there was in the present case silence, a breach of duty to disclose.[33]

Notes

This is the second of the two decisions cited in the *Tai Hing Cotton Mill* case as establishing the limits of the customer's duty in the operation of a current account.[34]

In the circumstances of the case the bank argued successfully that in view of the customer's failure to inform the bank of his wife's forgery of his cheques he was estopped from claiming that the bank was liable for paying the forged cheques.[35]

It may be remarked that *Greenwood's* case arose before the passing of the Law Reform (Married Women and Tortfeasors) Act 1935. As husbands were then still liable for their wives' torts, Greenwood would himself have been liable had the bank been able to bring an action against the wife. However, the fact that this "circular" effect would not arise today does not affect the important general principle of the decision.

Estoppel cannot normally be set up as a defence by the person whose negligence was the cause of the loss, and in the *Greenwood* case the trial judge found against the bank on the grounds that they had been negligent in not detecting the forgeries. The Court of Appeal and the House of Lords, how-

---

[31] At p. 58.
[32] [1932] 1 K.B. 371.
[33] At p. 381.
[34] See *ante*, p. 86.
[35] *cf.* Dictum of Kerr J. in *National Westminster Bank Ltd.* v. *Barclays Bank International Ltd.*, *post*, p. 137.

ever, considered that, while the bank's negligence was the proximate cause of their loss in paying the forged cheques, it was not the proximate cause of the loss of their right of action against the forger.

The facts were different, but no less favourable to the bank, in *Brown* v. *Westminster Bank Ltd.*[36] Here the bank had several times, through two successive managers of the branch concerned, drawn the attention of their customer, an old lady, to the number of cheques passing through her account payable to her servant, Carless. On the first such occasion she said that she was in the habit of asking Carless to cash cheques for her at the British Legion Club; and on other occasions she did not deny drawing the cheques. Eventually the second manager discussed the matter with the customer's son, who held her power of attorney; and in due course the present action was brought against the bank in respect of 329 cheques alleged to have been forged. Roskill J. held that the plaintiff was estopped from setting up the forgeries against the bank; even those that occurred before the bank first queried the cheques had been represented as genuine by the customer's statement to the manager, so that she was thereafter debarred from setting up the true facts.

The *Greenwood* and *Brown* cases may be compared with two older cases, where the bank failed in their defences based on their customers' negligence. In *Lewes Sanitary Steam Laundry Co. Ltd.* v. *Barclay & Co. Ltd.*,[37] the secretary of the company forged a large number of cheques on the company's account. The company sued the bank for the money paid out on the forgeries, and the bank alleged that the company had been negligent both in a system that did not provide for adequate scrutiny of the company's books and in their appointment as secretary of a person whom they knew to have been previously guilty of forgery. This defence failed, Kennedy J. remarking that "negligence to make an estoppel must be in, or immediately connected with, the transaction itself which is complained of."[38] And in *Kepitigalla Rubber Estates Ltd.* v. *National*

---

[36] [1964] 2 Lloyd's Rep. 187.

[37] (1906) 11 Com.Cas. 255.

[38] At p. 267. *cf.* Lord Finlay, in *London Joint Stock Bank Ltd.* v. *Macmillan and Arthur* (*ante*, p. 85): "Of course the negligence must be in the transaction itself, that is, in the manner in which the cheque is drawn. It would be no defence to the banker, if the forgery had been that of a clerk of the customer, that the latter had taken the clerk into his service without sufficient inquiry as to his character. Attempts have often been made to extend the principle of *Young* v. *Grote* [*ante*, p. 87] beyond the case of negligence in the immediate transaction, but they have always failed" (at p. 795). *cf.* also Scrutton L.J., quoted *post*, p. 171.

It is interesting to compare the courts' insistence on this point with the gradual extension of the scope of the banker's duty in the collection cases to circumstances far removed from the immediate transaction; *cf. post*, pp. 156 *et seq.*

Bank of India Ltd.,[39] where the secretary of a company over a period of two months drew cheques by forging the signatures of the directors, it appeared that during this period the directors had not examined the pass book or the company's cash book; but it was held that the plaintiffs were under no duty so to organise their business that forgery of cheques could not take place.

These two cases were decided before the *Macmillan* case had brought out the duty of care that the customer owes to his banker. But the facts in the *Macmillan* case, and in the *Greenwood* and *Brown* cases, were more favourable to the bank than those in the two earlier cases, and the courts so far have not extended the customer's duty of care to take in negligence less directly concerned with the transaction. It may be noted that McNair J. in *Brewer* v. *Westminster Bank Ltd.*,[40] expressly rejected the argument that *Greenwood's* case had weakened the *Kepitigalla* decision: "In my judgment," he said, "there is no inconsistency between the two decisions."

In *London Intercontinental Trust Ltd.* v. *Barclays Bank Ltd.*[41] the company's mandate required cheques to be signed by two directors. The company was managed by another company, Mitton, Butler Priest & Co. Ltd., and in accordance with that company's practice, cheques were signed by only one director. When M.B.P. went into voluntary liquidation, London Intercontinental claimed repayment of two cheques, for £100,000 and £95,000, as having been wrongly debited with only one signature. But their claim failed. Slynn J. held that the company had approved, and later ratified, the transaction in respect of which the cheques had been issued; and although the company owed no duty to the bank to examine their pass sheets,[42] the fact that they had done so and failed to notify the bank of the breach of the mandate was a representation that the cheques were validly drawn.

Tai Hing Cotton Mill Ltd. v. Liu Chong Hing Bank Ltd. and Others

[1986] A.C. 80

The customer owes his banker no duty to examine his bank statements, or to take precautions in his business to prevent forged cheques being presented for payment

[39] [1909] 2 K.B. 1010.
[40] [1952] 2 All E.R. 650, at p. 656, *post*, pp. 199 *et seq*.
[41] [1980] 1 Lloyd's Rep. 241.
[42] *cf. Tai Hing Cotton Mill Ltd.* decision, *infra*.

Facts

The plaintiff company had employed an accounts clerk who over a period forged cheques on the company's accounts with its three banks to a total of $ H.K. 5.5 million. When the fraud was discovered and the company claimed repayment from the banks, the banks argued that the company had been negligent in failing to supervise the work of their clerk, and in not checking their monthly statements. The Hong Kong Court of Appeal accepted their argument and rejected the company's claim, Cons J.A. saying that:

> After a great deal of hesitation, I find myself finally led to the conclusion that, in the world in which we live today, it is a necessary condition of the relation of banker and customer that the customer should take reasonable care to see that in the operation of the account the bank is not injured.

The company appealed to the Privy Council.

Decision

In the absence of express agreement to the contrary, the duty of care owed by a customer to his bank in the operation of his current account is limited to a duty to refrain from drawing a cheque in such manner as to facilitate fraud or forgery and a duty to inform the bank of any unauthorised cheques purportedly drawn on the account as soon as he, the customer, becomes aware of it.

Lord Scarman outlined the two duties laid down in the *Macmillan* and the *Greenwood* decisions of the House of Lords, and rejected both the argument that a term could be implied in the contract that would meet the banks' contention, and the suggestion that liability might be found in tort. He said:

> The argument for the banks is, when analysed, no more than that the obligation of care placed on banks in the management of a customer's account which the courts have recognised have become with the development of banking business so burdensome that they should be met by a reciprocal increase of responsibility on the customer.... One can fully understand the comment of Cons J.A. that the banks must today look for protection. So be it. They can increase the severity of their terms of business, and they can use their influence, as they have in the past, to seek to persuade the legislature that they should be granted by statute further protection. But it does not follow that because they may need protection as their business expands the necessary incidents of their relationship with their customer must also

change. The business of banking is the business not of the customer but of the bank.[42a]

Notes

The rule now confirmed by the Privy Council is of long standing although, as Lord Scarman remarked in the present case, "leading writers on banking law, notably Sir John Paget, and many of the banking community have never extended it a very warm welcome." As early as 1891, in *Chatterton v. London & County Banking Co. Ltd.*[43] Lord Esher M.R. expressed the opinion that customers were not bound to examine their passbooks. In that case the plaintiff claimed that the bank was liable for paying a number of cheques which the customer alleged were forged. The jury found that the plaintiff, who had seen and checked his passbook and not questioned the payment of the cheques, had contributed to the loss, and judgment was given for the bank. On the plaintiff's appeal a new trial was ordered, and the Court of Appeal upheld the order; and at the trial the jury this time found for the plaintiff.

The rule has been applied often since then,[44] but it may be noted that there have been cases in which the courts have seemed reluctant to accept the full rigour of the principle. Buckley L.J.'s comment in the *Morison* case[45] saw failure to examine the passbook as an element in the "lulling to sleep" finding, as did Lord Reading C.J., in the same case when he said:

It is true that the plaintiff owed no duty to the defendants to examine his passbook or check his accounts with them . . . but, when we are asked to find as a fact that the defendants were negligent, it is necessary to consider all the circumstances . . .

In *Bank of England v. Vagliano Brothers*[46] Lord Halsbury said:

The false documents were paid, duly debited to the customer, and duly entered in his passbook, and so far as the banker could know or

---

[42a] At pp. 105–106.

[43] *The Miller*, February 2, 1891. The case is fully reported only in *The Miller*, but the second trial is reported in *The Times*, January 21, 1891.

[44] In, *e.g.* the *Kepitigalla Rubber* case, *ante*, p. 92, and *Walker* v. *Manchester and Liverpool District Banking Co. Ltd.* [1952] 2 All E.R. 650.

[45] *Ante*, p. 172.

[46] *Ante*, p. 45.

conjecture, brought to his knowledge on every occasion upon which the payment was made and the bills returned.... Was not the customer bound to know the contents of his own passbook?

And in the *London Intercontinental Trust* case[47] Slynn J. said that although the company owed no duty to the bank to examine their pass sheets, the fact that they did so and yet failed to notify the bank of the breach of the mandate was a representation that the cheques were validly drawn.

But in *Wealden Woodlands (Kent) Ltd.* v. *National Westminster Bank Ltd.*[48] where the bank had contended that English law should be brought into line with the United States authorities, and that failure to examine and draw inferences from bank statements was negligence on which to found estoppel, McNeill J. said that without Parliamentary intervention, no triable issue arose as to the reconciliation of English and American principles.

The decision of the Hong Kong Court of Appeal seemed temporarily to strengthen the case for a stricter view of the customer's duty of care than the English courts had so far adopted. Now, in the light of the Privy Council decision, it is unlikely that there will be any substantial change in judicial attitudes in the foreseeable future. As regards the two courses of action which Lord Scarman suggested were open to the banks, it seems improbable that they will attempt the "persuasion" of Parliament[49]; and while there are overseas precedents for including the duty to examine statements in the banker/customer contract, the English banks are traditionally reluctant to introduce such a contract.[49a]

All three banks in the *Tai Hing Cotton Mill* case had written contracts which they had presumably hoped would cover the point in issue, but all three were rejected as falling short of the "clear and unambiguous provision" which their Lordships considered necessary to impose on the customer the binding obligation which the banks sought.

---

[47] *Ante*, p. 93.
[48] (1983) 133 N.L.J. 719.
[49] It is interesting to compare the position in the United States, where the Uniform Commercial Code imposes on the customer a duty to examine his bank statements.
[49a] The Jack Report recommends that legislation should enable the banker to plead contributory negligence.

Holland v. Manchester and Liverpool District Banking Co.

(1909) 25 T.L.R. 386

Where the customer acts, in good faith, upon a wrong entry made in the statement or passbook, so altering his position, the banker is estopped from claiming to have the error adjusted

Facts

The plaintiff had an account with the defendant bank. On September 21, 1907, after examining his passbook, which showed a balance to his credit of £70 17s. 9d., the plaintiff issued a cheque for £67 11s., in payment of a trade debt to Reynolds & Co. On presentation this cheque was dishonoured, as the actual credit balance was only £60 5s 9d., a credit for £10 12s. having been entered twice in the passbook. Although the bank apologised to Reynolds, when the circumstances were disclosed, this firm refused the plaintiff any further credit and, the facts becoming known, other creditors also refused him credit. The plaintiff brought the present action for damages.

Decision

The jury assessed the damages at £100, subject to the court's decision as to whether the plaintiff was entitled to draw the cheque in such circumstances. The Lord Chief Justice held that, although the bank were entitled to have the wrong entry ultimately adjusted, the plaintiff, not having been negligent or fraudulent, was entitled, until the correction was made, to act upon the bank's statement in the passbook. Having so acted, and suffered damage thereby, he was entitled to recover the amount of the damage.

In the course of his judgment, Lord Alverstone C.J. said that the effect of a passbook entry did not seem to have been clearly decided in the courts, but he considered that, whilst the bank in this case were entitled to have any wrong entry ultimately corrected, until the correction was made the customer had the right to act upon the bank's statements in the passbook, and to receive them as statements by the bank that there was so much money to his credit. The passbook in all cases although subject to adjustment was prima facie evidence against the bank of the amount standing to the credit of a customer, upon which that customer, in the absence of negligence or fraud on his part, was entitled to rely.

Notes

In *Skyring* v. *Greenwood & Cox*[50] the plaintiff was the

---

[50] (1825) 4 B. & C. 281.

administratrix of Major Skyring R.A. and the defendants were paymasters of the Royal Artillery. In error over a period of years the defendants had credited Major Skyring with pay in excess of the sums authorised. Early in 1821 a statement of running account between the parties was rendered, including pay not authorised. A few months later the defendants wrote claiming repayment of the excess. Major Skyring died in December, 1822, and the defendants rendered a statement to the plaintiff, carrying forward the balance from the previous statement, but showing the excess pay as a debit against that balance. Abbot C.J. in giving judgment for the plaintiff, said:

> It is of great importance to any man, and certainly not less to military men than others, that they should not be led to suppose their annual income is greater than it really is. Every prudent man accommodates his mode of living to what he supposes to be his income; it therefore works a great prejudice to any man, if after having had credit given to him in account for certain sums, and having been allowed to draw on his agent on the faith that those sums belonged to him, he may be called upon to pay them back.[51]

It will be noted, however, that in the *Holland* case Lord Alverstone considered that the bank had the right to call ultimately for adjustment of their mistake. Clearly, as had been established as long ago as 1860, in *Commercial Bank of Scotland* v. *Rhind*,[52] a credit entry to the customer's account is no more than prima facie evidence against the bank, which the banker can show to have been erroneous. But it is unlikely that Lord Alverstone intended to suggest (the point was not directly in issue in the *Holland* case) that the bank has any absolute right to adjust the error, irrespective of the customer's bona fide actions upon the strength of it.[53]

Some difficulty has been found in deciding whether or not the mere spending of the money wrongly credited can be such detriment to the customer as will estop the payer from reclaiming it. In *Holt* v. *Markham*,[54] where estoppel was one of the grounds of the decision against the bank, Scrutton L.J. said:

> I think this is a simple case of estoppel. The plaintiffs represented to the defendant that he was entitled to a certain sum of money and paid

---

[51] At p. 289.
[52] (1860) 3 Mac. 643 (H.L.).
[53] The point is also discussed *ante*, at pp. 138 *et seq.*
[54] *Post*, pp. 100 and 141.

it, and after a lapse of time sufficient to enable any mistake to be rectified he acted upon that representation and spent the money. That is a case to which the ordinary rule of estoppel applies.[55]

In *Lloyds Bank Ltd.* v. *Brooks*,[56] a case heard at Manchester Assizes on a question of amounts wrongly credited, counsel for the bank contended strongly that as the defendant had merely used the money for her own purposes the bank could not be estopped merely because she would not have so spent it had she not been misled. In his judgment in favour of the defendant, Lynskey J. reviewed the authorities, and quoted the judgment of Denning L.J. in *Larner* v. *L.C.C.*,[57] in which he said:

> This defence of estoppel, as it is called—or more accurately, change of circumstances—must, however, not be extended beyond its proper bounds. Speaking generally, the fact that the recipient has spent the money beyond recall is no defence unless there was some fault—as, for instance, breach of duty—on the part of the paymaster and none on the part of the recipient.[58]

Lynskey J. distinguished the cases upon which counsel for the bank had based his argument, on the grounds that in them the overpayment had been made by persons owing no duty to the persons paid; the bank, however, owed a duty not to over-credit their customer, and so induce her by their representation to draw more than she was entitled to.

In earlier editions of this book it was suggested that it would be difficult for a commercial customer to prove that he had acted on a wrong credit, especially if it was for a substantial amount. An attempt to do so in *United Overseas Bank* v. *Jiwani*,[59] exemplifies the difficulty created by the conditions that must be satisfied. Here the defendant, a resident in Uganda, had opened an account with the plaintiffs, a Swiss bank in Geneva, in order to build up assets outside Uganda. His balance in October 1972 was $10,000, when the bank received a telex message from Zurich that $11,000 had been paid to his credit. He was in process of buying a hotel, and in this connection he issued his cheque for $20,000. When the bank received written confirmation of the telex they mistakenly treated it as a second credit, credited the defendant's account and so advised him. He

[55] At p. 514.
[56] (1950) 72 J.I.B. 114.
[57] [1949] 2 K.B. 683.
[58] At p. 688.
[59] [1976] 1 W.L.R. 964.

issued a further cheque for $11,000 towards the hotel purchase; and when the bank discovered their mistake they sought to recover the resulting overdraft.

Mackenna J. in a judgment which bankers must welcome outlined the three conditions which the defendant must satisfy before he could resist payment: (a) that the bank had misrepresented the state of his account; (b) that he had been misled by the misrepresentation; and (c) that as a result "he changed his position in a way which would make it inequitable to require him to repay the money." The first condition was clearly satisfied; on the second the defendant's evidence was not accepted. But, more importantly for bankers generally, even if that evidence had been accepted, the third condition was held not to have been met. Had the mistake not been made the defendant would still have continued with his purchase (which "was in itself a benefit, and a continuing benefit, unlike the investment in *Holt's* case"), finding the money elsewhere, as he would on the evidence have been able to do. By the same token, he was now able to repay the money to the bank.[60]

The second of Mackenna J.'s conditions is important: the customer's good faith is essential to his claim. In *British and North European Bank Ltd.* v. *Zalstein*[61] the bank had credited the defendant with £2,000 in order to conceal his excess borrowing from the bank's auditors, and later debited the account with the same amount, neither entry being known to the defendant until he received his passbook. When the defendant was later sued for recovery of the overdraft on his account he claimed that the credit formed a payment to him, the bank having no right to make the later debit. Sankey J. rejected the claim: the credit and debit were book entries only, and "to treat a mere book entry as a payment some other circumstance must be present... either some express previous authority to pay, or some communication of the making of the entry to the customer and some acting on it by him."

It may be noted, however, that in normal circumstances of mistake as opposed to the unusual circumstances of the *Zalstein* case, it may well be difficult to prove that the customer knew the entry to be wrong, as indeed is indicated in the previous cases here noted.

---

[60] cf. *National Westminster Bank Ltd.* v. *Barclays Bank International Ltd.*, *post*, p. 136 for an example of detriment to the customer unsuccessfully pleaded in the context of money paid under a mistake of fact.
[61] [1927] 2 K.B. 92.

Tassell v. Cooper
(1850) 9 C.B. 509

Gray v. Johnston
(1868) L.R. 3 H.L. 1

The banker has a primary duty to honour his customer's mandates, and third party claims to the funds on the account must be established by legal process

Facts of Tassell v. Cooper

The plaintiff was an agent of Lord de l'Isle, and there passed through his account with the London and County Joint Stock Banking Co. (of which Cooper was the public officer) moneys of Lord de l'Isle as well as the private business of the plaintiff. Being dissatisfied with Tassell's work, Lord de l'Isle gave him instructions to stop acting for him, which Tassell observed, with the exception that a cheque received from a client for £180 4s. 8d. was paid into the account and collected.

Lord de l'Isle later visited the bank and asked to see Tassell's account. The manager refused to show it to him without head office sanction, so Lord de l'Isle wrote to head office and obtained permission. Having inspected the account he gave the manager a letter to the effect that all the money now standing to Tassell's credit, £128 1s. 10d., was his, and indemnifying the bank against any claim to it by Tassell. On the strength of this letter the bank dishonoured two cheques, and Tassell now brought an action against the bank (*a*) for the full balance of the account; (*b*) for dishonouring the cheques wrongfully; and (*c*) for exposing the account to a third party.

Decision

In giving judgment for the plaintiff on all three counts, Maule J. said:

...It seems to me that the banking company, having received the money on behalf of the plaintiff, and given him credit for it, became debtors to him for the amount; and that the circumstance that the receipt of the cheque by the plaintiff might have been blameable does not afford any answer to this action. The transaction was regular and lawful so far as the plaintiff and the bankers were concerned; it was a simple transaction of loan.[62]

---

[62] At p. 534.

Facts of Gray v. Johnston

The appellants were bankers of Dublin, and the respondent the son of one Thomas Johnston, a customer of theirs. The father by his will left a life interest in the whole of his property to his wife, with power of appointment amongst his children and grandchildren. At the time of his death, his business account was overdrawn against the security of his life policies; and in order to realise the policies, the bankers had first the will and later the probate from the widow, who was also the executrix. Upon receipt of the policy moneys, the overdraft was paid off and a balance of £853 17s. 5d. left to the credit of the account. This sum was then drawn off by a cheque signed by the widow in her capacity as executrix, and payable to Johnston and Mayston, in which name she was carrying on the business with her son-in-law. The cheque was then paid into the new account in this firm's name which had previously been opened with the Grays, and which at the time of the payment was overdrawn, although no complaint had been made by the bankers about the overdraft.

Johnston's son, the respondent here, brought the present action seeking a declaration that the money so transferred belonged to the estate of the deceased, and alleging that the transfer was a breach of trust by the widow, and that the bankers had known of and participated in the breach. The respondent bank denied all knowledge of the breach, and also contended that there was no custom amongst bankers of taking notice of trusts; that on the contrary they were bound to honour their customers' cheques, and not bound to inquire into the application of moneys so drawn.

Upon the Court of Chancery in Ireland deciding in favour of the plaintiff, the bank appealed.

Decision

The appeal was allowed. In the course of his judgment, Lord Cairns L.C. said:

In order to hold a banker justified in refusing to pay a demand of his customer, the customer being an executor, and drawing a cheque as an executor, there must, in the first place, be some misapplication, some breach of trust, intended by the executor, and there must in the second place . . . be proof that the bankers are privy to the intent to make this misapplication of the trust funds. And to that I think I may safely add, that if it be shown that any personal benefit to the bankers themselves is designed or stipulated for, that circumstance, above all others, will most readily establish that the bankers are in privity with the breach of trust which is about to be committed.

Applying these principles to the facts of the present case, the Lord Chancellor held that the respondent bankers had not been shown to be privy to the breach of trust, and that the benefit they had received in the reduction of the overdraft on the new firm account was incidental merely, and was not "designed or stipulated for."

Notes

It is unlikely that the circumstances of *Tassell* v. *Cooper* would be repeated today, but it provides a useful example of the banker's first duty, to honour the customer's cheques. *Gray* v. *Johnston*, is more typical of the kind of third party claim that occurs most frequently, based on the allegation that funds on an account are subject to a trust, and in the following pages it will be seen that they can raise problems of some difficulty.

It is often not clear whether or not an account is to be regarded as a trust account; a trust can be created without the use of any such words as "trust" or "confidence." The main difficulty in reconciling the decisions on third party claims is the question of what exactly is required to fix the banker with notice of the breach of trust which is taking place: the courts have recognised that it is not easy for the banker to decide whether in any particular case his duty to pay the customer's cheque is overridden by his duty to the *cestui que trust*; but it cannot be said that they have given very exact guidance as to what his decision should be.[62a]

Gray v. *Johnston* is the leading authority for what may be regarded as the moderate view of the banker's liability when trust funds are mishandled. In *Coleman* v. *Bucks and Oxon Union Bank*[63] Byrne J. took a similar view. There, a sum of money was paid to the defendant bank by a firm of solicitors for the credit of "James Gurney Trust." Gurney, who was a prosperous auctioneer and estate agent, was the sole trustee of the will of one Bovingdon, but he had no separate trust account with the bank, who placed the credit to Gurney's only account with them. This account was overdrawn by an amount in excess

---

[62a] *cf.*, *e.g. Neste Oy* v. *Lloyds Bank Ltd.*, *post*, p. 238 and *Barclays Bank Ltd.* v. *Quistclose Investments Ltd.*, *post*, p. 237; and see *Carreras Rothmans Ltd.* v. *Freemans Mathews Treasure Ltd.* [1985] Ch. 207.

[63] [1897] 2 Ch. 243.

of the credit. Three years later Gurney was adjudicated bankrupt, and new trustees of Bovingdon's will were appointed. The action was to recover the amount of the credit, the plaintiffs contending that the bank had notice of the existence of a trust, but despite this had taken the benefit of the moneys in reduction of the overdraft on Gurney's account.

Byrne J. did not accept the argument:

> If bankers have the slightest knowledge or reasonable suspicion that the money is being applied in breach of a trust, and if they are going to derive a benefit from the transfer and intend and design that they should derive a benefit from it, then I think the bankers would not be entitled to honour the cheque drawn upon the trust account without some further inquiry into the matter. But the present case is not that case at all, and... notwithstanding certain considerations which suggested themselves to me, as, for instance, if this money had first been carried to a trust account it may be that the trustee would not so readily have committed the breach of trust... and notwithstanding the fact that in point of law the money must be regarded as having been applied at the moment in reduction of the overdraft, I do not think that I can hold these defendants liable to make good this amount.[64]

In *John Shaw (Rayners Lane) Ltd.* v. *Lloyds Bank Ltd.*[65] an action was brought against the bank by the liquidator of a limited company for the recovery of moneys paid out on the signature of a person purporting to be the receiver of the company. In fact he was not the receiver, and there was even doubt as to whether there had ever been a debenture under which he could have been so appointed; but the only account with the bank had been in his name as receiver and there was nothing in the actual transactions or the account to put the bank on suspicion. On the point here under discussion Hallett J. said:

> [Counsel for the defendants] then says that... I should apply to this case the principle laid down in such cases as *Gray* v. *Johnston*,[66] *Coleman* v. *Bucks*,[67] *Bank of New South Wales* v. *Goulburn*[68]; in other words, that I should hold that the bank were not liable for allowing [the receiver] to draw from the account by means of cheques signed by him although they knew that it was an account which he had in a fiduciary capacity, unless it can be shown that the bank were privy to

---

[64] At pp. 253–254.
[65] (1944) 5 L.D.B. 396.
[66] *Supra*.
[67] *Supra*.
[68] [1902] A.C. 543.

the breach of trust on the part of [the receiver]. [Counsel] contends that such a case as *Bodenham* v. *Hoskins*[69] is clearly distinguishable, because there the decision depended upon the finding that the bank was in fact privy to the breach of trust. Taking the view that [he] is right upon this point, the question which I then have to decide is whether the bank was in fact... privy to the undoubted fraud...;

and in fact the learned judge found that it was not.

Comparison may also be made with *London Joint Stock Bank Ltd.* v. *Simmons.*[70]

It is to be noted that there is no presumption of a trust merely from the profession of the customer. Thus in *Thomson* v. *Clydesdale Bank Ltd.*[71] where the bank's customer was a stockbroker who absconded with the plaintiff's funds, the House of Lords held that knowledge of his profession imposed no duty of inquiry on the bank. Lord Herschell said:

It seems to me that if, because an account is opened with bankers by a stockbroker, they are bound to enquire into the source from which he receives any money which he pays in, it would be wholly impossible that business could be carried on, and I know of no principle or authority which establishes such a proposition.

In *Marten* v. *Rocke, Eyton & Co.*[72] there was a finding to the same effect as to an auctioneer's account; and in *Teale* v. *William Williams Brown & Co.*,[73] where the bank set off a credit balance on a solicitor's office account against the overdrawn private account, the court held that the bank was not called upon to assume that the money on an office account was affected by a trust. Now the position as regards solicitors' clients' accounts is governed by the provision in successive Solicitors' Acts (the most recent, section 85 of the Act of 1974) which excludes any such right of set-off between the clients' account and any other account of the solicitor. This is of course an exception to the general law, and *Teale's* case, while no longer applicable to solicitor's accounts, remains a good example of that general law.

It is to be noted, moreover, that section 85 also provides that the banker has no liability in connection with a clients' account, such as, for example, a duty to inquire as to the ownership of

---

[69] (1852) 2 De G.M. & G. 903, *ante*, p. 80.
[70] *Post*, p. 280.
[71] [1893] A.C. 282.
[72] (1885) 53 L.T. 946.
[73] (1893) 11 T.L.R. 56.

money on the account, that he would not have on an ordinary banking account. Similar protection is not provided in more recent statutes requiring other professions to establish separate banking accounts for clients' money: the Employment Agencies Act, 1973, the Insurance Brokers (Registration) Act, 1977, the Estate Agents Act, 1979. Clearly the establishment of separate clients' accounts should imply the necessary protection for bankers in connection with other accounts, but it is important that the general principle should also be kept in mind.[74]

In re Halletts Estate, Knatchbull v. Hallett

(1879) 13 Ch. 696

Banque Belge Pour L'Étranger v. Hambrouck and Others

[1921] 1 K.B. 321

When moneys on a customer's account are claimed by a third party, they can be followed into the account, so long as they are still traceable

Facts of Re Hallett's Estate, Knatchbull v. Hallett

Hallett was a solicitor who had paid into his banking account and there mixed with his own money funds which he held in a fiduciary capacity, (*a*) in respect of the property settled by him in his marriage settlement; and (*b*) as bailee of the property belonging to a client. The trustees of the settlement and the client whose property had been misappropriated each claimed to be entitled to the money in the hands of the bankers in preference to the general creditors of the estate.

Decision

It was held by the Court of Appeal that when money on an account is held in a fiduciary capacity, even though the customer is not a trustee proper, the person for whom he holds the money can follow it.

Jessel M.R. said:

If the bailee sells the goods bailed, the bailor can in equity follow the

---

[74] Although the point is not normally of concern to bankers, it may be noted that moneys in a solicitor's clients' account may be subject to the solicitor's prior charge for his professional expenses, and an order restraining the use of a defendant's assets does not cover any such assets in his solicitor's clients' account: *Prekookeanska Plovidba* v. *L.N.T. Lines S.R.L.* [1988] 3 All E.R. 897.

proceeds, and can follow the proceeds wherever they can be distinguished, either being actually kept separate, or being mixed up with other moneys. I have only to advert to one other point, and that is this—supposing, instead of being invested in the purchase of land or goods, the moneys were simply mixed with other moneys of the trustee, using the term again in its full sense as including every person in a fiduciary relation, does it make any difference according to the modern doctrine of Equity? I say none. It would be very remarkable if it were to do so. Supposing the trust money was 1,000 sovereigns, and the trustee put them into a bag, and by mistake or accident or otherwise, dropped a sovereign of his own into the bag. Could anyone suppose that a Judge in Equity would find any difficulty in saying that the *cestui que trust* has a right to take 1,000 sovereigns out of that bag? I do not like to call it a charge of 1,000 sovereigns on the 1,000 sovereigns, but that is the effect of it. I have no doubt of it. It would make no difference if, instead of one sovereign, it was another 1,000 sovereigns; but if instead of putting it into his bag, or after putting it into his bag, he carries the bag to his bankers, what then? According to law, the bankers are his debtors for the total amount; but if you lend the trust money to a third person, you can follow it. If in the case supposed the trustee had lent the £1,000 to a man without security, you could follow the debt, and take it from the debtor. If he lent it on a promissory note, you could take the promissory note; or the bond, if it were a bond. If, instead of lending the whole amount in one sum simply, he added a sovereign, or had added £500 of his own to the £1,000, the only difference is this, that instead of taking the bond or promissory note, the *cestui que trust* would have a charge for the amount of the trust money on the bond or the promissory note.[75]

Facts of Banque Belge Pour L'Étranger v. Hambrouck and others

A M. Pelabon, a customer of the plaintiff bank, was the owner of an engineering works, and Hambrouck was an accountant in his employ. Hambrouck by fraud obtained crossed cheques to the value of £6,000 payable to himself and drawn, or purporting to be drawn, by M. Pelabon. He paid them into his account at Farrow's Bank, who collected them from the plaintiff bank. Hambrouck drew cheques on his account in favour of the second defendant, Mlle. Spanoghe, with whom he was living, and who paid them to the credit of her account with the London Joint City and Midland Bank. When Hambrouck's frauds were discovered there was an amount of £315 to the credit of Spanoghe's account, the whole amount being part of the proceeds of the cheques in question. No consideration had been

[75] At pp. 710–711.

given for the cheques, beyond the illegal consideration of continuing to cohabit with Hambrouck.

The plaintiff bank claimed to recover the balance of £315, and brought the present action against the male and female defendants, joining the London Joint City and Midland Bank as defendants. The defendant bank paid the money into Court and were dismissed from the action.

Decision

The Court of Appeal held that the money was recoverable by the plaintiffs.

In the course of his judgment, Atkin L.J. said:

The appellant [the second defendant] however contends that the plaintiffs cannot assert their title to the sum of money which was on a deposit account: 1. because it has passed through one if not two bank accounts and therefore cannot be identified as the plaintiff's money. . . . First, does it make any difference to the plaintiffs' rights that their money was paid into Farrow's Bank, and that the money representing it drawn out by Hambrouck was paid to the defendant bank on deposit? If the question be the right of the plaintiffs in equity to follow their property, I apprehend that no difficulty arises. The case of *In re Hallett's Estate*[76] makes it plain that the Court will investigate a banking account into which another person's money has been wrongfully paid, and will impute all drawings out of the account in the first instance to the wrongdoer's own moneys, leaving the plaintiff's money intact so far as it remains in the account at all. There can be no difficulty in this case in following every change of form of the money in question, whether in the hands of Hambrouck or of the appellant, and it appears to me that the plaintiffs were . . . entitled to a specific order for the return of the money in question, and, as it is now represented by the sum in Court, to payment out of Court of that sum.[77]

Notes

Hambrouck's case is noteworthy for the clear tracing through one account and into another. It must be remembered that the money would not have been recoverable had the female defendant given valuable consideration for the money, as well as receiving it in good faith. Moreover, even in the circumstances of the case, had she paid it away, even to Hambrouck, she could not have been made liable to refund it.[78]

---

[76] *Supra.*
[77] At pp. 332–333.
[78] *Transvaal and Delago Bay Investment Co. Ltd.* v. *Atkinson & Wife* [1944] 1 All E.R. 579.

It does not often happen that the balance on the account into which funds are "followed" is composed entirely of such funds, as it was in *Hambrouck's* case. Where there has been mixing with other money, the question must arise whether the money sought is still in the account, and here the rule in *Clayton's* case[79] is applied. An important exception to this application of the rule, however, was established in the *Hallett* case,[80] where it was held that one who misappropriates trust funds is presumed to draw out from his banking account first his own money and only afterwards that of the trust. On this point Jessel M.R. said in his judgment:

> Now, first upon principle, nothing can be better settled, either in our own law, or, I suppose, the law of all civilised countries, than this, that where a man does an act which may be rightfully performed, he cannot say that that act was intentionally and in fact done wrongly.... When we come to apply that principle to the case of a trustee who has blended trust money with his own, it seems to me perfectly plain that he cannot be heard to say that he took away the trust money when he had a right to take away his own money.... His money was there, and he had a right to draw it out, and why should the natural act of simply drawing out the money be attributed to anything except to his ownership of money which was at his bankers?[81]

When, however, the point is reached at which all moneys which could be withdrawn from the account without breach of trust have been allowed for, and there are still further drawings, which amount to breaches of trust, *Hallett's* case shows that the rule in *Clayton's* case must be applied to these should there be a conflict between one *cestui que trust* and another. The result is that the money first misappropriated is deemed to be withdrawn before the money misappropriated later. One *cestui que trust* may therefore find the whole of his money paid away while that of another, paid in later, is intact. This was the decision of Fry J. in the court of first instance; his judgment on the first point was overruled by the Court of Appeal in the decision dealt with above, and in view of that decision on the first point no appeal was necessary on the second.

In *Chase Manhattan Bank N.A.* v. *Israel-British Bank (London) Ltd.*[82] where the plaintiff bank mistakenly duplicated

---

[79] *Post*, p. 150.
[80] *Supra*.
[81] At pp. 727–728.
[82] [1979] 3 All E.R. 1025.

a payment of $2 million to Mellon Bank International for the credit of the defendants, who thereafter were compulsorily wound up, Goulding J. allowed the plaintiffs' claim to refund of the mistaken payment; he said that "the equitable remedy of tracing is in principle available, on the grounds of continuing proprietary interest, to a party who has paid money in mistake of fact"—and he rejected the argument that whatever the rights were before the winding-up, when the winding-up began all the defendants' property was at the disposal of the liquidator. The "proprietary interest" was "persistent" and the money paid did not belong to the defendants beneficially.[83]

It must always be remembered that the right to trace misappropriated money to a banking account does not necessarily involve the banker in loss if the money has already been disbursed.[84]

Rogers v. Whiteley

[1892] A.C. 118

Plunkett v. Barclays Bank Ltd.

[1936] 2 K.B. 107

The effect of a garnishee order

Facts of Rogers v. Whiteley

There was standing to the credit of Rogers' account with the banking department of Whiteley's a balance of more than £6,800. One Elizabeth Holloway, a judgment creditor of the appellants for £6,000, obtained a garnishee order nisi ordering that "all debts owing or accruing due" from Whiteley's to Rogers be attached. In consequence the bank dishonoured cheques drawn by Rogers on the balance between £6,000 and his credit balance. Rogers brought action against Whiteley's for damages for injury to credit by these dishonours. Pollock B. found that the bank was bound by the order. An application to set aside this judgment on the ground, *inter alia*, of misdirection was refused by the Divisional Court, that decision was affirmed

---

[83] See *post*, p. 138 *et seq. re* money paid in mistake of fact; and *cf. Bankers Trust Company* v. *Shapira & Others, ante*, p. 17.

[84] But *cf. Aluminium Industrie Vaasen BV* v. *Romalpa Aluminium Ltd., post*, p. 358, in which the principle of *Re Hallett's Estate* was applied in a matter disconcerting to bankers.

by the Court of Appeal, and the appellant appealed to the House of Lords.

Decision

The House of Lords dismissed the appeal, holding that the whole balance was attached by the order. In his judgment Lord Halsbury said:

> The order appears to me to have been in such terms that it would have been a disobedience to the order on [the banker's] part if he had paid anything after it had been served upon him.[85]

In his concurring judgment Lord Morris discussed the evils possibly resulting from this judgment: for example, that of a credit balance of £50,000 attached for a £5 or £10 debt. He submitted that it was in fact competent for a judge to make an order attaching only a limited sum, although the order in this case was not so worded.[86]

Facts of Plunkett v. Barclays Bank Ltd.

In 1935 the plaintiff, a solicitor, opened two accounts at the Kingsway branch of the bank, one being distinguished as a "Client Account,"[87] in compliance with the Solicitors Act 1933, and the Solicitors' Accounts Rules 1935.[88] On September 7, 1935, £48 5s. was paid in, in cash, to the credit of the Client Account, this sum representing rent and costs due to a third party. On September 6, a cheque for the same amount was sent to the solicitor acting for the third party to whom the money was due. On September 9, application was made for a garnishee order by the plaintiff's former wife, for costs in her successful divorce proceedings against him. The order was made in the usual form, and served on the defendant bank. On September 10, the chief clerk of the branch informed the plaintiff that the bank must regard both accounts as being attached by the order; and on September 11, the bank dishonoured the cheque for £48 5s. with the marking "Refer to drawer." This action was

---

[85] At p. 120.

[86] It is now possible to word the order in this restrictive manner, and where it is so worded the banker can, of course, pay away any surplus over the amount expressly attached. Even if the costs prove unexpectedly high, and the amount attached is in fact insufficient, the bank cannot be held liable for paying away the surplus. cf. the emphasis of the courts on the need for care in the drafting of *Mareva* orders (*post* p. 117).

[87] cf. ante, p. 105.

[88] Now the Solicitors Act 1974 and the Solicitors' Accounts Rules, 1975.

brought for alleged breach of contract by the dishonour and alleged libel in writing the words "Refer to Drawer."

Decision

The court held that the balance of the Client Account was attached by the order, and that in the circumstances "Refer to Drawer" was not libellous.[89]

In his judgment du Parcq J. after holding that the £48 5s. was, to the knowledge of the defendants, trust money, went on to say:

> I find it impossible to say that money paid into a Client Account kept with a bank in the name of a solicitor is not a debt owing from the banker to the solicitor. It cannot be denied that the relation of debtor and creditor subsists between the banker and the solicitor. The solicitor may at any time draw a cheque upon the account and the bank must honour it. As a general rule, the bank is not entitled to set up a supposed *jus tertii* against the customer: see, *per* Lord Westbury, *Gray* v. *Johnston*.[90] The service of the order nisi gives the judgment creditor, in the words of Farwell L.J. in *Galbraith* v. *Grimshaw and Baxter*,[91] an equitable charge on the debt, and I cannot think that it was ever intended that the garnishee should be compelled to adjudicate upon conflicting equities, even though the problem presented by the conflict might appear to the lawyer to be a simple one.[92]

Notes[93]

A garnishee order is an order of the court granted to a judgment creditor, which attaches funds held by a third party who owes money to the judgment debtor. It is initially an order *nisi*—it is provisional, and the third party has the opportunity to show reason why the funds should not be attached, for example, because he has some counter-claim which he is entitled to set off against his own debt. If he cannot do so the order is made absolute. A garnishee order may thus attach the judgment debtor's banking account, the balance on which is money owing by the bank to its customer. A customer whose account is thus attached should be informed of the receipt of the order. The

---

[89] *cf. post*, pp. 133 *et seq.*
[90] (1868) L.R. 3 H.L. 1, 14; *ante*, p. 102.
[91] [1910] 1 K.B. 399 at p. 343.
[92] At pp. 118–119.
[93] In the cases discussed in these notes it is important to distinguish between those in which a bank is directly concerned, and those in which the parties are judgment creditor and judgment debtor. The latter do not concern the bank, which has observed the terms of the order nisi and awaits the issue, normally having paid the money attached into court.

decision of the House of Lords in *Rogers* v. *Whiteley* established the basic principle that an unrestricted garnishee order completely immobilises the designated banking account. It is for the customer to apply to the court for any modification that he can justify. Thus in *Harrods Ltd.* v. *Tester*[94] the respondent had opened an account with the Westminster Bank in the name of his wife. All credits to the account had been paid by him, he had authority to draw on the account, and his wife drew cheques on it only with his permission. The appellants obtained a garnishee order nisi against her, but the husband contended that in fact all the moneys on the account were his own, and the Court of Appeal upheld his contention: although payments into an account in the name of another are prima facie gifts, this is merely a presumption which can be rebutted.[95]

The importance of the decision in *Plunkett's* case is that it clarified the banker's position when funds that he knows are trust funds are attached by a garnishee order: the fact that he knows there is a trust does not entitle him to ignore the order. The judgment does not, of course, imply that the bank has, for example, any right of set-off between clients' and ordinary accounts, nor does it affect the rights of the *cestui que trust*[96]; upon representation being made, the court will amend the order to exempt the trust funds, and du Parcq J. emphasised that it is the bank's duty in such a case to make the position known to the court, as well as advising the customer of the receipt of the order. (The learned judge also emphasised the propriety of restricting the order where a client account is involved, and suggested that applicants for orders might properly be warned that extra costs may be incurred in the attachment of a trust account.) It need hardly be said that the trouble involved for the banks in this procedure is slight in comparison with that which would have resulted from a contrary decision.

The varying circumstances in which a garnishee order can give rise to problems have been seen in a number of cases. The order must clearly designate the judgment debtor, and where the designation is incorrect the bank is entitled to ignore the

[94] [1937] 2 All E.R. 236.
[95] It is to be noted that the order nisi binds the bank pending any successful objection by the customer, *e.g.* in *Harrods* v. *Tester*, the account was immobilised until the Court of Appeal discharged the order.
[96] *cf. Hancock* v. *Smith* (1889) 41 Ch.D. 456, where an account in the name of a stockbroker consisted entirely of clients' money, and *Lancaster Motor Co. (London) Ltd.* v. *Bremith Ltd.* [1941] 1 K.B. 675, where the creditors unsuccessfully sought to attach the liquidator's account.

order. In *Koch* v. *Mineral Ore Syndicate*[97] the bank informed the solicitors of the judgment creditor that they had no account in the name given. The solicitors asked them to attach a different account, which they said was the judgment debtor's, and the bank refused. Later the order was amended, but the bank was not liable for having paid cheques on the account in the meantime.

In *Heppenstall* v. *Jackson, Barclays Bank Ltd., Garnishees,*[98] moneys paid into the credit of the judgment debtor after service of the order nisi were held not to be attached; an accruing debt does not include "anything which *may* be a debt, however probable or however soon it may be a debt."[99] It is clearly convenient that upon receipt of the order the bank should rule off the account and start a new one for subsequent transactions, but it does not seem that this is a legal duty.

Similarly, money which has gone from the account at the time of the service of the garnishee order will not be attached; but the passing of such money from the account must have been completed before the service of the order. In *Rekstin* v. *Severo Sibirsko, etc., and the Bank for Russian Trade*[1] the first respondents instructed the second, their bankers, to transfer the whole of their credit balance to the account of the Trade Delegation of the U.S.S.R., a body enjoying diplomatic immunity. This transfer was completed in the books of the bank, and the account closed; but a quarter of an hour later a garnishee order nisi was served on the bank purporting to attach the balance which had been transferred. The bank had not communicated the transfer to the Trade Delegation, nor did this body have any knowledge that it was contemplated. On the question whether the bank was in fact still indebted to the first respondents when they received the order, the Court of Appeal held that mere book entries without communication to the transferee were recoverable, and that a garnishee order nisi operates to revoke any such transfer.[2]

---

[97] (1910) 54 S.J. 600.
[98] [1939] 1 K.B. 585.
[99] *Per* Lord Blackburn in *Tapp* v. *Jones* (1875) L.R. 10 Q.B. 591.
[1] [1933] 1 K.B. 47.
[2] But *cf. Momm* v. *Barclays Bank International Ltd. post*, p. 148, where the bank was held not to be entitled to reverse entries on the morning after they had been made, even though the credit had not been communicated to the beneficiary. Kerr J. considered that *Rekstin* must be confined to its special facts, and in the *Royal Products* case, *post* p. 403, Webster J. agreed with this view.

In *Hirschorn* v. *Evans*[3] the account which it was sought to garnishee was a joint account of a husband and wife. The garnishee order was against the husband only, and the Court of Appeal held, by a majority, that, as the debt owed by the bank was to husband and wife jointly, it could not be attached for the husband's debt.[4] Mackinnon L.J. said:

It is true that there was an authority on the bank to honour cheques upon that joint account if the cheques were signed by one or other of them. That simply means "Either of us has authority on behalf of and as agent for both of us to sign cheques." It would amount to no more than an authorisation to the bank: "Upon this our joint account you are authorised to honour cheques drawn by our clerk or agent, John Smith." But such an authorisation would not make the bank the debtor of John Smith.[5]

In *Bower* v. *Foreign and Colonial Gas Co. Ltd.*, *Metropolitan Bank, Garnishees*,[6] a garnishee order being served upon the bank they sought to reserve £500 of the balance attached to meet two bills under discount but not yet due. It was held that they could not do this; the discount of the bills was in effect a separate advance to the customer, which would have been nullified by any such lien as was claimed.

The question arising in *Fern* v. *Bishop Burns & Co. Ltd. and Lloyds Bank Ltd.*[7] seems, surprisingly, not to have been before the courts in any earlier case. Here the defendant company obtained a garnishee order against the plaintiff for £806. The balance on his account, £4,998, included a cheque for £4,700 paid in the day before the service of the order and not cleared. The bank transferred the £4,700 to a new account and claimed that only £298 was attachable. The District Registrar ruled against the bank but on the plaintiff's appeal O'Connor J., in Birmingham Crown Court held that the bank was right. On the basis of the *Underwood*[8] and *Zang*[9] decisions, in the absence of express or implied agreement by the bank to pay against uncleared effects the bank was merely an agent for collection, and the garnishee order did not attach any uncleared cheques. And he added that while in the rare situation where there is an

---

[3] [1938] 2 K.B. 801. *cf. post*, p. 196.
[4] But now see the Civil Liability (Contribution) Act 1978, *post* p. 202.
[5] At p. 814.
[6] (1874) 22 W.R. 740.
[7] New L.J. July 10, 1980.
[8] *Post*, pp. 158 *et seq.*
[9] *Post*, pp. 156 *et seq.*

express agreement it would be the bank's duty to inform the court, it would be quite wrong for the bank to volunteer such details of the customer's account as might support an implied agreement.

The judgment debtor in *Choice Investments Ltd.* v. *Jeromnimon*[10] had a current account balance of £44.45 and a deposit of £8.95 with the Midland Bank. He also had a U.S. dollar account with a balance of $2,524.59. The plaintiff company obtained a garnishee order against him, and he appealed against the county court judge's ruling that the dollars as well as the sterling were attached. But the Court of Appeal rejected the appeal. The *Miliangos* decision[11] established that the courts can give judgment for a sum owed in foreign currency, so the balance of an account in a foreign currency is a debt that can be attached by a garnishee order.

Lord Denning gave guidance as to how a bank should act in such a case, freezing a number of dollars which, converted at the buying rate for sterling at the time, would satisfy the sterling judgment.

The bank should *not* make a transfer into sterling at that stage. But, if and when the garnishee order is made absolute, the bank should exchange that stopped amount from dollars into sterling, so far as is necessary to meet the sterling judgment debt—and pay over that amount to the judgment creditor. But if and so far as the stopped amount (owing to exchange fluctuations) is more than enough to meet the judgment debt, the bank must release the balance from the stop and have it available for its customer on demand.

Presumably, if exchange fluctuations result in the stopped amount being less than the judgment debt, the creditor can apply for a further garnishee order to attach the balance.

In *Whitbread Flowers* v. *Thurston*[12] the Court of Appeal held that where a debtor is insolvent a garnishee order must not be used to give the garnishor precedence over the other creditors.

In *S.C.F. Finance Co. Ltd.* v. *Masri (No. 3)*[13] it was held that it was possible to garnish a debt that was not recoverable within the jurisdiction; and in *Interpool Ltd.* v. *Galani*[14] the Court of Appeal held that by analogy the Court had power under Order

---

[10] [1981] 2 W.L.R. 80.
[11] *Post*, pp. 241 *et seq.*
[12] (Unreported) (1979) C.L.Y. 22.
[13] [1987] 2 W.L.R. 81.
[14] [1988] Q.B. 738.

48 to discover the existence of such debts; the defendant here must answer questions as to his assets abroad, to enforce the judgment obtained by his judgment creditor.

Z Ltd. v. A. and Others
[1982] Q.B. 558

The Mareva injunction

Facts

A large company with its head office abroad and an office in London, was defrauded of £2 million by a wide ranging conspiracy, the proceeds of which were believed to have reached a number of bank accounts in London. The company obtained a *Mareva* injunction to freeze the balances on those accounts, and assets in the hands of other defendants—there were 35 in all. The case was settled after the High Court hearing, but the clearing banks, in order to obtain clarification of the position of banks receiving notice of a *Mareva* injunction, applied for leave to appeal against the injunction.

Decision

The Court of Appeal refused leave, but in their three considered judgments they reviewed the principal decisions in the injunction and provided detailed guidance not only as to the responsibility of banks (and other third parties) but also as to the principles on which the injunction should be implemented.

Notes

What has become known as the *Mareva* injunction was first granted by the Court of Appeal in *Nippon Yusen Kaisha* v. *Karageorgis*[15] in 1975, when they restrained a foreign company from removing funds from its banking account in England pending trial of an action for damages against it. Six weeks later the Court granted a similar injunction in the case from which it has taken its name: *Mareva Compania Naviera S.A. of Panama* v. *International Bulk Carriers S.A.*[16]

In the second case Roskill L.J., said that the courts should not be too ready to disturb the existing practice of not granting such injunctions, but in the event the courts have used the

[15] [1975] 1 W.L.R. 1093.
[16] [1975] 2 Lloyd's Rep. 509.

injunction freely and considerably expanded in its scope—notably, to include English as well as foreign defendants.[17] In 1979 Lord Denning said that so far from being exceptional applications were then being granted at the rate of about 20 a month, and the flow of reported cases of increasing complexity continues unchecked.

It may be noted that the *Mareva* injunction is normally granted before there is judgment in the dispute between the parties,[18] while the garnishee order[19] is made to give effect to a judgment already given. But the effect of the two orders on the banks is the same: until the order is discharged, the bank account is frozen, either completely or to the extent of any maximum sum named in the order. While it was evolving over a comparatively short time it produced uncertainties in the banks comparable to those resolved over many years in the case of garnishee proceedings. The Court of Appeal judgments, bringing together the effect of earlier decisions and adding their own points, went a good way towards resolving the banks' problems.

So, while a bank is in contempt of court in ignoring an injunction of which it has notice (whether or not the defendant—the bank's customer—knows that the injunction has been granted), there will not necessarily be a contempt when one official of the bank makes a payment out of the account in ignorance of an order of which another official has had notice; whether or not there is contempt will depend on the status and relationship of the officials. But Eveleigh L.J., said that while notice of an injunction to one official does not oblige a bank to make searches through its branches to discover whether any branch has the defendant's account, "it will obviously be prudent and in its own interests for the bank to take some steps in the matter." And he added, "the greater the difficulty in

---

[17] *Barclay-Johnson* v. *Yuill* [1980] 1 W.L.R. 1259; and s.27(3) of the Supreme Court Act 1981 now so provides. *cf.* also *The Pertamina* [1977] 3 W.L.R. 518 (the order can cover goods as well as money), *S.C.F. Finance Ltd.* v. *Masri* [1965] 1 W.L.R. 876 (the order may cover money in the name of the defendant's wife) and the *Third Chandris* decision that the fact that a bank account is overdrawn is no bar to the granting of the injunction: the existence of an overdraft does not prove that there are no assets [1979] 2 Lloyd's Rep. 184.

[18] But note *Stewart Chartering* v. *C. & O. Management S.A.* [1980] 1 W.L.R. 460 (the injunction may be extended after judgment to assist in the execution of the judgment); and *Orwell Steel Ltd.* v. *Ashphalt & Tarmac Ltd.* [1984] 1 W.L.R. 1097 (the order may be made after judgment for the same purpose).

[19] *Ante*, pp. 110 *et seq.*

discovering the account . . . the less likely the risk of contempt of court."

The Court should require the plaintiff to give an undertaking to indemnify the bank for any reasonable expenses involved in obeying the injunction. (Lord Denning considered that even without such an undertaking there is an implied duty on the plaintiff to indemnify third parties for such expenses).

The injunction does not prevent the debiting of cheque card and credit card payments for transactions effected before service of the order on the bank. (The bank obviously has also to meet such payments for transactions after receipt of the order, but to allow them to be debited against the frozen balance would defeat the whole purpose of the injunction, and such post-notice payments have to be placed to a new account—as have any credits received after notice.)

Other payments which the bank is bound to honour, *e.g.* under letters of credit or bank guarantees—are not inhibited by the injunction. It does not apply to shares or title deeds held as securities or (unless the order specifically refers to them) to articles held for safe custody. Joint accounts are affected only if the order specifies them—Kerr L.J., said that this was justifiable only in rare cases—and assets received after notice are also free unless the order specifically covers them.

The banks must of course observe the terms of the orders they receive, and the extent of the benefit they obtain from the Court of Appeal judgments depends on the extent to which the courts in granting future injunctions observe the principles the Court laid down. Much of that guidance does not directly affect the banks—for example, that the injunction should not be granted when the defendants are obviously of such standing and substance that there is virtually no possibility of their seeking to avoid an eventual judgment against them. But the Court of Appeal judgments included statements that the banks must welcome. Lord Denning said "The bank, or other innocent third parties, should be told with as much certainty as possible what they are to do or not to do." Kerr L.J., said the plaintiff "should make every effort to try to indicate (a) which bank or banks hold the accounts in question, (b) at what branches and (c) if possible under what numbers." And the plaintiff should serve notice of the injunction as quickly as possible on the defendant as well as the bank: it is a considerable embarrassment when a bank has to freeze the account of a customer who has not heard the granting of the injunction.

The first *Mareva* injunctions were comprehensive, covering all the defendants' assets wherever they were in the jurisdiction. It was soon appreciated that this could be unfair to a defendant with very substantial means, and the practice developed of naming a maximum sum—normally the amount of the plaintiff's claim—to be immobilised. A bank receiving such an order is in the difficulty that, its customer's balance being less than the maximum sum, it might dishonour a cheque although the customer has ample means elsewhere. The Court recognised the difficulty, and said that a maximum sum injunction should contain separate provisions covering assets believed to be in the hands of banks or other third parties, directing them to freeze such assets up to the maximum figure, thus relieving them of any responsibility to enquire as to the defendant's other means.

It was in connection with this difficulty that Eveleigh L.J., made a comment that the banks must hope applies to the whole *Mareva* area:

Carelessness or even recklessness on the part of the banks ought not in my opinion to make them liable for contempt unless it can be shown that there was indifference to such a degree that it was contumacious. A Mareva injunction is granted for the benefit of an individual litigant, and it seems to me to be undesirable that those who are not immediate parties should be in danger of being held in contempt of court unless they can be shown to have been contumacious.

The courts have given further guidance as to the proper range of *Mareva* orders in a number of cases not involving banks—for example, that while they provide protection for the plaintiff they should not offer him a weapon[20] and that a defendant's flagrant defiance of a *Mareva* order may justify a sentence of imprisonment[21]—while in several cases the rights of innocent third parties have been recognised.[22] Banks affected by the orders are of course such third parties, and the unusual circumstances of *Oceanica Castelana Armadora S.A.* v. *Mineral Importexport*; *Seawind Maritime Inc.* v. *Romanian Bank for Foreign Trade*[23] provided a further example of the care for third parties' rights. Barclays Bank International, on undertaking to provide a guarantee for customers seeking to free a cargo from a *Mareva* injunction in the first case, took a cash deposit

---

[20] *Per* Lawton L.J. in *C.B.S. (U.K.)* v. *Lambert* [1982] 3 All E.R. 237.
[21] *Pospischal* v. *Phillips, The Times,* January 20, 1988.
[22] *e.g. Galaxia Maritime S.A.* v. *Mineral Importexport* [1982] Com.L.R. 38.
[23] [1983] 1 W.L.R. 1294.

provided by the Romanian Bank for Foreign Trade. In the event the guarantee was not required but the plaintiffs in the second case had obtained a *Mareva* injunction against the Romanian bank, and Barclays applied for the court's direction as to what right of set-off they had against the deposit, the Romanian bank being substantially in arrears in interest payment on term loans made to them. Lloyd J. held that they were entitled to their right of set-off, and to debit the defendants' account in respect of liabilities on confirmed letters of credit opened before notice of the injunction. *Mareva* must not prejudice third parties' rights, and adding that "there is no doubt that by far the greatest burden of policing *Mareva* injunctions falls on the banks," he said that future injunctions to be served on banks should contain a suitable proviso that would avoid their having to come to court for variations.[24]

Two recent decisions carrying *Mareva* further are *Securities and Investment Board* v. *Pantell SA*[24a] and *X* v. *Y and Y Establishment*.[24b] In the first it was held that where it was alleged that a company was acting in contravention of the Financial Services Act 1986 a Mareva injunction would be granted to the SIB, even though the SIB had no beneficial interest in the company's assets and no private cause of action against the company. The second case concerned a dispute between a French bank and a Saudi Arabian businessman, in which the bank sought a *Mareva* injunction against the defendant restraining him from dealing with his assets in England. It was held that by virtue of section 25 of the Civil Jurisdiction and Judgments Act 1982 such interim relief could be granted where proceedings had been started in another country in the European Civil Jurisdiction Convention: section 25 had overridden the ruling in *The Siskina*[24c] that *Mareva* could be granted only where the dispute was triable in England.

———

The garnishee order freezes the banking account of a judgment creditor; the *Mareva* injunction freezes the account of a defendant in an action for damages pending trial of the action. In 1981 for the first time an order was granted freezing

[24] Further cases in which *Mareva* has been considered by the courts will be found at pp. 254 *et seq.*, *post.*
[24a] [1989] 2 All E.R. 673.
[24b] *The Financial Times*, May 16, 1989.
[24c] [1977] 3 W.L.R. 818.

an account suspected of containing funds that were the proceeds of crime.

The pioneering order was made by Forbes J., in *West Mercia Constabulary* v. *Wagener*[25] and in *Chief Constable of Kent* v. *V. and Another*[26] a similar order was upheld by a majority in the Court of Appeal. The defendant in this case was accused of defrauding an old lady of £16,000, which had been paid to his credit with the Bank of Credit and Commerce International. It was thought that the money might be removed from the bank, and the police sought and obtained an order on the lines of that granted by Forbes J., in the earlier case.

On the appeal against the order Lord Denning and Donaldson L.J., held that the order was justified. The Court had since 1968 allowed the right of the police to seize property suspected of being stolen.[26a] Donaldson L.J., said that in the 1968 decision:

> The common law came to the support of the common weal and invested the police with a right to seize goods which the courts could if necessary have enforced by mandatory injunction. In the instant appeal the common law could and should similarly invest the police with a right to "detain" monies standing to the credit of a bank account if and to the extent that they can be shown to have been obtained from another in breach of the common law. Only thus would a criminal be prevented from making the fruits of his crime immune from seizure by the simple expedient of banking the money.

The Supreme Court Act, 1981, in section 37(1), gave the High Court power to grant an injunction "in all cases in which it appears to the court to be just and expedient to do so." Slade L.J., in a dissenting judgment, did not accept, as Lord Denning had held, that the section had freed the courts from the requirement that injunctions could be granted only in the enforcement of a legal or equitable right, and he did not consider that the 1968 ruling on tangible property should be extended to cover intangible property. But it seems probable that following the majority decision, similar orders will be sought and granted in all appropriate cases.

However, the application in *Chief Constable of Leicestershire* v. *M. and Another*[27] was held by Hoffman J., to be outside the

[25] [1982] 1 W.L.R. 127.
[26] [1982] 3 W.L.R. 462.
[26a] See *Chic Fashions (West Wales) Lt.* v. *Jones* [1968] 1 All E.R. 229.
[27] [1989] 1 W.L.R. 20.

scope of the Court of Appeal ruling: here it was sought to prevent the defendant using the profits from mortgages obtained by fraud, and those profits were not themselves money "obtained from another in breach of the criminal law". In the similar facts of *Chief Constable of Surrey* v. *A. and Another*[28] where it was argued that the defendants were constructive trustees of the profits, Ognall J., following Hoffman J., refused the application.

The *Mareva* jurisdiction had been reinforced in 1976 when the Court of Appeal recognised a new restraint on defendants in the form of the Anton Piller order[29] which authorises a plaintiff and his solicitor to enter the defendant's premises to inspect documents, and which, although not matching the extraordinary growth of *Mareva*, has since been much used. And in 1985, in *Lipkin Gorman* v. *Cass (a firm)*[30] came the first modern grant of the ancient prerogative writ, *ne exeat regno*, denying to the defendant the right to leave the kingdom. It was issued again in *Al Nahkel for Contracting and Trading Ltd.* v. *Lowe*[31] and in *Bayer AG* v. *Winter*[32] where it was conceded that *ne exeat regno* was inappropriate, the Court of Appeal granted injunctions under section 37(1) of the Supreme Court Act 1981, having the same effect.

The injunctions were in support of *Mareva* and *Anton Piller* orders. But in *Bayer AG* v. *Winter (No. 2)*[33] Scott J. refused to extend the injunctions so as to authorise cross-examination of the defendant: "Star Chamber interrogatory procedure has formed no part of the judicial process in this country for several centuries." He repeated his criticism of *Anton Piller* procedure in *CBS* v. *Robinson*[33a] and it was endorsed by Hoffman J. in *Lock International plc* v. *Beswick and Others*.[33b]

---

[28] *The Times*, October 27, 1988.
[29] *Anton Piller KG* v. *Manufacturing Processes Ltd.* 1976 Ch. 55.
[30] *The Times*, May 29, 1985.
[31] [1986] 1 Q.B. 235.
[32] [1986] 1 W.L.R. 497.
[33] [1986] 2 All E.R. 43.
[33a] [1989] Ch. 38.
[33b] (1989) 139 N.L.J. 644.

Robarts v. Tucker

(1851) 16 Q.B. 560

Payment after a forged indorsement

Facts

A branch of the Pelican Life Insurance Company (of which company Tucker was secretary) drew on its head office a bill for £5,000 in settlement of a claim under a life policy. The indorsements to the bill were forged by the solicitor for the claimants under that policy, and the bill was presented at the head office of the company for acceptance. After scrutiny the bill was accepted payable at the firm's bankers, Robarts, Curtis & Co., and it was later paid there. Upon the forgeries being discovered, the insurance company paid £5,000 to the defrauded beneficiaries, and brought this action against the bank.

The bank in its defence argued (i) that they owed no duty, beyond that of reasonable care, in inspecting indorsements; (ii) that in this case the insurance company, in accordance with their usual practice, had inspected the indorsements before accepting the bill and so had vouched for them. Upon losing the case in the Queen's Bench Division, the bank appealed.

Decision

The Court of Exchequer Chamber dismissed the appeal.

In the course of his judgment, Parke B. said:

If this were the ordinary case of an acceptance made payable at a banker's, there can be no question that making the acceptance payable there is tantamount to an order, on the part of the acceptor, to the banker to pay the bill to the person who is according to the law merchant capable of giving a good discharge for the bill.... The bankers cannot charge their customer with any other payments than those made in pursuance of that authority. If bankers wish to avoid the responsibility of deciding on the genuineness of indorsements, they may require their customers to domicile their bills at their own offices and to honour them by giving a cheque upon the banker. [In the present case] reliance is placed on the evidence which shows that the company were accustomed to take precautions before accepting a bill. But that custom was never communicated to the bankers and there is no evidence, direct or indirect, of any communication to the bankers from which an authority to pay this bill without examination could be inferred.[34]

---

[34] At p. 579.

Notes

The banker's loss of the right to debit his customer arises, not from negligence in failing to detect the forgery of a signature which he cannot be expected to know, but from his failure to obey his customer's mandate: he has not paid to the designated payee.

This inability to debit the customer's account, clearly established in *Robarts* v. *Tucker*, would have been of considerable and ever-increasing danger to bankers as the use of cheques developed. It was this which gave rise to the statutory protection provided, *in the case of cheques*, by section 19 of the Stamp Act 1853,[35] later substantially re-enacted by section 60 of the Bills of Exchange 1882.

There are two cases, apart from section 60, when the banker can debit his customer's account with instruments on which the indorsement has been forged: (i) when the payee was fictitious or non-existing, and, as a result, the bill can be treated as payable to bearer under section 7(3) of the Act: the forgery of the indorsement is then irrelevant; (ii) when, rarely, the customer is estopped from denying the authenticity of the indorsement. *Bank of England* v. *Vagliano*[36] is an example of both exceptions; in addition to the finding already set out[37] the House of Lords held that by accepting the bill payable at his bank, Vagliano represented it to be genuine, although the bill was in fact a forgery throughout. The distinction on this point between *Vagliano's* case and *Robarts* v. *Tucker* is in the fact that in the latter case the bill itself was a good one, only the indorsements being forged, while in the former the whole instrument was forged save for Vagliano's signature; this alone gave the bill any value, as there was not even a drawer to whom recourse could be had.

In this connection, Lord Halsbury L.C. said:

I am not intending to throw any doubt upon the propriety of the decision in *Robarts* v. *Tucker*, nor am I prepared to assent to the proposition that it is a harsh decision. A customer tells his banker to pay a particular person; the banker pays someone else, and it would seem to follow as a perfectly just result that the banker should be called upon to make good the amount he has so erroneously paid. But what relation has such a decision to a case where a thing which bears the form and semblance of a known commercial document like a bill of

[35] *cf. post*, p. 143.
[36] [1891] A.C. 107.
[37] *Ante*, p. 45.

exchange gets by the act of the customer into the hands of a banker, where there is no real drawer, no real transaction between himself and the supposed drawer, and where, as a matter of fact, there is no person who in the proper and ordinary sense of the word is a payee at all? It seems to me that if all these cirumstances, acting upon and inducing the bankers to make the payments they did make, are acts which are the fault of the customer, it is the customer and not the banker who ought to bear the loss.[38]

It will be seen, however, how rarely such circumstances as those of the *Vagliano* case are likely to occur; for no protection can be drawn from that decision where the document is genuine apart from the forged indorsement. This must have been placed on the bill after the customer's acceptance, and he cannot be made responsible for it. It is to be noted, too that the banker will in such a case be liable to pay the true owner, and he will have no such protection as section 60 of the Bills of Exchange Act gives him with regard to cheques.

Curtice v. London, City & Midland Bank Ltd.
[1908] 1 K.B. 293

Westminster Bank Ltd. v. Hilton
(1926) 43 T.L.R. 124

Countermand of the payment is effective only when it is brought to the notice of the banker and when it is unambiguous in terms

Facts of Curtice v. London, City & Midland Bank Ltd.
The plaintiff was a customer at the Willesden Green branch of the defendant bank. He drew a cheque for £63 in payment for horses bought from one, Jones, but as the horses were not delivered, he sent a telegram stopping the cheque, and this telegram was delivered by the G.P.O. in the letter box of the bank at 6.15 p.m. On the next day the telegram was missed when the letter box was cleared, and during the day the cheque was paid. The following morning the telegram was found, together with the written confirmation of the countermand which the plaintiff had posted. He was notified that the "stop" had arrived too late to be effective, whereupon he drew a cheque for the whole of his balance, including the sum of £63, and, upon this cheque being dishonoured, brought the present

[38] At p. 117.

action for money had and received. In the county court, judgment was given for the plaintiff, and a Divisional Court dismissed the bank's appeal. The bank further appealed.

Decision

The Court of Appeal held that there had been no effective countermand of payment within section 75 of the Bills of Exchange Act; and this was so even though the negligence of the bank was the cause of it.

In the course of his judgment, Cozens-Hardy M.R. said:

> There is no such thing as a constructive countermand in a commercial transaction of this kind. In my opinion, on the admitted facts of this case, the cheque was not countermanded, although it may well be that it was due to the negligence of the bank that they did not receive notice of the customer's desire to stop the cheque. For such negligence the bank might be liable, but the measure of damage would be by no means the same as in an action for money had and received. I agree with the judgment of A. T. Lawrence J., on this point, and that is sufficient to dispose of the appeal. But as we have had an argument addressed to us as to the effect upon the duty of a bank of the mere receipt of a telegram, I wish to add a few words on that. A telegram may, reasonably and in the ordinary course of business, be acted upon by the bank, at least to the extent of postponing the honouring of the cheque until further inquiry can be made. But I am not satisfied that the bank is bound as a matter of law to accept an unauthenticated telegram as sufficient authority for the serious step of refusing to pay a cheque.[39]

And Fletcher Moulton L.J. said:

> It has long been held that an order must be unambiguous. If a master chooses to give an order to his servant that bears two meanings, he cannot find fault with his servant for having taken the meaning which it was not in fact intended to bear; and that applies to a banker when receiving orders as much as to agents generally. Now that principle which applies to the duty of conveying the mandate in a form in which the meaning is unambiguous applies, in my opinion, *mutatis mutandis*, to the question of its authenticity. If the mandate is sent in a form in which a servant, acting reasonably, has no security that the mandate comes from his employer, the employer cannot grumble that he did not act upon it. Authenticity and meaning appear to me, in the general law of agency, to stand on the same footing, subject, of course, to the broad difference

[39] At p. 298.

of circumstances which are due to the difference of nature of the two.[40]

Facts of Westminster Bank Ltd. v. Hilton

The plaintiff, who had an account with the defendant bank, drew a cheque for £8 1s.6d., payable to one, Poate. The cheque, which was drawn on July 31, 1924, was numbered 117285, and post-dated August 2. On August 1, the plaintiff wired to the bank to stop payment of cheque No. 117283, giving the payee and the amount of the cheque No. 117285. In fact, cheque No. 117283, to another payee and for another amount, had previously been paid by the bank. On August 6, cheque No. 117285 was presented and, the bank supposing that it had been drawn in the place of the one that had been stopped, paid it. The plaintiff brought an action for negligence against the bank, and when it was decided in favour of the bank he appealed. The Court of Appeal found in his favour, whereupon the bank appealed.

Decision

The House of Lords held that, as the one main certain item of identification was the number of the cheque, the bank was not guilty of negligence.

In the course of his judgment, Lord Shaw of Dunfermline said:

When a banker is in possession of sufficient funds to meet such a cheque from a customer, the duty of the bank is to honour that cheque by payment, and failure in this duty may involve the bank in serious liability to its customer. This duty is ended, and on the contrary when the cheque is stopped another duty arises—namely, to refuse payment. In a case of that character it rests upon the customer to prove that the order to stop reached the bank in time and was unequivocally referable to a cheque then in existence, and signed and issued by the customer before the notice to stop. It would, of course, be intolerable in business to permit the form of stoppage to be applied to a non-existent and non-issued cheque. Further, in the ordinary course of trade a cheque is signed on the date it bears. This being so the notice on reaching the bank will properly be treated as only applying to a cheque bearing a date the same as, or anterior to, the date of stoppage. To carry the scope of stoppage further and to make it apply to the case (exceptional and out of the ordinary course of business transactions)—the case of cheques which though subsequent to stoppage in date were yet anterior to stoppage at the time of signature and issue, namely, post-dated

[40] At pp. 299–300.

cheques—it is, in my view, necessary for the customer to prove and explain the post-dating, but further to prove that this fact was brought clearly home to the mind of the banker so as to bring the post-dated cheque within the order of stoppage. If these last things are not clearly proved (and the onus of doing so is no light one), then the bank acts rightly in declining to dishonour a cheque which *ex facie* bears a date subsequent to the stoppage.[41]

Notes

The validity of post-dated cheques is expressly established by section 13(2) of the Bills of Exchange Act, but they are both troublesome and dangerous for the banker,[42] and it is interesting to see, in *Kalish* v. *Manufacturers Trust Company*[43] an example of a common practice of banks in the United States whereby they obtain the agreement of new customers to the bank's exemption from certain liabilities, including any liability for the inadvertent payment of post-dated cheques.

It is to be remarked that, in the *Curtice* case, the opinions concerning the use of the telegram as a method of countermanding payment were *obiter*: the case was decided on the fact that the countermand was not in fact received. In *Westminster Bank* v. *Hilton* the *ratio decidendi* of Lord Shaw's judgment was not that of the four other Law Lords, which was based on the facts of the particular case. The judgments here quoted are valuable, however, in that they provide basic principles for the law of countermand of payment; and although not of binding force, they are yet of great authority.

It must be noted too in the *Curtice* case that the bank succeeded in the action brought against them for money had and received. An action on the same facts for negligence might well have had a different result.

A stop sent to one branch of a bank is not an effective stop of a cheque drawn on another branch of that bank.[44]

Gibbons v. Westminster Bank Ltd.

[1939] 2 K.B. 882

Upon the wrongful dishonour of his cheque a customer who is not a trader must prove special damage before he can be awarded substantial damages

[41] At pp. 129–130.
[42] *cf.* Paget's forceful comments, *op. cit*, pp. 186 *et seq.*
[43] 191 N.Y.S. (2d) 61 (1959); 7 L.D.B. 238.
[44] *London Provincial & South Western Bank Ltd.* v. *Buszard* (1918) 35 T.L.R. 142; *post*, p. 402 *cf. Burnett* v. *Westminster Bank Ltd. ante*, p. 35.

Facts

The plaintiff was a woman customer of the defendant bank, who, after paying in a sum of money to her account, drew a cheque which was dishonoured as a result of the bank's having put the credit to another account instead of to hers. Upon the dishonour, she called the manager of the branch at which the account was kept, and he paid her £1 1s.—in full satisfaction, as the bank claimed, of any claim she might have against them. The jury found, however, that she did not so accept the payment.

The defendant bank contended that the plaintiff was entitled to nominal damages only, as she had not pleaded special or actual damage. The jury awarded substantial damages, however, in the sum of £50, and after they had been discharged, the court heard further argument regarding damages.

Decision

It was held that as the plaintiff was a non-trader, who had not proved any special damage, she was entitled to nominal damages only and 40 shillings were awarded.

In the course of his judgment, Lawrence J. said:

> The authorities which have been cited in argument all lay down that a trader is entitled to recover substantial damages for the wrongful dishonour of his cheque without pleading and proving actual damage, but it has never been held that that exception to the general rule as to the measure of damages for breach of contract extends to any one who is not a trader. The cases cited in which this view has been taken are *Marzetti* v. *Williams*,[45] *Rolin* v. *Steward*,[46] *Bank of New South Wales* v. *Milvain*,[47] and *Kinlan* v. *Ulster Bank Ltd.*[48] The rule is so put in Grant's *Law of Banking* (7th ed.), at pp. 88–89, and in Smith's *Leading Cases* (13th ed.) Vol. 2, at p. 574, where it is also stated that the exception to the general rule is one which ought not to be extended, reference being made to the speech of Lord Atkinson in *Addis* v. *Gramophone Co. Ltd.*[49] In my opinion, this matter should be treated as covered by these authorities, and I hold accordingly that the corollary of the proposition laid down by them is the law—namely, that a person who is not a trader is not entitled to recover substantial damages

---

[45] (1830) 1 B & Ad. 415.
[46] (1854) 14 C.B. 595; *infra*.
[47] (1884) 10 V.L.R. 3.
[48] [1928] I.R. 171.
[49] [1909] A.C. 488 at p. 495.

for the wrongful dishonour of his cheque, unless the damage which he has suffered is alleged and proved as special damage.[50]

Notes

The rule that a trader, and so far only a trader, can recover substantial damages for the wrongful dishonour of his cheque without proof of actual damage is, as Lawrence J. pointed out, an exception to the general rule as to the measure of damages for breach of contract. It is of comparatively recent development, and may still be capable of extension; there are other classes of the community likely to suffer at least as serious damage as the trader.[51] It is to be noted that the rule does not apply in actions for defamation.

In *Evans* v. *London and Provincial Bank Ltd.*[52] the plaintiff, the wife of a naval officer, drew a cheque on her husband's behalf payable to a mess steward of the ship on which he was serving. This cheque was wrongfully dishonoured, and Lord Reading C.J. directed the jury that the only question was what damages were due to the lady for the bank's mistake, as she had not suffered any special damage. The jury returned a verdict of one shilling damages.

Rolin v. *Steward*[53] is an example of the trader's obtaining substantial damages without proof of special loss. In that case three cheques and a bill were dishonoured in error; they were re-presented the next day and paid. In the plaintiff's subsequent action a jury awarded him £500 damages, and on appeal it was held that, although in the circumstances this amount was excessive, yet he was entitled to substantial damages, and £200 was awarded.

In *Baker* v. *Australia and New Zealand Bank Ltd.*[54] the plaintiff, a company director, was awarded only nominal damages for breach of contract in the wrongful dishonour of her cheques, and a sum of £100 in her action for libel.

A recent example of the rule that a customer is entitled only to nominal damages for the dishonour of his cheques unless he is a trader is *Rae* v. *Yorkshire Bank plc.*[55] where Parker L.J. thought that even the £20 awarded in the court below might have been excessive.

---

[50] At p. 888.
[51] *cf.* Ellinger, *op. cit* p. 312.
[52] (1917) 3 L.D.B. 152.
[53] *Supra.*
[54] [1958] N.Z.L.R. 907; *post*, pp. 133, 134.
[55] [1988] F.L.R. 1.

Davidson v. Barclays Bank Ltd.

(1940) 56 T.L.R. 343

When a cheque is wrongfully dishonoured it may be possible to bring an
action for libel against the bank; and the defence of privilege cannot be
relied upon by the bank in such circumstances

Facts

The plaintiff, a bookmaker, drew a cheque for £2 15s. 8d.
upon the Kennington branch of the defendant bank. Owing to
the fact that the bank had previously paid in error a cheque
which the plaintiff had countermanded there were not sufficient
funds on the account to meet the later cheque, which was
accordingly returned marked "Not sufficient."

The plaintiff brought the present action against the bank,
complaining that the words meant that he had drawn a cheque
knowing that he had insufficient funds, that he was unable to
pay £2 15s. 8d., and that it was unsafe to transact business with
him and give him credit. The defendant bank pleaded, *inter alia*,
that the words were published only to the payee of the cheque,
who had an interest in knowing the reason why the cheque had
not been met, and to whom they were under a duty to
communicate that reason; that the words were published in the
honest though mistaken belief that they were true, and that the
occasion of publication was therefore privileged.[56]

Decision

It was held that the bank was liable. It owed no duty of
communication to the payee of the cheque; there was no
common interest between bank and payee calling for communication; and the occasion was not privileged.

In the course of his judgment, Hilbery J. said:

It seems obviously fallacious for the bank to say that, because they
had made a mistake as a result of which they thought the occasion to
be one when the cheque must be returned, therefore the occasion was
one where they had to make the communication explaining why the
cheque was returned.... What the bank seek to do here is to create an
occasion of qualified privilege after making a mistake which appeared

---

[56] In actions for libel or slander the defence of qualified privilege rests on there
being a duty to communicate in the interest of the party to whom the
communication is made, or the common interest of both parties, the
communication being made without malice.

to make a communication on their part necessary. That is where the essential difference lies between this case and that which counsel for the defendants instanced in argument—namely, where one person inquires of another about the character of a third person, or where the customer of a bank gives his bank manager as a reference to a person from whom he proposes to rent premises. In either of these examples, when the request for the information is made, the occasion of qualified privilege is already constituted. If on such an occasion . . . a communication is made which is mistakenly defamatory . . . the communication is privileged and, subject to the well-known qualification, no action will lie. In each of those examples the privileged occasion is already there when the communication is made . . . it is not the mistake which creates the occasion; it is the occasion which is followed by the mistake.[57]

Notes

It is open to the injured customer, in some cases, to frame his action in libel, either alone, as in the *Davidson* case, or jointly with his contractual claim, as in *Plunkett* v. *Barclays Bank Ltd.*[58] and *Baker* v. *Australia and New Zealand Bank Ltd.*[59] If the rule is established that only a trader can succeed in a claim for substantial damages without proof of special damage, this alternative course of action may be more used than it has been in the past. The banks are at risk in the matter only when cheques have been wrongfully dishonoured, but the risk then is a real one, and the cases suggest that it is now virtually impossible for them to avoid it.

For many years the banker could argue that his most common answer on dishonoured cheques, "Refer to drawer," had no necessarily defamatory meaning. In *Flach* v. *London and South Western Bank Ltd.*[60] the plaintiff's cheque was returned unpaid during the moratorium at the outbreak of the First World War. The bank succeeded in their first defence to her action against them, that they were protected by the terms of the moratorium; they succeeded also in their contention that the words "Refer to drawer" were not libellous, Scrutton J. saying on this point that in his opinion the words in their ordinary meaning amounted to a statement by the bank, "We are not paying; go back to the drawer and ask why," or else, "Go back to the drawer and ask him to pay."

In *Plunkett's* case[61] du Parcq J. adopted the view of Scrutton

---

[57] At p. 349.
[58] [1936] 2 K.B. 107; *ante* p. 111.
[59] *Ante*, p. 131.
[60] (1915) 31 T.L.R. 334.
[61] *Ante*, p. 111.

J. as to the libel issue before him, but as time passed it became increasingly unrealistic to expect contemporary opinion to agree; and by 1950 the decision of the Irish Supreme Court (not binding on English courts, but to be treated with respect) in *Pyke* v. *Hibernian Bank Ltd.*[62] was not unexpected. Three cheques were wrongly dishonoured with the answer "Refer to drawer," two of the cheques bearing also the word "re-present." A jury awarded £1 damages for breach of contract and £400 for libel, and this verdict was affirmed by the Supreme Court, where although two of the judges accepted the bank's argument that the words were incapable of a defamatory meaning, the other two rejected it, and distinguished the *Flach* decision on the grounds that there the dishonour was not in fact wrongful.

In England *Jayson* v. *Midland Bank Ltd.*[63] has probably settled the matter. Here the plaintiff claimed that the dishonour was wrongful and that "Refer to drawer" was libellous. The jury found that the words were (in the words of the question the judge put to them) likely "to lower the plaintiff's reputation in the minds of right thinking people." This did not avail the plaintiff, because the jury found also that the dishonour was justified, and the Court of Appeal dismissed the plaintiff's appeal on that point. But it seems unlikely that any bank could succeed in future in a plea that "Refer to drawer" is not defamatory, especially as the jury's view in *Jayson's* case is almost certainly shared by most people today.

The answer in the *Davidson* case, "Not sufficient," was clearly defamatory; so are such other answers as "Exceeds arrangements." It has been held by the Supreme Court of New Zealand (and again the decision is not binding in England, but is of great weight) that "Present again" is capable of bearing a defamatory meaning.[64] The decision of the Court of Appeal in 1906, in *Frost* v. *London Joint Stock Bank Ltd.*[65] that the absence of any stated reason for dishonour could not give rise to a presumption of one meaning rather than another especially when the meaning suggested is libellous, is of academic interest in view of the rule of the London Clearing House requiring written answers on all dishonoured cheques passing through the

---

[62] [1950] I.R. 195.

[63] [1968] 1 Lloyd's Rep. 409.

[64] *Baker* v. *Australia and New Zealand Bank Ltd.* [1958] N.Z.L.R. 907, *ante*, p. 131.

[65] (1906) 22 T.L.R. 760.

clearing. It may be questioned therefore whether any wording (other than those marking technical irregularities) can avoid the danger of a libel action if the dishonour is not in fact justified.

In *Russell* v. *Bank America National Trust and Savings Association*[66-67] O'Connor J. ruled that the words "Account closed" on four dishonoured cheques were capable of bearing a defamatory meaning, as implying that the plaintiff had drawn cheques without making arrangements for their payment and so was not to be trusted in business dealings. The plaintiff, a South American business man, said that when he transferred his account he had arranged with the bank for the handling of outstanding cheques. The bank's official who had dealt with the account transfer denied that any such arrangement had been made. The jury accepted the plaintiff's evidence and awarded £50,000 damages for the libel.

On the question of privilege, the "well known qualification" to which Hilbery J., referred is of course an allegation that the communication was activated by malice. The *Davidson* decision has not escaped criticism. In *Pyke's* case Black J., one of the judges finding for the bank, differed from Hilbery J.'s finding as to privilege in *Davidson's* case: he considered that Hilbery J.'s view of the authorities was too limited, and that on a wider range there was authority for holding that privilege can apply even when the occasion has arisen because of the mistake of the person claiming the privilege. But that opinion, persuasively reasoned as it was, can give the banker no comfort until it is followed in an English court.

In *Russell's* case the bank claimed privilege as one of their defences. The plaintiff cited *Davidson* in reply, but the judge considered that "whatever may be the law where a mistake is made by a bank," the present case was one of breach of contract, and once a finding of fact was made that the agreement had been made there could be no question of qualified privilege.

Barclays Bank Ltd. v. W. J. Simms Son and Cooke (Southern) Ltd. and Another

[1979] 3 All E.R. 522

[66-67] Unreported (1978).

National Westminster Bank Ltd. v. Barclays Bank International Ltd. and Another

[1975] Q.B. 654

The recovery of money paid under a mistake of fact

Facts in Barclays Bank Ltd. v. W. J. Simms Son and Cooke (Southern) Ltd. and Another

The defendant company had done work for a building association, and on September 12, 1977, the association sent them a cheque for £24,000 drawn on Barclays. On September 13 a receiver was appointed for the building company, and hearing of the appointment the association stopped payment of the cheque. The bank prepared the stop instruction for their computer, which was programmed accordingly, and the association confirmed the stop in writing. When the cheque reached the receiver he had it specially cleared, and the stop instruction was overlooked and the cheque paid. The bank claimed repayment from the receiver, who refused to repay, and the bank brought this action against the company and the receiver.

Decision

Robert Goff J. held that the bank was entitled to recover.

In a careful analysis of the authorities he said that while money paid under mistake of fact is prima facie recoverable, the payee has a defence (a) if the payer in making the payment was not influenced by the mistake; or (b) if there was good consideration for the payment; or (c) if the payee has changed his position in good faith on the strength of the payment. None of these applied on the facts of the case before him: but he pointed out that as to (b) the absence of consideration resulted from the fact that the payment having been made without the customer's mandate (they having stopped payment) it could not satisfy the liability to the payee. It would be otherwise if a cheque were paid in the mistaken belief that there were funds to meet it, for then it would be within the customer's mandate and would satisfy the liability.

Facts in National Westminster Bank Ltd. v. Barclays Bank International and Another

The second defendant was Mr. Ismail, a Nigerian businessman anxious to move susbtantial funds out of Nigeria, in evasion of the strict exchange control regulations in force there.

He bought, at a premium, a cheque for £8,000 on the National Westminster Bank, St. James's Square, London, but before paying for it he sent it to his own bank in London, Barclays Bank International, for special collection and advice of payment. The cheque was duly presented and paid, and Mr. Ismail paid for it in Nigeria. A fortnight later it was established that the cheque, which had been stolen from the owner's cheque book, was a clever forgery. The paying bank brought the present action for recovery of the money, which still stood to Mr. Ismail's credit in his London account. Barclays took no part in the trial, but Mr. Ismail resisted, arguing that (a) by paying the cheque the plaintiffs had represented that it was genuine, he had acted to his detriment on this representation and the plaintiffs were therefore estopped from recovering; (b) even apart from estoppel, the fact that he had acted to his detriment in reliance on the payment barred recovery; (c) the paying bank owes a duty of care to payees in honouring cheques, and the plaintiffs had been negligent in this duty; and (d) the plaintiffs were anyhow estopped by their negligence.

Decision

Kerr J. held that the plaintiffs were entitled to recover. He rejected all the defendant's arguments, and held further that even apart from the issues thus raised, in view of the suspicious circumstances in which the cheque had been obtained, which were not disclosed to the plaintiffs, he could not regard their payment of the cheque as a representation that it was genuine.

On the first of the defendant's arguments he said:

...Mr. Ismail can in the present case only succeed in raising an estoppel against the plaintiffs if the mere fact of a banker honouring a cheque on which his customer's signature has been undetectably forged carries with it an implied representation that the signature is genuine. I cannot see any logical basis for this. At most, it seems to me, the paying banker is thereby representing no more than that he believes the signature to be genuine.... Furthermore, I think that the law should be slow to impose on an innocent party who has not acted negligently an estoppel merely by reason of having dealt with a forged document on the assumption that it was genuine. In the context of forged share transfers this contention has been rejected as against companies which register a transfer in the belief of its authenticity; see *Simm* v. *Anglo-American Telegraph Co.*[68]

---

[68] (1879) 5 Q.B.D. 188; and *cf. The Lord Mayor of Sheffield* v. *Barclay and Others, post*, p. 351. *Per* Kerr J. at p. 674.

Notes

These two cases have served to clarify the position as to the recovery of money paid under mistake of fact.[69] The importance of the first is the fact that the bank was held entitled to recover from the payee of the cheque which they had paid despite their customer's stop order. In such circumstances the bank must of course refund the amount paid to their customer, but it had been thought previously that there was no right of subrogation against the payee. Robert Goff J., who had remarked on the importance of the case for bankers, "not only because it is an everyday hazard that customers' instructions may be overlooked, but because modern technology, rather than eliminating the risk, has if anything increased it," explained at the end of his long judgment why he was "happy to be able to reach the conclusion that the money is recoverable by Barclays." If the decision had been different the question whether the association was entitled to stop the cheque—"which ought to be the real dispute in the case"—would not have been ventilated, the bank would have had no recourse against the association, and there would have been

quite simply a windfall for the preferred creditors of the company at Barclays' expense. As however I have held that the money is recoverable, the situation is as it should have been, nobody is harmed, and the true dispute between the association and the receiver can be resolved on its merits.

It may be noted that Paget questions the relevance of the second of the judge's suggested defences: "it is not easy to see why the fact that the payee may have been entitled vis-a-vis the drawer should deprive the paying banker of the right to recover."[70] But even with that defence left available to future defendants, the decision is of obvious benefit to the banks. In earlier editions of this book *Chambers* v. *Miller*[71] was cited, as it has been in other textbooks, for the proposition that money paid in mistake of fact is recoverable only when the mistake is between payer and payee. Robert Goff J., said that the case, which turned on a different point, "provides, in my judgment, no basis for any such proposition, which was later to be authoritatively rejected by the House of Lords."

[69] See also *Chase Manhattan Bank N.A.* v. *Israel-British Bank (London) Ltd.*, *ante*, p. 109.
[70] *Op cit.* p. 322.
[71] (1862) 13 C.B.(N.S.) 125.

The second decision is noteworthy for the number of propositions, welcome to the bankers, for which the judgment is authority. Thus Kerr J. after carefully examining the several heads of the allegation of negligence, and holding that the bank had not in fact been negligent, rejected also the contention that the special presentation of the cheque should have put the paying bank especially on guard. "Special presentation," he said, "is usually the result of uncertainty as to the availability of funds, and does not 'imply anything sinister or suspicious which in itself should put the paying bank on guard.' "

He held also, rejecting the defendant's third argument, that the paying banker owes no "duty of care to a payee in deciding to honour a customer's cheque, at any rate when this appears to be regular on its face," while his comments on "the common aphorism that a banker is under a duty to know his customer's signature"—that it "is in fact incorrect even as between the banker and his customer. The principle is simply that a banker cannot debit his customer's account on the basis of a forged signature, since he has in that event no mandate from the customer for doing so"—should help the lay the recurrent superstition to rest.[72]

On the defendant's second argument, namely the detriment suffered, he said:

> The mere fact that the defendant has acted to his detriment by spending or paying away the money in reliance on having received the payment is not sufficient to bar the plaintiff's right to recover it: see e.g. Standish v. Ross,[73] Durrant v. Ecclesiastical Commissioners[74] and Baylis v. Bishop of London.[75] There are exceptions to this rule if in the circumstances the plaintiff represented to the defendant that he might treat the money as his own, or if he was under a duty as against the payee to inform him of the true state of account between them, or if the mistake was in some way induced or contributed to by the payee: see e.g. Holt v. Markham,[76] the review of the authorities by Asquith J. in Weld-Blundell v. Synott,[77] and Larner v. London County Council.[78] But none of these have any application here.[79]

---

[72] cf. Paget, op. cit. p. 319.
[73] (1849) 3 Ex. 527.
[74] (1880) 6 Q.B.D. 234.
[75] [1913] 1 Ch. 127.
[76] [1923] 1 K.B. 504; ante, pp. 98, 100, post, p. 141.
[77] [1940] 2 All E.R. 580.
[78] [1949] 2 K.B. 683; ante, p. 99.
[79] At pp. 675–676.

How far detriment to the defendant is relevant in resisting claims for repayment is essentially the point of apparent conflict between the decision of Mathew J. in *London and River Plate Bank* v. *Bank of Liverpool*[80] and that of the Judicial Committee of the Privy Council in *Imperial Bank of Canada* v. *Bank of Hamilton.*[81] The first case was one of bills bearing forged indorsements. By the time the forgery was discovered the defendant bank had lost their right to give notice of dishonour to other parties, and Mathew J., held that the plaintiffs could not recover. But basing his judgment on the earlier decision in *Cocks* v. *Masterman,*[82] he seemed to recognise no possibility of recovery of money paid by mistake except on immediate discovery of the mistake: it was not recoverable "where there is an interval of time in which the position of the holder may be altered." But in the *Imperial Bank of Canada* case Lord Lindley refused to accept that money was not recoverable "where notice of the mistake is given in reasonable time and no loss has been occasioned by the delay in giving it."

It is to be noted that the Privy Council was considering a strict interpretation of the principle, for in the Court of Appeal, Alberta, Armour, C.J. had said in his dissenting judgment, "The application of this rule does not at all depend on whether the holder of the bill is or is not prejudiced by the delay." It was this absolute application of the rule that the Privy Council was at pains to set aside; and it is unlikely that it will again be applied in its absolute form; Kerr J.'s statement of principle, that detriment is relevant only as an exception to the general rule, would seem to be the law as it now stands.[83]

In *Barclays Bank Ltd.* v. *W.J. Simms Son and Cooke (Southern) Ltd. and Another*[84] the defendants had argued, from a line of cases following *Cocks* v. *Masterman*, that the bank's failure to give immediate notice of the mistake (the bank having failed to observe their customer's instructions to stop payment of the cheque) invalidated their claim for repayment. But Robert Goff J., said that it was a prerequisite for that defence that the defendants should be under a duty to give notice of dishonour, whereas by section 50(2)(c) of the Bills of Exchange

[80] [1896] 1 Q.B. 7.
[81] [1903] A.C. 49. See Paget, *op. cit.* pp. 209 *et seq.* for discussion of the conflict.
[82] (1829) 9 B. & C. 902.
[83] *cf. ante*, pp. 97 *et seq.* for the relevance of detriment to the customer in cases on wrong entries in the customer's account.
[84] *Supra.*

Act, "Notice of dishonour is dispensed with . . . as regards the drawer . . . where the drawer has countermanded payment."

For money paid in mistake to be recoverable at all, the mistake must be one of fact, not law. Thus, in *Holt* v. *Markham*,[85] Holt & Co., acting as Army agents, overpaid Colonel Markham as a result of misinterpreting the relevant Army regulations. The Court of Appeal held *inter alia* that this was a mistake of law, and the money therefore not recoverable. But in *Admiralty Commissioners* v. *National Provincial and Union Bank of England Ltd.*,[86] where pay had been credited to an officer's account for some time after he had, first, been transferred to the Royal Air Force and, later, killed, the plaintiffs were held entitled to recover the money paid; the bank had contended that they were not entitled to release the amount in question until the consent of the personal representatives had been obtained, but this argument was rejected. It will be noted that the bank had not altered its position after receipt of the credits—for example, by paying out any part of them to, or on behalf of, their customer.

It is of course difficult, if not impossible, for the defendant to resist payment where he did not take in good faith. Kerr J.'s secondary finding in the *National Westminster Bank* case may be regarded as in part supporting this proposition.

The position of Barclays Bank International as collecting bank was not in issue, in view of their submission to whatever the court decided, but Kerr J. suggested that had they parted with the money they would have had a good defence "on the basis that as the collecting bank they were in the same position as agents who have parted with the money to their principal." As they had not parted with the money they could not have resisted the plaintiffs' claim.[87]

Carpenters' Company v. British Mutual Banking Co. Ltd.

[1938] 1 K.B. 511

The protection of section 60 of the Bills of Exchange Act 1882, may be lost if the paying bank is also the collecting bank, and through its negligence forfeits the protection of section 4 of the Cheques Act 1957

---

[85] [1923] 1 K.B. 504; *cf. ante*, pp. 98, 100.
[86] (1922) 38 T.L.R. 492.
[87] In *Chase Manhattan Bank N.A.* v. *Israel-British Bank (London) Ltd., ante*, p. 109, the plaintiff bank succeeded in recovering money paid in mistake on a different basis from that here discussed.

Facts

The plaintiffs were the trustees of a home, and kept an account in this connection with the defendant bank. The plaintiffs' clerk, Blackborow, was secretary of the committee administering the home, and as such regularly obtained cheques to pay tradesmen. Blackborow himself had an account with the defendants.

In 1920 he commenced to misappropriate the funds of the company, usually cheques drawn in favour of tradesmen who had supplied goods, in other cases cheques purporting to be in settlement of forged invoices. All cheques so misappropriated were crossed and properly drawn, Blackborow forging the indorsements of the payees and paying the cheques to the credit of his own account. These frauds continued over a period of years before they were discovered.

The company brought an action against the bank for the amount of the cheques, and Branson J. found as a fact that the bank did not act without negligence, and so had lost the protection of section 82 of the Bills of Exchange Act (now section 4 of the Cheques Act 1957), but that as they *paid* the cheques in good faith and in the ordinary course of business they were, notwithstanding their negligence in collection, protected by section 60. The company appealed.

Decision

The Court of Appeal held by a majority that the defendant bank had converted the cheques; as Branson J. had found that they did this negligently they could not rely on section 82, and were liable to the plaintiffs for the face value of the cheques so converted in the previous six years.

In his judgment, Greer L.J. said:

> ... when the cheques were presented to the defendant bank they had never ceased to be the property of the drawers, the Carpenters' Company, as they had never in fact been indorsed by the payees. The defendant bank was then asked by Blackborow to receive the cheques, and to place the amounts to the credit of his private account with it. This the bank did, and by so doing in my judgment converted the cheques to its own use and became liable to the Carpenters' Company, the drawers of the cheques, for the face value of the cheques.
>
> In my judgment section 60 of the Bills of Exchange Act, 1882, only protects a bank when that bank is merely a paying bank, and is not a bank which receives a cheque for collection.[88]

---

[88] At p. 529.

Notes[89]

The essential point of this decision, that a banker who acts as both paying and collecting banker cannot avoid his responsibility for negligence as collecting banker on the grounds that as paying banker he is protected by section 60, is a comparatively simple one.

It may be noted that the bank in this case claimed to be protected by section 19 of the Stamp Act 1853, which reads:

> ... any draft or order drawn upon a banker for a sum of money payable to order on demand, which shall, when presented for payment, purport to be indorsed by the person to whom the same shall be drawn payable, shall be a sufficient authority to such a banker to pay the amount of such draft or order to the bearer thereof; and it shall not be incumbent on such banker to prove that such indorsement, or any subsequent indorsement, was made by or under the direction or authority of the person to whom the said draft or order was or is made payable either by the drawer or any indorser thereof.

The lower court upheld this claim, but the Court of Appeal held that the section had been impliedly repealed, as regards cheques and bills, by section 60 of the Bills of Exchange Act. The effect of the present case, in this connection, is therefore to restrict the effect of section 19 of the Stamp Act to drafts other than cheques and bills.[90]

Raphael and Another v. Bank of England

(1855) 17 C.B. 161

The meaning of "good faith"

Facts

In November, 1852, some bank-notes issued by the defendants were stolen in Liverpool, and payment of the notes was stopped forthwith. The loss was advertised.

Raphael was the English correspondent of St. Paul, a money-changer in Paris, whose firm habitually changed English notes. There was some evidence that notice of the loss of the notes in question reached him in the spring of 1853. In June, 1854, one of the missing notes, for £500, was presented to St. Paul for changing, and after seeing the passport of the person presenting

---

[89] See *post*, p. 173, for the relevance of this case to the "lulling to sleep" doctrine.

[90] *cf. ante*, p. 125.

the note, and getting him to write his name and address on the note, he changed it into French money. St. Paul did not look at the file of notices of lost and stolen notes.

The plaintiffs now sued the defendants for the amount of the note and interest. The defendants pleaded *inter alia* that the plaintiffs were not bona fide holders for value of the note, because they had received notice that it was stolen. The jury found that St. Paul's firm gave value for the note; that they had notice of the robbery; that they had no knowledge of the loss when they took the note, although they had means of knowledge; and that they took the note bona fide. Judgment was entered for the plaintiffs, and the defendants appealed.

Decision

The Court of Common Pleas upheld the decision, and the appeal failed.

Cresswell J. said:

A person who takes a negotiable instrument bona fide for value has undoubtably a good title, and is not affected by the want of title of the party from whom he takes it. His having the means of knowing that the security had been lost or stolen, and neglecting to avail himself thereof, may amount to negligence: and Lord Tenterden at one time thought negligence was an answer to the action. But the doctrine of *Gill* v. *Cubitt*[91] is not now approved of. I think, therefore, there is no reason to find fault with the verdict on that ground. Then, the jury have found, in substance, that the note in question was taken by St. Paul bona fide and for value. He could not have taken it bona fide, if at the time he took it he had notice or knowledge that the note was a stolen note.[92]

And Willes J. said:

[In the case of *May* v. *Chapman*[93]] it is laid down by Parke B., that "notice and knowledge" means not merely express notice, but knowledge, or the means of knowledge to which the party wilfully shuts his eyes—a suspicion in the mind of the party, and the means of knowledge in his power wilfully disregarded.[94]

Notes

In sections 1 and 3 of the Cheques Act 1957, which provide

[91] (1824) 3 B. & C. 466.
[92] At p. 171.
[93] (1847) 16 M. & W. 355.
[94] At p. 174.

protection for respectively the paying and the collecting banker, that protection depends upon the banker having acted in good faith and (*a*) in the ordinary course of business, when he is the paying banker; (*b*) without negligence, when he is the collecting banker. Section 90 of the Bills of Exchange Act 1882 (with which the Cheques Act is construed as one) provides:

A thing is deemed to be done in good faith within the meaning of this Act, where it is in fact done honestly, whether it is done negligently or not.

Negligence by itself does not imply absence of good faith.

The possible relevance of constructive, as opposed to actual, notice was discussed in *Jones* v. *Gordon*,[95] where a person had taken bills (issued for a fraudulent purpose) at a gross undervalue and had deliberately refrained from making inquiries. Lord Blackburn said:

I consider it to be fully and thoroughly established that if value be given for a bill of exchange, it is not enough to show that there was carelessness, negligence, or foolishness in not suspecting that the bill was wrong, when there were circumstances which might have led a man to suspect that. All these are matters which tend to show that there was dishonesty in not doing it, but they do not in themselves make a defence to an action upon a bill of exchange. I take it that in order to make such a defence, whether in the case of a party who is solvent and *sui juris*, or when it is sought to be proved against the estate of a bankrupt, it is necessary to show that the person who gave value for the bill, whether the value given be great or small, was affected with notice that there was something wrong about it when he took it. I do not think it is necessary that he should have notice of what the particular wrong was.... But if the facts and circumstances are such that the jury ... came to the conclusion that he was not honestly blundering and careless, but that he must have had a suspicion that there was something wrong, and that he refrained from asking questions.... I think that is dishonesty.[96]

And in *Auchteroni & Co.* v. *Midland Bank Ltd.*[97] Wright J. quoted Lord Herschell in *London Joint Stock Bank* v. *Simmons*[98]:

I should be very sorry to see the doctrine of constructive notice introduced into the law of negotiable instruments. But regard to the

[95] (1877) 2 App.Cas. 616.
[96] At pp. 628–629.
[97] [1928] 2 K.B. 294; *cf. post*, p. 147.
[98] [1892] A.C. 201; *post*, p. 280.

facts of which the taker of such instruments had notice is most material in considering whether he took in good faith. If there be anything which excites the suspicion that there is something wrong in the transaction, the taker of the instrument is not acting in good faith if he shuts his eyes to the facts presented to him and puts the suspicions aside without further inquiry.[99]

An unusual example of a bank failing in its claim to be a holder in due course because of its manager's conspiracy with a fraudulent customer was *Bank of Credit and Commerce International S.A.* v. *Dawson and Wright.*[1] The manager knew that three cheques issued by the defendants in payment for goods were conditional on the goods being delivered. They were not delivered, the cheques were dishonoured, and the payee went bankrupt. The bank's claim as holder in due course failed, because the manager's financial arrangement with the payee was a lack of good faith within s.29 of the Bills of Exchange Act 1882.

Baines v. National Provincial Bank Ltd.

(1927) 32 Com.Cas. 216

The ordinary course of business

Facts

The plaintiff, a bookmaker, banked with the Harrogate branch of the defendant bank. On August 14, 1925, he drew a cheque for £200 payable to G. A. Wood, and handed it to the payee, shortly before 3 p.m. In the ordinary course the bank closed at 3 p.m., and the cheque could not have been presented before that time. Wood presented it, however, and for the purposes of this case the bank admitted cashing it at 3.5 p.m. The plaintiff later wished to stop payment of the cheque, and on the opening of the bank the next morning he sent his son to countermand payment. As the cheque had already been paid, the bank debited his account, however, and he then brought action for a declaration that they were not entitled to do so, and that in cashing it after closing time they had committed a breach of their duty to him as his bankers.

Decision

It was held that a bank is entitled to deal with a cheque

---

[99] At p. 302.
[1] [1987] F.L.R. 342.

within a reasonable business margin 'of time after their advertised time of closing, and that in cashing the cheque as they did in this case, the bank had acted within their rights. In the course of his judgment, Lord Hewart C.J. said:

> What precisely are the limits of time within which a bank may conduct business, having prescribed, largely for its own convenience, particular times at which the doors of the building will be closed, is a large question which is not raised here. What is contended on behalf of the defendants is that they are entitled within a reasonable business margin of their advertised time for closing to deal with a cheque, not of course in the sense of dishonouring it, but in the sense of doing that which the cheque asks them to do, namely, to pay it. In my opinion their contention is right, and the plaintiff's case fails entirely.[2]

Notes

In the *Joachimson* case[3] Atkin L.J. said that it was part of the banker's obligation to pay cheques of the customer in normal business hours. In the present case, the court was not prepared to make it part of the obligation *not* to pay the cheques outside normal banking hours. It seems certain, however, that the ordinary course of the banker's business could not reasonably be extended more than a short time after the advertised time of closing; it would not, for example, be within the ordinary course of business to pay a cheque at midnight.[4]

In practice it is, of course, impracticable to finish the counter work of the branch immediately upon the closing of the doors, and it frequently happens that a quarter of an hour, or longer, elapses before the last customer (who may be waiting to present a cheque) is attended to. A difficulty might arise if a person entered the bank unobserved, while there were still customers awaiting attention some minutes after closing time, and the bank cashed a cheque presented by such a person under the impression that he had been waiting since before closing time.

The ordinary course of business is so largely a question of what is reasonable in the particular circumstances that it is not possible to lay down firm rules.[5] Thus, in *Auchteroni & Co.* v. *Midland Bank Ltd.*[6] Wright J. said:

---

[2] At p. 218.
[3] *Ante*, p. 1.
[4] See Penn, Shea & Arora, *op. cit.* I 6.29, 18.124, and *cf. Royal Bank of Canada* v. *I.R.C.* [1974] Q.B. 76.
[5] *cf.* Reeday, *op. cit.* p. 394.
[6] [1928] 2 K.B. 294.

The law merchant has always recognised such presentation [of a bill, complete and regular on its face, and indorsed in blank by what the cashier knew to be the customer's genuine indorsement] as due presentation sufficient to require the bankers, in the absence of very special circumstances of suspicion, such as presentation by a tramp, or a postman or an office boy, to pay. To lay down any different principle and to treat that which is merely infrequent or unusual as irregular by the law merchant would be, I think, to make an inroad on the established rules of the law merchant without any sufficient ground.[7]

The encashment of cheques by open credit (*i.e.* "under advice"), at branches other than those at which the accounts are kept is so common a practice that it would almost certainly be held to be within the ordinary course of business.[8] The infrequency of litigation on open credits[9] seems to indicate that in practice little trouble arises; and in any event this service to customers is so popular that were any legal impediment to it to be discovered it is probable that it would be overcome by some such expedient as the opening of temporary accounts at the branches or banks at which it was desired to establish the credits.

The fate of cheques presented through the Bankers Clearing House must normally be decided on the day of presentation, but the rules of the Clearing House allow cheques which were dishonoured for other than technical reasons to be returned on the morning after presentation (with telephone advice if the cheque is over £30), where by inadvertence return has not been made on the day of presentation. This exception to the basic rule presumably originated with delayed posting and continues with computerisation; it was referred to by Bingham J. in his arbitration award in *Barclays Bank plc and Others* v. *Bank of England*.[10]

Automation was not accepted as justification for late dishonour in the special circumstances of *Momm* v. *Barclays*

---

[7] At p. 304.

[8] *cf. Questions on Banking Practice*, 11th ed., p. 125, as to the position where a cheque is cashed by another bank, as agent for the instructing bank.

[9] The circumstances of *Simons* v. *Barclays Bank Ltd.* (unreported) (1981) C.L.Y. 25 were unusual. Instructions to open a credit in Trinidad were delayed by a postal strike, and the confirmation of the credit to the plaintiff was not delivered until after he had left for his holiday. Lacking proof that he had resources he was refused admission and deported, and in the Court of Appeal, Stephenson L.J. held that he was entitled to reasonable compensation.

[10] [1985] 1 All E.R. 385.

Bank International Ltd.,[11] where Kerr J. held that the bank, having passed debit and credit entries between two customers' accounts on June 26, 1974, were not entitled to reverse those entries on the morning of June 27, even though the credit had not been communicated to the beneficiary. He rejected the bank's argument that the final balances for the day were not available from the computer until the following morning. He said:

A day is a day. For banking purposes it ends at the close of working hours, and otherwise at midnight. Commerce requires that it should be clearly ascertainable at the end of a day whether a payment to be made on that day has been made or not. Whether that has happened or not cannot be held in suspense until the following morning. The only result will be that the defendants will no longer be able to rely, as against their own payee customers, on the possibility of having second thoughts on the following morning.[12]

The judgment in this case is of considerable interest to bankers. It concerned an "in house" transaction[13]; two "out house" payments, made at the same time on the instructions of the debtor company, were "irrevocably despatched" before the close of business.

The case was not concerned with, and the judgment did not touch upon, the cheque clearing process, but that the same reasoning might be applied to postponed return of dishonoured cheques is clearly a possibility. But in the *Selangor* case,[14] Ungoed-Thomas J. said:

It is accepted that in the ordinary course of business, the decision what course to take with regard to a cheque presented for payment must be taken on the day of its receipt by the bank branch responsible for the decision. It seems to me, however, that a banker is not compelled at his risk to honour or dishonour his customer's cheques in the ordinary course, by the end of the day of its receipt, if there are circumstances requiring investigation.

---

[11] [1976] 3 All E.R. 588; also *sub nom. Delbreuck & Co.* v. *Barclays Bank International Ltd.* [1976] 2 Lloyd's Rep. 341.

[12] At p. 598. And *cf.* the House of Lords ruling in the *Afovos* case, *ante*, p. 75.

[13] *cf. The Brimnes, ante*, pp. 74 *et seq.*, considered by Kerr J. in the *Momm* judgment as not countering his view that communication to the payee is not an essential of a completed payment. See also *Royal Products* v. *Midland Bank Ltd. post*, p. 403.

[14] [1968] 2 All E.R. 1073.

Devaynes v. Noble, Clayton's Case

(1816) 1 Mer. 529, 572

In the case of a current account, payments in are, in the absence of any express indication to the contrary by the customer, presumed to have been appropriated to the debit items in order of date

Facts

Devaynes was the senior partner in a firm of bankers. Upon his death the surviving partners continued to carry on business under the former partnership name of Devaynes, Dawes, Noble & Co., despite written notice from Devaynes's son and from the trustees of the father that the continued use of the name Devaynes was without their consent. Upon the bankruptcy in the following year of the surviving partners, a number of questions of law fell to be argued in Chancery, one claimant being selected to represent each class of creditor.

In this way, Nathaniel Clayton represented those who, after Devaynes's death, continued to deal with the partners, both by paying in and drawing out, some withdrawals being made (after the death) before any credits were paid in, but the balance on the whole being increased by these transactions. In the case of Clayton himself, the balance of £1,713, at the death of Devaynes, was reduced within a few days to £453, no payments in being made in that time; and before the bankruptcy, withdrawals amounted to considerably more than the whole sum of £1,713. Clayton, however, claimed that the sum of £453 was due to him from Devaynes's estate, on the ground that subsequent withdrawals from the account were to be set against later credits.

Decision

Sir William Grant M.R. considered the general topic of appropriation of payments which, in the Civil Law, was primarily at the option of the debtor, and, in the absence of express appropriation by either debtor or creditor, was effected in the manner most beneficial to the creditor. In the English authorities there had been some conflict as to whether, instead, in the absence of appropriation by the debtor, the creditor had the option of appropriating whenever he thought fit, no matter how long after the payment. He continued:

But I think the present case is distinguishable from any of those in which that point has been decided in the creditor's favour. They were all cases of distinct insulated debts. . . . But this is the case of a banking account, where all the sums paid in form one blended fund, the parts of which have no longer any distinct existence. Neither banker nor customer ever thinks of saying, this draft is to be placed on the account of the £500 paid in on Monday, and this other to the account of the £500 paid in on Tuesday. There is a fund of £1,000 to draw upon, and that is enough. In such a case there is no room for any other appropriation than that which arises from the order in which the receipts and payments take place, and are carried into the account. Presumably, it is the sum first paid in, that is first drawn out. It is then the first item on the debit side of the account, that is discharged, or reduced, by the first item on the credit side. . . . You are not to take the account backwards, and strike the balance at the head, instead of the foot, of it. A man's banker breaks, owing him, on the whole account, a balance of £1,000. It would surprise one to hear the customer say, "I have been fortunate enough to draw out all that I paid in during the last four years; but there is £1,000, which I paid in five years ago, that I hold myself never to have drawn out; and, therefore, if I can find any body who was answerable for the debts of the banking-house, such as they stood five years ago, I have a right to say that it is that specific sum which is still due to me, and not the £1,000 that I paid in last week." This is exactly the nature of the present claim.[15]

Accordingly Clayton's claim was not substantiated.

Notes

In modern conditions the rule in *Clayton's* case is not likely to be applied again in the precise circumstances of *Devaynes* v. *Noble*. But the case is a landmark both in banking law and in the general law, and it is still constantly applied in a variety of circumstances in and out of banking. Many examples are to be found elsewhere in this book.[16]

The rule can of course work against as well as for the bank. In *Deeley* v. *Lloyds Bank Ltd.*[17] the bank had advanced money against a second mortgage. There was a subsequent mortgage to the borrower's sister, Mrs. Deeley, and the bank, which was held to have had notice of this third mortgage, did not break the account with their customer, despite the fact that it was a rule of the bank that this should be done. The account continued to work, and within three weeks credits paid in totalled more than the amount of the bank's mortgage, while within another fortnight credits totalled more than the whole of

[15] At pp. 608–609.
[16] *cf., e.g.* pp. 109, 316, 317, 343, 388, 395, 396.
[17] [1912] A.C. 756, *cf. post*, p. 343.

the indebtedness, secured and unsecured. Upon the customer's later bankruptcy the bank entered into possession of the mortgaged property, selling it for a sum just large enough to pay off the first and second mortgages. Mrs. Deeley subsequently claimed accounts as against a mortgagee in possession. Judgment was given for the bank, and a majority in the Court of Appeal dismissed the appeal, but the House of Lords allowed the further appeal, holding that payments to the credit of the account after notice of the third mortgage wiped out the advance outstanding at the time of the notice, while subsequent withdrawals had created a fresh advance to which Mrs. Deeley's mortgage had priority.

Lord Shaw of Dunfermline quoted with approval the words of Eve J. in the court of first instance:

I understand that to mean this: according to the law of England, the person paying the money has the primary right to say to what account it shall be appropriated; the creditor, if the debtor makes no appropriation, has the right to appropriate; and if neither of them exercises the right, then one can look on the matter as a matter of account and see how the creditor has dealt with the payment, in order to ascertain how he did in fact appropriate it.[18]

There can be other bars to the application of the rule besides the breaking of the account; in the *Deeley* case Lord Atkinson said:

It is no doubt quite true that the rule laid down in *Clayton's* case is not a rule of law to be applied in every case, but rather a presumption of fact, and that this presumption may be rebutted in any case, by evidence going to show that it was not the intention of the parties that it should be applied.[19]

and such evidence may be provided by the terms of the contract. Thus in *Westminster Bank Ltd.* v. *Cond*[20] the guarantor contended that, as the bank had continued the account unbroken after making demand on him, the advance he had guaranteed had been paid off by the payments into the account. But the bank's guarantee form contained a clause that was held to cover these circumstances and prevent the operation of the rule.

[18] At p. 783.
[19] At p. 771.
[20] (1940) 46 Com.Cas. 60. See *post*, pp. 293, 315, for facts and decision on main point at issue.

A clause of this kind is included in many bank guarantee forms, but is not usually relied upon, the account being usually broken. It is broken similarly on the death of one of the partners in a partnership; in *Royal Bank of Scotland* v. *Christie*[21] is seen an example of the application of the rule in *Clayton's* case upon failure to do so.

In the case of *The Mecca*[22] the House of Lords held that the rule in *Clayton's* case did not apply when, instead of an account current between the parties, there were a number of separate transactions, nor when, from an account rendered or other circumstances, it appeared that the creditor intended to reserve the right of appropriation. They also held that, whereas appropriation by a debtor must be made at the time of payment, appropriation by the creditor may be made as late as he wishes, "up to the last moment" (so long as he has not made earlier election), and might be declared by the creditor bringing an action, or by any other method so long as his intention was clear.

A trustee who has mixed trust money with his own by paying both into the same banking account cannot rely upon the rule in *Clayton's* case as against the beneficiaries, for it will be presumed in such a case that the moneys first drawn out by him from the banking account were his own, so as to leave any remaining balance available for the beneficiaries.[23] But the rule will apply as between two different beneficiaries whose moneys have both been paid into the same account, when the trustee later has drawn out part of the trust moneys.[24]

Douglass v. Lloyds Bank Ltd.

(1929) 34 Com.Cas. 263

Repayment after lapse of time

Facts

In going through the papers of her mother, lately deceased, a daughter found a deposit receipt dated May 12, 1866, issued at the Birmingham office of the defendant bank to a Mr. Fenwicke, her father, who had died in 1893. The receipt was for

---

[21] *Post*, p. 205.
[22] [1897] A.C. 286.
[23] See *Re Hallett's Estate, Knatchbull* v. *Hallett* (1879) 13 Ch.D. 696, *ante*, p. 106.
[24] See *Re Stenning, Wood* v. *Stenning* [1895] 2 Ch. 433 and *Re Hallett, supra*.

£6,000, with a memorandum of repayment of £2,500 indorsed upon it. No mention of the deposit was made in the will of the deceased, or in his papers. The present action was brought by the surviving executor of Mr. Fenwicke. The bank in their defence admitted that they could find no books of the Birmingham office before 1873, but contended that there was a presumption that the money had been repaid, and that in any event the plaintiff was debarred by his laches from bringing the action. The bank expressly disclaimed any intention of pleading the Statute of Limitations.

Decision

Roche J. giving judgment for the bank, decided the case on their first plea and the facts produced in evidence. He said:

On the facts I recognise to the full the strength of the fact that the plaintiff produces this deposit receipt, but I cannot ignore what experience tells me, and the evidence in this case shows, that people lose or mislay their deposit receipts at the time when they want to get their money back, and that money is paid over, if they are respectable persons and willing to give the necessary indemnity or receipt, without production of the deposit receipt; indeed, otherwise life would be intolerable and business impossible. . . . I am satisfied, and I so find, that the practice of this bank was such that no sum like this of £3,500, would have been treated by being carried to profit and loss account or to some reserve account, or to any of the other accounts which have been mentioned, within any such period as the short period between 1866 and 1873, or for long afterwards.[25]

Notes

This decision must not be given more than its proper weight: it was based upon the very special facts of a particular case. It is interesting, however, as a rare example of a bank successfully contesting (or indeed contesting at all) a claim against it, even though its books had been destroyed and it could not prove payment. The bank was allowed to produce its oldest surviving deposit ledgers, which showed no account in the name in question, and this was accepted as supporting the bank's claim that the deposit had been repaid. It need hardly be said that every bank keeps a strict account of "unclaimed balances," small or large, and it may be particularly noted that in the present case Lloyds Bank did not plead the Statute of

[25] At pp. 272, 276.

Limitations[26]; it is doubtful whether any bank would ever shelter behind the statute in such circumstances, for to do so would be, if not to admit the debt, at least not to deny it; while in any event time does not run against the customer until he has made demand for the debt owing to him.[27]

[26] cf. Holden, op. cit. I, 2–30.
[27] Joachimson v. Swiss Bank Corporation, ante, p. 1.

Chapter 4

THE COLLECTING BANKER

Westminster Bank Ltd. v. Zang

[1966] A.C. 182

The bank as holder for value

The effect of section 2 of the Cheques Act 1957

Facts

The defendant, having lost heavily at cards, borrowed £1,000 from a friend, Mr. Tilley, and gave him his cheque in exchange. The loan was money belonging to the company which Mr. Tilley controlled, and he subsequently paid the cheque to the credit of the company's account, together with others. He did not indorse any of the cheques, although the cheque for £1,000 was payable to him personally and not to the company. The clearing banks in 1957, after the passing of the Cheques Act, had laid down a rule that "indorsement will be required as heretofore if the instrument is tendered for the credit of an account other than that of the ostensible payee."

On the day the cheque was paid in the company account was overdrawn more than £1,000 in excess of the agreed overdraft limit, but not to an extent that caused the bank alarm; and further cheques were paid on the account on the same day. The cheque for £1,000 was dishonoured.

When their customer issued a writ against the defendant the bank surrendered the cheque to his solicitors, for the purpose of enabling him to enforce his claim, against their undertaking to return it on demand. This action was not proceeded with, and in due course the bank commenced their own action, claiming as holders in due course by virtue of section 2 of the Cheques Act. The defendant, having unsuccessfully pleaded the Gaming Act, took four further points—

(i) that the cheque was delivered to the bank by Mr. Tilley, not as the "holder" within section 2, but as the agent of the company;

156

(ii) that the words of the section, "which the holder delivers for collection," could not apply to an unindorsed cheque paid in to an account which was not that of the payee;

(iii) that the bank had not given value for the cheque; and

(iv) that the bank had ceased to be "holder" of the cheque when they gave it up to Mr. Tilley's solicitors.

Roskill J. having found for the bank, the defendant appealed. Upon the Court of Appeal finding for the defendant, the bank appealed further.

Decision

The House of Lords dismissed the appeal, holding that the bank had not established their claim to be holders for value. The respondent's first two points were rejected, and in view of their finding on the third point, their Lordships did not discuss the fourth.

Notes

The House of Lords decision in the *Zang* case is important both for its rejection of the bank's claim to be holder for value of the disputed cheque, and for its ruling on the effect of section 2 of the Cheques Act; and the finding of the Court of Appeal on the defendant's fourth point (on which the law lords did not pronounce) is also of concern to the banks.

The circumstances in which a bank can establish title as holder for value of a cheque collected for a customer was for many years a matter of debate in the text books,[1] and although much of that debate is now of only historic interest, the position is still not entirely clear. On the facts of the *Zang* case Viscount Dilhorne considered that (1) the reduction of the overdraft was irrelevant, in view of the fact that the bank charged interest on the amount of the cheque until it was cleared—"In those circumstances it is hard to see that by crediting it to the account and reducing the overdraft the bank gave value for it"[2]; (2) no implied agreement to pay against uncleared effects could be read into the circumstances of the case; (3) the printed words on the credit slip negatived such an agreement; and (4) no evidence was given "that cheques drawn by the company and presented between April 27 and May 2 were only honoured in consequence of the uncleared effects."

---

[1] For the history of this topic see Chorley, Gilbart Lectures, 1953, *The Law relating to the Collection of Cheques*, and *cf.* Paget, *op. cit.*, pp. 327 *et seq.*

[2] [1966] A.C. 182 at p. 219.

In *A.L. Underwood Ltd.* v. *Barclays Bank Ltd.*[3] where also the bank's claim was rejected, Atkin L.J. had said:

> I think it is sufficient to say that the mere fact that the bank in their books enter the value of the cheques on the credit side of the account on the day on which they receive the cheques for collection does not, without more, constitute the bank a holder for value. To constitute value there must be in such a case a contract between banker and customer ... that the bank will before receipt of the proceeds honour cheques of the customer drawn against the cheques ... neither [the *Gordon* decision[4]] nor the statute [the 1906 Act[5]] lays down the rule, judicial or statutory, that if a bank credits a cheque at once in its books that fact without more makes the bank a holder for value.[6]

That view was a little modified in the Court of Appeal hearing of *Zang*, when Salmon L.J. said:

> In *Underwood's* case there had been no drawings against the uncleared cheques. There had merely been book entries crediting the customer with their proceeds. It was in those circumstances that the Court was considering how a bank could become holders for value of the uncleared cheques. In my judgment this Court certainly did not lay down that in no circumstances could a bank become holders for value save by an express or implied contract to honour cheques drawn against the uncleared cheques. An obvious way of becoming a holder for value is to give value by honouring a cheque drawn against an uncleared cheque whether or not there is an antecedent contract to do so. Whether the bank has honoured a cheque drawn against uncleared effects is a matter of fact ... on the evidence of the bank manager and of the ledger to see how any such finding could have been made.[7]

But it will be noted that Viscount Dilhorne's judgment, at (4) above, if read strictly, set bounds to this argument: on this reading value is given only if it can be shown that cheques were paid that would have been dishonoured had the effects in question not been paid in.

An example of such circumstances is to be found in *Barclays Bank Ltd.* v. *Harding*,[8] where there was no doubt that the bank would have dishonoured substantial cheques unless covering effects had been provided. A further example is seen in

---

[3] [1924] 1 K.B. 775.
[4] *Capital and Counties Bank Ltd.* v. *Gordon* [1903] A.C. 240.
[5] Bills of Exchange (Crossed Cheques) Act 1906.
[6] At pp. 305–306.
[7] [1966] A.C. 182 at p. 210.
[8] (April 1962) 83 J.I.B. 109.

Barclays Bank Ltd. v. *Astley Industrial Trust Ltd.*[9] where Milmo
J. distinguished the *Zang* decision as being on materially
different facts—"in particular there was no question of the bank
having a lien such as there admittedly was in the present
case"[10]—but where in fact on one of the bank's contentions
there was no need to distinguish it. The bank's customers, a
garage company, had received cheques from the defendant
company in respect of hire purchase agreements. Upon
discovering that the agreements were fictitious the defendants
stopped payment of the cheques, but the bank had paid their
customers' cheques both before receipt of the Astley cheques
(upon the assurance that they were coming) and after they were
paid in, pending their clearance. The bank now claimed to be
holders for value (*a*) in respect of both the antecedent debt—the
overdraft—and the cheques paid pending collection; and (*b*) to
the extent of an overdraft, by virtue of section 27(3), as having
a lien on the cheques. They succeeded in all three contentions.
"The defendants took the cheques in good faith without notice
of any defect in [the plaintiff's] title, and the conditions in
section 29(1) of the [Bills of Exchange] Act to make them
holders in due course were satisfied."

It may be noted that Milmo J. expressly rejected the
defendants' argument that the bank could not be at once an
agent for collection of a cheque and a holder of that cheque for
value.

It seems to me that the language of section 2 of the Cheques Act
1957 negatives this proposition since it presupposes that a banker who
has been given a cheque for collection may nevertheless have given
value for it. It is, moreover, a commonplace occurrence for a banker to
allow credit to a customer against an uncleared cheque . . . I readily
accept that if a banker holds a cheque merely—and I emphasise the
word "merely"—as his customer's agent for collection he cannot be a
holder for value and still less a holder in due course; but that is an
entirely different proposition.[11]

He also refused to accept the argument that the fact of the
bank charging interest on the uncleared effects prevented them
from being holders for value. In the light of Viscount Dilhorne's
view this last finding cannot pass unquestioned; while the
reasoning based on section 2 of the Cheques Act may prove to

---

[9] [1970] 2 Q.B. 527, 9 L.D.B. 135, *cf. post,* p. 278.
[10] At p. 540.
[11] At p. 538.

have been an over-simplification. But one welcomes the reinforcement given to the finding of Ungoed-Thomas J. in *Re Keever*,[12] that the bank obtained a lien for the amount of the overdraft on cheques paid in for collection, the antecedent debt represented by the overdraft itself constituting consideration for the lien.

As to section 2 of the Cheques Act, Viscount Dilhorne said:

The acceptance of a paid unindorsed cheque as evidence of its receipt by the payee of the sum payable by the cheque does not appear to be as cogent evidence of receipt by the payee as production of a paid cheque indorsed by him. But this is, in my opinion, no ground on which one would be entitled to construe section 2 in the way contended for by the respondent. I regard the language of that section as clear and unambiguous. I can see nothing in the section nor in the other sections of the Act from which it is to be inferred that "collection" in section 2 means collection only for the payee's account. If that had been the intention of Parliament, it could easily have been expressed. If the protection given to the drawer by section 3 is inadequate, that is a matter for Parliament to rectify.[13]

There had been an earlier challenge to the banks on section 2. Thus in *Midland Bank Ltd.* v. *R.V. Harris Ltd.*[14] the argument was that as the bank were neither payees nor indorsees of cheques that they had received unindorsed, they could not be holders. Megaw J. had no difficulty in holding that the section was adequate to protect the bank, which in this case had received the unindorsed cheques for the credit of the payee.

The *Zang* case was more difficult, for here the respondent was arguing that an unindorsed cheque could be "collected" within the terms of section 2 only for the payee; and this argument had the attraction that any wider view must weaken the position of the drawer seeking to establish that the payee has received his money. As Lord Reid put it:

If the payee denies that he ever received the cheque, how is the payer to support the prima facie evidence afforded by section 3? There is no indorsement and no easy way to find out whether the payee ever received the cheque.[15]

---

[12] [1966] 3 All E.R. 631; but *cf. post*, p. 278.
[13] At p. 218.
[14] [1963] 1 W.L.R. 1021.
[15] At p. 222.

But only Lord Denning M.R. in the Court of Appeal was prepared to say that the Act required indorsement of cheques paid in to accounts other than those of the payee; while the rest of the Court, and Viscount Dilhorne and Lord Reid in the House of Lords, recognised the problem, they regarded the wording of the section as conclusive. It is for Parliament to amend the law if the drawer's position is regarded as seriously prejudiced. In practice, of course, the clearing banks' refusal to accept cheques for third party accounts without indorsement goes most of the way to redress the position, but the fact that this rule was inadvertently broken in the *Zang* case shows that the danger does exist.

The respondents' fourth point in the *Zang* case—that the bank had ceased to be holders of the cheque when they gave it up to Mr. Tilley's solicitors—is of more moment to bankers than their immunity in respect of third party cheques. The House of Lords, as has been pointed out already, did not pronounce on the point, but two of the judgments in the Court of Appeal found conclusive the argument that the cheques were returned to the payee in order that he should be able to sue—as holder. The bank thus lost its lien, and when the payee handed the cheque back it was not for collection. Even if the bank had then given value they would not have been holders in due course, for they would have known that the cheque had previously been dishonoured.

This point also had a preliminary airing in *Midland Bank Ltd. v. R.V. Harris Ltd.*[16] There the defendants were unable to produce evidence as to what had actually happened to the cheques (which, by the time the case came on for hearing, were in the possession of the bank). Megaw J. was therefore

unable to hold that the defendants have laid the foundation for any argument on this point, apart from any other difficulties (and I think they might have been formidable) in the way of the defendants in establishing the point.[17]

But any comfort the banks may have found in his comment in parentheses was removed by the finding of Lord Denning and Salmon L.J. in the *Zang* case.

In the normal course of business there is no problem: a cheque received back dishonoured is returned to the customer

---

[16] *Supra.*
[17] At p. 1029.

for whom it was collected and his account is debited. When trouble can be clearly foreseen it is open to the bank to retain the cheque, surrendering it, if at all, only subject to reservation of their own rights. But where trouble is not foreseen, as must often be the case, it would seem that the banks can find themselves at risk if they follow their normal routine.

NEGLIGENCE UNDER SECTION 4 OF THE CHEQUES ACT

Lloyds Bank Ltd. v. E.B. Savory & Co.

[1933] A.C. 201

Marfani & Co. Ltd. v. Midland Bank Ltd.

[1968] 1 W.L.R. 956

The negligence may refer back to the opening of the account

Facts of Lloyds Bank Ltd. v. E.B. Savory & Co.

The respondents were a firm of stockbrokers, who had in their employ two clerks, Perkins and Smith. In accordance with Stock Exchange practice, the firm was in the habit of issuing crossed bearer cheques representing payments to jobbers, and between March 1924 and March 1930 first Perkins and then Smith stole a number of these cheques and paid them into the appellant bank, in the case of Perkins for the credit of his account at Wallington, in the case of Smith for the credit of his wife's account at Redhill and later at Weybridge. Making use of the "branch credit" system used by all the large banks, the two clerks paid in the cheques at city branches of the bank and, while the cheques were cleared with the drawee bank, the credit slips were forwarded to the branches at which the accounts were kept. As the credit slips bore no particulars of the cheques, the branches receiving them through the post did not know the drawers of the cheques thus being credited. Moreover, neither branch had made enquiries as to who were the employers, in the one case of Perkins and in the other of the husband of Mrs. Smith.

When the frauds were discovered the respondents brought an action against the appellant bank for damages for conversion or, alternatively, for money had and received. The bank pleaded in defence section 82 of the Bills of Exchange Act, and sought to establish that they had not been negligent. It was shown in evidence that the "branch credit" system was commonly used by bankers' and had been so used for many years. The evidence as to the enquiries normally made upon the opening of a new account varied but the bank's rule book was shown to lay down that no new account should be opened "without knowledge of or full inquiry into the circumstances" of the customer.

Judgment was given for the bank (except in the case of one cheque, which had been paid in and collected before Mrs. Smith's account had been opened). The appeal of Savory & Co. was allowed by the Court of Appeal, and the bank appealed to the House of Lords.

Decision

The House of Lords held (Lord Blanesborough and Lord Russell of Killowen dissenting) that the bank had not discharged the burden of proving that they had acted without negligence, and the appeal was dismissed.

In his judgment in the Court of Appeal, Lawrence L.J. said:

Mr. Rayner Goddard [counsel for the bank]...submitted that to bring the bank within the protection of section 82 it was not necessary to do more than prove that it had acted according to the ordinary practice of bankers and that, whatever step might have to be taken in the future to guard against a repetition of similar frauds, it would not be right to convict the bank of negligence for having in good faith acted in accordance with such a long-established practice. In support of his argument, Mr. Rayner Goddard cited *Chapman* v. *Walton*[18] and *Commissioners of Taxation* v. *English Scottish and Australian Bank Ltd.*[19] In my judgment, neither of the pronouncements so relied on was intended to cover such a case as the present, where bankers, solely for the convenience of their customers, have adopted a system with an inherent and obvious defect which no reasonably careful banker could fail to observe.[20]

And in his judgment in the House of Lords, Lord Wright said:

I think...that at least where the new customer is employed in some position which involves his handling, and having the opportunity of stealing, his employers' cheques, the bankers fail in taking adequate precautions if they do not ask the name of his employers...because they fail to ascertain a most relevant fact as to the intending customers' circumstances. This is specially true of a stockbroker's clerk; it may be

[18] (1834) 10 Bing. 57.
[19] *Ante*, p. 30.
[20] [1932] 2 K.B. 122 at pp. 143–144.

different in the case of an employee whose work does not involve such opportunities, as, for instance, a technical employee in a factory. But in the case of a stockbroker's clerk or other similar employment, the bank are dealing with something which involves a risk fully known to them... It is clear that they ask information as to the man's occupation and if they find that he is (for instance) a stockbroker's clerk, they surely should go on and ask who his employers are, since otherwise they cannot guard against the danger fully known to them of his paying in cheques stolen from his employers. It is argued that this is not the ordinary practice of bankers and that a bank is not negligent if it takes all precautions usually taken by bankers. I do not accept that latter proposition as true in cases where the ordinary practice fails in making due provision for a risk fully known to those experienced in the business of banking.[21]

Facts of Marfani & Co. Ltd. v. Midland Bank Ltd.

The office manager of the plaintiff company introduced himself to a restaurant proprietor, Mr. Akaddas Ali, and in the course of several conversations, in which he said his name was Eliaszade, he spoke of his intention to open his own restaurant. Subsequently, on the eve of Mr. Marfani's departure on a visit to Pakistan, he drew a cheque for £3,000 on the company payable to Eliaszade, a London firm with which Marfanis did business, and obtained Mr. Marfani's signature to it. The cheque he paid into an account with the Midland Bank which he opened in the name of Eliaszade, giving as one of his two referees the name of Mr. Ali. When Mr. Ali, himself a good customer of the bank, who had introduced other satisfactory customers, confirmed that in his view the man would be good for the conduct of a bank account, the bank issued a cheque book, and over the following fortnight the balance of the account was withdrawn. When the fraud was discovered the company brought an action against the bank for damages for conversion of the cheque.

The company alleged negligence under several heads, in particular that the bank had not made sufficient inquiry upon the opening of the account, and that they should have had two references (the second referee did not reply to the bank's inquiry). Upon Nield J. finding that the bank had not been negligent the company appealed.

Decision

The Court of Appeal upheld the finding in the lower court. In his judgment Diplock L.J. said:

[21] At p. 231.

What the court has to do is to look at all the circumstances at the time of the acts complained of, and to ask itself where those circumstances such as would cause a reasonable banker possessed of such information about his customer as a reasonable banker would possess, to suspect that his customer was not the true owner of the cheque.[22]

Notes

The tort of conversion takes place wherever one person wilfully and without justification interferes with the chattel, *i.e.* movable property, of another in a manner inconsistent with that other's rights, and in such a way as to deprive him of possession of it.[23]

Section 4 of the Cheques Act 1957, which replaces section 82 of the Bills of Exchange Act 1882, confers protection on collecting bankers against the risk of action for conversion to which they are prima facie liable should the customer whose cheque is being collected turn out not to have a good title to it. This protection is, however, conditional upon the banker's being able to show (*inter alia*) that he conducted the collection ("received payment") without negligence.

Although the words of the section appear to refer only to the usual business of collection, the courts have held that the obligation to take care applies from the very beginning of the relationship, at which stage information must be obtained not only as to the customer's respectability but as to all matters relating to him which are obviously relevant to the possibility of his using his account to obtain payment of cheques which he has fraudulently converted to his own purposes. Such frauds can be guarded against only if precautions are taken, not only to see that everything is prima facie in order with the transaction at the time when it occurs—for example, that the indorsement is correct—but also that the surrounding circumstances, as discovered at the opening of the account and in the whole handling of it, do not throw any suspicion upon the transaction.

No more instructive illustration of the extreme responsibility which the courts have in the past put upon the banks can be found than the case of *Lloyds Bank Ltd.* v. *E.B. Savory & Co.*, which is perhaps the most important of all the section 4 cases. It will be observed that there were two distinct grounds upon which the bank failed to prove that due care had been taken.

---

[22] At p. 973.
[23] See Chorley, Gilbart Lectures, 1956; and *cf.* decision of McNair J. in *Marquess of Bute* v. *Barclays Bank Ltd.*, post, p. 181.

The judgments in the Court of Appeal were in the main based upon the deficiencies in the branch credit system[24]: that is to say, on negligence in connection with the handling of the account. In the House of Lords, however, all five judgments recognised in varying degrees that there was negligence involved in the use of the branch credit system only if the information concealed by it would put the bank on notice of irregularity if it were not so concealed: the negligence here in question was negligence occurring at the time the account was opened. The dissenting judgments were based on this point: since the customer's employer, and equally the employer of the husband of the woman customer, might admittedly be changed on the day after the account was opened, was there any useful purpose in inquiring about them? Lord Russell of Killowen said, in this connection:

> I know of no authority before the present case justifying the proposition, and I can conceive no logical basis on which one can rest an obligation on A to make an inquiry (for the purpose of regulating and guiding his future action during an indefinite period of time) the answer to which may cease to be correct immediately after it is given.[25]

But if there was no negligence in omitting to ask for the employer's name there was, *in the circumstances of the case*, no negligence in omitting to pass on the name of the drawers of the cheques paid in. It would be otherwise, of course, if, for example, a customer, the secretary or director of a company, paid into his account through the branch credit system cheques belonging to his company, for in such a case the information concealed by the system from the customer's branch would have put them on inquiry had it not been concealed, in that they would certainly have ascertained their customer's own employment.

The dissenting judgments in this case are of interest, for the case marks one of the extreme limits to which the courts have extended the duty of care in the collection of cheques, and it is still open to the House of Lords, in circumstances only a little different from those of the present case, to adopt the somewhat

---

[24] At least one of the large banks uses special credit slips for the branch credit system, and requires them to bear the names of the drawer and the payee of every cheque paid in in this way. The fact that this has not become general banking practice presumably indicates that this particular *Savory* risk is not found to be a serious one in practice; it does not appear to have come before the courts again in the 58 years since the *Savory* decision.

[25] (1932) 49 T.L.R. at p. 121.

broader outlook of Lords Blanesborough and Russell of Killowen. It may be remarked that in the *Orbit* case[26] Harman L.J. said:

> I must say that it seems to me to be a quite impossible obligation to put on the cashiers of a collecting bank to scrutinise the signatures of the drawers of incoming cheques, more especially the signatures to cheques of a limited company. Hundreds of these come in every day. In the latest case in the House of Lords on this subject, *Lloyds Bank Ltd. v. E.B. Savory & Co.*, it was held by the majority that a collecting bank had acted with negligence in not inquiring when two accounts were opened as to the employers of the customers. This seems to me a hard doctrine, but it has no application here . . . It cannot at any rate be the duty of the bank continually to keep itself up to date as to the identity of a customer's employer.[27]

The criticism of the *Savory* decision was, as is clear from this quotation, *obiter*, but it may perhaps be regarded as symptomatic of a rather less strict view of the banker's duty.[28]

This changing view has found its clearest expression so far in the *Marfani* case, where Diplock L.J. referred to the *Savory* decision and said:

> There were many other matters calculated to arouse suspicion in the social conditions of the 1920s. It was decided upon expert evidence, not of what is now current banking practice, but of what it was nearly 40 years ago. I find in it no more than an illustration of the general principle that a banker must exercise reasonable care in all the circumstances of the case.[29]

He also took a point that had been rejected in some of the earlier cases:

> It does not constitute any lack of reasonable care to refrain from making inquiries which it is improbable will lead to detection of the potential customer's dishonest purpose if he is dishonest, and which are calculated to offend him and maybe drive away his custom if he is honest.[30]

But the decision is perhaps principally significant for the Court of Appeal's endorsement of the principle that the current

---

[26] *Ante*, p. 41.
[27] [1963] 1 Q.B. 794 at pp. 824–825.
[28] *cf.* (June 1983) 103 J.I.B. 83.
[29] [1968] 1 W.L.R. 956 at p. 976, 9 L.D.B. 49.
[30] *Ibid.* at p. 977.

practice of careful bankers is not lightly to be considered negligent. Counsel for the plaintiffs had argued that the court should examine that practice and decide whether it complied with the standard of care expected of a prudent banker. Diplock L.J. agreed that this was so, "but I venture to think that this court should be hesitant in condemning as negligent a practice generally adopted by those engaged in banking business."[31] It is interesting to compare this view with that of Lord Wright in the *Savory* case: there is no contradiction between the two, but the difference in accent is noticeable.

In the *Selangor* case[32] Ungoed-Thomas J. after a long review of the cases on the negligence of both paying and collecting banker, saw the practice of bankers as one of the several factors in the assessment of the standard of care required. He said:

The standard of that reasonable care and skill is an objective standard applicable to bankers. Whether or not it has been attained in any particular case has to be decided in the light of all the relevant facts, which can vary almost infinitely. The relevant considerations include the prima facie assumption that men are honest, the practice of bankers, the very limited time in which banks have to decide what course to take with regard to the cheque presented for payment without risking liability for delay, and the extent to which an operation is unusual or out of the ordinary course of business.[33]

Of course, the *Marfani* decision is not to be regarded as removing all the dangers that await the careless banker. It recognises in part at least that negligence is to be measured by the standards of the present day; but every case must still be considered on its merits, and while the attitude of the courts today is different from that of half a century ago (as indeed is the banking system that they have to consider) bankers will have noted the warning sounded by Cairns J. With Diplock and Danckwerts L.JJ. he found for the bank, but with some hesitation: "if the defendant bank here exercised sufficient care, it was in my view only just sufficient."[34] And he remarked that the decision should not encourage any loosening of the rules that banks had made as a result of earlier, adverse, decisions. It is still necessary for the banker to study those decisions.

[31] *Ibid.* at p. 975.
[32] *Ante*, p. 83.
[33] At p. 1118.
[34] *Ibid.* at p. 982.

In them were set varying standards of care. As long ago as 1903, in *Turner* v. *London and Provincial Bank Ltd.*,[35] tried by Walton J. and a jury, carelessness in opening the account was one of the circumstances of the bank's negligence, and in *Ladbroke* v. *Todd*[36] the bank was held negligent for the same reason. Yet in the *Commissioners of Taxation* case[37] the bank successfully contested liability, despite apparent absence of inquiry regarding their customer, and Lord Dunedin went so far as to say: "It is not a question of negligence in opening an account, though the circumstances connected with the opening of an account may shed light on the question of whether there was negligence in collecting a cheque."[38]

In a later case, *Hampstead Guardians* v. *Barclays Bank Ltd.*[39] an account was opened in the name of Donald Stewart with the defendant bank. A reference was given, and in the course of the post a reply was received purporting to be from the referee but in fact a forgery. On the day the reply was received the customer brought in two orders drawn on the plaintiffs and payable to "D. Stewart & Company," with the explanation that this was his trading name. There was only one firm of the name in London, at an address different from that given when the account was opened. He later drew the proceeds of the orders and disappeared. Acton J. held that the bank had been negligent, and said that the reference, even had it been genuine, would have been good only for a genuine Donald Stewart. While this fact was not important on the day the account was opened, it became so when on the following day the orders were paid in. It is to be noted, however, that he went on to describe the negligence associated with the actual orders, and it is doubtful whether the circumstances of the opening alone would have been held to be sufficient negligence.

In *Nu-Stilo Footwear Ltd.* v. *Lloyds Bank Ltd.*[40] the circumstances were similar to those of the *Hampstead Guardians* case, the customer here opening his account in a false name, giving his own name as referee. Sellers J., however, distinguished the earlier decision on the grounds that in the present case the bank took up the reference by telephone and in

---

[35] (1903) 2 L.D.B. 33.
[36] *Ante*, p. 32.
[37] *Ante*, p. 31.
[38] *Ibid.* at p. 688.
[39] (1923) 39 T.L.R. 229.
[40] (1956) 7 L.D.B. 121.

writing, thus confirming that the referee was what he purported to be, and also inquired of the referee's bank (where he had earlier opened an account) as to his suitability as a referee. He found the bank negligent, nevertheless, in that the second cheque paid in to the customer's account, for £550 10s. 1d., payable to a third party, and other subsequent cheques, some of them payable to the customer, some to third parties, were of amounts inconsistent with his stated occupation of free-lance agent, newly started in business:

Each further personal cheque should have prompted an inquiry as to what the customer was doing as a free-lance agent, as the receipt by him of large sums was quite out of harmony with the description of his trade or prospects as revealed by him to the bank.[41]

The extent to which the bank's own rule book was cited in the *Savory* case in the judgments both in the Court of Appeal and in the House of Lords, is noteworthy. Viscount Buckmaster emphasised (as did Goddard J. in even more precise terms in the *Motor Traders* case[42]) that a bank's own rules do not themselves establish a legal standard of care; but "they afford a very valuable criterion of obvious risks against which the banks think it is their duty to guard."[43]

It may be remarked finally that Sir John Paget, in his note to the *Turner* case in the volume of *Legal Decisions affecting Bankers* cited above, said: "The lack of inquiry into the standing and habits of the customer seems somewhat remote from the actual transaction."[44] This comment has today some historic interest, in its reflection of the extent to which standards of negligence under section 82 have been tightened in the past 86 years. It is to be noted, however, that recently the taking up of references for new customers has been abandoned by some banks, presumably questioning the usefulness of the practice in modern conditions[45] which have changed further since Diplock L.J.'s comment of 20 years ago.

---

[41] At p. 127.
[42] *Post*, p. 177.
[43] At p. 117.
[44] (1903) 2 L.D.B. 33 at p. 34.
[45] *cf.* Ellinger, *op. cit.* 429.

Lloyds Bank Ltd. v. Chartered Bank of India, Australia and China

(1928) 44 T.L.R. 534

Negligence in collecting for agents or employees where the principal or employer is the drawer of the cheques

Facts

The plaintiff bank had as their chief accountant in their Bombay office one Lawson, who had authority to sign on behalf of his employers. He drew a series of 19 cheques, between March 1922, and January, 1924, to a total value of more than £17,000, all payable to the defendant bank, and these he sent to the bank, requesting them to credit the private account he kept with them. This they did, collecting the cheques (which were drawn on the Imperial Bank of India); and upon the fraud being discovered, the plaintiff bank brought an action for conversion. The defendants relied particularly upon section 131 of the Indian Negotiable Instruments Act 1881, corresponding to section 82 of the Bills of Exchange Act. Upon the main issue of negligence, judgment was given for the plaintiffs, and the defendants appealed.

Decision

The Court of Appeal held that, although the cheques were payable to the defendants themselves, they had received payment "for a customer"; but that they had not discharged the burden of proving due care, and the appeal failed.

In the course of his judgment, Scrutton L.J. said:

The learned judge finds, after careful consideration, that the defendant bank failed to prove absence of negligence. He rests his judgment on the payment by Lawson of large cheques of his bank into his private account, and failure to make inquiries of the manager of the plaintiff bank as to the regularity of the transactions. I agree in this finding, and would add that I think examination of Lawson's account (and I am sure that general examination of the accounts of every customer takes place from time to time in all well-managed banks) should, I think, have put the defendant bank on inquiry as to the source from which these heavy payments to stockbrokers were being made, in the case of an account generally in low water, except for these payments in, immediately reduced by payments out.

The only remaining defence was that the defendant bank was "lulled to sleep" by the failure of the plaintiff bank to detect these frauds. The learned judge has dismissed this on the ground that no one from the defendant bank came to say he was "lulled to sleep"; their attitude was that they remembered nothing about the matter. This is enough to dispose of the matter, but though a similar defence succeeded in *Morison's* case[46] I am not at all satisfied as to the grounds of such a decision. It does not seem consistent with the decisions in *Bank of Ireland* v. *Trustees of Evans' Charities in Ireland*,[47] and *Swan* v. *North British Australasian Company*,[48] that negligence, to act as estoppel, must be the proximate cause of the loss. If my butler for a year has been selling my vintage wines cheaply to a small wine merchant, I do not understand how my negligence in not periodically checking my wine book will be an answer to my action against the wine merchant for conversion. However, the ground of the learned judge's decision is enough to dispose of this point. This, I think, substantially exhausts the points taken on the appeal, which must be dismissed with costs.[49]

And Sankey L.J. said:

In my view, a bank cannot be held to be liable for negligence merely because they have not subjected an account to a microscopic examination. It is not to be expected that the officials of banks should also be amateur detectives. It is not easy, nor is it desirable. to define the degree of negligence which would render them liable. Many factors have to be taken into consideration, the customer, the account, and the surrounding circumstances. But, whilst it is difficult to draw the line, the problem upon which side of the line a particular case falls does not present such difficulties. Having regard to the uncommon nature of the cheques in question, having regard to the fact that Lawson was an employee of the plaintiffs, as was well known by the defendants, and having regard to the heavy payment made at crucial times to persons known to be brokers, I cannot come to any other conclusion but that the defendants were negligent in this case.[50]

Notes

In *Morison's* case, to which Scrutton L.J. referred—*Morison* v. *London County and Westminster Bank Ltd.*[51]—the manager of the plaintiff's insurance broking business, with authority to sign cheques for the firm, drew some fifty cheques which he paid into his account with the defendant bank. Some of the frauds were discovered by the plaintiff, others were probably known to the plaintiff's auditors: some of the cheques had

---

[46] *Infra.*
[47] (1855) 5 H.L. Cas 389.
[48] (1868) 10 Jur.(N.S.) 102.
[49] At pp. 536–537.
[50] At p. 540.
[51] [1914] 3 K.B. 356.

subsequently been the subject of an arrangement between the manager and the plaintiff, and the manager was re-employed by the plaintiff after the early frauds were discovered. Nothing of this was disclosed to the bank; but when the extent of the frauds was apparent an action for conversion in respect of all the cheques was brought against the bank. Lord Coleridge J., held that the bank had been negligent; but the Court of Appeal allowed the bank's appeal: there had been negligence in respect of the earlier cheques, but the plaintiff was held to have ratified them, while in the case of the later cheques Buckley L.J. said:

> The position... was such that any suspicion [the bank] ought to have had would have been lulled to sleep by the action of Morison himself. Such a sufficient time had then elapsed during which the customer had received back his passbook and his cheques, and had raised no question as to the validity of the cheques as that the defendants were entitled to assume that there was no cause for suspicion or inquiry.

The circumstances of *Morison* were clearly exceptional[52]: the behaviour of the plaintiff in continuing the employment of the fraudulent manager enabled him to continue his fraud with cheques that in fact formed the major part of the plaintiff's loss. But Buckley L.J.'s concept of "lulling to sleep" found no support in later cases. Scrutton L.J.'s comment is noted above; in the *Carpenters Company* case[52a] Greer L.J. said:

> It was suggested... the bank was entitled to suppose that the Carpenters Company had no objection to the long standing practice of [their clerk] paying cheques made out in favour of customers to the credit of his own account. It seems to me that this argument ought not to succeed. Each transaction... must fall to be determined on the facts relating to such transactions. It might well be that the earlier transactions were not fraudulent... There are some parts of the decision in *Morison's* case[53] which appear to indicate that after a number of transactions had appeared in the books of the defrauded company, and had been passed by the auditors of the defrauded company, the bank would be entitled to think when the next cheque came in that it was freed from the necessity of any inquiry, and its failure to inquire would not be negligence. This view is inconsistent with the case of *A.L. Underwood Ltd.* v. *Bank of Liverpool & Martins.*[54]

---

[52] *cf.* Penn, Shea & Arora *op. cit.* I, 7, 14, 15.
[52a] *Ante*, p. 141.
[53] *Supra.*
[54] [1924] 1 K.B. 775, *post*, p. 219. *Per* Greer L.J. at p. 540.

And Lord Wright's remark in *Lloyds Bank Ltd.* v. *Savory & Co.*[55] "no one from the bank came to say he was 'lulled to sleep,' or indeed had given his mind to the question at all"[56] applies with equal force in the circumstances of the *Morison* case. It must be considered doubtful whether even in similar circumstances the decision would now be in favour of the bank.[57]

But a bank is not defenceless in such circumstances. In the *Orbit Mining Co.* case[58] the Court of Appeal held that the bank had not been negligent, and Sellers L.J. said:

If the standard required goes beyond reasonable precaution in the interests of true owners of instruments which may, it must be admitted, be so readily converted where dishonesty holds sway... and goes to a standard which safeguards any fraud from being overlooked, it leaves a bank no remedy for conversion. It is clear in this case that, if Mr. Woolf had not filled in blank forms and disobeyed the requirements in Orbit's bank and had shown ordinary diligence in supervising what had happened to the cheques he had irregularly signed, these frauds would have been rendered at least more difficult and would probably never have arisen. It seems one-sided to blame the bank. Honest trading requires vigilance and proper conduct on the part of all involved.[59]

More recently the defence of contributory negligence, which was not available to the banks in the earlier cases, has been opened to them. The Law Reform (Contributory Negligence Act) 1945 was long held to have no application to the tort of conversion. (It will be remembered that negligence is relevant in conversion only in the negative, in the bank's defence). But Dr. Holden, in the first edition of his *Law and Practice of Banking*, had suggested that it did so apply, and had cited in support a New Zealand decision, based on the New Zealand equivalent of the English 1945 Act. In *Lumsden & Co.* v. *London Trustee Savings Bank*[60] where the plaintiffs' action was for the

---

[55] *Ante*, p. 163.
[56] At p. 236.
[57] And *cf.* the remarks of the Judicial Committee of the Privy Council in *Bank of Montreal* v. *Dominion Gresham Guarantee and Casualty Company Ltd.* [1930] A.C. 659: "In this connection the so-called doctrine of lulling to sleep has been invoked. Neglect of duty does not cease by repetition to be neglect of duty. If there be any doctrine of lulling to sleep it must depend upon and can only be another way of expressing estoppel or ratification" (at p. 666).
[58] *cf. ante*, p. 41 for facts and decision on another point.
[59] *Per* Sellers L.J. at pp. 817–818. *cf.* Harman L.J. quoted at p. 167, *ante*.
[60] [1971] 1 Lloyd's Rep. 114, 9 L.D.B. 198.

conversion of certain cheques, Donaldson J. accepted Dr. Holden's view of the Act and reduced the plaintiffs' damages by 10 per cent., holding that while the bank had been negligent in not fully establishing their customer's credentials when the account was opened, the plaintiffs had also been negligent in leaving spaces in their cheques which allowed additions to be made to the payees' names.[61]

Then, inadvertently, the new-found relief was removed. The Torts (Interference with Goods) Act 1977 provided in section 11(1) that "contributory negligence is no defence in proceedings founded on conversion or intentional trespass to goods," and "goods" must include cheques. However, it had not been intended that the defence should be removed from the banks, and the Banking Act 1979 specifically restored it, providing in section 47 that

> In any circumstances in which proof of absence of negligence on the part of a banker would be a defence in proceedings by reason of section 4 of the Cheques Act 1957, a defence of contributory negligence shall also be available to the banker notwithstanding the provisions of section 11(1) of the Torts (Interference with Goods) Act 1977.

In *Australia and New Zealand Bank Ltd.* v. *Ateliers de Construction Electriques de Charleroi*[62] the cheques in question were payable to, not drawn by, the agent's employers. He was the Australian agent of a Belgian company, and he paid into his own account cheques payable to the company and indorsed for them by himself. Before the Privy Council the bank's defence was not that there had been no negligence, but instead the assertion that there had been no conversion. The agent, the bank claimed, had implied authority to deal with the cheques; his employers knew that he had handled large sums for them previously by paying into his own account and later accounting to the company; they had given no instructions as to how cheques were to be handled, nor had they complained about the agent's methods; and they had no banking account in Australia. The Privy Council held that in the circumstances authority could, as the bank contended, be implied.[63]

---

[61] *cf. Slingsby and Others* v. *District Bank Ltd., ante*, pp. 63, 88.

[62] [1966] 2 W.L.R. 1216, 9 L.D.B. 1.

[63] On not dissimilar facts in an Australian case, *Souhrada* v. *Bank of New South Wales* [1976] 2 Lloyd's Rep. 444, the bank succeeded in the Supreme Court of New South Wales in their plea that there had been no conversion. Yeldham J. said: "There cannot be a conversion where the agent, on whose instructions the proceeds of the cheque were collected by the defendants, was authorised by the true owner of them to give such instructions" (at p. 452).

The banker is not freed from responsibility in his dealings with an agent by the fact that the agent acts under a power of attorney. In *Midland Bank Ltd.* v. *Reckitt and Others*,[64] a fraudulent solicitor, Lord Terrington, drew 15 cheques to a total value of close on £18,000 on the account of Sir Harold Reckitt. The cheques were signed "Harold G. Reckitt, by Terrington his attorney," and were paid to the credit of his account with the defendant bank, who were pressing him for reduction in his borrowing. In the action against them the bank relied upon section 82 and upon the ratification clause in the power of attorney. But the House of Lords rejected their appeal against the Court of Appeal's finding against them: the bank had been negligent in not questioning the crediting of the cheques, the form of which put them on notice that it was not Terrington's money; and they had never asked for or seen the power of attorney. The ratification clause, Lord Atkin said, did not appear to have been happily worded, but no such clause could preclude the principal "from objecting to a dealing with his property by a person who had notice . . . that the agent was exceeding his authority. . . ."

Unless a power of attorney is expressed to be given under section 10 of the Power of Attorney Act 1971 (when the attorney has authority to do anything that the donor of the power can lawfully do), the attorney must not act outside the powers granted in terms. Unless there is express power to borrow, the attorney must not do so—and power to draw on a banking account does not necessarily permit drawing on an overdrawn account, unless there is also a borrowing power; while a general clause in a power of attorney does not add to the powers given in the rest of the document.[65] But the principal danger to the banker remains that demonstrated in *Midland Bank Ltd.* v. *Reckitt*, the principle of which had already been applied in *Reckitt* v. *Barnett, Pembroke and Slater Ltd.*,[66] in which Lord Terrington had paid a personal debt to the respondents with a cheque drawn on Sir Harold Reckitt's account. It was held that the fact that the cheque was drawn by Lord Terrington as attorney, and the knowledge that the debt was a personal one, debarred the respondents from retaining the proceeds of the cheque.

---

[64] [1933] A.C. 1.
[65] *Attwood* v. *Munnings* (1827) 7 B. & C. 278.
[66] [1929] A.C. 176.

In the *Reckitt* case, as in *Morison's* case,[67] the effect of section 25 of the Bills of Exchange Act was considered. The section provides:

A signature by procuration operates as notice that the agent has but a limited authority to sign, and the principal is only bound by such signature if the agent in so signing was acting within the actual limits of his authority.

In both cases in question the bank had notice, not merely from the form of the signature, but from their knowledge of the parties, that the agent was paying his principal's money to his private account; and it may be presumed that a collecting banker who has no such knowledge need not make inquiries merely because his customer pays in a cheque drawn by an ostensible agent. The *Crumplin* decision[68] supports this view; the *Morison* case was there advanced in connection with two of the cheques in dispute, which had been signed "*per pro*"; but Pickford J. refused to hold that this form of signature, with no more, had any special concern for the collecting bank.

Motor Traders Guarantee Corporation Ltd. v. Midland Bank Ltd.

[1937] 4 All E.R. 90

Negligence in the collection of cheques payable to third parties

Facts

A certain motor trader in Bristol, by name Turner, had an account with the defendant bank. He induced the plaintiffs to make out a cheque for £189 5s., crossed "not negotiable," to a firm of car dealers in Bristol, Welsh & Co., representing that this sum was the purchase price of a car which was to be let on hire purchase to him. He forged the indorsement of Welsh & Co. and paid the cheque to his account with the defendants, saying that it had been negotiated to him. The cashier asked for an explanation, and a plausible one was offered; the cashier examined Turner's account in the ledger and saw that there had been several previous substantial transactions with Welsh & Co., including one payment to them of £484 10s., which Turner stated was in connection with the present transaction. In these

---

[67] *Supra.*
[68] *Post*, p. 187.

circumstances, the cashier accepted the cheque for Turner's credit, and it was duly presented and paid.

In the six months the account had been open, some 35 cheques had been dishonoured, only some of them being paid on representment.

The rules of the bank laid upon branch managers the duty of deciding whether or not such "third party" cheques should be accepted for the credit of customers.

The plaintiff brought this action for damages for conversion of the cheque, and the bank claimed to be protected by section 82.

Decision

It was held that (i) a breach of the bank's own rules is not conclusive proof of negligence, nor is even a customer entitled to demand literal performance of them, but (ii) in view of Turner's banking record, further inquiry should have been made before taking the cheque for his credit. The bank thus failed to prove that they had not been negligent within section 82 and so were liable.

In his judgment, Goddard J. said:

I am far from saying, and I do not intend to lay down until there is some authority which compels me to so hold, that it can be stated that there is an absolute duty upon a banker, even where he is put on inquiry, to inquire of the payee of the cheque or of the drawer of the cheque. The circumstances may be such that that is the only course that he can take to get satisfactory information. What I mean to say is that it would be going too far to hold that in every case a banker can discharge the onus which is upon him, if he wishes to take the protection of section 82, only by showing that he has inquired of one or other of these people. It may very well be that, in certain cases, the information that he gets is enough, and, as I have already said, I think that, if Turner's banking history had been different from what it is now shown to have been, I should have been inclined to hold, and I think that I probably should have held, that the inquiries which were made by [the cashier] were enough. But with a man who had this history of dishonoured cheques, and dishonoured cheques of considerable sums, I think it is obvious that [the cashier] should have consulted the manager, which is the course of conduct which the bank regulations set out. I again say that I am far from saying that the plaintiffs, or any other person whose property has been converted, are entitled to rely upon a literal performance, or are entitled to require a literal performance, by the bank of these regulations. The bank does not owe a duty to them to carry out this rule, that rule, or the other rule. Indeed, I doubt whether they owe their own customers the duty of carrying out all the rules which they may lay down as counsels of perfection. The question in every case is not whether the bank requires a particular standard of conduct, but whether the particular acts which are done are enough to discharge the onus which is upon the bank either in respect of their own customer or in respect of some other customer.[69]

Notes

This is one of the many examples which show the danger of accepting for the credit of private accounts cheques which are payable to companies, firms or public bodies.[70] The danger is now well recognised by bankers, and clear instructions are given by most banks to their employees as to the necessity for inquiry.

Some of the early cases on the point are based on circumstances which to the contemporary banker appear to represent the gross negligence of the defendant bank[71] and no bank would today defend an action based on similar facts. The circumstances of the *Motor Traders* case, however correspond to the regular practice for many banks.

The limits of the decision may be emphasised: it established, not that there is necessarily negligence in collecting a "third party" cheque for a customer, even where the customer has a doubtful banking record, but that in such a case the bank cannot be excused as it otherwise might, for not observing its own regulations. Even thus limited, however, the decision appears to go somewhat further than earlier cases, for it does provide a precedent for the view that a number of unpaid cheques on an account is a factor to be considered in deciding whether a particular cheque can safely be collected without further inquiry, a suggestion which had not previously appeared in the negligence cases.

The case is unusual in that it was concerned, not as are most of the negligence cases with whether the circumstances put the bank on inquiry—the cashier made inquiry at least as exhaustive as would appear reasonably possible, short of actually getting in touch with the drawer of the cheque—but with whether that inquiry was sufficient.

On the other hand, in the later case of *Smith and Baldwin* v. *Barclays Bank Ltd.*[72] we find inquiry by the bank of a character

---

[69] At p. 96.
[70] cf., e.g. A.L. Underwood Ltd. v. Bank of Liverpool and Martins, post, p. 219 and Penmount Estates Ltd. v. National Provincial Bank Ltd., post, p. 190.
[71] cf., e.g. Ross v. London County Westminster and Parr's Bank Ltd. [1919] 1 K.B. 678.
[72] (1944) 5 L.D.B. 370.

held by the court to be sufficient to satisfy the requirements of section 82. The plaintiffs were associates in a printing firm, the Argus Press, who took into an informal partnership one Bray. Over a period of two years Bray fraudulently paid into his private account with the defendants five cheques payable to the Argus Press, one of them representing an entirely fraudulent transaction of which the plaintiffs knew nothing, the others being genuine payments of debts owing to the firm. In October 1941 the manager of the branch at which Bray banked questioned him concerning the payment in of cheques payable to the firm, and Bray said that he had bought the business from the plaintiffs. The following day he showed the manager a certificate of registration under the Registration of Business Names Act 1916.[73] The plaintiffs, who themselves had never had a partnership agreement, had not registered the name of their business. It was held, with regard to the cheques other than the first (in respect of which the circumstances prevented any claim against the bank) that the bank had not been negligent, and were protected by section 82. Stable J. said:

> The plain fact of the matter was that there was his customer who, as [the manager] believed and as the fact was, was registered as the proprietor of the Argus Press. He was the only person in the wide world who was registered as the proprietor of the Argus Press, and what more natural than that into his account cheques made payable to that business should be paid. In my view, to say that if [the manager] had embarked on a prolonged and detailed scrutiny of every available piece of material that there was he might have discovered that Bray had not bought out Mr. Smith and Mr. Baldwin...seems to me to throw a wholly wrong standard of care on banks in a matter of this kind.[74]

To have gone further would have been to require the bank in the words of Sankey L.J. in the *Chartered Bank of India* case to play the part of "amateur detectives."[75]

But in *Baker* v. *Barclays Bank Ltd.*[76] the bank's inquiries were not sufficient. The plaintiff was in partnership with one Bainbridge, and each partner was authorised to indorse cheques

---

[73] Despite considerable opposition by business interests, the Registration of Business Names Act was repealed by s.119 of the Companies Act 1981, and the current statute, the Business Names Act 1985, makes no provision for their registration.

[74] *Ibid.* at p. 375.

[75] *Ante*, p. 171.

[76] [1955] 1 W.L.R. 822; see *post*, p. 199.

alone. Nine cheques payable to the firm were indorsed by Bainbridge and handed by him to a customer of the defendant bank, Jeffcott, who paid them to the credit of a previously dormant account in his name. The manager of the branch asked him how it happened that he was paying in these third party cheques, and he explained that Bainbridge was the sole partner in the firm and that he, Jeffcott, was helping him in the business with a view to becoming a partner. The manager accepted this explanation and made no inquiry of Bainbridge; and in the subsequent action for conversion of the cheques the bank was held to have been negligent in not making further inquiries (but the damages awarded were half the amount of the cheques collected because the plaintiff had been defrauded by his partner, with whom he shared profits and losses equally). It is interesting to note that Devlin J. came to this decision in spite of the fact, which he acknowledged, that inquiry of Bainbridge might well have been fruitless as far as the interests of the plaintiff were concerned; the manager should have inquired why Bainbridge had no account of his own into which to pay the cheques, and he should have recognised that in accepting the cheques in the way he did he was in effect opening an account for Bainbridge, who was not his customer.

And in *Thackwell* v. *Barclays Bank plc.*[77] the bank was saved by the maxim *ex turpi causa non oritur actio.* A cheque payable to the plaintiff, bearing his forged indorsement, was paid into the account of Riva Electronics (U.K.) Ltd. and the assistant manager, knowing that the plaintiff was in negotiation with Riva, did not question the credit. On Riva's insolvency the plaintiff brought his action for conversion, and Hirst J. held that the bank had been negligent: "It is no answer for a bank which has been guilty of negligence in the collection of a cheque to prove that even had the question, the omission to ask which constituted such negligence, been asked, a reassuring answer would have been given: see, for example, the *Selangor* decision."[78] However, he held also that the plaintiff had from the start been party to a fraudulent scheme in which the cheque was involved, and so he could not succeed in his action.

Marquess of Bute v. Barclays Bank Ltd.

[1955] 1 Q.B. 202

Negligence in the collection of cheques payable "to A for B"

---

[77] [1986] 1 All E.R. 676.
[78] But *cf.* Diplock, L.J.'s dictum, *ante*, p. 167.

Facts

The plaintiff had had in his employ as manager of three sheep farms in the Island of Bute one McGaw. McGaw resigned in April 1949 but in September 1949 the Department of Agriculture for Scotland sent him three warrants totalling £546 in respect of hill sheep subsidy which McGraw had quite properly claimed on behalf of the plaintiff four months before his resignation. The plaintiff had not notified the Department of Agriculture of the termination of McGaw's employment.

The warrants were re-addressed by the local post office and McGaw, who was now living at Barnsley, opened an account with the defendant bank, which received the three warrants as the first credit on the account and, after references had been taken up, allowed him to draw against them.

The warrants were expressed to be payment of hill sheep subsidy, and were drawn payable to Mr. D. McGaw, Kerrylamont, Rothesay, Bute. This name and address were in a printed rectangle, and outside this box, in brackets, were the words "for Marquess of Bute."

The plaintiff claimed the amount of the warrants as damages for conversion or as money had and received to his use. The defendant bank raised the defences (a) that the warrants were not the property of the plaintiff, or that they bore no indication that McGaw was not entitled to receive the proceeds; (b) that the plaintiff was estopped from denying that he had intended the warrants to be received by McGaw; and (c) that the bank was protected by section 82.

Decision

McNair J. rejected all three defences. He held that:

(a) (i) to claim in conversion the claimant need only establish that at the material time he was entitled to immediate possession, which (McNair J. held) the plaintiff here could do;

(ii) in any event, the test as to true ownership is the intention of the drawer, and here the Department of Agriculture knowing that the subsidy was due to the plaintiff had indicated their intention in the words in parentheses;

(b) the estoppel argument could succeed only if the documents were in a form that could reasonably be understood as an unequivocal representation that McGaw was entitled to the proceeds. Hill sheep subsidy from the Department of Agriculture in Scotland, tendered by a complete stranger in Barnsley, was not such a representation; and

(c) the same reasoning defeated any defence under section
82.

Notes

It is unfortunate that this decision,[79] on the peculiar facts of
a particular case, also extends the scope of negligence under
section 4 of the Cheques Act 1957.

Until the *Marquess of Bute* decision it was possible to argue
(as most bankers would have argued) that "Pay A for B"
entitled A to receive the proceeds, though he would be
accountable to B; that it was the drawer's intention that A
should have the money; and that A was entitled to immediate
possession—though always accountable to B. In the circumstances of the present case it would have seemed that the
Department of Agriculture, without notice that McGaw was
no longer entitled to receive the money, must have intended
him to receive it, even though they knew that the Marquess
of Bute was entitled to the ultimate benefit of it; otherwise
there seems little point in drawing the warrants in the form in
which they were drawn, instead of directly payable to the
Marquess of Bute with the intention that McGaw should
indorse *per pro*. McNair J.'s ruling, however, makes it more
difficult for a bank to argue on these lines, in circumstances
less unusual that those of this case.

It is to be noted that no question of the bank's negligence
could arise until the plaintiff had established conversion; had
McGraw indeed been the true owner of the warrants and
entitled to immediate possession of them the bank could not
have been negligent in collecting them for him.[80]

The form in which the warrants were drawn may be
compared with that of the cheque in *Slingsby* v. *District Bank
Ltd.*[81] As McNair J. said in his passing reference to that case,
however, there is a difference between the two. It will be
remembered that in the earlier *Slingsby* action on the cheque,

---

[79] The case is examined in some detail in Chorley, Gilbart Lectures, 1956.
[80] The *Marquess of Bute* decision was regarded by Sir David Cairns in
International Factors Ltd. v. *Rodiguez* [1979] Q.B. 351, as being "of some
assistance to the plaintiff...inasmuch as it shows that the fact that the
cheques were made out in favour of the company is not sufficient answer
to the claim of the plaintiffs that they were the persons who owned the
cheques in equity."
[81] *Ante*, p. 63.

against the collecting bank (Westminster Bank),[82] the plaintiff
lost—not on a form of drawing more in his favour than the "Pay
A for B" form, but on facts much more favourable to the bank.
Finlay J. said, in finding for the bank, that Mr. Cumberbirch
was of high repute and well known to the defendant bank.
There was nothing to arouse suspicion in the fact that Mr.
Cumberbirch was paying in the cheque to the account of the
company of which he was chairman, rather than to his private
account. Finlay J. felt that, with subsequent knowledge, it might
appear that inquiries ought to have been made, but, given the
large number of cheques with which banks have to deal every
day, they could not be expected to scrutinise each one with the
skill and care of detectives.

This decision represented what has been called[83] "a valiant
attempt to stem the stream" of "hard treatment" that the
collecting banker has received from the courts. But in *Slingsby*
v. *District Bank Ltd.*, Scrutton L.J. said:

There are, of course, difficulties as to how in law you should deal
with money claimed by a customer from a bank because the bank has
collected it from the customer's bank on a document which does not
authorise such collection, but I thought that all those difficulties had
been settled by the decision in *Morison's* case,[84] followed by this court
in *Underwood's* case[85]; in the *Lloyds Bank* case[86]; and in *Reckitt* v.
Midland Bank, lately affirmed in the House of Lords.[87] *Slingsby* v.
Westminster Bank Ltd.[88] is, in my opinion, wrongly decided and should
not be followed by any court in preference to those decisions of the
Court of Appeal....[89]

This emphatic disapproval checked the "stemming" at once;
the effect of this disapproval is no doubt as complete as though
the decision had been reversed on appeal. The words of Finlay
J. just quoted, were to find their first substantial echo, in other
circumstances, in the Court of Appeal in the *Orbit* case, 30
years later.[90]

---

[82] *Ante*, p. 64.
[83] Jacobs, *Bills of Exchange* (4th ed.), p. 248.
[84] *Ante*, pp. 172 *et seq.*
[85] *Ante*, pp. 158 *et seq.*
[86] *Ante*, pp. 171 *et seq.*
[87] (1932) 48 T.L.R. 271, *ante*, pp. 176 *et seq.*
[88] *Ante*, p. 64.
[89] [1932] 1 K.B. 544 at p. 558.
[90] *Ante*, p. 41.

House Property Co. of London Ltd. and Others v. London County and Westminster Bank Ltd.

(1915) 31 T.L.R. 479

Negligence in connection with cheques crossed "Account payee"

Facts

The plaintiff company were dealers in real property, the other plaintiffs being the trustees for the time being of a trust known as the Bingley Trust, to which the plaintiff company, in the course of their business, had mortgaged certain property. In 1912, Norman, the solicitor to the trustees, wrote to the company calling in the mortgage on grounds of depreciation. This was done fraudulently, no instruction having been given to him. After negotiation, the plaintiff company arranged to repay £800 of the mortgage moneys, and sent to the solicitor a cheque for this amount, payable to the trustees "or bearer" and crossed "Account payee." The solicitor paid the cheque to the credit of his account at the St. Mary Axe branch of the defendant bank, and it was collected for him.

The present action was brought on the grounds that the bank had been negligent in collecting a cheque so crossed for one who was not the named payee. The bank contended that (if the crossing had any effect as far as they were concerned) as the cheque was a bearer cheque they had in fact collected for the payee.

Decision

It was held that the bank had been negligent. In his judgment, Rowlatt J. said that:

[counsel for the defendants] had argued that the cheque was made out to Hanson and others or bearer, and that Norman was the bearer, and that the defendants in collecting it for his account were collecting it for the payee. That was a shallow argument, as "payee" did not mean the owner of a cheque at the time it was presented, but the name written across the face of the cheque—in this case, F.S. Hanson and others. No evidence had been called by the defendants, and they contended that they had not been guilty of negligence in allowing this cheque to be collected for a gentleman whom they knew to be a solicitor to be credited to his own account. The defendants offered no sort of excuse for so doing, and if he (his Lordship) were to say that they were entitled to do so without any explanation, he would be practically saying that a bank could not be negligent in respect of a cheque of that kind.[91]

---

[91] At p. 680.

Notes

The marking "Account payee" or "Account...only" is at least as old as *Bellamy* v. *Marjoribanks*[92] and is now widely used.[93] It is not part of the crossing (although it does not constitute an unlawful addition to an authorised crossing within section 79 of the Bills of Exchange Act),[94] and it does not restrict the negotiability of the cheque[95]; but the collecting banker ignores it at his peril.

The effect of the words is, however, merely to put the banker on inquiry, and he does not lose the protection of section 4 of the Cheques Act if his inquiries are reasonably answered. In *Bevan* v. *National Bank, Ltd.*,[96] for example, where some of the cheques payable to Malcolm Wade & Co. and collected for Malcolm Wade's private account were crossed "account payee," it was held that the bank had not been negligent in so collecting them, as it had been reasonable for them to accept Wade's statement that he was trading as Malcolm Wade & Co., although in fact he was only the manager of that firm. Again, in *Importers Co.* v. *Westminster Bank Ltd.*,[97] where the defendant bank collected as agents for a German bank, all the cheques concerned being payable to German payees, the plaintiffs' contention was that, as it was impossible for the Westminster Bank to know to what account "account payee" cheques had been credited, the bank accepted such business at their own risk. This was rejected by the Court of Appeal, and it was held that the bank had not been negligent so as to lose their statutory protection.

The crossing "Account payee" was at one time much criticised,[98] but it is clearly a useful additional protection for customers, however inconvenient it may be for bankers. However, its limitations are to be noted. In *Kenton* v. *Barclays Bank Ltd.*[99] the plaintiff was a licensed moneylender who was

---

[92] (1852) 7 Ex. 389.
[93] There has been some discussion as to whether the addition of "only" alters the effect of the crossing, by, for example, restricting the transferability of the cheque. There seems to be no English authority for the view that "only" has any separate significance: in *Universal Guarantee Property Ltd.* v. *National Bank of Australasia* ([1965] 1 W.L.R. 691) the Privy Council treated the two crossings as synonymous.
[94] cf. *Akrokerri (Atlantic) Mines Ltd.* v. *Economic Bank* [1904] 2 K.B. 465.
[95] *National Bank* v. *Silke* [1891] 1 Q.B. 435.
[96] (1906) 23 T.L.R. 65.
[97] [1927] 2 K.B. 297. *cf. ante*, p. 34.
[98] *cf.* Paget, *op. cit.* pp. 209, 348 *et seq.* for the effect of the crossing.
[99] *The Banker* Vol. 127 March 1977; p. 18.

persuaded by fraud to advance money against a promissory note. In order to ensure that the borrower had, as he claimed, a banking account, Mr. Kenton crossed his cheque "Account payee," but did not add "Not negotiable." The borrower passed the cheque to a customer of the bank, who paid it to the credit of her deposit account, the bank making no inquiry as to her title to the cheque. When the fraud was discovered and the payee could not be traced the present action was brought, but in the Mayor's and City of London Court, Leonard J. dismissed the plaintiff's claim. At the time the bank was dealing with the cheque he was not entitled to immediate possession of it so as to found a claim in conversion. The payee had a voidable, not a void, title, and this passed to the bank's customer, the plaintiff at that time having done nothing to avoid the payee's title.[1] And the judge added that the duty imposed on the collecting bank by the crossing is to ensure that the payee is not defrauded; it does not extend to protect the drawer against the payee's fraud, nor does it prevent the cheque's negotiation.

It may be noted that the addition of the words to *bearer* cheques, as in the *House Property Company* case, is a practice which is now less frequent than it was before the passing of the Cheques Act. Until 1957 many large concerns requested their customers to make out cheques in this way: the customer sending his cheque was protected from loss by the crossing (except in circumstances such as those in *Kenton*), while the creditor firm avoided having to indorse the cheques received by it, both at the expense of the collecting banker's vigilance.

Crumplin v. London Joint Stock Bank Ltd.

(1913) 30 T.L.R. 99

Negligence in connection with cheques crossed "Not negotiable"

Facts

The plaintiff was a stockbroker, who employed as manager, book-keeper and cashier one Rands. Rands from time to time introduced business, receiving half commission, and in 1909 he introduced in this way a Mr. Davies, for whom a small transaction was properly carried out. Between 1909 and 1913 Rands, speculating on his own behalf, used the name of Davies as a cover and, when the differences were in his favour, drew

---

[1] *cf.*, Paget, *op. cit.*, 207, 346 where it is argued that this finding was wrong.

cheques payable to Davies which were duly signed by the plaintiff and crossed "Not negotiable." Two of the cheques were signed "*Per pro*." Having endorsed Davies's name, Rands paid the cheques into his account with the Fenchurch Street branch of the defendant bank.

When the fraud was discovered the plaintiff brought this action, claiming that the bank had been negligent in accepting for the credit of one person cheques marked "Not negotiable" and payable to another person.

Decision

It was held that a "Not negotiable" crossing is merely one factor among others to be considered in deciding whether a collecting banker has been negligent, and that in the circumstances of the present case there had not been negligence.

In his judgment, Pickford J. said that:

...the mere taking of a "not negotiable" cheque ought not to be held to be evidence of negligence. It would be remarkable if, while the section provided that bankers were protected if they took a crossed cheque in good faith and without negligence that it should be possible to hold that the bankers were negligent merely from the fact that they took such a cheque, unless they gave rebutting evidence that they had made proper inquiries before taking it. It was a matter which ought to be taken into consideration together with all the other matters, and that it did not go higher than that. In the present case evidence was given by persons of importance in the banking world, who said that transactions of this kind were not uncommon... it was quite clear from that evidence that the practice for cheques of this description to be paid in was so common as not to raise suspicion. It came down to a mere question whether, looking at the total number of payments in, the number of these cheques that were paid in, their amount, and the period over which they were paid in, those circumstances were sufficient to put the defendants upon inquiry.... If the account had been opened with a small sum, followed by a succession of large cheques similar to Davies's cheques... this ought to have put the bank upon inquiry. But when, as in this case, the cheques were for small amounts, and when they were paid in at such long intervals, it was not negligence in the bank not to have made inquiry.[2]

Notes

Bankers are interested in negotiability in other ways besides their concern with cheques and bills of exchange, and the

---

[2] At p. 101.

principle is discussed earlier.[3] But it is in connection with cheques and bills that the principle is seen in its clearest form. It was widely canvassed in the discussion that preceded the passing of the Cheques Act[4]: the non-transferable instrument that was advocated then on grounds of safety would have taken the majority of money transfers out of the negotiable area.[4a] In the event the Cheques Act got rid of most indorsements while preserving the negotiability of cheques, and the effect of the limitation of that negotiability by the addition of restrictive wording is a matter of interest, though seldom of direct concern, to bankers.

The paying banker as such cannot normally know whether the cheque has been negotiated before it reaches him. The collecting banker who receives for the credit of A, a cheque payable to and duly indorsed by B, knows of the negotiation and may be, but usually is not, affected by that knowledge. In *Great Western Railway Co.* v. *London and County Banking Co. Ltd.*[5] there was a suggestion in Lord Brampton's judgment that section 82 might not give the same protection to the banker collecting "not negotiable" cheques as it does where the crossing is simple. The decision in the *Crumplin* case, in which the "not negotiable" was the main point at issue, was therefore important, even though it must not be given more than its proper weight. In the following year, in the *Morison* case,[6] Lord Reading referred to the question, *obiter*, in terms which left it open. He said:

It is certainly not conclusive evidence of negligence against a banker who collects crossed cheques so marked. Even if I assume that the taking of a crossed cheque bearing these words would be some evidence of negligence, it would not affect my decision upon the later cheques. . . . "[7]

There has been much discussion of the point.[8] The balance of argument is clear—as Paget puts it: "the 'not negotiable'

---

[3] *Ante*, pp. 38 *et seq.*
[4] See Holden, *Jones and Holden's Studies in Practical Banking* (6th ed.), pp. 287 *et seq.*
[4a] In the Jacks Report the creation of a non-transferable "bank payment order" is recommended as an *additional* means of money transfer.
[5] [1901] A.C. 414; *ante*, p. 30.
[6] *Ante*, p. 172.
[7] [1914] 3 K.B. 356 at p. 373.
[8] *cf.* Paget, *op. cit.*, pp. 347 *et seq.*

crossing has nothing to do with the collecting banker or he with it."[9]

Penmount Estates Ltd. v. *National Provincial Bank Ltd.*[10] is one of the more recent cases which may support the *Crumplin* decision. There a solicitor paid into his Clients' Account with the defendant bank a cheque crossed "not negotiable" payable to the plaintiff, whose indorsement had been forged. When the bank queried previous "third party" cheques paid in, the solicitor had told them that the payees had no accounts; on this occasion he said that he had arranged for the payees to indorse the cheque in order that he might pay it into his account and issue his cheque for the amount less his costs. The bank succeeded in their defence that they had not been negligent, Mackinnon J. saying: "It is true that, in the light of after events, the explanation given . . . may sound improbable to anyone in a suspicious frame of mind; but in my opinion the officials of the bank, doing their duty under section 82, have not to be abnormally suspicious."[11] The "not negotiable" crossing was not considered in the judgment, but it may be noted that the bank did not contest liability in respect of similar cheques crossed "Account payee only."

In the light of the above authorities it seems unlikely that a court would be prepared to hold a banker negligent merely because he collected a "not negotiable" cheque without inquiry.

In *Wilson & Meeson* v. *Pickering*[12]; it was held that the payee of a cheque crossed "not negotiable" is within section 81 of the Bills of Exchange Act 1882. In this case, a partner in the plaintiff firm handed a cheque so crossed, and signed in blank, to a secretary of the firm with instructions to complete it for £2, payable to the Inland Revenue. Instead the secretary made it out for £54 4s., payable to the defendant, to whom the secretary owed money. It was held that section 81 prevented the defendant from having any better right than the fraudulent secretary; and the plaintiffs were not estopped by their conduct from denying the validity of the cheque, as they owed no duty of care to the defendant. In any event, the defendant would not, in restoring the amount of the cheque, lose her original right against the secretary. The Court of Appeal pointed out also that the rule of estoppel as to the filling up of blanks in

[9] *Op cit.* p. 348.
[10] (1945) 173 L.T. 344.
[11] (1945) 173 L.T. 344 at p. 346. *cf. ante*, p. 184 for Finlay J.'s similar view.
[12] [1946] 1 All E.R. 394.

negotiable instruments applies only to such instruments; the cheque in this case was, on its face, not negotiable.

Because of its ineffectiveness *vis-à-vis* the collecting banker, the "not negotiable" crossing does not provide as complete protection to the drawer as is sometimes thought. If the drawer stops a cheque so crossed, whether because of a dispute with the payee or because it has been misappropriated, the crossing will prevent any third party into whose hands the cheque comes obtaining a right of action on it, as he might have if it were not so crossed. But if such a third party, innocent holder or thief, has paid it in for collection and it is paid before the stop becomes effective, the drawer normally has no recourse against either collecting or paying banker, and while he can, by reason of the simple crossing, discover to whose account it was credited, that may be of little value to him.

In practice virtually complete protection can be obtained only by using such words as "Pay John Smith only" (deleting "or Order"), or by a combination of "not negotiable" and "account payee only." (As to the rare failure, in the drawer's interest, of "account payee only," see *ante*, p. 186, where also its inconvenience to the banks is referred to). The non-transferable instrument mentioned earlier would of course have resolved the problem; in its absence it is not easy to explain to customers the differing consequences of additional crossings. But it remains unsatisfactory that the simple crossing of cheques is so widely regarded as providing drawers with protection much more complete than in fact it is.

Gowers and Others v. Lloyds and National Provincial Foreign Bank Ltd.

[1938] 1 All E.R. 766

The collection of pension warrants

Facts

A pensioner of the Colonial Service, named Gibson, lived in France and banked with the Paris branch of the defendant bank. His pension was paid by the Crown Agents for the Colonies, the plaintiffs in the present action, by warrant sent through the post to him, and the warrants were forwarded to the bank for collection, each with a certificate duly completed to the effect that Gibson was still living. Mrs. Gibson had a power of attorney to draw on Gibson's account.

Gibson died in 1929, but this fact did not become known to the defendants until 1935, when Mrs. Gibson also died. During the six years, pension warrants continued to be received by the bank, and were collected by them for credit of the Gibson account, the bank supposing Gibson to be living, as he had previously lived, as Vichy, whence the warrants were received. Each warrant bore the forged signature of Gibson, and a certificate of existence apparently regular. It was sought to recover from the bank the amount of the warrants wrongly paid on the ground, *inter alia*, that in presenting the documents for payment the bank implicity warranted the continued life of the pensioner.

Decision

The Court of Appeal affirmed the decision of the lower Court in favour of the bank, and on the point here dealt with Sir Wilfred Greene M.R. said:

What does the document on its face convey to such a bank? It conveys quite clearly, as it seems to me, that the evidence of life, and the evidence of the authenticity of the signature, which the Crown Agents required, which is the only evidence which they require, is the certificate, filled up and apparently in order. The alternative proposition, for which [counsel for the plaintiffs] contends involves that the bank whose case I am considering when a document of this kind is presented to it, with a certificate apparently in order, is bound at its peril before it forwards the certificate to the Crown Agents, itself to ascertain the very matters with which the certificate deals. It must ascertain whether or not the pensioner is alive, it must ascertain whether or not the signature upon the document is really his signature, and I apprehend that it must ascertain whether or not the person who purports to have signed the certificate is in fact the person who signed it, and that he held the necessary qualification.... It seems to me quite impossible to extract from this document, intended to be used in the way in which it is intended to be used, evidence of any such obligation upon the bank.[13]

Notes

In this case the bank successfully repelled the suggestion that by merely presenting a document for payment they had implicitly warranted the truth of a certificate which the document contained. Had the bank failed in this case the dangers of collecting such documents would have been greatly increased; already there are inherent risks in the more usual

[13] At pp. 771–772.

practice of the bank itself signing the certificate of existence of the payee. Often the latter lives abroad, and where this is so, and especially where the account concerned is a joint account, on which all recent drawings may have been by the other party, there is an obvious possibility that the banker may sign carelessly. It must be emphasised that the *Gowers* decision is not at all relevant to such facts, and would give the banker no protection. Where, as sometimes happens, the bank signs a standing certificate of existence (upon the understanding that a pension will be paid until the certificate is cancelled) the danger that the banker will be "lulled to sleep" is still greater.

Chapter 5

SPECIAL ACCOUNTS

JOINT ACCOUNTS

McEvoy v. Belfast Banking Co. Ltd.

[1935] A.C. 24

*Survivorship as applied to joint accounts is a presumption only and may
be rebutted*

Facts

In 1921 John McEvoy, who was in bad health and expecting
an early death, deposited £10,000 with the respondent bank on
a joint account in the names of himself and his son, then 15
years old, on the terms that either was to sign on the account,
and the balance was to go to the survivor. A little later he
executed his will, leaving the residue on trust for the son until
he reached the age of 25, and a month after the execution of
the will he died. The executors took possession of the deposit
receipt for £10,000, endorsed it and withdrew the money,
redepositing it in their own names. It was shown in evidence
that the deceased had wrongly imagined that by opening the
joint account death duties would be avoided; that in fact the
executors had concealed the deposit receipt in preparing their
accounts; and that the residue to be held in trust was very small,
in comparison with the deposit account.

Between the death of the father and the son's twenty-fifth
birthday the executors carried on the business of the father,
with the son taking an increasing part in the management.
Shortly before the son's twenty-first birthday, a sum of more
than £2,000 was withdrawn from the deposit for the purchase of
certain property by the executors, the son taking an active part
in the transaction. After he came of age, but before his twenty-
fifth birthday, the remaining amount on deposit was withdrawn
piecemeal and credited to the executors' account, which was
continually overdrawn and concerning which the bank frequently expressed anxiety.

Some months after the son's twenty-fifth birthday, he brought an action against the bank claiming that he was entitled to (a) the deposit account as at the time of his father's death, and (b) the interest thereon. He pleaded that he did not previously understand his rights in the matter. The bank denied that the son had ever been entitled to the money.

Decision

The House of Lords dismissed the son's appeal, a majority holding that the executors were entitled to receive the money and apply it in due course of administration as directed by the will. (Lord Atkin held that if the son on his majority had ratified the contract made by his father in opening the account the title would have been his, but that in fact his conduct had represented to the bank that he did not propose to ratify.)

In the course of his judgment, Lord Warrington of Clyffe said:

...I think the real question is not whether the appellant would, as the effect in law of the contract, have been held entitled to be paid the money by the respondents, but what in the view of a Court of Equity would be the position between him and the executors; would he be held entitled to retain the moneys, if so paid, for his own benefit, or must he hand them over to the executors to be dealt with as part of the testator's estate? The material circumstances are these: the money deposited was that of the father alone, the son was a mere volunteer. The intention of the father as to the disposition of his estate was clearly expressed at the interview of July 19, 1921. The form of the deposit receipt in no way operated to alter this intention; it was adopted for another purpose. The money was entirely at the father's disposal during his life. The will as actually made gives effect to the expressed intention of the father and there is no evidence of any *animus donandi* except subject to the testamentary directions. The residuary personal estate, including the deposit of £2,000, but excluding the £10,000 in question, was so small that it is impossible to suppose that the testator deliberately intended to withdraw so important an item as the £10,000 from the fund to be administered by the executors and trustees until the son should attain twenty-five. Finally the illegal proceedings of the executors, so much relied on by the trial judge, were entirely irrelevant, inasmuch as the testator was not in any way implicated in them. On the whole then I am satisfied that if the matter had been brought before a Court of Equity the decision would have been in favour of the executors... [1]

---

[1] At p. 50.

Notes

The bank succeeded in the *McEvoy* case only on its special facts, and they were severely criticised by the House of Lords, as having taken no steps to protect the interests of the infant son. Lord Warrington said:

> The proper course in my opinion would have been either to institute proceedings making the executors and the infant by his guardian *ad litem* defendants, and asking for directions as to the disposal of the money, or to refuse to act except under the directions of the court, leaving the executors or the infant to institute the necessary proceedings.

and he went on to explain how either course would have ensured that the son's interests would have been protected until he came of age.

It must be noted, in connection with the cases on joint accounts, that the survivor's *legal* title to the balance on the account, when the other party to the account has died, is never in question. Thus the banker is within his rights in paying out the balance to the survivor. Dispute arises only as to the *equitable* title—*i.e.* whether the survivor is entitled to keep the money or is rather to be regarded as holding it as trustee for others who claim the beneficial interest.

The presumption is that the equitable title follows the legal title; but this presumption can be displaced by showing that such was not the intention of the parties, and most of the cases are concerned with whether there is enough evidence to displace the presumed intention of survivorship. Such difficulties normally arise only when the joint account is not, in intention, a genuine joint account at all; in "survivorship" cases it is the intention of the person who provided the funds that is the principal issue.

Thus in *Marshal* v. *Crutwell*[2] there was a joint account in the names of husband and wife. It was shown that the husband was in failing health, and further that all the money paid into the account was provided by the husband, while the wife's withdrawals were all for household goods. It was held that the presumption of survivorship was displaced by these facts and that the balance of the account at the death of the husband went not to the widow but to the executors. However, there must be clear evidence as to the ownership of the money, and in *Hirschorn* v. *Evans*,[3] Greer L.J., while dissenting from the

---

[2] (1875) L.R. 20 Eq. 328.
[3] [1938] 2 K.B. 801; *ante*, p. 115.

majority view in the Court of Appeal that a garnishee order against the husband could not attach the joint account, held that in the circumstances of the case it could not do so as there was no clear evidence as to the beneficial ownership of the money in the account.

In *Jones* v. *Maynard*[4] a husband and wife had maintained a joint account fed by the husband's remuneration and investment income, the rent of a house owned by husband and wife jointly, and the wife's investment income of about £50 per annum. Periodically the surplus on the account was invested in the husband's sole name. The parties were later divorced and the wife now sought a declaration that she was beneficially entitled to half the investments so made. The husband contended that she was entitled only to such proportion as represented her own contributions to the joint account. In his judgment in favour of the wife, Vaisey J. said:

In my view a husband's earnings or salary, when the spouses have a common purse, and pool their resources, are earnings made on behalf of both . . . the money which goes into the pool becomes joint property.[5]

The reasoning of Vaisey J. was approved by the Court of Appeal in *Rimmer* v. *Rimmer*,[6] but in *Re Bishop, deceased*,[7] Stamp J. distinguished both these cases, regarding them as having been decided on their special facts; and on the facts before him—a joint account fed by funds from both husband and wife, and used in investments, variously in the name of the husband alone, of the wife alone and of both jointly—held that there was nothing to displace the legal titles so indicated. He said:

Where a husband and wife open a joint account at a bank on terms that cheques may be drawn on the account by either of them, then, in my judgment, in the absence of facts or circumstances which indicate that the account was intended, for some specific or limited purpose, each spouse can draw upon it not only for the benefit of both spouses but for his or her own benefit. Each spouse, in drawing money out of the account, is to be treated as doing so with the authority of the other and, in my judgment, if one of the spouses purchases a chattel for his own benefit, or an investment in his or her own name, the

[4] [1951] Ch. 572.
[5] At p. 575.
[6] [1953] 1 Q.B. 63.
[7] [1965] Ch. 450.

chattel or investment belongs to the person in whose name is it purchased or invested: for in such a case there is, in my judgment, no equity in the other spouse to displace the legal ownership of the one in whose name the investment is purchased.[8]

And this application of a principle enunciated as long ago as 1889, in *Re Young*,[9] was approved by Lord Upjohn in *Pettit* v. *Pettit*.[10]

In *Young* v. *Sealey*[11] Miss Jarman opened a deposit account in the joint names of herself and her nephew, on the terms that either was to sign and the balance was to go to the survivor; and she also made investments in the joint names. On her death the plaintiffs, her personal representatives, claimed that all such money formed part of her estate, arguing, *inter alia*, that the deceased had attempted to make a testamentary disposition not in conformity with the Wills Act, which was therefore invalid. Romer J., after reviewing the Irish and Canadian authorities which had been cited to him,[12] and "having regard to the disturbing effect which an acceptance of the argument might well have on titles already acquired," considered that any change in the current of authority should be left to the Court of Appeal to make. The nephew, he held, had a beneficial as well as a legal title to the moneys.

Jackson v. White and Midland Bank Ltd.

[1967] 2 Lloyd's Rep. 68

The holders of a joint account have a joint and several right of action against the bank

Facts

The first defendant induced the plaintiff to put up £2,000 for his failing business, under a loose arrangement envisaging the creation of a partnership; and an account was opened with the Midland Bank purporting to be a partnership account, cheques on which were to be signed by both parties. White thereafter forged the plaintiff's signature to a number of cheques, and obtained the plaintiff's signature to others which he represented as being in payment of trade debts; in fact he used all but three

[8] At p. 456.
[9] (1885) 28 Ch.D.
[10] [1970] A.C. 777.
[11] [1949] Ch. 278.
[12] The point does not appear to have been raised in any previous English case.

of them for his own purposes. The plaintiff brought this action against the first defendant in respect of all the cheques except three, and against the bank in respect of the forged cheques.

Decision

Park J. held that the bank's agreement with the two customers was with them jointly to honour cheques jointly drawn, and an agreement with each of them separately not to honour any cheques not drawn by him. The bank was therefore liable on the forged cheques, although it was entitled to be indemnified by the first defendant.

Notes

The nature of a bank's liability to customers on a joint account was a matter of controversy following the decision in *Brewer* v. *Westminster Bank Ltd.*[13] in 1952. Although *Jackson's* case, like *Brewer's*, was only at first instance it is generally accepted that the superior courts would agree with the line taken by Park J. and it is unlikely that the contrary view will reappear.

In *Brewer's* case the plaintiff was an executor and beneficiary of her father's will, her co-executor being the managing clerk of the solicitors who had managed her father's affairs. A joint account having been opened with the defendant bank, both parties to sign, the managing clerk forged the plaintiff's signature to cheques to a total of £3,000. Upon the plaintiff bringing this action against the bank, for payment of cheques bearing only one authorised signature, the bank contended *inter alia* (*a*) that action on the joint account could be brought only by the account holders jointly, and that as one of them could not, because of his forgeries, sue the bank, the other was also debarred; and (*b*) that it is an implied term of such a contract that each customer will act honestly. McNair J. accepted the first of these arguments, but rejected the second.

The decision provoked much criticism,[14] and in a succession of cases it was either distinguished or not followed.[15] And in *Catlin* v. *Cyprus Corporation (London) Ltd.*[16] what may

---

[13] [1952] 2 All E.R. 650.
[14] *cf.* Paget, *op. cit.* pp. 76 *et seq.*
[15] For example, by Devlin J. in *Baker* v. *Barclays Bank Ltd.* [1955] 1 W.L.R. 822, *ante* p. 180, and Harman J. in *Welch* v. *Bank of England and Others* [1955] Ch. 508, where he had said "I confess that I do not follow [the *Brewer*] decision."
[16] [1983] 1 All E.R. 809.

perhaps be the last attempt to rest a case on *Brewer* failed before Bingham J. The plaintiff and her husband had a joint account with the defendants, on the terms that cheques were to be signed by both. When the bank paid the husband all the funds on the account on his signature alone, the wife brought this action, and the bank argued that as their obligation was to the two account holders jointly, the plaintiff could bring no action by herself.

Bingham J. analysed the reasoning in *Brewer*, and the criticisms of the decision, and said that the bank's agreement to honour instructions by both account holders imported a negative agreement not to honour instructions not signed by both.

A duty on the defendants which could only be enforced jointly with the party against the possibility of whose misconduct a safeguard was sought, and where the occurrence of such misconduct through the negligent breach of mandate by the defendants would deprive the innocent party of any remedy, would be worthless. Indeed, it would be worse than useless, because a customer would reasonably rely on the two-signatures safeguard and refrain from active supervision of the account.[17]

It is to be noted, however, that the finding on the bank's second argument in *Brewer's* case, as to the implied guarantee by each customer of the other's honesty, has not been challenged. In this connection McNair J. quoted Scrutton L.J.[18] "a term can only be implied if it is necessary in the business sense to give efficacy to the contract" and went on:

Bearing in mind that the joint account was opened by the use of the bank's own form and... that the number of cases where bankers sustain losses by forgery is infinitesimal in comparison with the large business they do... I am unable to reach the conclusion that there is any necessity to imply such a term to give business efficacy to the contract.[19]

In view of his finding on the first argument this view was *obiter*, but it may well be taken as good law.

---

[17] At p. 817. *cf.* Martin J. in an Australian case, *Ardern* v. *Bank of New South Wales* (1956) 7 L.D.B. 85: "I consider that the view put by the plaintiff is the correct one—that the undertaking of the bank not to honour cheques unless they were signed by both partners was a condition which inured for the benefit of each partner."

[18] In *Reigate* v. *Union Manufacturing Co. (Ramsbottom)* [1918] 1 K.B. 592 at p. 595.

[19] [1952] 2 All E.R. 650 at p. 656.

PARTNERS

Alliance Bank v. Kearsley
(1871) L.R. 6 C.P. 433

A partner has no implied authority entitling him to open an account in his own name so as to bind the partnership

Facts

The defendant, William Kearsley, and his brother James were in partnership as coachbuilders, trading under the name of George Kearsley & Co. In 1864 James opened an account with the plaintiffs at Manchester, explaining that the account was a partnership account, but that as he was the only partner resident in Manchester it had better be in his name. In 1869, the account being then overdrawn, the plaintiffs sought to recover the amount of the overdraft from the defendant.

Decision

It was held that the bank could not recover. In his judgment Montague Smith J. said:

The partner has authority to do what is usual in the ordinary course of the business. It is established that in trade partnerships one partner may borrow money for the partnership, and will bind his co-partner by so doing. That is held to be within the implied authority of a partner because it has been found to be in the ordinary course of business necessary for the purposes of trade. But I do not think a judge can take it upon himself to assume, without evidence, that it is within the ordinary course of business for one partner to open a banking account in his own name on behalf of the partnership so as to bind his co-partners to the state of that account whatever it may be. That being so; the foundation of the implied authority entirely fails.... An account opened by a man in his own name is prima facie his private account, and it seems likely that such an implication of authority would give great facilities for mixing up private and partnership accounts so as to enable frauds to be committed with less chance of detection.[20]

Notes

The implied authority of a partner in a trading partnership to pledge the credit of the partnership extends only to transactions in the ordinary course of the firm's business, and when he attempts to do so outside this limit he makes himself liable. The

---

[20] At pp. 437, 438.

Alliance Bank case decided that the opening of an account in the partner's own name does not bind the co-partners, although it had been earlier decided, in *Beale* v. *Caddick*,[21] that one partner could effectively assent to the *transfer* of the partnership account when the business of the firm's bankers had been transferred to another bank.

Although there is no express authority in the cases it seems to follow from the fact that a partner has general authority to borrow money for the partnership business that he has power to open a banking account in the firm's name, and the importance attached by Montague Smith J. to the fact that James Kearsley opened the Manchester account in his own name and not that of the firm supports this view. In practice this important point is likely to arise only rarely, as the banker will normally obtain a mandate for the opening of an account signed by all the partners.

In *Brettel* v. *Williams*[22] the defendants were railway contractors and made a sub-contract with a firm of brick-makers. One of the partners guaranteed the payment by the brick-makers of the bills for the coal necessary to their work on the sub-contract. It was held that this guarantee was not binding on the other partners, Parke B. saying:

> To allow one partner to bind another by contracts out of the apparent scope of the partnership dealings, because they were reasonable acts towards effecting the partnership purposes, would be attended with great danger. Could one of the defendants in this case have bound the others by a contract to lease or buy lands, or a coal mine, though it might be a reasonable mode of effecting a legitimate object of the partnership business?[23]

In *Kendall* v. *Hamilton*[24] a creditor did not discover the existence of a third partner until he obtained judgment against two, and in the House of Lords, despite a strongly worded plea by Lord Penzance for substantial rather than formal justice, it was held by a majority of six to one that the creditor could not recover. A little over a hundred years later the Civil Liability (Contribution) Act 1978 has implemented Lord Penzance's plea in providing that judgment obtained against one person jointly

---

[21] (1857) 2 H. & N. 326.
[22] (1849) 4 Ex. 623.
[23] At p. 630.
[24] (1879) 4 A.C. 504.

liable is not a bar to an action against other persons jointly liable for the same debt.

A partner signing a cheque which bears the printed name of the partnership binds all the partners. In *Ringham* v. *Hackett and Another*[25] the first defendant, without the knowledge of his partner, signed a cheque for £500 under the printed name of the partnership. He subsequently disappeared, and his partner stopped payment of all cheques signed by him. In the action on this cheque the Court of Appeal rejected the partner's argument that by section 23 of the Bills of Exchange Act some such indication as "per pro" before the partnership name was necessary to bind the partnership. And in *Central Motors (Birmingham) Ltd.* v. *P. A. and S. N. Wadsworth*[26] where again a single partner signed a partnership cheque, the Court of Appeal did not accept the argument of the other partner that section 23 relieved him of liability: section 23(2) was reinforced by section 91(1) and by section 5 of the Partnership Act, 1890, and it must now be accepted that a person signing a cheque so printed is normally presumed to have signed in the name of the firm.

And in *United Bank of Kuwait* v. *Hammoud*[27] the Court of Appeal held that an undertaking given as security for a loan was within the ordinary business of a solicitor where there was an underlying transaction of a solicitorial nature. The bank was suing the partners of a solicitor who had fraudulently given such an undertaking, and they succeeded in their claim that the fraudulent solicitor had ostensible authority that bound his partners: banks were entitled to assume that admitted solicitors were of good character, whose statements did not need the degree of confirmation that might otherwise be appropriate.

It must be noted that in the case of partnerships, as in all others where there is any form of joint liability, it is common banking practice to take joint and several undertakings.[28]

Re Bourne, Bourne v. Bourne

[1906] 2 Ch. 427

Effect of a partner's death on the firm's bank account; duty of the surviving partners to realise the partnership assets, whether personalty or realty

---

[25] (1980) 124 S.J. 201; 10 L.D.B. 206; *ante*, pp. 51, 63.
[26] [1983] C.A.T. 82/231.
[27] [1988] 1 W.L.R. 1051.
[28] As to partnership generally, see Reeday, *op. cit.* pp. 87–113.

Facts

Bourne and Grove were in partnership, and in 1901, when Grove died, Bourne carried on the business in the partnership name until his own death in 1902. At the date of Grove's death the firm's account with their bankers, Berwick and Co., was £6,476 overdrawn, and some months later Bourne deposited with the bank deeds of certain real estate forming part of the partnership assets. Between Grove's death and the deposit of the deeds Bourne had paid into the account more than £10,000 and had drawn out more than £8,500. After further transactions the overdraft, at the date of Bourne's death, was £4,463. Bourne's estate proving insolvent, the question arose whether Grove's executors or the bank took priority against the proceeds of sale of the property charged.

Upon it being held that the bank took priority, Grove's executors appealed.

Decision

The Court of Appeal upheld the lower court's decision. In his judgment, Romer L.J. said:

When a partner dies and the partnership comes to an end, it is not only the right, but the duty, of the surviving partner to realise the assets for the purpose of winding up the partnership affairs, including the payment of the partnership debts. It is true that in a general sense the executors or administrators of the deceased partner may be said to have a lien upon the partnership assets in respect of his interest in the partnership on taking the partnership account, but that lien is not one which affects each particular piece of property belonging to the partnership so as to affect that property in the hands of any person dealing with the surviving partner in good faith. It is really what one may call a general lien upon the surplus assets.... Then the only question remaining is this: Was the debt of the bank which the surviving partner gave the charge to secure one that really to the knowledge of the bank was not a partnership debt? To my mind, on the contrary, the bank were entitled to consider it and treat it as a partnership debt. The account with them was a partnership account. It was continued under the partnership name, and apparently for the purposes of the partnership, and it appears to me impossible to say that it is not or may not be reasonable for a surviving partner to continue the partnership account for the purpose of winding up the estate.[29]

Notes

The Partnership Act 1890, s.38, provides that surviving partners after the death of their co-partner may bind the firm

[29] At pp. 431–433.

and continue business as far as it is necessary to do so in winding up the business of the firm. The importance of *Re Bourne* need not be emphasised: the attempt to impugn the right of the surviving partner to charge the firm's assets—the point made being that he could do this only with personal property—would, if successful, have made much more dangerous a bank's dealings with such a customer.

In *Royal Bank of Scotland* v. *Christie*[30] two surviving partners continued the partnership account after the death of the third partner, and made no arrangements to segregate from current business the amount due to the bank at the date of the death. It was held that the deceased partner's liability in respect of the indebtness to the bank was discharged at the point where the payings-in to the bank amounted to the total indebtedness at the time of his death; and security charged by the deceased partner to secure the borrowing of the firm was accordingly discharged, leaving the advance to that extent unsecured. It is, of course, now common practice to rule off an account which is overdrawn upon the death of a partner, or his bankruptcy or retirement.[31]

EXECUTORS

Farhall v. Farhall

(1871) 7 Ch.App. 123

Borrowing by an executor is always his personal responsibility and, if it is unauthorised, the estate of the deceased cannot be made liable for it

Facts

Farhall was a customer of the London and County Bank, and at the time of his death was overdrawn against the security of certain real property belonging to him. His widow, the executrix, borrowed further from the bank, and charged further property of the estate as security. A decree for the administration of the estate having been made, the bank sought to prove for these advances, and by consent the whole of the security charged to them was realised. This sale left an outstanding overdraft of £987, and the bank claimed to prove for this balance owing to them. Mrs. Farhall's own affidavit showed that to a great extent her withdrawals had been misappropriated, but the bank had no knowledge of the misappropriation.

---

[30] (1841) 8 Cl. & Fin. 214.
[31] *cf. ante*, pp. 150 *et seq.*

Decision

The Court of Appeal held that the bank was not entitled to prove, on the grounds that, although an executor can give a lien on a specific asset of the estate, he cannot create such a contract as will give the creditor a right to prove against the estate as a whole. In the course of his judgment Sir W. M. James L.J. said:

> ...to say that the executrix can, by borrowing money, enable the person who has lent it to stand as a creditor upon the estate, is a position supported by no authority and no principle. The contract is with the executrix; there is no loan to the estate; there is no credit to the estate; the credit is given only to the person who borrows, though the money may be borrowed for the purposes of the estate.
>
> It was argued for the respondents that they were, at all events, creditors to the extent to which the money was applied in payment of debts, and we were referred to *Haynes* v. *Forshaw*[32]... but there is nothing in that case to support the contention that, if a man lends money to an executor, who says "I am going to pay debts with it," and the debts are not paid, the lender is to stand in the same place as if the debts had been paid with the money. The bankers, no doubt, took it for granted that the executrix was going to apply the whole of the money which she borrowed from them for the purposes of the estate; but she did not do so; and I am of opinion therefore that their claim fails.[33]

Notes

The personal liability of executors and administrators is a fundamental of executorship law. Where the business of the deceased is carried on they are responsible for debts incurred even though they act ostensibly as personal representatives and even though they are authorised by the will to do so—although in the latter case they are entitled to indemnity from the estate. Similarly, in the case of unauthorised or misappropriated borrowing from a bank no contribution can be sought from the estate upon the failure of the personal representative to repay the advance.

Moreover, when there are two or more personal representatives they have in many respects similar powers to those of partners, and can deal with the assets without binding, and without the consent of, their co-representatives. In order therefore to make all the representatives liable for loans it is necessary for all to bind themselves, and this is especially important when, at the outset of the administration, borrowing

---

[32] (1853) 11 Hare 93.
[33] At pp. 125–126.

is sought to pay the death duties. The banker will normally satisfy himself as well as he can, from the will or from other available sources, that the advance is being made to the right persons; but in the event of their failure to obtain probate or letters of administration he will have no recourse against the estate beyond the extent to which such an advance has in fact been used to pay the duties due.

Just as one executor can act independently, so one can countermand another. In *Gaunt* v. *Taylor*,[34] when co-executors stopped payment of a cheque drawn by an executrix, the banker paid the money into court, and his action in doing so, and in refusing to pay the cheque, was not questioned.

A banker dealing bona fide with a personal representative may retain any security of the estate which has been lodged with him as security for an advance. In *Berry* v. *Gibbons*[35] an executrix borrowed in her capacity as executrix against the security of a picture belonging to the estate. It was held that the fact that, unknown to the bank, an administration order had been made in respect of the estate, did not invalidate the security. The decision in this case, however, was in part based on the facts that no receiver had been appointed, and no injunction had been granted to restrain the executrix from dealing with the assets. The picture was a possessory asset; the bank might not have been able to enforce a non-possessory security.

In the absence of express authority in the will or the unanimous approval of the creditors, a business may not be carried on by the personal representatives longer than is necessary for winding it up; and the personal representatives become personally liable if they carry it on for any longer period. Even when express authority is given in the will, a creditor who has not assented to the continuance is not bound. In *Re Elijah Murphy, deceased, Morton* v. *Marchanton*[36] the executors were given power to carry on the business, and it was carried on for two years, when the estate became insolvent. An unpaid creditor obtained judgment and a receiver was appointed; and the bank from which the estate had borrowed £3,000 sought a declaration that they had a charge on certain property ranking prior to the creditors at the date of the death. Judgment was given for the bank in the County Palatine Court,

---

[34] (1843) 2 Hare 413.
[35] (1873) 8 Ch.App. 747.
[36] (1930) 4 L.D.B. 328.

Manchester, on the grounds that the creditor had acquiesced in
the continuance of the business; had there been no such
acquiescence, the authority given to the executors in the will
would not have helped the bank.[37]

The executor or administrator of the estate of a deceased
customer has a clear legal title to the balance of the customer's
account, but he has to account to the beneficiaries under the
will or the persons entitled on an intestacy, and it is of course
only with this legal title that the banker is normally concerned.[38]
Paul v. *Constance*[39] is an unusual example of a successful
challenge to the title of widow-administratrix by the woman with
whom the deceased had been living, who established that the
money on the account (which the widow had withdrawn) had
been left on trust for her. The Court of Appeal rejected the
widow's argument that even though legal terminology is not
essential to establish an express trust, yet there must be words
clearly indicating that a trust is intended. Scarman L.J. said:

> [Counsel] was right to remind the court that we are dealing with very
> simple people, unaware of the subtleties of equity, but understanding
> very well indeed their own domestic situation.[40]

The rights and liabilities of the deceased customer normally
pass to his executor or administrator, to whom the banker must
look for the repayment of any money owing to him at the date
of death. *Re Amirteymour (deceased)*[41] is a quite exceptional
case of a bank's failure to recover overdrawn balances on the
death of an Iranian customer without personal representatives in
this country and of whom no personal representatives could be
traced abroad. Proceedings against the estate of a deceased
person are actions *in personam*, and in the absence of any
person, natural or artificial, recognised as a defendant, the
action cannot proceed. In the Court of Appeal, Lord Diplock

---

[37] *cf.* Trustee Act 1925, s.17.
[38] *cf.* Holden, *op. cit.* pp. 3–15 and 11–168 *et seq.*, as to the banker's
relationship with personal representatives.
[39] [1977] 1 W.L.R. 527.
[40] *cf.* Megarry J., in *Cresswell* v. *Potter* [1978] 1 W.L.R. 255: "the document
abounds in terms which, although speaking to the conveyancer in language of
precision, can hardly be expected to speak to a van driver and telephonist
lucidly or at all."
[41] [1979] 1 W.L.R. 63.

gave as a more general example of the rule the case where a sole defendant to an action dies and no executor or administrator has yet been appointed; the action may not abate, but it cannot continue.

UNINCORPORATED ASSOCIATIONS

Bradley Egg Farm Ltd. v. Clifford and Others

[1943] 2 All E.R. 378

The officers rather than the members of unincorporated associations are normally liable for the debts and contracts of the associations

Facts

The plaintiffs, poultry farmers, contracted to have their birds tested for disease. The defendants were the executive council of the Lancashire Utility Poultry Society, and the letters in which they contracted with the plaintiffs were on paper so headed, and signed by one Gates, as Technical Manager. The society was an unincorporated one, with a large number of members, each of whom paid a subscription of 7s. 6d., and was entitled to receive the publications of the society. The rules provided that on dissolution the funds were not to be distributed amongst the members but were to be given to some institution with similar aims to those of the society. No member as such had any interest in the funds of the society.

The test contracted for was carried out by an employee of the society, and through his negligence a number of the birds died. The plaintiffs claimed damages, and upon the decision being given in their favour, the defendants appealed.

Decision

The Court of Appeal, by a majority, upheld the lower court. In the course of his judgment, on behalf of Scott L.J. and himself, Goddard L.J. said:

The society thus has some analogy to a members' club, with this important difference, that, whereas the property of such a club belongs beneficially to the members jointly, the members of this society have no rights in the funds or property of the society at all. Its affairs are managed by a council composed of the defendants, who are entrusted with the management and administration of its affairs.... In view of the objects of the society as set out in the rules, it is plain that persons must be engaged to further them, and that this appointment and the

allocation of duties among them would be part of the duties of
management and administration conferred on the council. Gates was
appointed as technical manager and laboratory officer on April 21,
1939, at a meeting of the council. All of the defendant committee
either voted for or knew and approved of his appointment. In our
opinion, it is plain that Gates was employed by the council, and must
be regarded as their servant. Against whom but them could he claim
his salary? It was argued that if he was a servant of anyone it was of
the society, that is, of every member of the society, and that, if he in
the course of his duties made contracts, he made them as agent for the
members of the society jointly. In our opinion, this is an impossible
contention. Because members of a society, especially in a case where
they have no right or interest in the funds or property of the society,
entrust its affairs and management to a committee, that does not mean
that they thereby give the committee authority to make contracts
binding on them. Otherwise a person who pays a subscription of 7s. 6d.
to this society might find himself involved in liabilities of an unknown
amount. It is the defendant committee who are liable as Gates's
principals, and they are his principals, not because they are members of
the society, but because they are the committee entrusted with the
function of directing the activities of this unincorporated body, and
putting them into execution. That includes the making and performing
of contracts; and the manager appointed by them becomes their agent
and servant to act on their behalf in making such contracts as they may
direct and approve and appointing experts, etc.[42]

Notes

The unincorporated association, a collection of individuals
bound more or less loosely and with no single legal entity, is in
an anomalous position midway between that of the individual
and that of the corporate body, and lacking the legal
definiteness of either. In the relation of such bodies with their
bankers, however, there seems to have been little difficulty in
practice, and the leading case in which a bank was directly
involved is still *Coutts & Co.* v. *The Irish Exhibition in
London*.[43] In that case six prominent public men desired to set
on foot an Irish Exhibition in London, and, before any steps
had been taken to form a company for that purpose, they
opened an account with the plaintiff bank, with an arranged
overdraft of £10,000 against certain conditional guarantees,
which later proved worthless. Two months later the exhibition
was constituted a company, but, while the bank had notice of
the formation of the company, no change was made in the style

[42] At pp. 380–381.
[43] (1891) 7 T.L.R. 313.

of the account or in the arrangements for signature. A month later, upon pressure from the plaintiff bank, securities were lodged in support of the overdraft, and three months later still the bank obtained a memorandum of charge on debts owing to the company. Upon the project failing, the bank brought an action to recover the amount of the overdraft against the company, and against the six originators of the project. For these latter defendants it was contended, *inter alia*, that throughout the transactions it was not the intention of the bank to look to them personally for the amount borrowed. The Court of Appeal held that the bank was entitled to recover from the six promoters, Lindley L.J. saying:

> The ordinary relation of banker and customer must be held to have existed between Messrs. Coutts and these gentlemen, unless it could be made out that Messrs. Coutts were not to be the creditors of anybody until the exhibition was formed. But suppose, owing to some unforeseen cause, the exhibition had never been formed, was nobody to be liable to Messrs. Coutts?[44]

The effect of this decision and that in the Bradley Egg Farm case would seem to leave little doubt that the officers of an unincorporated association are personally liable for the debts which they incur in the name of the association. Paget contends[45] that the bank should obtain the personal undertaking of such persons as they wish to make liable; and it is clearly desirable in practice that any borrowing should be on the application and in the names of such persons, rather than in the name of the association alone, even though, on the authorities, it seems likely that the bank could recover against, *e.g.* the members of a committee of management even though they had not bound themselves individually and personally.

The distinction implied by Goddard L.J. between associations whose property belongs beneficially to the members and those in which the members have no rights in the property does not affect the point here discussed: the officers of the association are normally entitled to indemnity from such property, but the members as such are normally not liable personally for the acts of those officers.[46]

---

[44] At p. 314.
[45] *Op. cit.* pp. 26 *et seq.*
[46] *Wise* v. *Perpetual Trustee Co. Ltd.* [1903] A.C. 139.

LIMITED COMPANIES

Introductions Ltd. v. National Provincial Bank Ltd.

[1970] Ch. 199

A company's borrowing must not be for a purpose inconsistent with the company's objects set out in the memorandum of association

Facts

Introductions Ltd. was originally founded to provide services and facilities for overseas visitors to the Festival of Britain in 1951, and it subsequently provided deck chairs in seaside resorts. In 1960 it came under new management, and embarked upon a pig breeding venture, which was a failure, the company being wound up in 1965 with liabilities of £2 million including an overdraft with the bank of £29,500. The liquidator claimed that the two debentures given by the company as security for this advance were invalid. Pig breeding not being among the objects set out in the company's memorandum was *ultra vires*, and borrowing for that purpose must be *ultra vires* also.

The bank, which had knowledge of the memorandum, contended that the borrowing was covered by a clause in it empowering the company "to borrow or raise money in such manner as the company shall think fit," while a further clause provided that "each of the preceding sub-clauses shall be construed independently of . . . any other sub-clause, and that the objects set out in each sub-clause are independent objects of the company."

Decision

The Court of Appeal upheld Buckley J.'s finding against the bank. Harman L.J. said:

. . . borrowing is not an end in itself and must be for some purpose of the company; . . . you cannot convert a power into an object merely by saying so.[47]

---

[47] At p. 210 *cf. Thompson* v. *J. Barke & Co. (Caterers) Ltd.* [1975] S.L.T. 67, where the Court of Session held *inter alia* that the issue by the company of two cheques in repayment of a loan to a director of the company was *ultra vires*, despite a power in the memorandum to issue cheques: the nature of the transaction here was not the issue of cheques, but the repayment of a loan.

Notes

The *ultra vires* rule, now past its centenary, was established by the House of Lords in *Ashbury Carriage Co. v. Riche*,[48] when it was held that the company, whose memorandum of association included only such objects as the construction of railway carriages, did not have the capacity to contract to build a railway in Belgium, notwithstanding that the shareholders approved the project. The rule provides that a company incorporated and registered under the Companies Acts can lawfully do only the acts it was formed to do, as set out in the memorandum of association in what is known as the objects clause. Activities outside this scope are said to be *ultra vires*, or beyond its powers, and any contract in which the company seeks to pursue such activities is void.

The rule has been much criticised in recent years, both the Cohen Committee and the Jenkins Committee[49] having recommended changes in it. Originally designed to protect creditors and shareholders, its frequent effect was to prejudice innocent contractors with the company, while its operation became more arbitrary as the companies legislation made it progressively easier for a company to change its memorandum. The *Introductions* case is a good example of its unfortunate operation: "The company's *ultra vires* activity was known to, and presumably endorsed by, the company's shareholders; the memorandum could have been altered with no trouble at all to cover the new activity; the bank had lent the money to a respectably constituted concern. And yet at the end of the day their contract is invalid."[50] But the law was quite clear, and what may be called the "hard line" in the matter found expression in further words of Harman L.J. in the *Introductions* case:

It has always been the ambition apparently of the commercial community to stretch the objects clause of a memorandum of association, thus obtaining the advantage of limited liability with as little fetter on the activities of the company as possible. But still you cannot have an object to do every mortal thing you want, because that is to have no object at all.[51]

---

[48] (1875) L.R. 7 H.L. 653.
[49] Cmnd. 6659 (1945), Cmnd. 1749 (1962). These two reports on the operation of the companies legislation were the foundation of, respectively, the 1948 and the 1967 Companies Acts.
[50] *The Banker* (March 1969), Vol. 119, p. 255.
[51] At p. 209.

An attempt to alter the law was made by the European Communities Act 1972, which provides in section 9(1) that:

in favour of a person dealing with a company in good faith any transaction decided on by the directors shall be deemed to be one which it is within the capacity of the company to enter into, and the power of the directors to bind the company shall be deemed to be free of any limitation under the memorandum or articles of association; and a party to a transaction so decided on shall not be bound to enquire as to the capacity of the company to enter into it or as to any such limitation on the powers of the directors, and shall be presumed to have acted in good faith unless the contrary is proved.

This provision, now re-enacted as section 35 of the Companies Act 1985, is very similar to the proposals of the Jenkins Committee, and was intended to bring our *ultra vires* rule nearer to the Community's attempt in 1968 to introduce uniformity on the matter into the systems of the then member states. The effect of the provision is to protect persons who do not know that a transaction is *ultra vires*. It is important to note that it does not protect persons with actual knowledge that the *ultra vires* rule is being breached, for such a person cannot be acting in good faith. How the provision may affect a bank in a situation like that of the *Introductions* case remains to be tested in court, but it seems improbable that a banker who has received a copy of the memorandum and articles (as he will normally have done on opening the account) would succeed in a claim that he was without notice of its provisions.[52]

It is to be noted that criticisms of the *ultra vires* rule has recently developed to the extent that its abolition has become a real possibility. It remains for the time being however to give trouble to bankers and to others in avoiding its dangers.[53]

In *International Sales and Agencies Ltd.* v. *Marcus*[54] Lawson J. considered the effect of section 9(1) where the defendant, as he had held, had actual knowledge that payments to him by the company were *ultra vires*. He thought that the test of lack of "good faith" in the subsection lay "either in proof of his actual knowledge that the transaction was *ultra vires* the company or where it can be shown that such a person could not in all the circumstances have been unaware that he was a party to a

---

[52] s.9 has been widely criticised—see, *e.g.* Gowers, *Principles of Modern Company Law*, 4th ed., *passim*; as to section 9(1) especially, pp. 184–190.

[53] *cf.* Penn, Shea & Arora, *op. cit.*, I 17.08, where the Prentice proposals for reform are described and their adoption in the near future assumed.

[54] [1982] 3 All E.R. 551.

transaction *ultra vires*." He was satisfied that the subsection "was designed to deal, not with the operation of the doctrine of constructive trust, but only with the effect of the doctrines of *ultra vires*."

And in *TCB Ltd.* v. *Gray*[55] where a guarantor was contesting his liability for £1.8 million under his guarantee, he claimed *inter alia* that his guarantee had been given on the understanding that it was to be secured by a debenture, and that the debenture was not validly executed, the company's articles providing that debentures must be signed by a director not as here by an attorney for a director. But Browne-Wilkinson V.C. held that section 9(1) was a complete answer to the defence. "The manifest purpose of . . . the section is to enable people to deal with a company in good faith without being adversely affected by any limits on its capacity or its rules for internal management."

In *Charterbridge Corporation Ltd.* v. *Lloyds Bank Ltd.*[56] the bank successfully resisted a challenge to its security based on the *ultra vires* rule. The plaintiff company was the prospective purchaser of a property charged to the bank by a property development company. This latter company was one of a group, and its charge to the bank was in support of its guarantee of borrowing by the central company. The plaintiff company argued that the charge was void, as it had been created for purposes outside the scope of the company's business, and not for the company's benefit. But a clause in the memorandum covered the giving of guarantees and the lodgment of security in support, and Pennycuick J., finding for the bank, said:

> The memorandum of a company sets out its objects and proclaims them to persons dealing with the company and it would be contrary to the whole function of a memorandum that objects unequivocally set out in it should be subject to some implied limitation by reference to the state of mind of the parties concerned.[57]

It is to be noted that while a company's memorandum sets the limits of its activities, the inclusion of a particular activity as one of the objects does not in itself entitle the company to any

---

[55] [1986] Ch. 621.
[56] [1970] Ch. 62, 9 L.D.B. 111.
[57] At p. 69. *cf. Rolled Steel Products* v. *British Steel Corporation* [1982] 3 W.L.R. 715.

privileges associated with that activity. Thus in *United Dominions Trust Ltd.* v. *Kirkwood*[58] banking was one of the objects in the UDT memorandum, but this did not help the company to establish that they were bankers within the terms of the Moneylenders Act.[59]

The Royal British Bank v. Turquand

(1856) 6 E. & B. 327

Freeman and Lockyer v. Buckhurst Park Properties (Mangal) Ltd.

[1964] 2 Q.B. 480

The rule in Turquand's case

Facts of the Royal British Bank v. Turquand

A company was authorised by its deed of settlement (which at that time was the equivalent of the present memorandum and articles of association) to borrow, through its directors, such sums as might be authorised by a resolution passed at a general meeting of the company. The company arranged to borrow £2,000 from the plaintiff bank, and gave the bank a bond for that amount, under seal, and signed by two directors. The bank now sued the defendant as the official manager of the company, to recover the amount advanced, and it was contended for the company that as no resolution had been passed by the shareholders in general meeting the bank could not recover.

Decision

It was held by the Court of Exchequer Chamber that, as the power to borrow money on bonds was not inconsistent with the provisions of the deed of settlement, the bank were entitled to assume that the necessary resolution had been passed by the shareholders.

In the course of his judgment, Jervis C.J. said:

We may now take for granted that the dealings with these companies are not like dealings with other partnerships, and that the parties dealing with them are bound to read the statute and the deed of settlement. But they are not bound to do more. And the party here, on

[58] *Ante*, p. 27.
[59] As to companies generally, see Reeday, *op. cit.*, pp. 114–168; Penn, Shea & Arora, *op. cit.*, I 17.

reading the deed of settlement, would find, not a prohibition from borrowing, but a permission to do so on certain conditions. Finding that the authority might be made complete by a resolution, he would have a right to infer the fact of a resolution authorising that which on the face of the document appeared to be legitimately done.[60]

Facts of Freeman and Lockyer v. Buckhurst Park Properties (Mangal) Ltd.

The defendant company was formed in 1958 by Mr. Kapoor and Mr. Hoon, upon the latter's providing £40,000 to enable the former to buy the Buckhurst Park Estate. They became directors of the company, together with one nominee of each of them; and the articles of the company provided that a quorum of the company was to be four directors.

The first-named director acted throughout as managing director, to the knowledge of the other directors, but without express appointment, while for the greater part of the period in question in the case the second-named director was out of the country, so that the board was incapable of action as a board. Mr. Kapoor engaged the plaintiff firm of architects and surveyors to submit a planning application, and in this action they claimed their fees for work done.

The plaintiffs contended that Mr. Kapoor had actual authority to engage them on behalf of the company, or alternatively that he was held out by the company as having ostensible authority to do so. The defendant company argued that, in the absence of appointment generally as managing director or specifically for the purpose in question, his engagement of the plaintiff firm did not bind the company.

Decision

The Court of Appeal upheld the finding of the lower court in favour of the plaintiffs. In the course of his judgment, Diplock L.J. said:

If the foregoing analysis of the relevant law is correct, it can be summarised by stating four conditions which must be fulfilled to entitle a contractor to enforce against a company a contract entered into on behalf of the company by an agent who had no actual authority to do so. It must be shown: (1) that a representation that the agent had authority to enter on behalf of the company into a contract of the kind sought to be enforced was made to the contractor; (2) that such representation was made by a person or persons who had "actual"

[60] At p. 332.

authority to manage the business of the company either generally or in respect of those matters to which the contract relates; (3) that he (the contractor) was induced by such representation to enter into the contract, that is, that he in fact relied upon it; and (4) that under its memorandum or articles of association the company was not deprived of the capacity either to enter into a contract of the kind sought to be enforced or to delegate authority to enter into a contract of that kind to the agent.

The confusion which, I venture to think, has sometimes crept into the cases is in my view due to a failure to distinguish between these four separate conditions, and in particular to keep steadfastly in mind (a) that the only "actual" authority which is relevant is that of the persons making the representation relied on, and (b) that the memorandum and articles of association of the company are always relevant (whether they are in fact known to the contractor or not) to the questions (i) whether condition (2) is fulfilled, and (ii) whether condition (4) is fulfilled, and (but only if they are in fact known to the contractor) may be relevant (iii) as part of the representation on which the contractor relied.[61]

Notes

In earlier editions of this book the principles emerging from these cases were summarised thus:

> A person dealing with a registered company should satisfy himself that the proposed transaction is not inconsistent with the memorandum and articles of association, and that the person acting for the company is not one to whom power so to deal is unlikely to have been delegated; but he need not inquire whether all the necessary steps have been taken by the company to make the matter complete and regular.

This must now be read subject to the modification of the *ultra vires* rule by the European Communities Act. As was pointed out earlier,[62] the Act may be of little avail to the banker who holds a copy of the memorandum and articles of the company, while it might even be questioned whether a banker had acted in good faith within the terms of the Act if he had failed to obtain sight of the memorandum and articles of a company whose account he held. So the development and application of the rule in particular circumstances are still of concern to bankers, at least until the question is further considered by the courts; but the notes following must of course be read in the light of the 1972 Act.

---

[61] At pp. 505–506.
[62] *Ante*, p. 214.

A crucial aspect of the *ultra vires* problem is the question of delegated authority. This is of concern to bankers in their dealings with companies, especially in the drawing and indorsing of cheques and in borrowings by their company customers, for the companies' articles may well prescribe that certain formalities shall be observed which are laid down for the protection of the companies' assets. These cases are concerned with the position that arises when such formalities have not been observed.

The first decision above was the foundation of the important rule in *Turquand's* case. For many years after 1856 it was thought to be a principle of fairly simple application; for example in 1906 it was thus expressed[63]; "... where the regulations laid down by these documents, the memorandum and articles, appear to have been complied with, it is not the duty of the lender to see that the apparent conformity is a real conformity." More recent decisions have tended to restrict the wide terms of the original ruling, and there has been some doubt as to the present state of the law. The judgments in the *Freeman and Lockyer* case have gone far to resolve the confusion; of particular value is the judgment of Diplock L.J. in which he reconciled the decisions by reference to the four criteria set out above.

In a succession of cases the claim against the company has failed because the action of the agent was not of a kind that would normally be performed by a person occupying his position, so that "the conduct of the board of directors in permitting the agent to occupy that position ... did not of itself amount to a representation that the agent had authority to enter into the contract sought to be enforced, *i.e.* condition (1) was not fulfilled." *per* Diplock L.J. at pp. 507–508. The following two cases fall within this class.

In *A.L. Underwood Ltd.* v. *Bank of Liverpool and Martins*,[64] it was held that a director paying into his private account cheques drawn in favour of the company could not be considered to be acting within the scope of his apparent authority, even when he was the sole director and had authority to indorse cheques for the company as "sole director." In *Alexander Stewart & Son of Dundee Ltd.* v. *Westminster Bank*

[63] Tillyard, *Banking and Negotiable Instruments* (2nd ed.), p. 131.
[64] [1924] 1 K.B. 775. *cf. A.L. Underwood Ltd.* v. *Barclays Bank Ltd.*, ante p. 158. The two cases on the same facts came to the Court of Appeal together, but Barclays appealed also on their claim to be holders for value.

Ltd.[65] in similar circumstances, Bankes L.J. said that Stewart's authority in fact could be to indorse cheques only for the benefit of the company, whereas he intended when he made the indorsements to steal the proceeds of the cheques. By section 24 of the Bills of Exchange Act 1882, the signature was wholly inoperative, and the bank could acquire no rights under it in the absence of proof that Stewart had ostensible authority to indorse cheques. There was no ostensible authority in the circumstances of the case.

It may be remarked in connection with these two cases that the receipt of cheques payable to a limited company for the credit of a private or a firm's account may well be negligence in the bankers so receiving[66]; but in the latter case at least negligence was not relevant in view of the bank's defence that it was a holder for value. The question, which cannot be regarded as settled, whether a procuration signature becomes unauthorised merely because the signatory uses or intends to use the instrument signed unlawfully or fraudulently, is of some importance to the banker.

In *Cleveland Manufacturing Co. Ltd.* v. *The Muslim Commercial Bank Ltd.*[67] the bank paid a cheque under a letter of credit not to the plaintiffs but to their shipping agents, who had prepared the shipping documents and the cheque, signed the cheque over the name of the plaintiffs, and indorsed it in blank. The agents having subsequently gone into liquidation, the plaintiffs sued the bank, arguing that the agents were not authorised to receive payment on their behalf. The bank claimed, *inter alia*, that by authorising the agents to present the documents the plaintiffs had represented that the agents were authorised to receive payment.

Robert Goff J., citing Diplock L.J.'s judgment in *Freeman & Lockyer*, said that the representation of "ostensible" or "apparent" authority may be express or implied. Here there was no express representation, nor any evidence of any course of dealing from which such representation could be inferred.

Such authority would not, in my judgment, normally be implied in the case of a shipping agent authorised to prepare and sign such documents, because it could not be said that it would normally be

[65] (1926) 4 L.D.B. 40.
[66] *cf. Lloyds Bank Ltd.* v. *Chartered Bank of India, Australia and China, ante,* p. 171, and cases following.
[67] [1981] 2 Lloyd's Rep. 646; 10 L.D.B. 292; *ante,* p. 60.

implied that a shipping agent had authority to negotiate the bill... nor in my judgment... can it be said that where an individual is authorised to draw a draft on behalf of another, the indorsement of the draft in blank before delivery would normally be performed by such a person....

Moreover, to succeed on the argument of apparent authority the bank must show that they had relied on the representation. No evidence had been produced to show such reliance.[68]

It is clear that no representation under condition (1) can be relied upon when the person dealing with the company has been put on inquiry by other circumstances. Thus in *B. Liggett (Liverpool) Ltd.* v. *Barclays Bank Ltd.*[69] it was held that, although the two directors of the company had power to appoint a third, the fact that one of those directors had expressed continuing anxiety regarding the management of the business and had insisted on signing all cheques drawn on the account was sufficient to put the bank on inquiry regarding a notice they later received, signed by the other director as chairman of the company, notifying them that his wife had been appointed as third director.

A further example of this point is to be found in *Victors Ltd. (in liquidation)* v. *Lingard.*[70] There a company had an overdraft secured by the guarantee of the directors. Later the company gave further security in the form of debentures; but one of the articles of the company provided that no director should vote on a matter in which he had a personal interest, and all the directors had by virtue of their outstanding guarantees a personal interest in the improvement of the bank's security. In an action to enforce the debentures the bank contended that although they had notice of the company's articles, and, of course, of the directors' liability under their guarantees, and so could not assume that the resolution for the issue of debentures was validly passed, yet when they received the debentures under the company's seal they were entitled to assume that the seal had been properly affixed, for the company might have sanctioned the issue in general meeting; that is, they claimed that they were entitled to rely on the *Turquand* case. But Romer J. held that the resolution creating the debentures was a nullity (although in fact because of subsequent events the

[68] cf. *British Bank of the Middle East* v. *Sun Life Assurance Co. of Canada (U.K.) Ltd.* [1983] 2 Lloyd's Rep. 9.
[69] [1928] 1 K.B. 48. cf. *post,* p. 366.
[70] [1927] 1 Ch.D. 323.

company was held to be estopped from denying the validity of the debentures), and he rejected the argument of the bank on the facts of the case, holding that in fact they knew too much of the circumstances of the issue for their assumption to be justified.

Chapter 6

FINANCING BY BANKERS

Williams & Glyn's Bank Ltd. v. Barnes

[1981] Com.L.R. 205

Overdrafts and loans

Facts

The defendant was the founder, chairman and majority shareholder of Northern Developments Holdings Ltd., a property development company which from 1965 banked principally with the plaintiff bank. In 1972, when the company's overdraft limit was £6.5 million, the bank lent the plaintiff personally £1 million to enable him to buy more shares in the company; it was expected that the borrowing would be repaid out of funds owed to him by the company. But the collapse of the property market put the company in serious difficulties, and after a series of attempts to salvage the business, the bank appointed a receiver. The present action was for recovery of the personal lending to the defendant, who admitted the debt but raised a series of elaborate defences and counter-claims involving the manner in which the bank had dealt with the company.

Decision

Ralph Gibson J. held that no defence to the personal claim could be founded on the bank's conduct to the company; but in case he was wrong on that he went on to review each of the defendant's claims,[1] holding, *inter alia* that:

(a) it was not an express term of the advance that it should be repaid out of money owed to the defendant by the company, and there was no implied term that the bank would not damage the company so as to make payment impossible;

---

[1] In view of his rejection of all these claims, the action which Mr. Barnes had wanted the company to bring would also have failed.

(b) the bank owed no duty to the defendant, as a shareholder in the company, not to breach any duties it owed to the company; nor did the bank, as chargee of the defendant's shares, owe him any duty not to reduce the value of those shares by breaches of their duties to the company;

(c) the bank owed no duty to advise the defendant as to the prudence of buying shares in the company, when it ought to have known that the business was at risk;

(d) an overdraft is repayable on demand, unless it is expressly or impliedly agreed otherwise;

(e) the bank was under no implied obligation that it would on request raise the company's overdraft limit in relation to the company's retained profits.

Notes

The judgment in this remarkable case ran to 700 pages of typescript. It has not been fully reported, the single report here cited, representing the enterprise of a new series of official reports, being admittedly "extremely selective of facts and issues."[2] The case is probably the most wide ranging attack yet made on the banks' lending practices, and the fact that the attack failed hardly justifies the relative neglect of the decision.

The case is noteworthy for the number and variety of the borrower's unusual defences; the cases noted in this book include very many examples of the innumerable occasions on which banks have had recourse to the courts to obtain repayment of money lent to customers, but the challenges are more usually on alleged ineffectiveness of the security. The *Barnes* decision is notable also for the rejection of all the defences. The judgment was at first instance only, and it is possible that in other cases any one of the findings might be overruled or not followed, but the banks must regard as satisfactory the overall result of the case, and the judge's recognition of the realities of bank lending. He remarked that whereas a borrowing customer is free to replace the borrowing without notice if he can find accommodation on better terms, the financial state of the business may be such that no other lender will finance it, and then the difficulties of the borrower are likely to be shared by the bank: the expense and risks of receivership are clear, and the bank would often be forced to continue to support a customer from whom it would like to escape.

[2] See 10 L.D.B. 220.

The differences between loans and overdrafts are practical rather than legal and the *Barnes* decision is relevant to both. Both are advances to customers, granted normally at the discretion of the banker, although in the case of overdrafts unauthorised borrowing has always arisen when "cross firing" has been undetected, and in recent years cheque guarantee cards and credit cards have enlarged the area of unauthorised borrowing.[3]

The debiting of interest to overdrawn accounts, which gives the banker compound instead of simple interest, is justified, Paget suggests,[4] by the acquiescence of the customer, and it might be that a usage could be established. Lord Atkinson, in *Yuorell* v. *Hibernian Bank Ltd.*[5] considered it "a usual and perfectly legitimate mode of dealing between banker and customer."[5a]

The overdraft is often, though not of course always, less formal than the loan, especially in the possibility that there may be no agreed terms as to the borrowing. In the *Barnes* case it was the finding on overdrafts that attracted over-simplified attention in the popular press. In fact the judge held that one of the facility letters in the case would have required, to give it business effect, that the borrowing was *not* repayable on demand; in the event it was overtaken by another facility letter. His finding was that an overdraft is repayable on demand only when there is no express agreement as to the duration of the borrowing, and where no term can be implied to the contrary. And he held further that "on the usual banking conditions" does not necessarily mean that the overdraft is repayable on demand.[6] But his decision that overdrafts are normally repayable on demand was welcome to bankers as covering the very large number of simple overdraft advances.

Mr. Barnes had argued that a moratorium which the bank had supported during the salvage attempts was against public policy in that it encouraged the company to trade when, if its borrowing was repayable on demand, it could be brought down at any time by the bank. But the judge said that while a

---

[3] See *post*, pp. 230 *et seq.*
[4] *Op. cit.* p. 116.
[5] [1918] A.C. 372.
[5a] And the right to compound interest is not lost when demand for payment is made: *National Bank of Greece SA* v. *Pinios Shipping Co. No. 2, The Times*, December 1, 1989.
[6] Although the overdraft is normally repayable on demand, the banker must not dishonour cheques already issued in the belief that the facility is still available.

contract which encouraged a company to trade when it was clear that it could not meet its engagements would clearly be against public policy, this was not true of a contract which did no more than permit the directors of a company to trade, if they decided to do so with knowledge of all the facts, including the right of the bank to call in the advance. It is the directors' responsibility to ensure that trading is being carried on properly.

For an overdraft or a loan, as for other debts, the courts give summary judgment when there is no defence, and they have discretion to give it also when the defence is not considered to be "arguable." In *Paclantic Financing Co. Ltd.* v. *Moscow Narodny Bank Ltd.*[7] where the bank sought summary judgment for $14m lent to the defendant, Webster J. refused the application: although the plaintiffs' affidavits were almost incredible he considered that there was one issue that gave rise to an arguable defence.

In *Bank of Credit and Commerce* v. *Bawany*,[8] where the bank sought repayment of the defendants' overdraft of £95,000, the trial judge gave the defendants leave to appeal on the condition that they brought £45,000 into court. They appealed against the condition, but Lawton L.J. said that they had been lucky to get leave at all: their defence was that the company of which they were directors and guarantors had suffered loss by the bank's negligence in not opening an agreed letter of credit. As to bringing money into court, they said that the bank had second mortgages on their homes, but, his Lordship said, there was no evidence that they had any money at all, and their appeal was dismissed.

An even more unusual defence was rejected by the Court of Appeal in *Barclays Bank Ltd.* v. *Fisher.*[9] After long delay, the bank obtained summary judgment for the defendant's indebtedness on overdraft, and he appealed on the grounds that he had not been allowed to give evidence as to events since the debt was incurred, while the bank was allowed to claim interest accrued during that period. The appeal was dismissed.

Metropolitan Police Commissioner v. Charles

[1976] 3 All E.R. 112

Unauthorised borrowing

[7] [1983] 1 W.L.R. 1063.
[8] (Unreported) (1981) C.L.Y. 405.
[9] (Unreported) (1982) C.L.Y. 674.

Facts

The defendant had an account with the National Westminster Bank at Peckham Rye, where he had been allowed an overdraft limit of £100 and been given a cheque card. He had been instructed not to cash more than one cheque a day for £30. On one evening at a gaming club he issued all 25 cheques in a new cheque book, each for £30, and each backed by the cheque card, in exchange for chips. The bank of course had to honour the cheques, and the defendant was prosecuted under section 16(1) of the Theft Act 1968, with having "by deception" obtained for himself a pecuniary advantage "by deliberately or recklessly representing that he was entitled and authorised to use a cheque card." He was convicted, and the Court of Appeal upheld the conviction. The basis of his appeal, which was then pursued to the House of Lords, was that the use of a cheque card does not imply any representation by the drawer as to the state of his account, or his authoriy to draw on that account, nor can there be any inference that any such representation induces the recipient of the cheque to accept it: he relies entirely on the bank's guarantee to pay.

Decision

The House of Lords unanimously rejected the appeal. Lord Edmunds-Davies said:

> The card played a vital part for (as my noble and learned friend, Lord Diplock, put it during counsel's submissions) in order to make the bank liable to the payee there must be knowledge on the payee's part that the drawer has the bank's authority to bind it, for in the absence of such knowledge the all-important contract between payee and bank is not created; and it is the representation by the drawer's production of the card that he has that authority that creates such contractual relationship and estops the bank from refusing to honour the cheque. By drawing the cheque the accused represented that it would be met, and by producing the card so that the number thereon could be endorsed on the cheque he in effect represented "I am authorised by the bank to show this to you and so create a direct contractual relationship between the bank and you that they will honour this cheque."[10]

Notes

In an earlier case, *R.* v. *Kovacs*,[11] when it was argued that the deception in such a case was of the payees of the cheques, not

[10] At p. 121.
[11] [1974] 1 W.L.R. 370.

of the bank, the Court of Appeal held that section 16 requires, not that the person deceived should himself suffer any loss from the deception, but that there is a causal connection between the deception and the pecuniary advantage. The different defence in the *Charles* case—that in fact the payee had not been deceived—was heard with some sympathy by the Court of Appeal, but they considered themselves bound by their decision in *Kovacs*; and, as one must think fortunately, the House of Lords was able to put the matter beyond doubt.

R. v. *Lambie*[12] was concerned with the misuse, not of a cheque card but of a credit card, similarly capable of creating a borrowing which the bank has not authorised. The accused had used her Barclaycard substantially beyond her credit limit, and she was charged, also under section 16(1), in connection with one specific purchase, in a Mothercare shop. She was convicted, the jury finding that she had made a representation, which had induced the shop assistant to make the sale. But the Court of Appeal, albeit reluctantly, allowed her appeal, distinguishing the *Charles* case on the difference between credit card and cheque card, the former involving a contract between the credit card company and the trader, the latter being in the nature of an open offer to the world. The shop assistant had said in evidence that in a credit card transaction she was not concerned with the relation between the card holder and the credit card company: that company had guaranteed payment of the amount of the transaction.

The House of Lords overruled this decision. There had been a representation. Lord Roskill said[13]:

Following the decision of this House in *R.* v. *Charles*, it is in my view clear that the representation arising from the presentation of a credit card has nothing to do with the respondent's credit standing at the bank but is a representation of actual authority to make the contract with, in this case, Mothercare on the bank's behalf that the bank will honour the voucher upon presentation. Upon that view, the existence and terms of the agreement between the bank and Mothercare are irrelevant. . . .

And as to inducement, if the shop assistant had been asked whether she would have completed the transaction if she had known that the accused was acting dishonestly, "No" was the

---

[12] [1982] A.C. 449.
[13] At p. 94.

only possible answer. Although the question had not been asked, it was open to the jury to decide that the inference of inducement was irresistible.

There have been other card cases in which technical defences have been rejected. Thus in *R. v. Beck*,[14] the defendant had stolen a large number of Barclays Bank travellers cheques and a Diners Club card with which he obtained cash in France. He was convicted under section 20(2) of the Theft Act as having procured dishonestly with a view for gain the execution of a valuable security, and the Court of Appeal rejected his defence that no offence had been committed within the jurisdiction: execution takes place when a card or a travellers cheque is accepted by a payer, and also when final payment for either is made. And in *R. v. Bevan*,[15] where the defendant had cashed cheques with a cheque card in Belgium, so producing an unauthorised overdraft on his account, he appealed against his conviction under section 16 of the Act, claiming that he had not been "allowed to borrow by way of overdraft." But the Court of Appeal held that the paying bank, which had to pay the cheques, had in fact "allowed" the overdraft, however reluctantly; and as in *R. v. Beck* the jurisdiction plea as to the encashment in Belgium, was also rejected.

But in *R. v. Navvabi*[16] where the defendant, having cashed cheques with cheque cards, was convicted under section 3(1) of the Act of having assumed "the rights of an owner," his convictions for fraud and forgery were upheld, but his appeal on section 3(1) was allowed: his action "was not in itself an assumption of the rights of the bank," but only gave the cheques' payees a contractual right to be paid.[17]

Re Charge Card Services Ltd.[18] followed the liquidation of a card company and involved questions regarding the debts due to the company. The decision of Millett J., upheld by the Court of Appeal, is of interest to bankers as establishing that payment by credit card is not, like payment by cheque, conditional upon ultimate payment by the bank, but is complete when the sales voucher is signed.

Since early times bankers have been troubled by the misuse of cheques drawn upon them. The cheque that has been stolen and

[14] [1985] 1 W.L.R. 22.
[15] (1987) 84 Cr.App.R. 143.
[16] [1986] 1 W.L.R. 1311.
[17] *cf. Chan Man-Sin* v. *R.* [1988] 1 W.L.R. 196.
[18] [1988] 3 W.L.R. 764.

bears a forged signature is seen in such cases as *Greenwood* v. *Martins Bank Ltd.*[19] and *National Westminster Bank Ltd.* v. *Barclays Bank International Ltd.*[20] More commonly, cheques are presented for payment on accounts with insufficient funds to meet them and no pre-arrangement of overdraft facilities to cover them. Such a cheque is to be regarded as a request for a loan by way of overdraft,[21] and the banker is free to grant the overdraft or to refuse it and dishonour the cheque. But the decision which course to adopt can be a difficult one, and can have its own dangers.[22]

However, the banker in the past has relatively seldom been likely to suffer any legal wrong from such conduct by his customers. The payees of such cheques may or may not have been cheated by their issue, but they have had whatever civil action might be appropriate against the drawers. But the position has changed, on the one hand with the provision by the banks of credit cards and cheque cards, both of which enable the holders to draw on the banks' funds without authority, and on the other hand by the passing of the Theft Act 1968, which has facilitated prosecutions in such cases, so that the police have been more ready to take proceedings. In the result there has been a series of reported cases in courts of appeal which are of interest, and in some cases direct concern, to practical bankers. The decisions of the House of Lords in the *Charles* and *Lambie* cases are of course of particular significance for bankers.

By section 15 of the Theft Act, "a person who by any deception dishonestly obtains property belonging to another, with the intention of permanently depriving the other of it," is guilty of an offence, as is, by section 16, "a person who by any deception dishonestly obtains for himself or another any pecuniary advantage." The law lords discussed, in the *Charles* case, the nature of the representation made by the person who draws a cheque. The time honoured three representations in Kenny's *Outline of Criminal Law*[23]—that the drawer has an account, that he has authority to draw for the amount of the cheque, and that the cheque is a valid order for payment of that amount—they considered to be unnecessarily detailed, preferring a single representation, the equivalent of Kenny's third; in

---

[19] *Ante*, p. 90.
[20] *Ante*, p. 136.
[21] *cf.* Paget, *op. cit.* p. 115.
[22] See, *e.g. ante*, p. 129.
[23] 19th ed., p. 359.

the words of Pollock B., in *R*. v. *Hazleton*,[24] quoted by Lord Edmund-Davies, "the real representation made is that the cheque will be paid."[25]

It is unfortunate that the relevant sections of the Theft Act require, in the words of Lord Reid, in *Director of Public Prosecutions* v. *Turner*,[26] "elaborate and rarefied analysis to discover their meaning." In *Charles* and *Lambie* the representation involved in the use of the cards certainly produced a great deal of such analysis as the cases made their way through the courts; but it was not lacking in earlier cases, concerned with unsupported cheques (which, of course, the banks had the option of dishonouring).

In the *Turner* case the House of Lords had to resolve conflicting decisions of the Court of Appeal on prosecutions under section 16. In *R*. v. *Fazackerley*[27] the defence was that a debt is not evaded unless the creditor has been deceived into forgiving or cancelling the debt, which does not happen when a cheque is issued without funds. The Court of Appeal rejected the argument. But some weeks later, in *R*. v. *Turner*,[28] a differently constituted court was convinced by the apparent logic of the argument. On the appeal in the second case the House of Lords held that "debt" in the section means an obligation to pay immediately, and this obligation is evaded when a worthless cheque is given.

R. v. *Watkins*,[29] another section 16 case, turned on a different aspect of deception. The charge here was that the defendant had obtained a pecuniary advantage by understating his commitments in an application for an overdraft from Lombard North Central. His defence was that no offence was committed until borrowing actually took place, and there was no evidence that this had happened. But it was held in Warwick Crown Court that the granting of an overdraft is an advantage in that it makes the applicant free to draw on the account; the deception is when the application is made, not when the facility is drawn

---

[24] (1874) L.R. 2 C.C.R. 134.
[25] In *R*. v. *Gilmartin* [1983] Q.B. 953 the defendant argued that in giving a post-dated cheque, the only representation was that he had a banking account. But the Court of Appeal, after considering the House of Lords' analysis of representation, held that post-dating does not remove the implied representation that the cheque will be paid on or after the due date.
[26] [1974] A.C. 357.
[27] [1973] 1 W.L.R. 632.
[28] [1973] 1 W.L.R. 653.
[29] [1976] 1 All E.R. 578.

upon. And in the more complicated circumstances of *R.* v. *Governor of Pentonville Prison, ex parte Osman*[30] it was held, *inter alia*, by the Divisional Court that when a theft of funds in New York was initiated by a telex message from Hong Kong, the act of sending the Telex was the act of theft, and appropriation took place in Hong Kong.

It will have been noted that the defendants in these Theft Act cases were normally without merit, their defences resting to greater or less extent on "rarefied analysis" of the wording of the various sections, although some of those defences may well be considered logically sound. But few will regret that the general effect of the decisions is that the issue of a cheque without funds can be a criminal offence, as can, albeit indirectly, the enforced creation of an overdraft.[31]

Another area in which bankers can find themselves with unexpected overdrafts is that of cross-firing, on which there have been several cases in recent years. The comment of Lord Goddard C.J. in *R.* v. *Kritz*[32] is still relevant:

> Drawing against uncleared cheques is one of the oldest forms of fraud. Generally, bank managers are too much on their guard to let it go on, but in this case, because of the specious lies which the appellant told to the bank manager and of the fact that the bank manager did not have that degree of suspicion which bank managers ought to have, the appellant managed to defraud the bank to a very considerable extent.

The banker who pays against uncleared effects is granting an advance to a customer whom he believes to be credit worthy against the security of the cheques paid in. While such security, as we have seen elsewhere,[33] is not always to be relied upon, the banker is particularly vulnerable when his payments have formed part of a cross-firing operation. *Lloyds Bank Ltd.* v. *Suvale Properties Ltd.*[34] provides a notable example of the possible loss that a banker can suffer from the operation.

Cross firing was described by Leonard J. in the Mayor's and City of London Court, in *Arora* v. *Barclays Bank Ltd.*[35]

---

[30] *The Times*, April 13, 1988.
[31] See also *R.* v. *Greenstein* [1975] 1 W.L.R. 1353; *Halstead* v. *Patel* [1972] 1 W.L.R. 661; *R.* v. *Hamid Shadrok-Cigaril, The Times*, February 23, 1988.
[32] [1949] 2 All E.R. 406.
[33] *cf.*, *e.g. Westminster Bank Ltd.* v. *Zang, ante*, p. 156.
[34] Unreported (1981) C.L.Y. 271. *cf.* Penn, Shea & Arora, op.cit. I 19–06.
[35] (Unreported) (1979) C.L.Y. 20.

Cross firing has been described as the drawing of corresponding cheques by two persons on different branches of the same bank—or on different banks—unsupported by any consideration other than the mutual giving and receiving of cheques. This practice, due to the normal delay in clearing the cheques—if they are honoured—results in the temporary augmentation of the credit in each account. The practice is not illegal in itself, provided that it is not used for fraud or some illegal purpose. But it obviously can be used for some such purpose, and the defendants want to discourage it, so far as they can.

There may be, as there were in *Suvale Properties*, more than two accounts involved, and the greater the number of accounts, the more difficult it is to recognise the fraud, while the bank that breaks the ring is likely to be the one with the unexpected overdraft. It is, incidentally, not easy to see how the practice can ever be entirely innocent.

The plaintiff in *Arora* brought his action when the bank, suspecting cross-firing, dishonoured his cheque. He lost his case in the Mayor's Court, and the Court of Appeal dismissed what Stamp L.J. called "a quite hopeless frivolous appeal": the bank had a clear right to refuse payment against uncleared effects, and customers were so warned.

An unusual case on uncleared effects, not involving cross-firing, was *R.* v. *Hayat*[36] where the defendant was charged under section 155(*a*) of the Bankruptcy Act 1914, which prohibited an undischarged bankrupt from obtaining credit. He had drawn against uncleared effects on his account with the National Bank of Pakistan; the cheques were dishonoured, and his account was £704 overdrawn. He argued that "obtaining" credit requires words or conduct by the accused: to receive credit is not to obtain it. Unfortunately, the point was not decided, the Court of Appeal reversing the trial judge on his ruling that no conduct needed to be proved. Whether the jury would have convicted was therefore uncertain and the conviction was quashed.[36a]

COMBINATION OF ACCOUNTS

Barclays Bank Ltd. v. Okenarhe
[1966] 2 Lloyd's Rep. 87

The setting off of a credit balance against indebtedness on another account

[36] [1976] Crim.L.R. 508.
[36a] *R.* v. *Hayat* was distinguished in *Attorney General's Reference No 1/1988*, [1989] 2 W.L.R. 729; in s.1 of the Company Securities (Insider Dealing) Act 1985, information may be "obtained" by a person without any positive action on his part. But *contra*, *R.* v. *Fisher*, (1988) 4 B.C.C. 360.

Facts

The defendant stole a building society passbook belonging to a Mr. Crouch, and went to the Sloane Square branch of the plaintiff bank, where he claimed to be Mr. Crouch and said he wished to withdraw some £1,600 from the building society and open a deposit account at the bank. He later paid in the building society's cheque, and was allowed to withdraw almost the whole amount while it was still uncleared. On the same day he opened a current account at the plaintiff's Battersea Park branch, and paid in the cash he had withdrawn from Sloane Square. When the building society cheque was dishonoured, payment having been stopped, the bank sought to combine the defendant's accounts.

Decision

Mocatta J. held that although there cannot be an overdraft on a deposit account, and therefore the payment out to the defendant was not a loan on the deposit account, yet the loan had been made and was a banking transaction; and the bank was entitled to combine the defendant's indebtedness to them at Sloane Square with their indebtedness to him at Battersea Park.

In reviewing the authorities he said:

As regards the case in which the customer has separate running current accounts at each of two branches of a bank, it is plain that the general principle is that the bank is entitled to combine the two accounts. There is clear authority for this in the case of *Garnett* v. *McKewan.*[37] The learned Barons, in giving their judgments in that case, emphasised, of course, as one would have expected, that there was no right of combination in relation to accounts maintained with a banker by one person but in two different capacities; for example, one account might be a personal account of the customer and the other might be a trust account. Further, it was made clear by Baron Bramwell that the right to combine did not arise if there was an agreement between the customer and the banker that the two accounts should be kept separate, or if such an agrement should be implied from their conduct. Furthermore, in the case the learned judges dealt with what, at first sight, might seem the apparent anomaly that the customer cannot without the specific agreement of the bank draw on account A a sum in excess of his balance on that account but which is less than the combined balance at account A and account B. That limitation on the customer's rights, in other words, the inability of the customer without specific agreement to combine two accounts, is explained as necessary to business efficacy. It would make the task of the banker impossible if

[37] (1872) L.R. 8 Ex. 10, *infra*. See also *post*, pp. 235, 237, 363, 402.

every branch was expected to know the state of a customer's account at every other branch.[38]

Notes[39]

The setting off of a credit balance against an overdraft or loan of the same customer has sometimes been regarded as an example of banker's lien, but properly the two conceptions are distinct.[40] In *Garnett* v. *McKewan* a customer drew cheques against his credit balance at one branch of a bank. At another branch he was indebted to an amount almost as great as the credit balance at the first, and the bank, without notice to him, combined the balances and dishonoured his cheques. It was held that they were entitled to do so.

Some doubt arose as to this almost unqualified right of set-off as a result of a dictum of Swift J. in *Greenhalgh & Sons* v. *Union Bank of Manchester Ltd.*,[41] in which he rejected the possibility of any set-off between two accounts. The doubts raised by this dictum were finally laid to rest, when, in the *Halesowen Presswork* case,[42] Lord Kilbrandon in the House of Lords approved Lord Denning's express rejection, in the court below, of Swift J.'s view. There can no longer be any question as to the banker's right to combine accounts in appropriate circumstances.[42a]

While doubt continued, however, the banks introduced the letters of set-off which are signed by customers relying upon credit balances for borrowing on other accounts. These letters of set-off acknowledge the banker's right to combine, and are in effect no more than evidence of a right already existing; they are a useful precaution against a customer's possible protests, but do not themselves create any right.[43]

---

[38] At p. 95.
[39] As to combination of accounts generally, *cf.* Penn, Shea & Arora, *op. cit.* I 13, 31–36. As to the notice required upon closing an account, *cf. Prosperity* v. *Lloyds Bank Ltd., post,* p. 362.
[40] The distinction was discussed in the *Halesowen Presswork* case, *post,* p. 383, see in particular the judgment of Buckley L.J. in the Court of Appeal, quoted *post,* p. 278.
[41] [1924] 2 K.B. 153.
[42] *Post,* p. 383.
[42a] Thus, *e.g.* a bank may exercise its right of combination, or its right of set-off, without infringing a restraint order under the Drug Trafficking Offences Act 1986 *Re K., The Independent,* July 4, 1989.
[43] In *Midland Bank Ltd.* v. *Reckitt* (*ante,* p. 176) the bank took a document by which Terrington charged any credit balance on one account against any borrowing on another. Lord Atkin said about this document: "How this increased their rights if the money was the customer's money, or gave them any rights if the money was client's money, it is perhaps not necessary to discuss."

Buckingham v. *London & Midland Bank Ltd.*[44] was an example of one of the principal exceptions to the banker's right of set-off. The plaintiff had a current account, and also a loan account secured against house property. The branch manager had the property re-surveyed, and decided that the advance was too high. Thereupon he told the plaintiff that his account had been closed. The plaintiff protested that he had cheques outstanding, but the manager duly combined the accounts and dishonoured the cheques. The plaintiff suing the bank for damages, the jury found that the course of dealing between bank and customer was that the customer could draw upon the current account without reference to the loan account, and was entitled to reasonable notice of the ending of his arrangement. And in *Bradford Old Bank Ltd.* v. *Sutcliffe*,[45] where also a loan account and a current account were in question, Pickford L.J. took the same view and said: "If it were otherwise the company would be extremely hampered in its business, for it could never safely draw on the current account so long as the credit balance did not exceed the amount due on the loan account."

The principle of these decisions was applied in *Re E.J. Morel (1934) Ltd.*[46] to a "frozen" current account, which Buckley J. considered could not be properly regarded as a current account at all. But in the case of a similarly frozen current account in the *Halesowen Presswork*[47] case, the House of Lords held that the bank was entitled to combine such an account with the active current account when the banker/customer relationship was ended by the winding up of the company. The same principle clearly covers any other circumstances in which the banker/customer relationship is terminated.

The *Halesowen Presswork* decision also resolved any doubt that existed as to what notice, if any, the banker must give his customer of his intention to combine accounts. In the circumstances of that case, where the accounts were combined after the winding-up order, notice could serve no useful purpose. Had the bank decided to combine when they knew that a meeting of creditors was called, notice taking immediate effect would have been the right course, subject to the duty to pay cheques drawn before the customer received that notice. On this point, Lord Cross remarked that on the one hand a period

---

[44] (1895) 12 T.L.R. 70.
[45] *Post*, p. 314.
[46] [1962] Ch. 21.
[47] *Post*, p. 383.

of notice would enable the customer to defeat the combination by withdrawing the credit balance, while on the other hand if he had no notice at all he might continue to pay in to his account cheques that he could have paid in to another bank if he had known the true position. It will have been observed that in *Garnett's* case no notice was given; and Paget[48] argues that "in the absence of evidence to the contrary the right to combine without notice should be insisted upon, for the necessity for combination normally derives from some act or omission on the part of the customer." It is true that the customer usually knows well—and often before the banker—of his act or omission that justifies combining; it is true also that a banker will often have difficulty with customers who issue cheques after receiving notice, taking care to antedate them. But Lord Cross's view, although strictly *obiter*, must carry great weight, and it seems unlikely that bankers can rely in the future on the authority of *Garnett's* case in this matter of notice.

The right of set-off depends on the funds on the several accounts belonging to the same person. In *Bhogal* v. *Punjab National Bank*[49] the bank dishonoured cheques on two accounts in different names and claimed that both accounts were nominee accounts for a third party. But the Court of Appeal rejected their claim to a right of set-off. No firm evidence had been produced to support the bank's supicion that the accounts were nominee accounts, and a bank could not without warning dishonour a customer's cheque on a tenuous suspicion that the customer was a nominee.[50]

Barclays Bank Ltd. v. *Quistclose Investments Ltd.*[51] was an interesting example of a bank being refused the right of set-off because one of the accounts was held to be impressed with a trust.[52] Quistclose provided the money for a dividend that Rolls Razor could not meet, and the cheque for this amount was placed to the credit of a separate account with the appellant bank, Rolls' bankers. Rolls went into voluntary liquidation before the dividend could be paid, and the bank sought to combine the Rolls accounts, which, even combined, showed a substantial overdraft. But the House of Lords held that the

---

[48] *Op. cit.* p. 140.
[49] [1988] 2 All E.R. 296.
[50] The decision was followed in *Uttamchandani* v. *Central Bank of India, The Independent*, January 31, 1989.
[51] [1968] 3 W.L.R. 1097; 9 L.D.B. 105.
[52] And *cf. Re Gross, ante,* p. 78 and *Re Kayford Ltd. (In Liquidation)*, [1975] 1 W.L.R. 79.

dividend was subject to a trust in favour of the lender, and the balance on it was not available to other creditors, including, of course, the bank, which was held to have had notice of the trust.

In *Neste Oy* v. *Lloyds Bank Ltd.*[53] the bank's right of set-off was challenged in respect of six payments by the plaintiffs to their United Kingdom agents, customers of the bank, the plaintiffs claiming that they were held on trust for them. The payments by telex to the bank's head office had been credited to one of the customer's six accounts, and when the customers ceased trading, the bank set-off the credit and debit balances. As to five of the payments, the challenge failed, Bingham J. remarking that he was disinclined to see the intricacies of trusts introduced into everyday transactions. But he held that the bank should not include in their setting-off the last of the six payments, received after the bank had notice that their customers had ceased trading. That notice put them on inquiry, and inquiry would have shown that the customers were constructive trustees of that last payment.

DISCOUNT OF BILLS

Barclays Bank Ltd. v. Aschaffenberger Zellstoffwerke A.G.

[1967] 1 Lloyd's Rep. 387

The holder of a bill who sues as agent for another can be met by any defence available against his principal

Facts

An English company supplied the defendants, a German company, with machinery. Payment was by 18 bills of exchange drawn on the German company which accepted them. Barclays agreed to finance the transaction, and bought the bills, paying 73 per cent. of their face value and agreeing that when the bills were met at maturity the balance of 27 per cent. would also be paid to the company. In the event the last two bills were dishonoured, the German company alleging late delivery and defective materials. The bank, as holders for value, sought and obtained summary judgment on the bills, the court not being aware of the fact that the bank had not paid the face value of the bills. The defendants appealed.

[53] [1983] 2 Lloyd's Rep. 658.

Decision

The full facts of the case now becoming apparent, the Court of Appeal held that while there was no defence in law to the claim for the full amount of the bills, a stay of execution would be granted in respect of the 27 per cent., for which the bank was trustee for its customers. Lord Denning M.R. said:

> ...we have the authority of *Thornton and Others* v. *Maynard*[54] which shows that if the holder of a bill of exchange holds it in part as trustee for someone else, then when the holder sues upon the bill, the defendant can raise against the trustee any defence or set-off which he would have available against the person who was really behind the transaction. As it is said in Chalmers on Bills of Exchange,[55] "When the holder of a bill sues as agent for another person, or when he sues wholly or in part for the benefit of another person, any defence or set-off available against that person is available *pro tanto* against the holder."
>
> So it seems to me that any defence or set-off which the German company have as against Black Clawson International Ltd. is available against Barclays Bank Ltd., in so far as the proportion 26.839 per cent. is concerned; because to that extent they are trustees of Black Clawson International Ltd.
>
> What is to be done then? In point of law on the bills of exchange themselves, there is no defence in law to the whole amount. Judgment must go for the sum claimed with interest thereon. But, on the other hand, as the German company, it now appears, claim to have this set-off (because they claim liquidated damages which would be, if available, a true set-off) for more than this 26.839 per cent., they should be at liberty to have it available to them against that part of the claim, and no more.[56]

Notes

The decision is of interest, if seldom of direct concern, to bankers whose financing of commerce and industry by the discounting of bills is of very long standing; in the nineteenth century bankers found the discount of bills preferable to the early forms of overdraft as a method of lending to their customers,[57] and until the First World War the bill maintained its dominance in the finance of trade generally. As already noted,[58] the inland bill has now virtually disappeared, and while

---

[54] (1875) L.R. 10 C.P. 695.
[55] (13th ed.), p. 128.
[56] At p. 389.
[57] See Holden, *History of Negotiable Instruments in English Law*, p. 297.
[58] *Ante*, p. 62.

the bill of exchange is still of considerable importance in international trade, it is principally as the basis of the documentary credit, which gives the banker the additional security of the goods covered. But the simple discount, as seen in this case, is still frequently undertaken, and it is not unusual for the discounting bank to provide initially only a proportion of the value of the bills, the balance being credited when the bills are met at maturity.

When a bank makes an advance by way of discount, without any recourse against the goods involved, it looks first to the acceptor for payment, then to any indorser(s), and only failing them to the drawer, its customer. It is to be noted that even when, as in the present case, only a part of the value of the bills has been initially advanced, the bank becomes holder for value with a legal title to the whole amount. This legal title was not questioned in the *Aschaffenberger* case, and the judgments in the Court of Appeal were explicit that there could be no challenge to it.

In *Scholefield Goodman & Sons Ltd.* v. *Zyngier and Another*[59] the defendant had guaranteed, *inter alia*, any amounts owing on bills discounted by the Commercial Bank of Australia. The plaintiff company had drawn five bills on the defendant's company, which were discounted by the bank. On their dishonour the bank presented them to the plaintiffs, as drawers, and Scholefields paid the amounts due. In this action they claimed contribution from the defendant as co-surety, but the Privy Council dismissed their appeal. Lord Brightman said:

If a third party guarantees a bill of exchange for the benefit of a bank which discounts it, the normal understanding will be that the surety guarantees that payment will be made by one or other of the parties to the bill who are liable on it. It will not be the normal understanding that the surety intends to place himself on a level with the drawer so as to be equally answerable with the drawer if the acceptor defaults. There is no reason why he should . . .

The relevance of the *Aschaffenberger* decision to the rule that a bill of exchange is normally equivalent to cash, so that any counter-claim must not be set against it, is apparent[60]; it is unfortunate that this aspect of the matter seems to have been treated rather cavalierly by the Court of Appeal, as secondary in importance to the trusteeship issue.

[59] [1986] A.C. 562.
[60] cf. *ante*, pp. 66 *et seq.*

The judgments did not make it clear why the court was making an exception to a rule that they explicitly recognised. Salmon L.J. referred *inter alia* to the fact that arbitration proceedings were pending in Copenhagen, but in the *Nova (Jersey) Knit* case[61] the House of Lords refused an application for a stay of execution on the grounds of pending arbitration proceedings. The *Aschaffenberger* decision is significant in its finding on the trusteeship issue, but it would now seem to have little relevance to the cash equivalence principle.

EXCHANGE RATES

Miliangos v. George Frank (Textiles) Ltd.

[1976] A.C. 443

Payment of debts in a foreign currency

Facts

In 1971 the plaintiff, a Swiss national, contracted to sell polyester yarn to the defendants, an English company, the proper law of the contract being Swiss law, and the money of account and payment being Swiss francs. No payment was made for the yarn, and in April 1972 the plaintiff issued a writ claiming the sterling equivalent of the contract price at the date when payment should have been made ("the breach date"). But by the time of the hearing the value of sterling against the Swiss franc had fallen substantially, and the plaintiff obtained leave to amend his claim, and to claim payment in Swiss francs. The trial judge held that he was bound by precedent to order only payment in sterling, but the Court of Appeal ruled otherwise, and the defendants further appealed.

Decision

The House of Lords rejected the appeal. Lord Wilberforce reviewed the history of the rule that an English court could order payment only in sterling, which had been in force for centuries, and had been affirmed by the House of Lords as recently as 1960, in *Re United Railways of the Havana and Regla Warehouses Ltd.*[62] But in 1975, in *Schorsch Meier GmbH* v.

---

[61] *Ante*, p. 70.
[62] [1960] 2 All E.R. 332.

Hennin[63] the Court of Appeal by a majority held that an award in foreign currency could be made, and it was this decision that led the plaintiff in the present case to amend his claim.

Lord Wilberforce considered in some detail the circumstances that might justify their Lordships' reversal of their earlier decision, which was made possible by their declaration in 1966 that their earlier decisions might be reconsidered in the light of changing circumstances. In particular he noted the contemporary instability of exchange rates, and the recognition of that fact in arbitration awards. He said:

I do not for myself think it doubtful that, in a case such as the present, justice demands that the creditor should not suffer from fluctuations in the value of sterling; he has bargained for his own currency, and only his own currency. . . If means exist for giving effect to the substance of a foreign obligation, procedure should not unnecessarily stand in the way.[64]

And a majority of their Lordships agreed that the appeal should be dismissed, only Lord Simon of Glaisdale dissenting, on the grounds that so important a change should be left to Parliament.

Notes

This important decision concerned a contract "whose proper law is that of a foreign country and where the money of account and payment is that of that country." But like other such landmark decisions (for example, that in the *Mareva* case[65]), it has proved capable of extension. In *The Maratha Envoy*[66] Lord Denning said

once it is recognised that judgment *can* be given in a foreign currency, justice requires that it *should* be given in every case where the currency of the contract is a foreign currency, otherwise one side or the other will suffer unjustly by the fluctuations of the exchange.

[63] [1975] 1 All E.R. 152.
[64] At p. 465.
[65] *Ante*, p. 117.
[66] [1977] 1 Lloyd's Rep. 217, at p. 225.

So in later cases it has been held that damages can be given in foreign currency in an action for breach of contract[67], or in an action in tort.[68] One of the first cases to follow *Miliangos* was *Barclays Bank International* v. *Levin Brothers (Bradford) Ltd.*,[69-70] a decision with its particular interest for bankers. A New York supplier had drawn four bills on the defendants for $23,000 each. They were indorsed to the bank, and were subsequently dishonoured, and the bank obtained an order for summary judgment, the master applying the rate of exchange applicable on each of the four dates on which the bills were due. When the bank appealed against the limitation to sterling, the defendants argued that *Miliangos* did not cover the present case, and further, that even if it did, payment otherwise than in sterling was prevented by section 72(4) of the Bills of Exchange Act 1882. Mocatta J., rejected both arguments: *Miliangos* had revolutionised the position; and there was no justification for applying section 72(4) to cases where failure to pay at maturity is followed by legal action and currency fluctuations resulting from the delay. And he did not accept that his ruling would result in injustice if the pound had appreciated in the interval: "the plaintiff on either view gets the same number of dollars for which he has contracted."

It may be noted that both sections 57(2) and 72(4) were repealed by the Administration of Justice Act 1977. There is some historic interest in the temporary importance of a provision in the 1882 Act which had produced little litigation, and which was certainly not drafted in contemplation of the kind of exchange fluctuations familiar today. In *Miliangos* Lord Wilberforce was considering the difference between rates of 9.90 and 6.00 Swiss francs to the pound, which would have reduced the sterling result of the case from £60,000 to £42,000. Since 1976 the rate has changed even more dramatically to its present 2.45.

---

[67] *Kraut (Jean) A.G.* v. *Albany Fabrics* [1977] 2 All E.R. 116.
[68] *The Despina R.*, [1977] 1 Lloyd's Rep. 39. But in *Re Lines Bros. Ltd.* [1982] 2 W.L.R. 1010, where the liquidator had made interim payments to Lloyds Bank in respect of a debt in Swiss francs, the Court of Appeal refused to extend *Miliangos* so as to compel him to revalue the payments which had been made when sterling was depreciating against the Swiss franc. The liquidator had a surplus in hand after all debts; but Brightman L.J., said that if foreign debts could be recalculated in the course of a liquidation the potential dividend would have to be altered at each recalculation.
[69-70] [1976] 3 W.L.R. 852.

In *President of India* v. *Taygetos Shipping Co. SA*[71] the charter party provided that demurrage was payable in sterling "at the mean exchange rate ruling on the bill of lading date." The charterers appealed against the arbitration award in dollars, the currency of account, rather than sterling, the currency of payment. Staughton J. held that although normally, when the contract does not provide otherwise, payment should be in the currency of account, it was otherwise when as here the contract provides an agreed rate between money of account and money of payment; he had earlier remarked on the fact that the contract rate here was $2.2878 to the pound, and the rate at the date of judgment was $1.2390.

BANKER'S COMMERCIAL CREDITS

E. Clemens Horst Co. v. Biddell Bros.

[1912] A.C. 18

The effect of a c.i.f. contract

Facts

A contract for the sale of hops to be imported into this country provided for payment at "90s. per 112 lbs. c.i.f. to London, Liverpool or Hull. Terms net cash." There was no provision for payment against documents, and when the latter were in due course presented to them, with a request for payment, the buyers refused, contending that they were not bound to do so under the contract until they had been able to examine the goods.

Decision

It was held by the House of Lords that under a c.i.f. contract payment is due upon tender of documents, unless the contract expressly provides otherwise.

In the Court of Appeal,[72] which had upheld the buyers' contention, Kennedy L.J. delivered a dissenting judgment, which received the approval of the House of Lords, and may be regarded as of great authority. In it he said:

---

[71] [1985] 1 Lloyd's Rep. 155.
[72] [1911] 1 K.B. 934.

But in truth, the duty of the purchasers to pay against the shipping documents, under such a contract as the present, does not need the application of that doctrine of the inference in mercantile contracts that each party will do what is "mercantilely reasonable," for which we have the great authority of Lord Esher. The plaintiffs' assertion of the right under a cost freight and insurance contract to withhold payment until delivery of the goods themselves, and until after an opportunity of examining them, cannot possibly be effectuated except in one of two ways. Landing and delivery can rightfully be given by the shipowner only to the holder of the bill of lading. Therefore, if the plaintiffs' contention is right, one of two things must happen. Either the seller must surrender to the purchaser the bill of lading, whereunder the delivery can be obtained, without receiving payment, which, as the bill of lading carries with it an absolute power of disposition, is, in the absence of a special agreement in the contract of sale, so unreasonable as to be absurd; or, alternatively, the vendor must himself retain the bill of lading, himself land and take delivery of the goods, and himself store the goods on quay (if the rules of the port permit), or warehouse the goods, for such time as may elapse before the purchaser has an opportunity of examining them. But this involves a manifest violation of the express terms of the contract "90s. per 112 lbs. cost freight and insurance." The parties have in terms agreed that for the buyer's benefit the price shall include freight and insurance, and for his benefit nothing beyond freight and insurance. But, if the plaintiffs' contention were to prevail, the vendor must be saddled with the further payment of those charges at the port of discharge which *ex necessitate rei* would be added to the freight and insurance premium which alone he has by the terms of the contract undertaken to defray.[73]

Notes

In *T.D. Bailey, Son & Co.* v. *Ross T. Smyth & Co. Ltd.*[74] Lord Wright examined the effect of the c.i.f. contract and explained that:

The property which the seller retains while he or his agent or the banker to whom he has pledged the documents retains the bills of lading, is the general property, not a special property by way of security. But in general the importance of the retention of the property is not only to secure payment from the buyer but for purposes of finance. The general course of international commerce involves the practice of raising money on the documents so as to bridge the period between shipment and the time of obtaining payment against documents. These credit facilities, which are of first importance, would be completely unsettled if the incidence of the property were made a

[73] At pp. 958–959.
[74] (1940) 67 Ll.L.R. 147.

matter of doubt. By mercantile law the bills of lading are the symbols of the goods. The general property in the goods must be in the seller if he is to be able to pledge them. The whole system of commercial credits depends on the seller's ability to give a charge on the goods and the policies of insurance.[75]

"General property" in an article is that which the absolute owner has in it; "special property" is here the limited ownership exercised by, for example, a bailee, where the article can be put only to a particular use. The general property in goods can be fettered in various ways, as is the case when the documents of title are pledged with a banker; but subject to the particular restriction or restrictions it remains absolute ownership, while the special property which vests in him who exercises the restriction serves that limited purpose only.

Cape Asbestos Co. Ltd. v. Lloyds Bank Ltd.

(1921) 3 L.D.B. 314

Urquhart Lindsay & Co. v. Eastern Bank Ltd.

[1922] 1 K.B. 318

Revocable and irrevocable documentary credits

Facts of Cape Asbestos Co. Ltd. v. Lloyds Bank Ltd.

On the instructions of a Warsaw bank the defendant bank established a documentary credit in favour of the plaintiffs and advised them of its establishment. Their letter of advice ended with the words: "This is merely an advice of the opening of the above-mentioned credit, and is not a confirmation of the same." One draft was paid under the credit, and the credit thereafter withdrawn. The bank did not advise the plaintiffs of the withdrawal and they, in the belief that it was still operative, made a further shipment, and sent to the bank the relative documents, including an invoice for an amount larger than the balance of the credit and a bill of lading made out in favour of the buyers instead of the bank. The bank would not pay against these, and in the meantime, the goods having gone forward, the buyers obtained possession of them. It was not possible to collect payment from them, and the plaintiffs claimed from the defendant bank the balance of the credit.

---

[75] At p. 156.

It was shown in evidence that the bank normally advised the beneficiaries of the cancellation of credits and that on the present occasion the official concerned had forgotten to do so.

Decision

Bailhache J. held that the bank owed no duty to advise the beneficiaries of the cancellation; and further that the irregularity in the bill of lading and in the invoice would have justified the bank's refusal to pay.

In the course of his judgment he said:

It is to be observed that the notice that was given by the bank on the opening of the credit is of the opening of a revocable credit and not of a confirmed credit. That tells the person in whose favour the credit is opened that he may find that the credit is revoked at any time. That being the representation which is made by the bank to the person in whose favour the credit is opened, the seller in this case, are the bank under any legal obligation to him to inform him when the credit is revoked? . . . I have come to the conclusion that, however wise and however prudent, and however much in the interest of business, such a notice may be, there is no legal basis upon which I can found an obligation on the bank to give such a notice under such circumstances.[76]

Facts of Urquhart Lindsay & Co. v. Eastern Bank Ltd.

A credit was opened with the defendant bank in favour of the plaintiffs, who were manufacturers of machinery, on the terms that it was "confirmed and irrevocable." The contract in connection with which the credit had been opened contained, *inter alia*, the term that in the event of any increase in wages, cost of material or transit rates the plaintiffs' prices would be correspondingly increased.

Two drafts were drawn and paid under the credit. The buyers, finding that the plaintiffs were including in their invoices an addition to the prices already quoted, in respect of an increase in the cost of materials or wages, instructed the defendants to pay in future only so much of drafts presented as represented the original prices, the extra charges being referred to the buyers. The defendant bank advised the plaintiffs of this instruction, and then refused to meet the drafts in respect of the third shipment.

They paid these drafts later, under protest, but in the meantime the plaintiffs had issued a writ in the present action,

[76] At p. 315.

alleging breach of contract and consequent loss of profit. The defendants at first contended (but later abandoned the point) that the letter of credit must be taken to incorporate the original contract which, in the present case, on its true meaning, allowed increase in price only as a matter for subsequent independent adjustment.

Decision

Rowlatt J. held that the bank had committed a breach of contract. In his judgment he said:

> ...the defendants undertook to pay the amount of invoices for machinery without qualification, the basis of this form of banking facility being that the buyer is taken for the purposes of all questions between himself and his banker or between his banker and the seller to be content to accept the invoices of the seller as correct. It seems to me that so far from the letter of credit being qualified by the contract of sale, the latter must accommodate itself to the letter of credit. The buyer having authorised his banker to undertake to pay the amount of the invoice as presented, it follows that any adjustment must be made by way of refund by the seller, and not by way of retention by the buyer.[77]

Notes

A credit is termed irrevocable when the *issuing* bank gives an unqualified undertaking to honour drafts drawn under it; it becomes confirmed only when the *advising* bank adds its own guarantee to that of the issuing bank. It is obvious that, in this sense of the words, while irrevocable credits may frequently be unconfirmed, it is rarely that a revocable credit is confirmed; the advising banker is not eager to accept a liability which the issuing banker has seen fit to avoid.

A revocable credit can be cancelled at will, as was seen in the *Cape Asbestos* case, but an irrevocable credit can be varied or withdrawn only with the consent of all parties to it. Thus in *Hamzeh Malas & Sons* v. *British Imex Industries Ltd.*,[78] where the buyers, the plaintiffs in the case, sought an injunction to restrain the defendants from drawing on an irrevocable credit established with Midland Bank, the Court of Appeal upheld Donovan J.'s refusal. Jenkins L.J. said:

[77] At p. 323.
[78] [1958] 2 Q.B. 127.

A vendor of goods selling against a confirmed letter of credit is selling under the assurance that nothing will prevent him from receiving the price. That is no mean advantage when goods manufactured in one country are being sold in another. It is, furthermore, to be observed that vendors are often reselling goods bought from third parties. When they are doing that, and when they are being paid by confirmed letter of credit, their practice is—and I think it was followed by the defendants in this case—to finance the payments necessary to be made to their suppliers against the letter of credit. That system of financing these operations, as I see it, would break down completely if a dispute as between the vendor and the purchaser was to have the effect of "freezing," if I may use that expression, the sum in respect of which the letter of credit was opened.[79]

It is to be noted, however, that the court rejected the submission that they had no jurisdiction to interfere, Sellers L.J. saying:

I would not like it to be taken that I accept, or that the court accepts... that the court has no jurisdiction. There may well be cases where the court would exercise jurisdiction, as in a case where there is a fraudulent transaction.[80]

More recently, in *Discount Records Ltd.* v. *Barclays Bank Ltd. and Another*,[81] where Barclays had refused to accept instructions not to pay under an irrevocable credit, the court again refused the injunction sought by the plaintiffs. Here the plaintiffs had alleged, *inter alia*, fraud by the sellers, and while accepting that there was no English authority in support of their case, they cited an American decision, *Sztejn* v. *J. Henry Schroder Banking Corp.*[82] That decision was based on established rather than alleged fraud. Megarry J. did not reject the possibility that even alleged fraud might provide grounds for interference by the court, but the circumstances here he considered fell short of doing so. In any event, not all the parties were before the court; for an injunction to be granted the buyer would have to make the seller a co-defendant. And he said:

---

[79] *Ibid.* at p. 129. *cf.* Lord Wilberforce's comments on the bill of exchange, *ante*, p. 70.
[80] At p. 130.
[81] [1975] 1 W.L.R. 315.
[82] 31 N.V.S. 2d. 631 (1941). *cf. post*, pp. 252, 273.

I would be slow to interfere with bankers' irrevocable credits, and not least in the sphere of international banking, unless a sufficiently grave cause is shown; for interventions by the court that are too ready or too frequent might gravely impair the reliance which, quite properly, is placed on such credits.[83]

Transferable credits made a rare appearance in the law reports in *Bank Negara Indonesia 1946* v. *Lariza (Singapore) Pte. Ltd.*[84] A transferable irrevocable letter of credit subject to the Uniform Customs and Practice (1974 Revision) in favour of Lariza was opened by the bank, but when Lariza instructed the bank to transfer part of the credit to their suppliers, the bank refused, claiming that they were not bound to make any transfer themselves or, alternatively, any transfer except in a manner and to an extent to which they consented. In due course the dispute reached the Privy Council, who held that the provision of Article 46(b) of the Uniform Customs supported the bank's second argument, "whatever the commercial difficulties may be." It has been suggested that the effect of the decision is to destroy the whole purpose of the transferable letter of credit.[85]

United City Merchants (Investments) Ltd. v. Royal Bank of Canada and Others

[1983] A.C. 168

The nature of payment by letter of credit

Facts

Glass Fibres and Equipment Ltd. sold manufacturing equipment to a Peruvian company, the second defendants, and agreed to invoice for the order at twice the correct price, in order that the Peruvian company might exchange Peruvian currency to the total of the excess for United States dollars, in breach of the Peruvian exchange control regulations. Payment was to be made by confirmed irrevocable letter of credit, and this was issued by the buyers' bank, Banco Continental S.A. (the third defendants), and confirmed by the Royal Bank of Canada. Glass Fibres assigned their rights under the contract to the plaintiffs, their merchant bankers, as security for advances.

---

[83] At p. 320.
[84] [1988] 2 W.L.R. 374.
[85] See *Banking World*, May 1988, p. 53. As to transferable credits generally, see Penn, Shea & Arora, *op. cit.* II 13, 28.

Shipment of the goods was made a day later than the last day allowed by the credit, but the carriers' agent issued a received for shipment bill of lading dated as on that last day. On presentation of the documents the confirming bank refused to pay on the ground that they had information suggesting that shipment was not made as stated on the bill of lading. In the first hearing of the plaintiffs' action Mocatta J. held that the fraud of the agent was not known to the plaintiffs when the documents were presented, and the Royal Bank were not entitled to refuse payment against documents which on their face were in order. In the second hearing, when Banco Continental were given leave to amend the defence so as to raise the breach of the exchange control regulations, he held that the inflated price involved a monetary transaction in disguise, and that as the breach of the Peruvian exchange control infringed the Bretton Woods agreement[86] the credit was unenforceable and the bank's refusal of payment was justified.

The Court of Appeal reversed his first finding, holding that the bank was entitled to refuse payment when the documents included one containing a material misrepresentation of fact. On the second, they held that the credit was divisible, so that payment could have been allowed of the half that did not infringe the regulations, but in view of their first finding this second one did not help the plaintiffs, who further appealed.

Decision

The House of Lords held unanimously (1) (restoring Mocatta J.'s finding) that the bank were not entitled to refuse payment against documents in order on their face; the fraud of a third party, unknown to the beneficiary, was not a justification for refusal; (2) that the court should not enforce that part of the transaction which the Bretton Woods agreement made unenforceable; the plaintiffs' claim was enforceable to the extent that the contracts did not offend the Peruvian regulations.

Lord Wilberforce described the "four autonomous though interconnected contractual relationships" involved in the documentary credit:

---

[86] Bretton Woods Agreements Order in Council 1946, Art. VIII, s.2(b): "Exchange contracts which involve the currency of any member and which are contrary to the exchange control regulations of that member...shall be unenforceable in the territories of any member...."

(1) The underlying contract for the sale of the goods, to which the only parties are the buyer and the seller; (2) the contract between the buyer and the issuing bank under which the latter agrees to issue the credit and either itself or through a confirming bank to notify the credit to the seller and to make payments to or to the order of the seller (or to pay, accept or negotiate bills of exchange drawn by the seller) against presentation of stipulated documents; and the buyer agrees to reimburse the issuing bank for payments made under the credit. For such reimbursement the stipulated documents, if they include a document of title such as a bill of lading, constitute a security available to the issuing bank; (3) if payment is to be made through a confirming bank, the contract between the issuing bank and the confirming bank auhorising and requiring the latter to make such payments and to remit the stipulated documents to the issuing bank when they are received, the issuing bank in turn agreeing to reimburse the confirming bank for payments made under the credit; (4) the contract between the confirming bank and the seller under which the confirming bank undertakes to pay to the seller (or to accept or negotiate without recourse to drawer bills of exchange drawn by him) up to the amount of the credit against presentation of the stipulated documents.

... in contract (4), with which alone the instant appeal is directly concerned, the parties to it, the seller and the confirming bank, "deal in documents and not in goods," as article 8 of the Uniform Customs puts it. If, on their face, the documents presented to the confirming bank by the seller conform with the requirements of the credit as notified to him by the confirming bank, that bank is under a contractual obligation to the seller to honour the credit, notwithstanding that the bank has knowledge that the seller at the time of presentation of the conforming documents is alleged by the buyer to have, and in fact has already, committed a breach of his contract with the buyer ... that would have entitled the buyer to treat the contract of sale as rescinded. ... The whole commercial purpose for which the system of confirmed irrevocable documentary credits has been developed in international trade is to give the seller an assured right to be paid before he parts with control of the goods that does not permit of any dispute with the buyer as to the performance of the contract of sale being used as a ground for non-payment or reduction or deferment of payment.

And he went on to refer to the "one established exception" to these basic principles—fraud by the seller. The exception is well established in the American cases, but does not seem to have been applied in England[87]; and in any event it was not relevant here.

---

[87] *cf., ante*, p. 249, *post*, p. 273.

Notes

This case is notable for Lord Wilberforce's judgment, in which, in the passages quoted above, he re-stated comprehensively the basic rules of the documentary credit, and went on to apply them to the facts (including the novel problem of the application of the Bretton Woods agreement) which had produced contradictory findings in the courts below.

In rejecting the central argument of the bank—that a confirming bank owed no duty to pay the seller/beneficiary if the documents, although conforming to the terms of the credit, contain a material inaccuracy, even though it is unknown to the seller—he pointed out that its acceptance would involve a mismatch between contract (4) and the contracts with which it interacts. For

it is equally clear law, and is so provided by article 9 of the Uniform Customs, that confirming banks and issuing banks assume no liability or responsibility to one another or to the buyer "for the form, sufficiency, accuracy, genuineness, falsification or legal effect of any documents." This is well illustrated by the Privy Council case of *Gian Singh & Co. Ltd.* v. *Banque de l'Indochine*[88] where the customer was held liable to reimburse the issuing bank for honouring a documentary credit upon presentation of an apparently conforming document which was an ingenious forgery, a fact that the bank had not been negligent in failing to detect upon examination of the document.

He rejected also the narrower argument which the Court of Appeal had accepted. They had started

from the premiss that a confirming bank could refuse to pay against a document that it knew to be forged, even though the seller/beneficiary had no knowledge of that fact. From this premiss they reasoned that if forgery by a third party relieves the confirming bank of liability to the seller/beneficiary, fraud by a third party ought to have the same consequence....

He did not necessarily accept that the premiss was correct.

But even assuming the correctness of the Court of Appeal's premiss as respects forgery by a third party of a kind that makes a document a nullity, for which at least a rational case can be made out, to say that this leads to the conclusion that fraud by a third party which does not render the document a nullity has the same consequence appears to me, with respect, to be a non-sequitur....

[88] [1974] 1 W.L.R. 1234.

On the Bretton Woods question he said that it did not affect the contract between the seller and the confirming bank, which was merely "to pay currency for documents which included documents of title to goods." It was rather "a question of the substance of the transaction to which enforcement of the contract will give effect." There was no difficulty in identifying the monetary transaction that was sought to be concealed by the actual words used in the documentary credit and the underlying contract of sale; and there was nothing in the Bretton Woods agreement to prevent payment under the credit being enforceable to the extent of the genuine purchase price of the goods.[89]

But in the less unusual circumstances of *Etablissement Esefka International Anstalt* v. *Central Bank of Nigeria*[90] the contract was not separable. The Midland Bank had paid out $6 million on a part shipment to the Nigerian Ministry of Defence. When it was alleged that the documents submitted had been forgeries, the bank refused to make further payments, and the plaintiffs sued the Central Bank, who had established the credit. But the Court of Appeal rejected their argument that the part of the contract in which fraud was alleged was separable: the letter of credit covered the whole order—it was all one transaction.[91]

The liability of a confirming bank on a letter of credit subject to the Uniform Customs and Practice for Documentary Credits was in question in *Forestal Mimosa Ltd.* v. *Oriental Credit Ltd.*,[92] where payment was refused on account of alleged discrepancies, in drafts under the credit, and the plaintiffs claimed that the defendants, as the confirming bank, were responsible for acceptance and payment of the drafts on maturity. The credits contained a marginal insertion that they were subject to the Uniform Customs and Practice which provide, *inter alia*, that when an irrevocable credit is confirmed the confirmation is an undertaking "to accept drafts... or to be responsible for their acceptance and payment...," and the Court of Appeal upheld the plaintiffs' claim.

The finding in the *United City Merchants* case did not conflict with the principle that counter-claims are not admissible to

---

[89] *cf. Mansouri* v. *Singh* [1986] 1 W.L.R. 1393.

[90] [1979] 1 Lloyd's Rep. 445.

[91] The plaintiffs had also been granted a *Mareva* injunction at first instance, but the Court of Appeal also discharged this: the *Mareva* injunction should be granted only when there is danger of property being taken out of the jursidiction, and no such consideration applied to the Central Bank.

[92] [1986] 1 W.L.R. 631.

prevent payment under a documentary credit, which, as Lord Wilberforce had said, "does not permit of any dispute with the buyer as to the performance of the contract of sale" interfering with payment: the dispute here had nothing to do with performance of the contract of sale.

The principle of the non-admissibility of counter-claims had earlier been reaffirmed in *Power Curber International Ltd.* v. *National Bank of Kuwait S.A.K.*[93] where the Kuwaiti buyer lodged a counter-claim against the American seller, and obtained an order of the Kuwaiti court attaching the sum payable under the letter of credit. The plaintiffs obtained judgment for the amount in England, subject to a stay of execution, and the Court of Appeal allowed their appeal against the stay: the proper law of the contract was that of North Carolina, the Kuwaiti order did not affect the validity of the debt, and the stay was therefore not justified. And Lord Denning said:

> A letter of credit is like a bill of exchange given for the price of goods. It ranks as cash and must be honoured. No set off or counter-claim is allowed to detract from it. All the more so with a letter of credit. Whereas a bill of exchange is given by buyer to seller, a letter of credit is given by a bank to the seller with the very intention of avoiding anything in the nature of a set off or counter claim. . . .
>
> If the court of any of the countries should interfere with the obligation of one of its banks (by ordering it not to pay under a letter of credit) it would strike at the very heart of that country's international trade.[94]

And in *Domenica* v. *Shimco*[95] where a Mareva-type injunction[96] was granted at first instance restraining the plaintiffs from dealing with the proceeds of their judgment on dishonoured bills, the Court of Appeal allowed the plaintiffs' appeal, Bridge L.J. remarking that the granting of the injunction in such circumstances could have "the widest and most undesirable repercussions" by undermining the cash equivalence rule in bills of exchange. But the cash equivalence rule was held not to apply in the unusual circumstances of the bank's claim in *Hong*

---

[93] [1981] 1 W.L.R. 1233.
[94] The banker's duty to pay under a letter of credit may be compared with his duty to pay under performance bonds and guarantees, *post*, p. 271. See also the rule as to disputes between parties to bills of exchange, *ante*, pp. 66 *et seq.*
[95] *Montecchi* v. *Shimco*; *Domerica* v. *Same* [1980] 1 Lloyd's Rep. 50.
[96] See *ante*, p. 117.

Kong and Shanghai Banking Corporation v. *Kloeckner & Co. AG.*[96a] The bank sought to set-off against debts admittedly due to Kloeckners under a standby letter of credit, debts due to the bank on a separate transaction, which was the subject of a separate litigation. Hirst J., rejected Kloeckner's argument that the case was covered by the *Power Curber* decision: that decision, and by analogy the performance bond cases, were based on the principle that the bank's obligation to the beneficiary under the letter of credit was independent from any disputes between buyer and seller in relation to the underlying contract. It is only rarely that, as here, there is an antecedent connection between bank and beneficiary that can give rise to a separate dispute.

Lord Denning drew another parallel with bills of exchange in *W.J. Alan & Co. Ltd.* v. *El Nasr Export & Import Co.*[97] where he said:

I am of the opinion that in the ordinary way, when the contract of sale stipulates for payment to be made by confirmed irrevocable letter of credit, then, when the letter of credit is issued and accepted by the seller, it operates as conditional payment of the price.... It is analogous to the case where under a contract of sale, the buyer gives a bill of exchange or a cheque for the price. It is presumed to be given, not as absolute payment, nor as collateral security, but as conditional payment. If the letter of credit is honoured by the bank when the documents are presented to it, the debt is discharged. If it is not honoured, the debt is not discharged: and the seller has a remedy in damages against both banker and buyer.[98]

Curiously enough, there is little direct authority on the point.[99] In the *W.J. Alan* case the comments of the Court of Appeal were *obiter* but their unanimous view that payment is normally only conditional is clearly of considerable weight.

Midland Bank Ltd. v. Seymour

[1955] 2 Lloyd's Rep. 147

Payment by the banker under the documentary credit

[96a] *The Financial Times*, May 5, 1989.
[97] [1972] 2 Q.B. 189.
[98] At p. 212.
[99] See Gutteridge and Megrah, *op. cit.* pp. 34 *et seq.* for a review of the cases in England and abroad where the courts have discussed the question.

Facts

The defendant's business included the import of feathers from Hong Kong, and in 1952 he entered into a number of contracts with the Taiyo Trading Company, with whom he had not previously done business. Payment was to be made by means of confirmed irrevocable letters of credit, opened through the plaintiff bank. The goods shipped proved worthless, and the Hong Kong company could not thereafter be traced.

The bank, having paid out against documents apparently in order, claimed against the defendant, who in his counter-claim contended, *inter alia*, that the bank had not acted in accordance with the terms of the credits. The requests for the credits had authorised payment "against delivery of the following documents...evidencing shipment...of the undermentioned goods," and while the documents taken together included all the particulars required—the description, the quantity and the price—these particulars were not all to be found in the bill of lading.

Decision

Devlin J. held that, in the absence of a clear requirement that the bill of lading should contain all the particulars of the shipment, it was sufficient that the documents taken together should do so. In his judgment he said:

> ...no principle is better established than that when a banker or anyone else is given instructions or a mandate of this sort, they must be given to him with reasonable clearness. The banker is obliged to act upon them precisely. He may act at his peril if he disobeys them or does not conform with them. In those circumstances there is a corresponding duty cast on the giver of instructions to see that he puts them in a clear form. Perhaps it is putting it too high for the purpose to say that it is a duty cast upon him. The true view of the matter, I think, is that when an agent acts upon ambiguous instructions he is not in default if he can show that he adopted what was a reasonable meaning.[1]

Notes

It will be noted that the decision here is permissive, not mandatory; the bank was, in view of the ambiguity, justified in paying against the documents as a whole, but might not have

[1] At p. 153.

been at fault if they had refused payment on the grounds advanced by the plaintiff.[2]

The *Seymour* case is interesting for the long judgment of Devlin J. and its detailed examination of the machinery of the documentary credit. In particular he considered the contention of the plaintiff that the fact that the bill of lading contained a "weight unknown" clause itself invalidated it under the terms of the credit. By this very common clause the carrier disclaims responsibility for the weight, quality, contents and "possibly other particulars that are asserted in the bill of lading by the shipper as a description of the goods." The plaintiff argued that "in effect by virtue of this clause the bill of lading contains no description at all," but the argument was rejected:

"... I think it must be taken that what the letter of credit requires is the description in the body of the bill, whether or not it is accompanied by such a clause. If it were not so, then the bank would have to reject out of hand virtually every bill of lading that was tendered to it."[3]

There were two other findings in the *Seymour* case of importance to bankers. The plaintiff had further argued (*a*) that the bank had been wrong in accepting four of the drafts after the relevant credits had expired, even though the drafts had been negotiated in Hong Kong before the expiry dates; and (*b*) that the bank had been negligent in not passing on all the information they had received regarding the sellers. On the first point Devlin J. held that the words "available in Hong Kong" meant that the drafts could be accepted there, but not that negotiation without acceptance would meet the terms of the credit. The bank was thus at fault; but in fact the defendant was held to have later instructed the bank to accept the bills after the expiry dates. On the second point the defendants were awarded nominal damages; a bank is under a contractual duty in regard to inquiries made on behalf of its customers, and must not supply misleading information as the bank was here held to have done by not passing on the whole text of a cable received from their correspondents.

---

[2] *cf. European Asian Bank AG* v. *Punjab Sind Bank (No. 2)* [1983] 1 W.L.R. 642, 10 L.D.B. 411, where the plaintiffs were held at fault for not seeking interpretation of patently ambiguous instructions, but the defendants by their conduct had accepted the plaintiffs' interpretation and so were estopped from denying the plaintiff's claim.

[3] At p. 155.

The basic rule for the banker handling documentary credits is that the documents must conform with the credit. In his description in the *United City Merchants* case[4] of the interconnected contracts in the documentary credit, Lord Wilberforce said that the banker must pay the seller if on their face the documents presented conform with the requirements of the credit, and he later referred to "the contractual duty of each bank under a confirmed irrevocable credit...to examine with reasonable care all documents presented in order to ascertain that they appear *on their face* to be in accordance with the terms and conditions of the credit."

The principle was thus expressed by Lord Sumner in *Equitable Trust Company of New York* v. *Dawson Partners Ltd.*[5]

It is both common ground and common sense that in such a transaction the accepting bank can only claim indemnity if the conditions on which it is authorised to accept are in the matter of the accompanying documents strictly observed. There is no room for documents which are almost the same, or which will do just as well.... The bank's branch abroad, which knows nothing officially of the details of the transaction thus financed, cannot take it upon itself to decide what will do well enough and what will not. If it does as it is told, it is safe; if it declines to do anything else, it is safe; if it departs from the conditions laid down, it acts at its own risk.[6]

Lord Sumner's words were quoted by McNair J. in *Bank Melli Iran* v. *Barclays Bank (D.C. & O.).*[7]

The rule that documents must conform with the credit has been applied in varying circumstances in the cases.

Thus in *Rayner (J.H.) & Co. Ltd.* v. *Hambros Bank Ltd.*[8] the Court of Appeal held that the bank was entitled to refuse payment when the bill of lading referred to "machine-shelled groundnuts" when the credit called for "Coromandel groundnuts": the bank could not be expected to know that in the trade the two terms meant the same thing. In *Scott* v. *Barclays Bank Ltd.*[9] the bank refused payment on the grounds *inter alia* that the documents included a certificate of insurance, but not the insurance policy also called for by the credit and the Court of

[4] *Ante*, p. 250.
[5] (1927) 27 Ll.L.Rep. 49.
[6] At p. 52.
[7] [1951] 2 T.L.R. 1057, *post*, p. 263.
[8] (1942) 59 F.L.R. 21.
[9] [1923] 2 K.B. 1.

Appeal held that refusal was justified, Bankes L.J. pointing out that the certificate did not state the terms of the policy, so that it was impossible to know whether the policy complied with the terms of the credit. In *Kydon Compania Naviera S.A.* v. *National Westminster Bank Ltd.*[10] the letter of credit called for a sight draft on Euroasia Carriers, and the provision instead of a sight draft on the Janata Bank, was held by Parker J. *inter alia*, to be adequate reason for the bank's refusal to pay: it was not relevant that the draft served no specifically useful purpose.

But the rule is also that the banker need not for his own protection look beyond the documents themselves, and must not, as the *United City Merchants* decision itself showed, refuse payment when the documents do conform on their face. So in *Commercial Banking Co. of Sydney* v. *Jalsard Pty.*[11] where the credit called for a certificate of inspection and the bank's payment was challenged on the grounds that the document submitted was not a normal certificate of inspection, the Privy Council held that the phrase could cover documents containing a variety of information: if a particular method of inspection was required it must be specified. In *British Imex Industries Ltd.* v. *Midland Bank Ltd.*[12] the bank had refused payment on the ground that the bill of lading did not bear any acknowledgement that one of the printed clauses on the back had been complied with. Salmon J. held that their refusal was not justified: the credit called for "bills of lading" which meant "clean" bills, containing no indication that the goods or packing were defective, it did not call for acknowledgement that any particular clause had been complied with.

In these cases the courts have recognised that the duty of the paying bank must not be unduly extended. Thus in the *Commercial Banking Co.* case Lord Diplock said:

Both the issuing banker and his correspondent bank have to make quick decisions as to whether a document which has been tendered by the seller complies with the requirements of the credit at the risk of incurring liability to one or other of the parties to the transaction if the decision is wrong. Delay in deciding may in itself result in a breach of his contractual obligations to the buyer or to the seller. This is the reason for the rule that where the banker's instructions from his customer are ambiguous or unclear he commits no breach of his contract with the buyer if he has construed them in a reasonable sense,

[10] [1981] 1 Lloyd's Rep. 68.
[11] [1973] A.C. 279, 9 L.D.B. 281.
[12] [1958] 1 Q.B. 542.

even though upon the closer consideration which can be given to questions of construction in an action in a court of law, it is possible to say that some other reasoning is to be preferred.[13]

And in the *British Imex* case Salmon J., refusing to accept that the banker must read "the mutilfarious clauses in minute print on the back of these bills of lading," referred to the comment, *obiter*, of Scrutton L.J. in *National Bank of Egypt* v. *Hannevig's Bank*.[14]

I only say at present that to assume that for one-sixteenth per cent. of the amount it advances, a bank is bound carefully to read through all bills of lading presented to it in ridiculously minute type and full of exceptions, to read through the policies and to exercise a judgment as to whether the legal effect of the bill of lading and the policy is, on the whole, favourable to their clients, is an obligation which I should require to investigate considerably before I accepted it in that unhesitating form. . . . [15-16]

The *Seymour* decision is itself another example of the same tendency, welcome to the banker; and there are other examples in the cases. In the *Rayner* case one of the contentions of the plaintiffs was that when it would be unreasonable for the consignee to refuse to accept the documents, then it must be unreasonable also for the banker to refuse them; but the court held that the banker cannot be expected to be as familiar as the consignee with the terms and abbreviations of any particular trade. And in this connection the *Kydon* decision is of particular interest to bankers, Parker J. rejecting the plaintiffs' multiple attack. In addition to the point mentioned above he held that the duty imposed by article 7 of the Uniform Customs and Practice for Documentary Credits to examine documents to ensure that they conform with the credit does not imply any duty to the beneficiary; and further, that where there are more than a single presentation of the documents, the banker does not, in his first rejection of the documents, represent that they are acceptable apart from the reason given for that first rejection, and he is therefore not estopped from giving other reasons on subsequent presentations. He said:

[13] At p. 286.
[14] (1919) 3 L.D.B. 213.
[15-16] At p. 214.

To hold that they thereby made any representation would in my view involve a radical departure from the accepted legal position and would seriously undermine the whole system of documentary credits, for banks would be obliged, for their own protection and the protection of their customers, always to scrutinise with care every document presented from beginning to end, notwithstanding that they may find in the first few lines of the first document at which they looked one or more good and sufficient reasons for refusal to pay.

And in *Offshore International S.A.* v. *Banco Central S.A.*[17] where it was argued that the law to be applied was that of Spain, where the issuing bank was established, rather than that of New York, where the credit was opened. Ackner J. said that very great inconvenience would be caused if the law of the issuing bank was preferred in such a case: the advising bank would have consistently to be seeking to apply a whole variety of foreign law.[18]

However, some decisions present the banker with fresh questions. In *M. Golodetz & Co. Inc.* v. *Czarnikow-Rionda Co. Inc.*[19] Megaw L.J. quoted Lord Sumner's dictum in *Hansson* v. *Hamel & Horley Ltd.*[20] to the effect that documents must be "reasonably ready and fit to pass current in commerce." But the decision in *Golodetz* does not seem to square with that view. The case concerned a bill of lading acknowledging shipment of goods in good order but carrying a typed note that the cargo had subsequently been discharged because of damage by fire. The buyers rejected the bill as not being a clean bill, and the arbitrators agreed, but Donaldson J. allowed the appeal, saying that "if the buyers wanted bills which were not only 'clean' but 'in usual form' they could have contracted accordingly," and the Court of Appeal upheld his decision in favour of the plaintiffs: a clean bill of lading certifies that the goods were in apparent good order at the time of shipment, and the subsequent fate of the goods is not relevant.

The defendants had argued that even if this were the legal meaning of "clean," in practice the word also meant "marketable," and here two banks as well as the buyers themselves had rejected the bill. Megaw L.J. did not express his own opinion of the bill, confining himself to the fact that the arbitrators had

---

[17] [1977] 1 W.L.R. 399.
[18] *cf.* Gutteridge and Megrah, *The Law of Commercial Credits*, (5th ed.) pp. 211 et seq.
[19] [1980] 1 W.L.R. 495.
[20] *Post*, p. 265.

not mentioned marketability; had they held it to be unmarketable, the decision would have been different. But bankers cannot be happy with a decision that suggests that a notation which Donaldson J. said was new to both the courts and the text books may still leave a bill fit "to pass current in commerce."

Payment under reserve was considered by the Court of Appeal in *Banque de l'Indo-Chine et de Suez* v. *J.H. Rayner (Mincing Lane) Ltd.*[21] The plaintiffs, the confirming bank, had considered the documents submitted as defective in several respects, but had paid "under reserve." The buyers rejected the documents on one of the specified discrepancies, and the plaintiffs claimed repayment. The defendants argued, *inter alia*, that there was no obligation to repay unless one or more of the discrepancies was a valid ground in law for refusal of payment, while the bank contended that they were anyhow entitled to repayment. It was held there was here valid ground for refusal; but the appeal would anyhow have failed, for the Court rejected the defendants' argument—"a lawyer's view" rather than "a commercial view." "Under reserve," although widely used, had no generally accepted meaning, and banks using it should state precisely what they mean by it. Here, Kerr L.J. considered that the parties meant that there should be repayment if the issuing bank rejected the documents either on its own initiative or on the buyer's instructions.

Bank Melli Iran v. Barclays Bank (D.C. & O.)

[1951] 2 T.L.R. 1057

Undue delay may forfeit the right of the issuing bank to reject documents against which the confirming bank has paid

Facts

Bank Melli Iran, in late 1946, established an irrevocable credit for £45,000 with Barclays Bank (D.C. & O.) in favour of Eastern Development Co. in respect of the purchase by their customers Kharrazi & Co. of 100 new Chevrolet trucks, and Barclays confirmed the credit to Eastern Development. On January 17, 1947, Barclays advised Bank Melli that they had paid £40,000 against documents, and photostats of the documents reached Bank Melli on March 4. They included an

---

[21] [1983] 1 Lloyd's Rep. 228, 10 L.D.B. 376.

invoice for trucks "in new condition," and a certificate of purchase which referred to "new, good" trucks, but did not identify them as being those invoiced. Kharrazi questioned the wording, and the query was forwarded to Barclays without comment. Barclays obtained from Eastern Development, and forwarded to Bank Melli, confirmation that the trucks were new.

The first consignment of trucks needed a further payment for carriage, and on May 14 Bank Melli agreed to an appropriate increase in the credit. The further payment by Barclays was advised to them on June 15, and on that day they repudiated the first payment but said nothing on the second until July 23, when they repudiated that also, having meanwhile, *inter alia*, applied to Kharrazi for payment.

They brought the present action claiming a declaration that Barclays were not entitled to debit them in respect of either payment.

Decision

As to the first payment, McNair J. held "without hesitation" that the documents were not in accordance with the bank's mandate and that Barclays were not entitled to pay against them. But the plaintiffs' conduct, both in having authorised an increase in the credit and the failure to repudiate until June 15, amounted to "an overwhelming case of ratification." As to the second payment likewise, their conduct was "inconsistent with an intention to repudiate."

Notes

Article 8 of the Uniform Customs and Practice for Documentary Credits[22] provides:

(c) If, upon receipt of the documents, the issuing bank considers that they appear on their face not to be in accordance with the terms and conditions of the credit, that the bank must determine, on the basis of the documents alone, whether to claim that payment, acceptance or negotiation was not effected in accordance with the terms and conditions of the credit.

(d) The issuing bank shall have a reasonable time to examine the documents and to determine as above whether to make such a claim.

---

[22] 1974 Revision. *cf.* Penn, Shea & Arora, *op. cit.* II p. 292 as to the importance of the Uniform Customs and Practice for Documentary Credits.

The *Bank Melli* case is an example of the issuing bank's delay providing in part a defence for the confirming bank which had paid against documents not meeting the requirements of the credit. What amounts to "reasonable time" for examination of the documents must depend on the circumstances, but in practice refusal must be prompt, and it is unfortunate that McNair J., in the case of the second payment, seemed to accept that had it not been for Bank Melli's conduct in the surrounding circumstances their defence of pressure of work in the documentary credits departments might have justified their six weeks' delay in repudiation.

This suggestion has been widely criticised,[23] and is to be contrasted with, for example, Lord Sumner's statement in *Hansson* v. *Hamel & Horley Ltd.*,[24] where he said:

> These documents have to be handled by banks, they have to be taken up or rejected promptly and without any opportunity for prolonged examination... they have to be such as can be re-tendered to sub-purchasers, and it is essential that they should so conform to the accustomed shipping documents as to be reasonably and readily fit to pass current in commerce[25]

or with the Privy Council's similar attitude in *Commercial Banking Co. of Sydney* v. *Jalsard Pty.*[26] Certainly six weeks would seem to be considerably in excess of the "reasonable time" of the Uniform Customs, while in any case unusual pressure of work would not normally be accepted as a defence for apparent inefficiency.[27]

Pavia & Co. S.P.A. v. Thurmann-Nielsen

[1952] 2 Q.B. 84

The time within which credits must be opened

Facts

In a contract for the sale c.i.f. of shelled Brazilian groundnuts payment was to be by confirmed irrevocable credit, the contract

---

[23] *cf.* the editor's note to the case in 6 L.D.B. 227; Paget, *op. cit.* p. 543; Gutteridge and Megrah, *op. cit.* p. 162.
[24] [1922] 2 A.C. 36.
[25] At p. 46. *cf. ante*, p. 262.
[26] See the quotation from the judgment, *ante*, p. 260.
[27] *cf., e.g. Ross* v. *London County and Westminster Bank Ltd.* [1919] 1 K.B. 678.

providing that the shipping periods should be from February 1 to May 31. Despite repeated requests by the sellers for the credit to be opened it was not in fact made available until April 22. Only a small portion of the quantity of the groundnuts covered by the contract was shipped, and the sellers claimed damages for breach of contract by delay in opening the credit.

Decision

The Court of Appeal, upholding the judgment of McNair J., held that the credit should have been established on February 1. In his judgment Denning L.J. said:

In the absence of express stipulation, I think the credit must be made available to the seller at the beginning of the shipment period. The reason is because the seller is entitled, before he ships the goods, to be assured that, on shipment, he will get paid. The seller is not bound to tell the buyer the precise date when he is going to ship; and whenever he does ship the goods, he must be able to draw on the credit. He may ship on the very first day of the shipment period. If therefore, the buyer is to fulfil his obligations he must make the credit available to the seller at the very first date when the goods may be lawfully shipped in compliance with the contract.[28]

Notes

It had been argued for the buyers that the only obligation was to establish the credit by such time as the seller was in fact ready to ship; but Somervell L.J. said on this point:

...the contract would be unworkable if...the buyer under it was under no obligation until a date, which he could not possibly know, and which there is no machinery for his finding out, namely, when the seller actually has the goods down at the port ready to put on the ship.[29]

A gloss on the *Pavia* decision was provided in *Sinason-Teicher Inter-American Grain Corporation* v. *Oilcakes and Oilseeds Trading Co. Ltd.*,[30] a case in which the contract called for a bank guarantee. Denning L.J. said with reference to the *Pavia* case:

It does not decide that the buyer can delay right up to the first date for shipment; it only decides that he must provide the letter of credit

[28] At p. 88.
[29] At p. 88.
[30] [1954] 1 W.L.R. 1394.

by that time at the latest. The correct view is that, if nothing is said about time in the contract, the buyer must provide the letter of credit within a reasonable time before the first date for shipment. The same applies to a bank guarantee, for it stands on a similar footing.[31]

In *Bunge Corp.* v. *Vegetable Vitamin Foods (Private) Ltd.*[32] the plaintiffs claimed that the credit agreed to be established was not open by the due date, and purported to cancel the contract. The defendants said that on the wording of the contract it was enough that they had arranged with their bank for the credit to be opened; it was not necessary for the credit to reach the plaintiffs. They also claimed that the credit was in fact opened and notified in time. Neill J. held that on the evidence the second defence was proved, but he rejected the first argument. There were three contracts in a letter of credit: between the buyer and the issuing bank; between issuing bank and beneficiary; and between confirming bank and beneficiary. On the defendants' argument, only the first was needed, and that could not be correct; all three were needed.[33]

The *Pavia* contract was c.i.f. The time in which the credit should be opened under an f.o.b. contract was the issue in *Ian Stach Ltd.* v. *Baker Bosley Ltd.*,[34] the argument of the buyers being that as, under a "classic f.o.b. contract," the buyer can himself fix the date of shipment at any time within the shipping period, the time at which the credit must be opened is reasonable time before the date of shipment fixed by the buyer. Diplock J. refused to accept this argument, and held that the credit must, like the credit under a c.i.f. contract, be opened at latest by the earliest shipping date. (He doubted the extension of the *Pavia* principle in Denning L.J.'s remarks in the *Sinason-Teicher* case quoted above, and said he considered that those remarks were *obiter*.) He said:

The alternative view . . . that the credit has to be opened a reasonable time before the actual shipping date, seems to me to lead to an uncertainty on the part of buyer and seller which I should be reluctant to import into any commercial contract.[35]

---

[31] At p. 1400.
[32] [1985] 1 Lloyd's Rep. 613.
[33] *cf.* Lord Wilberforce's analysis in the *United City Merchants* case, *ante*, p. 250.
[34] [1958] 2 Q.B. 130.
[35] At p. 143.

He went on to point out that such "reasonable time" might depend on circumstances known to the parties at the time of the contract, or on circumstances discovered later before instructions to ship were given, or even on circumstances as they actually were, whether known to the parties or not.

It would therefore appear that under both c.i.f. and f.o.b. contracts the rule is the same: the credit must be opened by the first possible date for shipment. But it is still perhaps open to question whether it must be a reasonable time before that date.

Trendtex Trading Corporation Ltd. v. Central Bank of Nigeria

[1977] 1 All E.R. 881

Government agencies and commercial contracts

Facts

In 1975 the plaintiffs, a Swiss company, sold cement to an English company, Pan African Export Co. Ltd., who had contracted to supply cement to the Ministry of Defence in Nigeria. The Central Bank issued a letter of credit for $14.28 million in favour of Pan African; it was issued through, but not confirmed by, Midland Bank in London, the Central Bank having assured the suppliers that confirmation was not necessary as the money would be available.

As a result of gross over-ordering of cement the Nigerian ports became congested, and a new military government imposed import controls and instructed the Central Bank not to make any payments that were not authorised under the controls. The bank refused payment under the letter of credit and the plaintiffs brought the present action. The bank claimed that it was a department of the state of Nigeria, and so was immune from action by the doctrine of sovereign immunity. Donaldson J. accepted the argument and the plaintiffs appealed.

Decision

The Court of Appeal held that the bank had not established that it was a department of state. They held further, by a majority, that in any event the doctrine of sovereign immunity did not cover commercial, as opposed to governmental, acts of a sovereign state. Lord Denning reviewed the position in international law and the law of the European Community which provided "a great cloud of witnesses" that the rule of sovereign immunity had changed. It was time that England followed. In the present case it had been argued that the fact that the cement was ordered for the building of army barracks made the purchase of a governmental nature, like the purchase of boots for the army.

But I do not think this should affect the question of immunity. If a government department goes into the market places of the world and buys boots or cement—as a commercial transaction—that government department should be subject to all the rules of the market place.[35a]

And in any event the plaintiffs were suing not on the contract of purchase but on the entirely separate contract of the letter of credit, a straightforward commercial transaction.

Both Shaw and Stephenson L.JJ. agreed with him, the latter dissenting on the immunity ruling only because he thought that so important a change in the law should be left for the House of Lords or Parliament.

Notes

Like the *Hedley Byrne* decision[36] in another area, the *Trendtex* case was of much wider significance than its banking relevance. It was the most notable of the small group of cases in which the absolute rule of sovereign immunity was challenged in the years preceding the State Immunity Act of 1978.[37] That Act removed from the area of immunity state transactions of a commercial nature, with the exception that the property and assets of "a state's central bank or other monetary authority" are immune from any process for the enforcement of a judgment.

Hispano Americana Mercantil S.A. v. *Central Bank of Nigeria*[38] was concerned with facts virtually identical with those of *Trendtex* but it came to court after the passing of the 1978 Act, and Lord Denning considered the central bank exemption, and the similar exemption in the earlier American legislation of 1976. But the court held that the Act had no retrospective effect, while in the American Act the central bank exception is restricted to "funds held for governmental purposes," which would not have covered the present case even if it had been relevant.

[35a] At p. 893.
[36] *Ante*, p. 18.
[37] See *The Philippine Admiral* [1976] 1 All E.R. 78; *Thai-Europe Tapioca Service* v. *Government of Pakistan* [1975] 3 All E.R. 961.
[38] [1979] 2 Lloyd's Rep. 277.

Neither *Trendtex* nor *Hispano Americana* was appealed to the House of Lords, but in *I Congreso del Partido*[39] where the state immunity question concerned claims to two cargoes of sugar, and had no banking implications, Lord Wilberforce reviewed the cases, including *Trendtex* ("the other landmark authority") and said:

The case was not appealed to this House and since there may be appeals in analogous cases it is perhaps right to avoid commitment to more of the admired judgment of Lord Denning than is necessary. Its value in the present case lies in the reasoning that, if the act in question is of a commercial nature, the fact that it was done for governmental or political reasons does not attract sovereign immunity.

In the light of the Act and its central bank exemption the *Trendtex* decision would not be repeated today. But the general principle of the decision, confirmed in legislation, is of interest to bankers: governmental trading is likely to involve agencies other than central banks, and the Act has done nothing to ease the difficulty, experienced for example in *Hispano Americana*, of deciding whether a particular action is in fact governmental or commercial.

Czarnikow C. Ltd. v. *Centrala Handlu Zagranicznego Rolimpex*[40] is an interesting example of an English plaintiff's unsuccessful attempt to prove that the foreign agency was an arm of government. A government directive having forbidden the export of sugar from Poland the defendants pleaded *force majeure* as a defence to the English importer's claim for the sugar they had failed to deliver. The plaintiffs claimed that as an arm of the government imposing the ban the defendants could not so plead, but the House of Lords found on the evidence that Rolimpex was an independent body.

In *Alcom Ltd.* v. *Republic of Columbia*[41] the plaintiffs had obtained a garnishee order against the Colombian embassy, freezing their banking account. The State Immunity Act provides that "commercial purposes" are not entitled to immunity, and the High Court set aside the order on the grounds that the purpose of the account was the running of the embassy, which was prima facie non-commercial. The Court of Appeal reversed this decision: the purpose of money in a bank

[39] 3 W.L.R. 328.
[40] [1978] 3 W.L.R. 274.
[41] [1984] A.C. 580.

account was to pay for goods and services, and there was no evidence here of any non-commercial use. But the House of Lords overruled the Court of Appeal. The account would be used for many purposes outside the widest definition of "commercial"; while in any event the ambassador had given a certificate that the account was not used or intended to be used for commercial purposes, and this was conclusive by section 13(6) of the Act.

Lord Diplock added that the present action was not an attempt to avoid a judgment; it was owing to a misunderstanding that the embassy had failed to enter an appearance in time, so that judgment in default had been given. It is unfortunate that an innocent misunderstanding has produced a decision which must make enforcement of judgments against embassy accounts more difficult, if not impossible, in circumstances that may be less innocent.

In *Gur Corp.* v. *Trust Bank of Africa*[42] a hospital was to be constructed in the territory of Ciskei, and a dispute arising between the plaintiff and the bank, the bank sought to join Ciskei as third party. South Africa had declared that Ciskei was a sovereign and independent state, but the Foreign Office had issued their certificate that Ciskei was not recognised as an independent state by the UK. The Court of Appeal held that the certificate was conclusive, but that the court could give effect to acts which did not contravene the certificate, and as South Africa was entitled to delegate legislative power to Ciskei the court could properly regard Ciskei as a subordinate body with *locus standi* to sue and be sued.

Edward Owen Engineering Ltd. v. Barclays Bank International Ltd.

[1978] 1 All E.R. 976

Performance bonds and guarantees

Facts

The plaintiffs contracted with Libyan buyers to supply and erect a substantial glasshouse installation covering five acres, at a cost of some £500,000. The buyers called for a performance bond for ten per cent. of the contract price, and the plaintiffs instructed their bank, the defendants, to provide the bond

[42] [1986] 3 W.L.R. 583.

against their counter guarantee. The defendants asked the Umma Bank in Libya to issue the required bond, undertaking to pay the amount on demand.

The buyers had agreed to supply a confirmed irrevocable letter of credit, but the letter of credit supplied was not confirmed, and the plaintiffs repudiated the contract. The buyers, however, claimed under the guarantee from the Umma Bank, who in turn claimed payment from the defendants. The plaintiffs sought an injunction to restrain the defendants from paying. An interim injunction was granted by Peter Pain J. but it was discharged by Kerr J. and the plaintiffs appealed.

Decision

The Court of Appeal dismissed the appeal, holding that a bank which issues a performance guarantee is bound to honour it, and is not concerned with disputes between the parties unless there is notice of established fraud by one of the parties to the underlying contract. Here it was clear that the plaintiffs were not in default, but the facts, although indicating the possibility of sharp practice, did not come anywhere near establishing fraud.

Lord Denning said that a performance bond has many similarities to a letter of credit. "It has long been established that when a letter of credit is issued and confirmed by a bank, the bank must pay if the documents are in order and the terms of the credit are satisfied." And he adopted a passage in the judgment of Kerr J. in *R.D. Harbottle (Mercantile) Ltd.* v. *National Westminster Bank Ltd.*[43]:

It is only in exceptional cases that the courts will interfere with the machinery of irrevocable obligations assumed by banks. They are the life-blood of international commerce. Such obligations are regarded as collateral to the underlying rights and obligations between the merchants at either end of the banking chain. Except possibly in clear cases of fraud of which the banks have notice, the courts will leave the merchants to settle their disputes under the contracts by litigation or arbitration as available to them or stipulated in the contracts. The courts are not concerned with their difficulties to enforce such claims; these are risks which the merchants take. In this case the plaintiffs took the risk of the unconditional wording of the guarantees. The machinery and commitments of banks are on a different level. They must be allowed to be honoured, free from interference by the courts. Otherwise trust in international commerce could be irreparably damaged.

[43] [1977] 2 All E.R. 862; *infra.*

One of the plaintiffs' arguments was that as the document between the two banks was expressed to be a guarantee the bank was not liable to pay unless there was a principal debtor and some default by him in his obligations under the contract. On this point Geoffrey Lane L.J. said:

> Although this agreement is expressed to be a guarantee, it is not in truth such a contract. It has much more of the characteristics of a promissory note than the characteristics of a guarantee.

Notes[44]

It would appear from all three judgments that the court extended the analogy with letters of credit to include the one possible exception to the letters of credit rule that the bank must pay—the case where fraud is established. Here, as with letters of credit, the fraud must be established: allegation of fraud is not enough. It is of course only seldom that the bank can have notice of proven fraud; it is significant that the only authority is the American decision in *Sztejn* v. *J. Henry Schroder Banking Corp.*, noted earlier in the letters of credit section,[45] and cited again in the present case.

In *Bolivinter Oil SA* v. *Chase Manhattan Bank and Others*[46] where the plaintiffs unsuccessfully sought to restrain Chase Manhattan and the Commercial Bank of Syria from paying under, respectively, a letter of credit and a performance bond, Sir John Donaldson, while recognising the similarity between performance bonds and letters of credit, emphasised that only in a "wholly exceptional case," where fraud is clearly proved, would an injunction preventing payment be justified. And in *United Trading Corporation SA* v. *Allied Arab Bank Ltd.*[47] Ackner L.J. said that such clear proof required that the buyer should have been given an opportunity to answer the allegation and have failed to give any adequate answer.

The facts of the *Harbottle* case were virtually identical with those of *Edward Owen Engineering*. The buyers there were Egyptian, and the plaintiffs obtained injunctions against both the English and the Egyptian banks, and the buyers, to prevent payment being made. The National Westminster Bank

---

[44] As to performance bonds generally, see Penn, Shea & Arora, *op. cit.* II 12.17 *et seq.*
[45] *Ante*, pp. 249, 252.
[46] [1984] 1 W.L.R. 392.
[47] [1985] 2 Lloyd's Rep. 554.

appealed, and Kerr J. discharged all three injunctions on the grounds set out in the passage from his judgment adopted by Lord Denning and set out above.

In *Howe Richardson Scale Co. Ltd.* v. *Polimpex-Cekop and Another*[48] the plaintiffs' attempt to prevent payment under their performance bond was on the grounds that arbitration proceedings were pending in Zurich. Their action was not against the bank to stop them paying but against the beneficiaries to stop them claiming; the National Westminster Bank were the second defendants. It was the bank, not Polimex, that appealed, and the Court of Appeal considered that their intervention was justified. The Court held that the circumstances here were different from those in cases where they had intervened on the grounds of pending arbitrations[49]: here the plaintiffs were seeking to interfere in a contractual relationship to which they were not a party.

A different attack on the performance bond was also unsuccessful in *The State Trading Corporation of India* v. *E.D. & F. Man (Sugar) Ltd. and Another*,[50] where a contract for the purchase of sugar was only part performed when export of sugar was forbidden by the Indian government. The buyers therefore proposed to give notice of default to the State Bank of India, but the plaintiffs obtained an interim injunction to prevent the giving of notice. The Court of Appeal held that the fact that the plaintiffs had challenged the allegation of default before notice had been given made no difference to the position; nor could a term be implied in the contract that notice of default would only be served when there was reasonable cause or evidence of default. Such a term would mean that the bank could be prevented from paying by the mere assertion of the party that he was not in default.

In *Potton Homes Ltd.* v. *Coleman Contractors (Overseas) Ltd.*[51] where the plaintiffs sought to prevent payment of a performance bond by the Midland Bank, alleging disputes with the defendants, the Court of Appeal discharged the injunction granted at first instance, but Eveleigh L.J., while concurring in the decision, questioned the extent to which the performance

---

[48] [1978] 1 Lloyd's Rep. 161.
[49] *cf. Elian & Rabbath* v. *Matsas and Matsas and Others* [1966] 2 Lloyd's Rep. 495, where an injunction was granted in what Lord Denning called a "special case." Here Roskill L.J., said "It should in my view be regarded as a very special case."
[50] [1981] Com.L.R. 235.
[51] (1984) 128 S.J. 282.

bond is to be regarded as independent of the underlying contract; "I would wish at least to leave it open for consideration how far the bond is to be treated as cash in hand as between buyer and seller." The comment was *obiter* and has not so far been followed in other cases.

In *Settebello Ltd.* v. *Banco Totta and Accores*[52] the plaintiffs had contracted with Portugese shipbuilders for the building of a large tanker, and the defendant bank had guaranteed payments due if the tanker was not completed by April 30, 1982. On April 20 the Portugese government decreed that companies in a critical economic condition could suspend the right of cancellation of contracts. When no payment was made, the bank denied liability under the decree, and the plaintiffs challenged the decree's validity, and asked that letters of request be issued to Portugal and West Germany to investigate the background. But the Court of Appeal upheld the refusal of Hirst J. to make the order. In the absence of a failure to meet the standards of civilised nations English courts must give effect to the decree: letters of request would be offensive to the courts of Portugal and West Germany, and judicial comity between friendly states prevents the making of such requests.

The decision here may be compared with that in *Williams & Humbert* v. *W&H Trade Marks (Jersey) Ltd.*,[53] a case concerning the compulsory acquisition by the Spanish government of three companies, where the motives of the legislation and the good faith of the administration were attacked. Lord Templeman said that no English judge could properly entertain such an attack on a friendly state.[54]

---

[52] [1985] 1 W.L.R. 105. The case is discussed in Penn, Shea & Arora, *op. cit.* II 3–17, in the context of a wide ranging study of sovereign risk.

[53] [1986] A.C. 368.

[54] *cf.* also *Intraco Ltd.* v. *Notis Shipping Corp. of Liberia*, [1981] Com.L.R. 184, *United Trading Corp. SA* v. *Allied Arab Bank Ltd.* [1985] 2 Lloyd's Rep. 554 *Esal (Commodities) Ltd.* v. *Oriental Credit Ltd. and Wells Fargo Bank N.A.* [1985] 2 Lloyd's Rep. 546, and *J.H. Rayner (Mincing Lane) Ltd.* v. *Bank fur Gemeinwirtschaft AG* [1983] 1 Lloyd's Rep. 462.

Chapter 7

SECURITIES FOR ADVANCES

BANKERS' LIEN

Brandao v. Barnett

(1846) 12 Cl. & Fin. 787

The scope of bankers' lien

Facts

The plaintiff was a Portuguese merchant whose London
agent, Burn, habitually purchased exchequer bills for him,
received the interest upon them on his behalf, and at proper
intervals exchanged them for others. Burn had an account with
the defendant bankers, and there kept several tin boxes in
which he lodged the plaintiff's and other such bills, and of which
he held the keys. On December 1, 1836, Burn took out several
bills, delivered them to the defendants and, as was his custom,
asked them to get the interest upon them and to exchange
them. This the defendants did, but, before Burn returned to
pick up the new bills, acceptances were presented on his
account in excess of the credit balance upon it, and paid. Upon
Burn's failure the defendants claimed a lien on the bills in his
hands. The Court of Common Pleas found for the plaintiff and
the Court of Exchequer Chamber on appeal reversed this
decision. The plaintiff further appealed.

Decision

The House of Lords restored the verdict for the plaintiff. In
the course of his judgment Lord Campbell said:

I am of opinion that the general lien of bankers is part of the law-
merchant, and is to be judicially noticed...But I am humbly of
opinion that, upon the facts found, there was no lien and that the
judgment ought to be reversed. I do not, however, proceed upon the
ground taken by the Court of Common Pleas—that these exchequer
bills being the property of Brandao there was no lien as against him,

although there might have been as against Burn...; the right acquired by a general lien is an implied pledge, and where it would arise (supposing the securities to be the property of the apparent owner), I think it equally exists if the party claiming it has acted with good faith, although the subject of that lien should turn out to be the property of a stranger....

Bankers most undoubtedly have a general lien on all securities deposited with them, as bankers, by a customer, unless there be an express contract, or circumstances that show an implied contract, inconsistent with lien... Now it seems to me, that, in the present case, there was an implied agreement on the part of the defendants, inconsistent with the right of lien which they claim.... [The bills] not only were not entered in any account between Burn and the defendants, but they were not to remain in the possession of the defendants; and the defendants, in respect of them, were employed merely to carry and hold till the deposit in the tin box could be conveniently accomplished.... Nor, I presume, can any weight be attached to the circumstance that the tin box... remained in the house of the defendants.... I think that the transaction is very much like the deposit of plate in locked chests at a banker's.... In both cases a charge might be made by the bankers if they were not otherwise remunerated for their trouble.[1]

Notes

The ordinary right of lien is a right merely to retain possession. A banker's lien is exceptional in that it carries with it the right of sale,[2] and as such approximates more closely to pledge: it is, in Lord Campbell's words, an "implied pledge." It applies, however, irrespective of the customer's knowledge of its existence: it exists by mercantile usage, and the customer is assumed to know of it.

The essential factor in deciding what property may and what may not be subject to the lien is whether or not it came to the banker's hands in the course of his business as a banker. It has sometimes been suggested that the dividing line is between items intended for collection and those deposited for safe custody, and while this is a little too broad a statement to be always accurate it does provide an approximate guide. It may be noted that in *Re United Service Co., Johnston's Claim*,[3] Sir William James considered that the securities there would have

---

[1] At pp. 805–809.
[2] Although it is considered by some that this "right of sale" arises only in the case of negotiable instruments, the most frequent objects of bankers' lien.
[3] (1870) 6 Ch.App. 212.

formed the subject of bankers' lien. Paget[4] cites Sir Mackenzie Chalmers's doubts on this point, and suggests that, possession of the certificates not being necessary for collection of the dividends, safe custody is more likely to have been the primary purpose of the deposit, in which case there would probably be no lien.[5]

The concept of bankers' lien was examined in the *Halesowen Pressworks* case, where, as was pointed out earlier,[6] the confusion between lien and set-off was finally resolved: set-off is a right independent of lien. In that case also, doubt was cast on the possibility of money, in particular in the form of cheques paid in for collection, becoming subject to bankers' lien.

Earlier cases had seemed to accept the possibility without question. Thus, in *Misa* v. *Currie*[7] where the question related to an order to pay money, Lord Hatherley said:

A good deal of argument has arisen as to whether this document is to be treated as a bill of exchange, or whether it is to be treated simply as an authority authorising Messrs. Glyn & Co. to collect this debt due to Lizardi from Misa.... Supposing it to be necessary to hold it to be an authority, I do not see, regard being had to the lien which bankers have upon all documents which are placed in their hands by customers who are indebted to them in the course of their banking transactions, that it would make any important difference whether it should be held to be an authority or a bill of exchange.[8]

And in *Re Keever*[9] and in *Barclays Bank Ltd.* v. *Astley Industrial Trust Ltd.*[10] the banks were held to have obtained a lien on the cheques that had been paid in for collection. But the idea had already been questioned. Thus Paget had argued that money paid into a bank becomes the property of the bank, which thereafter owes a corresponding debt to the customer, and a debt is not a suitable subject for lien.[11]

In *Halesowen Pressworks* in the Court of Appeal Buckley L.J. took the same view:

---

[4] *Op. cit.* p. 411.
[5] See *Questions on Banking Practice* (11th ed.), question 628; and generally, 629, where securities "probably subject" and "probably not subject" to bankers' lien are listed.
[6] *Ante*, p. 235.
[7] (1876) 1 App.Cas. 554.
[8] At p. 567.
[9] *Ante*, p. 160.
[10] *Ante*, p. 159.
[11] *Law of Banking* (7th ed.), p. 485; *op. cit.* p. 411.

The money or credit which the bank obtained as the result of clearing the cheque became the property of the bank, not the property of the company. No man can have a lien on his own property and consequently no lien can have arisen affecting that money or that credit.... It has of course long been recognised that a banker has a general lien on all securities deposited with him as a banker by a customer unless there be an express contract or circumstances that show an implied contract inconsistent with lien.... The term "securities" is no doubt used here in a wide sense, but does not, in my judgment, extend to the banker's own indebtedness to the customer.[12]

This passage was *obiter*, but it was expressly approved by Viscount Dilhorne in the House of Lords hearing of the same case, and on this point the earlier decisions must be viewed with considerable reserve.

It may be said that there is one clear ruling possible as to when bankers' lien does not arise. Any property which is handed to a banker for an express purpose cannot be subject to lien, even when the purpose itself has failed; in the old case *Lucas* v. *Dorrien*[13] for instance, deeds were left with a banker as security for an advance. The advance was not granted, but the deeds were not picked up by the depositor; and it was later held that they could not be subject to lien in the banker's hands.[14]

The rule is reasonably clear that bankers' lien can only attach to property that comes to the banker in the course of his banking business. The fact that safe custody does not give rise to bankers' lien may be regarded as illogical, as implying that safe custody is not a part of banking business, but the division is well established, and safe custody occupies its own small section of the wide area of banking law.

Its main concern to bankers is now of little more than historical interest. For many years it was held that a banker providing safe custody for reward might be held guilty of negligence, while a banker doing so gratuitously could be guilty only of gross negligence. Apart from difficulties of definition as to what was gross and what was ordinary negligence, there was

---

[12] [1971] 1 Q.B. 1, at p. 46; 9 L.D.B. 253.

[13] (1817) 7 Taunt. 278.

[14] *cf. Siebe Gorman & Co. Ltd.* v. *Barclays Bank Ltd. post*, p. 347, where bankers' lien on bills held for collection was held to have become ineffective by the operation of the rule in *Clayton's* case. Fuller discussion of the topic will be found in Penn, Shea & Arora, *op. cit.* I 13, 02–20 and in Paget, *op. cit.* pp. 405 *et seq.* Here, and throughout this chapter, reference should be made to Holden, *Securities for Bankers' Advances.*

considerable discussion as to whether in normal banking practice safe custody was or was not gratuitous.

It is now fairly generally accepted that the so-called "free" services of banking involve at least indirect reward; and as to ordinary and gross negligence, it may be hoped that Ormerod L.J. in a case unconnected with banking, *Houghland* v. *R.R. Low (Luxury Coaches) Ltd.*[15] has given the point its quietus when he said that he had always found some difficulty in understanding what "gross negligence" meant: "the question we have to consider in a case of this kind...is whether in the circumstances of this particular case a sufficient standard of care has been observed by the defendants or their servants."

PLEDGE

London Joint Stock Bank v. Simmons

[1892] A.C. 201

The pledgee of a negotiable instrument becomes the holder for value to the extent of the sum he has advanced

Facts

A firm of stockbrokers had for many years received advances from the appellant bank against various stocks, shares and bonds, these securities frequently changing. One of the partners in the firm, without the knowledge of his partner or the authority of the owner, sold certain negotiable bonds belonging to the respondent, Simmons, which the firm was holding for safe custody. The sale was in the name of the firm, as was the repurchase of securities for the next account, but the cheque on the firm's account representing the purchase money was paid against a temporary advance by the bank against additional security including, *inter alia*, the bonds thus repurchased.

The fraudulent partner having absconded, the firm suspended payment and the bank sold the bonds to repay the advance. Simmons brought an action against the bank claiming the value of the bonds, and the Court of Appeal, upholding the lower court, considered themselves bound by authority and held the bank liable. The bank appealed.

---

[15] [1962] 1 Q.B. 694.

Decision

The House of Lords allowed the appeal, and held the bank entitled to retain the value of the bonds.

In his judgment Lord Herschell said:

...I desire to rest my judgment upon the broad and simple ground that I find, as a matter of fact, that the bank took the bonds in good faith and for value. It is easy enough to make an elaborate presentation after the event of the speculation with which the bank managers might have occupied themselves in reference to the capacity in which the broker who offered the bonds as security for an advance held them. I think, however, they were not bound to occupy their minds with any such speculations. I apprehend that when a person whose honesty there is no reason to doubt offers negotiable security to a banker or any other person, the only consideration likely to engage his attention is, whether the security is sufficient to justify the advance required. And I do not think the law lays upon him the obligation of making any inquiry into the title of the person whom he finds in possession of them; of course, if there is anything to arouse suspicion, to lead to a doubt whether the person purporting to transfer them is justified in entering into the contemplated transaction the case would be different, the existence of such suspicion or doubt would be inconsistent with good faith. And if no inquiry were made, or if on inquiry the doubt were not removed and the suspicion dissipated, I should have no hesitation in holding that good faith was wanting in a person thus acting.[16]

Notes

The pledge with a banker of a negotiable security had been for some time before the *Simmons* case the subject of what has been called the "pernicious theory" that the banker was affected by constructive notice of any defect in the title of a customer whose business was that of agency, as, for example, a stockbroker. This inference had been drawn from the decision, also of the House of Lords, in *The Earl of Sheffield* v. *London Joint Stock Bank*,[17] where a money dealer had advanced large sums against securities belonging to the Earl of Sheffield, and pledged on his behalf by his agent. The money dealer in his turn pledged these and other securities with the London Joint Stock Bank as security for certain advances, and when he went into liquidation the owner of the securities and his agent brought this action against the bank to recover the stocks or their value. The Court of Appeal supported the lower court in dismissing the

[16] At p. 223.
[17] (1888) 13 App.Cas. 333.

action, but the House of Lords reversed this decision and held that the bank were not entitled to retain the stocks.

In the *Simmons* case the *Sheffield* decision was distinguished on the point that there the bank not only might have suspected but did in fact know that the securities pledged were not the property of the pledgor. The value of the *Simmons* decision lies in the emphasis with which the theory of constructive notice is rejected where the subject of the pledge is negotiable.

The importance of negotiability in the law of pledge as it affects bankers is considerable. It is not, strictly, necessary to have a memorandum of deposit of the instrument pledged where it is negotiable, as the deposit of it establishes prima facie the fact of the pledge.[18] Moreover, although it is desirable for the banker to have such a memorandum, to show that the securities were not left with him merely for safe custody, their negotiability makes them easily realisable, and this liquidity is of course of the greatest value in banking securities.

Sewell v. Burdick

(1884) 10 App.Cas. 74

Brandt v. Liverpool Brazil and River Plate Steam Navigation Co. Ltd.

[1924] 1 K.B. 575

A pledgee of a bill of lading does not take the general property in it unless and until he presents the bill to enforce his security

Facts of Sewell v. Burdick

Upon the shipment of certain goods to Russia, the shipper pledged the bill of lading to the appellant banker as security for a loan, and indorsed the bill to him. The goods were seized in Russia and sold to pay customs duties on them, the amount realised on the sale not covering the duties. The banker did not present his bill of lading, nor take possession of the goods.

Freight was unpaid on the consignment, and the shipowner brought the present action against the banker, contending that under the Bills of Lading Act the liability to pay the freight had

---

[18] Of course, in the case of quasi-negotiable documents of title, such as bills of lading, and of other forms of security, entirely lacking negotiability, the mere deposit of the documents of title without any form of charge gives a good *equitable* title to the property.

passed to the banker when he became indorsee of the bill of lading. The shipowner won in the lower courts, and the banker appealed.

Decision

The House of Lords allowed the appeal, holding that the obligations under the contract pass to the indorsee only when he takes the general property in the bill of lading, and not when he takes only such special property as a pledgee takes.[19]

In his judgment, Lord Blackburn said:

No one, in ordinary language, would say that when goods are pawned, or money is raised by mortgage on an estate, the property, either in the goods or land, passes to the pledgee or mortgagee, and I cannot think that the object of the enactment was to enact that no security for a loan should be taken on the transfer of bills of lading unless the lender incurred all the liabilities of his borrower on the contract. That would greatly, and I think unnecessarily, hamper the business of advancing money on such security which the legislature has, by the Factors Acts, shown it thinks ought rather to be encouraged.[20]

Facts of Brandt v. Liverpool Brazil and River Plate Steam Navigation Co. Ltd.

A consignment of zinc ashes was sent from Buenos Aires to Liverpool. The bill of lading stated that the goods had been shipped in apparent good order, but in fact a part of the consignment had been wetted by rain before loading, and began to swell. The master of the vessel, in the interests of the safety of his ship, discharged most of the consignment to a warehouse in Buenos Aires where, after unnecessary delay, they were reconditioned and reshipped to England, arriving three months after the arrival of the first ship. In the meantime the price of zinc had fallen, and the charges involved for warehousing and for the reconditioning amounted to £748.

The bill of lading had been indorsed to pledgees who had made an advance against it to the shipper. On arrival of the cargo the pledgees paid the freight due and, under protest, the charges of £748 for which the shipowners claimed a lien on the goods. They then brought an action against the shipowners for damages for delay, and for repayment of the sum of £748.

[19] As to general and special property, see *ante*, p. 245.
[20] At p. 95.

Decision

The Court of Appeal held that as the plaintiffs had taken delivery of the goods under the bill of lading they had acquired the rights and obligations under the contract of which the bill of lading was evidence, and could uphold a claim for the delay, and for the reconditioning of the goods.

In the course of his judgment, Scrutton L.J. said that in *Sewell* v. *Burdick*[21]:

Lord Selbourne expressed the view that if the bankers did present the bill of lading they might then be liable on the contract contained in the bill of lading. It seems to me that such a case is to be governed by the old law which existed before the passing of the Bills of Lading Act. When a holder of a bill of lading, who has some property in the goods, presents the bill of lading and accepts the goods, can there be inferred a contract on each side to perform the terms of the bill of lading? The view that Greer J. has taken is that such a contract can and ought to be implied in this case, and I take the same view.[22]

Notes

The Bills of Lading Act 1855, s.1, provides that:

Every consignee of goods named in a bill of lading, and every endorsee of a bill of lading to whom the property in the goods therein mentioned shall pass, upon or by reason of such consignment or endorsement, shall have transferred to and vested in him all rights of suit, and be subject to the same liabilities in respect of such goods as if the contract contained in the bill of lading had been made with himself.

The point decided by these two cases is that while the pledgee of a bill of lading does not, as such, acquire the rights or incur the liabilities of the original consignee, and is not, even when the bill of lading is indorsed to him when it is pledged, such an indorsee as is included within section 1 of the Act, yet when he enforces his security he does in doing so step into the shoes of the consignee. The protection given to the banker (among others) by the first decision is much diminished by the second.

Another possible danger to the pledgee of a bill of lading lies in the fact that such bills are normally issued in sets of three. This danger was exemplified in *Glyn Mills Currie & Co.* v. *East and West India Dock Co.*,[23] where the consignees indorsed to

[21] *Supra*.
[22] At p. 596.
[23] (1882) 7 App.Cas. 591.

the plaintiff bank the first of such a set of bills in consideration of a loan made to them. The consignees later presented to the dock company to whom the cargo had been discharged the second bill in the series, and the dock company in good faith and without notice of the bank's claim delivered the goods to the order of the consignees. Upon the bank's action against the dock company for conversion the House of Lords held that the bank could not maintain any action. The danger can be, and now commonly is, met by the pledgee obtaining the complete set.

In *Barclays Bank Ltd.* v. *Commissioners of Customs and Excise*[24] the bank's security was unsuccessfully challenged with the argument that the bill of lading, charged to the bank after the goods had been unloaded and warehoused, was no longer at that time a document of title capable of being pledged by delivery and indorsement. But Diplock L.J., sitting as an additional judge of the Queen's Bench Division, held that the contract evidenced by a bill of lading is not discharged by the completion of the carriage by sea alone, but continues until the shipowner actually surrenders possession. The bill of lading remains a document of title until that time.

Re David Allester Ltd.

[1922] 2 Ch. 211

Re Hamilton, Young & Co., ex p. Carter

[1905] 2 K.B. 772

The pledgee does not necessarily cease to be pledgee because he ceases to hold the goods or the documents of title

Facts of Re David Allester Ltd.

David Allester Ltd. were wholesale seed merchants whose banking account was with Barclays Bank. They were in the habit of borrowing from the bank against the pledge of goods; and when it became necessary to sell the goods, they issued to the bank a form of trust receipt, against which the bank released the documents of title. The trust receipt read as follows:

---

[24] [1963] 1 Lloyd's Rep. 81.

...I/we receive the above [documents of title] in trust on your account, and I/we undertake to hold the goods when received, and their proceeds when sold, as your trustees. I/we further undertake to keep this transaction separate from any other and to remit you direct the entire net proceeds as realised, but not less than...within...days from this date....

Upon David Allester Ltd. going into liquidation, the liquidator took out a summons to determine whether the bank was entitled to priority in respect of its claim to the proceeds of the sale of the goods. He contended that the documents were not valid against him as they had not been registered under section 93(1)(c) and (e) of the Companies (Consolidation) Act 1908, which refer to "a mortgage or charge created or evidenced by an instrument which, if executed by an individual, would require registration as a bill of sale," and to "a mortgage or charge on any book debts of the company." (Similar provisions are now contained in sections 395/6 of the Companies Act 1985).

Decision

The court gave judgment in favour of the bank. Astbury J. said:

With regard to the first point the liquidator contends, though I think without much confidence, that these letters of trust would, if executed by an individual, require registration as bills of sale. He relies on the definition in the Bills of Sale Act 1878, s.4, and contends that the letters of trust are "declarations of trust without transfer" within that Act, and that they are not covered by the exception "documents used in the ordinary course of business as proof of the possession or control of goods."

In my judgment these letters of trust do not fall within the bills of sale definition at all. The pledge rights of the bank were complete on the deposit of the bills of lading and other documents of title. These letters of trust are mere records of trust authorities given by the bank and accepted by the company stating the terms on which the pledgors were authorised to realise the goods on the pledgees' behalf. The bank's pledge and its rights as pledgee do not arise under these documents at all, but under the original pledge: see *Ex parte Hubbard*.[25] The bank as pledgee had a right to realise the goods in question from time to time, and it was more convenient to them, as is common practice throughout the country, to allow the realisation to be made by experts, in this case by the pledgors. They were clearly

[25] (1886) 17 Q.B.D. 690.

entitled to do this by handing over the bills of lading and other documents of title for realisation on their behalf without in any way affecting their pledge rights: see *North Western Bank* v. *Poynter.*[26]

If I am right about this it is unnecessary to consider the exception in the Bills of Sale Act 1878, s.4, but if it were necessary to deal with it, it seems to me that *In re Hamilton Young & Co.*[27] is an authority for saying that these letters of trust are documents used in the ordinary course of business as proof of the possession or control of the goods in question. . . .

The second point taken by the liquidator is a more difficult one. . . . The answer however to this point is, that these letters of trust really create no mortgage or charge on book debts in any true sense of the word at all. The bank had its charge before these letters came into existence. The object of these letters of trust was not to give the bank a charge at all, but to enable the bank to realise the goods over which it had a charge in the way in which goods in similar cases have for years and years been realised in the City and elsewhere.[28]

Facts of Re Hamilton Young & Co., ex parte Carter

A mercantile firm in Manchester had periodical advances from the National Bank of India against letters of lien in the following form:

We beg to advise having drawn a cheque on you for £—, which amount please place to the debit of our loan account No. 2, as a loan on the security of goods in course of preparation for shipment to the East. As security for this advance we hold on your account and under lien to you the undermentioned goods in the hands of . . . as per their receipt enclosed. These goods when ready will be shipped to Calcutta, and the bills of lading duly endorsed will be handed to you, and we then undertake to repay the above advance either in cash or from the proceeds of our drafts . . . to be negotiated by you and secured by the shipping documents representing the above-mentioned goods. . . .

Accompanying such letters of lien the borrowers gave the bank the receipts specified. Upon the bankruptcy of the firm the trustee in bankruptcy contended, *inter alia*, that the letters of lien were bills of sale, and that as they were not in the form set out in, nor registered as required by, the Bills of Sale Acts, they were void. Upon judgment being given for the bank, the trustee appealed.

[26] [1895] A.C. 56.
[27] *Infra.*
[28] At pp. 215–218.

Decision

The Court of Appeal dismissed the appeal. In his judgment, Cozens-Hardy L.J. said:

> The general policy of the Bills of Sale Act, 1878, was not to interfere with ordinary business transactions. In so far as they might be hit by the general words in the definition of "bill of sale," they are taken out by the express exception. I think the letter of lien, coupled with the deposit of the bleachers' receipt, was a "document used in the ordinary course of business as proof of the control of goods" within the meaning of s.4 of the Act of 1878. It enabled the bank to prevent the bankrupts by injunction from dealing with the goods in any manner inconsistent with the arrangement contemplated by the parties—an arrangement which would result in the handing over of bills of lading when the goods were ready for shipment to Calcutta. It thus gave the bank a "control" of the goods.[29]

Notes[30]

There is always a prima facie danger in parting with documents of title which are security for an advance, but the advantages of doing so are so great to a banker, who cannot in practice be also a merchant, that it has become to all intents and purposes essential for him to release the documents to his customer when sale of the goods is necessary: his advance cannot normally be repaid until the goods are sold, and the person best fitted to sell them is the merchant handling them. The trust receipt was evolved to meet this need, and the decision in *Re David Allester Ltd.* is important in that it effectively dispelled one of the attendant dangers of the practice: upon the customer's bankruptcy, the banker is as completely secured as if he had retained the documents.

A comparable decision was that of the Privy Council in *Official Assignee of Madras* v. *Mercantile Bank of India Ltd.*,[31] where the bank had been in the habit of making advances against letters of hypothecation backed by railway receipts covering consignments of groundnuts. The goods were taken into possession in warehouses leased to the borrowing firm, but in doing so the bank first released the railway receipts to the firm, who arranged the unloading into the warehouse. At the time of the firm's bankruptcy goods covered by 46 railway

---

[29] At pp. 789–790.
[30] The character and operation of trust receipts and letters of hypothecation are explained in Penn, Shea & Arora, *op. cit.*, II 13, 97–9.
[31] [1935] A.C. 53.

receipts were in transit, and the Official Assignee contended that the bank had no title to the goods, and that until they were reduced into possession in the warehouse the pledge was a pledge of the documents only. The Privy Council held that the receipts were documents of title within the terms of the Indian Contract Act of 1872, that their delivery to the bank constituted a pledge of the goods,[32] and that the pledge was effective even though the bank handed the documents back to the pledgor as trustee. Moreover, (i) even if the bank "did not get a good pledge at law by the delivery of the railway receipts, still that delivery, considered on all the facts of the case, was evidence of a good equitable charge at least as between the immediate parties, even ignoring the accompanying letters of hypothecation" and the assignee in bankruptcy must be subject to the same equity; (ii) apart from the pledge of the goods, the letter of hypothecation constituted a good equitable charge, so as to bind both lender and borrower and the assignee in bankruptcy, who could here have no better right than the insolvent firm could have had.

With regard to the second case above, *Re Hamilton, Young & Co.*, it may be remarked that it would not be safe for the banker to use a novel form of letter of hypothecation, lest it might be held to be outside the ordinary course of mercantile business, and so require registration as a bill of sale. In *R. v. Townshend*[33] the defendant, a fruit broker, had advances from his banker against goods consigned to him which were still at sea. He deposited as security indorsed bills of lading, but before making the advance the bank called for a letter of hypothecation. In this letter the defendant undertook to hold the goods in trust for the bankers, and to hand over the proceeds as and when received. It was held that this was a

---

[32] The judgment of the Privy Council, delivered by Lord Wright, included a valuable analysis of the English law of pledge, and emphasised the distinction, on the present point, between English and Indian law. In English law a pledge of documents (except a bill of lading) is not deemed to be a pledge of the goods themselves. An exception to this rule is made by s.3 of the Factors Act, which applies only to mercantile agents: pledge of documents by such agents is deemed to be a pledge of the goods. Thus the anomaly arises that an agent can, perhaps in fraud of his principal, do what his principal cannot do—obtain an advance against documents of title without notification to the warehouseman. In practice the banks are understood not to rely on this distinction, but to obtain in all cases registration of the goods in their own name. *cf. Beverley Acceptances Ltd. v. Oakley* [1982] R.T.R. 417.

[33] (1884) 15 Cox C.C. 466.

bill of sale within the terms of the Bills of Sale Acts 1878 and 1882, as being a declaration of trust without transfer. It would thus have been unenforceable for lack of registration as a bill of sale, had it not been also held that for another reason it was exempt from the necessity for registration.

The other noteworthy danger in the handling of trust receipts was seen in *Lloyds Bank Ltd.* v. *Bank of America National Trust and Savings Association.*[34] Here the plaintiff bank advanced £57,000 to Strauss & Co. Ltd. against merchandise, took a letter of hypothecation from the company, and surrendered the documents of title against trust receipts. Instead of selling the goods the company pledged the documents with the defendant bank, who advanced against them in good faith. On the company going into liquidation, Lloyds Bank claimed the value of the goods from the Bank of America. The Court of Appeal held that in the circumstances Strauss & Co. had been constituted mercantile agents within section 2(1) of the Factors Act 1889,[35] and as such were able to make a valid pledge to the Bank of America; and judgment was accordingly given for the Bank of America.

An unusual challenge to a bank on its delivery orders was unsuccessful in *Alicia Hosiery Ltd.* v. *Brown Shipley & Co. Ltd.*[36] Cascade Stockings Ltd. had an overdraft with the defendant bank, and in 1964 they secured a further advance against a shipment of stockings from Italy, the warehousemen being instructed to hold them to the order of the bank. The plaintiff company were prospective purchasers of the stockings, and the bank, upon receiving the agreed purchase price of £11,500, issued a delivery order, but the warehouse refused to release the stockings until they received a further sum of £3,000 in respect of unpaid customs duty and purchase tax. Both Alicia Hosiery and the bank had believed that duty and tax had been paid. The plaintiffs now sought to recover the money paid to the bank on the grounds (i) that the bank was in breach of its agreement to procure delivery to them and (ii) that the company having the right to immediate possession was being denied it by the bank. But Donaldson J. held that

---

[34] [1938] 2 K.B. 147.
[35] The effects of this subsection of the Factors Act, and of section 3 (*supra*), together with the further exception to the common law rule created by section 25(2) of the Sale of Goods Act 1893 (now the 1979 Act), are noted in Penn, Shea & Arora, *op. cit.* II 13–93, 94.
[36] [1970] 1 Q.B. 195.

there was no contractual relationship between the plaintiffs and the bank: there were rather two contracts, between the bank and its customers, and between the customers and Alicia Hosiery. Moreover, the issue of a delivery order by the bank as pledgee (as contrasted with delivery orders issued by the sellers of goods) did not involve an undertaking by the bank that the goods would be delivered. And on the second point, while the bank was in constructive possession of the goods until the delivery order was issued, this was no longer true after the warehouse had received the order; from then onwards the warehouse held the goods to the order of the purchasers.

GUARANTEES

Hamilton v. Watson

(1845) 12 Cl. & Fin. 109

The contract of guarantee is not one uberrimae fidei . . .

Facts

In 1835 Peter Elles obtained from his bank a loan of £750 against a bond by himself, his father and two other sureties. Upon the death of one of them in the same year, the bank pressed for payment or fresh security, but neither was forthcoming. After continuous pressure by the bank, in 1837 a new bond was signed, in which the appellant joined as surety. The appellant knew nothing of the previous history of the advance. When Elles died, insolvent, and the appellant was called upon to pay to the bank the amount of the loan, he contended, *inter alia*, that he was not liable, as the full facts had not been disclosed at the time of his signing.

Decision

The House of Lords found for the respondent (the public officer of the bank). Lord Campbell said:

Your Lordships must particularly notice what the nature of the contract is. It is a suretyship upon a cash account. Now the question is, what, upon entering into such a contract, ought to be disclosed? And I will venture to say, if your Lordships were to adopt the principles laid down, and contended for by the appellant's co⁻ here, that you would entirely knock up those transactions in S of giving security upon a cash account, because no bankers would rest satisfied that they had a security for the advance they made, if, as it is contended, it is essentially necessary that every thing should be disclosed by the creditor that it is material for the surety to know. If such was the rule, it would be indispensably necessary for the bankers to whom the security is to be given, to state how the account had been kept: whether the debtor was in the habit of overdrawing; whether he was punctual in his dealings; whether he performed his promises in an honourable manner; for all these things are extremely material for the surety to know. But unless question be particularly put by the surety to gain this information, I hold that it is quite unnecessary for the creditor, to whom the suretyship is to be given, to make any such disclosure; and I should think that this might be considered as the criterion whether the disclosure ought to be made voluntarily, namely, whether there is anything that might not naturally be expected to take place between the parties who are concerned in the transaction, that is, whether there be a contract between the debtor and the creditor, to the effect that his position shall be different from that which the surety might naturally expect; and, if so, the surety is to see whether that is disclosed to him. But if there be nothing which might not naturally take place between these parties, then, if the surety would guard against particular perils, he must put the question, and he must gain the information which he requires.[37]

Notes

A contract *uberrimae fidei*—a contract in which the utmost good faith must be observed—is one in which one of the parties is presumed to have knowledge not accessible to the other, and is bound to disclose fully and truthfully any such knowledge which might affect the other's judgment whether or not it does in fact do so. The most common of such contracts is that of insurance, which is voidable at the option of the insurer if any fact is withheld the withholding of which might affect his judgment, even though in the particular case it does not do so.[38] It is clearly of the utmost importance to the banker that the guarantee should not be so regarded, as Lord Campbell made clear in his judgment here quoted.

But the fact that so early as 1845 the position as to disclosure had been so clearly laid down by Lord Campbell has not prevented a number of sureties from seeking to escape from this liability on the ground that they had not

[37] At p. 118.
[38] *cf., post*, p. 356.

been told the material circumstances. Thus, in *National Provincial Bank of England* v. *Glanusk*[39] Lord Glanusk had guaranteed the overdraft of his brother-in-law, who was also his agent, at the plaintiffs' Crickhowell branch. The guarantee was on the face of it for all moneys which might be owing to the plaintiffs, but the guarantor contended that there was an antecedent agreement that it should cover only the estate account, and that the bank knew, and should have informed him, that his brother-in-law was using the overdraft for purposes not contemplated by him. It appeared that the branch manager was informed by his customer that the guarantor knew of the cheque in question and Horridge J. held that, even had it been proved that the bank had been suspicious of the transaction, they owed no duty to communicate their suspicions to the guarantor.

In *Westminster Bank* v. *Cond*[40] the issue was even simpler. There the customer had an overdraft guaranteed by two sureties and, wishing to increase his borrowing, was told that he must first produce additional security. The defendant agreed to guarantee the account for £300, and in an interview with the branch manager inquired whether the latter considered his customer's prospects good. The manager replied that in view of his customer's salary he did not think he would have difficulty in paying off the overdraft. The defendant did not ask the manager whether there was any existing overdraft, and the manager did not volunteer the information. Upon the customer's later insolvency the defendant refused to pay under the guarantee, contending that the manager owed him a duty to disclose that there was a previous overdraft, even though he did not ask him for that particular information. Tucker J. held that there was no such duty.

Again, in *Cooper* v. *National Provincial Bank Ltd*[41] the plaintiff contended that the bank should have told him that (*a*) the husband of the person guaranteed was an undischarged bankrupt who had (*b*) been given power to draw on the account; and (*c*) the account had been irregularly conducted in that some dozen cheques had been "stopped" by the customer. Lawrence L.J., basing his judgment on the

[39] [1913] 3 K.B. 335.
[40] (1940) 46 Com.Cas. 60, *ante*, p. 152, *post*, p. 315.
[41] [1945] 2 All E.R. 641.

judgment of Lord Campbell quoted above, found that there was nothing in the contract between the bank and its customer which could be regarded as unusual, and that there was therefore no duty of disclosure.

The guarantors in these cases were probably encouraged to seek to avoid their liabilities by the fact that it is not easy to define what exactly is unusual conduct, between the banker and his customer, that would require disclosure to a proposing guarantor; and every guarantor hopes, when he is called upon to pay, that there may be something in the previous history of the account which needed such disclosure. In *Royal Bank of Scotland* v. *Greenshields*[42] the law on this point was outlined in terms which are themselves clear, but which emphasise the difficulty in which the bank manager may find himself. Lord Mackenzie said:

> It is well settled law that there is no obligation upon a bank agent to disclose the position of his customer's account unless he is asked a specific question which imposes that obligation upon him or unless circumstances emerge which put upon him the duty of making a full disclosure. The circumstances may be either that he volunteers a statement which is only half the truth, in which case the cautioner [guarantor] is entitled to say "I was misled; I was entitled to assume that you were disclosing the whole truth," or ... if the intending cautioner makes a statement to the bank agent, or in his presence, which plainly shows that he is entering into a transaction in an entire misapprehension of the facts of the case, then the bank agent equally would be under an obligation, arising out of the circumstances of the case, to prevent the cautioner from being misled.[43]

In *Lloyds Bank Ltd.* v. *Harrison*[44] the customer was in difficulties and the bank had insisted that he should for six months accept only such business as would reduce his stock. The guarantor contended that this was a material and unusual fact which should have been disclosed to him when he signed the guarantee upon which this action was brought. The Court of Appeal unanimously dismissed the guarantor's appeal. In his judgment, Sargant L.J. said:

> It must be remembered that in this case, as in most cases, the

---

[42] 1914 S.C. 259.
[43] At p. 271.
[44] (1925) 4 L.D.B. 12.

surety is approached in the first instance by the principal debtor, and is brought to the bank as a person who is willing to accept a certain responsibility in connection with the banking affairs of the principal debtor. Speaking generally, I should think the bank would be wrong in disclosing, without some very special direction by the customer, the whole particulars of the state of account of that customer to the surety.... Then, taking the test of *Hamilton* v. *Watson*,[45] which is undoubtedly the leading case on the subject, Lord Campbell pointed out very clearly what an extraordinary and unpractical obligation would be cast upon bankers if they were to be forced to disclose to a person becoming a surety for a cash account all the circumstances of the business relations of the customer whose account was proposed to be guaranteed. Of course, in every case there must be a large number of particular circumstances which do not occur in other cases, but,...there is no obligation on the banker to disclose anything that might naturally take place between the parties.[46]

Paget suggests[47] that the customer, in seeking the guarantee, has given implied permission for replies to be given, when the intending guarantor asks direct questions of the bank manager, but it has been suggested that a "more cautious approach may be justified"[48] and it may well be that the manager should at least obtain his customer's express authority before answering the questions.[49]

Mackenzie v. Royal Bank of Canada

[1934] A.C. 468

...but misrepresentation, whether innocent or otherwise, may avoid the guarantee

Facts

In 1920 the plaintiff, Mrs. Mackenzie, hypothecated to the defendant bank certain shares to the value of $10,000, as

---

[45] *Supra.*
[46] At p. 216.
[47] *Op. cit.* p. 501.
[48] Penn, Shea & Arora, *op. cit.* I, 19.22, where a more cautious approach is described.
[49] *cf. ante*, pp. 6 *et seq.* concerning disclosure generally. As to guarantes generally, see Reeday, *op. cit.*, pp. 300–328 and Penn, Shea & Arora, *op. cit.*, I.20.

security for borrowing by Mackenzie Ltd., a company in which her husband was interested. The company later became bankrupt, and in the proceedings that followed, under Canadian bankruptcy law, the bank took over such of the company's property as had been charged to them, and the bank was thereby discharged. In the meantime, however, the bank had also taken a letter signed by the plaintiff and her husband, which referred to the proposed arrangements in bankruptcy and added: "...we hereby agree that your so doing shall not in any way release us from our obligation under guarantees to the bank, nor shall our personal securities be in any way affected until the amount due to the bank by Mackenzie Ltd. has been actually paid."

The company was now reconstructed, and the bank and Mackenzie required the plaintiff to guarantee the borrowing of the new company, the bank manager and Mackenzie assuring her that her shares were still bound to the bank, but that this was an opportunity of regaining them. After she had signed the guarantee and the accompanying form of hypothecation she was asked to take to a solicitor a form for him to sign, stating that he had independently advised her. This the solicitor signed, although in fact he had not so advised her.

The present action was for recovery of the shares, the plaintiff alleging that she had been induced to hypothecate them by misrepresentation. The trial judge gave judgment for her, which was reversed on appeal. She now appealed to the Privy Council.

Decision
The Privy Council allowed the appeal. Lord Atkin said:

It may very well be that in procuring the plaintiff's signature to this document [the letter quoted above] the bank had in mind to extend their obligations so as to cover a contemplated reconstruction. If so they failed in their purpose, for it appears to their Lordships that the terms of this letter cannot be construed to give any right to the bank over securities once the debt had been discharged in the manner above mentioned....

A contract of guarantee, like any other contract, is liable to be avoided if induced by material misrepresentation of an existing fact, even if made innocently.... The evidence conclusively establishes a misrepresentation by the bank that the plaintiff's shares were still bound to the bank with the necessary inference, whether expressed or not, and their Lordships accept the plaintiff's evidence that it was expressed, that the shares were already lost, and that the guarantee of the new company offered the only means of salving them. It does not seem to admit of doubt that such a representation made as to the plaintiff's private rights and depending upon transactions in bankruptcy, of the full nature of which she had not been informed, was a representation of fact. That it was material is beyond discussion. It consequently follows that the plaintiff was at all times, on ascertaining the true position, entitled to avoid the contract and recover her securities.[50]

Notes

The law of misrepresentation and mistake in contract (and a guarantee is merely one form of contract) is somewhat involved, and is best studied in the framework of general contract law.[51] It may be said here that a misrepresentation of fact, whether innocent or fraudulent, makes the contract voidable at the option of the person misled, and an action for damages may also lie. A mistake of fact, if it goes to the root of the contract, may make it void *ab initio*; and the effect of misrepresentation is often, of course, extremely difficult to distinguish from that of mistake.

It is essential for the banker that the guarantee should not be vitiated either by misrepresentation or by mistake. It is not always easy for him to observe his duty to his customer and at the same time avoid any suspicion of misleading the surety, and the cases dealt with in the preceding heading show how often the surety, at any rate, considers that he has been misled.

In *Stone* v. *Compton*[52] the defendant became surety for an advance made by the plaintiff banker to a customer. The misrepresentation here was in a recital in the mortgage entered into by the debtor, which suggested that at the time of the advance the customer did not owe the bank anything, although in fact there was a considerable advance outstanding, for the clearance of which the new advance was partly designed. The mortgage deed was read in the presence of the defendant before he had bound himself, and it was held that as a result of this misrepresentation he was not liable.

For many years *Carlisle and Cumberland Banking Co.* v. *Bragg*[53] stood as warning of the danger of allowing the

---

[50] At pp. 473, 475–476.
[51] *cf.* Reeday, *op. cit.* pp. 25–28.
[52] (1838) 5 Bing.N.C. 142.
[53] [1911] 1 K.B. 489.

guarantee form to be taken away by the customer in order that he may obtain the signature of the surety to it. In that case the customer gave a form of guarantee to the defendant and, fraudulently representing that it was an insurance paper, obtained his signature. The customer then forged the signature of a witness and returned the form to the bank, who allowed him the advance he sought. The Court of Appeal held that the defendant had signed in complete ignorance of the nature of the transaction, and that as he owed no duty of care to the bank he was not bound as against them. This decision was expressly overruled in *Saunders* v. *Anglia Building Society*[54] when the House of Lords redefined the scope of the principle of *non est factum* (it is not his deed).

The effect of this important decision (sometimes cited as *Gallie* v. *Lee*, the parties to the action in the lower courts) is that there is a heavy burden of proof on the person relying on the principle; that there must be a fundamental difference between what he signed and what he thought he signed; and, perhaps most important, that he must show that he acted carefully. Only in quite exceptional circumstances can any person of full age and understanding disavow his signature so as to prejudice the rights of an innocent third party.

In *United Dominions Trust Ltd.* v. *Western*,[55] the Court of Appeal closed a possible loophole in the *Saunders* ruling when they refused to accept the defendant's argument that signing a document in blank is of different effect from signing a completed form: this was neither good sense nor good law. If another person is authorised to complete the form the signatory takes his chance of the blanks being filled in fraudulently.[56]

It is to be noted that the overruling of the *Carlisle and Cumberland Banking Co.* decision on the particular point of the carelessness of the signatory lessens but does not remove the danger of allowing the customer to take the guarantee away for the signatory to sign, a practice that is normally forbidden by the banks.

---

[54] [1970] 3 All E.R. 961; 9 L.D.B. 180.
[55] [1976] 2 W.L.R. 64.
[56] The plea of *non est factum* was rejected in the unusual circumstances of *Credit Lyonnais* v. *P.T. Barnard & Associates* [1976] 1 Lloyd's Rep. 557 where the defendants' managing director, knowing no French, accepted two bills of exchange drawn in that language in the belief that they were receipts. Mocatta J., applying the *Saunders* rule, held that the defendants had not shown that they acted carefully.

A guarantee is a contract which is strictly construed by the courts, and it is important that its terms should be carefully observed. In *Burton* v. *Gray*,[57] for example, the plaintiff's brother had taken to his banker certain securities belonging to the plaintiff. He had shown the banker a letter purporting to be signed by the plaintiff and charging the securities "in consideration of your lending F. Burton the sum of £1,000 for seven days from this date." The banker allowed the brother to overdraw his account in a series of cheques which in aggregate were less than £1,000, and it was held that as no loan of £1,000 had been made, and as no term had been assigned to the overdraft that had been granted, the plaintiff was not bound, and the securities must be released.

Another rule of contract law to which particular attention has to be paid in dealing with guarantees is that relating to consideration. This is essential to the validity of the guarantee, unless it is under seal; and if a guarantee is given for an advance already granted it is essential that there should be some such consideration as an extension of time or forbearance to sue.

A case demonstrating the necessity for consideration for a guarantee not under seal, as well as, incidentally, the fact that there must be no misrepresentation, is *Provincial Bank of Ireland* v. *O'Donnell*.[58] Here a wife guaranteed the payment of premiums on a life policy of her husband's which was charged to the bank as security for an advance on his account. The guarantee was expressed to be in consideration for advances "heretofore made or that may hereafter be made from time to time." In fact the bank had no intention at the time of making any further advances, but the wife was not told this, nor was she informed of the state of the account. It was held that the existing debt could not form the consideration necessary to support the guarantee, that there was therefore no effective consideration, and that as a result the guarantee failed.

The banker needs to ensure that the guarantee is not weakened by any dispute as to the amount of the debt that has been guaranteed and the guarantee normally includes a "conclusive evidence" clause, by which the guarantor agrees to accept as conclusive, in the event of demand being made, the bank's statement of the amount due. *Bache & Co. (London)*

---

[57] (1873) 8 Ch.App. 932.
[58] [1934] N.I. 33.

Ltd. v. *Banque Vernes et Commerciale de Paris*[59] was unusual in
that there it was a bank that challenged the effectiveness of such
a clause. The defendant bank had guaranteed their customers'
contract with the plaintiffs, London commodity brokers, and
upon being called upon to pay under the guarantee (which
contained a "conclusive evidence" clause) argued (*a*) that their
customers disputed the amount due, and (*b*) that in any case the
clause was against public policy in purporting to oust the
jurisdiction of the courts. The Court of Appeal rejected both
arguments. There was no public objection to the clause; and if
the figures proved wrong the bank's customers had an action
against the brokers and the bank could claim indemnity against
their customers. And Lord Denning added:

> ... this commercial practice ... is only acceptable because the
> bankers or brokers who insert them are known to be honest and
> reliable men of business who are most unlikely to make a mistake.
> Their standing is so high that their work is to be trusted. So much so
> that a notice of default given by a bank or a broker must be honoured.
> It ranks as equivalent to, if not higher than, the certificate of an
> arbitrator or engineer in a building contract.[60]

This decision appears to make it unlikely that any challenge
to the clause, as being unreasonable under the Unfair Contract
Terms Act 1977, would succeed.

It may be noted that in *O'Hara* v. *Allied Irish Bank Ltd. and
Another*,[61] where the second defendant had guaranteed a
company of which she was a director, Harman J. rejected her
defence that the bank, of which she was not a customer, had
given her no advice:

> I cannot see that a stranger, invited to sign a guarantee ... is owed
> any duty whatever at that point of time. It seems to me that at that
> point they are mere prospective contracting parties. ... In such a case
> as the present, where the only evidence is that nothing was said, and
> therefore no representation by words could have been made, and no
> representation by conduct is alleged, I can see no duty of care by one
> stranger to another.[61a]

[59] [1973] 2 Lloyd's Rep. 437. *cf. ante*, pp. 271 *et seq.* for guarantees provided by
banks, for their customers.
[60] At p. 440.
[61] [1985] B.C.L.C. 52.
[61a] But the Jack Report recommends that banks should explain the legal effect
of guarantees to guarantors, whether or not they are customers.

National Westminster Bank PLC v. Morgan
[1985] A.C. 686

Liability in cases of undue influence

Facts

The bank had agreed to lend Mr. and Mrs. Morgan £14,500 against the mortgage of the matrimonial home, in order to pay off a mortgage to the Abbey National Building Society, which had threatened possession proceedings. The branch manager took the mortgage form to Mrs. Morgan for her signature. She expressed concern that the loan might be used in her husband's business, and the manager assured her that it would not be so used; and in fact, although the mortgage was actually unlimited, the bank only sought to enforce it when the loan was not repaid, as security for the refinancing loan. But Mrs. Morgan resisted the bank's action, alleging that the manager had put pressure on her, and that her signature had been obtained by the undue influence of the bank.

The bank contended that the defence of undue influence could only be raised when a defendant had entered into a transaction which was manifestly disadvantageous. Here the husband had died without business debts, and the transaction had benefited the wife by averting proceedings for possession by the prior mortgagor. The trial judge rejected the wife's defence, but he was overruled by the Court of Appeal, which held that there was here a special relationship which raised the undue influence defence, and the bank could not resist it because they had failed to advise the wife to seek independent advice. The bank appealed to the House of Lords.

Decision

Allowing the appeal, their Lordships held that, as the bank had argued, the undue influence defence must show that the transaction challenged was disadvantageous to the defendant. That was not shown here. The principle of the defence was not public policy, but the prevention of the victimisation of one party by another, so a presumption of undue influence would not necessarily arise from the fact that a confidential relationship existed between the parties. The bank manager had not crossed the line between an ordinary business relationship and a special relationship in which he had a dominating position, and there was therefore no duty to ensure that Mrs. Morgan had independent advice.

Lord Scarman, after reviewing the relevant decisions, added a cautionary note:

There is no precisely defined law setting limits to the equitable jurisdiction of a court to relieve against undue influence.... It is the unimpeachability at law of a disadvantageous transaction which is the starting point from which the court advances to consider whether the transaction is the product merely of one's own folly or of the undue influence exercised by another. A court in the exercise of this equitable jurisdiction is a court of conscience. Definition is a poor instrument when used to determine whether a transaction is or is not unconscionable: this is a question which depends on the particular facts of the case.[61b]

Notes

Bankers are concerned with questions of undue influence principally in connection with guarantees and mortgages. In either case they may be challenged as having exerted undue influence on a guarantor or a mortgagor, or on the grounds that a guarantee or a mortgage is ineffective because it was given under the influence of a third party.

In their appeal in the present case the bank asked the House to review the decision of the Court of Appeal in *Lloyds Bank Ltd.* v. *Bundy*[62] and this Lord Scarman did, pointing out that while Lord Denning had based his decision on inequality of bargaining power as founding undue influence, Sir Eric Sachs and Cairns L.J. had held that the undue influence stemmed from the special relationship between the manager and his elderly customer. He had crossed the line between the ordinary business relationship and the special relationship which may found undue influence. In *Morgan* the line was not crossed.

Misunderstanding of *Bundy* encouraged attempts by guarantors and mortgagors to allege undue influence when it was sought to realise the security. *Morgan* too is misunderstood when it is said that it overruled *Bundy*. Lord Scarman restated clearly the principle of undue influence established in *Allcard* v. *Skinner*[63] and applied, for example, by the Privy Council in *Bank of Montreal* v. *Stuart*,[64] for long regarded as the leading case on the topic.

There Mrs. Stuart had guaranteed lending to the company of which her husband was the president, the guarantee being

[61b] At p. 709.
[62] *Ante,* p. 22.
[63] (1886–90) All E.R. 9.
[64] [1911] A.C. 120.

arranged by a director of the company, who was also solicitor to the company and Mr. Stuart's legal adviser. When the company went into liquidation Mrs. Stuart sought to set aside her guarantees, claiming that her husband, under whose influence she had acted, was the bank's agent, and that she had received no independent advice: she had acted of her own free will and would have scorned to consult anyone in the matter. The Privy Council dismissed the bank's appeal against the finding of the Supreme Court of Canada that the bank, having left everything to the director, was liable for the fact that he had failed to advise Mrs. Stuart of the obvious risks of what she was doing.

This was an example of the bank's liability for the undue influence exercised by a third party; in *Bundy* and in *Morgan* the banks were challenged on the undue influence which it was claimed they had exercised themselves. In a succession of cases in which *Morgan* has been applied,[65] we see demonstrated a variety of circumstances in which the banks and other lenders may find themselves at risk through an allegation that the surety has been subjected to undue influence. It can be difficult for the lender to recognise the existence of the risk, but clearly when there is any doubt he should ensure that independent advice is given.

Bank of Baroda v. *Shah*[66] is an example of an unsuccessful challenge to the bank in this area of independent advice. The defendants had charged their home as security for an advance to Seasonworth Ltd. under the influence of the second defendant's brother, a director of the company, and the company's solicitor, who represented himself as acting also for the defendants, although they had not instructed him to act for them. When the company defaulted and the bank sought possession of the house, the defendants resisted the bank's claim, but the Court of Appeal gave the bank their case. Dillon L.J. said that when the bank's solicitors sent the charge to the company's solicitor for execution, they were entitled to assume that he would act honestly and give proper advice to the defendants. The defendants' argument that by so dealing with the charge the

---

[65] See, *e.g. Kings North Trust Ltd.* v. *Bell* [1986] 1 W.L.R. 119; *Coldunell Ltd.* v. *Gallon and Another* [1986] Q.B. 1184; *Woodstead Finance Ltd.* v. *Petrou* (1985) 136 New L.J. 188; *Goldsworthy* v. *Brickell and Others* [1987] 1 All E.R. 853; *Midland Bank plc* v. *Shephard* [1988] 3 All E.R. 17. These cases are discussed at 10 L.D.B. 525. And see *Chetwynd-Talbot* v. *Midland Bank, post*, p. 328.
[66] [1988] 3 All E.R. 24.

bank's solicitors had effectively sent it to the second defendant's brother could not be accepted.

The existence of independent advice may be a difficulty for the lender; even less in his control is judgment as to the disadvantage to the surety. In *Bank of Credit and Commerce International SA* v. *Aboody*[67] Mrs. Aboody was an Iraqi Jew who was born in Baghdad and lived within the local community, in which business was a man's exclusive province. She and her husband moved to Manchester, where the husband established a company, Eratex. Mrs. Aboody became a co-director and secretary of the company, and was told that she would have no duties in those capacities. In due course she signed three guarantees and three charges on her house to secure the company's debts. When, after massive frauds, the company collapsed, the bank claimed under the joint and several guarantees of Mr. and Mrs. Aboody, and she strongly contested the claim on the grounds that her signature had been obtained by the undue influence of her husband. But the Court of Appeal upheld the trial judge's view that although there had clearly been undue influence, there was no manifest disadvantage to Mrs. Aboody in view of the fact that at the time of signing the company was supporting the Aboodys in considerable comfort and there was reasonable prospect that the company would succeed.

Standard Chartered Bank v. Walker and Another

[1982] 1 W.L.R. 1410

Other conduct that may free the guarantor

Facts

The defendants, husband and wife, were directors of Johnny Walker (Developments) Ltd., a company dealing in metal pressing machines. In 1977 the company took a loan from the plaintiff bank against the security of a debenture, and in 1978 the defendants guaranteed the borrowing to a limit of £75,000. The company's business suffered in the depression, and the borrowing at one time reached £250,000. Under pressure from the bank it was reduced to £80,000 by November 1980, when the bank appointed a receiver.

The receiver arranged for a sale of the machinery, estimated as likely to produce £90,000, but the auction, in February 1981,

---

[67] [1989] 2 W.L.R. 759.

in severe weather, was in Lord Denning's words "a disaster," producing only £42,000, which left little for the preferred creditors and nothing for the bank. The bank then claimed against the guarantors, and the registrar, and on appeal Bristow J. gave judgment for the bank. The guarantors appealed, seeking leave to defend. They said that the assets had been sold at a gross undervalue, the auction was held at the wrong time of the year, none of the customers on the company's large mailing list had been informed, and the bank had instructed the receiver to hold a quick sale.

Decision

The Court of Appeal allowed the appeal, giving the defendants leave to issue a counter-claim and to join other parties to it. Lord Denning said that the duty of a mortgagee in possession, set out in the *Cuckmere Brick* case,[68] to take reasonable care to obtain a proper price on the sale of the property mortgaged, was owed both to the mortgagor and to the guarantor, who are both in close proximity to the circumstances of the sale.

As to the receiver, he too owed a duty to get the best possible price, and although he was the agent of the company and not the debenture holder, this duty was owed to the guarantor as well as the company, for the guarantor was only liable to the extent of the company's liability.

On the present facts, which the bank has not controverted, there are two triable issues of fact. First, did the bank interfere with the sale so as to take away some of the receiver's discretion, not only as to the time of the sale, but also perhaps as to the advertising and other matters? Second, was the disastrous sale due to faults in the arrangements made for it, without proper care for those interested in the proceeds?

Notes

This decision expressly overruled *Barclays Bank Ltd.* v. *Thienel*[69] and *Latchford* v. *Beirne*[70] in which attempts to extend the principle of the *Cuckmere Brick*[71] decision to guarantors were unsuccessful. Lord Denning said that in *Thienel's* case the trial judge relied on a wide clause in the guarantee which

---

[68] *Post* p. 324.
[69] (1978) 122 S.J. 472.
[70] [1981] 3 All E.R. 705.
[71] *Post,* p. 324.

authorised the bank "to realise any securities in such manner as you think expedient."

But any clause which makes the guarantor liable for a bigger sum than the mortgagor is liable for is repugnant or unreasonable and cannot be right. It would be invalid under the Unfair Contracts Terms Act 1977.

And in the *Latchford* case the trial judge "treated the guarantor almost as a creditor, and held that no duty of care was owed to him." Both decisions were erroneous in holding that the guarantor was liable for more than the mortgagor would have been, and they were not to be followed.

Challenges to guarantees founded on the conduct of the creditor have been most frequent in the areas of misrepresentation and undue influence.[72] But guarantees can be attacked also on more technical grounds, as in the *Standard Chartered* case, and in cases where the challenge has been on the grounds that the terms of the contract have been varied to the disadvantage of the guarantor.

Thus in *Barclays Bank Ltd.* v. *Trevanion*[73] the bank had released two of three guarantors upon their entering into an arrangement to pay a fixed sum each; the third, the defendant in the case, failed to come to terms, and was sued by the bank, under the guarantee. The contract of guarantee being joint as well as several, the release of some of the guarantors would discharge the others in the absence of a clause expressly permitting it, and the bank contended that certain clauses in their guarantee form did so permit, especially one which read:

As a separate and independent stipulation . . . I/we agree that all sums of money which may not be recoverable from the undersigned on the footing of a guarantee whether by reason of any legal limitation disability or incapacity on or of the principal or any other fact or circumstance and whether known to you or not shall nevertheless be recoverable from the undersigned as sole or principal debtor(s) in respect thereof. . . .

It was held that the bank was not protected by this form of words, which, it will be noted, did not refer to the co-sureties at all. Swift J. said:

[72] *Ante*, p. 295 *et seq.*
[73] (1933) *The Banker*, p. 98.

In my view, when they released two [of the guarantors] they altered the contract between themselves and the third guarantor in such a way as to prevent it being enforceable. They deprived him of his rights against his co-sureties, and I think that they then did something that released him from his bargain altogether.

And in *James Graham & Co. (Timber)* v. *Southgate-Sands*,[74] where three directors of a company had guaranteed the company's account, one of the directors was bankrupt when the company went into liquidation and the signature of the second guarantor was shown to have been forged. The third guarantor denied liability under the guarantee, and the Court of Appeal accepted his argument that he had lost his right of contribution against his co-guarantors: the parties had intended that the guarantee should be by three guarantors, and the document signed by the third guarantor was not the guarantee intended by the parties, and could not be enforced against him.

The plaintiffs in *Burnes* v. *Trade Credits Ltd.*[75] had guaranteed a mortgage in New South Wales, the guarantee providing, *inter alia*, that "any further advances" were covered and that the mortgagor might be granted time "or any other indulgence or consideration" without the guarantors' consent. In the event the term of the mortgage was extended, and the interest rate increased; and when on default by the mortgagor $8,583 interest was claimed from the guarantors, the Privy Council allowed the guarantors' appeal from the New South Wales Court of Appeal.

Where the term for repayment... is extended it is true to say that the sum remains advanced for a further period, but it is a distortion of language to say that a further advance has been made....

The granting of an indulgence to a debtor may have the effect of prejudicing the rights of the guarantor vis-à-vis the debtor, and accordingly, in the absence of a provision such as this one, it had the effect of releasing the guarantor from liability. The purpose and effect of the provision in question is merely to safeguard the creditor against that eventuality. It does not enable the debtor and the creditor, by agreement between themselves, to require the guarantor to shoulder an added liability.

But a clause providing that the bank might "vary, exchange or release any other securities held... and accept compositions

---

[74] [1986] Q.B. 80.
[75] [1981] 1 W.L.R. 805; 10 L.D.B. 276.

from and make any arrangements with the debtors" defeated the guarantor in *Perry* v. *National Provincial Bank of England Ltd.*[76] He had guaranteed an advance to a firm, mortgaging some of his property in support, and the clause was contained in the mortgage deed. The firm became insolvent, a company was formed to take over the business, and the bank accepted in full settlement of the claim against the firm debenture stock in the company to the value of the indebtedness on the account less the firm's securities which they held. Later, when interest on the debentures was not paid and the securities were not expected to realise the figure at which they had been valued, the bank proposed to sell the mortgaged property. The guarantor claimed that the release to the principal debtor freed him from liability under his guarantee, but the Court of Appeal rejected the claim, Cozens-Hardy M.R. saying " . . . it is perfectly possible for a surety to contract with a creditor . . . that notwithstanding any composition, release or arrangement, the surety shall remain liable although the principal does not.

And in *Bank of India* v. *Trans Continental Commodity Merchants*[77] a more general challenge to the bank failed. The second defendant, Jashbai Nagjibhai Patel, had guaranteed performance of 12 foreign exchange contracts by Trans Continental. Judgment was entered against the company, but the bank claimed also against the guarantor, who said that the bank's negligence in not ensuring that all the contracts were signed had prejudiced his position as guarantor: he argued that "if the creditor acts in such a way as to prejudice the interests of the surety, the surety will be discharged unless he consented to the course of conduct." But Bingham J. did not accept the argument. He said:

The true principle is that while a surety can be discharged if the creditor acts in bad faith towards him, or is guilty of concealment amounting to misrepresentation, or causes or connives at the default of the debtor in respect of which the guarantee was given, or varies the term of the contract in such a way as to prejudice the surety, other conduct on the part of the creditor, even if irregular, and even if prejudicial to the interests of the surety in a general sense, does not discharge the surety.[77a]

Ford & Carter Ltd. v. Midland Bank Ltd.

(1979) 129 New L.J. 543

The effectiveness of the guarantee depends on its terms

[76] [1910] 1 Ch. 464.
[77] [1982] 1 Lloyd's Rep 506.
[77a] At p. 515.

Facts

Wilson Lovett & Sons Ltd., with four associated companies, gave a mutual guarantee to the bank, all five companies executing a memorandum indorsed on the guarantee. Later another member of the group, Ford & Carter Ltd., purported to join the guarantee. Their name was added to the memorandum, with the signatures of two of their officers, but no fresh signatures were obtained from the first five companies. Ford & Carter gave the bank a floating charge in support of their guarantee.

In 1971 all six companies were called upon to pay under the guarantee, and believing that they were liable, Ford & Carter asked the bank to appoint a receiver under the floating charge. They subsequently went into liquidation, and the liquidator then questioned whether in fact they had been liable under the guarantee. The bank claimed that the memorandum envisaged the addition of further members of the group, and that all the companies were members of the same group, with a common financial adviser. The trial judge held that the company were not liable; the Court of Appeal reversed that decision, finding in favour of the bank.

Decision

The House of Lords unanimously restored the first finding: Ford and Carter were not liable. The wording of the memorandum did not support the bank's first argument, while although the second corresponded with the commercial reality of the situation, it was important that where creditors are involved "the separate legal existence of the constituent companies of the group has to be respected." Ford & Carter were in credit when the guarantee was called in, so the appointment of the receiver was not justified and the moneys he had taken in must be repaid; and damages were awarded against the receiver, who had become a trespasser when the service of the writ in the present action first effectively called upon him to give up his position.

Lord Salmon said:

It has been argued that if Ford & Carter succeeds in its claim against the bank this will produce an artificial and unreal result—and so in a sense it may. I am confident that probably all the signatories to this so-called interlocking guarantee believed that they were each bound by it and had always intended that they should be. I find great difficulty, however, in reading the language of that document as creating an agreement between the five parties who signed it in October, 1967 that, in future, Wilson Lovett or its chairman or financial director should have the power to authorise any new subsidiary company (wholly owned by Wilson Lovett) to become a party to the guarantee by signing it. To give it such a meaning would, in my view, stretch the language of the document to breaking point. There is no evidence that anyone in October, 1967 anticipated that Ford and Carter or any other company was likely to become a member of the Wilson Lovett group of companies. Had it been intended to cater for such an event so that any new wholly-owned subsidiary should automatically become a party to the guarantee merely by signing it, nothing would have been easier than to have written that guarantee in language which would clearly have had that effect.

Notes

This decision is an instructive example of the fact that the effect of a guarantee, like that of other contracts, depends on the words of the contract. Several cases illustrating the point have already been discussed in the preceding sections; and through the years there have been many other cases in which a variety of hidden dangers in the existing forms of guarantee have been revealed. The banks' standard forms have steadily grown larger as successive stable doors have been closed after successive escapes; but the law is not changed when the dangers have been met, and earlier cases in which banks have been challenged, not always successfully, are still useful in reminding us of the purpose of the complicated documents that have developed.

The decision in *Ford & Carter* was an application in more complicated circumstances of the principle seen many years earlier in the simpler facts of *National Provincial Bank of England* v. *Brackenbury*,[78] that a joint and several guarantee is not effective until it is executed by all the intending parties. There the intention was that a guarantee should be signed by four guarantors, and the form was so drawn. In the event only three signed, and it was held that they were not liable, Walton J. remarking that although the old adage of equity "might lead to results that ordinary people might not call equitable," it was well established: the present case was "a hard case for the bank, and a curious result of the equitable doctrine."

In a more recent case of cross-guarantees, *Brown* v. *Cork and Another*,[79] six companies in a group executed joint and

[78] (1906) 22 T.L.R. 797.
[79] [1985] B.C.L.C. 363.

several mutual guarantees in favour of the Midland Bank, and gave the bank debentures. The bank appointed a receiver when the group owed £750,000, and after liabilities to the bank were paid, a surplus of £195,000 resulted from overpayments by companies under their guarantees. All the companies now being in liquidation, the receiver, and the liquidator of one of the companies, proposed that the surplus should be distributed on the basis that each company had discharged its liability and borne so far as it could an equal share of the liability to the bank. The other liquidators said that inter-company trading debts should also be taken into account. The Court of Appeal upheld the first suggestion. The second would have been applicable in the ordinary way, but not, as here, where the liability to the creditor was secured: see the Mercantile Law Amendment Act 1856, section 5, which provides that a surety who has paid more than his share of the debt can enforce the rights of the creditor against his co-sureties; it is not necessary for the overall state of the accounts to be considered.

In *Offord* v. *Davies and Another*[80] the right of a guarantor to terminate his liability by notice, in the absence of an express stipulation to the contrary in the contract, was established. The guarantee there was expressed to be "for the space of 12 months." Before the end of that period the guarantors countermanded the guarantee, and when the bank claimed payment for money advanced after the notice but within the year, it was held that the defendants were not liable.

The two defendants in *Garrard* v. *James*[81] guaranteed the performance of an agreement by which the company of which they were directors borrowed £1,500 from the plaintiff. When the company was called upon to implement the agreement it appeared that to do so would be *ultra vires*, requiring them to purchase their own shares. The plaintiff then called on the guarantors for payment and they pleaded that their guarantee was only in the event of default by the company, and "default" meant failure to do what they could legally do. But it was held that they were liable, Lawrence J. saying:

> The word "default" is a word of wide general import, and includes "failure" and "omission." it seems to me immaterial whether the failure or omission by the company to perform its obligations is attributable to its financial inability or to statutory disability.... The

[80] (1862) 12 C.B.(N.S.) 748.
[81] [1925] 1 Ch. 616.

gist of the bargain entered into by the defendants, in my opinion, was: "If you, the plaintiff, will advance this £1,500, we, the defendants, will pay you, if the company does not pay."[81a]

No question arises as to the guarantee of an *illegal* transaction[82]: the guarantee in such cases is entirely ineffective. But in *Coutts & Co.* v. *Browne-Lecky*[83] the guarantee of an advance to an infant was ineffective because the advance was itself void, and there has been some doubt whether a borrowing which is *ultra vires* a limited company can be any more effectively guaranteed than a borrowing which is entirely void. Either type of advance can be brought within the contract of guarantee by a clause making the guarantor liable as principal debtor in the event of failure of the guarantee itself. A clause of this type is quoted in *Barclays Bank Ltd.* v. *Trevanion.*[84]

In *Lloyds and Scottish Trust Ltd.* v. *Britten and Another*[85] the defendants, directors of a company, guaranteed a loan by the plaintiffs to enable the company to buy two properties. The guarantees were limited to £64,000 for such time as one property, Balfour Place, formed part of the security. After the appointment of a receiver the plaintiffs obtained an order for the sale of Balfour Place, and a foreclosure on the second property, and in due course both properties were sold, Balfour Place realising £47,000. As the total indebtedness was not covered the plaintiffs brought this action for the deficiency. The judge accepted the guarantors' argument that the guarantee was no longer effective when Balfour Place ceased to "form part of the security."[86]

A challenge on the wording of the guarantee failed in *Amalgamated Investment and Property Co. Ltd.* v. *Texas*

[81a] At pp. 622–623.

[82] *cf., e.g.* Swan v. *Bank of Scotland* (1836) 10 Bli.(N.S.) 627, where the customer was allowed to draw unstamped documents.

[83] [1947] K.B. 104; reversed by the Minors' Contracts Act 1987.

[84] *Ante,* p. 306.

[85] (1982) 44 P. & C.R. 249.

[86] The guarantors' further argument, of wider significance than the wording of the contract, was that the plaintiffs could no longer sue the company, and so the defendants could not be sued as guarantors. This argument was also accepted: the authorities established that after a foreclosure a mortgagee can sue the mortgagor only if he retains the property; none of the authorities was concerned with the effect of the foreclosure on a guarantee, but if money is not recoverable from the principal debtor it cannot be recovered from the guarantor.

Commerce International Bank Ltd.[87] The company had guaranteed the borrowing of a subsidiary, and the bank had made the loan not directly, but through their own subsidiary. The company claimed that the guarantee covered only loans made by the bank directly, but throughout the transaction both sides had acted on the assumption that the guarantee covered the loan, and it was held in the Court of Appeal that the company was estopped from denying the efficacy of the agreement, Eveleigh L.J. remarking that it ran counter to all principles of construction to give the words a meaning that would defeat the clear intention of the parties as revealed by the rest of the evidence.

And in *Perrylease Ltd.* v. *Imecar AG*[87a], where the guarantors claimed that their guarantees did not make the extent of their liability clear, the court rejected their argument that section 4 of the Statute of Frauds made extrinsic evidence on the point inadmissible, and admitted such evidence.

The terms of the guarantee in *First National Finance Corporation* v. *Goodman*[88] produced what Bingham J. admitted was a "harsh result" for the guarantor. Here he had guaranteed, with his co-directors, an advance to their company renewable after one year, by Cassel Arenz, a wholly-owned subsidiary of First National. The borrowing was increased after the first year; in 1972 Cassel Arenz was merged with First National; about the same time the defendant ceased to be a director of the company and had no further connection with the business; and thereafter the borrowing increased further. In 1977 the company was wound up and First National were left with a liability of £338,000, for payment of which they called upon the defendant as guarantor. The judge accepted that when the larger advances were made the defendant had no interest in the company and no knowledge of the advances; and he accepted too that "a guarantor should not be exposed to liability beyond what is normal without very clear language, and that any ambiguity in the guarantee should be resolved in his favour." But the words of the guarantee were against the defendant, defeating also his further argument that he could be made liable only for advances made by Cassel Arenz: the guarantee provided that "the bank" included its successors and assigns and any company with which it might amalgamate. And the Court of Appeal dismissed the guarantor's appeal.[89]

---

[87] [1982] Q.B. 84.
[87a] [1987] 2 All E.R. 373.
[88] [1983] Com.L.R. 184.
[89] *cf. Bradford Old Bank* v. *Sutcliffe, post*, p. 314.

The amendment to the memorandum in *Ford & Carter*, at the instance of the bank, was an alteration in the terms of the contract which did not have the effect that the parties—including the group companies—thought it would have: the case is a dramatic example of the danger of meeting a changed situation by altering existing documentation instead of the more troublesome creation of new documents. Even simple alterations can have unexpected effects. In *Westminster Bank Ltd.* v. *Sassoon*[90] the defendant wanted to limit her liability to a period of a year, and the words "This guarantee will expire on June 30, 1925" were added to the guarantee. The account was broken on that date, but when demand was made on the guarantor some three months later she claimed that she was not liable after June 30. The bank argued that the words merely restricted her liability to advances made before June 30, and the Court of appeal accepted that argument, but the case has its obvious lesson.

Bradford Old Bank v. Sutcliffe

[1918] 2 K.B. 833

Demand under a guarantee

Facts

The defendant, Frank Sutcliffe, and his brother Albert, directors of Samuel Sutcliffe & Co. Ltd., in 1894 gave a joint and several guarantee as security for the company's borrowings from its bankers. In August 1898 the defendant became insane and the bank received formal notice of this fact in December 1899. The company's two accounts continued as before. In 1912 the bank demanded payment of the company's indebtedness, and enforced the debentures held as part security; and in 1915 the present action was commenced against the committee in lunacy of Frank Sutcliffe. The defendants contended, *inter alia*, that the claim was now barred by the Statute of Limitations. When in the court of first instance the decision went against them they appealed.

Decision

The Court of Appeal dismissed the appeal. On the present point Pickford L.J. said:

[90] (1927) 5 L.D.B. 19.

But another answer was given by the plaintiffs—*i.e.* that the cause of action did not accrue until demand by them and that no demand had been made until the realisation of the debentures in 1912, less than six years before the beginning of the action. This seems to depend upon the construction of the document.... It was argued on behalf of the defendant that the words "on demand" should be neglected because the money was due, and therefore a demand was unnecessary and added nothing to the liability. This proposition is true in the case of what has been called a direct liability—for example, for money lent. There the liability exists as soon as the loan is made, and a promise to pay on demand adds nothing to it, as in the case of a promissory note for the amount payable on demand, and the words "on demand" may be neglected. It has, however, been held long ago that this doctrine does not apply to what has been called a collateral promise or collateral debt, and I think that a promise by a surety to pay the original debt is such a collateral promise or creates a collateral debt.

The only question, therefore, is whether on the construction of the guarantee the parties meant the words "on demand" to mean what they say. I cannot doubt that they did.[91]

Notes

This decision may be compared with that in *Lloyds Bank Ltd.* v. *Margolis*,[92] which turned on demand under a mortgage.

In an earlier case, *Parr's Banking Company Ltd.* v. *Yates*[93] it was held, also by the Court of Appeal, that in a case of a guarantee that had no demand clause, in the words of Vaughan Williams L.J. "the right of action on each item of the account arose as soon as that item became due and was not paid, and the statute ran from that date in each case." The decision was criticised at the time,[94] and it may be that in similar circumstances today the matter would be viewed differently[95]; but in practice a demand clause is of course included in all bank guarantee forms.

The breaking of the account, which was in question in *Westminster Bank Ltd.* v. *Cond*,[96] was not discussed in the Court of Appeal in the present case, although one of the defences, that credits to the current account after the notice of lunacy should be considered to have paid off the indebtedness on the loan account, raised a cognate point. The court rejected the argument, Pickford L.J. saying, "The facts clearly show that

[91] At p. 840.
[92] *Post*, p. 321.
[93] [1898] 2 Q.B. 460.
[94] *cf.* Sir John Paget's comment at 1 L.D.B. 278.
[95] *cf. post*, p. 323.
[96] *Ante*, pp. 152, 293.

the accounts must be kept distinct. . . . If it were otherwise the company would be extremely hampered in its business, for it could never safely draw on the current account so long as the credit balance did not exceed the amount due on the loan account. The effect of this arrangement is that payments to the credit of the current account are appropriated to that account and cannot be taken in reduction of the loan account."[97]

In *Thomas* v. *Nottingham Football Club*[98] the plaintiff had guaranteed the club's overdraft with Lloyds Bank. In 1967 he gave notice to the bank to determine the guarantee, and thereafter he called upon the club to free him from his liability by paying off the advance guaranteed. Under the terms of the guarantee his liability was to arise when demand was made, and here the bank had made no demand, so the club argued that he was not entitled to the declaration he sought—that he had a right in equity to require the club to free him from his liability by paying off the overdraft. But Goff J. held that he was so entitled "it being quite unreasonable" (in the words of a judgment of 1683) "that a man should always have such a cloud hang over him."

Re Sherry, London & County Banking Company v. Terry

(1884) 25 Ch. 692

The death of the guarantor

Facts

John Sherry, who died in 1880, had guaranteed the account of his son-in-law, Edward Terry, with the Sandwich branch of the plaintiff bank. When they received notice of the guarantor's death, the bank ruled off Terry's account, then overdrawn £677 17s. 2d., and opened a new one, through which Terry's later transactions passed. In 1881 Terry filed a liquidation petition, and the bank sought to recover against the estate of Sherry. It was contended by the executors that breaking the account was ineffective, and that the guarantee for "all moneys which shall at any time be due" covered the whole account; but, the guarantee terminating at death, fresh advances could not be

---

[97] The current account was not in fact broken, and it was held in the lower court and not disputed on appeal that the small overdraft at the date of notice of lunacy was, by the rule in *Clayton's* case, paid off by the subsequent credits to the account.

[98] [1972] Ch. 596; 9 L.D.B. 245.

covered by it, and payments into the account, under the rule in *Clayton's* case,[99] went in reduction of the overdraft. The bank did not dispute the termination of the guarantee, but claimed that the appropriation of payments effected by the breaking of the account was a bar to the operation of the rule in *Clayton's* case.

Decision

The Court of Appeal found for the bank. In his judgment, the Earl of Selborne L.C. said:

Then, is there an implied contract [to appropriate payments received subsequently to the termination of the guarantee towards the secured or guaranteed debt]? A surety is undoubtedly and not unjustly the object of some favour both at law and in equity, and I do not know that the rules of law and equity differ on the subject. It is an equity which enters into our system of law, that a man who makes himself liable for another person's debt is not to be prejudiced by any dealings without his consent between the secured creditor and the principal debtor. If, therefore, it could be shewn that what has been done here was done without the consent of the surety in prejudice of an implied contract in his favour, I quite agree that he ought not to suffer from it. But there being no express contract, on what ground is to be said that there is an implied contract? I am unable to find any such contract, unless we are to hold that the mere fact of suretyship takes away from the principal debtor and the creditor those powers which they would otherwise have of appropriating payments which are not subject to any particular contract with the surety.[1]

Notes

It cannot be said with any certainty whether a guarantee is in fact determined by the death of the guarantor, but it is generally assumed that notice of the death operates as notice of determination[2] and it is for this reason that the decision in *Re Sherry* is important to the banker; had the court decided otherwise, and ruled that the breaking of the account was ineffective, he would not be able to continue business with his customer without the danger of losing the benefit of the guarantee as payments into the account were set off against the indebtedness at the date of death.

It must be noted, however, that there was no argument in *Re Sherry* on the question of the termination of the guarantee, and

---

[99] *Ante.* p. 150.
[1] At pp. 703–704.
[2] *cf.* Penn, Shea & Arora, *op. cit.* I 20.39. and Paget, *op. cit.* p. 511 for discussion of the point.

all three judgments were therefore based on the assumption that
it had in fact terminated. It had been suggested, for the
executors, that there was no difference between breaking an
account during the guarantor's lifetime so as to deprive him of
the benefit of subsequent payments in, and breaking it upon his
death. The court distinguished the two on the assumption that
the guarantee was terminated by the death, and so, in the
unlikely event of its ever being decided that there is no such
determination, the executors' suggestion might be made again.

In practice, of course, the point can be covered in the bank's
guarantee forms by a provision that the guarantee shall be a
continuing one notwithstanding the death of the guarantor. If
the guarantee binds the personal representatives of the deceased
guarantor by a clause calling for notice of determination, the
account of the borrower can be continued unbroken until the
expiration of such notice, and it would appear that the estate
will be liable for further advances until notice is given. It is the
practice of banks to notify the personal representatives of the
liability.

In *Bradford Old Bank Ltd.* v. *Sutcliffe,*[3] it was held by
Lawrence J., and not disputed on appeal, that notice of the
lunacy of a guarantor determines the guarantee.

It may be added that, when the guarantee is joint and several,
neither the death[4] nor the mental disorder[5] of one surety ends
the continuing liability of his co-sureties. And in *Egbert* v.
National Crown Bank[6] it was held that a joint and several
guarantee which was to continue "until the undersigned . . . shall
have given the bank notice in writing to make no further
advances . . . " remained in force against all the guarantors until
each and all of them, or their respective executors or
administrators gave notice to determine it. It was not
determined by notice by one of the guarantors alone; Lord
Dunedin said that had the intention been that notice by one
guarantor should determine the guarantee, "nothing would have
been easier than to express such an intention by such words as
'all or any of the undersigned.' "

In the unusual circumstances of *Dow Banking Corporation* v.
Bank Mellatt[7] Lloyd J. held that demand on the guarantor was

---

[3] *Ante,* p. 314. At 3 L.D.B. 195, the case is discussed wrongly as one concerning
the lunacy of the principal debtor.
[4] *Beckett* v. *Addyman* (1882) 9 Q.B.D. 783.
[5] *Bradford Old Bank Ltd.* v. *Sutcliffe, supra.*
[6] [1918] A.C. 903.
[7] *The Financial Times,* January 12, 1983.

invalid in that no effective prior demand had been made on the borrower, and the demand on the guarantor did not make clear what sum the guarantor was called upon to pay. It was held further that notice of default by the borrower which is given to the guarantor and not to the borrower does not entitle the lender to call in the advance.

MORTGAGES

Barclays Bank Ltd. v. Beck

[1952] 2 Q.B. 47

The nature of a bank's mortgage

Facts

The defendants were overdrawn with the plaintiff bank, and in 1949 executed in the bank's favour a charge on their farm under the Agricultural Credits Act 1928. Clause 1 of the charge read:

The farmer hereby covenants with Barclays Bank Limited (hereinafter called "the bank") that the farmer will on demand or upon the death of the farmer without demand pay to the bank the balance of all moneys now or hereafter owing by the farmer under any account current... and all other moneys and liabilities now or hereafter due or to become due from the farmer to the bank in respect of any advance made or to be made by the bank to the farmer or upon any account or in any manner whatever....

In 1950 the bank appointed a receiver under the charge, and the defendants, who were anxious to avoid a forced sale of their property, arranged to sell privately. Their solicitors confirmed to the bank that they had been instructed to authorise the purchaser to pay direct to the bank the sum of £4,000, part of the purchase price, against the bank's discharge of their charge. This sum was duly paid, but as a result of charges made by the receiver and other expenses there remained an outstanding overdraft of nearly £600, and it was for this sum that the present action was brought.

The defendants argued that where a higher security, such as a bond, is given for a simple contract debt, the two are merged so that only the higher security is enforceable. On this argument the debt on the banker/customer relationship of the overdraft was merged in the covenant in the charge, and, the latter having been enforced, the bank had lost its right to sue on the overdraft.

Decision

The Court of Appeal upheld the finding of Barry J. in favour of the bank. In his judgment Denning L.J. said (at p. 54):

... a future debt on a running account is a debt created by parol, and it remains a simple contract debt, even though the customer has previously given a charge to secure it, which includes a covenant under seal. The future debt on running account is not created under the deed. It may be that it would never have been created but for the deed, but that is a different thing. It only means that the deed is collateral security for its repayment.

And Somervell L.J. said (at p. 52):

The question here, as it seems to me, is whether the ordinary contractual position as between banker and customer, which would be usual in respect of advances apart from this clause, is merged in and destroyed by being replaced by what appears in clause 1. In my opinion that clause, so far from doing that, indicates that the position is the contrary.

Notes[8]

The decision here was followed by Upjohn J. in *Lloyds Bank Ltd.* v. *Margolis and Others*,[9] though in that case the point at issue was decided on other grounds, the fact that the security was collateral being a subsidiary point.

The fact that the charge in the *Beck* case was executed under the Agricultural Credits Act does not affect the generality of the decision; the challenge might have been made in respect of an ordinary bank charge, and the decision would have equally applied. That decision confirms the long-standing practice of the banks; it is perhaps surprising that no borrower seems to have challenged a bank on the same grounds before.

The merging of a simple contract debt into a specialty debt is seen when a debt is sued for and, judgment being given, the debt is merged in the judgment. Somervell L.J. gave the further example of a creditor giving time for payment of an existing debt, and taking a bond for it.

---

[8] See Penn Shea & Arora *op. cit.* I 24 and Reeday, *op. cit.*, Chap. 6 for the problems of bankers lending against land as security.

[9] *Post*, p. 321.

There, again, it is plain that the whole basis of that is that it is in substitution for the simple contract debt. It would make nonsense of the transaction if, having entered into that arrangement...the man the next day could sue upon the simple contract debt.[10]

But, as Denning L.J. put it, merger depends on the intention of the parties as expressed in the documents they have signed, and bank forms of charge are clear enough on the point at issue.

It is to be noted that in banking practice the word "collateral" is more often used of third-party security than in the sense in which Denning L.J. used it here.[11]

The question whether a bank's standard form of mortgage covers contingent liabilities as well as the principal debt was answered in *Re Rudd & Son Ltd.*; *Re Fosters and Rudd Ltd.*[12] where the two companies, as a partnership, had charged property to the Midland Bank. When they went into liquidation, and in due course the overdraft was repaid, the bank refused to vacate the mortgages as there were contingent liabilities on counter-indemnities for performance bonds to local authorities. It was held at first instance that no liability to the bank was covered by the mortgages after the liquidator had called on the bank to vacate them. But the Court of Appeal allowed the bank's appeal. The mortgage cover included "all moneys for which the firm...shall be liable to the bank as surety...," and a surety's liability was contingent until called upon. It did not make commercial sense that the mortgage covered contingent liabilities once they were called but not otherwise.

Lloyds Bank Ltd. v. Margolis and Others

[1954] 1 W.L.R. 644

Demand under a mortgage

Facts

In 1936 the plaintiff bank took a mortgage on Winterslow Farm to secure the overdraft of George Lyster, its owner, the third defendant in this action. On December 19, 1938, when their customer was in process of selling the farm, the bank made demand upon him. In the years that followed the farm was sold

---

[10] At p. 51.
[11] As to the various meanings of "collateral" see Holden, *Securities for Bankers' Advances*, (6th ed.), pp. 353 *et seq.*.
[12] *The Times*, January 22, 1986.

to the first defendant, and subsequently by him to Reginald King, the second defendant, in both cases subject to the bank's mortgage; and on November 29, 1950, the bank issued a summons claiming to enforce their mortgage. The defendants claimed that the charge was no longer enforceable, being barred by the Limitation Act 1939; no advances had been made after October 1938, more than 12 years before the date of the summons.

Decision

Upjohn J. held that time began to run from the date of the demand, not from the dates of the various advances, so that the bank were just within the statutory 12 years. In his judgment he said (at p. 649):

> ... where there is the relationship of banker and customer and the banker permits his customer to overdraw on the terms of entering into a legal charge which provides that the money which is then due or is thereafter to become due is to be paid "on demand," that means what it says. As between the customer and the banker, who are dealing on a running account, it seems to me impossible to assume that the bank were to be entitled to sue on the deed on the very day after it was executed without making a demand and giving the customer a reasonable time to pay. It is indeed a nearly correlative case to that decided in *Joachimson* v. *Swiss Bank Corporation*[13] where the headnote was this—
>
> "Where money is standing to the credit of a customer on current account with a banker, in the absence of a special agreement, a demand by the customer is a necessary ingredient in the cause of action against the banker for money lent."
>
> In this case the agreement has provided quite clearly what is to be done before the bank can sue. They must demand the money.

Notes

This decision may be compared with that in *Bradford Old Bank Ltd.* v. *Sutcliffe*,[14] which turned on demand under a guarantee.

Under the Limitation Act 1980 time runs from the date at which a right of action is acquired, and the question here was whether the bank had a right of action before they made demand; if they had, then they would have lost it by the time the summons was issued. The case here was stronger in their

---

[13] *Ante*, p. 1.
[14] *Ante*, p. 314.

favour than it was in the *Joachimson* case, for here, as Upjohn J. remarked, the agreement specified demand; in the current account with a credit balance it needed the *Joachimson* decision to establish the need for demand.

The demand clause is usually included in standard bank forms of charge, so that it is a largely academic question whether by analogy with *Joachimson* it might not now be held that demand by the bank is necessary in the absence of such a clause.[15] The words of Upjohn J., quoted above, "it seems to me impossible to assume that the bank were to be entitled to sue on the deed...without making a demand," would be apt to cover such a situation, and would indeed be widely accepted as the justice of the matter.

In *Barclays Bank Ltd.* v. *Kiley*[16] the borrowing customer died and no personal representatives were appointed. The bank purported to make demand upon the customer six months after his death, and thereafter appointed a receiver of the rents of the property charged. The present action was on an originating summons by the bank, asking for delivery of the property, and Pennycuick J. held, *inter alia*, that the demand was good, nothing in the form of charge restricting the conditions of demand to the borrower's lifetime.

The importance of proper demand before the exercise of any rights of sale or foreclosure is emphasised by the decision in *Hunter* v. *Hunter and Others*,[17] where demand properly made was held by the House of Lords to have been waived by the taking of further security and the resumption for a year of normal working on the account. Viscount Hailsham L.C. said:

I have felt some regret in reaching this conclusion. I have no doubt that the bank acted in perfect good faith, and that the plaintiff had full notice of what they were doing; and if he had objected at the time, the bank would undoubtedly have served a formal demand which he could not have met. But the right of sale is a very drastic remedy, and it is essential for the due protection of borrowers that the conditions of its exercise should be strictly complied with.[18]

---

[15] In so far as the banks are now lending for terms of years, care is needed to reconcile a covenant to repay on demand with the provisions of the term loan.

[16] [1961] 1 W.L.R. 1050.

[17] [1936] A.C. 222.

[18] At p. 247.

Cuckmere Brick Co. Ltd. v. Mutual Finance Ltd.

[1971] Ch. 949

Western Bank Ltd. v. Schindler

[1976] 2 All E.R. 393

The mortgagee's rights, and restrictions upon them

Facts of Cuckmere Brick Co. Ltd. v. Mutual Finance Ltd.

The plaintiffs borrowed £50,000 from the defendants against the mortgage of a site in Maidstone with planning permission for 100 flats. Later, with the agreement of the defendants, they obtained permission for 33 houses instead. In the event no building was put in hand for five years, and the defendants called in the advance and advertised the site for sale.

The estate agents included in the advertisement mention of the planning permission for houses, but omitted the permission for flats. The plaintiffs protested that the permission for flats should have been included, but the sale went ahead, realising £44,000. In this action the plaintiffs claimed that more would have been realised if the particulars had included the permission for flats. The defendants denied liability, and counter-claimed for the balance of the advance.

Decision

The Court of Appeal held unanimously that a mortgagee is not a trustee of the power of sale for the mortgagor, and where there is a conflict of interests he is entitled to give preference to his own over those of a mortgagor. But in exercising the power of sale he is under a duty to take reasonable care to obtain the true value of the property. The court held further, by a majority, that the defendants here had been negligent. Salmon L.J. said:

> I accordingly conclude, both on principle and authority, that a mortgagee in exercising his power of sale does owe a duty to take reasonable precaution to obtain the true market value of the mortgaged property at the date on which he decides to sell it. No doubt in deciding whether he has fallen short of that duty, the facts must be looked at broadly, and he will not be adjudged to be in default unless he is plainly on the wrong side of the line.[19]

---

[19] At pp. 968–969. *cf.* Sched. 4, 1(1) of the Building Societies Act 1986, requiring the exercise of reasonable care to ensure that the price obtained for a mortgaged property is the best that can be reasonably obtained.

Facts of Western Bank Ltd. v. Schindler

The defendant had mortgaged his house on terms that no interest was payable until the loan became repayable in 10 years' time. By a separate agreement he also charged a life policy as collateral security. When he allowed the policy to lapse the bank claimed possession of the property, although there had been no breach of the mortgage agreement, and there could therefore be no exercise of the power of sale. The defendant argued that an implied term must be read into the mortgage that the bank could not exercise its right to possession in the absence of default in the terms of the mortgage.

Decision

The Court of Appeal rejected the defendant's argument, and found for the plaintiff. Buckley L.J. said:

A legal mortgagee's right to possession is a common law right which is an incident of his estate in the land. It should not, in my opinion, be lightly treated as abrogated or restricted. Although it is perhaps most commonly exercised as a preliminary step to an exercise of the mortgagee's power of sale, so that the sale may be made with vacant possession, this is not its only value to the mortgagee. The mortgagee may wish to protect his property: see *ex parte Wickens*.[20] If, for instance, the mortgagor were to vacate the property, the mortgagee might wish to take possession to protect the place from vandalism. He might wish to take possession for the purpose of carrying out repairs, or to prevent waste. Where the contractual date for repayment is so unusually long delayed as it was in this case, a power of this nature to protect his security might well be regarded as of particular value to the mortgagee.[21]

Notes

In the first case Salmon L.J., while setting out clearly the duty of the mortgagee in exercising his power of sale, set out equally clearly the wide extent of that power.[22] Once it has accrued the mortgagee can exercise it when he likes—"it matters not that the moment may be unpropitious and that by waiting a higher price could be obtained." He can properly accept the best bid at even a poorly-attended auction at which the bidding is

---

[20] [1898] 1 Q.B. 543.
[21] At p. 396.
[22] *cf. Barclays Bank plc* v. *Tennet* (unreported) [1985] C.A.T. 84/242, where, applying *Samuel Keller (Holdings)* v. *Martins Bank Ltd.* (1970) 114 S.J. 951; 9 L.D.B. 169, it was held that the mortgagee's power of sale cannot be defeated or postponed by a counter-claim (in that case that the bank's conduct had caused the failure of the mortgagor's business) for unliquidated damages.

exceptionally low. "Providing none of those adverse factors is due to any fault of the mortgagee, he can do as he likes."[23] But absence of fault, on which the mortgagee's freedom of actions depends in all aspects of the sale, may be difficult to establish: "the facts must be looked at broadly."[24]

In *Bank of Cyprus (London) Ltd.* v. *Gill*,[25] where the bank claimed the balance of indebtedness after their sale of the property lodged as security, the defendant counter-claimed, alleging that the bank had sold at less than the true value. But the Court of Appeal upheld Lloyd J.'s finding for the bank. The mortgagee's duty to get the best possible price did not require that they should wait for a depressed market to rise. The bank had taken independent advice, and the mortgagor had been given the opportunity to sell by his own efforts.

The duty of the mortgagee to seek to obtain the true market value of the property when exercising his power of sale was considered by the Privy Council in *Tse Kwong Lam* v. *Wong Chit Sen*[26] where the mortgaged property was sold by auction, the only bid received being that of the mortgagee's wife, for the reserve price. The mortgagor's claim that the sale had been improper, and the mortgagee's counter-claim, came in due course to the Privy Council, and Lord Templeman said that while a sale at auction does not itself show that the true market value has not been obtained, here the mortgagee had not consulted estate agents, only 15 days had been allowed between the first advertisement and the sale, and the reserve price had been fixed by the mortgagee, himself a property investor who, unlike an independent bidder, knew all about the property. The mortgagee argued that a mortgagee may sell to a company in which he is interested at a price fixed by himself, if the property is advertised and sold by auction. But:

a decision to this effect would expose borrowers to greater perils than those to which they are now exposed as a result of decisions which enable a mortgagee to choose the date of the execution of his power.

However, the borrower had been guilty of inexcusable delay

---

[23] *cf.* the position of the receiver under a debenture, *ante*, p. 305.
[24] *cf. Standard Chartered Bank Ltd.* v. *Walker, ante*, p. 304, where the principle of the *Cuckmere Brick* case was extended to protect guarantors. But in *Parker-Tweedale* v. *Dunbar Bank plc The Times*, December 29, 1989 no such extension was allowed to protect a third party with a beneficial interest in the mortgaged property.
[25] [1980] 2 Lloyd's Rep. 51 (at first instance).
[26] [1983] 1 W.L.R. 1394.

in his counter-claim, so achieving the position that if the property decreased in value he could either abandon his action or seek damages, while if it increased in value he could pursue his claim to set the sale aside. So he was entitled only to the alternative remedy of damages.

The mortgagee's right to possession is independent of the power of sale, but section 36 of the Administration of Justice Act 1970 gave the court discretion to suspend an order for possession if it appears that the mortgagor can within a reasonable time make good his default. The defendant in the *Western Bank* case raised a further defence under the section, claiming that read strictly it makes the discretion dependent on default by the mortgagor, with the absurd result that a mortgagor not in default could not be so protected. As Parliament could not have intended this result, the defendant argued that the effect of the section must be to exclude altogether, except in the case of default, the common law right of possession. But Scarman and Buckley L.JJ. held that the section must be treated as giving the discretion whatever the grounds on which possession is sought, and Goff L.J., preferring the literal reading (which is supported by section 8 of the Administration of Justice Act 1973), held that on this reading the section was irrelevant in the present case, where there had been no default.[27]

The strict wording of the mortgage was unsuccessfully invoked in *Barclays Bank Ltd.* v. *Parry*,[28] where the defendant had guaranteed the accounts of two companies, supported by a mortgage on her house. When the bank claimed possession under the mortgage, she argued that the first covenant of the mortgage deed referred to her account with the bank, and as she had no such account, the second covenant, which depended on the first, could not apply. The Court of Appeal rejected the argument: the guarantee and the mortgage must be seen together. Eveleigh L.J. said:

> To put a construction on the [mortgage] as contended for by the appellant would make that document serve no purpose at all.... In those circumstances I regard it as permissible to ignore a word in the mortgage if that word would make the document wholly inapplicable to the transaction which was being undertaken.

---

[27] *cf.* as to the application of s.8 of the 1973 Act, *Royal Trust Company of Canada* v. *Markham* [1975] 1 W.L.R. 1416; 9 L.D.B. 399; *Centrax Trustees Ltd.* v. *Ross* [1979] 2 All E.R. 952; *Habib Bank Ltd.* v. *Tailor* [1982] 1 W.L.R. 1218; and *Bank of Scotland* v. *Grimes* [1985] Q.B. 1179.

[28] (Unreported) (1980) C.L.Y. 260.

A challenge to the mortgagee's rights on the grounds of undue influence was successfully resisted in *Chetwynd-Talbot* v. *Midland Bank Ltd.*[29] The plaintiff was joint owner with her husband of the matrimonial home, which was charged to secure an advance to the husband and his business partner. When the wife signed the form of charge the bank had wanted to arrange for a local solicitor to advise her as to its effect, but no solicitor being then available she said that she was happy to accept the bank's explanation. But when eventually the bank called in the advance and sought to realise the security she claimed that in signing she had been under the undue influence of her husband and the bank.

McCullogh J., after analysing the nature of undue influence, rejected the claim. Every case had to be considered individually; here the plaintiff was an intelligent woman with some business experience, who was familiar with the partnership's affairs, and in his view she knew the nature of a mortgage. She had not sought the bank's advice, and there was no special relationship between the bank and herself, nor was there any relevant special relationship between her and her husband. Although the bank had not expressly stated that the matrimonial home might be sold if the bank enforced their security, their explanation had been accurate and adequate.[30]

Williams & Glyn's Bank Ltd. v. Boland and Another;

Williams & Glyn's Bank Ltd. v. Brown

[1980] 2 All E.R. 408

The rights of an occupier against the mortgagee

Facts

Each case concerned the mortgage to the bank of a property which was the matrimonial home of the defendants. In each case the wife had contributed to the purchase of the property or the paying off of the mortgage on it; each house was registered land, registered in the sole name of the husband. The husbands had mortgaged the houses to the bank, and on default being made the bank obtained orders for possession in the High Court and the county court respectively. The Court of Appeal

---

[29] (1982) 102 J.I.B. p. 214.
[30] *cf. Lloyds Bank Ltd.* v. *Suvale Properties Ltd.*, *ante*, pp. 232, 233; *Bank of Montreal* v. *Stuart and Another*, *ante*, p. 302.

discharged the orders for possession on the grounds that the wives, being in actual occupation of the properties, had an overriding interest within section 70(1)(*g*) of the Land Registration Act 1925, to which the bank's interest was subject, and were entitled to remain in possession as against the bank. The bank appealed, arguing that the wives' interests were minor interests within section 3 of the Act, and further that they were not persons in actual occupation within the meaning of section 70(1)(*g*).

Section 3(xvi) defines "overriding interests" as "all. . . the interests. . . not entered on the register but subject to which registered interests are by the Act to take effect."

Section 70(1)(*g*) provides that "the rights of every person in actual occupation of the land" are overriding interests "save where enquiry is made of such person and the rights are not disclosed."

Decision

The House of Lords affirmed the decision of the Court of Appeal. The equitable interest of the wives under a trust for sale was a minor interest in itself, but when protected by actual occupation was also capable of being an overriding interest. As to "actual occupation" their Lordships rejected the bank's arguments (a) that the mortgagor's occupation excluded the possibility of occupation by others; (b) that the wives' occupation was a mere shadow of the husband's; and (c) that "occupation" in section 70 must be apparently inconsistent with that of the mortgagor, which would exclude the wife of a husband mortgagor whose apparent occupation would be accounted for by his.

On the wives' interests as co-owners Lord Wilberforce said:

It is clear, at least, that the interests of the co-owners under the statutory trusts are minor interests: this fits with the definition in section 3(xv). But I can see no reason why, if these interests or that of any one of them, are or is protected by "actual occupation" they should remain merely as "minor interests." On the contrary, I see every reason why, in that event, they should acquire the status of overriding interests. And moreover, I find it easy to accept that they satisfy the opening, and governing, words of section 70, namely, interests susbsisting in reference to the land. As Lord Denning M.R. points out, to describe the interests of spouses in a house jointly bought to be lived in as the matrimonial home as merely an interest in the proceeds of sale. . . is just a little unreal.[30a]

[30a] At pp. 414–415.

Lord Scarman said:

The courts may not . . . put aside as irrelevant the undoubted fact that if the two wives succeed the protection of the beneficial interest which English law now recognises that a married woman has in the matrimonial home will be strengthened, whereas if they lose this interest can be weakened, and even destroyed by an unscrupulous husband. Nor must the courts flinch when assailed by arguments to the effect that the protection of her interest will create difficulties in banking or conveyancing practice. The difficulties are, I believe, exaggerated; but bankers, and solicitors, exist to provide the service which the public needs. They can, as they have successfully done in the past, adjust their practice, if it be socially required.[30b]

Notes

This is the most important decision of recent years on mortgages, remarkable not least for the fact that it was merely the application of legislation more than half a century old. The issue in the case was the rights of the two wives in the matrimonial home, and those rights were clearly central to the decision. But the decision was much wider ranging than the problems of the matrimonial home. At the start of his judgment Lord Wilberforce said:

Although this statement of the issue uses the words "spouse," "husband and wife," "matrimonial home," the appeals do not, in my understanding, involve any question of matrimonial law, or of the rights of married women or of women as such. Exactly the same issue could arise if the roles of husband and wife were reversed, or if the persons interested in the house were not married to each other. The solution must be derived from a consideration in the light of current social conditions of the Land Registration Act 1925 and other property statutes.[30c]

In his judgment in the High Court Templeman J., rejecting the wife's case on section 70, had said that the consequences of accepting it must be "wide and almost catastrophic," but the Court of Appeal did not see them as so formidable. Lord Scarman's view was quoted above; Lord Wilberforce said that "what is involved is a departure from an easy-going practice of dispensing with enquiries as to occupation beyond that of the vendor and accepting the risks of doing so."

Bankers were not able to regard the matter in this relaxed manner, seeing as they did the possibility of the ruling being applied not merely to Lord Wilberforce's "persons not married

[30b] At p. 416.   [30c] At p. 411.

to each other," (a common example would be the elderly parent pooling resources with a married son or daughter to share a larger house) but also to individuals or companies with competing interests in commercial property. And when the Law Commission examined in considerable detail the implications of the decision they did not see adjustment of the practice of bankers and solicitors as adequate to meet the practical difficulties. Their Report[31] suggested that while the decision improves the protection of co-owners, that protection is far from complete, while the difficulties of house purchasers are unacceptable. Their principal recommendation was that the Matrimonial Homes (Co-ownership) Bill, which they had drafted earlier, should be extended to include a registration requirement for all co-owners, whereby "an equitable co-ownership interest... is enforceable against a purchaser or lender if, but only if, the interest is registered in the appropriate manner."

But pending legislation, the pressure for which appears to have slackened as lenders have come to terms with the new conditions, the banks have made what "adjustments" they have considered necessary and practical. It is to be noted that the decision protects the existing *rights* of occupiers: it is not a blanket protection to all occupiers, even when they are spouses in the matrimonial homes. In *National Provincial Bank Ltd.* v. *Ainsworth*[32] the Court of Appeal's decision in favour of the deserted wife—the "deserted wife's equity"—was that she had an overriding interest under section 70. But she had made no contribution to the home on which a right could be founded, and the House of Lords overruled the Court of Appeal, to what has now proved to be the temporary relief of the banks.

After *Ainsworth* Parliament restored part of the wife's protection which the Court of Appeal had tried to provide. Under the Matrimonial Homes Act 1967 the wife (or, as must always be remembered, the husband) who lacks a legal title to the house is given a statutory right of occupation, but this binds a purchaser or mortgagee only if it has been registered, while it is expressly *not* an overriding interest.

It is also to be noted that *Boland* covers only registered land: in the case of unregistered land an equitable interest can affect a purchaser or mortgagee only if he has actual or constructive notice of it. But bankers can take only partial comfort from this

---

[31] Property Law; the implications of *Williams & Glyn's Bank Ltd.* v. *Boland*, Cmnd. 8636.

[32] [1965] A.C. 1175.

fact: where the house is unregistered land they may not be affected by the occupation of relatives or friends of the legal owner, but it seems likely that in the more common case concerning the matrimonial home the bank would now be held to have had notice because they knew, or ought to have known, that the wife was living in the house.

In the many cases on *Boland* many of the implications of the decision have been worked out.[33] We may here consider two cases that have made their way to the House of Lords: *Winkworth* v. *Edward Baron Development Co. Ltd. and Others*[34] and *City of London Building Society* v. *Flegg and Others*.[35] In the first, a company controlled by Mr. and Mrs. Wing bought for £70,000 the couple's matrimonial home. Later their former home was sold and after charges on the property were paid, a balance of £8,600 was paid into the company's account, where it reduced the company's overdraft. Later the house was mortgaged to the plaintiff, the charge appearing to have been signed by the Wings, but in fact it was signed only by Mr. Wing, who forged his wife's signature. The company went into liquidation, and the plaintiff sought possession of the house, which was now occupied only by Mrs. Wing. The Court of Appeal held, by a majority, that Mrs. Wing had an equitable interest in the property, the payment of £8,600 being referable to the acquisition of the property, but the House of Lords overruled them: there was no connection between the payment for the property and the incurring of the overdraft, while since both the Wings breached their duty to the company as directors and Mrs. Wing had not discovered her powers as a director, equity would not allow the company to hold part of its property in trust for Mrs. Wing, to the detriment of its creditors.

In the second case, too, the House of Lords overruled the Court of Appeal to give judgment for the building society. The case concerned a property, Bleak House, bought with the funds provided by the Fleggs and their daughter and son-in-law, the latter obtaining a building society loan to raise their share of its purchase price, and with this in view the house was transferred

---

[33] *cf.* the discussion in 10 L.D.B. 256 where, as well as the Lords cases here noted, *Bristol and West Building Society* v. *Henning* [1985] 1 W.L.R. 778, *Paddington Building Society* v. *Mendelsohn* (1985) 50 P. & C.R. 244, *Midland Bank Ltd.* v. *Dobson* [1986] 1 F.L.R. 171, *Grant* v. *Edwards* [1987] 1 All E.R. 426, and *Kingsnorth Trust Ltd.* v. *Tizard* [1986] 2 All E.R. 54 are considered.

[34] [1987] 1 All E.R. 114.

[35] [1987] 3 All E.R. 435.

to the daughter and son-in-law, on trust for sale for themselves and the parents. When they defaulted the building society sought possession, and the question in dispute was whether the parents' interest as occupiers was prevented by the overreaching provisions of the Law of Property Act 1925 from becoming an overriding interest under section 70. The Court of Appeal held that *Boland* was not restricted to cases where there was only one registered proprietor. But the House of Lords held otherwise: the building society loan, being an advance to two trustees overreached the Fleggs' interest, which transferred to the capital money in the hands of the children.

The fact that in these two cases the House of Lords differed from the Court of Appeal may fairly be seen as reflecting some of the considerable difficulties the banks experience in the *Boland* area.

As was remarked above, the *Boland* decision is of much wider significance than the matrimonial home, but while legislation is awaited it must considerably enlarge the mortgagees' exposure, with which they have long been familiar, to challenge in matrimonial cases. The challenge can come in a variety of forms.[36] In *Whittingham* v. *Whittingham, National Westminster Bank Ltd. intervening*[37] the wife was living in a house, not the matrimonial home, of which the husband was the legal owner. In divorce proceedings she applied under section 24 of the Matrimonial Causes Act 1973 for a transfer of property, but she did not register a pending land action. The husband executed a legal charge to the bank, and the wife sought to have the charge avoided under section 37 of the Act, arguing that only existing interests were registrable, and her action was not an existing interest. But the Court of Appeal held that claims for transfer of land were pending land actions registrable under the Act, and without registration her action did not bind the bank.[38]

Green v. *Green (Barclays Bank Ltd. third party)*[39] is another example of how a mortgagee can be indirectly at risk in matrimonial disputes. The husband and wife had sold land, part of the matrimonial home, to a company, which had thereafter charged it to the bank as security for an advance. The marriage

---

[36] *cf., e.g. Halifax Building Society* v. *Clark and Another*, [1973] Ch. 307; *Chetwynd-Talbot* v. *Midland Bank Ltd.*, *ante*, p. 328; and *First National Securities Ltd.* v. *Hegarty*, *post*, p. 337.

[37] [1978] 3 All E.R. 805; 10 L.D.B. 89.

[38] *cf. Backhouse* v. *Backhouse*, *ante*, p. 208.

[39] [1981] 1 All E.R. 97.

broke down, and after the divorce, the wife claimed financial relief against the husband. She had not received any part of the purchase price of the land, and she claimed to have the conveyance set aside under section 37, arguing further that if this claim succeeded against the husband, the court could direct the setting aside or the reduction of the charge. But Eastham J. rejected the claim on the grounds, *inter alia*, that if it succeeded the bank would be deprived of their defence under section 37, if they were themselves sued under the section, that the disposition was made for valuable consideration.

But in *Leeman* v. *Leeman*[40] where after the marriage had broken down the husband had mortgaged the house to the bank and the bank had entered into possession and arranged a sale, the wife obtained an injunction under section 37, restraining the husband from dealing with the proceeds until the outcome of the matrimonial proceedings. No injunction was made against the bank, Brandon L.J. remarking:

> Provided the bank has notice of the injunction against the husband, as it has by being present by its solicitor and counsel at the hearing of this appeal, it seems to me that the result will be the same.... It is unthinkable that an institution such as Barclays Bank would allow a husband to deal with a balance in his account.

The equity of exoneration makes relatively few appearances in the law reports. It was in question in *Re Pittoriou (a bankrupt)*[41] where the bankrupt and his wife had charged their jointly-owned house to the National Westminster Bank to secure the bankrupt's borrowing. The marriage broke up, the husband moving to live with another woman, and upon his bankruptcy the trustee sought the sale of the property. The question arose as to how, as between the trustee's share and the wife's share, the bank's secured indebtedness should be met.

Scott J. quoted *Halsbury's Laws* as to the equity of exoneration:

> If the property of a married woman is mortgaged or charged in order to raise money for the payment of her husband's debts, or otherwise for his benefit, it is presumed, in the absence of evidence showing an intention to the contrary, that she meant to charge her property merely by way of security, and in such case she is in the position of surety, and is entitled to be indemnified by the husband, and to throw the debt primarily on his estate to the exoneration of her own....

[40] (1979) C.L.Y. unreported, 124.
[41] [1985] 1 W.L.R. 58.

But he held that it was necessary to take the circumstances of each case into account (noting that the Victorian cases were of limited value as a guide in the changed circumstances of the present); and here payments from the account included payments for the benefit of the wife and family. But "payments made by the bankrupt purely for business purposes and, a fortiori, any payments made by him for the purposes of the second establishment it seems he was supporting" should be charged on his half-share of the property. There must be an inquiry as to the relative shares, and there should be no sale until the wife could judge whether she could make an offer to purchase the husband's interest, which she would be able to consider when the result of the inquiry was known.

Roberts Petroleum Ltd. v. Bernard Kenny Ltd.

[1983] 2 A.C. 192

Charging orders

Facts

The plaintiffs supplied petroleum products to the defendants, who owned two petrol stations and who in 1978 were in financial difficulties. In March 1979 the plaintiffs issued a writ against them claiming £74,000, and on March 23 obtained judgment, the district registrar on the same day imposing a charging order nisi on the defendants' land. On April 2 the defendants' shareholders resolved that the company should be placed in voluntary liquidation, and on April 4 the district registrar made the charging order absolute.

The defendants appealed and Bristow J. discharged the charging order; as the company was insolvent, paramount consideration must be given to obtaining equal treatment for all the company's creditors. The Court of Appeal reversed this decision: there must be some other factor present, such as a scheme of arrangement with some prospect of success, to give "sufficient cause" not to make the charging order absolute. The defendants appealed to the House of Lords.

Decision

The House of Lords allowed the appeal. Lord Brightman, remarking that the issue raised had not been before the court in any reported case, reviewed what authority there was, and the "formidable," but as he thought mistaken, argument of the plaintiffs based on section 325 of the Companies Act 1948, now replaced by section 183 of the Insolvency Act 1986. No discredit to either party was involved in the facts that the plaintiffs applied for the charging order in the hope of obtaining an advantage over the other unsecured creditors, and that the voluntary liquidation of the defendants was sought at short notice to deprive the plaintiffs of that advantage; each had every right to defend himself. But he concluded that Bristow J. had been correct:

> I reach this conclusion without any regret. First, it may help to avert an unseemly scramble by creditors to achieve priority at the last moment. Second, it establishes a clear working rule, and avoids the uncertainties of an inquiry whether or not a scheme of arrangement "has been set on foot and has a reasonable prospect of succeeding."[41a]

Notes

In order, as Cross L.J. put it in *Irani Finance* v. *Singh*,[42] "to make sure, by shifting the equitable interests away from the land and into the proceeds of sale, that a purchaser of land takes free from the equitable interests," the Law of Property Act 1925 provided that property held by two or more persons, whether as tenants in common (s.34) or joint tenants (s.36) is held on the statutory trusts for sale, and the equitable interest of each individual holder is in the proceeds of sale, not in the land itself.

As to charging orders, which, by section 35 of the Administration of Justice Act 1956, were to be granted only on interests in land, the position of mortgagees was improved by the Charging Orders Act 1979, which provided that a charging order may be made on, *inter alia*, "any interest held by the debtor beneficially ... (ii) under any trust." In *Irani Finance* v. *Singh*[43] a charging order on beneficial interests in the statutory trusts was refused, under section 35; but in *National Westminster Bank Ltd.* v. *Stockman*[44] Russell J. held that the 1979 Act removed the restriction of the 1956 Act.

Bankers, like other lenders against land, have an obvious interest in charging orders, and *Roberts Petroleum* is an example of a question arising in the circumstances of a normal commercial transaction. But a group of cases demonstrate the

[41a] At p. 213.
[42] [1970] 3 All E.R. 199.
[43] *Supra*.
[44] [1981] 1 W.L.R. 67.

frequency with which charging orders are involved in cases where houses are jointly owned by husband and wife. Thus in *Cedar Holdings Ltd.* v. *Green*,[45] where the wife's signature was forged on a charge on property jointly owned by husband and wife and the husband had charged his beneficial interest, the Court of Appeal held that the charge was ineffective: it was a charge on land, and could not extend to cover his interest in the proceeds of sale, which was not an interest in land. However, in *Boland*[46] Lord Wilberforce considered that *Cedar Holdings* was wrongly decided, and although the comment was strictly *obiter*, in *First National Securities* v. *Hegarty*,[47] Bingham J. at first instance thought it justified him in differing from the Court of Appeal's ruling in *Cedar Holdings*, and the Court of Appeal upheld his judgment.[48]

The decision of the House of Lords in *Roberts Petroleum* was applied in the *First National Securities* case, where the company had been prompt in seeking their remedy against the husband's share in the house, and had done so before the wife commenced divorce proceedings. But this decision was distinguished in *Harman* v. *Glencross*[49] where the wife had commenced divorce proceedings and served notice of severance of the joint tenancy before the judgment creditor obtained a charging order on the husband's interest. The Court of Appeal, varying the order at the request of the wife, said that hardship to either party had to be weighed. The judgment creditor here had not given evidence as to his means, but it would have been proper to consider potential hardship to him also had he so argued.

Harrold v. Plenty

[1901] 2 Ch. 314

Equitable mortgages

---

[45] [1979] 3 All E.R. 117.
[46] *Ante*, p. 328.
[47] [1985] Q.B. 850.
[48] Lord Wilberforce's statement that in his view *Cedar Holdings* was wrongly decided referred to the finding that the proceeds of sale were not an interest in land. It did not cover the dictum of Goff L.J. that even had there been an interest in land, no order would have been granted that would prejudice the interests of third parties such as the wife. In *Thames Guaranty* v. *Campbell*, *post*, p. 342, *Cedar Holdings* was cited in support of the finding there on the wife's potential hardship.
[49] [1986] 1 All E.R. 545 applied in *Austin-Fell* v. *Austin-Fell*, *The Independent*, July 19, 1989.

Facts

The plaintiff made a loan of £150 to the defendant against the security of a share certificate. In the present action the plaintiff claimed an order for the transfer of the shares to himself by foreclosure. The defendant made default in appearance, and the question before the court was whether the deposit of the share certificate amounted to an equitable mortgage carrying a right to foreclosure, or whether it was a mere pledge.

Decision

It was held that the plaintiff's security was a good equitable mortgage, and that he was entitled to foreclosure.

In his judgment, Cozens-Hardy J. said:

The only material allegation in the statement of claim is that in March, 1897, the defendant deposited with Harrold the certificate of ten ordinary shares in a limited company as security for the repayment to Harrold of the sum of £150, then owing to him from the defendant, with interest thereon at the rate of £6 per cent. per annum.... The deposit of the certificate by way of security for the debt, which is admitted, seems to me to amount to an equitable mortgage, or, in other words, to an agreement to execute a transfer of the shares by way of mortgage. The result is that the plaintiff is entitled to a judgment substantially in the form which would be given if, instead of the certificate of shares, the document had been a title-deed of real estate or a policy of assurance.[50]

Notes

The simple deposit of deeds as security for an advance has been recognised as creating an equitable mortgage since *Russel* v. *Russel*.[51] At the time this decision was regarded as an unfortunate limitation on the effect of the Statute of Frauds, and Lord Eldon, who refused to apply the new rule except in the clearest cases, said in *Ex p. Haigh*,[52] "The case of *Russel* v. *Russel* is a decision much to be lamented; that a mere deposit of deeds shall be considered as evidence of an agreement to make a mortgage." The rule became established law, however, and was extended to apply to other documents: in *Spencer* v. *Clarke*,[53] for example, the deposit of a life policy was recognised as creating an equitable mortgage, and in *Harrold* v. *Plenty* the deposit of a share certificate was treated in the same way.

[50] At p. 316.
[51] (1783) 1 Bro.C.C. 269.
[52] (1805) 11 Ves.Jr. 403.
[53] (1878) 9 Ch.D. 137.

The essential element in mortgage by deposit of documents, unsupported by any written evidence such as is provided by the ordinary memorandum of deposit, is intention to give security: without the intention, of course, no such mortgage is created. Thus, the deposit of deeds with a banker for safe custody does not give him even a lien upon them.[54]

The equitable mortgagee is necessarily in a less favourable position than the legal mortgagee. A legal mortgage has preference over an equitable one,[55] and although the old maxim of equity, "where the equities are equal the law prevails" has been weakened by the property legislation of 1925—in particular, registration has important effects on the priorities of charges registered—an equitable mortgagee will still be postponed to a later legal mortgagee without notice of the equitable charge.

It is also a maxim of equity that when the equities are equal the first in time prevails. Thus in *Coleman* v. *London County and Westminster Bank Ltd.*[56] 45 debentures in a private company were issued to Mrs. Coleman, who, under a family arrangement, settled them upon trust for herself for life with remainder to her three sons equally. The trustee did not register the transfer of the debentures to himself. One of the sons assigned his interest to his wife for value. Some years later the settlor obtained possession of the debentures and charged them to the defendant bank as security for an advance. The bank inspected the company's register and found the settlor registered there as the owner of the debentures; and they then gave notice of their interest to the trustee of the debenture trust deed, who was also trustee of the settlement. At this time the bank had of course no knowledge of the existence of the settlement; and the trustee merely acknowledged the notification of their interest. The trustee and the settlor later died, and the present action was by the wife of the trustee, to whom 15 debentures had been assigned, and his executors, claiming a declaration that the bank had no title to the debentures. The bank in their defence pleaded the trustee's negligence in not registering his transfer,

---

[54] *Ante*, p. 276.
[55] *cf. Northern Counties of England Fire Insurance Co.* v. *Whipp* (1884) Ch.D. 482. The company had lent against a legal mortgage supported by the deeds. The mortgagor abstracted the deeds and borrowed from the defendant against deposit of the deeds. The Court of Appeal held that the legal charge had precedence, despite the carelessness of the company.
[56] [1916] 2 Ch. 353.

and his non-disclosure of the existence of the settlement when he received, in his other capacity, notice of their interest.

It was held that the omission to register the transfer did not bar the trustee's title, but that, even if it did, the wife's equitable title, prior in time to the equitable title of the bank, must succeed.

When a banker takes an equitable mortgage of stocks and shares he normally seeks to register his interest with the company. The company may be prevented by its articles from accepting such notice, as in *Société Générale de Paris and Another* v. *Walker and Others*,[57] and other companies frequently refuse to accept notice because they consider that section 360 of the Companies Act 1985 similarly prevents them from doing so. The section provides that a company may not accept notice of any trust, and whether it has the effect thus claimed for it, of preventing the registration of an equitable charge, has been doubted.[58] It is to be noted that in *Bradford Banking Co. Ltd.* v. *Briggs, Son & Co. Ltd.*[59] (which is authority for the view that notice to the company gives the banker priority over subsequent advances by the company to the mortgagor), the House of Lords said that the notice of deposit which the bank had sent to the company was not a notice of trust within section 30 of the Companies Act 1862, the section now replaced by section 360 of the 1985 Act.

When notice is in question the priority of equitable interests is normally according to the time of the notice. *Re Wallis*[60] is an interesting example of an exception to this rule. It was there held that although the wife had not given notice to the insurance company of her husband's deposit with her of the insurance policy as security for a loan her right was not affected by the subsequent notice by the trustee in bankruptcy, who was a statutory assignee, and not an incumbrancer for value, and in whom the policy vested subject to all rights existing at the commencement of the bankruptcy.

In *Barclays Bank Ltd.* v. *Taylor*[61] the bank had made an advance against an equitable mortgage of their customer's property, and notice of deposit of the land certificate was duly registered. Later the customer executed a legal mortgage in the

[57] (1866) 11 A.C. 20.
[58] *cf.* Paget, *op. cit.* p. 453.
[59] (1886) 12 App.Cas. 29.
[60] [1902] 1 K.B. 719; see also *Spencer* v. *Clarke, supra.*
[61] [1974] Ch. 137; 9 L.D.B. 322.

bank's favour; this was not registered, the bank instead lodging a Notice of Deposit of a Land Certificate. Later again the defendants in this action contracted to buy the property, and registered a caution in respect of their contract. When the bank sought to register their legal mortgage the defendants claimed priority for their contract, and Goulding J. found in their favour, basing his decision on section 106(2) of the Land Registration Act 1925, which provides that a mortgage of registered land "may, if by deed, be protected by a caution in a specifically prescribed form and in no other way." This decision caused alarm in the banks, for it seemed to render ineffective a time-honoured, simple and economic method of charging their customers' property. However, on appeal the decision was reversed. Russell L.J. said:

> ... quite apart from the fact that the land certificate was in the possession of the bank, (a) failure by the bank to lodge a caution in special form was irrelevant, (b) the Taylors' caution did not and could not confer on their equitable entitlement or interest any priority over the bank's equitable charge, (c) ordinary rules of priority between persons equitably interested in the land must apply.... [62]

And section 106 has now been replaced by a new section 106, set out in section 26 of the Administration of Justice Act 1977, providing *inter alia* that the equitable mortgage is protected by a Notice of Deposit.

The bank's possession of the land certificate in the *Taylor* case, although not there the deciding factor, is relevant in that without it a third party cannot create a legal interest that would defeat the bank's equitable charge.

An unusual example of the failure of the deposit of a land certificate as security was seen in *Re Alton Corporation*[63] where Merrill Lynch International Bank lent Alton, a Liberian company, £1 million to buy a property in London. Alton deposited the land certificate with the bank, and Planwed SA deposited £1 million with the bank as security. Later, when there was a successful petition for the winding up of Alton, Merrill Lynch called in the loan and appropriated the cash deposit. When Planwed, now subrogated to the rights of the bank, sought to enforce the mortgage which they claimed had

---

[62] At p. 147.
[63] [1985] B.C.L.C. 27.

been created by the deposit of the land certificate, their claim was rejected. Sir Robert Megarry said that to establish the existence of the equitable mortgage there must be evidence of an agreement to create the charge, and here there was no such evidence; it was the deposit of £1 million that was expressed to be security for the loan.

In *Thames Guaranty Ltd.* v. *Campbell and Others*[64] the plaintiff company made a loan against the deposit of the land certificate of what was in fact the jointly-owned matrimonial home, the wife knowing nothing of the transaction. When Thames claimed that they had an equitable charge on the husband's beneficial interest the wife counter-claimed for the delivery to her of the land certificate, and the Court of Appeal agreed with the trial judge's view that "the hardship principle" displaced the normal rule which would have given Thames their case: the couple had no income but their retirement pension, the wife was 61, and as an innocent third party her hardship would far outweigh that of Thames, who were at fault in not requiring the husband to perfect the charge. Moreover, even if the husband had had a beneficial interest he would not have been permitted to part with the land certificate without his wife's consent.

Hopkinson v. Rolt

(1861) 9 H.L.Cas. 514

The position of a mortgagee making further advances after notice of a second mortgage

Facts

The appellant was the public officer of the Commercial Bank of London. A customer of the bank, a shipbuilder named Mare, had mortgaged to them certain property as security for an advance. The respondent, Rolt, was Mare's father-in-law, who made Mare a loan against a second mortgage of the property. He knew of the bank's earlier mortgage, and the bank were notified of his second mortgage. The bank's mortgage for £20,000 was expressed to be for the "sums and sum of money which then were or was, or at any time and from time to time thereafter, should or might become due or owing." The bank continued to make advances, by discount and otherwise. On

---

[64] [1985] Q.B. 210.

Mare's bankruptcy Rolt claimed that the bank's advances since his mortgage were postponed to his own claim.

Decision

It was held that the bank's further advances were postponed to the second mortgagee's. In his judgment, Lord Campbell L.C. said:

Although the mortgagor has parted with the legal interest in the hereditaments mortgaged, he remains the equitable owner of all his interest not transferred beneficially to the mortgagee, and he may still deal with his property in any way consistent with the rights of the mortgagee. How is the first mortgagee injured by the second mortgage being executed, although the first mortgagee having notice of the mortgage, the second mortgagee should be preferred to him as to subsequent advances? The first mortgagee is secure as to past advances, and he is not under any obligation to make any further advances. . . . The hardship upon bankers from this view of the subject at once vanishes when we consider that the security of the first mortgage is not impaired without notice of a second, and that when this notice comes, the bankers have only to consider . . . what is the credit of their customer and whether the proposed transaction is likely to lead to profit or to loss.[65]

Notes

When a banker grants a loan on current account against a mortgage, it is normally intended that the security shall be against future as well as present advances. It was established in *Hopkinson* v. *Rolt* that if a subsequent mortgage is obtained of which he has notice it takes priority over any further advances he may make against his mortgage; and, as was settled in *Deeley* v. *Lloyds Bank Ltd.*,[66] which was itself a case of competing mortgages, the rule in *Clayton's* case operates on a current account to wipe out the overdraft at the time of notice by subsequent payments into the account, leaving further withdrawals postponed to the later mortgage.

The decision in *West* v. *Williams*[67] was a development of the rule in *Hopkinson's* case. There the mortgagees *covenanted* to make advances at certain times, and did so both before and after receiving notice of another mortgage; and it was held that even so the advances made after notice were postponed to the other mortgage, Lord Lindley M.R. saying:

[65] At p. 143.
[66] *Ante*, p. 151.
[67] [1899] 1 Ch. 132.

Whatever prevents the mortgagor from giving to the first mortgagee the agreed security for his further advances releases the first mortgagee from his obligation to make them.[68]

The argument that by creating a second mortgage the mortgagor weakens the security of the first mortgagee is hardly a good one, in that, had the court not decided as it did in *West* v. *Williams*, there would be no such weakening.

How far the Law of Property Act makes the whole question academic is not clear. Section 94 of the Act provides that further advances shall have priority:

(*a*) by arrangement with later mortgagees;

(*b*) where the prior mortgagee has no notice of the subsequent mortgage (and, while registration constitutes notice, the mortgagee is not fastened with it where the prior mortgage was expressly made to secure a current account or further advances unless the later mortgage is registered at the time when the original mortgage was created or when the last search was made);

(*c*) whether or not he had such notice as aforesaid, where the mortgage imposes an obligation on him to make such further advances.

The relevance of the last proviso to such circumstances as those of *West* v. *Williams* has been debated, and the reader is referred to Paget[69] for a fuller discussion of the point. Cheshire[70] considers that the Act reverses the *West* case, so that where the first mortgagee binds himself to make further advances, they will take priority. Paget disagrees, largely on the same grounds as the Master of the Rolls in the *West* case, the diminishing of the first mortgagee's security; but, it may be repeated, if in fact the law is that such further advances have priority, there is no diminishing of the security, while if the subsection in question is not intended to reverse the *West* decision it is not easy to see what purpose it serves.

In practice it would be only in the most exceptional circumstances that a bank mortgage would *bind* the bank to make further advances; and the normal bank advance is fully protected by the combination of proviso (*b*) and the banks' established practice of "breaking" the account on receipt of notice.

---

[68] At p. 144.
[69] *Op. cit.* pp. 439 *et seq.*
[70] *Modern Law of Real Property* (14th ed.), p. 692.

Re Kent & Sussex Sawmills Ltd.

[1947] Ch. 177

Registration of charges under the Companies Acts

Facts

The company had contracted with the Ministry of Fuel and Power to supply cut logs, and the Westminster Bank agreed to allow them overdraft facilities in connection with this contract, provided the company wrote to the Ministry in the following terms:

With reference to the above-mentioned contract, we hereby authorise you to remit all moneys due thereunder direct to this company's account at Westminster Bank Ltd., Crowborough, whose receipt shall be your sufficient discharge. These instructions are to be regarded as irrevocable unless the said bank should consent to their cancellation in writing, and are intended to cover any extension of the contract in excess of 30,000 tons if such should occur.

The company wrote this letter, and the Ministry accepted the instructions; and in due course, there being an extension of the contract, the bank agreed to further advances, and the company wrote a further, similar, letter to the Ministry.

Upon the company going into voluntary liquidation, the liquidator contended that the two letters of authority constituted a charge on the book debts of the company which should have been registered under section 79 of the Companies Act 1929 (now replaced by ss.395, 396(1) of the Companies Act 1985), and that as they had not been so registered they were void against him. The bank claimed that they must be regarded rather as a sale to the bank of the whole of the company's interest in the moneys due under the contract.

Decision

It was held that no sale was intended, but an equitable assignment by way of security; and this not having been registered was void against the liquidator.

Notes

The liquidator had argued that there was no assignment at all, basing his case on *Bell* v. *London and North-Western Railway Co.*,[71] where a railway contractor gave his bankers a letter

---

[71] (1852) 15 Beav. 548.

directing the railway company to pass cheques due to him to his account with the bank. It was there held that the letter did not constitute an assignment, although it would have done so if payment had been directed to the bank and not to the customer's account with the bank: as it stood the order (in the words of Lord Romilly M.R.) "would always be revocable by the person giving it...." Wynn-Parry J. distinguished this earlier decision: the case before him would have been covered by that decision had it not been for the second part of the letter, which made the order irrevocable except with the bank's permission.[72]

With the *Kent & Sussex Sawmills* case may be compared *Re David Allester Ltd.*,[73] an example of circumstances in which it was held that no charge registrable under section 95 had been created.

In *Re C. L. Nye*[74] the bank's charge was inadvertently registered out of time, the date of the charge being wrongly stated to the registrar. But the Court of Appeal held, against the liquidators, that once the registrar's certificate is issued, it is, by section 98(2) of the 1948 Act (now section 401 of the 1985 Act), conclusive evidence that all the requirements of the Act have been complied with. The decision at first instance in *R.* v. *Registrar of Companies, ex p. Central Bank of India*[75] distinguished that decision, but the Court of Appeal re-affirmed it: no evidence is admissible that the statutory requirements of registration have not been satisfied.

When a company is in liquidation a creditor is not normally allowed to register a charge out of time, under section 404 of the Companies Act 1985,[76] but Harman J. in an "odd and unusual case," *Re R. M. Arnold & Co. Ltd.*,[77] allowed late registration. The company had created a debenture in favour of Lloyds Bank on land which they might acquire. The bank agreed to a fixed charge being granted on the land to another company which was providing funds for the purchase, but that

---

[72] *cf.* the question whether communication to the customer is essential to the completion of payment to his account: the *Rekstin* decision and the *Momm* and *Royal Products* cases, *ante*, p. 114.

[73] [1922] 2 Ch. 211, *ante*, p. 285.

[74] [1971] Ch. 442.

[75] [1986] Q.B. 1114.

[76] *cf., e.g.* Re Resinoid and Mica Products Ltd. [1983] Ch. 132 where the Court of Appeal upheld the rejection of an application for late registration of a charge due to inadvertence: extension should not be granted after liquidation, because the rights of the parties were determined at the liquidation date.

[77] (1984) 128 S.J. 659.

charge was not registered. When, on Arnold becoming insolvent, the bank appointed a receiver, the lending company sought registration of their charge, although liquidation had begun. The only creditor who could be affected by the registration was the bank, and they did not object to it; and it was granted subject to a proviso protecting the rights of a "possible but unlikely" claimant who might have acquired an interest in the land between its acquisition and the date of registration.

Section 106 of the 1948 Act (now section 409 of the 1985 Act) extended the requirement for registration to charges by companies incorporated outside England which had established places of business in England. The effect of this provision was demonstrated in *Re Oriel Ltd.*[78] where the company was incorporated in 1978, in the Isle of Man, with the purpose of operating garage sites in England. The two directors, husband and wife, lived in Wigan. Seven sites were established, financed by Conoco, and were not registered in England as it was believed that registration was not required for Isle of Man companies. But when the company was wound up the liquidator claimed that the charges to Conoco were void against him, the directors' residence being a place of business in England. At first instance he succeeded but the Court of Appeal held that each charge had to be considered separately as to evidence of the place of business at the date each charge was created. In the present case the place of residence as such was irrelevant, and on the first four charges the liquidator again succeeded, but there was evidence on the three later charges that business was by then being conducted from the residence, and for them Conoco's appeal was allowed.

A case of considerable interest regarding registration of charges is *Siebe Gorman & Co. Ltd.* v. *Barclays Bank Ltd.*[79] where the bank's customer, R. H. McDonald Ltd., had executed a debenture in favour of the bank, charging, *inter alia*, "by way of first fixed charge" all book debts present and future. McDonalds later made an absolute assignment to Siebe Gorman, to whom they owed money for goods supplied, of bills of exchange to the value of £8,500 which were held by the bank for collection. The bank was notified of the assignment, and Siebe Gorman were notified of the debenture, which had been

[78] [1986] 1 W.L.R. 180; 10 L.D.B. 528.
[79] [1979] 2 Lloyd's Rep. 143; 10 L.D.B. 94.

registered under section 95, but it was not until after the assignment was made that they learned its precise terms.

When a compulsory winding-up order was made against McDonalds, the bank claimed that as against Siebe Gorman they had a prior claim to the bills by virtue of their debenture and their bankers' lien, while they contended that the plaintiffs' failure to register their assignment invalidated their claim. But Slade J., having first accepted that the bills of exchange were book debts within the terms of the debenture, held (1) that the debenture was effective to give the bank its first fixed charge, but the bank's claim on the debenture failed because Siebe Gorman had not been given notice of its full relevant terms, and so did not know that McDonalds could not dispose of their interest in the bills; (2) that the bank could have exercised their right under the lien when they received notice of the assignment, but after that date credits to the account, which was not broken, had almost cleared the indebtedness, and by the rule in *Clayton's* case the bank could not rely on the lien to cover the further indebtedness which further withdrawals had created; and (3) that the absolute assignment was not a security, and did not require registration.

The decision provided yet another example of the importance of breaking the account when the bank's security is threatened; and the third finding is interesting in confirming that not every kind of assignment requires registration.

The decision that the bank had a right to a fixed charge on the book debts resolved, at least at first instance, the question whether such a fixed charge was effective, and so would take priority over preferential creditors, or whether it would be regarded as a floating charge under another name, and so fall behind the preferential creditors. Slade J. was clear on the point: the bank's claim under the debenture failed, but "as I hope has already been made clear, this does not involve the conclusion that the fixed charge on future book debts comprised in the bank's standard form of debenture is no more effective than a floating charge."

William Brandt's Sons & Co. v. Dunlop Rubber Co. Ltd.

[1905] A.C. 454

The equitable assignment of choses in action

Facts

Kramrisch & Co., who were rubber merchants in Liverpool, were financed by Brandts, who were London bankers. When Kramrisch's made a purchase, Brandts provided the necessary funds, and by way of security they/took delivery of the goods. When the goods were sold, they were released by Brandts, who received the purchase money direct from the purchasers. Kramrisch & Co. had entered into a similar arrangement with another firm of bankers.

Kramrisch & Co. sold certain rubber to the defendant company, and sent with the goods an invoice on which was stamped a request that the amount thereof should be sent to Brandts. There was an error in the invoice, and it was returned; the corrected invoice later sent out did not bear the instructions for remittance to Brandts. There was also sent to the defendant company a letter signed by Kramrisch & Co. requesting the Dunlop company to sign another letter, which was enclosed, promising to remit the price of the goods in question to Brandts; and this letter was signed by the defendants and sent to Brandts.

The whole correspondence was handled by the Birmingham office of Dunlops, but cheques were sent out from their London office. Only the corrected invoice was sent from Birmingham to London, and the cheque was therefore sent to the second firm of bankers, who had not in fact had anything to do with this particular transaction. When Brandts wrote to Dunlops pressing for a remittance, they were informed that the amount had been paid; and Brandts then brought the present action to recover the amount from them, claiming that the money in question had been assigned to them, and that Dunlops had notice of the assignment.

Decision

The House of Lords held that there was evidence of an equitable assignment of the debt, with notice to the defendant company, and that the plaintiffs were therefore entitled to recover the amount claimed.

Lord Macnaghten considered it immaterial that the document did not on the face of it purport to be an assignment, and said:

An equitable assignment does not always take that form. It may be addressed to the debtor. It may be couched in the language of command. It may be a courteous request. It may assume the form of mere permission. The language is immaterial if the meaning is plain.

All that is necessary is that the debtor should be given to understand that the debt has been made over by the creditor to some third person. If the debtor ignores such a notice, he does so at his peril. If the assignment be for valuable consideration and communicated to the third person, it cannot be revoked by the creditor or safely disregarded by the debtor.[80]

Notes

A chose in action[81] is a right which can be enforced only by legal action, and is opposed to a chose in possession. One example is the life policy, certain special features of the assignment of which are dealt with later; but the most familiar ordinary example is the simple debt.[82] A chose in action can be (but seldom is) mortgaged, and the appropriate formal charge is by way of deed of assignment; but any expression of intention by the creditor to charge the chose in action in favour of a third party may constitute a valid equitable assignment.

Section 136 of the Law of Property Act 1925 provides that an assignment of a chose in action must be absolute, and not by way of charge only, in writing signed by the assignor, and that written notice must be given to the debtor. If these provisions are satisfied the assignment is a legal assignment; if they are not satisfied there may be a good equitable assignment according to the principles outlined by Lord Macnaghten in the passage quoted above.

There is an important distinction to be observed between an assignment of a debt and an order to pay money, such as a cheque or a bill of exchange, which by section 53 of the Bills of Exchange Act is never an assignment of the debt due to the customer.[83] The distinction was formerly of especial significance in view of the danger that an assignment in the form of written instructions might be objected to as being in effect a bill of

---

[80] At p. 462.
[81] Now sometimes termed "thing in action."
[82] In *R.* v. *Kohn* [1979] Crim.L.R. 675; C.L.B. 8, the Court of Appeal, holding that the defendant had been properly charged with the theft of choses in action, held that a cheque drawn on an account in credit, or within an agreed overdraft limit, was a chose in action: the customer could enforce by action the bank's obligation to pay. But this did not apply to one of the cheques in issue, which was drawn in excess of the overdraft limit, and the conviction on that cheque was quashed.
[83] *cf. Schroeder* v. *Central Bank* (1876) 34 L.T. 735.

exchange, and not properly stamped as such.[84] But in *Buck* v. *Robson*[85] Cockburn C.J. said:

> In our acceptation of the term an order for the payment of money presupposes moneys of the drawer in the hands of the party to whom the order is addressed, held on the terms of applying such moneys as directed by the order of the party entitled to them. No such obligation arises out of the ordinary contract of sale. If a purchaser buys goods of a manufacturer or tradesman, he undertakes to pay the price to the seller, not to a third party, who is a stranger to the contract, nor will the mere order or direction of the seller to pay to a third party impose any such obligation upon him; it is only when and because the right of the seller to the price has been transferred to the third party by an effectual assignment that the assignee becomes entitled as of right to the payment.[86]

The *Brandt* case, as well as illustrating the effect of an assignment of a chose in action, provides an illustration of the importance of notice by the assignee to the debtor. Notice, as we have seen above, is an essential element of a legal assignment of a chose in action; it is not essential to an equitable assignment, but it is always most desirable, for without it the debtor may discharge himself by paying the creditor, while priority among several assignees of otherwise equal equities is determined by the dates of notice.[87]

The Lord Mayor, etc., of Sheffield v. Barclay and Others

[1905] A.C. 392

The mortgage of stock exchange securities

Facts

Timbrell and Honeywill were the joint owners of certain Corporation of Sheffield stock. Timbrell applied to the defendant bankers for an advance against this stock, and in order to obtain it executed a transfer in favour of a member of the bank, forging Honeywill's name on the transfer. The bank forwarded the transfer to the registrar of the corporation, and were duly registered as owners. Upon repayment of the advance

---

[84] The Finance Act 1970 freed bills of exchange (including cheques) from stamp duty.

[85] (1878) 3 Q.B.D. 686.

[86] At pp. 691–692.

[87] *Dearle* v. *Hall* (1828) 3 Russ. 1.

the stock was transferred to two third parties and they were in due course registered as the new owners of the stock.

Upon Timbrell's death the fraud was discovered, and Honeywill brought an action against the corporation for rectification of their register, payment of back dividends and other relief. He won this action, and as this involved the corporation in a loss of more than £11,000, they in turn brought the present action against the bank, claiming the amount of their loss on the grounds that by sending in the forged transfer for registration they had either warranted it as genuine or had by implication undertaken to indemnify the corporation against any claim that might result from registration of it. The Lord Chief Justice found against the bank, but the Court of Appeal allowed the bank's appeal. The plaintiffs further appealed.

Decision

The House of Lords allowed the appeal and restored the Lord Chief Justice's decision. In the course of his judgment the Lord Chancellor, Lord Halsbury, said:

[The bank] have a private bargain with a customer. Upon his assurance they take a document from him as a security for a loan, which they assume to be genuine. I do not suggest that there was any negligence—perhaps business could not go on if people were suspecting forgery in every transaction—but their position was obviously very different from that of the corporation. The corporation is simply ministerial in registering a valid transfer and issuing fresh certificates. They cannot refuse to register, and though for their own sake they will not and ought not to register or to issue certificates to a person who is not really the holder of the stock, yet they have no machinery, and they cannot inquire into the transaction out of which the transfer arises. The bank, on the other hand, is at liberty to lend their money or not. They can make any amount of inquiries they like. If they find that an intended borrower has a co-trustee, they may ask him or the co-trustee himself whether the co-trustee is a party to the loan, and a simple question to the co-trustee would have prevented the fraud. They take the risk of the transaction and lend the money. The security given happens to be in a form that requires registration to make it available, and the bank "demand"—as, if genuine transfers are brought, they are entitled to do—that the stock shall be registered in their name or that of their nominees, and are also entitled to have fresh certificates issued to themselves or nominees. This was done and the corporation by acting on this "demand" have incurred a considerable loss.[88]

---

[88] At pp. 396–397.

Notes

The *Sheffield Corporation* case is an example of the principal danger to which the lending banker is liable when he advances against stocks or shares.[89] It may be noted that in the case of a legal mortgage such a danger could be avoided by requiring the mortgagor himself to carry out the formalities of transfer, for it is only on their implied warranty of genuineness that the bank becomes liable to indemnify the company, and if the transferor himself forwards the transfer to the company there can be no warranty by the bank. The fact that the banks do not normally adopt this practice may probably be taken as evidence that the danger is not a serious one. In the case of equitable mortgage by way of blank transfer the transfer is usually registered only when the security is to be realised, and here it would anyhow often be difficult to insist upon the mortgagor completing the formalities himself.

Equitable mortgages of stocks and shares are more common than legal ones, and here there is the further danger of there being other, prior, equitable interests. The security charged may, for example, be subject to a trust.[90] In *Peat* v. *Clayton*[91] the plaintiffs were trustees of a trust under which a debtor had assigned all his property for the benefit of his creditors. Part of the property consisted of shares in a company, and the trustees, having asked the debtor for the shares and been unable to obtain them from him, gave notice to the company of the assignment. Later the debtor sold the shares through his brokers, executed a transfer and received the purchase money. In spite of the notice the company registered the purchaser as owner of the shares, but later removed her name from the register and refused to issue a certificate. The brokers provided the purchaser with other shares in the company, and then claimed to have a lien on the shares they had sold. The present action was by the trustees who sought a declaration that they were entitled to the shares, and it was held that the brokers' lien could not be upon more than the interest which the debtor himself had in the shares, and that this interest was subject to the right of the plaintiffs.

The principle of the *Sheffield Corporation* case was applied in *Yeung and Another* v. *Hong Kong and Shanghai Banking*

---

[89] *cf. Williams and Glyn's Bank Ltd.* v. *Barnes, ante*, p. 223, for an unusual (and unsuccessful) challenge to the bank's stock exchange security.

[90] *cf. National Provincial Bank of England* v. *Jackson*, (1886) 33 Ch.D. 1.

[91] [1906] 1 Ch. 659.

Corporation,[92] where the bank was the registrar, not the presenter of the transfers. Certificates for shares in the bank were stolen in Hong Kong, and later presented with completed share transfers by a firm of stockbrokers who had no knowledge that the signatures were forged. The bank failed to check the signatures against the specimen which they held; the transfers were registered, new certificates were issued, and the shares were sold soon afterwards. The true owner claimed against the bank, and the bank claimed indemnity from the stockbrokers. The Privy Council, upholding the decision of the Hong Kong courts, rejected the appeal of the stockbrokers, who argued that the *Sheffield Corporation* decision applies only when the person presenting the transfers does so for his own benefit. The bank was entitled to the indemnity, and as the contract of indemnity allows no claim for contribution, the bank's own negligence was not relevant. But it is to be noted that their Lordships suggested that in a similar case in England the Civil Liability (Contribution) Act 1978 might have let in a claim for contribution.

Beresford v. Royal Insurance Co. Ltd.

[1983] A.C. 586

The mortgage of life insurance policies

Facts

In 1925 Major Rowlandson insured his life with the Royal Insurance Co. Ltd. for £50,000. Each of the policies contained the following clause:

If the life or any one of the lives assured (being also the assured or one of them) shall die by his own hand, whether sane or insane within one year from the commencement of the assurance, the policy shall be void as against any person claiming the amount hereby assured or any part thereof, except that it shall remain in force to the extent to which a bona fide interest for pecuniary consideration, or as a security for money . . . shall be established. . . .

In 1934 a premium became due which the assured was unable to pay, and he obtained several extensions of the time for payment. The last of these ended at 3 p.m. on August 3, and a few minutes before that hour he shot himself.

The appellant, who was the niece and the administratrix of Major Rowlandson, brought this action against the company

[92] [1980] 2 All E.R. 599; 10 L.D.B. 208.

claiming the amount of the policies. The jury found as a fact that the deceased was sane at the time of the suicide, and the court held that the plaintiff was entitled to the policy moneys. The Court of Appeal reversed the decision of the lower court on grounds of public policy and the plaintiff further appealed.

Decision

The House of Lords upheld the decision of the Court of Appeal: it was against public policy for the contract to be enforced. In his judgment, Lord Atkin said:

Anxiety is naturally aroused by the thought that this principle may be invoked so as to destroy the security given to lenders and others by policies of life insurance which are in daily use for that purpose. The question does not directly arise, and I do not think that anything said in this case can be authoritative. But I consider myself free to say that I cannot see that there is any objection to an assignee for value before the suicide enforcing a policy which contains an express promise to pay upon a sane suicide, at any rate so far as the payment is to extend to the actual interest of the assignee. It is plain that a lender may himself insure the life of the borrower against sane suicide; and the assignee of the policy is in a similar position so far as public policy is concerned. I have little doubt that after this decision the life companies will frame a clause which is unobjectionable; and they will have the support of the decision of the Court of Queen's Bench in *Moore* v. *Woolsey*,[93] where a clause protecting bona fide interests was upheld.[94]

Notes

Life policies are a popular form of security, with the merit of simplicity, and, in the case of endowment policies, an increasing surrender value as long as the premiums are paid regularly. There are relatively few legal difficulties: the *Beresford* case is an example of one of them.[94a]

The decision in this case was significant in establishing for the first time that a policy was unenforceable after a sane suicide even where it contained a clearly implied term that if the suicide took place more than a year after the date of the policy the insurers would pay under it.

The case was decided when suicide was a crime. Since the passing of the Suicide Act 1961 this is no longer so, but it might still be held to be against public policy to allow the personal representative of the suicide to receive the policy moneys, and it

[93] (1854) 4 E. & B. 243.
[94] At pp. 599–600.
[94a] Penn, Shea & Arora, *op. cit.* I, 26.

would be unsafe to assume that the Act has materially altered this aspect of the matter; it might now be held that there is an implied condition that the insured will not himself end the life assured.

The principle covers a wider area than suicide: the policy is invalidated if the event is the result of the assured's own criminal act. It was applied (when death was still the penalty for murder) when the insured was executed.

It is the personal representatives who are defeated by the principle; the banker is normally concerned not with the position of the personal representative, but with that of the assignee of the policy. Lord Atkin's view here quoted was expressly *obiter dictum*, but it carried great weight, and is supported by the much older decision to which he referred. The policy in *Moore* v. *Woolsey* contained a clause excluding liability in the case of persons dying "by duelling or by their own hands or by the hands of justice," but expressly exempting from the terms of the clause "any bona fide interest which may have been acquired by any other person." On grounds of strict logic it would still be open to the courts to hold even such a clause to be against public policy: in the *Beresford* case it is clear on the facts that the insured committed suicide with the definite purpose of gaining for his personal representatives the benefit of the policies which he could no longer maintain, and if in similar circumstances the insured was seeking to protect his mortgagee the inducement to suicide would be equally apparent. But the risk to the mortgagee seems remote, and the common sense of the decision in *Moore* v. *Woolsey* is unlikely to be upset by the application of logic to what is anyhow so rare an event.

It will be noted that Lord Atkin's opinion and the *Moore* v. *Woolsey* decision both concern policies with clauses protecting third-party interests. And it may be worth pointing out that the whole discussion regarding suicide is concerned only with sane suicide: in the case of mental disorder no question of avoiding the policy arises.

Another danger to mortgagees is the possibility that the person taking out the policy has no insurable interest in the life insured.[95] The banker is seldom at risk in this way, for where the policy is on the mortgagor's own life, or that of his or her spouse, an insurable interest is presumed.

A third risk of more general concern is that all contracts of insurance are *uberrimae fidei* (*i.e.* they have an implied

---

[95] *Harse* v. *Pearl Life Assurance Co. Ltd.* [1904] 1 K.B. 558.

condition of "utmost good faith"[96]). The validity of the policy depends on the accuracy of the representations made by the insured in his proposals to the company, and this fact, even more than the possibility of suicide, makes it impossible to value the security with perfect certainty.[97]

An example of the strict application of this principle, which applies to all contracts of insurance, including life policies, was seen in *Woolcott* v. *Sun Alliance & London Insurance Ltd.*[98] where the plaintiff had an advance from a building society, secured by the mortgage of his house. The house was to be insured by the defendant company, and the form of application for the loan required him to state the amount of insurance he wanted, but made no other inquiry regarding the insurance. The insurance was effected in the names of the plaintiff and the society, as mortgagor and mortgagees. When the house was destroyed by fire the company paid the amount of the mortgage to the society, but refused to pay the balance to the plaintiff on the grounds that he had not disclosed that 12 years before he had been sentenced for robbery.

The plaintiff's action against the company failed, despite the court's acceptance of his evidence that he had led an honest life since he left prison, and that he would have disclosed his conviction if he had been asked a relevant question. It was held that the applicant for insurance owes a duty to disclose such facts as a reasonable insurer might treat as material, even though he is not asked or, as here, where there is no separate proposal form.[99]

It may be said again that all these risks, including the last named, are of infrequent relevance to bankers. It is significant that the accepted definition of what representations are material in insurance is found in section 18 of the Marine Insurance Act 1906: "a representation is material which would influence the judgment of a prudent insurer in fixing the premium, or determining whether he will take the risk." This has been held

---

[96] *Ante*, p. 291.

[97] This is one of the "slight risks" listed by Holden, *op. cit.* II.11, 24–9, in "what are regarded by bankers as one of the most satisfactory forms of security."

[98] [1978] 1 W.L.R. 493.

[99] But in *Woolcott* v. *Excess Insurance Co. Ltd.* [1979] 2 Lloyd's Rep. 210; a similar defence by the insurance company failed, because the policy had been effected through brokers who knew the plaintiff's record and did not disclose it to the company. The plaintiff was given judgment against the company, and the company was granted their claim for indemnity from the brokers.

to be applicable to all insurance contracts; but it may be noted that in a case directly concerned with section 18[1] it was held that to avoid a policy the underwriter must show not merely that the mind of a prudent insurer might have been affected by the undisclosed facts, but that the insurer would have declined the risk or increased the premium.

Aluminium Industrie Vaasen BV v. Romalpa Aluminium Ltd.

[1976] 2 All E.R. 552

When a supplier of goods to a company expressly reserves the property in the goods until payment for them is effected, he may, in the winding up of the company, have the right to trace the proceeds of resale of the goods in priority to secured creditors

Facts

The plaintiffs, Dutch manufacturers of aluminium foil, supplied foil to the defendants, an English company. The contract provided, in clause 13, that the ownership of the foil would remain with the plaintiffs until the defendants had paid all sums owing to the plaintiffs. It provided further that where the foil was used in the manufacture of other products, the ownership of such products was to be transferred to the plaintiffs as security for full payment. The defendants were entitled to sell such "mixed" goods on condition that, while any money was owing to the plaintiffs, the defendants would on request assign to the plaintiffs the benefit of any claim against the sub-purchasers.

When the defendants' bankers, Hume Corporation, appointed a receiver under its debenture there was an outstanding debt owing to the plaintiffs of £122,000. The plaintiffs claimed that they were entitled, in priority to all creditors, to (*a*) £35,152, representing proceeds of resale of foil supplied by them, and (*b*) redelivery of foil worth £50,235, still in the possession of the receiver. The second claim was admitted by the company. On the first, Mocatta J. gave judgment for the plaintiffs, and the defendants appealed.

Decision

The Court of Appeal dismissed the appeal. Roskill L.J. said:

I see no difficulty in the contractual concept that, as between the defendants and their sub-purchasers, the defendants sold as principals,

---

[1] *C.T.I. International Inc.* v. *The Oceans Mutual Underwriting Association (Bermuda)* [1982] Com.L.R. 68.

but that, as between themselves and the plaintiffs, those goods which they were selling as principals within their implied authority from the plaintiffs were the plaintiffs' goods which they were selling as agents for the plaintiffs to whom they remained fully accountable.

... Like the learned judge, I find no difficulty in holding that the principles in *Re Hallett's Estate*,[2] to which I have already referred, are of immediate application, and I think that the plaintiffs are entitled to trade these proceeds of sale and to recover them. . . .[3]

Notes

Reservation of title, familiar on the Continent, has been possible in England since at least 1893,[4] but it has seldom been seen in practice, and its appearance in the *Romalpa* case, and its increased adoption, in part as a result of the decision in that case, has been a matter of concern to bankers.

The implications of the decision are wide ranging. The banker is concerned as a lender: the stock-in-trade of a company may be the only asset not incumbered by a fixed charge, and the possibility that even the stock is not wholly the property of the company must affect the banker's risk assessment. In particular, a floating charge could be of substantially less value than had seemed to be the case. Moreover, a supplier of goods protected as the plaintiffs were here takes precedence over preferential creditors, so that advances to pay wages[5] could be similarly at risk.

There are of course other implications: for example, a receiver's work is more difficult when the company's apparent assets are in fact the property of others; and taxes as well as wages are preferential debts. These matters are not of direct banking interest, but they reinforce the concern with which accountants as well as bankers have viewed the matter.[6] "Mixed goods," which clause 13 purported also to cover, were not in issue in the case, but it does not appear from the judgments that the court would have found for the defendants if they had been. And while the court had difficulty with the wording of clause 13, it will be comparatively easy for similar clauses to avoid the complication for which translation was partly responsible in *Romalpa*. It is reasonable to assume that a well-drafted clause

[2] *Ante*, p. 106.
[3] At p. 563.
[4] *cf.* Sale of Goods Act 1893, s.19.
[5] As to which, see *post*, p. 394.
[6] The accountancy bodies issued a statement of guidance to their members which recommended, *inter alia*, that there should be a note in the accounts indicating that goods are affected by reservation of title.

will cover the whole area of goods supplied and not paid for, and it must be further assumed that a provision so clearly useful to suppliers will be increasingly used as it becomes more widely known.

So far no such clause has been before the courts. In *Borden (U.K.) Ltd.* v. *Scottish Timber Products Ltd.*,[7] where under a retention of title clause the suppliers of resin to chipboard manufacturers claimed to trace the resin into the manufactured chipboard, the Court of Appeal, overruling the lower court, held (1) that the effect of the retention clause was to reserve property in the resin as long as it remained unused; once incorporated in the chipboard it ceased to exist as resin and there was nothing to trace; (2) that there was no fiduciary relationship between the sellers and the buyers that could found a right to trace; and (3) that even if the sellers had acquired an interest in the chipboard it would have been by way of charge requiring registration under section 95 of the Companies Act 1948.[8] Bridge L.J. said:

> the essence of the [*Romalpa*] decision . . . was that on the facts found or admitted Romalpa were selling the plaintiffs' material, the aluminium foil, as agents for the plaintiffs. It seems to me quite impossible to say here that in using the sellers' resin in their own manufacturing process to manufacture their own chipboard, the buyers could possibly be described as acting in any sense as agents for the sellers.[8a]

And he questioned whether there can ever be a right to trace where heterogeneous goods are mixed, as opposed to the mixing of homogeneous goods envisaged in *Re Hallett's Estate*[9] and whether, even if such a right was admitted, there could be any practicable method of quantifying the value of the manufactured goods that could be claimed by the seller. "If [the seller] wishes to acquire rights over the finished product, he can only do so by express contractual stipulation."

Such a stipulation was considered in *Re Bond Worth Ltd.*,[10] where there was no retention of title clause, but in one clause the sellers claimed until payment "equitable and beneficial ownership" of the goods supplied, ownership of any products in

---

[7] [1979] 3 All E.R. 961.
[8] *Ante*, pp. 345 *et seq.*
[8a] At p. 968.
[9] *Ante*, p. 106.
[10] [1979] 3 All E.R. 919.

which the goods were incorporated, and, where there was resale, entitlement to the proceeds. But Slade J. held that the nature of the contract deprived "equitable and beneficial ownership" of its primary meaning. The clause created an equitable charge, created by the buyers by way of an implied grant back: and it was a floating rather than a fixed charge, and as such required registration under section 95.

In *Clough Mill Ltd.* v. *Martin*[11] the plaintiffs' claim was simpler—for unsold goods still in possession of the buyers. The plaintiffs had contracted to sell yarn to the buyers, and their retention clause had provided "that ownership of the material shall remain with the seller, which reserves the right to dispose of the material until payment in full for all the material has been received." When a receiver was appointed for the buyers they still owed part of the purchase price and held a quantity of unused yarn. The plaintiffs told the receiver that they intended to repossess the yarn, but he said the the retention clause was a charge on the yarn, and void for non-registration; and he allowed the buyers to use the yarn themselves.

The plaintiffs claimed damages for conversion, and when the trial judge allowed the receiver's claim they appealed. The appeal was allowed, Robert Goff L.J. rejecting the argument that a charge had been created: "the buyer did not by way of security confer an interest in the property. On the contrary, the seller retained the property in that material." The clause provided for retention of property until all the material had been paid for, so that title could be retained even if part had been paid for. Title could be retained even if the material had been used by the buyers, provided that it remained separate and identifiable; only when its identity was lost was it to be assumed that the ownership had passed to the buyer, subject to a charge in favour of the seller by virtue of the retention clause.

But in *Tatung (UK)* v. *Galex Telesure Ltd.*,[12] where again the relevant clause provided that property would not pass until all sums due from the buyer had been paid, it was held that a registrable charge had been created. There would still seem to be doubt as to whether such retention of title clauses can be effective without registration.

[11] [1985] 1 W.L.R. 111.
[12] [1989] 5 B.C.C. 25.

Chapter 8

TERMINATION OF RELATIONSHIP BETWEEN BANKER AND CUSTOMER

NOTICE

Prosperity Ltd. v. Lloyds Bank Ltd.

(1923) 39 T.L.R. 372

Termination by notice by the banker

Facts

The plaintiff company was formed in 1922 with the object of setting on foot a "snowball" insurance scheme. The scheme was explained to the manager of the Victoria Street branch of the defendant bank, who agreed to open an account in the name of the company, to receive applications from subscribers and to allot the moneys subscribed as provided in the rules of the company. The account was accordingly opened and payments received until there was a credit balance on the account of some £7,000.

The publicity which the scheme attracted was brought to the notice of the head office of the bank, and it was decided that it was undesirable for the bank to be associated with the project. A letter was sent from the head office on February 14, 1923, informing the plaintiffs that after March 14, the bank would cease to act as bankers to the company. The plaintiffs brought the present action seeking (*a*) a declaration that the bank were not entitled to close the account without reasonable notice; and (*b*) an injunction restraining the bank from closing the account.

Decision

It was held that an injunction was not an appropriate remedy in the circumstances; but that the plaintiffs were entitled to the declaration sought. In his judgment McCardie J. said:

With respect to all accounts there might be a special contract between banker and customer which bound both of them and that special contract might provide that the banking relationship should last for a given period. It might, however, provide that no notice should be given at all. If, however, there was no special contract, then, in his (his Lordship's) view, it was the law that the bank could not close an account in credit without reasonable notice. . . .

It was obvious that the question of reasonableness must depend on the special facts and circumstances of the case. An account might be a small account drawn upon only be cheques cashed by the customer for his own purposes. In that case a comparatively short notice might be all that was needed. . . . A customer might also deal with his account by sending cheques, to the knowledge of the bank, to different parts of the Continent. In that case . . . the existence of such outstanding cheques might place upon the bank a larger burden as to notice. . . . He had come to the conclusion that, having regard to the knowledge and approval in the first place of Lloyds Bank of this scheme, and having regard to their knowledge as to the far extent to which the pamphlets and forms were being sent throughout the world, one month was not an adequate notice, because it did not give the plaintiffs a sufficient opportunity of dealing with the position created by the decision of Lloyds Bank to end the account.[1]

Notes

In his judgment in *Joachimson* v. *Swiss Bank Corporation*[2] Atkin L.J. said: "It is a term of the contract that the bank will not cease to do business with the customer except upon reasonable notice." The customer can at any time close his current account without notice to the banker, but if the banker closes it without giving the customer time to make other arrangements, the subsequent dishonour of the customer's cheques may leave him liable for damage to credit.

The only question in any particular case is the length of notice required. It is seldom that an account which the banker desires to close has such extensive ramifications as those discussed in the *Prosperity* case; but while the case is an exceptional one, it serves to underline the necessity for "reasonable" notice.

Garnett v. *McKewan*[3] is an example of the banker's right to combine two accounts, and so in effect close one of them, without notice. It may be remarked, however, that even in circumstances like those of that case the banker would be cautious in dishonouring a cheque on the closed account with

---

[1] At p. 373.
[2] *Ante*, p. 1.
[3] (1872) L.R. 8 Ex. 10; *ante*, pp. 234, 235, *post*, p. 402.

the answer "Account closed," or "No account"; indeed it is difficult to imagine a banker today dishonouring a cheque at all in such a case.[4]

MENTAL DISORDER

Re Beavan, Davies, Banks & Co. v. Beavan
[1912] 1 Ch. 196

Customer of unsound mind; bank advance for necessaries

Facts

For many years the plaintiffs, who were bankers, had had a current account in the name of J.G. Beavan. For two years before his death in 1906 the customer was of unsound mind, following a paralytic stroke, and the bank, with the approval of the other members of the family, agreed to continue his account, to be worked by his eldest son, who signed cheques "for J.G. Beavan, S.S. Beavan." The account was operated in these two years for the maintenance of the customer's household in its accustomed manner, rents being collected and credited, and necessary outgoings being debited.

Upon the death of the customer the account was overdrawn, the amount including bank charges for interest and commission. The bank claimed the amount owing to them from the four executors, and the eldest son and one of his brothers, considering that the claim should not be resisted, severed from the two other executors and did not appear.

Decision

It was held that the bank were entitled to recover from the estate, by the doctrine of subrogation, all amounts paid out by them for necessaries; but that interest and commission charges could not be so recovered. In his judgment, Neville J. said:

Now it is not disputed that the law is that a person maintaining another of unsound mind is entitled to recoupment from his estate in respect of necessary expenditure, having regard to the position in life of the person of unsound mind. Starting with that, the question is, what is the right of one who lends money to the person who is maintaining the lunatic where that money is applied in the provision of necessaries for the maintenance of the lunatic? It appears to me that no legal right arises as a result of the lending in favour of the lender, but I think an

---

[4] But see *Russell* v. *Bank America National Trust*, *ante*, p. 135.

equity arises, and that that equity is to stand in the shoes of those creditors who, being creditors for necessaries supplied for the maintenance of the lunatic, have been paid out of the money advanced by the lender. That is an equity which applies in many cases, and I think that it also applies in the present case. Then it was argued that, in addition to that, there was a right on the part of the bank to recover the charges for interest and commission which, had they been dealing with a person of sound mind, they would have been entitled to charge. It does not seem to me that the contention can prevail. I think that, inasmuch as the equity which is to be applied is merely the right to stand in the shores of the creditors who are paid off, it is impossible that in addition to that there should be a right to receive the charges which have been paid for obtaining the loan.[5]

Notes

It is to be noted that the Mental Health Act 1959 (now replaced by the Mental Health Act 1983) repealed the earlier statutes governing the affairs of the mentally disordered. There has been no judicial consideration of how far the "mental disorder" of the 1959 Act equates with the "lunacy" of the earlier legislation, under which the relevant cases were decided.

There have in fact been very few cases in which a question has arisen concerning the banker's relationship with a customer of unsound mind, and this may probably be taken as an indication that in practice difficulties do not often occur. It is not clear whether it is mental disorder or notice of mental disorder that does in fact end the relationship[6]; in any case, the student must seek the theory of the matter in the general law of contract, and *Re Beavan* itself is an example of the application of this law to the banker-customer relationship. It can certainly be said at least that notice of mental disorder revokes the mandate to pay the customer's cheques.

It need hardly be pointed out that no banker wishes to rest upon his right of subrogation only, and that today, in circumstances like those of *Re Beavan*, the account would be stopped pending an order of the Court of Protection. Should immediate business be necessary it would be conducted through a new account in the name of the son.

In *Scarth* v. *National Provincial Bank Ltd.*[7] the bank's customer became of unsound mind and the bank stopped his account, even though the wife had authority to sign "*per pro.*"

---

[5] At pp. 201–202.
[6] *cf.* Holden, *op. cit.*, I.3.34.
[7] (1930) 4 L.D.B. 241.

She opened a separate account, and later, against the indemnity of herself and another, the bank transferred the balance of the husband's account to the wife's. Later the husband recovered from his disability, and claimed the balance of the account from the bank. The case was heard at York Assizes, and Humphreys J., applying the equitable principle[8] stated by Wright J. in *Liggett's* case,[9] decided in favour of the bank on the grounds that before the balance had been transferred the wife had used a larger sum than that balance in paying the husband's debts.

There are many circumstances in which the mental disorder of the customer, or the suspicion of it, can be a matter of extreme embarrassment to the banker.[10] It may be added here that in practice the banks would not be likely to stand on their legal rights in matters of this kind, and the necessities of the dependants must often be met immediately, without any legally satisfactory arrangement being possible.

INSOLVENCY

The Insolvency Act 1986 has consolidated the enactments relating to company insolvency and winding-up and enactments relating to the insolvency and bankruptcy of individuals, and has made sundry amendments and additions to the earlier legislation. Some of the pre-1986 cases are now of historic interest only, but many are of course still relevant, while the first cases originating under the Act, for example those on the administration order, have made their appearance.[10a]

Re Wigzell, Ex p. Hart

[1921] 2 KB 835

Payments on an account before the banker has notice of the making of a bankruptcy order

Facts

Wigzell was a customer at the Stoke Newington branch of Barclays Bank. A receiving order was made against him on October 8, 1919, but on his application the County Court

---

[8] "Under which a person who has, in fact, paid the debts of another without authority is allowed to take advantage of his payment."

[9] *Ante*, p. 221.

[10] *cf.* Holden, *op. cit.*, I,3,26–37.

[10a] For the considerable complications of the new legislation, see Penn, Shea & Arora, *op. cit.*, I.28.

granted a stay of the advertisement of the order and of all proceedings thereunder, pending his appeal against the order. On November 10, the appeal was dismissed with costs.

Between the date of the order and the dismissing of the appeal against it, the debtor had paid into his account with the bank sums totalling £165 2s. 3d., and he withdrew from the account sums totalling £199 19s. 7d. The bank had no knowledge of the bankruptcy proceedings.

The trustee claimed that he was entitled, as against the bank, to the sum of £165 2s. 3d., and that the bank was not entitled to deduct any of the debtor's withdrawals. The County Court and a Divisional Court held that the trustee's claim was justified, and the bank further appealed.

Decision

The Court of Appeal dismissed the appeal. Younger L.J. said that the bank had to concede that their transactions with their customer were on all fours with other transactions of the debtor in the period between the act of bankruptcy and the advertisement, and to allow the appeal would have had the result that those other transactions would also escape, so that "this court would in substance be ignoring that necessary condition for protection which is imposed by section 45 of the Act."

Notes

The Insolvency Act 1986 brought more closely into line the previously separate provisions covering individual bankruptcy and corporate insolvency. One notable change was the abolition of the "act of bankruptcy" as a controlling factor in bankruptcy proceedings, and thus of the problems of "relating back," which had been left open to challenge by the trustee transactions of the bankrupt between the first act of bankruptcy and the making of the bankruptcy order. Now, by section 278 of the 1986 Act, bankruptcy begins when the bankruptcy order is made.[11]

Re Wigzell is an example of the danger to the banker that as a result of the postponement of the advertisement of a receiving order he might make payments on the bankrupt's account which

---

[11] As to the problems of the banks with the relating back rules, *cf., e.g. Re Seymour* [1937] 1 Ch. 668 and *Re Simms* [1930] 2 Ch. 22. As to the comparable difficulty in winding up, between the presentation of the petition and the making of the order, see *post*, p. 390 *Re Grays Inn Construction Co. Ltd.*

would not be protected by section 45 or 46 of the Bankruptcy Act, 1914. The bank cited a line of precedents which tended to establish that, in the words of Farwell L.J. in *Re Tyler, ex parte Official Receiver*[12] "it would be insufferable for this court to have it said of it that it has been guilty by its officer of a dirty trick." But in *Re Wigzell* the court did not consider that the trustee's conduct had been at all at fault, especially as the postponement had naturally been sought by the debtor, not by the trustee himself.

Section 4 of the Bankruptcy (Amendment) Act 1926 went some way to remedy the position in providing that where money or property was transferred between the date of the receiving order and the date of the advertisement and the transfer was void under the principal Act as against the trustee in bankruptcy, the trustee should not proceed against the transferor unless the court was satisfied that it was not "reasonably practicable" to recover from the transferee. It is to be remarked that this enactment would not have helped the bank in *Re Wigzell*: there the payments in question were made to the bankrupt himself, and it is obviously not "reasonably practicable" for the trustee to recover from the debtor. The Act of 1926 was repealed in the new insolvency legislation, and a similar provision to the old section 4 appears in section 284(5) of the 1986 Act. Where a payment is made from an account at the order of the customer after the commencement of his bankruptcy the debit is provable unless the bank had earlier notice of the bankruptcy, or it is not reasonably practicable to recover the amount involved from the payee.

In *Re Byfield, ex p. Hill Samuel & Co. Ltd.*[13] the customer's bankruptcy was gazetted on April 4, 1979. On April 5 the bankrupt instructed the bank to transfer £19,500 to her mother's account at another bank, and the mother used £12,000 of that amount to pay off some of the bankrupt's creditors. When the trustee claimed the £12,000 the bank paid the money over, and then sought to prove for £12,000 as the creditors paid by the mother might have done had they not been paid. But Goulding J. held that the bank were not entitled to an extension of the relief under the Bankruptcy (Amendment) Act, while the principle that a trustee in bankruptcy should not take unfair advantage of a mistake did not apply here, where the mistake had nothing to do with the conduct of the trustee.

[12] [1907] 1 K.B. 865.
[13] [1982] 1 All E.R. 249; 10 L.D.B. 301.

Re Dutton, Massey & Co., Ex p. Manchester and Liverpool District Banking Co. Ltd.

[1924] 2 Ch. 199

Proof of debt in bankruptcy

Facts

Two of the partners of a firm deposited with the bank at which the firm's account was maintained certain of their own securities to secure the indebtedness of the firm. They also gave the bank their personal guarantees for the joint debt of the firm.

Later the firm entered into a deed of arrangement under which the firm's property was assigned to a trustee for the benefit of the creditors of the firm. The property was to be divided in proportion to the debts of the various creditors, and was to be administered in all respects in accordance with the general law of bankruptcy as though the firm had been adjudged bankrupt.

The bank sought to prove against the separate estates of the partners for their individual guarantees, and the trustee contended that they could not do so without taking into account the proceeds of the deposited securities. The trustee had already admitted the bank's claim against the partnership property in respect of the firm's overdraft.

Decision

The Court of Appeal held that, as the securities were not charged in respect of the partners' obligations under the contracts of guarantee, they need not be taken into account in the bank's proof against the partners individually.

In the course of his judgment Sargant L.J. said:

In my judgment, when the matter is looked at carefully, it seems perfectly plain that the security which was given by the two partners was not in any sense at all a security for the guarantee given by each of them, but was a guarantee simply and solely for the joint debt of the partnership. And when once that is appreciated, and also the fact that in these questions as to the administration of the joint and separate estates of partners, the partnership is to be regarded as a separate juridical entity from each of the partners individually, it seems to me to follow that there can be no obligation on the bank to give credit against the guarantee by each of the partners for a security which was given for the debt of a separate juridical entity—namely, the partnership.[14]

---

[14] At p. 213.

Notes

When a creditor seeks to prove against the estate of a bankrupt, it would obviously be inequitable to allow him to retain the benefit of any security he may hold which, if not charged, would go to augment the debtor's general estate, while at the same time proving for the full amount of his debt. The bankruptcy rules under the 1914 Act, and now under the Insolvency Act 1986, cover this point, and the present decision.

The decision, of obvious importance to bankers, establishes that in the application of these rules the creditor need not bring into account securities lodged for what is properly a different debt from that sought to be proved. The bank here had only one overdraft, but in the circumstances the debt of the firm was entirely distinct from the obligations of the partners individually under their guarantees; and as there was no possibility of the bank's recovering the whole of the overdraft, no question arose as to the position if, with the separate securities, the bank had been in a position to receive more than twenty shillings in the pound. Clearly they could not do so; and the question which would arise in such a case would be between the estates of the firm and the partners respectively.

Re Rushton, ex p. National Westminster Bank Ltd. v. *Official Receiver*[15] saw an application of the principle in the different circumstances of a charge on property owned by joint tenants, the bankrupt and his wife. After the bankruptcy the bank realised the security, which did not cover the indebtedness, and proved for the balance. The trustee said that the bank was only entitled to claim for half the balance, and the divisional court agreed, rejecting the bank's argument that the debtor, as one of two joint tenants, was not the owner of the entirety, so that the entirety was not the property of the debtor within section 167 of the Bankruptcy Act 1914. In a careful examination of the authorities Goff J. said that in *Re Dutton Massey*, on which the bank had in part relied, "the court was entirely influenced by the peculiar rules relating to partnerships," by which the partnership is regarded as a separate juridical entity from each of the partners individually.

Another question of importance to bankers regarding proof in bankruptcy was settled as long ago as 1896 in *Re Sass, ex p. National Provincial Bank of England.*[16] There the debtor's guarantor had guaranteed the whole of the borrowing, but with

---

[15] [1971] 2 All E.R. 937; 9 L.D.B. 202.
[16] [1896] 2 Q.B. 12; 1 L.D.B. 234.

a limit on the amount recoverable. On the debtor's bankrutpcy the bank made demand on the guarantor, and he paid £303, the amount for which he was liable. The bank then proved for the whole debt, and the trustee rejected the proof, claiming that it should be reduced by £303. But the court held that the bank's proof must be accepted: the guarantee was in respect of the whole debt, and Vaughan Williams J. said "it would be wrong to hold that the surety could, as against the bank, get any right to dividend by reason of the payment of a part of what was to be treated, as between him and the bank, as the whole of the debt, unless the bank had received the whole of the debt."

PREFERENCES

Re Joseph Samson Lyons, ex p. Barclays Bank Ltd. v. The Trustee

(1934) 51 T.L.R. 24

Preference as it affects the banker in bankruptcy and winding up proceedings

Facts

The bankrupt had an account with Barclays Bank with an agreed overdraft of £2,000. This advance was secured by the guarantee of the bankrupt's father. It was shown in evidence that early in 1932 the bankrupt knew that he was insolvent. In August 1932 he ceased payments to his general creditors, but continued to pay into his account, with the result that by October 22, when a bankruptcy petition was presented, the overdraft had been reduced to a little over £1,300. He was adjudicated bankrupt in December, and the trustee sought a declaration that the payments in reduction of the overdraft constituted a fraudulent preference of the bank and/or the guarantor.

Clauson J. held that the facts justified the inference that the bankrupt had intended to relieve his father of his liability, and that there was therefore fraudulent preference. He made an order against the bank for the sum involved, but made no order against the guarantor. The bank appealed.

Decision

The Court of Appeal held that the facts did not justify the inference drawn from them in the lower court, and allowed the appeal.

In his judgment Lord Hanworth M.R. said that the bankrupt's banking account was an ordinary business account into which cheques were paid, and on which cheques were drawn. Clauson J. had said that the account was operated in such a way that the only possible inference was that an effort was being made by the bankrupt to prefer his father. But was that so? The bankrupt continued to operate the account after September 12, in exactly the same way as he had done before that date, when there was admittedly no intention to prefer anyone. He paid money in and he drew money out. To deduce from that that the only explanation was that the debtor was minded to relieve his father from liability was to misread the evidence and not to look at it in its proper perspective. It overlooked the essential nature of a fraudulent preference as indicated by Lord Tomlin in *Peat* v. *Gresham Trust Ltd.*[17] as follows:

The onus is on those who claim to avoid the transaction to establish what the debtor really intended, and that the real intention was to prefer. The onus is only discharged when the Court, upon a review of all the circumstances, is satisfied that the dominant intent to prefer was present. That may be a matter of direct evidence or of inference, but where there is not direct evidence and there is room for more than one explanation it is not enough to say there being no direct evidence the intention to prefer must be inferred.[17a]

Notes[18]

One of the changes in the insolvency legislation was the omission of "fraudulent" from the "fraudulent preference" which had been familiar to bankers for so many years. It had long been recognised that the word was misleading[19] but it has been familiar for so long that it may take bankers a little while to remember that it has gone.

This case is of double interest to bankers. It emphasises that intent to prefer is an essential element in fraudulent preference, but it left untouched the doctrine that when a guarantor had been preferred recovery could be obtained from the bank, the guarantor escaping liability at least as far as the particular action goes—for it must be noted that the Court of Appeal reversed the decision of the lower court only on the facts of the case, not

---

[17] (1934) 50 T.L.R. 345 at p. 349.
[17a] At p. 25.
[18] In the following notes preference is seen in the context of winding up proceedings as well as bankruptcy.
[19] *cf.* The comment of Roskill L.J. *post* p. 376.

on the law involved. The bank can, of course, still sue the guarantor, but this is often not worth doing, and must always be more troublesome than the joining of the guarantor in the first proceedings.

Section 44 of the Bankruptcy Act 1914, (now section 340 of the Insolvency Act 1986) first extended the legislation against fraudulent preference to prevent such preference of a guarantor. The section has not been consistently applied, however. In *Re G. Stanley & Co. Ltd.*[20], Eve J. held that the section was designed to enable the liquidator to proceed against the person actually preferred; but in *Re Lyons*, as we have seen, only the banker's liability was in question, and in *Re Conley*,[21] which established that a person charging property to secure the debt of another is a surety within the terms of section 44, Luxmore J. in the Court of Appeal expressly approved the decision of Farwell J. in the court below when he followed *Re Lyons* rather than *Re Stanley*.

The provisions against fraudulent preference in the Companies Acts (now s.239 of the Insolvency Act 1986) have similar effects *vis-à-vis* the banker. In *Re M. Kushler Ltd.*[22] the guarantor and co-director of a private limited company had professional advice that the company was insolvent. Between the date of that advice and the date, a fortnight later, of the resolution for voluntary winding up, the company's overdraft of £600 had been completely repaid, although only two trade bills had been paid in the meantime, and an important trade creditor had been pressing for payment of an account due for three months. The Court of Appeal held that on these facts fraudulent preference was established, the inference, otherwise incomplete, being completed by the pressure of the important creditor.

The trustee in bankruptcy or the liquidator in winding up proceedings can always be more sure of obtaining repayment from a bank than from a guarantor, and there is thus no inducement for him to bring an action against the latter. And when the bank sought, in *Re Singer A. & Co. (Hat Manufacturers) Ltd.*[23] to join the two guarantors involved as parties, the Court of Appeal upheld the trial judge's refusal to order the liquidator to do so: the courts had no jurisdiction "to

---

[20] [1925] 1 Ch. 148.
[21] [1938] 2 All E.R. 127.
[22] [1943] 2 All E.R. 22.
[23] [1943] 1 Ch. 121.

settle disputes between persons who are for the purpose of those disputes altogether outside the winding up."

Following the *Singer* case the Committee of London Clearing Bankers made strong representations to the Company Law Amendments Committee (The Cohen Committee)[24]; and the Companies Act 1948 gave partial protection to the banker in section 321(3), which provided that:

> On any application made to the Court with respect to any payment on the ground that the payment was a fraudulent preference of a surety or guarantor, the Court shall have jurisdiction to determine any questions with respect to the payment arising between the person to whom the payment was made and the surety or guarantor and to grant relief in respect thereof, notwithstanding that it is not necessary to do so for the purposes of the winding up, and for that purpose may give leave to bring in the surety or guarantor as a third party as in the case of an action for the recovery of the sum paid.

This subsection deals with the point in question in *Re Singer Ltd.*, but it does not exempt the banker from liability. In practice, as was pointed out above, it is of course invariably easier and sometimes only possible to recover from the banker; but the provision does make possible the joining of the guarantor in the action, and to that extent the banker's position *vis-à-vis* the guarantor is restored. The protection of section 321(3) may be compared with that given in other circumstances by section 4 of the Bankruptcy (Amendment) Act 1926.[25]

Section 321(1) of the Companies Act 1948, provided as follows:

> Where, in the case of a company wound up in England, anything made or done after the commencement of this Act is void under the last foregoing section as a fraudulent preference of a person interested in property mortgaged or charged to secure the company's debt, then (without prejudice to any rights or liabilities arising apart from this provision) the person preferred shall be subject to the same liabilities, and shall have the same rights, as if he had undertaken to be personally liable as surety for the debt to the extent of the charge on the property or the value of his interest, whichever is the less.

This subsection made the third party mortgagor of property in favour of a company liable in the same way, upon a

---

[24] *Ante*, p. 213.
[25] *Ante*, p. 368.

fraudulent preference, as a guarantor. It may be noted that it restores only a personal liability, as compared with the right *in rem* which has been lost upon the surrender of the security charged; but although the protection to the banker is thus not by any means complete it is, like that of section 321(3), valuable so far as it goes.[26]

As regards bankruptcy, it is important to note that section 115 of the Companies Act 1947, one of the sections not repealed in 1948 by the consolidating Act, extends to bankruptcy law the provisions regarding the fraudulent preference of sureties and guarantors, which are now embodied in section 321. This is now contained in somewhat different terms in section 241(1)(*e*) of the Insolvency Act 1986 in respect of companies, and section 342(1)(*e*) in respect of individuals, whereby the court order may provide for any surety or guarantor whose obligations to any person were released or discharged (in whole or in part) by the giving of the preference to be under such new or revived obligation to that person as the court thinks fit.

A banker's difficulties with fraudulent preference are normally the result of a customer's attempt to ease the position of a guarantor, rather than any wish to benefit the bank directly. An example of an alleged preference of the bank was *Re F.L.E. Holdings Ltd.*[27] where the company had borrowed from the bank against the deposit of deeds, which was not registered under section 95 of the Companies Act 1948. Neither the bank's manager nor the company realised that the charge was defective. The company later got into difficulties, and a second charge was arranged for one of the creditors. The bank manager, hearing of this proposal, called on the company to execute a legal charge in favour of the bank, and this was done on the day before the second charge was executed. When the company went into liquidation the liquidator claimed that the legal mortgage was a fraudulent preference of the bank, but Pennycuick J. rejected the claim: although there was no consideration for the legal mortgage, nor pressure from the bank in the sense of a threat to call in the advance, this was not conclusive as to an intent to prefer, and in the circumstances he held that there was no intention beyond that of keeping faith with the bank.

Similarly in *Re William Hall (Contractors) Ltd.*,[28] where the company had borrowed against security lodged with memoranda

---

[26] *cf.* Paget, *op. cit.* 68.
[27] [1967] 1 W.L.R. 1409; 9 L.D.B. 34.
[28] *Post*, p. 397.

of deposit, and on the brink of insolvency had executed legal mortgages, it was held that there had been no fraudulent preference, the company's intention being merely to complete its existing obligation to the bank.

But in *Re F.P. and C.H. Matthews Ltd.*,[29] where the company had borrowed against the guarantee of Mr. Matthews and his wife, the sole shareholders, the overdraft of some £10,000 was cleared by the payment in of two cheques on the day after Mr. Matthews had decided that the company would have to stop trading. When some months later the company went into liquidation the liquidator's claim that the two credits were a fraudulent preference of the bank was allowed by the Court of Appeal. At the date of the payments in the debtor had honestly believed that all his creditors could be paid in full within three to six months, and the bank had argued that therefore no intention to prefer could be inferred. But section 44 was concerned only with "a person unable to pay his debts as they become due," and whatever the debtor's belief as to the future, he knew that the could not pay his debts as they arose.

The nature of fraudulent preference was discussed in *Osterreichische Landerbank* v. *S'Elite Ltd*[30] where Austrian bankers claimed as holders for value of a bill drawn by their customers, Eisart A.G., on the defendants, and dishonoured on presentation. They were given summary judgment, and the defendants appealed, alleging that Eisart were to the knowledge of the bank insolvent when the bill was drawn; the bank's title was defective under section 29(2) of the Bills of Exchange Act 1882, which provides that the title of a person negotiating a bill is defective if, *inter alia*, he has obtained it by "fraud"; and that this amounted to a fraudulent preference. But the Court of Appeal, dismissing the appeal, overruled an earlier decision which had equated "fraud" in section 29 with fraudulent preference in section 44 of the Bankruptcy Act; and Roskill L.J. said:

A fraudulent preference, as has often been pointed out, is a misleading term. A preference can be "fraudulent" within the statute without there being any element of common law fraud involved.…

It has often been pointed out that the phrase is an inept one, and that a better phrase than "fraudulent preference" is "voidable preference"…I take the view that in the relevant sections of the 1882 Act "fraud" means common law fraud.[30a]

[29] [1982] 1 All E.R. 651.
[30] [1980] 2 All E.R. 651.   [30a] At p. 654.

And in the present case there were no "relevant allegations of fraud, let alone any relevant allegations of fraud to which the bank was party."

ADMINISTRATION ORDERS

Re Consumer and Industrial Press Ltd.

[1988] B.C.L.C. 177

The basis on which the court will make an administration order

Facts

The company published a knitting and needlework magazine which had been established in 1949 and had a considerable reputation. But by April 1987 after incurring substantial trading losses, it was heavily insolvent, and independent auditors reported that it would not be possible to trade out of its difficulties. In July 1987 the Commissioners of Inland Revenue sought an order for the compulsory winding up of the company; and in October the company sought an administration order, and the dismissal of the winding-up petition. The company claimed that administrators could continue publication of the magazine, and so be likely to obtain a higher price on its sale than could a liquidator.

Decision

Peter Gibson J. set out the conditions which by section 8(1) of the Insolvency Act 1986 must be met for the court to make an administration order—that (a) the company is or is likely to become unable to pay its debts and (b) the court is satisfied that the making of an order would be likely to achieve one or more of the purposes specified in section 8(3). The word "likely" was important; it was not enough that it was "possible" that a purpose might be achieved. In the present application he was not satisfied on the evidence that an order would ensure the survival of the company, or obtain approval of a voluntary arrangement. But on the fourth of the four purposes of the subsection, effecting a more advantageous realisation of the company's assets than would be possible in a winding up, there was more satisfactory evidence, including the profit obtained, after cutbacks in overheads, by the most recent issue, and the fact that four purchasers had expressed interest in the magazine. So the statutory preconditions for the exercise of discretion were satisfied.

This was not necessarily enough. The Revenue had argued that a liquidator could examine, as an administrator could not, the facts that the company had continued to trade when insolvent and even after the making of the winding-up order; moreover, the true beneficiaries of an administration order were likely to be the secured creditors, who might have put in a receiver and had chosen not to do so. The court should ignore them, and allow the Revenue to prevail over the opposing unsecured creditors.

But although feeling the force of the Revenue's submissions, his Lordship did not accept them:

I do not think I should ignore the benefit that would accrue to secured creditors... although I accept that their interests weigh lighter in the scales than the other creditors. But the administration order, in addition to benefiting the secured creditors, will give at least the possibility of achieving more benefit for the preferential creditors and other unsecured creditors than would a liquidation.

Notes

The administration order is an important innovation of the Insolvency Act 1986.[31] Its purpose is to facilitate rescue operations for ailing companies, and there has been considerable use of it in its first years of operation.[32] Its effect is to freeze the company's position, so that actions against the company are suspended, there can be no winding-up petition, and no fresh legal process can be commenced. The administrator has normally three months in which to formulate proposals for reorganisation for submission to the creditors.

Banks are generally not likely to welcome the making of administration orders, which can delay the realisation of their security. The appointment of an administrator can be blocked by the holder of a floating charge, if the charge and other charges cover virtually the whole of the company's assets, and banks are likely to extend their use of the floating charge.

---

[31] Insolvency Act 1986, ss.8–27.
[32] See, *e.g.* *Re Harris Simons Construction Ltd.* [1989] 1 W.L.R. 368. *Re Newport County F.C.* [1987] B.C.L.C. 582, and *Re St Ives Windings* [1987] 3 B.C.C. 634.

RECEIVERS

Gomba Holdings U.K. Ltd. and Others v. Homan and Another

[1986] 1 W.L.R. 1301

The powers of a receiver

Facts

The plaintiffs had granted fixed and floating charges to Johnson Matthey Bankers Ltd. The bank appointed receivers under the charges who realised various assets to the value of about £11 million, but the current indebtedness was still about £11 million. The sole and controlling director of the plaintiffs claimed to have entered into an agreement with an undisclosed third party on undisclosed terms which would provide funds to pay off the outstanding debt, and the plaintiffs claimed that they therefore required information about the current state of the receivership and details of disposals made or proposed to be made; and further they sought an order that five days' notice should be given of any commitment to dispose of further assets.

Decision

On the last point Hoffman J. saw no arguable cause of action: no claim by the plaintiffs that they could shortly redeem could give them a right to limit the receivers' unrestricted right to sell at any time. As to the request for further information, he reviewed in some detail the duties of a receiver and manager who, although nominally the agent of the company, has a "primary duty to realise the assets in the interests of the debenture holder, and his powers of management are really ancillary to that duty." There are certain principles which can be deduced from the nature of receivership. "The first is that the receiver and manager should have the power to carry on the day-to-day process of realisation and management of the company's property without interference from the board." The second is that "in the absence of express contrary provision made by statute or the terms of the debenture, any right which the company may have to be supplied with information must be qualified by the receiver's primary duty to the debenture holder."

In the present case, after briefly reviewing the relationship between the plaintiffs' solicitors and the receivers and their solicitors—with frequent accusations of bad faith against the receivers and the bank, letters of complaint to the receivers' professional body, and two-and-a-half months of heavy litigation challenging the validity of the receivers' appointment—and detailing the course of the present action, he was willing to accept that a mortgagor in the process of redeeming was entitled to particulars of the amount still due.

But I do not think that for this purpose it is sufficient for the mortgagor merely to say that he wants to redeem or that he had some mysterious third party who will put up £12m. The history of this case, both before and after the appointment of the receivers, is a chronicle of unfulfilled assurances by Mr Shamji that someone was about to provide the money to pay his debts to the bank. In my judgment the receivers were under no obligation to provide any information until they had firmer evidence that there was a realistic prospect of redemption.[32a]

Notes

The long course of litigation to which Hoffmann J. referred is of legal interest, aside from its relevance as an important footnote to the Johnson Matthey collapse; the "two and a half months of heavy litigation" produced in *Shamji* v. *Johnson Matthey Bankers Ltd.*[33] another notable receivership decision when Hoffmann J., affirmed by the Court of Appeal, rejected the plaintiff's claim to stop the appointment of receivers on the grounds that negotiations for a sale were near completion. He rejected too the argument that the bank owed a duty to consider "all relative matters" before appointing receivers, and further to maximise their recovery from the group so as to minimise their call on the plaintiff's guarantee: the bank's power of appointment was unqualified, and there was no room for such implied terms.

A receiver's appointment was challenged on other grounds in *Re Potters Oils Ltd. (No. 2)*[34] The company had borrowed from Lloyds Bowmaker Ltd. to finance the purchase of plant from France. Later a winding-up order was made against the company, and a liquidator appointed. Lloyds Bowmaker notified the liquidator of their charge, and he confirmed that the "alleged debenture" would be notified to the court, but that he and the court would have to be satisfied of its validity. Lloyds Bowmaker then appointed a receiver, and in due course the plant was sold back to the French company, the proceeds being

[32a] At p. 1309.
[33] [1986] B.C.L.C. 278.
[34] [1986] 1 W.L.R. 201.

enough to satisfy the bank's claim. But the liquidator now challenged the receiver's remuneration, claiming that the appointment had been unnecessary, he being capable of handling the whole business. But Hoffmann J. rejected his claim. The liquidator might well have been right in saying that the French claim was bound to fail, but there was no reason why Lloyds Bowmaker, who had a cast iron claim, should have taken any chances; and the liquidator's sceptical reception of the debenture, and his threat to sue for patent infringement, could only confirm their view that they needed to look after themselves.

It is important that the formalities of the appointment be strictly observed. In *Windsor Refrigerator Co. Ltd.* v. *Branch Nominees Ltd.*[35] a receiver was appointed by Branch Nominees, a subsidiary of the National Provincial Bank, under a debenture conferring a power to appoint a receiver "by writing." Such appointments are normally under seal, and Branch Nominees had affixed its common seal to an undated document appointing a receiver. Some days later demand was made on the company and the day's date inserted on the document; and when payment was not forthcoming the document was handed to the named receiver. The appointment was challenged on the grounds that the deed was, in view of the circumstances of its making, invalid; but the Court of Appeal held that the document was valid as an appointment by writing, because an appointment by writing could properly be made out before it was intended to take effect.

In the more complicated circumstances of *Cripps (Pharmaceuticals) Ltd.* v. *Wickenden and Another*,[36] the *Windsor Refrigerator* decision was applied on the question of the pre-dating of the appointments, and the National Westminister Bank successfully resisted further challenges to the appointments in question, Goff J. holding, *inter alia*, that they could not be impugned on the ground that no reasonable time was given after the demand for it to be met: where a debt is payable on demand the creditor need give the debtor no more time than is needed to fetch the money. But there had been confusion over the appointments. When the initial appointments were challenged on the dating point the bank purported to make fresh appointments "to rectify this unfortunate error" (which, as was now held, was not in fact an error); and the judge's

---

[35] [1961] Ch. 375.
[36] [1973] 1 W.L.R. 944; 9 L.D.B. 306.

comment on the position that would have arisen had his finding been different serves as a warning of the danger of failing to observe the rule:

> ... if I had held the first appointments bad I would have had to have found the second appointments to be bad also, because no person can take advantage of his own wrong. In my judgment the bank could not appoint a receiver until it had restored the company to possession of its assets and renewed its demands. If it could not do that because it had sold the assets, then there might be a serious question whether it had forfeited its right altogether, or would be entitled to appoint a receiver after restoring the proceeds, the company having an action for damages for conversion for any loss not recouped by return of the proceeds. ...
> Even if that were wrong and the second appointments were good, still the bank would be liable for damages down to [the date of the second appointments] for the first wrongful appointments, and that would include damages for loss of the opportunity to avoid the second appointments occasioned by the wrongful freezing of assets under the first.[37]

The receiver is not automatically displaced by the making of a winding up order. In *Barrows and Others* v. *Chief Land Registrar*[38] where the power of receivers to complete the disposal of assets after the making of the winding up order was in question, Whitford J. held that the winding up order might terminate the agency of the receiver *vis-à-vis* the company but it did not terminate his power to act in the name of the company. And he quoted Goulding J. in *Re Satis House Datchett Bucks: Sowman* v. *David Samuel Trust Ltd.*[39]

> Winding up deprives the receiver, under such a debenture as that now in suit, of power to bind the company personally by acting as its agent. It does not in the least affect his powers to hold and dispose of the company's property comprised in the debenture including his power to use the company's name for that purpose, for such powers are given by the disposition of the company's property which is made (in equity) by the debenture itself. That disposition is binding on the company and those claiming through it, as well in liquidation as before liquidation.

And exceptionally the receiver may himself petition for the winding up of the company of which he is the receiver. In *Re Emmardart Ltd.*[40] he was allowed to do so as the only way in

---

[37] At pp. 956–957.
[38] *The Times*, October 20, 1977.
[39] (1977) Unreported.
[40] [1979] 2 W.L.R. 868.

which exemption from rates could be obtained on a vacant shop property, Brightman J. remarking that the protection and preservation of the assets of the company are incidental to the receiver's possession of them.

When the appointment of a receiver proves to have been unjustified, he must repay money received, and may be liable for damages for trespass.[41]

The Insolvency Act 1986 contains the term "administrative receiver," meaning a receiver or manager of the whole, or substantially the whole, of the company's property appointed by the holders of a debenture secured by a charge which when it was created was a floating charge. The Act sets out the specified powers of the administrative receiver.[42] Receivers under fixed or partial floating charges remain simply "receivers."

WINDING UP

National Westminster Bank Ltd. v. Halesowen Presswork & Assemblies Ltd.

[1972] A.C. 785

A winding-up order terminates the banker-customer relationship and any ancillary agreements dependent on that relationship

The set-off provisions of the Bankruptcy Act 1914, and the Companies Act 1948, cannot be excluded by agreement between debtor and creditor

Facts

Early in 1968 the company had an inactive and overdrawn account with the appellant bank, the company's trading account being with Lloyds Bank. In April, 1968, the trading account was moved to the appellants, the inactive account being then frozen; and the bank agreed that the two accounts should not be combined within the following four months "in the absence of materially changed circumstances." In May a meeting of creditors was called, and on June 12, a winding up order was made. The bank then sought to combine the accounts, arguing that the agreement to keep them separate terminated at the moment when the customers' mandates were terminated. The liquidator contended, *inter alia*, (*a*) that the agreement to keep

---

[41] *Ford & Carter Ltd.* v. *Midland Bank Ltd., ante,* p. 308.
[42] As to these powers, and receivers generally, see Penn, Shea & Arora, *op. cit.* I.23.

the accounts separate continued after the winding up, and (b) that by the agreement the bank had contracted out of section 31 of the Bankruptcy Act 1914, as applied to companies by section 317 of the Companies Act 1948.

Decision

The House of Lords held unanimously (a) that the agreement terminated with the ending of the banker-customer relationship and (b) that the agreement did not purport to contract out of section 31. They held further, Lord Cross dissenting, that such contracting out is anyhow not possible: section 31 is mandatory.

In his judgment Viscount Dilhorne said:

The weight of opinion in the cases to which I have referred appears to me to be in favour of the conclusion that it is not possible to contract out of section 31. The word in that section is "shall" not "may". . . . I think that the terms of section 31 and of the sections that follow it show that "shall" was used in all those sections in its directory and mandatory sense. . . .

If, contrary to my view, it is possible to contract out of section 31, the agreement made in this case did not, in my opinion, purport to do so. . . . The agreement was, to use the words of Lord Macnaghten in *British Guiana Bank* v. *Official Receiver*[42a] only "intended to be operative so long as the accounts were alive," that is to say, while the relationship of banker and customer existed and the company was a going concern. In my opinion the agreement came to an end when the winding up resolution was passed.[42b]

Notes

The importance of this decision lies in its clarification of a number of points that had earlier been in some doubt. Thus it confirmed that the banker has, in the absence of agreement express or implied to the contrary, a long established common law right to combine accounts of a customer[43]; that this right is not strictly a lien; and that it can be exercised without notice to the customer, again unless the contract provides otherwise.[44]

More specifically, the decision established that an agreement ancillary to the bank-customer relationship is terminated when the relationship is ended by a winding up order; and that the statutory set-off provisions in bankruptcy and winding up proceedings cannot be excluded by agreement. As to the first of

[42a] (1911) 104 L.T. 754.
[42b] At pp. 805 and 807.
[43] cf. *Hong Kong & Shanghai Banking Corporation* v. *Kloeckner & Co A.G., The Financial Times*, May 5, 1989.
[44] cf. *ante*, pp. 235, 278.

these two points, the importance of the decision is its reversal of the Court of Appeal's unanimous view that the agreement survived the winding up order. It is to be noted, however, that the decision depended on the wording and purpose of the agreement, designed to help keep the company solvent and so without further purpose when the winding up order was made. An agreement expressly designed to continue in force after a winding up might still be effective, though not, in view of the further finding, to exclude section 31, were any bank to enter into so unlikely an agreement.

Section 31 of the Bankruptcy Act 1914 provided for the setting off of claims between bankrupt and creditor where there have been "mutual credits, mutual debts or other mutual dealings"; and section 317 of the Companies Act 1948 extended this and other bankruptcy rules to the winding up of insolvent companies. Section 323 of the Insolvency Act 1986 replaced section 31 in somewhat rearranged terms as regards individual insolvency, and in relation to company insolvency section 317 has been repealed, and under schedule 8 of the 1986 Act various provisions in relation to insolvency or winding up of companies may be made by delegated legislation. These are currently contained in S.I. 1986 No. 1925, of which r. 4.90 repeats the provisions as to mutual credits, mutual debts and mutual dealings, so that the *Halesowen* case remains good law, resolving any doubt that had existed as to whether the provision was mandatory or merely permissive.

In the Court of Appeal it had been held, Buckley L.J. dissenting[45] that section 31 did not apply, the frozen account not being within the mutual dealings of the section. The House of Lords was unanimous in reversing this finding: the dealings here were not comparable with those in other cases where a debtor had deposited money with his creditor to be applied for a special purpose. It is submitted that the same reasoning would cover a loan account, although some of the speeches based this point on the temporary nature of the separation of the current account balances.

The House of Lords resolved also the questions raised in the judgments of the Court of Appeal as to the notice required (*a*) had the bank chosen to terminate the agreement when the meeting was called (admittedly a material change of circumstances) and (*b*) when the winding up order was made. As to (*a*) it is now clear, as bankers would have wished, that notice taking

---

[45] [1971] 1 Q.B. 1.

immediate effect is the right course, subject to the obligation to pay cheques drawn before the customer receives the notice.[46] In the case of (b) notice of any kind could serve no useful purpose.

Another case on section 317 was *Re Islington Metal and Plating Works Ltd.*[47] The section applied bankruptcy rules to insolvent companies in liquidation, allowing no unliquidated claims, whereas section 316, covering solvent companies, admitted all claims. Here there were assets to pay a substantial, but not a full, dividend to creditors, and there were outstanding claims for misfeasance against directors. But there were also large claims against the company for nuisance, so the liquidator might find that all the creditors had been paid in full, when the company would again be solvent, and section 316 would let in the nuisance claims, which might make the company again insolvent. Harman J., remarking that this might be the secret of perpetual motion, could not accept that it was the law, and he held that once a company passed into the control of section 316, all claims had to be admitted, even though they might not be paid in full; in such a case a just estimate of each claim must be made.

A different section 317 question arose in *Re Lines Bros Ltd. (in Liquidation)*,[48] where the liquidator, after the proved debts had been paid in full, sought guidance as to how creditors' interest should be paid. Section 317 provided that in the case of insolvent companies, interest at four per cent. should be paid on proved debts, and the surplus here would have covered all the creditors at four per cent. But there were also contractual debts, which were interest-bearing, and payment of these would have required substantially more than was available. Was the liquidator here still winding up an insolvent company? Mervyn Davies J., after reviewing the authorities, and referring to section 10 of the Supreme Court of Judicature Act 1873, held that the company was no longer insolvent under section 317: debts and liabilities at the commencement of the winding up had been met in full, no interest was payable under section 317, and contractual interest could be paid to the extent the surplus would allow.

---

[46] *cf. ante*, p. 235.
[47] [1984] 1 W.L.R. 14.
[48] [1984] B.C.L.C. 215. There is some confusion in the reporting of the Lines Brothers cases. The case here noted is not to be confused with the earlier decision at [1982] 2 W.L.R. 1010 (*ante*, p. 243), or with *Re Lines Bros Ltd. (in Liquidation) No. 2* [1984] B.C.L.C. 227. The present case appears to have not been so widely reported.

Re Yeovil Glove Co. Ltd.

[1965] Ch. 148

Floating charges

Facts

In January, 1958, the company created a floating charge on its property and assets in favour of the National Provincial Bank, with whom it was overdrawn to the extent of nearly £70,000. The bank did not undertake to make any further advances in consideration for this charge being given.

An arrangement had earlier been made that the No. 1 account fed into the No. 3 account and the No. 4 account the exact amounts respectively of the wages paid 18 weeks before and of the salaries paid four months before, thus providing a method by which the bank's preferential rights in a winding up in respect of money advanced for the payment of wages and salaries could be ascertained at any time.[49] All the accounts were at all times overdrawn.

In August the bank appointed a receiver, and there was no more working on the accounts. In January 1959 a petition for the compulsory winding up of the company was lodged by trade creditors, a winding-up order was made and a liquidator appointed. The liquidator claimed that the floating charge was invalid against him by virtue of section 322 of the Companies Act 1948, which provided that:

> Where a company is being wound up, a floating charge on the undertaking or property of the company created within twelve months of the commencement of the winding up shall, unless it is proved that the company immediately after the creation of the charge was solvent, be invalid, except to the amount of any cash paid to the company at the time of, or subsequently to the creation of, and in consideration for, the charge together with interest. . . .

Decision

The Court of Appeal affirmed the decision of Plowman J. that the bank could rely on the charge. Drawings from No. 1 account after January 1958 were cash paid by the bank in consideration for the charge; in accordance with the rule in

---

[49] *cf. post,* p. 394.

Clayton's case[50] money credited to No. 1 account after January 1958 was to be set against the earliest advances, *i.e.* those before the charge.

In his judgment Harman, L.J. said:

> The fallacy in the appellant's argument lies, in my opinion, in the theory that, because the company's payments in to the bank after the date of the charge were more or less equal to the payments out by the bank during the same period, no "new money" was provided by the bank. This is not the fact. Every such payment was in fact new money having regard to the state of the company's accounts, and it was in fact used to pay the company's creditors. That the indebtedness remained approximately at the same level was due to the fact that this was the limit set by the bank to the company's overdraft.[51]

Notes

Section 322 has been repealed, and new provisions of a wider nature are now contained in section 245 of the Insolvency Act 1986. In particular, the invalidity period in respect of a charge in favour of a "connected person" is two years before the date of the presentation of a petition for an administration order, or the date of the commencement of the winding–up.

This decision is of unusual interest in that the only authority directly in point, and extensively considered in the judgments, was *Re Thomas Mortimer Ltd.*,[52] a 39-year-old decision unreported otherwise than in the *Journal of the Institute of Bankers* and *Legal Decisions affecting Bankers*. In that case the company had an overdraft of some £58,000 with the National Provincial Bank. In January 1924 a debenture of £50,000 was created in favour of the bank. Two months later the company went into liquidation, but in the meantime £40,000 had been paid into the account and £50,000 paid out. Romer J. held that section 212 of the Companies (Consolidation) Act 1908 (which was substantially re-enacted in section 322 of the 1948 Act), did not invalidate the payment.

In *Re Yeovil Glove Ltd.*, Plowman J. at first instance, and all three Lords Justices in the Court of Appeal, approved the decision of Romer J. in 1925. It may be noted that the Court of Appeal, again unanimously, refused to accept the bank's argument that, even if they disagreed with the *Mortimer* decision, they could not properly allow the appeal when the

---

[50] *Ante*, p. 150.
[51] At p. 174.
[52] (1925) 4 L.D.B. 3.

decision had stood so long, and two subsequent statutes had re-enacted the provision unaltered. Instead, after full consideration, they approved the earlier decision on its merits.

In *Re G.T. Whyte & Co. Ltd.*[53] Lloyds Bank made an advance to the company against specified security through their subsidiary, Lloyds Associated Banking Co. Ltd. The arrangements were later changed, the advance was called in, and the bank provided a replacement advance, this time against the company's floating charge. When 10 months later the company was compulsorily wound up the liquidator successfully challenged the floating charge: the bank and the subsidiary could not be regarded as separate entities, and the replacement advance was not "cash paid" under section 322, but was in effect to secure past indebtedness.[54]

Two recent decisions have done something to resolve the questions which have arisen regarding the crystallisation of floating charges. Crystallisation occurs on the appointment of a receiver, but there have been doubts as to whether, or when, it can predate that appointment. Thus in *Re Woodroffes (Musical Instruments) Ltd.*[55] the company created fixed and floating charges in favour of the Hong Kong and Shanghai Banking Corporation and later, in breach of the terms of the lending, a second floating charge was given in favour of the principal shareholder. In due course she gave notice crystallising her charge, and a few days later the bank appointed a receiver. A dispute on priorities arose between the bank, the shareholder and the preferential creditors, and Nourse J. held that a floating charge can crystallise without intervention when a company ceases to do business. But here there was no evidence that this had happened before the receiver was appointed, and crystallisation at that date gave priority to: (1) the bank, to the extent of the shareholder's claim; (2) the preferential creditors; (3) the bank, as to the rest of its claim; and (4) the shareholder.

In *Re Brightlife Ltd.*[56] where a debenture provided that the chargee could by notice crystallise the floating charge if he believed that his security was in danger, and in the event he gave notice, Hoffmann J. was not prepared to interfere with the contractual freedom of the parties to a debenture to agree their

---

[53] *The Financial Times*, December 14, 1982.
[54] The changes in the law effected by section 245 of the Insolvency Act 1986 are discussed in Penn, Shea & Arora, *op. cit.* I.21–38–42. The cases here described remain good law.
[55] [1986] Ch. 366; 10 L.D.B. 497.
[56] [1986] 3 All E.R. 673.

own terms, and here notice had converted the floating charge into a fixed charge. This gave the chargee priority over the preferential creditors; but the insolvency legislation of 1986 restored the position of the preferential creditors *vis-à-vis* the earlier crystallisation of a floating charge, and *to this extent only* superseded these two cases.

Re Gray's Inn Construction Co. Ltd.

[1980] 1 W.L.R. 711

The operation of the account after the commencement of the winding–up

Facts

The company had its banking account with the National Westminster Bank. When, on August 3, 1972, a petition to wind up the company was presented there was an overdraft, against the guarantee of the managing director, of £5,322. The petition was advertised on August 10, and the bank became aware of it at head office some time before the branch manager, who had notice on August 17. A compulsory winding up order was made on October 9, the account having been continued until then without breaking, as was permissible by the bank's internal rules; and between August 3, and October 9, £25,313 had been paid in and £24,129 paid out.

The liquidator claimed payment of either the credits received or the payments out, as dispositions of the company's property within section 227 of the Companies Act, 1948, (now replaced by section 127 of the Insolvency Act 1986) which provided that

In a winding up by the Court, any disposition of the property of the company, including things in action, and any transfer of shares, or alterations in the status of the members of the company, made after the commencement of the winding up, shall, unless the Court otherwise orders, be void.

However, in the proceedings neither claim was pressed, and the claim was restricted to the loss suffered as a result of the continued trading, an amount agreed at the trial as £5,000. Templeman J. held that the credits were not dispositions of the company's property within section 227, and exercising his discretion under the section he validated the payments out, holding that the decision to allow banking facilities for normal trade was made after proper consideration by a prudent and conscientious bank manager who prescribed and enforced proper safeguards for the operation of the account. The liquidator appealed against this decision.

Decision

The Court of Appeal allowed the appeal. Buckley L.J., reviewed, in a judgment with which Goff L.J. and Sir David Cairns concurred, the principles upon which the courts should exercise their discretion under section 227, and said that it should be within the context of the liquidation provisions of the 1948 Act, a basic concept of which was that the free assets of the insolvent company should be distributed rateably amongst the unsecured creditors. So no payment should be validated which resulted in a pre-liquidation creditor being paid in full at the expense of other creditors who would receive only a dividend.

Templeman J. had spoken of banks facing a dilemma when asked to continue banking facilities after the presentation of a petition. But the bank can seek or get the company to seek, a validation order from the court. If this is not done the bank is at risk of the court's later refusal to validate transactions involved, and so should have in mind the considerations that would influence the court. The court is more likely to validate a transaction if it does not reduce the value of the company's assets; *a fortiori* if it increases their value.

If a bank decides to continue to afford facilities to a corporate customer against whom a winding-up petition has been presented, having an account in debit at the date of the presentation of the petition, the bank can itself freeze that account and insist on all subsequent dealings being dealt with on a separate account. It can require personal assurances from the directors of the company that no payments out of the new account will be made in discharge of pre-liquidation debts, and that all payments out of the new account shall be in respect of liabilities incurred in the ordinary course of business subsequent to the presentation of the petition. It can institute such checks on the profitability of the company's trading as it thinks fit.[56a]

Even when the bank has obtained a validation order, allowing the business and the account to continue, it will be subject to the condition that continued trading is at a profit, and is for the benefit of creditors generally.

A bank cannot of course spend all or even a great deal of its time in conducting a day-to-day surveillance of a customer's business, and the court, if asked to make a prospective order, must do its best to make a

[56a] At p. 720.

realistic assessment of the risk involved of any system of safeguards falling short of failing safe.[56b]

He held that both credits and debits were dispositions within section 227. The credits in the present case received before the advertisement should be validated, as should a credit paid in on August 11, a total of £2,670. The credit paid in on August 15, by which date the bank must be assumed to have known of the petition, was not validated. The validations would reduce the pre-liquidation overdraft to £2,652. The bank was not entitled to appropriate later credits to discharge this debt, so validation was refused also to credits after August 11, to that amount. The bank was vulnerable also to a further £4,824 in respect of sums paid out on pre-liquidation debts, but recovery of these sums should be sought first from the recipients of the payments.[57]

As to the trading loss, had the bank applied for a prospective validating order the court might have authorised continued banking facilities subject to precautions to ensure as far as possible that the company was not supported in unprofitable trading, unless this was for the benefit of creditors. The bank took the risk of going on without such an order, and must restore to the company the amount lost in post-liquidation trading.

Notes

This important decision has marked a change in the attitude of the courts to relief under section 227. The decision of Templeman J. in favour of the bank was in line was a respectable body of precedent, and although the reversal of that decision by the Court of Appeal did not overrule such earlier decisions, it seems probable that some of them would now be decided differently.

In *Re Wiltshire Iron Co., ex p. Pearson*[58] Lord Cairns L.J. said:

But where a company actually trading, which it is in the interest of everyone to preserve, and ultimately to sell, as a going concern, is made an object of a winding-up petition, which may fail or may succeed, if it were to be supposed that transactions in the ordinary

---

[56b] At p. 720.

[57] *cf.* the view of Street C.J. in the Australian case, *Re Mal Bowers Macquarie Electrical Centre Pty. Ltd.* [1974] 1 N.S.W.L.R. 254, whose judgment is cited at some length in Paget, *op. cit.* 62: that "disposition" in s.227 involves a disponee, from whom alone recovery can be claimed, a cheque being merely the vehicle by which the disposition is made.

[58] (1868) L.R. 3 Ch.App. 443.

course of its current trade, bona fide entered into and completed, would be avoided, and would not, in the discretion given to the court, be maintained, the result would be that the presentation of a petition, groundless or well-founded, would, *ipso facto*, paralyse the trade of the company, and great injury would be done to those interested in the assets of the company.[58a]

This dictum has influenced later decisions[59] as justifying the continuation of banking facilities with the object of saving the business. Buckley L.J., remarking that the trial judge in the present case had Lord Cairns' remarks in mind in coming to his decision, went on:

It will be observed that Lord Cairns there supposes a case of a company actually trading which it is in the interests of everyone to preserve and ultimately to sell as a going concern. It has not been suggested in the present case that anyone ever addressed his mind to the question whether it would be in the interests of the unsecured creditors that the company's business should be continued with a view to a sale as a going concern notwithstanding the possibility of trading losses meanwhile.[59a]

In previous editions of this book the comment of Phillimore L.J. (in *Re Clifton Place Garage Ltd.*[60]) on banking practice in the matter was quoted:

I question also whether this rigid practice of the banks in all cases is right, or whether, particularly if they were aware that the court would look with indulgence on such cases, it would not be possible, after proper enquiry, at any rate in some cases, to cash cheques for a company, even if only against current receipts on a day-to-day basis.[60a]

It was noted then that in fact the banks' practice was not as rigid as had been suggested, at least one of the clearing banks being on record[61] as allowing accounts, whether in credit or debit, to continue after the presentation of a petition "provided they are conducted in the ordinary course of business."

[58a] At p. 447.

[59] *cf., e.g. Re T.W. Construction Ltd.* [1954] 1 W.L.R. 540.

[59a] At p. 724.

[60] [1970] Ch. 477.

[60a] At p. 494.

[61] (October, 1970) J.B.L. 253. The bank also "allowed credit accounts of individuals to continue in the ordinary course of business notwithstanding that the bank has received notice of an available act of bankruptcy, relying on the decision of the court in *Re Dalton* [1963] C.L. 336 to pay third-party cheques."

This would now seem to be of historic interest only. The fact that credits as well as debits to the account are at risk, and that future losses of the company may be relevant, make it virtually certain that banks will now increasingly seek validation orders, and not rely on the optimistic view of the courts' eventual decision which Phillimore L.J. had seemed to encourage and which clearly influenced those banks whose practice had been less than rigid.

National Provincial Bank Ltd. v. Freedman and Rubens

(1934) 4 L.D.B. 444

The bank as preferential creditor for wages cheques

Facts

The defendants were receiver and debenture holder respectively of a company, N. Bach Ltd., whose account had been kept with the plaintiff bank. The company's overdraft having increased to an extent which the bank could not approve, the practice was followed, for a period of more than a year, of paying in cheques received at the time in each week at which it was desired to draw wages, the branch manager refusing to pay the wages cheque until he was satisfied that about the same amount was being paid into the credit of the company. Upon the winding up of the company the bank claimed that these payments had been in fact advances for wages, the corresponding credits to the account having been reductions of the existing indebtedness; and that by virtue of section 264(3) of the Companies Act 1929 (subsequently s.319(4) of the 1948 Act and now s.386 and Schedule 6 of the Insolvency Act 1986) they, the bank, were therefore entitled to stand in the shoes of the employees of the company to whom the wages had been paid, and to rank as preferential creditors to that extent in the winding up of the company. The defendants contended that no advances had been made to the company for wages, that what had happened represented the mere exchange by the bank of the cheques which the company took to them weekly, and that therefore the bank could not be preferential creditors in this connection.

Decision

It was held that the bank were entitled to the declaration they sought. In the course of his judgment, Clauson J. said:

There is a suggestion that there were conversations of a somewhat loose character, from which it can be inferred that there was an arrangement that the cheques paid in were to be used simply to provide the cash to pay the wages. What seems to me to be most important is the way in which the account was kept. The way the account was kept shows perfectly clearly that that was not the transaction at all. The transaction was that these cheques reduced the overdraft and that is the meaning of the bank account as it appears.... The bank manager, whatever loose language he may have used, was not going to let the overdraft be permanently increased, and accordingly it was necessary for him to take care that the wages cheque was not paid until these cheques had gone into the account. But those cheques did not provide the wages; those cheques reduced the overdraft, and the wages cheque was paid by money which was advanced by the bank for the purpose.... The truth of it is that danger always occurs when loose expressions used by the people whose business it is to carry on the details of business are regarded with more attention than the real settled methods of business which appear in the books kept by banks and other responsible persons.[62]

Notes

The Insolvency Act 1986, replacing earlier legislation, provides in section 330 for priority in winding-up proceedings to wages and salaries paid by a company in the four months before the winding-up, to a maximum of £800 (S.I. 1986 No. 1996). Similar priority is given by section 40 when a receiver is appointed but the company is not in the course of being wound up.

Section 264 of the Companies Act 1929, virtually re-enacted in section 319 of the 1948 Act, gave priority in winding-up proceedings to wages and salaries paid by a company in the four months before the winding-up, to a maximum of £200 per employee. (This maximum was increased to £800 by the Insolvency Act 1976).

The *Freedman and Rubens* case, reported only in *Legal Decisions affecting Bankers*, was the first action brought under the 1929 Act. Clauson J.'s decision was founded on the principle of the rule in *Clayton's* case, and in *Re Primrose Builders Ltd.*,[63-65] where the facts were almost identical with *Freedman and Rubens*, Wynn-Parry J., following Clauson J., expressly based on *Clayton's* case his ruling that the bank were entitled to rank as preferential creditors. It may be repeated that the rule

---

[62] At p. 445.
[63-65] [1950] Ch. 561.

in *Clayton's* case raises a presumption only, and the presumption can be displaced by the facts of a particular case. That is the reason why in this case it was so strenuously argued that there was an arrangement for the bank to pay the wages out of the proceeds of the cheques paid in. In both the cases here considered the facts were held not to be sufficient to displace it.

In *Re James R. Rutherford & Sons Ltd.*[66] there were two accounts, one of them being a wages account, and both being overdrawn. Transfers were made to the wages account weekly, each one being expressed to be "in repayment of the earliest advances made on (wages) account and still outstanding, utilised in payment of salaries and/or wages to persons whose salaries and/or wages since the date of such advances have exceeded £200 to the extent of that excess." On the company going into voluntary liquidation it was held that the bank was entitled to rank as a preferential creditor for the amount transferred from current to wages account as well as for the overdrawn balance of wages account, the effect of such transfers not being to repay the bank or to alter the nature of the borrowing; but, the rule in *Clayton's* case applying to credits paid in to the current account after the opening of the wages account, such credits served to reduce the indebtedness as at that date, and the amount transferred from current to wages account must be reduced accordingly.[67]

Re Rampgill Mill Ltd.[68] is of twofold interest, on the one hand as an example of the importance of the separate wages account in establishing preferential status, and on the other as a finding by the court that this status can be established without either a separate account or even a specific agreement as to the purpose of a borrowing. The circumstances were that the company had a borrowing facility for general purposes with Lloyds Bank. In order that the company might obtain cash for wages in another town open credit facilities were established with a branch of the Midland Bank, no Lloyds branch being available. Cheques were cashed under this arrangement, and debited to the company's ordinary overdrawn account. When the company went into liquidation the bank claimed that some £5,000 of the overdraft ranked as a preferential debt; but applying the rule in *Clayton's* case this was reduced to a little

---

[66] [1964] 1 W.L.R. 1211.
[67] *cf.*, as to preferred creditors under s.319, Paget, *op. cit.* 59 *et seq.*
[68] [1967] Ch. 1138.

over £2,000. The liquidator resisted this smaller claim, on the basis that in order to prove that an advance is entitled to preference the banker must have exercised a discretion in relation to it, and decided to make it because, as far as he knew, it was to be used for the particular purpose. But Plowman J. said that this was too rigid a test; he preferred a "benevolent construction," which gave the bank its case.

And in *Re William Hall (Contractors) Ltd.*[69] where four properties had been separately charged to secure the company's borrowing from Lloyds Bank, that borrowing totalled £7,922 at the date of the company's voluntary liquidation, £2,274 being preferential under section 319. The bank realised £5,780 by the sale of the properties, appropriated that sum to clear the non-preferential debt of £5,648 with the balance appropriated to the preferential debt, and proved for the balance of £2,142. The liquidator rejected the proof, on the grounds that the proceeds of the security should have been first appropriated to the preferential debt. But Plowman J. held that even if the mortgages had not contained the usual clause entitling the mortgagees to appropriate as they wished, they were entitled to do so as a general principle of law.

But in *Re C.W. and A.L. Huges Ltd.*[70] the company were building contractors who sometimes employed as sub-contractors on a labour only basis groups of workers—"gangs"—payment being made to the leader of the group. When on the company's voluntary liquidation Midland Bank claimed to rank as preferential creditors for moneys advanced to pay the gangs, Plowman J. rejected the claim: it was necessary that there should be a contract of employment between the company and the men so as to create the relation of master and servant, and there was no such contract in the case before him.

R v Grantham

[1984] Q.B. 675

Fraudulent trading

Facts

The appellant was at the time of the alleged offence a director of East Midlands Potato Company Ltd., and in association with

---

[69] [1967] 2 All E.R. 1150. See also *ante*, p. 375.
[70] [1966] 2 All E.R. 702.

three others arranged for the importation of a quantity of potatoes from France at an agreed price of £88,000. The collapse of the potato market within days of the commencement of the arrangement did not halt the organisers, and in the event the French supplier received only £19,688 of his entitlement of £88,000. The appellant and one of his associates were convicted of fraudulent trading under section 332 of the Companies Act 1948. He appealed against conviction, claiming that the judge had misdirected the jury as to what constituted the offence of fraudulent trading under section 332.

Decision

The Court of Appeal, Criminal Division, dismissed the appeal. It was not necessary for the prosecution to prove that when the debts were incurred there was no prospect of the creditors ever receiving payment; belief that funds might become available in the distant future was no defence. Lord Lane C.J. said:

In the present case it was open to the jury to find, if not inevitable that they would find, that whoever was running this business was intending to deceive, or was actually deceiving, the French supplier into believing that he would be paid in 28 days or shortly thereafter, when they knew perfectly well that there was no hope of that coming about. He was plainly induced thereby to deliver further potatoes on credit. The potential or inevitable detriment to him is obvious.[70a]

Notes

Section 332 is now replaced, as to criminal liability, by section 458 of the Companies Act 1985. Civil liability for fraudulent trading, which was also covered by section 332, is now dealt with, in slightly changed form, in sections 213 and 215 of the Insolvency Act 1986.

Section 332 was in question also in *In Re Augustus Barnett & Sons Ltd.*[71] where the company, a subsidiary of Rumasa, a Spanish company, was in liquidation, and the liquidator claimed that Rumasa, which had issued letters of comfort to the company, had been knowingly a party to carrying on the company's business with the intent to defraud creditors. As to section 332, Hoffman J. held that liability must be of somebody involved in the carrying on of the business, and here there was no allegation of intention to defraud against the directors of the

[70a] At p. 683.
[71] [1986] P.C.C. 167.

company. The liquidator said that this implied that the letters of comfort were legally worthless, but his Lordship, while agreeing that the law might be inadequate on the point, said the matter was one for wider investigation than was open to the judge on an interlocutory application to strike out the liquidator's claim.[72]

There has been some inconsistency in the decisions on section 332 which must now be relevant in the operation of the new legislation. Thus in *Re Gerald Cooper Chemicals Ltd.*[73] Templeman J. held that there was fraudulent trading when an individual creditor was cheated in a single transaction, whereas Oliver J. held in *Re Sarflax*[74] that a transaction intended to give one creditor an advantage over his fellow creditors was not fraudulent trading. Another difficulty has been the question whether knowledge that the company is trading fraudulently is essential to a director's liability, or whether it is enough that a reasonable man in his position would have drawn the conclusion from the circumstances. This latter point is somewhat eased by the appearance in section 214 of the Insolvency Act of the new concept of wrongful trading.

In this unfamiliar area there are new possibilities of danger for bankers. Liabilities can arise for negligent as well as fraudulent conduct, and "shadow directors" can be liable; so that a banker whose advice shades into control can be at risk.[75]

---

[72] In *Kleinwort Benson Ltd.* v. *Malaysia Mining Corporation Berhad, The Financial Times*, February 1, 1989, the Court of Appeal held that the letters of comfort there involved entailed a moral responsibility, but no contractual liability.

[73] [1978] Ch. 262.

[74] [1979] Ch. 592.

[75] *cf., e.g. Re a Company (No. 005009 of 1987)* (1988) 4 B.C.C. 424, where the liquidator claimed that the bank was liable for wrongful trading as a shadow director, and Knox, J. dismissed the bank's application to strike out the claim and said the matter should go to trial.

Chapter 9

BANKING ADMINISTRATION

R. v. Grossman

[1981] Crim.L.R. 396

The relationship between a bank and its branches

Facts

The Inland Revenue, investigating a case of alleged tax evasion, wished to inspect the account with a Manx bank of the company involved. They were refused an order under the Isle of Man Bankers Books Evidence Act 1935. They now applied for an order under the English Act[1] to inspect the account of the Manx bank with the Douglas branch of Barclays Bank, their clearing agents. Barclays took a neutral stance, but the Manx bank said that they were merely customers of Barclays, and the order requiring Barclays to produce their customer's account was unjustified.

Decision

The Court of Appeal rejected the application: the branch of Barclays in another jurisdiction was to be regarded as a separate legal entity, not amenable to the English Act.

Lord Denning said:

I do not think that Barclays' branch in Douglas should be considered any differently from an Irish or American branch bank which is not subject to our jurisdiction. Barclays had to get a licence to operate there. The branch there should be considered a separate entity.

Notes

In *Power Curber International* v. *National Bank of Kuwait SAK*[2] Lord Denning referred to the *Grossman* decision and elaborated on the point here discussed:

---

[1] *Ante*, p. 11.
[2] *Ante*, p. 255.

Many banks now have branches in many foreign countries. Each branch has to be licensed by the country in which it operates. Each branch is treated in that country as independent of its parent body. The branch is subject to the orders of the courts of the country in which it operates, but not to the orders of the country where its head office is situated. We so decided in the recent case about bankers' books in the Isle of Man.[2a]

It was applied also in *McKinnon* v. *Donaldson, Lufkin and Jenrette Securities Corporation*[3], Hoffman J. recognising that the principle was applicable even though, as had been established the previous year in *Bonalumi* v. *Secretary of State for the Home Department*,[4] the decision in *Re Grossman*, like several others, had been given in ignorance of the relevance of the provision in the Supreme Court Act 1981 (repeating previous legislation) barring appeals to the Court of Appeal from the High Court in criminal causes.

The head office of a bank and its branches are in law a single entity, but the courts have recognised a variety of circumstances in which practical expediency requires that they should be treated as if this were not so. The Court of Appeal ruling in the two cases noted above provides one example; others are found, as we have seen earlier, in the service on head office of garnishee orders[5] and *Mareva* injunctions[6], such notice not acting as notice to the branches involved (although in both cases the head office must use its best endeavours to locate the relevant bank accounts).

It has long been established that payment of a cheque can be demanded only at the branch on which it is drawn.[7] The rule has been applied in such special circumstances as those of *Clare & Co.* v. *Dresdner Bank*[8] and *Zivnostenska Banka* v. *Frankman*.[9] In the first case the plaintiffs had an account with the Berlin branch of the defendant bank, and, after the outbreak of war between England and Germany, sought payment of the balance of their account from the London branch of the bank. Upon this being refused they brought the present action, in which it was held that they could not demand payment except at the branch at which the account was kept.

[2a] At p. 1241.
[3] [1986] Ch. 482.
[4] [1985] Q.B. 675.
[5] *Ante*, p. 110.
[6] *Ante*, p. 117.
[7] *cf. Woodland* v. *Fear* (1857) 7 E. & B. 519.
[8] [1915] 2 K.B. 576.
[9] [1950] A.C. 57.

In *Zivnostenska Banka* v. *Frankman* a Prague resident became by inheritance in 1935 the owner of securities, held for safe custody by the London branch of the bank. She was advised of the position by the Prague office of the bank, with which she had an account. The action was brought by her son, as administrator of her estate, for delivery of the securities. Such delivery was forbidden by the current Czech exchange control regulations as the daughter was resident in this country, although it was not against English law. It was held by the House of Lords that the contract of deposit was with the Prague office, and that delivery could therefore be properly demanded only in Prague. Delivery in London could have been arranged with the consent of the Prague office, but this could not be given because of the regulations. In his judgment Lord Macdermott spoke of the "established banking practice that a customer who does business with one branch of a bank cannot, in the absence of some special provision, call as of right on another branch to complete or clear that business."

Similarly, countermand of payment is effective only at the branch on which the instrument to be "stopped" is drawn. In *London Provincial & South Western Bank Ltd.* v. *Buszard*[10] the defendant drew a cheque on the Oxford Street branch of the plaintiff bank, at which he had an account. The payee took it to the Victoria Street branch of the same bank, where she had an account, and was allowed to draw against it. In the meantime the defendant had stopped payment of the cheque, and in due course it was returned to the Victoria Street branch marked "Ordered not to pay." The bank brought this action as holders in due course against the drawer of the cheque, who contended that the bank had notice of the "stop," notice to one branch being notice at all; but it was held that the countermand of payment was effective only at the branch on which the cheque was drawn, and judgment was given for the bank.

But the essential unity of the bank in all its branches remains, where it is not clearly impracticable to insist upon it; *Garnett* v. *McKewan*[11] is a good example of the application of this principle.

The position with subsidiary companies, which are separate legal entities, is different from the position of branches, which as was pointed out above, are legally a single entity with their head office. Thus, in *Bank of Tokyo Ltd.* v. *Magid Karoon*,[12]

---

[10] (1918) 35 T.L.R. 142.
[11] *Ante*, pp. 234, 235, 237, 363.
[12] [1986] 3 W.L.R. 414.

where the Iranian government was seeking the recovery of $685,000 which Mr. Karoon had transferred from his personal account with Bank of Tokyo Trust Company in New York to his personal account with Bank of Tokyo in London, and B.T. was now seeking an injunction to restrain him from further action in New York in his case alleging violation of his privacy. B.T. had inquired of B.T.T.C. how the sum of $685,000 was made up; and they now claimed that the information disclosed by B.T.T.C. must be treated as having been in the possession of B.T., the parent company. The injunction was refused, and dismissing the appeal Ackner L.J. said that the reality of the matter was that B.T.T.C. was not a branch of B.T. "That is not the way B.T. has chosen to organise its business as a bank. There is no valid basis and no authority was provided for the contention that the court must ignore B.T.T.C.'s separate existence."

But it may be noted that in the *Amalgamated Investment and Property* case[13] where the bank had made a loan through its subsidiary and the Court of Appeal held that in the circumstances the plaintiffs were estopped from denying the validity of their guarantee, Lord Denning also said that it was a case where a wholly-owned subsidiary was to be regarded as the alter ego of the parent company.[14]

Royal Products Ltd. v. Midland Bank Ltd. and Another

[1981] Com.L.R. 93

The relationship between a bank and its correspondents

Facts

The plaintiffs had current accounts with the defendants, with the National Bank of Malta, and with the Bank of Industry, Commerce and Agriculture Ltd. (BICAL) in Malta. They instructed the Midland to transfer £13,000 by cable to BICAL, and the Midland cabled the National Bank, their correspondents in Malta, to pay the money to BICAL. The National Bank credited the money to a suspense account in the name of BICAL and advised BICAL. The National Bank knew that BICAL were in difficulties, but they had been told by the Central Bank of Malta that they would be open the following

---

[13] *Ante*, p. 312.
[14] *cf. Re G.T. Whyte & Co. Ltd., ante*, p. 389.

day. In fact they ceased business the following day, and by this action the plaintiffs claimed that they were entitled to the return of their money on the grounds (1) that the transfer had not been completed because it had not been communicated to BICAL; (2) that the National Bank were their agents and were in breach of their duty of care in making the transfer when they knew of BICAL's difficulties, and further that the Midland were liable for National's breach; and (3) that even if National were not their agents, Midland owed them a duty of care of which they were in breach.

Decision

Webster J. rejected all three arguments. As to (1), he held that a payment was not necessarily incomplete because the payee had not consented to receive it. This might be true when payment to a third party is ordered, but here it was a bank that had been told to credit the customer. He distinguished the *Rekstin* decision[15]: there a judgment debtor sought to transfer from its account to another customer's account, with diplomatic immunity, and to which the judgment debtor owed nothing; here the transfer was of a customer's money from one of its banks to another.

As to (2) he cited Chorley[16] on the difference between a correspondent and a branch. The National were agents of the Midland, but the Midland could not create privity of contract between National and Royal so as to make National the agents of Royal. And as to (3), Midland would have been liable for National's negligence, but here there had been no negligence. National's knowledge of BICAL's position was confidential; there could be no liability for carrying out a normal banking transaction in a normal banking manner.

Notes

The effect of the contract between a bank and its correspondent bank was in question in *Mackersy* v. *Ramsays Bonar & Co.*,[17] where the appellant was a customer of the respondent banking firm, who gave them for collection a bill of exchange drawn on a person in Calcutta. They sent it to their agents, Coutts & Co., who in turn forwarded it to their own agent in Calcutta. The bill was paid by the acceptor, but the

---

[15] *Ante*, p. 114.
[16] *Law of Banking*, (6th ed.), p. 374.
[17] (1843) Cl. & Fin. 818.

Calcutta agent went bankrupt, and the respondent bank did not receive the money, and refused to credit their customer. But it was held that they were liable to the customer, and in the House of Lords Lord Cottenham was very clear as to the position:

If I send to my bankers a bill or draft upon another banker in London, I do not expect that they will themselves go and receive the amount, and pay me the proceeds; but that they will send a clerk in the course of the day to the clearing house and settle the balances, in which my bill or draft will form one item. If such clerk, instead of returning to the bankers with the balance, should abscond with it, can my bankers refuse to credit me with the amount? Certainly not.

But while the banker is clearly responsible for the acts of his correspondent bank, the contract is between the two banks, and the fact that the banker initiating the business does so on behalf of a customer, does not make that customer a party to the contract. In the *Royal Products* case Webster J. referred to *Calico Printers Association* v. *Barclays Bank Ltd. and Anglo-Palestine Co. Ltd.*[18] where the plaintiff association were in the habit of handing to Barclays Bank parcels of bills of exchange and bills of lading on one Ydlibi, of Beirut. At their request these bills were collected through the Anglo-Palestine Co. although this company was not Barclays' usual agents. If the goods were not taken up Barclays were requested to warehouse and insure them, and Barclays instructed their agents accordingly. In fact certain goods were destroyed by fire, and it was found that they had not been insured. The plaintiffs claimed against the first defendants that they had accepted a liability to insure and had been negligent in not seeing that this was effective. They claimed against the second defendants that they had been negligent in similarly failing.

It was held by Wright J. that the Palestine agents had been grossly negligent in their conduct, but that their only liability, in the absence of any privity of contract with the plaintiff, was to their principals, Barclays Bank. There had also been some degree of negligence by Barclays, but they were protected by a clause in the plaintiffs' instructions excluding liability. Upon the plaintiffs appealing only against the decision in Barclays' favour, the Court of Appeal upheld the lower court.

---

[18] (1931) 36 Com.Cas. 71 and 197.

In *Kahler* v. *Midland Bank Ltd.*,[19] which may be regarded as a complementary case to the *Zivnostenska Banka* case,[20] the plaintiff was in 1938 a customer of a bank in Prague, and arranged with them that they should hold certain of his securities on his behalf in London. Their correspondent bank in London, with which these arrangements were made, was the Midland Bank. After the shares had been virtually expropriated by the occupying power during the war, the plaintiff's title had been restored in 1946 by the Czech authorities, but as the plaintiff was no longer a Czech citizen the Czech exchange control regulations prevented him from obtaining the securities. The present action was a claim to possession as sole and unfettered beneficial owner. The House of Lords held that the Midland Bank was not a party to the contract of deposit; and, by a majority of one, that, although the plaintiff was the sole owner, yet the contract envisaged delivery in London only with authorisation from the Prague bank (which could not now be given); and that the Midland Bank could not be required to give up the securities to the plaintiff.

Barwick v. English Joint Stock Bank

(1867) L.R. 2 Ex. 259

A bank is liable for the actions of is officers in the ordinary course of banking business if those actions are within the apparent scope of their authority

Facts

The plaintiff had supplied oats on credit to J. Davis & Son, who were working under government contract. When Barwick asked for better security Davis arranged for the manager of the defendant bank, where he had his account, to write a letter undertaking to honour the firm's cheque in favour of the plaintiff on receipt of government payment for forage supplied, "in priority to any other payment except to this bank." Davis owed the bank £12,000, but the plaintiff did not know this. The government payment amounted to £2,676, but Davis's cheque for £1,227 payable to the plaintiff was dishonoured, the bank claiming the whole of the government payment in reduction of their lending. The plaintiff brought this action against the bank for false representation and for money had and received.

---

[19] [1950] A.C. 24.
[20] *Ante*, p. 402.

Decision

The Court of Exchequer Chamber held (i) that there was evidence to go to a jury that the manager knew and intended the guarantee to be unavailing and fraudulently concealed from the plaintiff the fact that would make it so; and (ii) that the bank would be liable for such fraud in their agent.

In the course of his judgment, Willes J. said:

> The general rule is, that the master is answerable for every such wrong of the servant or agent as is committed in the course of the service and for the master's benefit, though no express command or privity of the master be proved. That principle is acted upon every day in running down cases. It has been applied also to direct trespass to goods, as in the case of holding the owners of ships liable for the act of masters abroad, improperly selling the cargo. It has been held applicable to actions of false imprisonment, in cases where officers of railway companies, ... improperly imprison persons who are supposed to come within the terms of the bye-laws. ... In all these cases it may be said, as it was said here, that the master has not authorised the act. It is true, he has not authorised the particular act, but he has put the agent in his place to do that class of acts, and he must be answerable for the manner in which the agent has conducted himself in doing the business which it was the act of his master to place him in.[21]

Notes

The act complained of must be within the ostensible authority of the officer before the bank can be made liable for it. Thus in *Bank of New South Wales* v. *Owston*,[22] where the complaint was of wrongful arrest and malicious prosecution, the Judicial Committee of the Privy Council held that the act was not one for which the bank was to be held liable. Sir Montague Smith said:

> The duties of a bank manager would usually be to conduct banking business on behalf of his employers, and when he is found so acting, what is done by him in the way of ordinary banking transactions may be presumed, until the contrary is shown, to be within the scope of his authority; and his employers would be liable for his mistakes, and, under some circumstances, for his frauds, in the management of such business. But the arrest, and still less the prosecution of offenders, is not within the ordinary routine of banking business, and when the question of a manager's authority in such a case arises, it is essential to inquire carefully into his position and duties.[23]

---

[21] At p. 265. The bank had not pleaded the Statute of Frauds defence (see *ante*, p. 25).

[22] (1879) 4 App.Cas. 270.

[23] At p. 289.

The liability of a bank for the acts of its officers is a particular application of the principle developed from *Turquand's* case,[24] but that principle is unlikely to be explored in this context. Indeed, even the kind of question that arose in the two cases here considered is unlikely to arise in modern conditions: a bank may argue, as the bank did in *Woods* v. *Martins Bank Ltd.*,[25] that an action is outside the scope of the bank's business, but it would be reluctant to disclaim responsiblity for an action by one of its officers merely on the grounds that it was outside the scope of his authority.[26] No such claim appears to have been made in *Selangor United Rubber Estates Ltd.* v. *Cradock*.[27]

[24] *Ante*, p. 216.
[25] *Ante*, pp. 22, 33.
[26] But see *UBAF Ltd.* v. *American Banking Corp. ante*, p. 26.
[27] *Ante*, p. 83.

INDEX

Account payee,
  cheques crossed,
    negligence, and, 185–187
Accounts,
  combination of, 233–238. *See also*
    Combination of accounts.
Act of bankruptcy,
  abolition of, 367
Administration orders, 377, 378
  basis for making, 377, 378
  conditions for making, 377, 378
  purpose of, 378
Administrators, 205–209. *See also*
  Executors.
Agents,
  negligence in collecting for,
    principal drawer of cheques,
      where, 171–177
  ostensible authority, 406–408
Antecedent debt,
  meaning in Bills of Exchange Act,
    54–55
Anton Piller order, 123
Assignment,
  choses in action, of, 348–351
Automated book-keeping, 35–36
Automation,
  ordinary course of business, and,
    148–149

Bank,
  liability for actions of staff, 406–408
  relationship with branches, 400–403
  relationship with correspondents,
    403–406
Bank statements,
  duty of customer to examine,
    whether, 93–96
  wrong entry made in,
    customer acting in good faith upon,
      97–100
Banker,
  definition, 27–30
Banker and customer, 1–36 *et seq.*
  account, 30–35
  automated book-keeping, 35–36
  bank as customer of another bank, 34
  debtor and creditor, 1–6

Banker and customer—*cont.*
  disclosure of information, 6–11, 11–18
  duration of relationship, 30–35
  implied contract, 1–6, 6–11
  money lent to banker not payable
    except on demand, 1–6
  negligence, and, 20–24. *See also*
    Negligence.
  special relationship, 18–27
  Statute of Frauds, 25, 26–27
Bankers' commercial credits, 244–275.
  See also Letter of credit.
  banker need not look beyond
    documents, 260
  clarity of, 257
  documents must conform with credit,
    259
  government agencies, 268–271
  irrevocable, 246–250
  machinery of, 258
  payment by banker under, 256–263
  rejection of documents,
    undue delay, and, 263–265
  revocable, 246–250
  time within which opened, 265–268
Banker's draft,
  negotiability, 40
Bankers' lien, 276–280
  nature of, 277
  negligence, and, 279–280
  property subject to, 277–278, 279
  set-off, and, 278
Banking administration, 400–408
Bankruptcy,
  act of, abolished, 367
  bankruptcy order,
    payments on account before bank
      has notice, 366–371
  preferences, 371–377
  proof of debt in, 369–371
Bill of exchange,
  cash equivalence, 66–71
    defences, 68–69
    importance in international trade,
      68
    pending arbitration proceedings,
      and, 70–71
  consideration, 54–56

Bill of exchange—*cont.*
consideration—*cont.*
  fraud, and, 55–56
  third party, and, 55–56
definition, 41–44, 45
due on non-business day, when
  payable, 73
holder for value, 57
holder in due course, 56–61
  importance of status, 58–60
indorsement in blank, 60–61
international commerce, use in, 62
liability of acceptor,
  drawer of cheque compared, 89
material alteration, 63–66
negotiability, 38
notice of dishonour, 61–63
payee fictitious or non-existing
  person, 45–50
presentation for payment, 63
regular indorsement, requirements
  of, 56–61
signature in representative capacity,
  50–54
  companies, 52–53
  option of holder, 53–54
stay of execution, and, 69–71
unconditional, bill must be, 44
validity of indorsements, 59
void, payment of, 64
Bill of lading,
clean, 262–263
negotiability, 39
pledge of,
  presentation of bill to enforce
   security, 282–285
Borrowing,
unauthorised, 226–233
Branch credit system, 162–163
Branches,
relationship with bank, 400–403
Breach of trust, 103–106

Charging orders, 335–337
matrimonial property and, 336–337
Cheque. *See also* Bill of exchange.
bank as holder for value, 156–162
countermand, 126–129
crossed,
  "opening" of, 66
crossed "Account payee,"
  negligence, and, 185–187
crossed "Not negotiable,"
  negligence, and, 187–191

Cheque—*cont.*
dishonour of,
  wrongful, damages for, 129–135.
   See also Dishonour of cheque.
dual function, 87
forged,
  duty of customer to inform bank,
   90–93
  duty of customer to prevent,
   whether, 93–96
legal nature of, 86
liability of drawer,
  acceptor of bill of exchange
   compared, 89
misuse of, 229–230
money paid under mistake of fact,
  recovery of, 136–141
negotiability, 38, 41–44
order to "pay cash or order," 41–44
payable "to A for B," collection of,
  negligence, and, 181–184
payable to third parties, collection of,
  negligence in, 177–181
payment of debt by, when effected,
  71–74
post-dated, validity of, 129
reasonable precautions against
  possible alteration, 85–90
receipt form on, 45
undated,
  refusing payment of, 66
unreasonable delay in completing,
  66
Cheque card,
unauthorised use, 226–233
Cheques Act 1957,
neglegence may refer back to opening
  of account, 162–170
section 2,
  effect of, 156–162
Choses in action,
equitable assignment of, 348–351
C.i.f. contract,
effect of, 244–246
Clayton's case, rule in, 150–153
Collecting banker, 156–193
Combination of accounts, 233–238
notice of intention to combine,
  236–237
setting off credit balance against
  indebtedness on another
  account, 233–238
Companies, 212–222
authority of agent, 216–222

Companies—*cont.*
 borrowing,
  memorandum of association, and,
   212–216
  personal liability of signatory of
   cheque, 52–53
  Turquand's case, rule in, 216–222
   facts, 216
  ultra vires rule, 213–216
   delegated authority, and, 219
   modification by European
    Communities Act, 218
Conclusive evidence clause, 300
Consideration,
 bill of exchange, and, 54–56
 guarantee,and, 299
Constructive trust, 79, 83–85
Contempt of court,
 Mareva injunction, and, 118
Contributory negligence, 174–175
Correspondents,
 bank liable for acts of, 405
 relationship between bank and,
  403–406
Countermand of payment, 126–129
 branches, and, 402
 brought to notice of banker, 126–129
 must be unambiguous, 126–129
Credit card,
 misuse of, 228, 229
Cross firing, 232–233
Customer,
 definition, 30–35
 duty of banker to honour mandates,
  101–106

Death,
 guarantor, of, 316–319
 partner, of,
  effect of, 203–205
Debenture,
 bearer, negotiability, 38
Deception,
 obtaining by, 230–233
Disclosure of information concerning
 customer's affairs, 6–18, 291–295
Discount of bills, 238–241
 holder of bill suing as agent for
  another,
  defence available against principal,
   238–241
Dishonour of cheque, 129–135
 wrongful, liability in contract,
  129–131

Dishonour of cheque—*cont.*
 wrongful—*cont.*
  liability for libel, 132–135

Employees,
 negligence in collecting for,
  employer drawer of cheques,
   where, 171–177
Estoppel,
 customer acting in good faith upon
  wrong entry made in statement
  or passbook, 97–100
 forgery, and, 90–93
 mistake, and, 97–100
 negligence, and, 91–93
Executors, 205–209
 legal title to balance of customer's
  account, 208
 personal liability, 206–207
Exchange rates, 241–244
 payment of debts in foreign currency,
  241–244

Fictitious or non-existing person,
 meaning, 45–50
Financing by bankers, 223–275
Floating charges, 387–390
 crystallisation, 389–390
Foreign currency,
 garnishee order, and, 116
 payment of debts in, 241–244
Forgery,
 duty of customer to inform bank,
  90–93
 duty of customer to prevent, whether,
  93–96
 estoppel, and, 90–93
 payment after, 124–126
 precautions against, 85–90
Fraudulent preference, 372–373,
 374–375, 376
Fraudulent trading, 397–399

Garnishee order, 110–117
 balance of account in foreign
  currency, 116
 debt not recoverable within
  jurisdiction can be garnished,
  116–117
 effect of, 110–117
 joint account, and, 115
 money gone from account at time of
  service, 114
 money paid in after service of, 114

Garnishee order—*cont.*
  not to be used to prefer garanishor
    over other creditors, 116
  property attached by, 111–117
  trust funds, and, 113
Good faith,
  meaning, 143–146
Government agencies,
  letters of credit, 268–271
Guarantees, 271–275, 291–319
  additional security, 293
  carelessness of signatory, 298
  conduct of creditor, and, 306–308
  conduct that may free guarantor,
    304–308
  consideration for, 299
  contract,
    not *uberrimae fidei*, 291–295
  death of guarantor, 316–319
    co-sureties, and, 318
    notice of, 317–318
  demand under, 314–316
  dispute as to amount of debt, 299–300
  duty to obtain proper price on sale of
    property, 305
  effectiveness of,
    terms, and, 308–314
  further advances, and, 307
  illegal transaction, of, 312
  interlocking, 309–310, 311–312
  mental disorder of guarantor, 318
  misrepresentation, and, 295–300
  release of co-sureties, and, 306–307
  Statute of Limitations, and, 314–315
  terms of, 308–314
    alteration, 314
  undue influence, and, 301–304
  unusual conduct, and, 294
  words of, 310, 312–313
    extrinsic evidence, 313

Holder,
  for value, 156–162
  in due course, 57–58
Hypothecation. *See* Guarantees.

Immediate use of funds,
  meaning in money transfer, 76
Indorsement,
  forged,
    payment after, 124–126
  requirements of, 56–61
Insolvency, 366–399. *See also*
  Bankruptcy and Winding up.

Joint accounts, 194–200
  garnishee order, and, 115
  joint and several right of action
    against bank, 198–200
  survivorship,
    rebuttable presumption, 194–198

Lapse of time,
  repayment of balance after, 153–155
Letter of credit. *See also* Bankers'
  commercial credits.
  fraud by seller, and, 252
  nature of payment by, 250–256
  non-admissibility of counter claims,
    255
Letters of hypothecation,
  advances against, 288–290
Libel,
  cheque wrongfully dishonoured,
    where, 132–135
  privilege, defence of, 132–135
  "refer to drawer," and, 111–112,
    133–134
Life insurance policies,
  death result of accused's own criminal
    act, 356
  mortgage of, 354–358
Limited companies, 212–222. *See also*
  Companies.

Mareva injunction, 117–123
  comprehensive initially, 120
  contempt of court, and, 118
  effect of, 118, 121–122
  grounds for, 122
  proper range of, 120
  reasonable expenses of obeying, bank
    should be indemnified, 119
  SIB, granted to, 121
Material alteration,
  meaning, 63–66
Matrimonial home,
  rights of occupier against mortgagee,
    328–335
Mental disorder, 364–366
  customer, of, 364–366
    bank advance for necessaries,
      364–366
  guarantor, of, 318
Mercantile usage,
  negotiability, conferring, 37–41
Misrepresentation,
  guarantee, and, 295–300
  law of contract, and, 297

Mistake,
  estoppel, and, 97–100
  fact, of,
    recovery of money paid under,
      136–141
Mortgages, 319 *et seq.*
  contingent liabilities, and, 321
  demand under, 321–323
  equitable, 337–342
  equitable assignment of choses in
    action, 348–351
  life insurance policies, 354–358
  limitation of actions, and, 321–323
  mortgagee making further advances,
    notice of second mortgage, after,
      342–344
  nature of, 319–321
  power of sale, 324–328
  priorities, 339–340
  registration,
    Companies Act, under, 345–348
    companies incorporated outside
      England, 347
    out of time, 346–347
  reservation of title, and, 358–361
  retention of title to goods, and,
    358–361
  rights of mortgagee, 324–328
    restrictions upon, 324–328
  rights of occupier against mortgagee,
    328–335
    equity of exoneration, 334–335
    matrimonial disputes, 333–335
    unregistered land, and, 331–332
    wives' interests as co-owners,
      329–330
  second, notice of,
    mortgagee making further
      advances after, 342–344
  stock exchange securities, 351–354
  undue influence, and, 328

Necessaries,
  bank advance for,
    mental disorder of customer, and,
      364–366
Negligence,
  banker and customer, 20–24
  breach of bank's own rules, and, 178
  Cheques Act 1957, and, 162 *et seq.*
  cheques crossed "Account payee,"
    185–187
  cheques crossed "Not negotiable,"
    187–191

Negligence—*cont.*
  collection for agents or employees, in,
    principal or employer drawer of
      cheque, where, 171–177
  collection of cheques payable "to A
    for B," 181–184
  collection of cheques payable to third
    parties, 177–181
  contributory negligence a defence,
    174–175
  conversion of cheques, and, 141–143
  correspondents, of, 405
  estoppel, and, 91–93
  factors to be taken into consideration,
    172
  may refer back to opening of account,
    162–170
  objective standard, 168
  power of attorney, and, 176–177
  reasonable banker test, 165
  section 60, Bills of Exchange Act
    1882, and, 141–143
Negotiability, 38
Negotiable instruments, 37–77
  Bills of Exchange Act 1882, 40–66.
    See also Bill of exchange.
  mercantile usage, and, 37–41
  pledgee as holder for value, 280–282
Normal business hours, 147
Not negotiable,
  cheques crossed,
    negligence, and, 187–191
Notice,
  constructive, 145–146. *See also*
    Constructive trust.
Notice and knowledge,
  meaning, 144

Obtaining by deception, 230–233
Occupier,
  rights against mortgagee, 328–335
Officers of bank,
  actions in ordinary course of banking
    business, 406–408
  scope of authority, 406–408
Ordinary course of business, 146–149
  automation, and, 148–149
Overdrafts, 223–226
  loan distinguished, 225–226

Partners, 201–205
  death, effect of, 203–205
  duty of surviving partners to realise
    partnership assets, 203–205

Partners—*cont.*
  implied authority, 201–203
  partner has no implied authority to
    open partnership account,
    201–203
Passbook. *See* Bank statements.
Pay cash or order,
  meaning, 41–44
Paying banker, 78–155
Payments in to account,
  presumed to have been appropriated
    to debit items in order of date,
    150–153
  time at which effected, 74–77
Pension warrants,
  collection of, 191–193
Performance bonds, 271–275
  fraud, and, 273
  nature of, 272–273
Pledge, 280–291
  bankruptcy, and, 287
  bill of lading, of,
    presentation of bill to enforce
      security, 282–285
  negotiable instrument, of,
    constructive notice of defect in
      title, and, 281–282
    pledgee as holder for value,
      280–282
  pledgee ceasing to hold goods or
    documents of title, 285–291
  trust receipt, and, 285–291
Power of attorney, 176–177
Preferences, 371–377

Receivers, 379–383
  challenge to appointment, 380–381
  duty of, 304
  formalities of appointment, 380–381
  predating of appointments, 381–382
  winding up order, and, 382
Repayment of balance,
  lapse of time, after, 153–155
Reservation of title, 358–361
Retention of title to goods, 358–361
Romalpa clause, 358–361
Rule book,
  relevance of to negligence, 170, 178

Securities for advances, 276–361
Set-off. *See* Combination of accounts.
Signature,
  representative capacity, in, 50–54

Sovereign immunity, 268–271
Special accounts, 194–222
Statement of Account. *See* Bank
  statements.
Stock exchange,
  securities,
    mortgage of, 351–354
Suicide,
  life insurance, and, 354–358
Suretyship. *See* Guarantees.

Termination of relationship between
    banker and customer, 362–399. *See
    also* Bankruptcy and Winding up.
  administration orders, 377, 378
  insolvency, 366–399
  mental disorder, 364–366. *See also*
    Mental disorder.
  notice by banker, 362–364
  preferences, 371–377
  receivers, 379–383
Third party,
  collection of cheques payable to,
    negligence in, 177–181
  moneys claimed by,
    followed into account, 106–110
Trust,
  breach of, 103–106
  constructive, 79, 83–85
  dealing in manner inconsistent with,
    78–85
  following funds into account, 106–110
  garnishee order, and, 113
  inference of knowledge of, 80–81
Trust receipt,
  pledge, and, 285–291

Unauthorised borrowing, 226–233
Undue influence, 301–304
  guarantees, and, 301–304
  independent advice, and, 303–304
  mortgage, and, 328
  ordinary business relationship, and,
    302
  third party, and, 303
Uniform Customs and Practice for
    Documentary Credits, 254,
    264–265
Unincorporated associations, 209–211
  contracts of, 209–211
  debts of, 209–211
  members, liability of, 209–211
  officers, liability of, 209–211

Wages cheques,
  bank as preferential creditor for,
    394–397
Winding up, 383–399
  ancillary agreements, and, 383–386
  bank as preferential creditor for
    wages cheques, 394–397
  company as going concern,
    392–394
  continuation of banking facilities,
    and, 390–394

Winding up—*cont.*
  effect of order, 383–386
  floating charges, 387–390
  fraudulent trading, and, 397–399
  operation of account after
    commencement, 390–394
  payment of creditors' interest, and,
    386
  preferences, 371–377
  set-off provisions, and, 383–386
  validation order, 391–392